WEST ORANGE PUBLIC LIBRARY
46 MT. PLEASANT AVENUE
WEST ORANGE, N.J. 07052

Antonio

JOHN A. RICE

Antonio Salieri

AND VIENNESE OPERA

For Mariza de Andrade

CONTENTS

ILLUSTRATIONS

Salieri

AND VIENNESE OPERA

THE UNIVERSITY OF CHICAGO PRESS / CHICAGO AND LONDON

WEST ORANGE PUBLIC LIBRARY
46 MT. PLEASANT AVENUE
WEST ORANGE, N.J. 07052

782.1092
SAL
RIC

JOHN A. RICE is the author of *W. A. Mozart: La clemenza di Tito* and of many articles on eighteenth-century music.

TITLE PAGE ILLUSTRATION: Costume design for Altamor in *Axur re d'Ormus,* executed by F. A. Lohrmann for Wojciech Bogusławski's production in Polish, Warsaw, 1793. (Courtesy of Warsaw University Library.)

The University of Chicago Press, Chicago 60637
The University of Chicago Press, Ltd., London
© 1998 by The University of Chicago
All rights reserved. Published 1998
Printed in the United States of America

07 06 05 04 03 02 01 00 99 98   1 2 3 4 5

ISBN: 0-226-71125-0 (cloth)
ISBN: 0-226-71126-9 (paper)

A publishing subvention from the American Musicological Society is gratefully acknowledged.
Music autography by Jürgen Selk, Music Graphics International.

Library of Congress Cataloging-in-Publication Data

Rice, John A.
Antonio Salieri and Viennese Opera / John A. Rice.
p. cm.
Includes bibliographical references and index.
ISBN 0-226-71125-0 (alk. paper).—ISBN 0-226-71126-9 (pbk.: alk. paper)
1. Salieri, Antonio, 1750–1825—Criticism and interpretation.
2. Opera—Austria—Vienna—18TH century. I. Title.
ML410.S16R53 1998
782.1′092—dc21
[B]   97-32585
CIP
MN

♾ The paper used in this publication meets the minimum requirements of the American National Standards Institute—Permanence of Paper for Printed Library Materials, ANSI Z39.48-1992.

ACKNOWLEDGMENTS

My acquaintance with Salieri's music goes back to 1974, when, at the age of eighteen, I bought a recording of his festive concerto for flute and oboe. But it was only later, during graduate study at the University of California, Berkeley, between 1980 and 1987, that the possibility of a book on Salieri's operas first suggested itself. To my teacher, Daniel Heartz, I am grateful not only for guiding my education but for remaining a generous and inspiring friend. He read early drafts of several chapters of this book and allowed me to read his *Haydn, Mozart, and the Viennese School* before publication.

Bruce Alan Brown and Michel Noiray read the entire typescript. Their comments, corrections, and suggestions—as voluminous as they were thoughtful and incisive—went well beyond what any scholar can reasonably expect from busy colleagues.

Dexter Edge, in the course of stimulating conversations, drew my attention to many sources of information on Viennese musical life; he also read an early version of chapter 2, which has greatly benefited from his comments. Richard Armbruster read several chapters and let me in on many of his important Salieri discoveries before their publication. Thomas Bauman's comments on some of the early chapters helped me improve them greatly.

John Platoff shared with me his photocopies and microfilm of Salieri librettos and scores. Dorothea Link sent me a copy of a recording of *La grotta di Trofonio* and allowed me to study and to use her transcriptions of Viennese documents. Lorenzo della Chà and James Webster sent me advance copies of their publications about Salieri's operas. I am grateful to Roberta Visentin, *Sindaco* of Legnago (Salieri's birthplace), for copies of two recent books about Salieri. Monika Woitas, Ronald Rabin, Marita McClymonds, Walther Brauneis, Irene Adrian, Federico Pirani, Jane Girdham, Caryl Clark, Matthew Cron, Albert Rice, Elizabeth Dunstan, Bertil van Boer, Julian Rushton, Mary Hunter,

Eva Badura-Skoda, and Don Neville generously gave me the benefit of their knowledge and experience.

A Research Initiation Grant from the University of Houston (1991) and a Summer Stipend from the National Endowment for the Humanities (1992) supported some of the preliminary research for the book. With the help of a travel grant from the American Philosophical Society I worked with the Keglevich papers in the National Archives of Hungary (1993). A generous fellowship from the Alexander von Humboldt–Stiftung enabled me to spend a year in Europe (1993–94): a month of research in Vienna and the rest in Würzburg, where, under the guidance of Wolfgang Osthoff, I wrote much of the book.

At The University of Chicago Press Kathleen Hansell oversaw the book's production, demonstrating, at every stage, equal expertise as an editor and a musicologist. My profound thanks to Margaret Dybala for reading the page proofs.

The directors and staffs of many libraries have allowed me to use their collections: the New York Public Library at Lincoln Center, the Wiener Stadtbibliothek, and the libraries of the University of California, Berkeley, the University of Washington, Harvard University, the University of Houston, Rice University, the Universität Würzburg, and the Conservatorio Santa Cecilia in Rome. I am grateful to the archivists at the Haus-, Hof- und Staatsarchiv and the Hofkammerarchiv in Vienna, the Kärntner Landesarchiv in Klagenfurt, and the National Archives of Hungary in Budapest for their guidance.

Günter Brosche and his staff at the music collection of the Austrian National Library made their vast holdings of Salieri materials available to me whenever I was able to get to Vienna. I will always remember with pleasure and gratitude my many hours in the Musiksammlung. Enjoying the warm summer breezes that drifted through open windows, I looked out at the Staatsoper: the ornate building that in 1869 replaced the Kärntnertortheater, where many of Salieri's operas were first performed. In the Musiksammlung I took advantage of a research tool that, in our computer-fixated age, is becoming increasingly rare and valuable: an elegantly prepared and painstakingly maintained card catalogue. I do not need to describe to scholars the delightful anticipation that I felt when, still panting from four flights of stairs, I beheld the beautifully bound manuscripts that I had ordered the day before now neatly stacked in front of me.

Houston
January 1998

ABBREVIATIONS

A-Wn Vienna, Nationalbibliothek, Musiksammlung

A-Wst Vienna, Stadtbibliothek

A-Wth Vienna, Bibliothek des Österreichischen Theatermuseums

Am *Analecta musicologica*

AmZ *Allgemeine musikalische Zeitung*

Angermüller, *Fatti* Rudolph Angermüller, *Antonio Salieri: Fatti e documenti* (Legnago, 1985)

Angermüller, *Leben* Rudolph Angermüller, *Antonio Salieri: Sein Leben und seine weltlichen Werke unter besonderer Berücksichtigung seiner "großen" Opern,* 3 vols. (Munich, 1971–74)

Badura-Skoda *Joseph Haydn: Bericht über den Internationalen Joseph Haydn Kongress, Wien, Hofburg, 5.–12. September 1982,* ed. Eva Badura-Skoda (Munich, 1986)

BmZ *Berlinische musikalische Zeitung*

COJ *Cambridge Opera Journal*

Convegno *Da Beaumarchais a Da Ponte: Convegno su Antonio Salieri, Verona, 9 Aprile 1994,* ed. Rudolph Angermüller and Elena Biggi Parodi (Turin, 1996)

D-Dlb Dresden, Sächsische Landesbibliothek

D-F Frankfurt am Main, Stadt- und Universitätsbibliothek

D-Mbs Munich, Bayerische Staatsbibliothek

D-Mth Munich, Theatermuseum

D-MHrm Mannheim, Reiss-Museum

Da Ponte Lorenzo da Ponte, *Memorie,* ed. Cesare Pagnini (Milan, 1960)

Della Croce/Blanchetti Vittorio Della Croce and Francesco Blanchetti, *Il caso Salieri* (Turin, 1994)

DTÖ *Denkmäler der Tonkunst in Österreich*

EM *Early Music*

F-Pn Paris, Bibliothèque Nationale

GB-Lcm London, Royal College of Music

Goldoni *Tutte le opere di Carlo Goldoni,* ed. Giuseppe Ortolani (Milan, 1935–56)

Gt *Gazzetta toscana*

Hadamowsky, *Hoftheater* Franz Hadamowsky, *Die Wiener Hoftheater (Staatstheater) 1776–1966,* 2 vols. (Vienna, 1966–75)

HHStA Vienna, Haus-, Hof-, und Staatsarchiv

GH Generalintendanz der Hoftheater

HKF Handarchiv Kaiser Franz

HMK Hofmusikkapelle

HP Handbilleten-Protokoll

OKäA Oberstkämmereramt

OMeA Obersthofmeisteramt

Sb Sammelbände

HKA Vienna, Hofkammerarchiv

I-Fc Florence, Conservatorio di Musica Luigi Cherubini

I-Rsc Rome, Conservatorio di Musica Santa Cecilia

JM *Journal of Musicology*

Joseph II *Joseph II. als Theaterdirektor: Ungedruckte Briefe und Aktenstücke aus den Kinderjahren des Burgtheaters,* ed. Rudolf Payer von Thurn (Vienna, 1920)

Khevenhüller *Aus der Zeit Maria Theresias: Tagebuch des Fürsten Johann Josef Khevenhüller-Metsch, Kaiserlichen Obersthofmeisters, 1742–1776,* 8 vols. (Vienna, 1907–72)

MBA *Mozart: Briefe und Aufzeichnungen,* ed. Wilhelm A. Bauer, Otto Erich Deutsch, and Joseph Heinz Eibl, 7 vols. (Kassel, 1962–75)

MDL *Mozart: Die Dokumente seines Lebens,* ed. Otto Erich Deutsch (Kassel, 1961)

Michtner Otto Michtner, *Das alte Burgtheater als Opernbühne von der Einführung des deutschen Singspiels (1778) bis zum Tod Kaiser Leopolds II. (1792)* (Vienna, 1970)

ML *Music and Letters*

MOL Budapest, Magyar Országos Levéltár (National Archives of Hungary)

Mosel Ignaz von Mosel, *Ueber das Leben und die Werke des Anton Salieri* (Vienna, 1827)

Muraro, *Mozart* *I vicini di Mozart,* ed. Maria Teresa Muraro and David Bryant, 2 vols. (Florence, 1989)

Muraro, *Venezia* *Venezia e il melodramma nel Settecento,* ed. Maria Teresa Muraro, 2 vols. (Florence, 1978–81)

NG *New Grove Dictionary of Music,* ed. Stanley Sadie, 20 vols. (London, 1980)

NGDO *New Grove Dictionary of Opera,* ed. Stanley Sadie, 4 vols. (London, 1992)

NMA *Neue Mozart Ausgabe* (Kassell, 1955–)

NOHM *New Oxford History of Music,* ed. J. A. Westrup et al., 10 vols. (London and Oxford, 1954–90)

PEM *Pipers Enzyklopädie des Musiktheaters,* ed. Carl Dahlhaus, Sieghart Döhring et al., 7 vols. (Munich, 1986–97)

RISM *Répertoire International des Sources Musicales,* Einzeldrucke vor 1800 (Kassel, 1971–)

Sadie *Wolfgang Amadé Mozart: Essays on His Life and Music,* ed. Stanley Sadie (Oxford, 1996)

Sartori Claudio Sartori, *I libretti italiani a stampa dalle origini al 1800: Catalogo analitico con 16 indici,* 7 vols. (Cuneo, 1990–94)

Swenson Edward Swenson, "Antonio Salieri: A Documentary Biography" (Ph.D. diss., Cornell University, 1974)

US-NYp New York, Public Library at Lincoln Center

US-Wc Washington, D.C., Library of Congress

WZ *Wiener Zeitung*

Zechmeister Gustav Zechmeister, *Die Wiener Theater nächst der Burg und nächst dem Kärntnerthor von 1747 bis 1776* (Vienna, 1971)

Zinzendorf The diary of Count Carl von Zinzendorf, manuscript in Vienna, Haus-, Hof- und Staatsarchiv

A NOTE ON THE TERMINOLOGY OF ITALIAN OPERATIC POETRY

Italian poetic theory categorizes a line of verse according to two interacting criteria: (1) the distance from the end of the line of the last accented syllable and (2) the number of syllables.

Lines in which the penultimate syllable is accented, *versi piani* (flat, plain verses), are by far the most common in operatic poetry. *Versi tronchi* (truncated verses) end with an accented syllable; the term suggests versi piani from which the last syllable has been cut off. In *versi sdruccioli* (steep, slippery verses) the antepenultimate syllable is accented.

In counting the numbers of syllables in a line, students of Italian poetry consider versi tronchi and versi sdruccioli as departures from the norm represented by versi piani. They assign the term *quinario* to a verso piano of five syllables:

Il mio padrone

(Adjacent vowels, as in "mio," are normally counted as one syllable.) But they also apply the term *quinario* to a verso tronco of four syllables (*quinario tronco*—the theoretical fifth syllable cut off):

Non voglio dir

And *quinario* is also used for a verso sdrucciolo of six syllables (a *quinario sdrucciolo*):

Sono una giovine

(This line contains an example of elision: when a word ending with a vowel is followed, in the same line, by a word beginning with a vowel, the vowels are normally considered a single syllable for the purposes of scansion.)

The most common kinds of lines in eighteenth-century opera are *quinari, senari, settenari, ottonari, decasillabi,* and *endecasillabi.* (*Novenari* are very rare.) I have generally left these terms untranslated. It is tempting to translate *quinari* as "five-syllable lines," *senari* as "six-syllable lines," and so forth; but to do so oversimplifies. Although the aria "Sono una giovine" in Goldoni's *La buona figliuola,* from which the lines quoted above were extracted, is in quinari throughout, it would be misleading—indeed incorrect—to say that it consists entirely of five-syllable lines.

KREUZER, GULDEN, AND DUCATS

In Austria during the second half of the eighteenth century most payments, prices, and salaries were expressed in terms of Gulden and Kreuzer.[1] The Kreuzer (normally abbreviated Kr. or xr.) was the smallest monetary unit in common use. A Gulden (abbreviated fl. or f.) was worth sixty Kreuzer.

Three gold coins known as ducats also circulated. During most of the second half of the century they differed very slightly from one another in value according to the purity of the gold with which they were made. Until September 1783 the official exchange rate fixed the ordinary ducat at 254 Kreuzer (4 Gulden, 14 Kreuzer), the imperial ducat at 256 Kreuzer, and the Kremnitz ducat at 258 Kreuzer.

At the royal-imperial court in Vienna salaries and gifts were frequently expressed in ducats, but both those who gave and those who received them rarely specified what kind were involved in any particular transaction. It was left to court accountants, who preferred to keep their records in Gulden and Kreuzer, to ascertain the type of ducats paid or to be paid before expressing their value in more practical terms. For example, in 1776 Emperor Joseph II granted Salieri a salary of 200 ducats from the theatrical administration. Financial records for that year, in Vienna's Haus-, Hof- und Staatsarchiv, tell us that Salieri received 853 Gulden and 20 Kreuzer, the equivalent of 200 imperial ducats.[2]

1. This note is based primarily on the very useful discussion of Austrian currency in Dexter Edge, "Mozart's Fee for *Così fan tutte*," *Journal of the Royal Musical Association* 116 (1991): 218–19.

2. Franz Hadamowsky, *Die Josefinische Theaterreform und das Spieljahr 1776/77 des Burgtheaters* (Vienna, 1978), 16, 105.

As inflation gradually lowered the value of Kreuzer, the value of ducats as expressed in Kreuzer increased. In 1786 Joseph II recognized the effects of inflation and simultaneously rationalized the relation between Kreuzer and ducat by decreeing that the imperial and Kremnitz ducats were equal in value and by fixing the rate of exchange at 270 Kreuzer (precisely four and a half Gulden) to the ducat.

INTRODUCTION

The last third of the eighteenth century saw extraordinary achievement and rapid change in Viennese opera. Comic opera in Italian, which had attracted almost no attention from Viennese composers before 1765 and was to attract just as little after 1800, dominated Vienna's court theaters for most of the period in between. Several talented composers and librettists produced works of great originality and solid craftsmanship, of dramatic power and musical beauty. In doing so they transformed the sound and character of opera in the Habsburg capital, causing one traveler to remark in 1785: "after having left Vienna, it is not an easy matter to be pleased with an opera."[1]

Our understanding of this achievement is based largely on our knowledge of two great composers, Gluck and Mozart. But Gluck wrote his last Viennese opera in 1770, and he wrote no opere buffe. The adult Mozart was active as a composer in Vienna for a single decade only, 1781–91. Study of their lives and works can provide us with only a fragmentary view of the evolution of Viennese opera during the crucial period of more than thirty years that separated Gluck's *Paride ed Elena* from Beethoven's *Fidelio.* Nor can our knowledge of the musical environment in which Gluck and Mozart worked help us understand the important changes that occurred in Viennese musical institutions during the 1770s and 1790s.

The life and works of Antonio Salieri offer us an opportunity to fill the gaps: to view the last third of the eighteenth century as a single, coherent period in the evolution of Viennese opera and operatic life. Salieri's career was more closely and consistently connected with Viennese opera than were those of his more celebrated and more gifted

1. James Dawkins, an English traveler, quoted in Jeremy Black, *The British Abroad: The Grand Tour in the Eighteenth Century* (New York, 1992), 256.

contemporaries, and over a longer period. He settled in Vienna in 1766, when he was sixteen years old; he remained, except for relatively short periods abroad, for the rest of his life. As protégé of Emperor Joseph II he enjoyed imperial patronage from his arrival in Vienna until Joseph's death in 1790; he continued to compose operas for the court theaters until the turn of the century. His operas and his career reflect changes in Viennese opera and musical life during the Classical Period more fully than do the operas and careers of Gluck and Mozart.

Salieri's operas, of which a few have been staged or recorded in recent years but most still lie silently on library shelves, are worthy of study and performance not only for what they tell us about their composer and Viennese opera but also as musical dramas of intrinsic value and interest: works that delighted and moved audiences in many parts of late-eighteenth- and early-nineteenth-century Europe. "I shed tears ten times; it was too strong for me," wrote the poet Heinrich von Gerstenberg after hearing *Armida* in Hamburg in 1776.[2] Of a performance of *Axur re d'Ormus* in Königsberg in 1795 the young E. T. A. Hoffmann wrote: "The music of this opera, as always with Salieri, is outstanding: its wealth of ideas and its perfection of declamation put it on the same level as Mozart's. My friend, if I could compose one such opera it would make my life a success!"[3] Not all of Salieri's operas drew reactions as enthusiastic as these, of course. Northern Germany was particularly susceptible to their charms; but many of them won applause in Paris, London, Prague, Warsaw, Lisbon, and Milan.

That these works are so little known today is surprising in light of the interest that many scholars and musicians have shown in the relations between Mozart's musical and theatrical language and the common practice of his time. Wye Jamison Allanbrook, in her pathbreaking study of *Le nozze di Figaro* and *Don Giovanni,* assumed the extramusical connotations of Mozart's rhythmic vocabulary to be part of the common musical language.[4] But by largely ignoring Mozart's operatic contemporaries she left readers wondering if the assumption was justified. Nor did she attempt to show how Mozart's handling of rhythmic conventions differed from that of other operatic composers.[5] Those who have studied the opere buffe of Mozart's contemporaries have until recently tended to focus their attention on music by Italian composers not resident in Vienna and to consider only superficially, or not at all, music written in Vienna, for the singers and the audience for whom Mozart wrote. Sabine Henze-Döhring, for example, con-

2. Gerstenberg to his wife Sophie, 15 April 1776, in *Briefe 1776–1782* (Hamburger Klopstock Ausgabe), ed. Helmut Riege, 3 vols. (Berlin, 1982), 1:383.

3. Hoffmann to Teodor Gottlieb von Hippel, in *Briefwechsel,* ed. Friedrich Schnapp, 3 vols. (Munich, 1967–69), 1:70.

4. Wye Jamison Allanbrook, *Rhythmic Gesture in Mozart: Le nozze di Figaro and Don Giovanni* (Chicago, 1983), 2.

5. Allanbrook referred to only one aria by Salieri (p. 52). Her more detailed discussion of an aria by Salieri's teacher Florian Gassmann (p. 27) mentions neither the date nor the title of the opera in which the aria appears.

sulted ten operas by Giovanni Paisiello and twelve by Niccolò Piccinni in tracing the "convergence of genres" that led to *Don Giovanni.* But she apparently examined not a single opera by Salieri, whose oeuvre includes several works in which this convergence could usefully be studied.[6] Michael F. Robinson, in a fine essay on the opera buffa tradition within which Mozart wrote *Le nozze di Figaro,* mentioned Salieri as the author of some of the most often performed Viennese operas of the 1780s but showed much more interest in the music of Pasquale Anfossi, Domenico Cimarosa, and Paisiello.[7]

The scholarly emphasis on Mozart's Italian contemporaries at the expense of those active in Vienna may reflect the influence of Hermann Abert. His pioneering investigation, in his great biography of Mozart, of the operatic culture from which Mozart's operas sprang is based almost entirely on the operas of Italian composers who rarely if ever worked in Vienna—Piccinni and Paisiello in particular—and he seems not to have distinguished between works performed often in Vienna and those never performed there. Composers active in Vienna, including Salieri, are almost entirely absent from Abert's very influential account.[8]

During the last fifteen years or so scholars and performers have become more interested in Mozart's Viennese contemporaries. Dissertations on the opera buffa finale during the 1780s, on the comic operas of Vicente Martín y Soler, and on the dramaturgy of Viennese opera buffa have been complemented musically by recordings of operas by Salieri, Martín, and Florian Gassmann. It has become increasingly obvious that the musical context of Mozart's operatic achievement was primarily Viennese: that the Italian operas most likely to help us understand Mozart's are those written for and first performed in Vienna.[9]

The history of Salieri scholarship begins shortly after the composer's death. Ignaz von Mosel, Viennese composer, librarian, and friend of Salieri during his last years, wrote the first substantial biography, *Ueber das Leben und die Werke des Anton Salieri.* Published in Vienna in 1827, Mosel's book is based partly on reminiscences recorded and collected by Salieri himself. The present location of Salieri's papers is unknown; they may have been destroyed or lost. (It does not bode well for their future reappearance that even Mosel referred to them in the past tense.) Their disappearance leaves

6. Sabine Henze-Döhring, *Opera seria, Opera buffa und Mozarts Don Giovanni: Zur Gattungskonvergenz in der italienischen Oper des 18. Jahrhunderts* (Laaber, 1986).

7. Michael F. Robinson, "Mozart and the Opera Buffa Tradition," in *W. A. Mozart: Le nozze di Figaro,* by Tim Carter (Cambridge, 1987), 11–32.

8. In addition to Piccinni and Paisiello, Hermann Abert, *W. A. Mozart,* 2 vols. (Leipzig, 1955–56), discusses Tommaso Traetta, Pietro Guglielmi, Anfossi, Domenico Fischietti, Baldassare Galuppi, and Gassmann, of whom only the last lived in Vienna for more than a few months. Abert's brief consideration of Gassmann (1:381–82) differs from his treatment of Italian composers in lacking musical examples.

9. An excellent collection of essays appeared too late for me to take account of its contents here: Mary Hunter and James Webster, eds., *Opera Buffa in Mozart's Vienna* (Cambridge, 1997), testifies to the wealth of new ideas about opera to which recent study of Mozart's contemporaries has given rise.

Mosel's biography as an indispensable primary source of information about Salieri and a foundation for all studies of his life and works, including this one.

Mosel supplemented Salieri's autobiographical materials with the composer's correspondence and with the scores of his operas, which he studied with more care and musical insight than most of Salieri's more recent biographers, but the book contains no musical examples.

Mosel's biography served as the basis for the first account of Salieri's life in English. During the early 1860s the great Beethoven scholar Alexander Wheelock Thayer published, in several installments, a long article on Salieri in *Dwight's Journal of Music.* It consists largely of excerpts of Mosel (sometimes labeled as such, sometimes not), into which Thayer wove some useful commentary and translations of documents. Thayer largely ignored Mosel's remarks about Salieri's music and made no attempt to study it himself.

The next hundred years revealed very little about Salieri's life and works that was not already known to Mosel. Two scholars did attempt brief surveys of the operas; but the vastness of Salieri's oeuvre—thirty-six operas performed during his life, three more left unperformed—largely doomed both surveys to superficiality.[10]

During the 1970s two scholars and a playwright laid the groundwork for the revival of interest in Salieri of which this book is a product. Working simultaneously but independently, Edward Swenson and Rudolph Angermüller wrote dissertations on Salieri that made available for the first time an immense quantity of information, both biographical and bibliographical. Peter Shaffer's *Amadeus* (1979) and the movie based on it (1984) brought Salieri and his rivalry with Mozart into the public eye by returning to themes first explored by Pushkin in his one-act play of 1830, *Mozart and Salieri.*

Several biographers have taken advantage of documentary material made accessible by Angermüller and Swenson and of curiosity piqued by Shaffer. Volkmar Braunbehrens has written a thoughtful life and works whose brevity, however, has not allowed him to discuss Salieri's operas in much detail. It contains no musical examples. Vittorio Della Croce and Francesco Blanchetti have subjected Salieri's scores to more sustained examination than anyone since Mosel; their musical biography contains a wealth of new insights. But their project of covering all of Salieri's musical output (not just the operas) necessarily forced them to leave many important points about the operas unmade. And the absence of musical examples leaves readers without a glimpse of what Salieri spent so much of his life doing: putting notes on paper.

The present book spins three threads. The first is biographical: a life of Salieri up to the end of his career as an opera composer in 1804 that relies as much as possible on archival and other primary sources. I have made frequent use of documents published

10. Andrea della Corte, *Un italiano all'estero: Antonio Salieri* (Turin, 1936); Werner Bollert, "Antonio Salieri und die italienische Oper," in *Aufsätze zur Musikgeschichte* (Bottrop, 1938), 43–93.

by Angermüller and Swenson but have also used many documents unknown to them, some published here for the first time. The second thread is institutional: a study of Viennese operatic organizations within which Salieri's career unfolded, and of the people who shaped them and who worked within them. The third is musico-dramatic: a study of a representative sample of Salieri's operas, amply illustrated with examples of his music. Woven together, these threads produce a biography that can also be read as a history of Viennese opera from the primacy of Gluck in the 1760s to the period in which the operas of Luigi Cherubini and Nicolas Dalayrac (in German translation) triumphed in Vienna, Beethoven wrote the first version of *Fidelio,* and Salieri, at the age of fifty-four, gave up the composition of opera.

Instead of attempting to cover in equal detail all of Salieri's operas, I have focused on works that were performed often or widely, that reveal significant aspects of the composer's creative personality, or that illustrate important developments in Viennese opera. The book mentions briefly or not at all works to which Salieri contributed only part of the music (such as *La moda,* a pasticcio of 1771, and the first version of *Il talismano,* of which he set act 1 only). It mentions but in most cases does not discuss in depth operas that did not reach performance during Salieri's life and operas that were performed rarely (in a few cases never) after their initial production (such as *L'amore innocente, Les Horaces,* and *Eraclito e Democrito*). Readers disoriented by these omissions may wish to turn occasionally to the chronological list of all of Salieri's operas at the end of the book.

Throughout his life Salieri guarded his autograph scores. Now in the Austrian National Library, these manuscripts constitute one of the largest and most complete collections of eighteenth-century operatic autographs. But they present dangers as well as opportunities to scholars and performers, because of the revisions they contain. Salieri considered his operas to be works in progress long after they were first performed, always subject to revision according to changing public taste, changing circumstances of performance (different singers, different orchestras, and so forth), and his own artistic development. In this attitude he was no different from many (probably most) eighteenth-century composers. Gluck, when he presented his Viennese operas *Orfeo ed Euridice* and *Alceste* in Paris, accepted revision as a necessary part of revival. So did Mozart when he presented *Idomeneo* and *Don Giovanni* in Vienna and revived *Figaro* three years after its first performance.

Salieri differed from some of his contemporaries, however, in the extent of his revisions. Mosel, in pointing out a change that Salieri made in *La grotta di Trofonio,* referred to his tendency to revise as something that distinguished him from other composers: "already then [1785] Salieri gave in to an inclination to change his best compositions after a certain time: an inclination that he took too far in later years."[11] Salieri often made

11. Mosel, 88–89.

revisions in his autographs, which rendered many of them unreliable records of the operas as they were first performed.

Revivals inspired and often required Salieri, like Gluck and Mozart, to revise. But one cannot safely assume that the autograph of an opera that was revived rarely or not at all will present the work as it was originally performed. *L'amore innocente,* a very early work of which only a few revivals are known to have taken place, is preserved in an autograph that, to judge by watermarks and writing style, contains several numbers copied out by Salieri many years after the first production.

Generally speaking, however, operas performed most widely, and over the longest time, are those that Salieri revised most heavily. The autographs of *Armida, La fiera di Venezia, La scuola de' gelosi,* and *Axur,* operas that made his name known throughout Europe, are full of alterations, cuts, and additions. To horns he added trumpets; to flutes and oboes he added clarinets. He replaced arias, shortened recitative, enriched textures, changed tempos, and changed or added instructions for dynamics. It is often impossible to tell from the autograph what is original and what is revision or to distinguish revisions made before the first performance from those made afterward.

Not all of Salieri's revisions were made with the intention of preparing operas for revivals. In 1822, after most of his operas had disappeared from the repertory, Salieri read through his collection of autographs. For his own satisfaction, and perhaps also with posterity in mind, he revised his operas yet again: "I am delighted to find in them more good than bad, and when I sometimes succeed in improving something that always displeased me and that I have earlier tried in vain to improve, nobody is happier than I am. It will be said that I am easily satisfied. But what I do is evidence of the passion of an artist for his art, without which passion one can never accomplish something good."[12]

An admirable sentiment, to be sure, but scholars and performers need to treat it as a warning. A conductor preparing a production of *La fiera di Venezia* (first performed in 1772) based on the autograph score needs to know that the performance may include "improvements" made by Salieri fifty years after the opera was first performed.

A study of Salieri's revisions, particularly as they reflect the evolution of musical style during his long career, would require extensive preparatory investigation of librettos, paper types, copyists, and the evolution of the composer's handwriting. Such a study would be extraordinarily interesting and useful, but for the purposes of this book I have focused my attention on what I have identified as an early version of each opera, following Salieri's artistic development as reflected in successive operas rather than in successive versions of a particular opera. I say "an early version" rather than "the original version" because in many cases it is impossible to know exactly the state of the operas as they were first performed. (The same, of course, can be said for most operas performed before the advent of recorded sound.)

12. Mosel, 199–200.

I have identified an early version of each opera with the help of the libretto for the first production, assuming that an early version of the score will correspond closely, if not exactly, to this libretto. (Identifying the libretto for the first production is itself not always an easy task; in the case of *Axur,* for example, two different versions of the opera are preserved in librettos with identical title pages bearing the year of the first performance.)[13] I have followed other clues as well, such as the note that Salieri left on the title page of a manuscript copy of *Armida* in which he informed prospective readers and performers that he could supply them with a score that was "corrected and improved."[14] The manuscript copy, presumably made from the autograph before Salieri "corrected and improved" it, represents a version of the opera earlier than the autograph's; and in such cases I have usually based my discussion primarily on copies. The list of Salieri's operas in the appendix mentions the sources—manuscripts, printed scores, and librettos—that I have consulted in the course of this study. My remarks about an opera pertain to the version transmitted in the source or sources cited there. A study of other sources will certainly lead, in some cases, to different conclusions.

It was probably in 1822, when he read through his operas, that Salieri made extensive annotations on the empty pages at the beginning and end of many of his autographs. Often written with a shaky hand, these didactic and often superficial remarks show an old artist-teacher looking back proudly, but also self-critically, at his life's work. I have quoted often from Salieri's annotations, which occasionally contain important information about the circumstances of composition and performance, the singers for whom he wrote, and the success or failure of individual numbers. But it must be kept in mind that Salieri wrote most if not all of these notes long after the operas to which they refer. They generally tell us more about the composer as an old man than about operas he wrote many years earlier.

Limitations of space have kept me from including as many texts in the original language as I would have liked. Excerpts from librettos are given in the original language and in English translation. In regard to other quotations from sources in languages other than English, I have adopted (with very few exceptions) the following policy. Where I quote from unpublished archival documents or from books or journals published during Salieri's life, the original is given in a footnote. Where I quote from a book, dissertation, or article published after 1825, I refer to the source in a footnote without quoting the text in the original language.

13. Bruno Brizi, "Da Ponte e Salieri: A proposito dell''Axur re d'Ormus,'" in *Omaggio a Gianfranco Folena,* 3 vols. (Padua, 1993), 2:1405–29.

14. A-Wn, Mus. Hs. 17837.

1

FROM VENICE TO VIENNA

Antonio Salieri served a single institution, the Viennese court, throughout his career. Vienna became his home, and he absorbed its musical language so completely that Empress Maria Theresa, only six years after his arrival and three years after the performance of his first opera, could not think of him as an Italian. She wrote her daughter-in-law Maria Beatrice in 1772: "For the theater, I confess that I prefer the least Italian to all our composers: Gassmann, Salieri, Gluck, and others. They can sometimes write one or two good pieces, but on the whole I always prefer the Italians."[1] Salieri had already become, for the Viennese, one of "our composers"; and so he remained. He won the friendship of leading musicians and the patronage of Emperor Joseph II, Maria Theresa's son; he married a Viennese; he climbed a career ladder within the court from an unpaid place in Joseph's private chamber ensemble to Vienna's most prestigious musical position, that of Hofkapellmeister; he retired and died in Vienna.

The popularity of Italian opera in many parts of eighteenth-century Europe led to the engagement of Italian composers and music directors by rulers and impresarios throughout the continent. But most of these musicians stayed only a few years before moving to another job or returning to Italy. Andrea Bernasconi's thirty-one years of service (1753–84) to the electors of Bavaria represented an exceptionally long engagement. At the other extreme, Antonio Tozzi stayed only about a year (1774–75) in Munich as opera composer and director; he was dismissed because of an affair with a married noblewoman. ("You may tell everyone the story of Tozi and Countess Seefeld, so that

1. Maria Theresa to Maria Beatrice, 12 November 1772, in *Briefe der Kaiserin Maria Theresia an ihre Kinder und Freunde,* ed. Alfred von Arneth, 4 vols. (Vienna, 1881), 3:149.

people will see that the Italians are rascals everywhere," gloated Leopold Mozart when he spread the news of Tozzi's dismissal to Salzburg.)[2] The Russian court in St. Petersburg, a thriving center of Italian opera that attracted the services of such great composers as Baldassare Galuppi, Tommaso Traetta, Giovanni Paisiello, and Giuseppe Sarti, discouraged them from settling in Russia by engaging most of them on three-year contracts. Although they could, and sometimes did, renew their contracts, only one of them (Sarti) stayed in Russia more than seven years.

Even if Catherine the Great did not share Leopold Mozart's opinion of Italians as rascals, she may have feared that if Italians stayed too long in Russia their music would lose the qualities that made it so distinctive and attractive. The idea that a prolonged stay in northern Europe could adversely affect an Italian's music led to criticism of more than one composer on his return to Italy. Niccolò Jommelli's friend and admirer Saverio Mattei defended his late Neapolitan operas (composed after sixteen years of service to the duke of Württemberg) against charges that the music was "harsh and of German inspiration."[3] When Paisiello returned from Russia in the mid 1780s, an Italian critic, writing of a production of *Le gare generose,* blamed what he considered unpleasant aspects of Paisiello's style on his seven years in Russia: "During his long sojourn in the northern countries of Europe, where harshness of climate cannot give birth in a composer's imagination to very cheerful ideas, he unfortunately developed a very strong inclination for minor keys, for unprepared dissonance and for forced and frequent changes of key. The novelty of this style transformed opere buffe into funerals, and finales into lugubrious psalmody and funeral chants."[4]

Only one of Salieri's operas—one of the few that he wrote for an Italian theater—received more than a few scattered productions in Italy: *La scuola de' gelosi.*[5] Italian audiences may have heard (or expected to hear) in his music the same "German inspiration" that supposedly marred the operas that Jommelli wrote on his return from Stuttgart, the same influence of northern climates that one listener thought he heard in *Le gare generose.* Italians would probably have agreed with Maria Theresa: Salieri's residence and training in Vienna made him Viennese, despite his place of birth.

That Salieri was an orphan may have helped him establish a strong position at the Habsburg court. Maria Theresa, in dissuading her son Archduke Ferdinand, governor of Lombardy, from giving Mozart a position at his court, saved her best argument for

2. Leopold Mozart to his wife, 1 March 1775, in *MBA,* 1:525.

3. Saverio Mattei, *Saggio di poesie latine, ed italiane* (Naples, 1774), 2:271; quoted in Marita McClymonds, *Niccolò Jommelli: The Last Years, 1769–1774* (Ann Arbor, Mich., 1980), 758.

4. Letter dated Padua, 18 August, and signed "M," *Gazzetta urbana veneta,* 1789, p. 533; quoted in John A. Rice, "Emperor and Impresario: Leopold II and the Transformation of Viennese Musical Theater, 1790–1792" (Ph.D. diss., University of California, Berkeley, 1987), 174.

5. Elena Biggi Parodi, "La fortuna della musica di Salieri in Italia ai tempi di Mozart," in *Convegno,* 41–71.

last: "Besides, he has a large family."[6] Mozart was fifteen at the time, only one year younger than Salieri had been when he arrived in Vienna. His family was not large, but close; potential employers had to consider that with Mozart came a strong-willed father, a mother, and a sister, two of them musicians who might themselves seek patronage in the future. Some of the Italian musicians who occupied positions in Germany and Russia were drawn back to Italy by members of their family. Jommelli left Stuttgart in 1769 to accompany his sick wife back to his native city of Aversa, near Naples, where he hoped the climate would be healthier for her; he ended up staying in Aversa himself. Salieri, born on 18 August 1750 in the town of Legnago, on the Venetian *terraferma,* left several brothers and sisters there; but he had no parents, wife or children to return to in Italy.[7]

"Antonio Salieri Veneziano"

Despite Vienna's fondness for Italian opera, during the second half of the eighteenth century almost all the leading court musicians were natives of Austria, Bohemia, or German-speaking territories nearby. Georg Reutter, Hofkapellmeister from 1769 to 1772, was born in Vienna; so were Joseph Bonno, Hofkapellmeister from 1774 to 1788, and Joseph Weigl, music director in the court theaters from 1791. Joseph Starzer, court composer from the 1750s, was Austrian. The Salzburg into which Mozart, court chamber composer from 1787 to 1791, was born, although not officially part of the Austrian monarchy, was politically and culturally close to Vienna. Florian Gassmann, Hofkapellmeister from 1772 to 1774, and Leopold Kozeluch, court chamber composer from 1792, were Bohemian. Gluck, who served the court in a variety of posts (including that of court composer from 1774 until his death in 1787), was born in Bavarian territory but spent much of his childhood in Bohemia. Salieri, Hofkapellmeister from 1788 but a leading figure in Viennese opera from the early 1770s, stood out among Viennese court musicians of the last thirty years of the eighteenth century as the only Italian in a position of leadership above that of concertmaster.

To understand Salieri's unique position in Vienna, we must remember that Legnago was in Venetian territory. Although not born in the city of Venice, Salieri considered himself a Venetian. He went to Venice, not Milan, Rome, or Naples, after his parents'

6. Maria Theresa to Ferdinand, 12 December 1771, in *Briefe der Kaiserin Maria Theresia,* 1:93; quoted in *MDL,* 124. Harrison James Wignall, "L'avversario imperiale di Mozart," *Nuova rivista musicale italiana* 28 (1994): 1–16, discusses the letter and reproduces it in facsimile.

7. Swenson, 24, and Angermüller, *Leben,* 3:1, quote a baptismal record stating that Salieri was born at "the 22d hour" (hora 22) of 18 August 1750. The late hour of Salieri's birth apparently led the composer to celebrate his birthday on 19 August, which is the date cited by Mosel.

death. "Antonio Salieri Veneziano": thus he identified himself on the librettos printed for the first productions of several of his operas.[8]

By the time Salieri came to Vienna in 1766, special cultural relations had long linked his native land to his new home. Several important Venetian composers had served Habsburg emperors during the late seventeenth century and the first half of the eighteenth, including Marc'Antonio Ziani, Kapellmeister under Leopold I and Charles VI, and Antonio Caldara, who spent the last twenty-three years of his life at the Habsburg court as Vice-Kapellmeister under Johann Joseph Fux. Venetian librettists—Apostolo Zeno, Lorenzo da Ponte, Caterino Mazzolà, and Giovanni Bertati—found employment in Vienna.

Several of the Italian singers engaged in Vienna had sung in Venice immediately before traveling north across the Alps. Venice served on more than one occasion as a convenient place for Viennese theater directors to recruit singers, whose subsequent performances often represented a transfer of Venetian musical culture to Vienna. Such was the case when bass Baldassare Marchetti and soprano Caterina Consiglio joined the Viennese opera buffa troupe during spring 1775. Having created leading roles in Paisiello's *La frascatana* in Venice the previous fall, they made their Viennese debuts in the same opera, which became one of the two operas most often performed in Vienna during the rest of 1775.[9]

Another sign of cultural ties between the two cities was the extraordinary popularity in Vienna of the plays and librettos of the Venetian Carlo Goldoni.[10] Between 1750 and 1780 various German troupes presented no fewer than thirty-four productions of translations or adaptations of Goldoni's spoken plays. Martín y Soler's setting of Da Ponte's libretto *Il burbero di buon cuore* (1786), based on Goldoni's play *Le Bourru bienfaisant,* was one of the last in a series of Viennese comic operas derived from Goldoni's librettos and plays, to which Mozart (*La finta semplice,* 1768), Gassmann, and Salieri also contributed.

Operatic connections between Vienna and Venice had to do partly with geography: Venice was the Italian operatic center closest to Vienna (significantly closer than Milan or Florence, both of which had much stronger political connections to Vienna). Count Giacomo Durazzo, who had supervised Viennese opera during the late 1750s and early 1760s, served as Austrian ambassador to Venice during much of Salieri's career. As an informal agent for the Viennese court opera he played a crucial role in the formation of

8. Including *La partenza inaspettata, La dama pastorella,* and *Il ricco d'un giorno.*

9. On the Viennese debuts of Marchetti and Consiglio see Khevenhüller, 8:75. *La frascatana* was performed forty times in Vienna before the end of Carnival 1776 (*Geschichte und Tagbuch der Wiener Schaubühne,* ed. Johann Heinrich Friedrich Müller [Vienna, 1776]; and MOL, Keglevich Cs., V/16, 17, 21).

10. This paragraph is based on data in Zechmeister and Hadamowsky, *Hoftheater.*

Joseph II's opera buffa troupe in 1783, engaging in Venice several of the troupe's most important singers.[11]

A Venetian composer at a court steeped in tradition and respect for precedent, Salieri represented the continuation or reestablishment of a succession of Venetian musicians who had devoted much of their careers to the cultivation of Italian opera at the Habsburg court. Just as Francis II's abdication of the throne of the Holy Roman Empire in 1806 brought to a close a great era in the history of the Habsburg dynasty, so Salieri's death nineteen years later marked the end of a dynasty of Venetian musicians that had served the Habsburgs since the seventeenth century.

Childhood

Legnago lies on the Adige River some eighty-five kilometers southwest of Venice, almost equidistant (about forty kilometers) from Mantua to the west, Verona to the northwest, and Vicenza to the northeast. In the midst of flat, rich agricultural country, Legnago enjoyed some prominence in the eighteenth century as a center of grain trading. Salieri's father, also named Antonio, was a prosperous merchant. Young Antonio grew up in a middle-class home with several brothers, sisters, and half siblings (his father's two children from a previous marriage). Showing early signs of musical talent, he received training in violin from his older brother Francesco, who was a student of the great Paduan violinist Giuseppe Tartini (whether this Francesco was Antonio's half brother Francesco, born in 1737, or his full brother Francesco, born in 1741, is unknown). Giuseppe Simoni, organist in the Cathedral of Legnago and a student of Padre Martini, taught Antonio keyboard.[12]

Mosel's short account of Salieri's childhood mentions sacred rather than operatic music. Legnago was one of the smallest Italian towns to have its own public theater, but operas were rarely performed there.[13] As in most small Italian towns the church provided Legnago with its main access to elaborate music, including violin concertos, a common feature of church services in eighteenth-century Italy. In his autobiography the Viennese violinist and composer Carl Ditters von Dittersdorf recalled the performance by him and other violinists of concertos in church during his visit to Bologna in 1763. Dittersdorf played concertos during both mass and vespers.[14]

11. Michael Kelly, *Reminiscences*, ed. Roger Fiske (London, 1975), 97.

12. Mosel, 13–14, and Swenson, 20–21, which includes the names and dates of birth of one half brother, one half sister, eight brothers, and one sister.

13. Swenson, 19. Sartori (Indici, 1:70) lists only seven librettos recording performances in Legnago, all comic operas performed between 1763 and 1786.

14. Carl Ditters von Dittersdorf, *Lebensbeschreibung seinem Sohne in die Feder diktiert*, ed. Norbert Miller (Munich, 1967), 115–22.

Mosel tells us that Francesco Salieri, Antonio's older brother (or half brother), often played concertos at church festivals in and around Legnago. Antonio, "who from infancy was passionately fond of music," came along with Francesco whenever there was a place for him in the carriage. But on one occasion the carriage was full, and that led to trouble in the Salieri household when Antonio, expressly forbidden to go off on his own to such festivals without telling his parents, disobeyed his father.[15]

Another anecdote recorded by Mosel shows a side of young Salieri's musical personality that would be characteristic of the man: a preoccupation with musical genre and the style appropriate to particular genres. Perhaps one can sense here too a pedantic streak and a tendency to oversimplification, both of which would serve him well later in life in his important work as teacher of singers and composers:

> While walking with his father he met a monk who was the organist of his monastery. Young Salieri often visited this monastery's church, especially when high mass or vespers were celebrated with music, and he heard how, "as was then the almost universal practice in Italy," the monk improvised in a playful style, unworthy of the sacred place. Salieri's father greeted the holy man and conversed with him a short time; the boy greeted him too, but with a kind of reluctance and with such coldness that it struck his father even more than it had on previous occasions. When the conversation was over and Antonio and his father were alone again, his father asked him why he did not greet the monk with more respect. He answered: "I wanted to greet him properly, but I don't like him because he is a bad organist." Laughing, Salieri's father answered: "How can you, a boy, judge in such matters, you who have just begun to study music?" But the boy answered proudly: "It is true, I am still a beginner, but if I were in his place I think I would play the organ with more solemnity." [16]

Salieri's point of view was far from original. To accuse church music of sounding too secular, too operatic, was a commonplace of eighteenth-century musical criticism. Dittersdorf, in Bologna in 1763, criticized a setting of vespers on exactly the same grounds.[17] In the boy who censured a monk for not playing the organ with enough solemnity we can recognize the old man at the first Viennese performance of Rossini's *Tancredi* in 1816 who insisted, after hearing the cheerful overture, that the opera must be comic, not serious.[18]

Salieri's comfortable childhood came to an end suddenly with his mother's death in 1763 and, shortly thereafter, his father's. After living briefly with an older brother in Padua, he was taken in by the Venetian nobleman Giovanni Mocenigo, a friend of his father, who brought him to Venice early in 1766. Mocenigo arranged for further musi-

15. Mosel, 14–17. 16. Mosel, 17–18.

17. Dittersdorf, *Lebensbeschreibung*, 115–16.

18. *Flora: Ein Unterhaltungsblatt* 8 (1828): 540, quoted in Angermüller, *Leben*, 3:225.

cal instruction for his sixteen-year-old ward, with the intention of sending him eventually to one of the conservatories of Naples. Giovanni Battista Pescetti, second organist at San Marco and a well-known composer of operas, gave Salieri lessons in figured bass (that is, the rudiments of composition). Pescetti could not have instructed him for long, however; he died on 20 March 1766. Ferdinando Pasini (also known as Pacini), a tenor at San Marco and singer in serious opera who had lodgings in Mocenigo's palace, taught him singing.

Gassmann at the Ascension Fair

In the events that brought Salieri from Venice to Vienna we find an illustration of the operatic connections between the two cities. Shortly after his arrival in Venice Salieri met Florian Gassmann. The encounter, one of the most important events of Salieri's life, took place during the annual fair with which Venice celebrated the Feast of the Ascension.

Born in Brüx (now Most), Bohemia, in 1729, Gassmann ran away from home when he was about twelve years old to devote his life to music. He found generous patronage in Venice, where he received musical training and where his first opera, *Merope,* was performed during Carnival 1757. During the next five years he wrote at least five more operas, both serious and comic. These must have earned him a fine reputation, because in 1763 he was called to Vienna to succeed Gluck as composer and conductor in the court theaters. He directed a Burgtheater performance from the keyboard for the first time on 10 April 1763[19] and presented his first Viennese opera, *L'Olimpiade,* the following year.

The death of Emperor Francis in August 1765 occasioned a long period of mourning, and Vienna's court theaters were closed. During the closure the responsibility of running the theaters was assumed by an impresario who transformed the repertory into one in which, for the first time, opera buffa predominated. Remembering these events fifty years later, Salieri placed Gassmann's trip to Italy in the context of this repertorial shift: "In the first months of the year 1766 Maestro Gassmann, who had been appointed chamber composer and music director of the theaters of Vienna in 1764, was instructed by the theatrical administration [probably the impresario Franz Hilverding] to go to Italy to form an Italian opera company, which subsequently ['after the period of mourning that followed the death of Emperor Francesco I,' explained Salieri], in the course of the same year, began its performances in this city."[20] Three years after leaving Venice for Vienna Gassmann returned to the city where his career had begun, and where he

19. Bruce Alan Brown, *Gluck and the French Theatre in Vienna* (Oxford, 1991), 91.

20. Salieri to Count Ferdinand Kueffstein, 20 May 1816, in Angermüller, *Leben,* 3:162–63, and Angermüller, *Fatti,* 185–86.

FIGURE 1.1 Canaletto, *The Bacino di S. Marco on Ascension Day.* (Courtesy of The Royal Collection, Her Majesty Queen Elizabeth II.)

now won a commission from the venerable Teatro di S. Giovanni Grisostomo to make a new setting of Pietro Metastasio's *Achille in Sciro* for the forthcoming Ascension fair.

On Ascension Day, a great religious and civic holiday, the doge renewed Venice's wedding to the sea by throwing a ring into the water from his gorgeously decorated galley, the Bucintoro. Merchants set up market stalls in the Piazzetta in front of the Doge's Palace. The Bucintoro and the market can be seen in Canaletto's view of the Piazzetta during the Ascension fair (fig. 1.1). Evenings were devoted to revelry: two carnivalesque weeks of balls, masks, and theater. Salieri would later make the Ascension fair the backdrop of one of his most popular Viennese operas, *La fiera di Venezia.*

From the libretto published for the production of Gassmann's *Achille in Sciro* we learn that the relatively minor role of Licomede was sung by none other than Pasini, young Salieri's singing teacher and fellow resident in Mocenigo's palace. Pasini introduced his student to Gassmann, and Salieri gave him a demonstration of his skills at the keyboard and in singing. Gassmann must have found the sixteen-year-old a talented and attractive youth. Perhaps too he noticed the similarity between Salieri's situation as an orphan in Venice looking forward to a career in music and his own condition when he first arrived in Venice, alone and helpless, and even younger than Salieri.[21] Doubtless aware of the recent death of Salieri's composition teacher Pescetti, Gassmann asked for and received permission from Mocenigo to take him as his student and apprentice.

21. Swenson, 29.

Instead of going south to Naples for musical training, Salieri went north to Vienna, making the same trip that Gassmann had made three years earlier.

Musical Education under Gassmann

Gassmann, a thirty-seven-year-old bachelor, all but adopted Salieri, who within a few days of their arrival in Vienna was to describe Gassmann as his father. Salieri was not the only young musician to benefit from relations with an older Viennese composer close enough for the younger man to think of his mentor as a surrogate father. Dittersdorf tells us that during the early 1760s Gluck (married but childless) "loved me as his own son."[22] Salieri would later consider himself a second father to the young Joseph Weigl. Gassmann's "adoption" of Salieri exemplifies a practice according to which Viennese composers acted as fatherly mentors to young musicians (a practice from which the young Mozart, closely bound to his real father, could not benefit).

Salieri arrived in Vienna on 15 June 1766. His first memory of the city where he would spend most of the rest of his life was of being taken by Gassmann to the Italian church:

> Here I cannot pass over an event always present in my grateful memory. The day after my arrival in the capital, my teacher took me into the Italian church so that I might offer my devotions. As we were going home he said to me, "I thought that I should begin your musical education with God. Now it will depend on you whether its outcome will be good or bad; I shall in any case have done my duty." Such men are rare! I promised him eternal gratitude for all the good he should do me, and—praise be to God!—I can boast that I honestly proved myself grateful to him as long as he lived and, after his death, to his family.

"A truth which all Vienna can confirm," added Mosel, "and which, no less than his exceptional talent, won him universal respect."[23] And yet Salieri did not let his gratitude keep him from associating himself with a name more celebrated than Gassmann's. After his teacher's death he called himself Gluck's pupil when it was to his advantage to do so.

As an old man Salieri remembered with pleasure the first residence he shared with Gassmann: "an old house by the so-called Wasserkunstbastey, before whose windows lay a marvelous view of the widespread suburbs."[24] Gassmann married in 1768, but his student continued to live with him. A financial document of 1772 records the residence of both Gassmann and Salieri (still described as Gassmann's student) as "Im neuen Häusel an der Bürger Spittal Kirche."[25]

22. Dittersdorf, *Lebensbeschreibung,* 107.

23. Mosel, 20. 24. Mosel, 199.

25. HKA, Hofzahlamtsbuch no. 378, fol. 12. The Bürgerspittal-Kirche was located, very conveniently for Gassmann and Salieri, next to the Kärntnertortheater.

Almost immediately after Salieri arrived in Vienna he began intensive studies designed and supervised by Gassmann. An Italian priest led him through the intricacies of Latin and Italian poetry. With another teacher he studied German and French. A musician described by Mosel only as "a young Bohemian" gave Salieri lessons in continuo realization, score reading, and violin. Gassmann himself, a Bohemian educated in Italy, instructed him in counterpoint, basing his lessons on Fux's *Gradus ad Parnassum*. Salieri's musical education represented a synthesis of Italian, Bohemian, and Viennese traditions similar to the ingredients of Gassmann's own education.

The *Gradus* served as the basis for the counterpoint studies of Haydn, Beethoven, and countless other composers of the classical period.[26] The respect that musicians felt for Fux's treatise (perhaps especially in Vienna) can be sensed in the recollections of the aged Haydn, who "kept a hard-used copy." Haydn's early biographer Georg August Griesinger recounted the composer's youthful struggles to master Fuxian counterpoint: "With tireless exertion Haydn sought to comprehend Fux's theory. He worked his way through the whole method, did the exercises, put them by for several weeks, then looked them over again and polished them until he thought he had got them right. 'I did, of course, have talent. With that and with great diligence I progressed.'"[27]

Much the same attitude toward Fux's treatise is expressed in a conversation reported by Dittersdorf. The court composer Bonno, having agreed to teach the young violinist counterpoint, showed him a copy of *Gradus,* which "is written in Latin, and consists throughout of dialogues between teacher and pupils. . . . Bonno . . . said: 'I assume you understand Latin?' I turned a page or two and read through a couple of passages here and there, and answered: 'That is such kitchen-Latin that any schoolboy in second grade could understand it!' 'Oh indeed!' he replied, in his usual schoolmaster's tone. 'We don't want elegant Latinity here, but good sound theory—and that the book contains.' Of course he was right."[28]

Salieri seems to have known less Latin than Dittersdorf. In an effort to ensure that the various parts of his education reinforced one another (and showing no more concern for the quality of Fux's Latin than Bonno), Gassmann required that part of each Latin lesson be devoted to translation of a passage from the *Gradus.*

In 1768 Salieri took over some of the operatic work that Gassmann would normally have done. He became less a pupil and more an apprentice, developing a knowledge of musical theater by composing replacement arias for operas to be performed under Gassmann's supervision and directing rehearsals and performances from the keyboard.

26. There seems to be no direct evidence that Mozart studied Fux's book, but he made use of it in teaching Thomas Attwood. See Alfred Mann, "Johann Joseph Fux's Theoretical Writings: A Classical Legacy," in *Johann Joseph Fux and the Music of the Austro-Italian Baroque,* ed. Harry White (Aldershot, 1992), 63.

27. Georg August Griesinger, *Biographische Notizien über Joseph Haydn,* ed. Franz Grasberger (Vienna, 1954), 10; translation (used here) by Vernon Gotwals, *Haydn: Two Contemporary Portraits* (Madison, 1968), 10.

28. Dittersdorf, *Lebensbeschreibung,* 85.

He also composed much church music (a *Missa a stylo a cappella,* the autograph score of which is dated 12 August 1767, a *Tantum ergo* dated 1768, a *Salve regina,* and several graduals and offertories) and instrumental music (Mosel mentions six string quartets, two symphonies, and several pieces for wind instruments).[29]

Salieri's later activities as teacher and mentor of promising young musicians had roots in the education and fatherly support that Gassmann gave him. He made explicit the connection between his own education and his teaching of others when he agreed, around 1783, to take Joseph Weigl as a student. When Weigl's father (Haydn's principal cellist at Eszterháza before becoming a member of the Burgtheater orchestra) asked Salieri for advice about his son's musical training, he offered to take charge of it himself: "Since you were the best friend of my teacher Gassmann, I will repay through your son what I owe to my teacher; I will be his second father."[30] He took his fatherly role seriously, signing a letter to Weigl, in which he congratulated his former student on the success of a new opera, "Most affectionate Papa Salieri."[31] Weigl was not alone in bringing out Salieri's paternal instincts. One of his later students, Anselm Hüttenbrenner, called him "Papa," and Salieri, in return, called Hüttenbrenner "the young Salieri": striking evidence of how closely he identified the roles of teacher and father.[32]

Weigl's account of Salieri's pedagogical methods suggests that they largely duplicated those of Gassmann. Like Salieri, Weigl underwent an apprenticeship in the court theaters, writing replacement arias and directing rehearsals and performances. Weigl's description, more detailed than Mosel's account of Salieri's own education, can thus help us understand what Salieri himself learned from Gassmann:

> Now I put my mind on my studies and, under the excellent guidance of my teacher, concentrated entirely on composition. Every day at nine in the morning he gave me a lesson in theater craft, musical declamation, and score reading. He took me to all rehearsals and performances, and in a short time I had to accompany rehearsals at the keyboard. At every evening performance I watched his every movement, and during the summertime, when audiences in the theater were small, he began to let me sit at the keyboard during the second and third acts. . . .
>
> After I had written several individual arias, duets, concerted pieces [i.e., ensembles], etc., owing to my diligence under Salieri's guidance (for I did not resent composing a piece of music five or six times, until my teacher was satisfied), he gave me a libretto, *La sposa collerica,* to set to music. In a short time I was finished with it. At that time I thought that if every page of the score was full of notes, then the composition must be excellent, because I always had

29. Mosel, 29.

30. "Zwei Selbstbiographien von Joseph Weigl (1766–1846)," ed. Rudolph Angermüller, *Deutsches Jahrbuch der Musikwissenschaft* 16 (1971): 53.

31. For the letter, dated 1820 in an unknown hand, see Angermüller, *Leben,* 3:191.

32. Anselm Hüttenbrenner to Ferdinand Luib, 7 March 1858, in "Anselm Hüttenbrenners Erinnerungen an Schubert," ed. Otto Erich Deutsch, *Jahrbuch der Grillparzer-Gesellschaft* 16 (1906): 142–43.

> Mozart's excellent instrumentation in my head, but I did not have the wisdom to decide where full instrumentation belonged, where one must consider the singer, where one can play around with instrumentation, and so forth. The score of my *Sposa collerica* was thus completely black with notes, and I was very happy with it and could not wait for the moment of performance.
>
> But Salieri was of a better opinion. So as not to discourage me, he did not reject my work, but made me understand that it would be better if I wrote pieces for various operas that were scheduled to be performed, in which musical numbers were either lacking or unsuited to the voice of the singers. Thereby I would learn how one must write for the voices of various singers and at the same time become familiar with the effects of instrumentation. Since I unconditionally submitted to my teacher's will in every respect, I composed a great quantity of such arias, duets, etc., according to need, and I learned to recognize what the singer is in a position to do, how declamatory singing should be handled, where the instrumentation can be powerful, where the vocal part should be delicately accompanied, where the expression should be intensified, and so forth.[33]

Mosel mentioned an opera composed by Salieri in 1768, *La vestale:* "a little Italian opera for four voices and chorus"[34] that has apparently not survived, and of which nothing further is known. It does not seem to have been publicly performed. Gassmann probably assigned the composition of *La vestale* to Salieri as an exercise, just as Salieri, about two decades later, assigned Weigl the composition of *La sposa collerica,* another student opera that does not seem to have survived and of which we have no record of a performance. But Salieri, like Weigl, did not have to wait long to see his operas staged in the court theaters.

Metastasio and Gluck

Gassmann supplemented Salieri's education and at the same time helped him establish a reputable place in Viennese society by introducing him to some of Vienna's most distinguished theatrical artists. Salieri came to know Metastasio by participating in the poet's regular Sunday-morning salons; he later became a more frequent visitor, taking part in musical entertainments of the Martinez family, with whom Metastasio lived. He was thus exposed to a musical and literary milieu that had contributed much to the artistic development of Haydn, who lived during the early 1750s in a garret above the Martinez apartment and taught music to the talented young daughter of the house, Marianne von Martinez.

The great poet of *dramma per musica* befriended Salieri, according to Mosel: "When

33. Weigl, "Selbstbiographien," 54. *La sposa collerica* may have been the libretto of the same title set by Piccinni for the Roman Carnival of 1773 (Sartori no. 2241).

34. Mosel, 29.

they were alone, Metastasio often had him read whole scenes from his operas and oratorios, 'which,' says Salieri, 'served me as an extremely useful school of declamation, a school that (in Metastasio's opinion) was absolutely necessary to anyone who wanted to become a composer of vocal music.' "[35] The young musician benefited much from these readings: "It is clear that Salieri did not neglect this important aspect of a composer's education, and one of the finest features of his vocal works is their perfectly correct and highly energetic declamation, which every attentive reader or listener must notice with delight."[36] About forty-five years later the setting of Metastasio's verse was to occupy an important place in Schubert's studies with Salieri.

It says something noteworthy about Salieri's ability to get along with important and influential people that he developed this friendship with Metastasio, of whom Charles Burney, in Vienna in 1772, wrote: "he is very difficult of access, and equally averse to new persons, and new things."[37] Even more remarkable, Salieri managed to maintain good relations with Metastasio while developing ties to a musician—Gluck—whose conception of opera was becoming radically different from and indeed incompatible with Metastasio's. "Party runs high among poets, musicians, and their adherents, at Vienna as elsewhere," wrote Burney. "Metastasio and Hasse, may be said, to be at the head of one of the principal sects; and Calsabigi and Gluck of another." Young Salieri succeeded in being a member of both sects.

Writing in 1809, Salieri boasted of close relations with Gluck from shortly after his arrival in Vienna until the older composer's death more than twenty years later: "Thanks to favorable circumstances, I not only knew Gluck but enjoyed his trust and his hospitality from 1766 (my sixteenth year) to his death in November 1787."[38] On the title page of the score of Salieri's first French opera, *Les Danaïdes*, first performed as the product of collaboration between Gluck and Salieri, he identified himself as Gluck's pupil; but that he received any formal or systematic teaching from Gluck is unlikely.

Joseph's Chamber Group

By assigning to Salieri the composition of replacement arias and the direction of rehearsals and performances, Gassmann gave his student an important role within the court's musical establishment. He strengthened Salieri's position by seeing to it that the young musician was paid for his work. From 1772 (and perhaps earlier, but a lack of surviving financial records from the years 1766–72 leaves us with no way of knowing) Salieri received an annual salary of 480 Gulden from the theatrical management.[39] The salary

35. Mosel, 26. 36. Mosel, 26.

37. Charles Burney, *The Present State of Music in Germany, the Netherlands, and United Provinces*, ed. Percy A. Scholes (London, 1959), 80.

38. Letter by Salieri published in *AmZ* 12 (1809–10): cols. 196–98; quoted in Swenson, 31.

39. MOL, Keglevich Cs., V/18, fol. 611.

meant that he was no longer merely Gassmann's apprentice but a professional composer in his own right; the document recording the payment refers to him as "compositeur." Salieri later helped Weigl obtain a similar position.[40]

Gassmann also found his pupil a place at court. Within days of their arrival in Vienna in June 1766, Gassmann introduced Salieri to Emperor Joseph II, who was to be his most important patron during the next twenty-five years.

Few rulers have exercised more control over the production of opera in their capitals than Joseph; few have contributed to the creation of more operatic masterpieces. He ruled the Habsburg monarchy from 1765 to 1790, sharing the throne with his mother Maria Theresa until her death in 1780 and thereafter reigning alone. During the first decade of the coregency he had little to do with the management of the court theaters, leased out from 1766 to 1776 to a succession of impresarios who kept him at arm's length. The emperor made his most important contributions to Viennese opera during the late 1770s and the 1780s, with his founding of a Singspiel company in 1778 and an opera buffa company in 1783. Of concern here are his musical activities other than those of operatic manager, which brought Salieri into frequent contact with him and contributed much to Salieri's early success on the operatic stage.

Joseph belonged to a long line of musical rulers: generous patrons who themselves played, sang, or composed. Emperor Leopold I, his great-grandfather, played several instruments and composed much vocal music. Joseph's grandfather Charles VI played the keyboard with skill and wrote a considerable amount of keyboard music. Charles saw to it that his daughter Maria Theresa received training in music (with instruction from Johann Adolf Hasse and Georg Christoph Wagenseil she became a fine singer); she in turn provided for the musical education of her own numerous children. Joseph became a cellist and keyboard player; his brother Leopold played keyboard, as did his sister Marie Antoinette and many of his other siblings.

One of the ways in which Joseph expressed interest in music was his participation in performances several times a week, whenever he was in Vienna, with a small group of court musicians. A report published shortly after his death discusses in some detail these private concerts, the musicians who took part in them, and their repertory. It depicts the emperor as an enthusiastic and well-practiced musician.

> If one person in our imperial capital was a connoisseur of music, if one person prized and loved it, that person was he. Every afternoon he enjoyed the pleasure of performing a little concert with three of his chamber musicians and his valet, [Johann Kilian] Strack, who possessed the full confidence of our immortal monarch, and was also a musician. . . . The first violinist in this private concert of the emperor was Herr [Franz] Kreibich. . . . Strack . . . played the cello and was also entrusted with the music library.

40. Weigl, "Selbstbiographien," 54–55; Dexter Edge, "Mozart's Viennese Orchestras," *EM* 20 (1992): 76.

Among other members of the group were the violinists Thomas Woborzill, Johann Baptist Hoffmann, and Heinrich Bonnheimer (all members of the Burgtheater orchestra), the violist and composer Ignaz Umlauf, and the organist, singer, and composer Joseph Krottendorfer.

> All these gentlemen assembled only in extraordinary cases. Usually there were only three of them, with Strack and Joseph. The latter sometimes played the *Klavier,* sometimes the cello, and he often took a vocal part as well. Very seldom were quartets played and when they were, only those recommended by Kreibich or Strack as palatable dishes. . . . The emperor was fond of the pathetic and sometimes had music by Gassmann, Ordonez, and so forth performed. But generally excerpts from serious operas and oratorios were played from the score. Joseph had the fault of greatly enjoying it when the performance fell apart; and the more Kreibich strained and overworked himself and grew angry, the more heartily Joseph laughed. This imperial private concert therefore often had a double object: artistic enjoyment and congenial fun.
>
> This private concert took place daily in the emperor's room. It generally began after dinner and lasted until theater time. If public business interfered, it began later but lasted so much the longer, especially when nothing of interest was given in the theater. Strack was always part of the group, but the other chamber musicians took turns: three one day, three the next.[41]

Mosel gives us a few more details about Joseph's musical abilities—especially his versatility—and the performances in which he took part, contradicting the earlier account only in saying that the group met three times a week rather than every afternoon: "Joseph II had a very deep knowledge of music, and could read at sight both vocal and instrumental music with great skill. At these chamber concerts, which took place three times a week, lasted about an hour, and to which no listeners were invited, he normally played either the cello or the viola; or he accompanied at the keyboard from the score, and at the same time sang a tenor or bass part; and he pointed out with real expertise the good passages in a composition and those that deserved criticism."[42]

Joseph's music making was important for Salieri's career because it provided him with access to court patronage. It was during a chamber-music session that Salieri, soon after his arrival in Vienna, was first presented to the emperor. Gassmann, as Joseph's chamber composer, took part in the concerts, contributing not only compositions

41. "Auszug eines Schreibens aus Wien vom 5ten Jul. 1790," in *Musikalische Korrespondenz der teutschen Filarmonischen Gesellschaft,* 28 July 1790, cols. 27–31; in Angermüller, *Leben,* 3:55–58. Throughout the book I have generally left untranslated the words *Klavier, Spinett,* and *cembalo* because they were used freely in the eighteenth and early nineteenth centuries to mean both harpsichord and piano.

42. Mosel, 71–72. Joseph had a good bass voice, according to Dittersdorf, *Lebensbeschreibung,* 230.

but also his skills as a performer.[43] Especially warm relations linked the emperor and Gassmann, who was "loved and treasured by his monarch," according to Mosel.[44] This helps explain the warmth with which Joseph welcomed and befriended Gassmann's young Venetian pupil. Mosel presumably based his account of the occasion on Salieri's reminiscences:

> the monarch received him most graciously and addressed him in his own kind way: "Ah, good day! How do you like Vienna?" Salieri, frightened, embarrassed, and accustomed from his stay in Venice to address men of rank with the title of Excellency, replied: "Well, Your Excellency!" But correcting himself quickly, he added: "Exceptionally well, Your Majesty!" Some of the musicians of the court ensemble who were present laughed at the youth's embarrassment and simplicity. The emperor, in contrast, asked with graciousness about his homeland, his parents, and so forth; and Salieri answered him with growing self-possession, without embarrassing himself further. He even used the opportunity to express his gratitude to his teacher, who was present, and whom he described as his father and benefactor. Now the emperor wanted to hear the young music student sing and play something from memory, in which he succeeded in winning the monarch's applause.
>
> The regular chamber concert now began; it consisted of vocal pieces from the opera *Alcide al bivio* by Kapellmeister Hasse. Since Salieri sang with security and ease from the score, and at sight, not only the alto part in the choruses but also some solo passages, his teacher was commanded always to bring Salieri with him to these musical entertainments; and so began Salieri's service to the imperial court, service that would subsequently never be interrupted.[45]

In Hasse's richly scored *festa teatrale,* first performed in 1760 in celebration of Joseph's marriage to Isabella of Parma, young Hercules must choose between a life of pleasure and one of virtue. Since Salieri sang the alto part in Hasse's choruses, we might suppose that among his solo passages were parts of the role of Hercules, written by Hasse for the contralto Giovanni Manzuoli. In light of Gassmann's recent statement of the choice that lay before Salieri ("it will depend on you whether [the] outcome [of your musical education] will be good or bad"), Salieri may have recognized the relevance of Hercules' choice to his own situation.

Late in life Salieri recalled fondly his music making with Joseph, leading Hüttenbrenner to believe that sometimes just the two of them played together: Joseph "often read through Italian scores for hours at a time. Salieri played Klavier, Emperor Joseph the cello, on which he expertly performed the melodies of the operas."[46] Although Sa-

43. Salieri wrote that Gassmann "as court composer was obliged to go three times a week to the chamber music of H. M. the Emperor Joseph II" (Salieri to Kueffstein, 20 May 1816, in Angermüller, *Leben,* 3:162–63, and Angermüller, *Fatti,* 185–86).

44. Mosel, 22.

45. Mosel, 22–23.

46. Hüttenbrenner to Ferdinand Luib, 7 March 1858, in Hüttenbrenner, "Erinnerungen," 145.

lieri did not at first receive a salary for his performances with the chamber-music group, he received something more valuable: the sovereign's good will, symbolized by the generous presents, first 50 ducats, later 80, that Joseph gave him every New Year's Day.[47]

Gassmann's early death on 20 January 1774 left Salieri an orphan once again. Joseph took over as father figure: a diffident but generous benefactor and confidant. On 3 February he dictated a memorandum to his Obersthofmeister (chief steward), Prince Johann Joseph Khevenhüller:

> Dear Prince Khevenhüller,
> Since, following the death of Kapellmeister Gassmann, I have bestowed the position occupied by Gassmann in my chamber group, now vacant, on Antonio Saglieri, together with the annual salary of 100 ducats, you will prepare a decree for him as [you did] for Gassmann and give the treasury notification of the amount of his salary.
>
> Vienna, 3 February 1774
> Joseph[48]

The emperor did not clearly designate Salieri's new position. Salieri himself, as quoted in translation by Mosel, referred to it as that of *Kammer-Kompositor.*[49] He continued to occupy this position until March 1788, when, at Bonno's retirement, he was finally promoted to the position of Hofkapellmeister.

Favors bestowed by the emperor led to further favors. The impresarios running the court theaters were obliged, by custom and perhaps also by contract, to hire Joseph's chamber composer as music director. Salieri's appointment as chamber composer was thus followed shortly by his appointment as Gassmann's replacement as music director of the court theaters, with an additional salary of 300 ducats.

In a painting by Joseph Hauzinger, Emperor Joseph sits at the keyboard of what is probably a grand piano, about to accompany his sisters Anna and Elisabeth in a duet (fig. 1.2). On the music stand, documenting Joseph's predilection for Italian vocal music, is a manuscript score entitled "Duetto" (fig. 1.3). At the bottom right of the title page an inscription can be made out: "del Sig. Salieri / Scholare del [the following two words are hardly legible:] rinomato Sig. / Gasman."

Musical title pages rarely mention a composer's teacher. It was probably the painter

47. Mosel, 25–26.

48. Lieber Fürst Khevenhüller. Da ich nach Absterben des Capell Meisters Gassmann, die bey meiner Cammer Music von ihm besessene und jetzo erledigte Stelle dem Antonio Saglieri, samt dem von dem Gassmann genossenem Gehalte von jährlichen Hundert Ducaten verliehen habe, so werden sie ihm, so wie dem Gassmann das Decret ausfertigen, und die Anweisung zu Erhebung seines Gehaltes bey der Hof Cammer machen. Wienn den 3t Februar 1774 (HHStA, OMeA 1774, Kart. 78, no. 11). I am grateful to Julia Moore, who discovered this document, for sharing it with me.

49. Mosel, 57.

FIGURE 1.2 Joseph II at the keyboard, preparing to accompany his sisters the archduchesses Anna and Elisabeth in the performance of a duet by Salieri. Painting by Joseph Hauzinger. (Courtesy of Kunsthistorisches Museum, Vienna.)

FIGURE 1.3 Joseph II at the keyboard, detail. (Courtesy of Kunsthistorisches Museum, Vienna.)

rather than a music copyist who put Gassmann's name on the cover of Salieri's duet. In bringing Gassmann and Salieri together in a painting of Joseph, Hauzinger neatly alluded to the emperor's fondness for these men and for their music. Looked at from Salieri's point of view, the painting documents two of the most important relationships in his life: those that linked him firmly to a generous teacher of great musical talent and to an enthusiastic and powerful patron.

Courtship and Marriage

The death of the man Salieri called his second father and the achievement of a position at court may have encouraged him to think of marriage and a family. It was probably shortly before Gassmann's death that Salieri met a young Viennese woman, Therese Helferstorfer, who would soon become his wife. He remembered his brief courtship as having taken place during the winter, and that Therese's father died less than a week after he declared his love to her. Carl Jacob Helferstorfer, retired from a career in the court treasury, died on 24 January 1774.[50] Salieri's courtship thus presumably took place (or culminated) in January 1774, the very month in which Gassmann also died. According to the wedding contract Antonio married Therese on 10 October 1774.[51] But Mosel, quoting Salieri, placed his courtship and marriage in the following year, 1775. How can we explain Salieri's apparent misdating of these crucial events? A simple lapse of memory is possible; or did he feel uneasy that his courtship and marriage had taken place so close to the time of Gassmann's death?

Salieri's account of his courtship and of his efforts to gain the approval of Therese's guardian is the longest of the autobiographical sketches that Mosel included in his biography. Its quotation of Italian operatic verse and its colorful references to music lessons in a convent, conversations in French, and weekly mass in St. Stephen's Cathedral all reflect life in the Catholic, cosmopolitan, music-loving city in which Salieri grew to adulthood.[52]

Therese died in 1807, at the age of fifty-two. Four or five of Antonio and Therese Salieri's eight children died young; only three are known to have outlived their father. All but one were girls. Salieri's only son, Alois, died in 1805 at the age of twenty-three.[53] As an old man Salieri remembered him as having had "a most beautiful voice and a great talent for composition."[54]

50. Wiener Stadtarchiv, Totenbeschauprotokoll, 1774.

51. The contract, in the Wiener Stadtarchiv, is transcribed in Swenson, 57–58, and Angermüller, *Leben,* 3:4–5.

52. Mosel, 56–59. Translation in Alexander Wheelock Thayer, *Salieri, Rival of Mozart,* ed. Theodore Albrecht (Kansas City, Mo., 1989), 55–61.

53. Angermüller, *Leben,* 2:44–46.

54. Hüttenbrenner to Ferdinand Luib, 7 March 1858, in Hüttenbrenner, "Erinnerungen," 143.

The year 1774 marked an important turning point in Salieri's life. Gassmann's death near the beginning of the year led directly to Joseph's decision to give Salieri a position at court. This decision, in turn, made it possible for him to marry. At the beginning of 1774 the twenty-four-year-old musician had already seen eight of his operas performed in the court theaters, but his place in Viennese society was still that of Gassmann's student and apprentice. By the end of 1774 he had become an independent man and musician: music director of the court theaters and Joseph's chamber composer, married to a Viennese woman of respectable middle-class family, and soon to be master of house number 1115 in central Vienna (on what is now the Seilergasse), where he would live for the rest of his life.[55]

Appearance and Character of "the Talleyrand of Music"

In reading Mosel's biography we must keep in mind that he knew Salieri only during the composer's old age and that the book, published shortly after Salieri's death, was intended as an encomium to be read by an audience whose opinion of him had been influenced by his supposed hostility to Mozart. If Mosel found some aspects of Salieri's personality unpleasant, he kept these largely to himself. But despite his good intentions, and perhaps precisely because of his one-sidedness, his depiction is difficult for us to admire. What he praised as virtue and piety we are tempted to condemn as sanctimoniousness and intolerance:

> Salieri was more short than tall in stature, neither fat nor thin; he had a dark complexion, lively eyes, black hair. He was of choleric temperament: he flew easily into a rage, but could, like Horace, say of himself: "Tamen ut placabilis essem" [But let me be calm]. Reflection always quickly replaced anger. He loved order and cleanliness; he dressed according to fashion, but his clothes were always appropriate to his age. He was indifferent to every kind of game. He drank only water, but was uncommonly fond of pastries and sweets. Reading, music, and solitary walks were his favorite pastimes.
>
> He hated ingratitude; he considered the expression of gratitude his most pleasant obligation. He did good deeds when he could, and his purse was always open to those in need. He liked to talk, especially about music, a subject on which he was inexhaustible. Idleness disgusted him; [religious] disbelief horrified him. . . . But normally he was vigorous and lively; his kindness, jolly humor, and cheerful wit (which was never offensive) made him most pleasant company in society.[56]

Michael Kelly, engaged to sing in Joseph's opera buffa troupe in 1783, met Salieri on his arrival in Vienna. His memory of Salieri's appearance and character agrees in some

55. My thanks to Walther Brauneis for helping me trace the location of Salieri's Viennese residences.
56. Mosel, 207–8.

respects with Mosel's: "He was a little man, with an expressive countenance, and his eyes were full of genius. I have often heard Storace's mother [that is, the mother of the soprano Nancy Storace] say, he was extremely like Garrick."[57] Kelly elsewhere stated that Salieri "would make a joke of anything, for he was a very pleasant man, and much esteemed in Vienna; and I considered myself in high luck to be noticed by him."[58]

To his students Salieri showed paternal generosity and loyalty; to the poets with whom he collaborated, respect and collegiality. He treated the singers who performed his works (if Kelly is typical) with politeness and friendliness. But his relations with leading composers of the day—composers who were neither his mentors nor his students—do not seem to have been close or warm. Of his opinion of their music we know very little, and the absence of evidence is itself somewhat troubling. The reminiscences on which Mosel based his biography must have contained little if anything about what Salieri thought of his compositional contemporaries. Surely if he had left comments on the music of Gassmann, Mozart, or Paisiello, Mosel would have quoted or paraphrased them. But Mosel was almost completely silent about such matters.

Of the few favorable opinions about the music of other composers that can be attributed to Salieri, some were expressed in contexts in which uncritical praise was necessary. His conventionally adulatory bow to Gluck in an open letter printed shortly after the premiere of *Les Danaïdes* tells us nothing about what he really felt about the older composer and his music; equally uninformative is his exaggerated praise of Joseph's Singspiel troupe and its performance of André Grétry's *Lucile* as "wonderfully perfect in every respect," when asked by Joseph himself for his opinion in 1780.

The lack of interest that Salieri showed in music other than his own may have partly to do with his positions of authority in Viennese musical life and his expectation that he would rise further. Already in 1774 he "had hope of becoming Hofkapellmeister one day," as he put it to Therese Helferstorfer's guardian.[59] For political reasons he probably became used to keeping his opinions to himself. Hüttenbrenner may have had this tactful reticence in mind when he wrote: "Salieri seemed to me to be the greatest musical diplomat; he was the Talleyrand of music."[60] But politics alone cannot explain his silence. Busily immersed in composition, conducting, teaching, and administration, he seems to have remained largely indifferent to the magnificent flowering of musical and operatic culture that occurred during his lifetime and of which his own operas were but one product.

Visual depictions of Salieri are few, and most of them, like Mosel's verbal depiction, show him as an old man. The earliest surviving image seems to be a silhouette by Hier-

57. Kelly, *Reminiscences*, 99.
58. Kelly, *Reminiscences*, 101.
59. Mosel, 57.
60. Hüttenbrenner to Ferdinand Luib, 7 March 1858, in Hüttenbrenner, "Erinnerungen," 142.

FIGURE 1.4 Salieri, silhouette by Hieronymus Löschenkohl, published in 1786. (Courtesy of Historisches Museum der Stadt Wien.)

FIGURE 1.5 Te Deum in the court chapel, April 1790, detail of a colored engraving by Hieronymus Löschenkohl. Wiener Stadtbibliothek.

onymus Löschenkohl published in 1786, a valuable suggestion of his appearance in his midthirties, at the peak of his influence and creative power (fig. 1.4). Another picture by Löschenkohl, this one a colored engraving, shows a performing musician who is almost certainly Salieri. The engraving records the performance of a Te Deum in celebration of an oath of allegiance to Archduke Leopold (soon to be Emperor Leopold II) that took place in the Hofkapelle (court chapel) in April 1790. Chorus and orchestra, split into two groups, occupy balconies on opposite sides of the chapel.[61] On the left, surrounded by musicians, a conductor lifts his hand (fig. 1.5). Although Löschenkohl did not portray the conductor with much detail, it may be possible to recognize in him Hofkapellmeister Salieri, paying musical homage to a ruler to whose family he owed much of his success.

61. The engraving is reproduced in John A. Rice, "Vienna under Joseph II and Leopold II," in *The Classical Era,* ed. Neal Zaslaw (London, 1989), 160.

2

OPERA IN VIENNA, 1766–76: THEATERS, MANAGEMENT, PERSONNEL

The city that Salieri made home in 1766 was, linguistically at least, the most cosmopolitan in Europe: capital of a monarchy whose subjects spoke German, French, Flemish, Czech, Polish, Hungarian, Serbo-Croatian, and Italian. Vienna's nobility corresponded and conversed in French as well as German, and in the city's streets all the monarchy's languages could be heard. The babble must have sounded something like the words that the aged and partially paralyzed Gluck, whose mother tongue was Czech, spoke when Salieri left Vienna on a journey to Paris in 1786: "Ainsi . . . mon cher ami . . . lei parte domani per Parigi. . . . Je vous souhaite . . . di cuore un bon voyage . . . Sie gehen in eine Stadt, wo man schätzet . . . die fremden Künstler . . . e lei si farà onore . . . ich zweifle nicht."[1] Thirty-five years later, when Salieri himself was an old man, his speech resembled Gluck's. Friedrich Rochlitz, editor of the *Allgemeine musikalische Zeitung* of Leipzig, visited Salieri in 1822: "When German escaped him in the heart of conversation, it was replaced by Italian, mixed with French; whereupon he smilingly excused himself: 'I have only been in Germany for over fifty years! How could I have learned the language yet?' "[2]

Vienna in the eighteenth century consisted of two distinct parts. The walled city (corresponding roughly to what is now the first district, inside the Ringstrasse) had

1. Mosel, 93. See Daniel Heartz, "Coming of Age in Bohemia: The Musical Apprenticeships of Benda and Gluck," *JM* 6 (1988): 524.

2. Letter from Friedrich Rochlitz to Gottfried Christoph Härtel, 9 July 1822, *AmZ* 30 (1828): cols. 5–16, part of which is quoted in translation (used here) in Thayer, *Salieri*, 166–69.

some 52,000 residents during the 1770s and 1780s (fig. 2.1). It was surrounded by rapidly growing suburbs where most of the people lived—140,000 in 1772, 165,000 in 1785.[3] Vienna and its suburbs together represented by far the largest urban area in the German-speaking part of Europe.[4]

The Habsburg court dominated the inner city and all its activities. Around the Hofburg (the imperial palace) clustered the offices of government. Ministries, treasuries, and lawcourts were surrounded by palaces of the high nobility, churches, monasteries, and convents; apartments of court officials, bureaucrats, lawyers, accountants, and secretaries; and shops, restaurants, and coffeehouses. Also inside the walls were the two court theaters, the Burgtheater and the Kärntnertortheater, where Vienna's cosmopolitanism bore its most significant artistic fruit.

These theaters enjoyed a virtual monopoly over professional theatrical activity open to the public within the walls of Vienna. Outside the walls professional theater for public audiences was almost nonexistent on all but the most temporary stages until Emperor Joseph's theatrical reorganization of 1776 led to the founding of several permanent suburban theaters during the 1780s.[5] Although the suburbs played an increasingly important role in Viennese musical life from the late eighteenth century on, Salieri had little to do with them. As a court musician he devoted his attention to the court theaters and those who patronized them. His daily walk along the walls of Vienna circumscribed the area to which he limited most of his professional musical activity.

Salieri came to the Habsburg capital shortly after the end of a great era in the history of Viennese opera. Under the leadership of Count Durazzo, the court's *Musikgraf* (supervisor of musical activities), the court theaters had presented during the early 1760s a wide variety of musico-dramatic genres: opéra-comique, opera buffa, ballet, and serious opera in Italian combining aspects of opera seria, tragédie lyrique, and ballet. Durazzo had brought together daring and original artists—the composers Gluck, Traetta, and Gassmann, the poet Ranieri de' Calzabigi, the choreographer Gasparo Angiolini, and the contralto Gaetano Guadagni—to make Vienna a center of operatic innovation and excellence.

By the time of Salieri's arrival Durazzo had resigned under pressure from the court (April 1764). Even more important for the fate of Viennese opera, on 18 August 1765

3. These estimates of population are from Otto G. Schindler, "Das Publikum des Burgtheaters in der Josephinischen Ära: Versuch einer Struckturbestimmung," in *Das Burgtheater und sein Publikum,* ed. Margret Dietrich (Vienna, 1976), 91.

4. Vienna and its suburbs had a population of about 230,000 in 1789; Berlin, by way of comparison, had about 172,000 people in 1800. But not even Vienna approached the population of Europe's largest cities: London (861,000 in 1800), Paris (547,000), and Naples (430,000). See Tertius Chandler and Gerald Fox, *3000 Years of Urban Growth* (New York, 1974).

5. On the suburban theaters see Emil Karl Blümml and Gustav Gugitz, *Alt-Wiener Thespiskarren: Die Frühzeit der Wiener Vorstadtbühnen* (Vienna, 1925).

FIGURE 2.1 Bird's-eye view of Vienna, 1785, by Joseph Daniel Huber. (Courtesy of Historisches Museum der Stadt Wien.)

Emperor Francis had died. It was probably the death of her husband more than anything else that persuaded Maria Theresa, during the period of mourning that followed, to put the theaters in the hands of an impresario who was nominally independent of the court. She withdrew from many aspects of court life, the theater among them. Leasing the theaters had the effect of distancing their management from herself and the court. She may also have hoped to discourage her son and coregent Joseph from involving himself in theatrical affairs; she succeeded in doing so, for the most part, until 1776.

During the decade between 1766 and Joseph's founding of the Nationaltheater in 1776 a series of impresarios presented opera, ballet, concerts, and spoken drama within the institutional framework of the court; for them Salieri wrote his first ten operas. The impresarios were hindered by restrictions imposed on them by the court, which insisted on maintaining some control over the theaters, their personnel, and repertory. In areas not under the court's control, financial constraints limited the impresarios' choices and eventually hurt the quality of the troupe and its performances. That, in turn, led the emperor to decide (or provided him with an excuse) to dissolve the contract by which the last impresario was running the court theaters and to bring them once again under the direct control of the court.

The Court Theaters and Their Audience

The Burgtheater, which adjoined the imperial palace, was sometimes called the French Theater during the several periods between the mid-1750s and the mid-1770s when French troupes presented plays, opéras-comiques, and ballets on its stage (figs. 2.2 and 2.3). The Kärntnertortheater (also called the German Theater when, as often during the eighteenth century, it was the home of German troupes) was located nearby, at the Kärntnertor (the Carinthian Gate, where the road south to Carinthia and hence to Italy began; in Italian it was sometimes called Porta d'Italia; fig. 2.4).

The Burgtheater and the Kärntnertortheater were intimate spaces, smaller than most of the major Italian theaters.[6] The Burgtheater's seating capacity has been estimated to have been somewhere between 1,000 and 1,350.[7] By comparison, La Scala in Milan, built in the late 1770s as one of Europe's largest theaters, seated about 3,300. Burney, in Vienna in 1772, witnessed a performance of Salieri's *Il barone di Rocca Antica* at the Kärntnertor. His comments about the singing of the prima donna, whom he had previously heard in Italy, refer to the size of the hall: "I cannot attribute all the improvement I now found in her voice to time; something must be given to the difference of theatres; those of Florence and Milan, are, at least, twice as big as this at Vienna, which is about the size of our great opera-house, in the Hay-market."[8]

Burney also left us a description of the Kärntnertor's admission policies and design:

> The admission into this theatre is at a very easy rate; twenty-four *Creuzers* only are paid for going into the pit; in which, however, there are seats with backs to them. A *Creuzer* here, is hardly equal to an English halfpenny; indeed, part of the front of the pit is railed off, and is called the amphitheatre; for places there, the price is doubled, none are to be had for money, except in the pit and the slips, which run all along the top of the house, and in which only sixteen *Creuzers* are paid. The boxes are all let by the season to the principal families, as is the custom in Italy.

6. On the size and shape of the court theaters see Mary Sue Morrow, *Concert Life in Haydn's Vienna: Aspects of a Developing Musical and Social Institution* (Stuyvesant, N.Y., 1989), 71–81; and for further discussion see Dexter Edge's review of Morrow's book in *Haydn Yearbook* 17 (1992): 117–19.

7. Schindler, "Das Publikum des Burgtheaters," 34.

8. Burney, *Germany*, 85.

FIGURE 2.2 The Michaelerplatz with the Burgtheater at the far right, ca. 1785. Drawing by Carl Schütz. (Courtesy of Historisches Museum der Stadt Wien.)

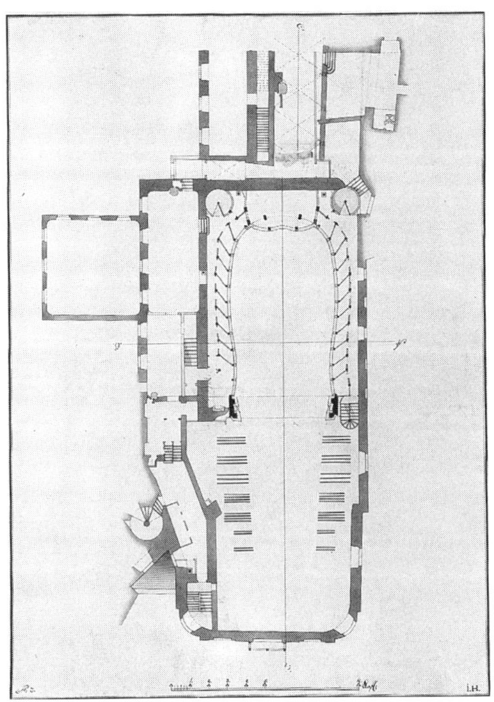

FIGURE 2.3 Groundplan of the Burgtheater, 1778. (Courtesy of Graphische Sammlung Albertina, Vienna.)

FIGURE 2.4 The Kärntnertortheater, ca. 1772. Engraving by J. E. Mansfeld.

> The size of this theatre may be nearly imagined, by comparing with any one of our own, the number of boxes and seats in each. There are in this five ranks of boxes, twenty-four in each; in the pit there are twenty-seven rows of seats, which severally contain twenty-four persons.

Burney's statement that no seats "are to be had for money" in what he called "the amphitheatre" alludes to the court theaters' segregation of audiences by social class. Certain parts were off-limits to the commoner Burney (except as the guest of a nobleman) no matter how much money he might offer for a ticket. In the Burgtheater, for example, the *parterre noble,* directly in front of the stage (that is, the equivalent of Burney's "amphitheatre"), was reserved for the nobility and the diplomatic corps (most of whose members were noble), as were the first two tiers of boxes, except those belonging to the imperial family. The second parterre (behind the parterre noble), parts of the third tier of boxes, and the upper gallery were open to anyone who could pay the substantial ticket prices. These were for the most part wealthier members of Vienna's middle class, along with foreign visitors like Burney.

That Burney found admission to the Kärntnertortheater "at a very easy rate" does not mean that Vienna's lower classes could easily afford to attend the court theaters. The price of seats in the Burgtheater in 1775 ranged from 20 Kreuzer in the uppermost section of the theater, the so-called Paradies, to 1 Gulden 42 Kreuzer for a reserved seat (*chaise fermée*) in the parterre.[9] A domestic servant earning 7 Gulden a month (14 Kreuzer a day) would have to spend more than a day's earnings for an evening in the theater. A seamstress in the suburbs making 3½ Kreuzer a day would have to work six days to be able to attend a performance in the Burgtheater.[10] It has been estimated that although the nobility and upper strata of the middle class together may have made up only about 7 percent of the population of Vienna and its suburbs, they represented 90 percent of the Burgtheater's audience.[11]

A major source of income for the management of the court theaters was the rental of boxes to the nobility, who paid dearly for their privilege. The annual fee for a box in the Burgtheater in 1775 ran from 700 to 1,000 Gulden, as can be seen in a partial list of subscribers for the period October 1774–Carnival 1775, for which they paid half the annual fee.[12] This list also shows that the audience of the Burgtheater included many of Vienna's most illustrious families—Esterházy, Palffy, Auersperg—as well as the ambassadors of Russia, Naples, and Spain. The purchasing power of 700 Gulden can be appreciated if one considers that, according to the estimate of one visitor, a single man of

9. Ticket prices for the court theaters during 1773–75 are well documented in box-office receipts in MOL, P 421 (Keglevich Cs.), V/15–22.

10. These wages are reported in Johann Pezzl, *Skizze von Wien,* ed. Gustav Gugitz and Anton Schlossar (Graz, 1923), 203, 344.

11. Schindler, "Das Publikum des Burgtheaters," 92.

12. MOL, P 421 (Keglevich Cs.) V/19, fol. 320v. This was the second half of the theatrical year, which extended from the day after Easter to the end of Carnival in the following calendar year.

the middle class could live comfortably in Vienna during the 1780s on an annual income of 550 Gulden.[13] Yet many noblemen renewed their subscriptions year after year. Count Carl von Zinzendorf attended concerts and the theater several times a month whenever he was in Vienna, over a period of more than fifty years, from the early 1760s until his death in 1813. His feat is remembered today because he recorded it in his diary,[14] but there is no reason to doubt that other Viennese went to the theater as often as Zinzendorf and for as many years.

The court theaters of Vienna educated their audience well by exposing it to some of Europe's finest musicians. Having become accustomed during the 1760s to theatrical music of high quality through performances of the operas of Gluck, Hasse, and Traetta, the Viennese public expected the same level of quality from composers and performers during subsequent decades. It thus helped maintain the court theaters' tradition of musical excellence even during the early 1770s, when the court itself did very little to foster operatic activity.

Impresarios and the Court

The impresarios who managed the court theaters between 1766 and 1776—Franz Hilverding from 1766 to 1767, Giuseppe Affligio (also spelled Afflisio) from 1767 to 1770, Johann Kohary from 1770 to 1772, and Joseph Keglevich from 1772 to 1776[15]—had responsibilities that went well beyond the production of plays, operas, and ballets. They organized concerts during evenings when dramatic productions were prohibited by the court and supervised balls in the Redoutensäle (the palace ballrooms) and in the Kärntnertortheater. They also ran the Hetztheater, the animal baiting arena in the suburbs, where Viennese of every rank watched oxen being attacked by dogs and various wild beasts to the sound of Turkish music and fireworks.[16]

Although nominally independent, the impresarios could do little that was not subject to the court's approval or veto. Count JohannWenzel Sporck, who replaced Durazzo

13. Pezzl, *Skizze von Wien*, 344.

14. According to Ulrich Harbecke, "Das Tagebuch des Grafen Karl von Zinzendorf und Pottendorf als theatergeschichtliche Quelle" (diss., University of Cologne, 1969), the diary records 4,148 evenings at the theater experienced by Zinzendorf between 1761 and 1813, not only in Vienna but in Paris, London, Dresden, Trieste, and many other cities.

15. Zechmeister, 397. The names in this list are those of the active managers of the court theaters. In some cases these managers acted in the name of an officially designated impresario. For example, Kohary's contract remained in force until 1776, although Keglevich in fact managed the theaters from 1772 to 1776. When Joseph dissolved Kohary's contract in 1776 it was Keglevich who lost his job.

16. The impresarios' responsibilities, which of course changed during the course of the decade, are recorded in court documents in HHStA, OMeA, SR, Kart. 369. For excerpts and summaries of some these documents see Eduard Wlassack, *Chronik des k. k. Hof-Burgtheaters* (Vienna, 1876), 17; and Franz Hadamowsky, *Wien, Theatergeschichte: Von den Anfängen bis zum Ende des ersten Weltkriegs* (Vienna, 1988), 220.

as Musikgraf in 1764 and occupied that position until 1775, retained a supervisory role, and he could on occasion exercise considerable authority over repertory and personnel.[17]

The court theaters continued to present, as in Durazzo's time, magnificent operatic spectacles in Italian that combined solo song, chorus, and often ballet. Members of the opera troupe assembled by the impresarios performed in these works, but the court probably subsidized many if not all of them. The cast of Gassmann's *Amore e Psiche,* first performed on 5 October 1767 in celebration of the ill-fated betrothal of Archduchess Maria Josepha to King Ferdinand of Naples, included only one member of the impresario's troupe. The four other roles (including the two title roles) were created by opera seria singers brought to Vienna especially for this production, presumably at the court's expense.[18] In 1767 Calzabigi wrote to Prince Wenzel Anton Kaunitz, the powerful minister of state and one of Vienna's leading operatic patrons, about preparations for Gluck's *Alceste.* The letter clearly implies that the production had the court's backing.[19] Three years later the court paid the theatrical management 5,000 Gulden as a subsidy for theatrical performances and balls organized in celebration of the marriage of Archduchess Marie Antoinette to the dauphin of France.[20]

The court had long forbidden the performance of plays and operas on certain days, and these rules applied to the impresarios. As of 1774, no theatrical productions could be given on Fridays (considered penitential days); during the last nine days of Advent (16–24 December) and the whole of Lent; or on Christmas, Easter, Pentecost, and the Feasts of the Assumption, the Immaculate Conception, All Saints, and All Souls. Performances on the eves of several important feast days were also forbidden, and several days were set aside in memory of Maria Theresa's parents and husband.[21] These restrictions may have contributed to the financial problems that often hindered the impresarios. An evening without a performance was an evening without receipts, yet the performers received salaries even when they did not perform.

The court also intervened in decisions about personnel. The contract by which the former dancer-choreographer Hilverding became impresario at the end of 1765 required him to honor already-existing contracts with the German troupe, as well as those with the composers Gassmann and Starzer, the stage designer Quaglio (either Giovanni

17. Zechmeister, 79.

18. For the cast of *Amore e Psiche* see Zechmeister, 288.

19. Calzabigi alludes, in a passage quoted in Brown, *Gluck,* 430, to the court's role as well as Kaunitz's in the production of *Alceste:* "If therefore Her Imperial Majesty [and] Your Highness should decide that Alceste go on stage . . ." For an annotated translation of Calzabigi's letter see Daniel Heartz, *Haydn, Mozart, and the Viennese School, 1740–1780* (New York, 1995), 729–32.

20. Andrea Sommer-Mathis, *Tu felix Austria nube: Hochzeitsfeste der Habsburger im 18. Jahrhundert* (Vienna, 1994), 187.

21. This information on days when the theaters were closed is derived from the anonymous *Almanach des Theaters in Wien* ([Vienna], 1774)

Maria Quaglio or his son Carlo), the stage machinist Pietro Rizzini, the librettist Marco Coltellini, and the oboist Carlo Besozzi.[22] Restrictions like these produced a situation in which it was normal for some of the musicians hired to compose and direct music at court also to receive a salary from the impresarios as operatic composers and music directors.

Salieri enjoyed this kind of dual appointment. On Gassmann's death in 1774 Joseph appointed Salieri to the position of court chamber musician left vacant by Gassmann, with its salary of 100 ducats. Joseph's letter announcing his decision makes no mention of the theater, and yet, according to Mosel, Salieri's appointment as music director of the court theaters, with a salary of 300 ducats, was granted "at the same time" as his court appointment. This strongly suggests that the impresario Keglevich was (or felt) obliged to engage Salieri as music director as a result of his court appointment.

The status of Salieri's employment is clarified in his account (quoted by Mosel) of his efforts to persuade his future bride's guardian of his financial dependability. The guardian, as if straight out of an opera buffa, wanted to marry Therese himself, but was at least willing to consider the wishes of his ward and of Salieri. He asked Salieri about his income.

> I replied that I earned three hundred ducats as Kapellmeister of the Italian opera, one hundred ducats as imperial chamber composer, and had hope of becoming Hofkapellmeister one day; that, moreover, my compositions and music lessons brought me in another three hundred ducats annually, so that I could estimate my total income at seven hundred ducats. The guardian answered: "That would be more than sufficient if it were certain; but, of all this, you can count with certainty only on the one hundred ducats that you receive from the court; and I must therefore ask you to wait until your position improves in some reliable way before I, as guardian, can give my consent to this marriage."[23]

The guardian implied that Salieri's theatrical position depended to some extent on the impresario. If Keglevich were to resign or be dismissed by the court (as indeed happened two years later), the salary that Salieri received as music director might be discontinued. His court appointment, on the other hand, was for all practical purposes permanent.

When Joseph found out that Salieri had been denied the hand of his beloved, he looked for a way to help his young protégé, so as to provide this little operatic drama with a *lieto fine.* He raised Salieri's court salary to 300 ducats, on two conditions: that he assist Hofkapellmeister Bonno (recently appointed to Gassmann's place) and that he

22. Zechmeister, 273–74; for further documentation see HHStA, OMeA, SR, Kart. 369.
23. Mosel, 67.

"direct the Italian opera, and will continue to do so if His Majesty brings the opera under his own management."[24]

This second condition is of interest because it brings to the surface yet again the ambiguous position of the impresario, who was here having his music director appointed for him by Joseph, apparently for the second time. The fact that Salieri was already "Kapellmeister der italienischen Oper" (as he himself put it when he added up his income for Therese's guardian) was less important than the source of his salary. By giving him a court salary for the position, Joseph extended his influence over the management of the theaters. The emperor's reference to the possibility that he might bring the opera "under his own management" anticipated an action that he took two years later, when he swept away the arrangement by which impresarios managed the theaters and took control of them himself.

The impresario represented a useful excuse for the emperor and court officials when they did not want to get involved in theatrical affairs or when they wanted to withdraw their support from a project that they had initiated. Leopold Mozart learned this in 1768, through the bitter experience of trying to persuade the impresario Affligio and later the emperor to perform his twelve-year-old son's opera buffa *La finta semplice.* Leopold was so angry and confused when he wrote from Vienna to his friend Lorenz Hagenauer in Salzburg that he seems not to have noticed his letter's contradictions. Having claimed that "the court cannot say a word to this Affligio," a few sentences later he implied that the commission for *La finta semplice* resulted from a request by the emperor to the impresario. Also contradictory: Joseph and his courtiers "cannot command" Affligio to perform Mozart's opera; yet "they would perhaps command him at some other time."[25] The court could indeed command the performance of an opera, as it had with Gluck's *Alceste.*

Joseph seems to have used his influence to get the commission for Wolfgang, but he then failed to support the Mozarts through the whole process of bringing the opera to performance. He could probably have induced the impresario to cooperate with the Mozarts had he wanted to and had he been able to do so quietly and discreetly. (One need only think of how quickly Joseph raised Salieri's court salary six years later.) It is likely that the more vehemently and publicly Leopold Mozart struggled to have his son's opera performed, the more reluctant Joseph became to support him.[26]

Eighteen-year-old Salieri, unmentioned in Leopold Mozart's letter, had been in Vienna only two years when the controversy over *La finta semplice* arose. He may have

24. Mosel, 58.

25. *MBA,* 1:269–74.

26. For a somewhat different interpretation of the controversy, see Heartz, *Viennese School,* 512–16. Leopold Mozart's appeal to Joseph is published in *MBA,* 1:279–83, and, in English translation, in Heartz, *Viennese School,* 733–36.

learned from Leopold's mistakes. Always aware of who was really in charge, he depended on Joseph fully and openly but never tried to embarrass his patron or to force his hand. He rarely involved himself in public quarrels with impresarios and other theatrical personnel. And he was rarely disappointed in the support that Joseph gave him. When the time came, less than two years later, for the composition of his first opera buffa, Salieri brought it to performance with a tact that contrasts strongly with Leopold Mozart's self-righteous aggressiveness.

The Rise of Viennese Opera Buffa

When Salieri moved in 1766 from the Venice of Goldoni and Galuppi to the Vienna of Metastasio and Gluck, in the company of a musician who had composed more serious operas than comic and whose only Viennese operas were settings of Metastasio's *L'Olimpiade* and *Il trionfo d'Amore,* he might have supposed that he was leaving opera buffa behind in Venice. Events proved otherwise. A few months after Salieri's arrival in Vienna Gassmann directed the performance of his first Viennese comic opera, *Il viaggiatore ridicolo.* During the decade that followed, under Gassmann's musical direction, opera buffa emerged for the first time as Vienna's most important operatic genre.

The contract stipulating the conditions under which Hilverding took over the Kärntnertortheater in 1765 did not require him to produce works in any particular genre, insisting only that "the spectacles must be worthy of an Imperial-Royal capital."[27] Hilverding and his successors favored opera buffa over the various kinds of serious Italian opera because it was economically more viable. Its singers generally demanded less money than those of opera seria,[28] and it was more popular with theatergoing Viennese. Leopold Mozart explained the choice of genre that led to the composition of *La finta semplice:* "It is not an opera seria, however, for there is no opera seria here now, and moreover people do not like it. . . . There are no singers here for serious operas. Even Gluck's tragic opera *Alceste* was performed entirely by opera buffa singers."[29]

Opera buffa had only recently established itself in Vienna. Traveling troupes of Italian comic singers had given the Viennese a taste of Neapolitan intermezzi between 1746 and 1748 and of Venetian opera buffa in 1759.[30] But it was not until near the end of

27. Quoted in Hadamowsky, *Wien, Theatergeschichte,* 220.

28. John Rosselli, *Singers of Italian Opera: The History of a Profession* (Cambridge, 1992), 124.

29. Letter of 30 January–3 February 1768 to Lorenz Hagenauer, in *MBA,* 1:258. Leopold Mozart exaggerated the participation of opera buffa singers in the first production of *Alceste.* The tenor Giuseppe Tibaldi, who was in the middle of a career devoted almost entirely to opera seria, created the role of Admeto. Antonia Bernasconi, who created the role of Alceste, was a member of the Viennese opera buffa troupe, but she had extensive experience in Italy as a singer of opera seria. See Heartz, *Viennese School,* 230–31.

30. Zechmeister, 240–42. The leader of the buffa troupe, Angelo Mingotti, had helped to introduce Neapolitan opera buffa to Venice in 1743 with his production of Gaetano Latilla's *La finta cameriera.* See Daniel Heartz, "Vis Comica: Goldoni, Galuppi, and *L'Arcadia in Brenta* (Venice, 1749)," in Muraro, *Venezia,* 2:70.

Durazzo's tenure that opera buffa began to earn a solid place in the repertory. In 1763, under the direction of the impresario Giacomo Maso, a troupe of Italian *buffi* presented a series of Venetian comic operas, beginning with Domenico Fischietti's celebrated *Il mercato di Malmantile.*[31] Zinzendorf's reaction to the first performance of Fischietti's opera was that of someone confronted with a theatrical genre for the first time: "At 7 o'clock to the opera buffa, entitled *Il mercato di Malmantile.* . . . the troupe is good: it consists of Romans and Bolognese. The genre is singular. I was annoyed at the beginning, at all these trivial things, which they sing to you with such emphasis; but after all the same thing happens in French opéra-comique."[32]

Maso seems to have ended his association with the court theaters in September 1763, but opera buffa soon returned to Vienna. Shortly after Sporck replaced Durazzo, he dismissed the troupe of French singers and actors assembled and cultivated by his predecessor. It was probably Sporck who assembled Vienna's first resident opera buffa troupe in 1764.

Giuseppe Scarlatti's *Gli stravaganti,* performed by this troupe in 1765, was possibly the first opera buffa written for performance in Vienna by a resident composer.[33] As such it would mark the beginning of a tradition that continued until the end of the century, one to which Salieri contributed far more operas, over a longer period, than any other composer.

All the Viennese impresarios gave opera buffa a prominent place in the repertory, limiting the performance of serious opera in Italian to a few works, some of great artistic and historical importance but hardly representative of the daily fare. Performances by French troupes were limited to two periods, the first from 1768 to early 1772 and the second from 1775 to early 1776. Opera buffa, on the other hand, could be enjoyed throughout the decade: it was often the only kind of opera available to Viennese audiences. A contemporary observer saw it as the cause of the decline of French musical theater, which, he wrote in 1772, "held its own in Vienna for a long time, and its operettas and its music were once beloved; but the Italian opera buffa has driven it away."[34] The

31. Zechmeister, 252.

32. A 7h. du soir a l'opera buffa, intitulée, Il mercato di Malmantile. . . . La troupe est bonne composée de Romains et de Bolonois. Le genre est singulier, je fus faché au commencement de toutes ces choses triviales, qui on vous chante avec emphase, mais enfin, la même chose arrive dans les Operas comiques françois (Zinzendorf, 15 May 1763). My thanks to Bruce Alan Brown for sharing with me his transcription of this passage.

33. According to Gustav Donath, "Florian Leopold Gassmann als Opernkomponist," *Studien zur Musikwissenschaft* 2 (1914): 76, Scarlatti wrote several opere buffe for Vienna much earlier, including *Il mercato di Malmantile* and *L'isola disabitata* (both 1757). But he cited no evidence for these performances and dates. Nor did Abert, *Mozart,* 1:381, back up his statement that Scarlatti introduced opera buffa to Vienna in 1757, leaving the reader to decide what the word "introduced" (*eingeführt*) means in this context.

34. Es hat sich lang in Wien erhalten, auch liebte man einmal sehr ihre Operetten, und ihre Musik; die wälsche *Opera buffa* verdrang sie (*Theatralkalender von Wien, für das Jahr 1772* [Vienna, [1772]], 82).

year of Salieri's arrival in Vienna saw the beginning not only of a decade of impresarial management but also of a thirty-year epoch in which opera buffa, imported from Italy and of local authorship, dominated the Viennese operatic stage.[35]

The House Poet

In Goldoni's play *L'impresario delle Smirne* (1759), one of many eighteenth-century dramas that find comedy behind the scenes of a theater, the theatrical agent Nibbio and the librettist Maccario explain to a Turk the duties that a librettist is expected to fulfill:

> NIBBIO: Believe me. An impresario must always have a poet at hand. As the need arise, he will write new librettos, or make old ones over if convenient. If the composer introduces an old aria, no one will recognize it once the words have been changed. Believe me, a poet is useful for a number of reasons.
>
> MACCARIO: Tell him, too, that I teach the singers how to act, that I direct the staging, and that I run from box to box to warn the prima donna that she must come post-haste. That I take part in the mob scenes, and that I may be relied on to whistle when the scenery is to be changed.

Maccario exaggerates, perhaps, but on the whole this conversation accurately reflects the responsibilities of operatic poets in eighteenth-century Italy.[36]

A house poet not only wrote new librettos but also revised old ones to fit the requirements of a particular cast and the tastes of a particular city. Such revision was normal whether the opera had already been produced elsewhere or was to be a new setting of an existing libretto. The house poet also staged operas, directing the movements and gestures of the singers and coordinating various aspects of the production—costumes, scenery, and so forth.[37]

The impresarios of Vienna did not differ from those of Italy in their need for house poets, at least two of whom described themselves as "Poeta de' Cesarei Teatri." This and similar terms have caused confusion between the impresarios' house poet on the one hand and the court poet, sometimes called the *poeta cesareo,* on the other. The court poet from 1730 until his death in 1782 was Metastasio, who took on the duties of house poet to the extent of directing the staging of his own librettos. His position was granted for life, but by the time the impresarios took over the court theaters in 1766 he had

35. Joseph's theatrical reform of 1776 was followed by a period of seven years in which opera buffa was not supported by the court, but during most of this period opere buffe continued to be performed at the Kärntnertor (and during the theatrical years 1776–77 in the Burgtheater as well) by various independent troupes.

36. Goldoni, *L'impresario delle Smirne,* original version in verse (1759), in Goldoni, 7:1362–63. The passage is quoted in translation (used here) and discussed as evidence of the activities of a theatrical poet in Piero Weiss, "Carlo Goldoni, Librettist: The Early Years" (Ph.D. diss., Columbia University, 1970), 47–48.

37. Daniel Heartz, *Mozart's Operas* (Berkeley, 1990), chap. 5.

largely withdrawn from theatrical life. In any case, he would not have wanted to get involved in the staging, revising, or writing of Goldonian comedies.

Marco Coltellini, who served the Viennese impresarios as the first of three house poets, owed his engagement to his earlier work at court. *Ifigenia in Tauride,* with music by Traetta (1763), and *Telemaco,* with music by Gluck (1765), must have pleased: Coltellini was among the theatrical artists whose employment Hilverding had to guarantee before he could take over the Kärntnertortheater. Hilverding and his successors, with their interest in opera buffa, would probably have preferred someone other than Coltellini. Salieri, writing in 1783, listed several of Coltellini's serious librettos and continued: "In addition to these he also wrote some comic librettos, but in this genre he was never successful."[38]

Coltellini's main duty as house poet was the adaptation of comic librettos by other poets in preparation for their performance in Vienna. Working behind the scenes, he rarely left evidence allowing us to attribute to him with certainty the adaptation of any particular libretto. We know from Leopold Mozart that he revised Goldoni's *La finta semplice* for Wolfgang in 1768. His name on several editions of the libretto of Gassmann's *La contessina* attests to his responsibility for the complete rewriting of Goldoni's early libretto. He collaborated with Salieri only once. The work they produced, *Armida,* is of the serious, spectacular type to which Coltellini was well suited.

Giovanni Gastone Boccherini, who succeeded Coltellini in 1772, was born in Lucca in 1742, a year before his brother Luigi, the distinguished cellist and composer.[39] Like several of his sisters, Giovanni Gastone became a dancer; he was a member of the Viennese court theaters' ballet troupe from 1759 to 1767 and from 1769 to 1771. His literary ambitions were encouraged in Vienna by Calzabigi, who praised his first libretto, *Turno re de' Rutoli,* when it was published in Vienna in 1767. In spite of Calzabigi's endorsement this *dramma tragico per musica* received no musical setting. But Boccherini had better luck when he turned two years later to comic opera and to Salieri. His first comic libretto, *Le donne letterate,* was the basis of Salieri's first publicly performed opera and marked the beginning of a collaboration that produced four more operas.

Boccherini's engagement as house poet at the beginning of 1772 formalized an arrangement already in force. The contract that he signed on 15 January 1772 confirmed the variety of tasks that a house librettist was expect to do. In exchange for a salary of 1,200 Gulden he agreed

> First. To shorten or otherwise accommodate all the librettos of the Italian operas that the administration wishes to present in these theaters.

38. Salieri to Carl Friedrich Cramer, 25 February 1783, in Angermüller, *Leben,* 3:17–18, and Angermüller, *Fatti,* 115–17.

39. Gabriella Biagi Ravenni, "Calzabigi e dintorni: Boccherini, Angiolini, la Toscana e Vienna," in *La figura e l'opera di Ranieri de' Calzabigi,* ed. Federico Marri (Florence, 1989), 29–71.

Second. To supervise the preparation of scenery, costumes, and everything necessary for the performance of said operas.

Third. To be present at all the rehearsals held before the opera is staged; and to be present in the theater where the operas are being presented at all the premieres that may occur, in order to observe and to make sure that everything happens in an orderly fashion and with the greatest possible precision.

Fourth. To compose three new librettos every year; these, if the theatrical administration so desires, must be written by him on the subjects that it pleases the same administration to give him; and otherwise he is free to write them on any subject he pleases.[40]

Boccherini moved to Spain after this contract expired at the end of Carnival 1775; his position was taken during Lent by Giovanni de Gamerra (fig. 2.5).

Born in Livorno in 1743, De Gamerra was one of several eighteenth-century Italian poets whose adventurous lives combined romance, literature, and theater. After studying law at Pisa he joined the Austrian army, in which he served from 1765 to 1770. His legal studies and military service did not keep him from literary work: he produced many plays and poems, including a *poema eroicomico* in seven volumes, *La corneide* (1781). His service in the Austrian army may have helped him win the position of house poet at the Regio Ducal Teatro of Milan (an Austrian possession) in 1771 and a similar position in Vienna four years later.[41]

Like Coltellini, De Gamerra found more success in serious opera than comic. Some of his early serious librettos were set repeatedly by leading composers of the age. Mozart, J. C. Bach, and at least two others set *Lucio Silla;* at least ten composers set *Medonte re d'Epiro.* When a setting of his *Erifile* was performed in Florence in 1779, the *Gazzetta toscana* praised him as "one of the best dramatic poets of Italy, who brings great honor to Tuscany, his native land."[42]

40. Primo. A scortare, o sia accomodare tutti i Libri delle Opere Italiane, che dalla Direzione si vorranno dare sù questi Teatri.

Secondo. Di ordinare le Decorazioni, Vestiario, e tuttociò che sarà necessario per le rappresentazioni di dette Opere.

Terzo. Di assistere a tutte le ripetizioni, o siano prove, che si faranno prima che vadano in scena; come altresì di ritrovarsi sul Teatro, ove si rappresentaranno le Opere tutte le prime sere, che si daranno, per osservare, e procurare, che tutto vada con buon ordine, e con la possibile esattezza.

Quarto. Di comporre tre libri nuovi per ogni anno, e questi, se la Direzione Teatrale vorrà, devono da esso esser fatti secondo il soggetto, che alla medesima piacerà di dargli; e in caso diverso potrà esso stenderli a suo capriccio (MOL, P 421 [Keglevich Cs.], V/22, fol. 9–10).

41. On De Gamerra's activities as librettist (with special reference to *Lucio Silla*) see Kathleen Kuzmick Hansell, "Opera and Ballet at the Regio Teatro of Milan, 1771–1776: A Musical and Social History" (Ph.D. diss., University of California, Berkeley, 1980), 200–203; and Rosy Candiani, *Libretti e librettisti italiani per Mozart* (Rome, 1994).

42. *Gt,* 1779, pp. 22–23 (article dated 6 February). A review of Francesco Bianchi's *Erifile* describes De Gamerra as "uno de' migliori drammatici Poeti della nostra Italia e che gran decoro apporta alla Toscana sua patria."

FIGURE 2.5
Giovanni de Gamerra. Engraving by Pompeo Lapi after a painting by F. M. Berio.

In Vienna De Gamerra began a brief period of collaboration with Salieri that resulted in two operas, *La finta scema* (1775) and *Daliso e Delmita* (1776), neither of which achieved much success. He left Vienna sometime after the production of *Daliso;* he returned much later, in 1794, reclaiming his position as house poet and reestablishing his collaboration with Salieri.

The Operatic Music Director

The impresario's music director, referred to by Salieri, in Mosel's translation, as "Kapellmeister der italienischen Oper," supervised the composition, arrangement, and performance of Italian opera in the court theaters. He answered to the impresario, not the court: his position differed from that of the Hofkapellmeister, the court music director, who occupied the most prestigious musical post in Vienna. Since the Hofkapellmeister, like the court poet, had what amounted to a lifelong appointment, the position tended to become an honorary one as he grew older and less active. An old Hofkapellmeister might have very little or nothing to do with opera. This was certainly the case during most of the impresarial decade. Reutter, Hofkapellmeister from 1769 to his death in 1772, took no part, as far as we know, in operatic activities during this time. He was succeeded by Gassmann, whose short term as Hofkapellmeister (1772–74) was an unusual period in which the activities of operatic music director and the prestige of Hofkapellmeister were joined in one person. The aged and inactive Bonno succeeded Gassmann as Hofkapellmeister in 1774, while Salieri took over the duties of operatic music director.

As operatic music director from the beginning of the impresarial decade to his death in 1774, Gassmann fully earned his annual salary of 840 Gulden.[43] He served as resident composer, enjoying an almost exclusive privilege to compose new comic operas for the court theaters. He wrote nine opere buffe between 1766 and 1774, at a rate of one per year. During his tenure his comic operas and those of his assistant Salieri were—with one exception—the only newly composed full-length opere buffe to reach the stage of the court theaters.[44] Gassmann also revised operas that had been performed elsewhere, a task often involving the composition of new arias and ensembles.[45] He probably advised the impresario on the choice of operas to be performed and the distribution of roles among members of the troupe. Finally, he or his assistant supervised rehearsals and directed performances from the keyboard.

During Salieri's apprenticeship he gradually took over many of his mentor's duties. He wrote substitute arias and ensembles, directed rehearsals and performances, and, from 1770, shared in Gassmann's privilege to compose new comic operas for the court theaters. By the time of Gassmann's death Salieri had composed and conducted eight operas, and had in many other ways demonstrated his ability to serve as operatic music director.

43. Gassmann's salary for 1772 is mentioned in one of the few documents in the Keglevich papers that refers to the period before 1773: MOL, P 421 (Keglevich Cs.), V/18, fol. 611.

44. The exception was Joseph Bartha's *La diavolessa* (Vienna, 1772). Giuseppe Scarlatti, although active as an operatic composer in Vienna during the 1760s, seems to have written no new opere buffe for the court theaters after 1765. *La moglie padrona,* performed in the court theaters in 1768, is a revision of *Gli stravaganti,* according to Eva Badura-Skoda, "Giuseppe Scarlatti und seine Buffa-Opern," in *Musik am Hof Maria Theresias,* ed. Roswitha Karpf (Munich, 1984), 58. *Dov'è amore è gelosia,* also performed in the court theaters in 1768, is an intermezzo, not a full-length opera buffa. *L'amor geloso* (a revision of *Dov'è amore è gelosia*) was performed at Schönbrunn by noble amateurs in 1770 (see Khevenhüller, 7:37). The failure of Leopold Mozart to bring his son's *La finta semplice* to the stage in 1768 probably had something to do with Gassmann's monopoly.

45. Zechmeister, 509–34.

In assuming Gassmann's position in 1774 Salieri simply continued to do what he had done since 1770. But unlike Gassmann he had no student to whom he could delegate responsibility and with whom he could share privilege. During the last two years of the impresarial decade Salieri acted alone. Taking advantage of the music director's monopoly on the composition of opere buffe, he wrote two more works for the court theaters, *La calamita de' cuori* and *La finta scema*, the only operas composed for the court theaters during these years. The second of these was the last opera that Salieri wrote before Joseph canceled the arrangement by which the impresarios ran the court theaters and set up his Nationaltheater early in 1776.

Orchestras

During most of the first half of the 1770s the impresarios presented programs simultaneously in the two court theaters, requiring two orchestras, one often referred to in almanacs and financial records as the French orchestra or the orchestra of the Burgtheater, and the other as the German orchestra or the orchestra of the Kärntnertortheater.[46] These names are somewhat misleading because, according to an almanac recording the state of the theaters in 1771, the orchestras did not always stay in one theater but moved from one to the other according to the requirements of particular programs, which were themselves usually presented in both theaters.[47] Furthermore, during part of the impresarial decade some musicians seem to have played in both orchestras when their special abilities were needed. For example, a list of players in the Kärntnertortheater during 1774 includes the names Wolfram (no first name) among the second violins, Maderer (no first name) among the violas, and Thomas Heger among the cellos. But annotations next to their names indicate that all three were expected to play in both theaters: Wolfram and Maderer as trumpeters and Heger as timpanist.[48] For the sake of convenience, however, the two orchestras will be referred to here as the "Burgtheater orchestra" and the "Kärntnertortheater orchestra," with the understanding that their personnel may have overlapped.

Both orchestras changed slightly in size during the first half of the 1770s, but the Burgtheater orchestra was generally larger than that of the Kärntnertortheater. In 1771

46. During the period in 1772 when Burney visited Vienna, reporting that on most nights only one of the theaters was open, only one orchestra was under permanent contract with the impresario. When two orchestras were needed simultaneously, the second one consisted of musicians hired on a daily basis, according to *Theatral-Neuigkeiten* (Vienna, 1773), 128.

47. "Diese Orchester wechseln in beyden Theatern, nachdem es die Opern und Ballette erfodern, ab" (*Genaue Nachrichten von beyden kaiserlich-königlichen Schaubühnen*, ed. Johann Heinrich Friedrich Müller [Vienna, 1772], 89).

48. MOL, P 421 (Keglevich Cs.), V/18, fol. 654–55. For a discussion of orchestral and choral forces in the Kärntnertortheater in 1774, based on documents in MOL, see Edge, "Mozart's Viennese Orchestras," 68–71.

the Burgtheater, according to one almanac, had thirty-one players: fifteen violins (including the concertmaster, who is listed separately, and two "Ballet-Geiger," violinists who played during ballet rehearsals but probably also participated in performances), four violas, two cellos, two double basses, two oboes, two flutes, two bassoons, and two horns. In the same year the Kärntnertortheater had twenty-six players: it lacked full-time flutists and had fewer strings.[49] Four years later, in December 1775, the Burgtheater had thirty-two players and the Kärntnertortheater thirty.[50]

Neither orchestra had full-time trumpeters or timpanists. As if in tacit recognition of this, many Viennese operas of the impresarial decade (including Mozart's *La finta semplice,* Gassmann's *La contessina,* and Salieri's *Le donne letterate* and *La locandiera*) do not require trumpets or timpani. But trumpets and timpani were available when needed. The three players cited above may have played trumpet and timpani in operas or ballets that required these instruments, or violin, viola, and cello on evenings when the programs in neither theater required trumpets and drums. Similarly, the lack of flutists in several lists of players in the Kärntnertortheater does not mean that its orchestra never used flutes: the same orchestra list that refers to three string players as trumpeters and drummer describes violinists Martin Menschel and Michael Kaffer also as flutists.

Who played trumpet and timpani in the Kärntnertortheater when Wolfram, Maderer, and Heger were busy in the Burgtheater? Horn players may have played trumpet when necessary (and when a score did not call for both trumpets and horns).[51] A list of players in the Kärntnertortheater orchestra, dated 1773, contains two names under the rubric "corni e clarini," as if the same two musicians played both instruments (fig. 2.6). At other times trumpeters and timpanists were hired from outside the orchestras. A record of the theatrical administration's expenses during 1772 and early 1773 includes references to several payments "für Trompeten, und Pauken" between October 1772 and March 1773.[52] Salieri's *La secchia rapita,* performed during this period, makes very heavy use of trumpets and timpani (three drums instead of the normal two).[53] In the extraordinary concertante aria "Sulle mie tempie in dono" these instruments (and others) have elaborate solo parts. The theatrical administration probably engaged trumpeters and timpanist specifically to perform in Salieri's opera.

The list of orchestral musicians engaged to play in the two court theaters during 1773, reproduced as figure 2.6, shows that in size and composition the orchestras did not differ much from those of 1771 and 1775. The Burgtheater orchestra in 1773 consisted of

49. *Genaue Nachrichten,* 86–89.

50. MOL, P 421 (Keglevich Cs.), V/16, fols. 47–49.

51. This was normal practice in several Italian cities, documented by hornists' contracts that require them to play trumpet as needed (Kathleen Hansell, personal communication).

52. MOL, P 421 (Keglevich Cs.), V/18, fols. 649–51.

53. David Charlton, "Salieri's Timpani," *Musical Times* 112 (1971): 961–62.

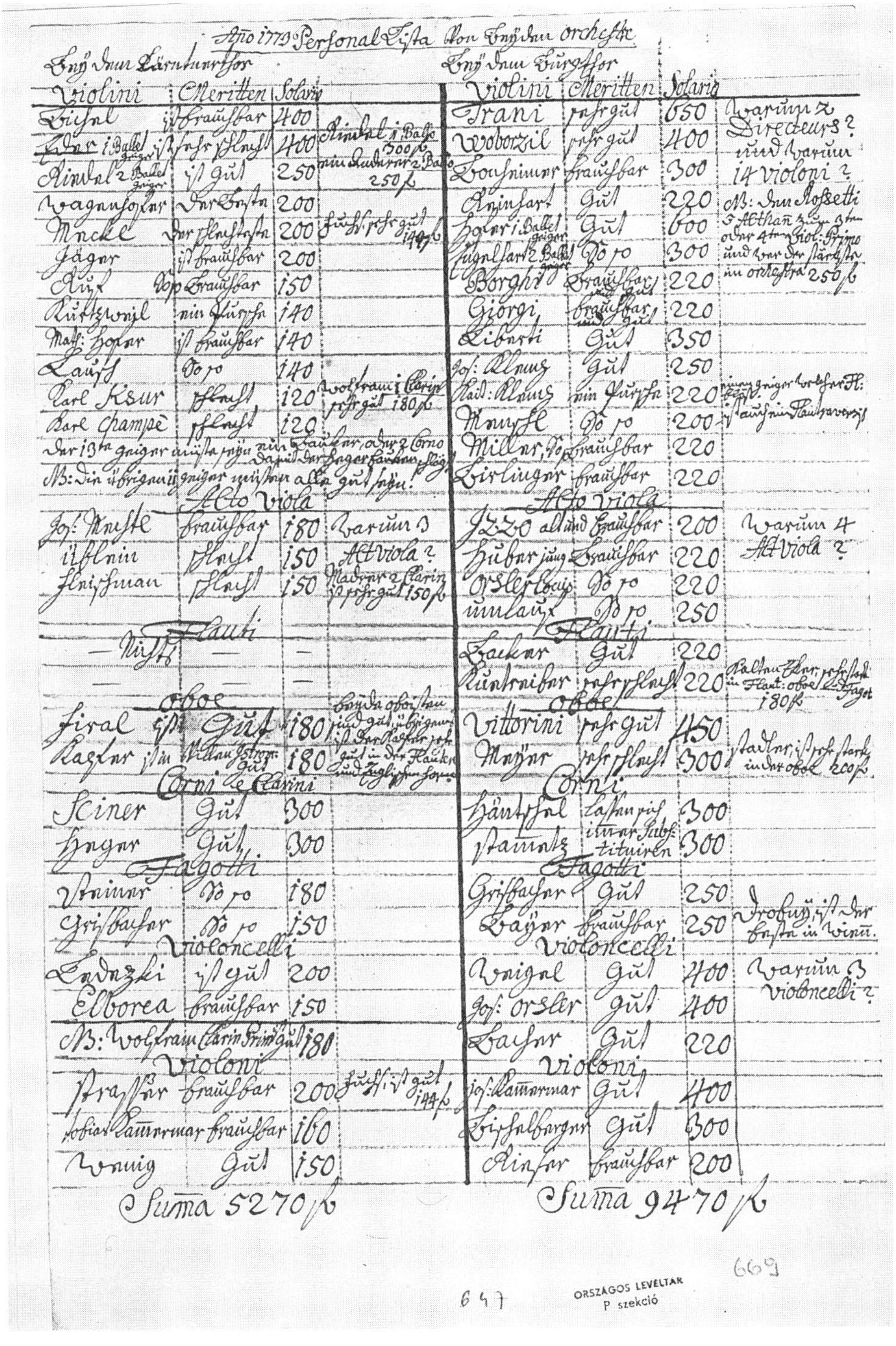

Ano 1773 Personal Lista von beyden orchester

Bey dem Kärntnerthor

Violini	Meritten	Solario	
Tischl	ist brauchbar	400	
Huber 1 Ballet geiger	sehr schlecht	400	Rindel 1 Basso 300 fl ein [illegible] 2 Basso 250 fl
Rindel 2 Ballet geiger	ist gut	250	
Wagenhofer	der beste	200	
Mucke	der schlechteste	200	Fuchs sehr gut 144 fl
Jäger	ist brauchbar	200	
Ruff	Do so brauchbar	150	
Kurtzweil	ein Pfuscher	140	
Math: Hofer	ist brauchbar	140	
Lauss	Do so	140	
Carl Kaur	schlecht	120	Wolfram 1 Clarin sehr gut 180 fl
Carl Champè	schlecht	120	
der 13te geiger müsste sehr ein brauchbar, oder 2 Corno [illegible]			
NB: die übrigen geiger müssen alle gut seyn.			
Alto viola			
Jos: Muste	brauchbar	180	warum 3 Alt viola?
Üblein	schlecht	150	
Fleischman	schlecht	150	Madner 2 Clarin ist sehr gut 150 fl
Flauti			
— Nichts	—	—	
—	—	—	
Oboe			
Firal	ist gut	180	beyde oboisten sind gut, übrigens ist der Kagler sehr gut in der Flauten und zugleich [illegible]
Kagler	ist ein [illegible] gut	180	
Corni e Clarini			
Steiner	gut	300	
Hugar	gut	300	
Fagotti			
Steiner	Do so	180	
Grießbacher	Do so	150	
Violoncelli			
Ladazki	ist gut	200	
Elborea	brauchbar	150	
NB: Wolfram Clarin Prim gut		180	
Violoni			
Strasser	brauchbar	200	Fuchs ist gut 144 fl
Tobias Lammermar	brauchbar	160	
Wenig	gut	150	

Suma 5270 fl

Bey dem Burgthor

Violini	Meritten	Solario	
Trani	sehr gut	650	warum 2 Directeurs? und warum 14 violoni?
Woborzil	sehr gut	400	
Hoffmann	brauchbar	300	
Reinhart	gut	220	NB: der Rossetti [illegible] Althan [illegible] oder 4ten Viol: Primo und war der stärkste im orchestra 250 fl
Hofer 1 Ballet geiger	gut	600	
Huglhart 2 Ballet geiger	Do so	300	
Borghi	brauchbar	220	
Giorgi	brauchbar und gut	220	
Liberti	gut	350	
Jos: Alung	gut	250	
Rud: Alung	ein Pfuscher	220	ein geiger welcher [illegible] auch ein Pfuscher [illegible]
Mauser	Do so	200	
Miller	Do brauchbar	220	
Hirlinger	brauchbar	220	
Alto viola			
Izzo	alt und brauchbar	200	warum 4 Alt viola?
Huber jung	brauchbar	220	
Orsler	Do so	220	
Umlauf	Do so	250	
Flauti			
Zacker	gut	220	
Kuntreiber	sehr schlecht	220	[illegible] Flaut: oboe [illegible] Fagot 180 fl
Oboe			
Vittorini	sehr gut	450	Stadler ist sehr stark in der oboe 200 fl
Mayer	sehr schlecht	300	
Corni			
Hantschel	lassen sich immer substituiren	300	
Stamitz		300	
Fagotti			
Grießbacher	gut	250	Drobney ist der beste in Wien.
Bayer	brauchbar	250	
Violoncelli			
Weigel	gut	400	warum 3 violoncelli?
Jos: Orsler	gut	400	
Bauer	gut	220	
Violoni			
Jos: Lammermar	gut	400	
Fischelberger	gut	300	
Kinser	brauchbar	200	

Suma 9470 fl

669

647

ORSZÁGOS LEVÉLTÁR
P szekció

FIGURE 2.6 List of players in the two theater orchestras, 1773, with evaluations of their ability. Keglevich papers. (Courtesy of National Archives of Hungary, Budapest.)

thirty-two players: fourteen violins, four violas, three cellos, and three double basses made up a string ensemble of twenty-four, reinforced by pairs of flutes, oboes, bassoons, and horns. The orchestra at the Kärntnertor was of similar size but lacked full-time flutists (under the rubric "Flauti" is written "Nichts").

This list is of special interest because it shows how one person, perhaps a court official or the impresario Keglevich, judged the quality of musicians who made up the orchestras: each name is followed by a very brief opinion of the player's ability.[54] Only three players in the Burgtheater, the violinists Giuseppe Trani (concertmaster) and Thomas Woborzill and the oboe virtuoso Vittorino Colombazzo (referred to here as "Vittorini"), were rated "very good"; about one-third of the players were rated "good"; the rest were judged "usable," "so-so," and (two musicians) "very bad." The quality of the players at the Kärntnertor, if we are to trust the anonymous opinions in the manuscript, was somewhat lower than that of the Burgtheater players. Their lower quality is consistent with their lower pay, documented in the same list. As of 1773, Keglevich paid the Burgtheater orchestra 9,470 Gulden per annum, the Kärntnertor orchestra only 5,270 Gulden.

"The Best Buffi of Italy"

Leopold Mozart, greatly impressed by the comic singers he heard in Vienna during his visit in 1767–68, described several of them as "excellent people" before he began to suspect that they had joined in a conspiracy against the performance of *La finta semplice.*[55] Few of those he named stayed in Vienna very long, however. The same financial problems that encouraged the turnover of impresarios may have discouraged the formation of a troupe whose members stayed together for several years, developing a sense of ensemble and a sense of identity: the kind of company assembled by Prince Nicolas Esterházy and by Joseph II during the 1780s. Only two of the singers mentioned by Mozart were still singing in Vienna in 1773; of those singing in 1773, only one was still in Vienna after Carnival 1775. And yet a small group stayed in Vienna long enough (or returned often enough) to have served as a kind of core that gave the troupe some degree of continuity.

One of the most important members of the core group was the Tuscan *buffo* Domenico Poggi, whose career spanned the 1760s, 1770s, and 1780s.[56] Poggi sang in Vienna during most of the life of the opera buffa troupe, from 1767 to Carnival 1775, with the exception of the theatrical year 1770, which he spent in Italy. When he married the so-

54. I am grateful to Dexter Edge for pointing this out to me during a conversation in Vienna in 1991.

55. Letter dated 30 January–3 February 1768 to Lorenz Hagenauer, in *MBA,* 1:258.

56. The libretto printed for a production of a pasticcio, *Le pescatrici* (Florence, spring 1763; Sartori no. 18604), describes Poggi as being "di Firenze." He is also said to be Tuscan in *Genaue Nachrichten,* 73.

prano Clementina Baglioni in late 1765 or early 1766, he became part of a family of singers of crucial importance for Viennese opera buffa during the late 1760s and early 1770s.[57]

Joseph von Sonnenfels devoted a letter in his *Briefe über die Wienerische Schaubühne* (1768) to the singers of the opera buffa troupe. In warmly praising Poggi's singing and acting, he presented a useful panorama of the opera buffa repertory near the beginning of the impresarial decade:

> He never exaggerates; and no matter how closely I have observed him, I have never been able to find a fault in him. His acting is always under control and his unforced gestures, never exaggerated, seem to follow only his own feelings. True, the old man in *Il vecchio geloso* [an alternative title of Galuppi's *L'amante di tutte,* Venice, 1760; Vienna, 1767] was not a good role for him. A healthy, lively man is too far out of character when forced to represent a stiff old man. His best roles are peasants, middle-aged fathers, and also servants.
>
> In *La contadina in corte* [by Antonio Sacchini, Rome, 1765; Vienna, 1767], where he played the former lover of a peasant girl who finds herself at court, and where the various scenes offered him opportunity to make use of all his cunning and sense of humor and to display the peasant's bashfulness and simplicity, he won special praise from connoisseurs.
>
> In *Il marchese villano* [by Galuppi, Venice, 1762; Vienna, 1767] he was the only one who did not overstep the bounds that separate the humorous from the farcical. . . .
>
> In *La notte critica* [by Gassmann, 1768], where he plays the servant in love with the maid, I was almost completely convinced by his portrayal of a French servant, with the exception of this fellow's impudence, which has begun to be repugnant to me since I have been in Germany. [In his *Briefe* Sonnenfels initially adopted the persona of a French visitor to Vienna.][58]

In addition to his skills as an actor and singer, Poggi was also a poet. He collaborated with Salieri in *La locandiera,* transforming Goldoni's prose play into a libretto. Poggi sang the role of the servant Fabrizio in Salieri's opera, the kind of role that (according to Sonnenfels) suited him. Another servant part probably written for him was that of Simone in Mozart's *La finta semplice;* but the original distribution of roles in Mozart's opera is not known for certain, contrary to what some recent discussions of the opera suggest.[59]

57. When Clementina Baglioni sang in Guglielmi's *I rivali placati* in Milan during fall 1765, she still used her maiden name (Sartori no. 20037), but in Rutini's *L'olandese in Italia* (Bologna, Carnival 1766; Sartori no. 16907) she appeared under her married name: Clementina Baglioni Poggi. The editors of *MBA* (5:188) state mistakenly that Clementina Baglioni was Domenico Poggi's daughter.

58. Joseph von Sonnenfels, *Briefe über die Wienerische Schaubühne* (Vienna, 1884), 71.

59. In the introduction to their edition of *La finta semplice* in *NMA,* Rudolph Angermüller and Wolfgang Rehm attribute the roles to specific singers without citing evidence or the apparent source of their information, Abert, *Mozart,* 1:104–11. They thereby turn Abert's attributions, which he presented for the most part as reasoned guesses, into apparent facts (see Heartz, *Viennese School,* 518). The editors of *MBA* also attribute the roles to specific singers, again without evidence; as one might expect, their attributions differ

During the early years of the impresarial decade the buffo Francesco Carattoli, who sang in Vienna from 1764 until sometime before his death in March 1772, was one of the troupe's most distinguished members. Born in Rome in 1704 or 1705, Carattoli began singing professionally in the mid-1740s.[60] His career coincided with a crucial period in the history of opera buffa.[61] His earliest roles included at least one in Neapolitan dialect,[62] through which he helped introduce Neapolitan musical comedy to Rome, whence it spread to northern Italy. Singing in works by Gaetano Latilla, Galuppi, and Fischietti, he contributed much to the growing prestige and popularity of opera buffa during the 1740s and 1750s. He created roles in several of Galuppi's earliest and most important collaborations with Goldoni: Foresto in *L'Arcadia in Brenta,* Cecco in *Il mondo della luna,* Furibondo in *Arcifanfano re de' matti,* and Tritemio in *Il filosofo di campagna.* Later, in Rome during Carnival 1760, he played the first Tagliaferro, the German soldier in Piccinni's *La buona figliuola.* Within little more than a decade he thus created many of the finest comic bass roles of the mid-eighteenth century.

Carattoli began singing in Vienna in May 1764, within a few weeks of Durazzo's resignation. In one of his first appearances he sang Tagliaferro in *La buona figliuola;* Khevenhüller described him in his diary as "one of the best buffi I have ever heard."[63] When Sonnenfels wrote of him in 1768 he was already about sixty-three years old. Well suited to parts that were not right for Poggi, Carattoli excelled in roles written for him by Gassmann in his settings of Goldoni's librettos:

---

somewhat from those of Angermüller and Rehm. Leopold Mozart's "Species facti," a statement of his version of the affair, names the four male singers who were going to perform *La finta semplice:* the basses Francesco Carattoli and Domenico Poggi and the tenors Gioacchino Caribaldi and Filippo Laschi. But we do not know the distribution of their roles. Leopold's letter to Lorenz Hagenauer of 30 July 1768 (*MBA* 1:269–74) discloses that two of the three female roles were to have been sung by Antonia Bernasconi and "die Baglioni" (singular): either Clementina or Rosa Baglioni, both of whom were in Vienna in 1768. But what roles they were to sing, and who the third female singer was to be, is unknown.

60. Librettos printed for productions of Giuseppe Scarlatti's *Il giocatore* (Florence, Carnival 1747; Sartori no. 11955) and Latilla's *Madama Ciana* (Livorno, fall 1748; Sartori no. 14562) describe Carattoli as "di Roma." That he was born in 1704 or 1705 follows from the fact that he was sixty-seven years old when he died in Vienna on 22 March 1772; see Gustav Gugitz, "Die Totenprotokolle der Stadt Wien als Quelle zur Wiener Theatergeschichte des 18. Jahrhunderts," *Jahrbuch der Gesellschaft für Wiener Theaterforschung* (1953–54), 120.

61. Daniel Heartz, "The Creation of the Buffo Finale in Italian Opera," *Proceedings of the Royal Musical Association* 104 (1977–78): 67–78, discusses Carattoli's roles in *L'Arcadia in Brenta* and *Il mondo della luna,* both by Goldoni and Galuppi. See also Piero Weiss, "La diffusione del repertorio operistico nell'Italia del Settecento: Il caso dell'opera buffa," in *Civiltà teatrale e Settecento emiliano,* ed. Susi Davoli (Bologna, 1986), 241–56.

62. Carattoli sang the role of Cuosemo in Antonio Aurisicchio's *L'inganno deluso* (Rome, 1743; Sartori no. 13157). The libretto states: "Cuosemo e Ciomma parlano Napolitano." The rest of this paragraph is based on Sartori.

63. Khevenhüller, 6:35 (19 May 1764).

> Caratoli is no longer much of a singer; but he is an actor all the more; and he knows how to render singing superfluous. His roles are old men. In *Il viaggiatore ridicolo* and in *L'amore artigiano* he revealed himself in all his power. Hogarth could stand constantly before the stage drawing this actor's posturings: in every drama he would have a series of outstanding caricatures to collect. His face especially is expressive: true, like nature itself; his acting varied and changeful; his intelligence great—but he disowns this intelligence too often in the interest of superficial laughter, by which an audience expresses not approval but foolishness. In *La notte critica,* where the set depicts a flourishing garden where the maid and the daughter of the house await their lovers at night, and therefore the season is clearly defined, I have seen him come on stage dressed in a fur coat; in another piece I saw him decorate his coat with little round mirrors instead of buttons. Generally he tries in his dress to look as unseemly as possible, with a vest that is longer than his coat, and so forth.[64]

Mozart probably wrote the role of Cassandro, the stingy landowner in *La finta semplice,* for Carattoli, who certainly took part in preparations for the production. When Mozart finished the first act, his father showed it to the great buffo and several other male members of the troupe. Carattoli responded with enthusiasm: "What? What? This is a miracle! This opera will be immortal! It is a marvel! Do not fear: keep writing!"[65] The Mozarts must have valued this praise highly, coming from one of the finest comic basses of his time and one who had created so many important roles.

Of several tenors who belonged at various times to the impresarios' opera buffa troupe, Gioacchino Caribaldi was probably the best. A shop assistant in Rome before he found success on the operatic stage at the age of twenty-four, Caribaldi made some early attempts in opera seria (Rome, Carnival 1759) but soon devoted himself entirely to comic opera. Mozart wrote a role for him in *La finta semplice,* but whether it was that of the foolish gentleman Polidoro or that of the Hungarian officer Fracasso, both fine tenor roles, we do not know.

Caribaldi's acting did not please Sonnenfels, who felt that he lacked Carattoli's skill and judgment, and described as "forced and monotonous" his portrayals of Marchese Giorgino in *Il marchese villano,* Giannino in Gassmann's *L'amore artigiano,* and the servant Carlotto in *La notte critica.* "But the mediocre actor has a throat that delights: a tenor voice that has something positively moving and sweet in it, and over which he has such control that he can bring to it, when required, the proper relaxation [*Nachlassung*] and tension [*Anspannung*] that constitute the chiaroscuro of singing and thus the soul of expression. . . . His *passaggi* and coloratura are smooth and flowing, but without art: only the scale in stepwise motion, always the same thing."[66]

64. Sonnenfels, *Briefe,* 69–70.
65. *MBA,* 1:280.
66. Sonnenfels, *Briefe,* 72.

Burney, who heard Caribaldi in Milan in 1770, also praised his singing: "Garibaldi, the first man, . . . sung very well. He has a pleasing voice, and much taste and expression; was encored, *alla Italiana,* two or three times."[67]

Caribaldi created a role in Salieri's first publicly performed opera, *Le donne letterate,* but not without controversy. The plainness of his coloratura may have had something to do with his lack of formal musical education, a deficiency that brought him into conflict with Salieri, as we shall see in chapter 4.

Among the female members of the opera buffa troupe, a single family accounted for much of the talent and achievement: the sisters Clementina, Costanza, and Rosa Baglioni, among the many musical daughters of the Roman buffo Francesco Baglioni.

Clementina Baglioni started singing professionally in the mid-1750s and rose to fame in comic operas, especially the collaborations of Goldoni and Galuppi.[68] Like Carattoli, she created roles in some of Galuppi's most successful operas: Lesbina in *Il filosofo di campagna* and Clarice in *L'amante di tutte.* She also sang in several opere serie, which suggests a capacity for virtuoso singing and for the expression of intense emotions greater than was expected of opera buffa singers, who rarely entered the world of opera seria.

Clementina was first engaged in Vienna to sing serious opera, not comic. During spring 1762 (when opera buffa was, as far as we know, entirely absent from the repertory) she created the role of Larissa in Hasse's *Il trionfo di Clelia.* She resumed her career in Italy, but in 1766 returned to Vienna, now singing under her married name, Clementina Baglioni Poggi.[69] Like her husband she stayed in Vienna until Carnival 1775, except for engagements in Italy in 1770.

Taking advantage of her experience in opera seria, the impresarios occasionally assigned Clementina heroic roles, such as that of Venere in Gassmann's *Amore e Psiche*. In comic operas she specialized in bravura singing. Salieri gave her opportunity to demonstrate those talents in *Le donne letterate,* in which (according to Mosel) she created the role of Artemia. Mozart may have written the prima-donna role of Rosina in *La finta semplice* for her; it is often attributed to her in discussions of Mozart's first opera buffa, but without documentary evidence.

Sonnenfels praised Clementina's voice but thought little of her acting: "This singer's voice is silvery, as flexible as one could want, and it floats beautifully; she sings not with boldness but with truth. Her gestures are decorous, free, and noble. But what good are

67. Charles Burney, *The Present State of Music in France and Italy,* ed. Percy A. Scholes (London, 1959), 69–70.

68. Clementina Baglioni is described as "di Roma" in librettos printed for productions of a pasticcio, *Ciro riconosciuto* (Pisa, Carnival 1764; Sartori no. 5719), and Fischietti's *Il mercato di Malmantile* (Florence, summer 1764; Sartori no. 15456). The rest of this paragraph and the following one are based on Sartori.

69. Clementina Baglioni sang in the premiere of Gassmann's *Il viaggiatore ridicolo* on 25 October 1766 (Zechmeister, 280, 500; Sartori no. 24755).

these gifts when an obviously ill-tempered singer makes no use of them? So often she acts with so little effort, with such negligence, as if she were doing the public a favor."[70]

Clementina was joined in Vienna by her sisters Costanza and Rosa (also called Rosina) Baglioni, who were probably younger than Clementina because they began singing in public much later. Costanza made one of her first public appearances in Venice in 1762. Although she sang briefly in Vienna in 1765, she did not join the troupe until 1771. Burney witnessed her performance in Florence in 1770: "her voice is clear, and always in tune, her shake open and perfect, and her taste and expression left nothing to wish."[71] Rosa began singing professionally in 1764 or shortly before. She was probably quite young when she arrived in Vienna sometime between Carnival 1766 and the premiere of Gassmann's *Il viaggiatore ridicolo* later the same year.[72]

Both Rosa and Costanza won praise from the *Theatralkalender* of 1772:

> Mademoiselle Constantia Baglioni, sister of the above-mentioned [Clementina], has a stronger voice, but not so pleasing and accurate. Her acting has much fire, but also the weaknesses of Italian acting.
>
> Mademoiselle Rosina, her younger sister, has the makings of a pleasing singer. A beautiful voice, good appearance, intelligence, and a truly natural style of acting. But she is too timid, and a bashful modesty keeps her from bringing fire and emotion to her performance. If she had enough courage to give herself over to her roles, she would be one of the best opera singers. Furthermore she is an exceptionally good learner, without thirst for glory, presumption, and caprice.[73]

A contract signed by Costanza and Rosa on 13 April 1772 states the conditions under which they were employed during the theatrical years 1773–74 (see fig. 2.7). The two sisters undertook "to sing in the licenced theaters of the city of Vienna and in the imperial villas [i.e., Laxenburg and Schönbrunn] in all the operas, both serious and comic, and in the academies [i.e., concerts] that will be presented at the expense of the Theater Management. And the above-mentioned Sig[a] Costanza agrees to alternate with the other Prima Donna [probably Clementina Baglioni] both in the comic and in the

70. Sonnenfels, *Briefe*, 74.

71. Burney, *France and Italy*, 173.

72. Rosa Baglioni sang in Venice during Carnival 1766 (Sartori nos. 4276 and 16635). In Vienna during 1766 she created a role in *Il viaggiatore ridicolo* (Sartori no. 24755).

73. Mademoiselle Constantia Baglioni, eine Schwester der Vorigen, hat eine stärkere, aber nicht so angenehme und richtige Stimme. Viel Feuer in ihrer Aktion, aber mit den Fehlern des italiänischen Spieles.

Mademoiselle Rosinen, ihrer jüngern Schwester, fehlt nichts zu einer angenehmen Sängerinn. Eine schöne Stimme, gute Gestalt, Einsicht, und ein recht natürliches Spiel. Aber sie ist zu furchtsam, und eine blöde Schamhaftigkeit hindert sie Feuer und Empfindung anzubringen. Wenn sie Muth genug hätte, sich ihrer Rolle zu überlassen, sie würde eine der besten Operistinnen seyn. Im übrigen ist sie ungemein gelehrig, ohne Ruhmgierde, Einbildung und Eigensinn (*Theatralkalender von Wien, für das Jahr 1772*, 86–87).

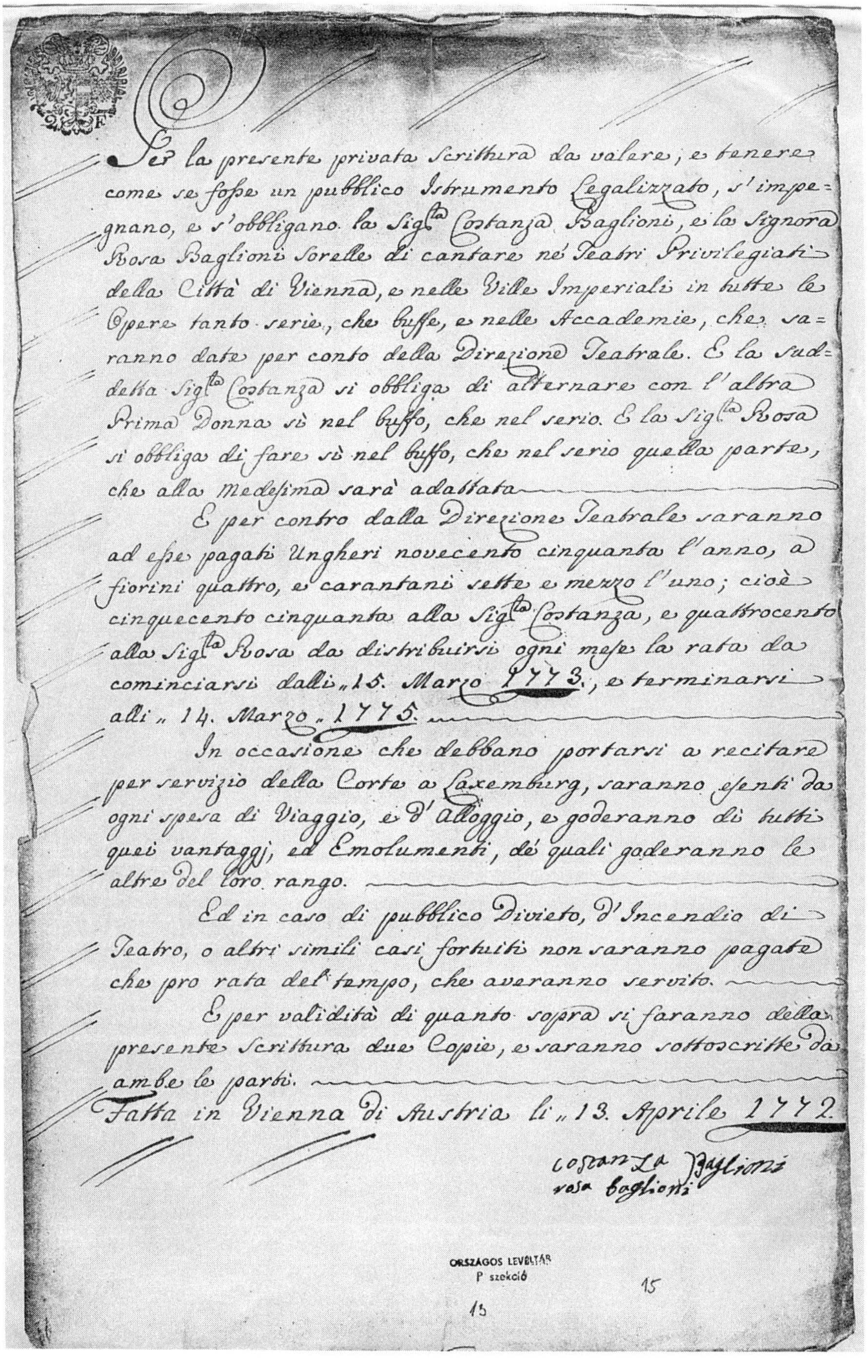

Per la presente privata Scrittura da valere, e tenere come se fosse un pubblico Istrumento Legalizzato, s'impegnano, e s'obbligano la Sig.ra Costanza Baglioni, e la Signora Rosa Baglioni Sorelle di cantare ne' Teatri Privilegiati della Città di Vienna, e nelle Ville Imperiali in tutte le Opere tanto serie, che buffe, e nelle Accademie, che saranno date per conto della Direzione Teatrale. E la suddetta Sig.ra Costanza si obbliga di alternare con l'altra Prima Donna sì nel buffo, che nel serio. E la Sig.ra Rosa si obbliga di fare sì nel buffo, che nel serio quella parte, che alla Medesima sarà adattata.

E per contro dalla Direzione Teatrale saranno ad esse pagati Ungheri novecento cinquanta l'anno, a fiorini quattro, e carantani sette e mezzo l'uno; cioè cinquecento cinquanta alla Sig.ra Costanza, e quattrocento alla Sig.ra Rosa da distribuirsi ogni mese la rata da cominciarsi dalli 15. Marzo 1773., e terminarsi alli 14. Marzo 1775.

In occasione che debbano portarsi a recitare per servizio della Corte a Laxemburg, saranno esenti da ogni spesa di Viaggio, e d'Alloggio, e goderanno di tutti quei vantaggj, ed Emolumenti, de' quali goderanno le altre del loro rango.

Ed in caso di pubblico Divieto, d'Incendio di Teatro, o altri simili casi fortuiti non saranno pagate che pro rata del tempo, che averanno servito.

E per validità di quanto sopra si faranno della presente Scrittura due Copie, e saranno sottoscritte da ambe le parti.

Fatta in Vienna di Austria li 13. Aprile 1772.

Costanza Baglioni
rosa baglioni

ORSZÁGOS LEVÉLTÁR
P szekció
15
13

FIGURE 2.7 Contract signed by Costanza and Rosa Baglioni with the terms of a two-year engagement in Vienna (March 1773–March 1775). Keglevich papers. (Courtesy of National Archives of Hungary, Budapest.)

serious. And Sig^a^ Rosa agrees to sing the part prepared for her, both in the comic and in the serious."

The roles assigned to Costanza and Rosa in Salieri's *La locandiera,* first performed on 8 June 1773 (and one of the few Viennese operas of the early 1770s whose complete cast we know with some degree of certainty) agree exactly with the requirements of their contract. Costanza, as prima donna, sang the title role of the innkeeper Mirandolina. Rosa sang the only other female role in the opera, that of the servant girl Lena, a part not requiring the "fire and emotion" that shyness kept her from expressing.

The contract's recurring phrase "sì nel buffo, che nel serio" points to a characteristic feature of Italian opera in Vienna, not only during the impresarial decade, but during the 1780s and 1790s as well: a tendency to break down some of the distinctions between opera seria and opera buffa. In Italy singers were expected to specialize in one type of opera or the other. In Vienna such distinctions were less important, as one might guess from the performance of several roles in Gluck's *Alceste* by members of the opera buffa troupe and from the contract signed by Costanza and Rosa Baglioni, whose careers in Italy had been devoted almost entirely to comic opera. Those who produced opera in Vienna, furthermore, seem to have made special efforts to engage singers with experience in opera seria even at times when the genre was not represented in the repertory. And we will see that Viennese composers, even when writing opere buffe, often reacted to the presence of such singers with music inspired by the grandeur and pathos of opera seria.

Burney witnessed performances of some of the Baglioni sisters in Milan in 1770 and called them "midling"; he saw one of them two years later in Vienna and praised her singing in Salieri's *Il barone di Rocca Antica:*

> She is very much improved since that time [i.e., since Burney heard her in Italy in 1770], and her voice is now one of the clearest, truest, most powerful, and extensive I ever heard. In compass, it is from B♭, on the fifth space in the base [i.e., a whole step below middle C], to D in alt [D above high C], full, steady, and equal; her shake is good, and her *Portamento* admirably free from the nose, mouth, or throat. There is such a roundness and dignity in all the tones, that every thing she did became interesting; a few plain slow notes from her, were more acceptable to the audience, than a whole elaborate air from any one else.
>
> This singer is young, has good features, the *embonpoint charmant,* and is upon the whole a fine figure.[74]

We do not know the cast of this production, and Burney did not specify by name which sister he heard in it. Although some modern scholars have assumed it was Costanza, it is more likely to have been Clementina. The qualities Burney ascribed to the sister who

74. Burney, *Germany,* 84–85.

sang in *Il barone,* especially the large compass, were not those Salieri emphasized in music he wrote for Costanza in *La locandiera.*

The Viennese opera buffa troupe took shape in Italy: some of its most important members had sung there together before coming to Vienna. Francesco Baglioni, the father of Clementina, Costanza, and Rosa, had helped to assure the success of comic operas by Latilla and Rinaldo di Capua in Rome during the late 1730s; he had played an equally important role in the formative years of Goldonian opera buffa, creating many important parts in Goldoni's librettos.[75] During the 1750s and 1760s he often shared the stage with one or more of his daughters, including Clementina and Costanza, and with Francesco Carattoli. Although he never sang in Vienna, as far as we know, Francesco Baglioni was at the center of a group of comic singers that included several who would later contribute to Viennese opera buffa. The playwright Vittorio Alfieri remembered a performance of an opera buffa in Turin during the early 1760s as having been "sung by the best buffi of Italy: Carattoli, Baglioni and his daughters."[76] The employment of several of these singers in Vienna shows that the impresarios, despite their financial problems, were committed to presenting the very finest of comic opera in the court theaters.

75. See Weiss, "La diffusione del repertorio operistico," 254–56, on Francesco Baglioni's role in the success of Latilla's *La finta cameriera.* For a discussion of Baglioni's contribution to Goldoni and Galuppi's *L'Arcadia in Brenta,* in which he as well as Carattoli created roles, see Heartz, "Vis Comica."

76. "Vita di Vittorio Alfieri da Asti scritta da esso," in *Opere di Vittorio Alfieri,* ed. Vittorio Branca (Milan, 1968), 34.

3

GOLDONIAN OPERA BUFFA IN VIENNA BEFORE SALIERI

The Venetian dramatist Goldoni contributed much to the shape and content of opera buffa during the second half of the eighteenth century and to the popularity of the genre in much of Europe. In settings of his librettos by Galuppi, Latilla, Piccinni, and Fischietti the most characteristic elements of midcentury opera buffa came to dramatic life. Goldoni did not invent most of these elements, but he helped to transform the genre nevertheless, bringing to the operatic stage the charm, lightness of touch, and vividness of characterization that distinguish his spoken comedies from those of his contemporaries.

Goldoni derived many of his characters from comic opera in Neapolitan dialect—*commeddeja pe mmuseca*—that infiltrated northern Italy during the 1730s and 1740s; from the Neapolitan comic intermezzo; from great spoken comedies of the past, most notably those of Molière; and from commedia dell'arte. Following the lead of Neapolitan librettists he introduced noble, serious characters into many librettos; these contributed elegance and pathos and sometimes provided him and his composers with an easy object of parody. He brought these characters together in well-crafted plots, some of which unfold against the colorful background of contemporary Italian life (the ballroom, the inn, the village square, the drawing room) while others present elaborately conceived worlds of fantasy (a kingdom of madmen, an island ruled by women). With a delicate mixture of wit, sensibility, and silliness, Goldoni exposed vice to gentle mockery, whether he found it in the aristocracy, in the bourgeoisie, or among servants and peasants.

Goldonian opera buffa appealed to audiences outside Italy more strongly than earlier Italian comic opera. While Pergolesi's intermezzo *La serva padrona* delighted audiences in midcentury Paris, it could never on its own represent a full evening's entertainment in Paris or elsewhere. Neapolitan comic operas and operas created in imitation of them in Rome and northern Italy were more successful in Italy than north of the Alps. Latilla's *La finta cameriera* (Rome, 1738; an adaptation of his Neapolitan comedy *Gismondo*) delighted audiences in Italy during the 1740s but was rarely performed outside Italy.[1]

Opera buffa had to overcome, with Goldoni's help, the consensus among operagoers outside Italy that its plots were childish and that its characters offered little more than senseless caricature. The German man of letters Christian Felix Weiße, remembering his experiences in Paris in 1759, compared opera buffa unfavorably to opéra-comique. French singers "did not attempt to arouse loud applause through farcical actions or grotesque caricature, like most of the Italians."[2] Friedrich Melchior Grimm recognized the musical richness of opera buffa but could not accept its ridiculous plots and characters: "the only thing that keeps us from going crazy over Italian opera buffa is that the librettos generally lack common sense."[3]

In discussing Carattoli, whom he heard in Milan in 1770, Burney alluded to an Italian taste for (as he saw it) exaggerated farce as a barrier to the appreciation of opera buffa in England, calling Carattoli "a baritone at whom they laugh very much *here,* but his humour is too national to please in England, he is always noisy and blustering in comic character."[4] Goldoni's librettos were the primary vehicles through which Carattoli, near the end of his life, won applause in Vienna as well as in Italy.

Goldoni's transformation of opera buffa led to its rapid spread to many parts of Europe. Attempting to explain the success in London of Piccinni's setting of Goldoni's *La buona figliuola,* Burney pointed to a feature that contributed to its popularity and to that of many other settings of the librettos of Goldoni and his followers: "The celebrated Buona Figliuola . . . rendered the name of [Piccinni], which had scarcely penetrated into this country before, dear to every lover of music in the nation. . . . And some

1. On the popularity of *La finta cameriera* in Italy, see Piero Weiss, "La diffusione del repertorio operistico," 254–56, and "Opera Buffa," in *NGDO,* where some of the few productions outside Italy are cited as well. *La finta cameriera* (under an alternate title, *Don Colascione*) failed to find appreciative audiences in London when it and other opere buffe were performed by a traveling troupe between 1748 and 1750. See Richard G. King and Saskia Willaert, "Giovanni Francesco Crosa and the First Italian Comic Operas in London, Brussels and Amsterdam, 1748–50," *Journal of the Royal Musical Association* 118 (1993), 246–75.

2. Sie suchten nicht, wie die meisten Italienischen durch Possenreißereyen und groteske Carrikaturen lautes Lachen zu erregen (Christian Felix Weiße, *Selbstbiographie,* ed. Christian Ernst Weiße and Samuel Gottlob Frisch [Leipzig, 1806], 103; quoted in translation in Karin Pendle, "Opéra-Comique as Literature: The Spread of French Styles in Europe, ca. 1760 to the Revolution," in *Grétry et l'Europe de l'opéra-comique,* ed. Philippe Vendrix [Liège, 1992], 230).

3. Pendle, "Opéra-Comique as Literature," 245, quoting Friedrich Melchior Grimm, *Correspondance littéraire,* 16 vols. (Paris, 1877–82), 2:136–37.

4. Charles Burney, *Music, Men and Manners in France and Italy, 1770,* ed. H. Edmund Poole (London, 1974), 52.

of the success of the opera, particularly in England, must be ascribed to the drama, which has more character, and much less ribaldry and buffoonery, than usual in Italian burlettas."[5]

The establishment of opera buffa as a central part of the Viennese operatic repertory during the mid-1760s coincided with the spread of the genre through Europe. All the opere buffe performed in Vienna as the genre gained a foothold at the end of Durazzo's theatrical regime were imported from Italy, and most were settings of librettos by Goldoni: Fischietti's *Il mercato di Malmantile,* Giuseppe Scolari's *La conversazione,* Giuseppe Scarlatti's *La serva scaltra,* and Galuppi's *Il filosofo di campagna* in 1763; Fischietti's *Il signor dottore* and *Il mercato di Malmantile,* Piccinni's *La buona figliuola* and *La buona figliuola maritata,* and Galuppi's *Le nozze* in 1764.[6]

Durazzo, to whom the appeal of Goldonian opera buffa must have been clear, may have tried to bring Goldoni himself to Vienna. In a letter of 4 January 1764 Charles-Simon Favart wrote to Durazzo: "I congratulate Your Excellency on your acquisition of the divine Goldoni. . . . I dare say Vienna will be no less happy with his productions than Venice and Paris."[7] Durazzo's apparent attempt to engage Goldoni was unsuccessful. But that did not keep Viennese composers, when they began writing their own opere buffe, from using Goldoni's librettos more often than not.

Gassmann, trained in Venice during the period in which Goldoni established his reputation as the leading poet of opera buffa, had probably worked with the librettist there. He had made the first settings of Goldoni's librettos *Gli uccellatori* (1759) and *Filosofia ed amore* (1760), presumably in consultation with Goldoni and with the librettist acting as stage director. For the Viennese opera buffa troupe he wrote four comic operas during the second half of the 1760s: *Il viaggiatore ridicolo* (1766), *L'amore artigiano* (1767), *La notte critica* (1768), and *L'opera seria* (1769). Goldoni wrote the librettos for all but the last (by Calzabigi).

Other composers working in or near Vienna similarly favored Goldoni. Mozart set *La finta semplice,* as adapted by Coltellini for the Viennese stage.[8] (In Vienna during the early 1780s Mozart turned again to a drama by Goldoni, planning a German opera based on the play *Il servitor di due padroni.*)[9] At nearby Eisenstadt and Eszterháza Haydn

5. Charles Burney, *A General History of Music,* ed. Frank Mercer, 2 vols. (New York, 1957), 2:871–72.

6. Zechmeister, 485–95.

7. Charles-Simon Favart, *Mémoires et correspondances,* ed. A. P. C. Favart, 3 vols. (Paris, 1808); quoted in Brown, *Gluck,* 80–81.

8. The libretto of *La finta semplice,* first performed in Venice during Carnival 1764 with music by Salvador Perillo, was first published anonymously, and attributed to Goldoni only thirty years later (by Zatta in his edition of Goldoni's collected works, 1788–95). Ortolani accepted the attribution and included the libretto in his edition of the complete works (abbreviated here as "Goldoni").

9. Mozart mentioned the project in a letter to his father dated 5 February 1783, in *MBA,* 3:255.

wrote three opere buffe during the second half of the 1760s, two of them, *Lo speziale* and *Le pescatrici,* settings of librettos by Goldoni.[10]

Salieri, born shortly after Goldoni began his collaboration with Galuppi in 1749, passed his childhood as Goldonian opera buffa spread through Italy and Europe. One of the few operatic productions known to have taken place in his hometown of Legnago was of Piccinni's *La buona figliuola* in 1763, when he was thirteen.[11] He received his operatic training from a musician who was busy, at the same time, setting Goldoni's librettos to music and directing their performance. The spirit of Goldonian comedy pervades Salieri's opere buffe. We cannot hope to understand Salieri as musical dramatist without some knowledge of Goldoni's librettos and the music that they inspired in Gassmann and his Italian contemporaries.

Two Goldonian Operas in Italy and Vienna: Fischietti's *Il mercato di Malmantile* and Piccinni's *La buona figliuola*

Fischietti's setting of Goldoni's libretto *Il mercato di Malmantile* and Piccinni's of *La buona figliuola* were both enormously popular during the 1760s in Italy and abroad. Both were performed in Vienna by casts that included a singer who had created roles in the original productions. These works can help us understand operatic taste and practice in Vienna as well as in Italy at the time when Salieri received his operatic training, Goldonian opera invaded and conquered Vienna, and Gassmann established opera buffa as a genre that Viennese composers could cultivate with success.

After its premiere in Venice during Carnival 1758 *Il mercato di Malmantile* spread quickly throughout northern Italy, with performances in Bologna, Piacenza, Florence, Livorno, and Milan before the end of the year.[12] *Il mercato* also enjoyed great popular-

10. Pierluigi Petrobelli, "Goldoni at Esterhaza: The Story of His Librettos Set by Haydn," in Badura-Skoda, 314–18.

11. Sartori no. 4190.

12. Some copies of the libretto printed for the first production of *Il mercato di Malmantile* attribute the music to Giuseppe Scarlatti; at least one copy (in US-Wc) "gives Fischietti as the composer, but his name may have been added later, for it is not perfectly aligned with the other type on that page" (Howard Mayer Brown, preface to a facsimile edition of *Il mercato di Malmantile* [New York, 1983]). Most other editions of the libretto and most surviving scores attribute the opera to Fischietti. This suggests that the initial attribution to Scarlatti was an error. Gordana Lazarevich, "Mercato di Malmantile, Il," in *NGDO,* accepts Fischietti as author.

The present discussion of *Il mercato di Malmantile* is based on three manuscript scores, all naming Fischietti as composer: F-Pn MSS D.4140–42 and GB-Lcm, MS 4045 (reproduced in the facsimile edition), and US-NYp, Signature *MSI. Where these scores conflict, I have generally preferred the reading in the Paris MS.

On Fischietti's life and comic operas see Richard Engländer, "Domenico Fischietti als Buffokomponist in Dresden," *Zeitschrift für Musikwissenschaft* 2 (1919–20): 321–52, 399–422. Goldoni's libretto is discussed in Ronald J. Rabin, "Mozart, Da Ponte, and the Dramaturgy of Opera Buffa: Italian Comic Opera in Vienna, 1783–1791" (Ph.D. diss., Cornell University, 1996), 73–80; and, more briefly, in David Newton Marinelli,

ity abroad. Bonn saw it in March 1758, within a few months of its premiere; London in 1761; Dublin in 1762; Vienna in 1763; Lisbon and Warsaw in 1765; Dresden in 1766; and Hannover in 1770. One of the last documented performances occurred in Salzburg in 1773.[13] Alfieri seems to have expressed the opinion of many opera lovers when he wrote of a performance of *Il mercato* in Turin during the early 1760s: "The spirit and the variety of that divine music made the profoundest impression on me, leaving in my ears and in my imagination a furrow of harmony, so to speak, and stirring my innermost fibers, so that for several weeks I remained immersed in an extraordinary but not unpleasant melancholy."[14]

Performed in Vienna on 15 May 1763, *Il mercato* was the first of several opere buffe presented there by Maso and his traveling troupe.[15] Since his performances mark the beginning of opera buffa as a permanent part of the Viennese repertory, *Il mercato* has a place of particular importance in the history of Viennese opera. One evening in July 1763 an audience at the Kärntnertor showed its enthusiasm for Fischietti's opera by demanding the repetition of two arias, much to the annoyance of Durazzo, who may have sensed that opera buffa would soon dominate the repertory at the expense of the genres and composers that he favored.[16] *Il mercato* did indeed outlast the Musikgraf; it was performed again in Vienna in 1764, following Durazzo's resignation.

La buona figliuola, first performed in Rome during Carnival 1760, took Italy by storm during the early 1760s.[17] Within a decade of its premiere it reached the stages of Bologna, Milan, Venice, Turin, and several smaller cities. At the same time audiences in

---

"Carlo Goldoni as Experimental Librettist: The *Drammi Giocosi* of 1750" (Ph.D. diss., Rutgers University, 1988), 112–13; and Ted Emery, *Goldoni as Librettist: Theatrical Reform and the Drammi Giocosi per Musica* (New York, 1991), 172.

13. Sartori nos. 15431–470.

14. "Vita di Vittorio Alfieri da Asti scritta da esso," 34. Alfieri remembered the opera's title as *Il mercato di Malmantile* and the year as 1762; but Mercedes Viale Ferrero, "Torino e Milano nel tardo Settecento: Repertori a confronto," in Muraro, *Mozart,* 1:103–4, points out that, in the absence of other evidence that *Il mercato di Malmantile* was performed at the Teatro Carignano in 1762, Alfieri may have erred in the date of the performance or the title of the opera.

15. Zechmeister, 252.

16. "Au Theatre allemand a la representation du *Mercato di Malmantile.* On s'avisa de faire repeter deux airs, ce qui fut fort ressenti par M. Durazzo" (Zinzendorf, 16 July 1763; quoted in Harbecke, "Das Tagebuch des Grafen Karl von Zinzendorf," 58; and Brown, *Gluck,* 105).

17. This discussion of *La buona figliuola* is based on a manuscript score in I-Fc (reproduced in facsimile, New York, 1983). On the libretto and its literary antecedents see William C. Holmes, "Pamela Transformed," *Musical Quarterly* 38 (1952): 581–94; Mary Hunter, "'Pamela': The Offspring of Richardson's Heroine in Eighteenth-Century Opera," *Mosaic* 18 (1985): 61–76; and Ted Emery, "Goldoni's *Pamela* from Play to Libretto," *Italica* 64 (1987): 572–82. On Piccinni's score see Anna Amalie Abert, "Italian Opera," in *NOHM* 7:59–61; Reinhard Strohm, *Die italienische Oper im 18. Jahrhundert* (Wilhelmshaven, 1979), 265–77; Heartz, *Mozart's Operas,* 197–99; and, on the finales, Wolfgang Osthoff, "Die Opera buffa," in *Gattungen der Musik in Einzeldarstellungen: Gedenkschrift Leo Schrade,* ed. Wulf Arlt, Ernst Lichtenhahn, and Hans Oesch (Bern, 1973), 727–29; and Henze-Döhring, *Opera seria, Opera buffa und Mozarts Don Giovanni,* 72–74.

many other parts of Europe became familiar with it through performances in Prague, Brunswick, Vienna, Dresden, Mannheim, Barcelona, Copenhagen, and Paris.[18]

Piccinni's opera enjoyed extraordinary popularity in London, where a performance in 1774 gave rise to this touching encomium: "The music of this favourite opera appears always new; and we may venture to affirm that it will for ever remain the standard of true harmonical taste. The first motion of the overture never fails to call on the countenance of the audience the most radiant symptoms of cheerfulness and heart-felt satisfaction; and it continues so to the end of the opera."[19]

That both *Il mercato* and *La buona figliuola* found success in Vienna suggests that Viennese audiences were eager for the best in contemporary Italian comic opera. These productions also point to the interdependence of repertory and personnel.[20] Carattoli created the role of Lampridio in *Il mercato* in Venice; six years later, in 1764, he sang the same role in Vienna. Having created the role of Tagliaferro in *La buona figliuola* in Rome and sung it in Bologna and Milan, he portrayed the same character in Vienna in 1764 and probably again in 1768 (the distribution of roles in the 1768 production is unknown). During the second half of the 1760s he was joined in Vienna by several singers who had sung roles in *Il mercato* and *La buona figliuola* in Italy. Clementina Baglioni had sung both Lena and Brigida in Fischietti's opera; she had frequently portrayed Marchesa Lucinda in Piccinni's. Caribaldi had displayed his vocal and dramatic versatility by portraying two very different characters in *La buona figliuola:* the noble Armidoro (singing the part an octave lower than written) and the peasant Mengotto.

Large-Scale Form

Early in his career Goldoni had hoped to make his name as a writer of serious librettos. His failure to do so did not dampen his admiration for Metastasio, whose strengths he enumerated in his *Mémoires:* "his pure, elegant style; his flowing, harmonious verses; an admirable clarity in the expression of feeling; an apparent facility that hides the hard labor of being precise; a moving energy in the language of passions; his portraits; his tableaux; his pleasing descriptions, his gentle ethics."[21] The many Metastasian features of Goldoni's comic librettos show that he absorbed some of the precepts of Metastasian

18. Sartori nos. 4171–240.

19. *Westminster Magazine* 2 (1774): 635; quoted in Frederick C. Petty, *Italian Opera in London 1760–1800* (Ann Arbor, Mich., 1980), 142. As late as 1789 a London critic could compare Piccinni's work favorably to the new operas of the day: "The opera of La Buona Figliuola . . . was received throughout with the greatest and well-deserved approbation. Among all the Italian operas, none can be compared with this. . . . Therefore, we doubt not, if the manager will consider his interest as well as the public's pleasure, this charming opera ought to be repeated in preference to all the stuff of the other Italian comic productions" (unidentified clipping, from a collection in US-NYp, quoted in Petty, 269–70).

20. The rest of this paragraph is based on Sartori.

21. *Mémoires de M. Goldoni,* critical edition in Goldoni, 1:187; Heartz, "Vis Comica," 50.

dramaturgy; but since the librettists of commeddeja pe mmuseca also learned much from Metastasio and his predecessors, it is hard to tell which of these influenced Goldoni more strongly. In using the terms *dramma giocoso per musica* and *dramma comico per musica* (rather than *commedia per musica,* the Tuscan equivalent of *commeddeja pe mmuseca*) to describe most of his comic librettos written after 1750, Goldoni acknowledged—and called attention to—his debt to Metastasian dramma per musica.[22]

Like Metastasio's drammi per musica (and most commeddeje pe mmuseca) Goldoni's librettos are divided into three acts, the third normally somewhat shorter than the first two. Most of the interaction between characters and the advancement of the plot take place in *versi sciolti* (blank verse of settenari and endecasillabi) set by composers as simple recitative. Characters express their state of mind to the audience or communicate their feelings to one another in arias, during which the plot does not normally move forward. Many of these arias, like the great majority of those in Metastasian opera, are exit arias, sung by a character before leaving the stage. Although most Goldonian opere buffe have at least one ensemble, and those written after 1750 generally have several, their musical content is concentrated in arias. Goldoni's librettos typically have many more arias than all other orchestrally accompanied numbers combined.[23]

One of the most characteristic features of Goldonian opera buffa is the finale: the long, complex musical number at the end of an act, in which most—sometimes all—of the opera's characters take part, often with several sections that reflect a changing dramatic situation with differing tempos, meters, keys, and numbers of singers. Goldoni, in collaboration with Galuppi, persuasively demonstrated the finale's comic, dramatic, and musical potential in such operas as *L'Arcadia in Brenta* (1749).[24] Thirty-five years later the finale presented Lorenzo da Ponte with one of the most difficult challenges he faced as a novice librettist. His well-known description is part of an account of his struggle to write his first libretto (*Il ricco d'un giorno,* with music by Salieri). He exaggerated, as often, for comic effect; and he based his description on finales of the 1780s rather than on those that Salieri might have studied or heard as he was learning

22. The tendency of modern scholars to use only part of the generic designation—*dramma giocoso*—has obscured the relation between the Metastasian term *dramma per musica* and the Goldonian term *dramma giocoso per musica.* Goldoni emphasized the closeness of his generic term to Metastasio's by inverting the order of the first two words in the preface to his libretto *I portentosi effetti della madre Natura* (Venice, 1752): "Questi giocosi Drammi per Musica" (original capitalization preserved). "'A frolic with serious elements' would be one paraphrase of *dramma giocoso*" (Heartz, *Mozart's Operas,* 196). Keeping the genre's full name in mind, another rendering might be "a comic dramma per musica." Goldoni did not invent the term *dramma giocoso per musica;* see Weiss, "La diffusione del repertorio operistico," 247.

23. Osthoff's emphasis on the importance of ensembles in opera buffa ("Die Opera buffa," 681–82) does not fully apply to opera buffa of the mid-eighteenth century. Emery, *Goldoni as Librettist,* 68, likewise exaggerates the importance of ensembles and chorus in Goldoni's librettos and underplays the prevalence of exit arias. Rabin, "Mozart," 146–47, on the other hand, usefully emphasizes the predominance of arias.

24. Weiss, "Carlo Goldoni, Librettist," 130; Heartz, "Vis Comica," and "The Creation of the Buffo Finale"; and Marinelli, "Goldoni," 72–80.

his craft. Yet Da Ponte's account accurately conveys the essence of the finale as cultivated throughout the second half of the century:

> This finale, which must moreover be intimately connected with the rest of the opera, is a kind of little play, a little drama in itself, and requires a new development in the plot and activity of great interest. Here above all the composer's genius, the singers' bravura, and the drama's greatest effects must shine. Recitative is excluded from it, everything is sung, and every type of singing must be found: the adagio, the allegro, the andante, the lyrical [*l'amabile*], the harmonious, the loud, the very loud, the loudest of all, with which the finale always ends; musicians call this the *chiusa* or the *stretto*. . . . In this finale theatrical custom requires that all the singers appear on stage . . . and if the drama's plot does not permit it, the poet has to find a way to make it possible despite the rules of logic and of all the world's Aristotles; and, if it still does not win approval, so much the worse for him.[25]

Gasparo Gozzi, writing in 1760 of Latilla's setting of Goldoni's *L'amore artigiano,* singled out the finales as particularly attractive parts of the opera and attributed to Goldoni himself an important role in their development: "he can call himself the first inventor of closing the acts with this novelty of pleasing and varied action."[26]

The first and second acts of most opere buffe written after 1750 end with finales. These and the increasing number of other ensembles progressively differentiated the structure of Goldonian dramma giocoso per musica from those of dramma per musica and commeddeja pe mmuseca. The finale also helped distinguish Goldonian opera from another comic genre. Opéra-comique of the 1760s and 1770s borrowed many features from opera buffa, but its librettists and composers wrote finales only sporadically.

After three-movement overtures (fast-slow-fast), *Il mercato di Malmantile* and *La buona figliuola* unfold over three acts, the first two considerably longer than the last. *Il mercato* has twenty-four arias, of which all but five are exit arias. With one duet, three trios, two finales, and a concluding *coro* for all the soloists, Fischietti's work has a ratio of arias to ensembles of just over 3 : 1. Twenty-four arias (including seventeen exit arias), two duets, and three finales give Piccinni's opera a higher aria-to-ensemble ratio, almost 5 : 1. *La buona figliuola* is as heavily dominated by arias as many serious operas of the time.

Opere buffe written for performance in Vienna during the 1760s share with *Il mercato* and *La buona figliuola* many aspects of form: three-movement overtures, three acts, finales. In some Viennese comedies the numerical predominance of arias over ensembles is as obvious as in *La buona figliuola.* Giuseppe Scarlatti's *Gli stravaganti* (a set-

25. Da Ponte, 96–97.

26. Quoted by Ortolani (Goldoni, 11:1327), and in translation (followed here, with some changes) in Heartz, "The Creation of the Buffo Finale," 73.

ting of a revision of a Neapolitan libretto first performed, under the title *La moglie padrona,* in 1748) has twenty arias, one duet, one trio, an introduzione (an ensemble, in this case a quartet, at the beginning of the opera), and three finales, for an aria-to-ensemble ratio of just over 3 : 1.[27] Gassmann's first comic opera for Vienna, *Il viaggiatore ridicolo,* with sixteen arias and seven ensembles, is exceptional in its large number of ensembles and relatively few arias, but his next opera buffa is more typical of its time. *L'amore artigiano* has twenty-four arias, an introduzione, a quartet, and three finales, for a ratio of arias to ensembles almost identical to that of *La buona figliuola.*[28]

Parti Buffe and Buffi Caricati

The popularity of midcentury opera buffa owed much to the complexity and depth of the characters that Goldoni created and that his composers developed musically. Many of his characters have more than one side. A young woman may be playfully alluring and yet virtuous, a nobleman both heroic and ridiculous, a servant both comic and pathetic, a soldier both violent and tender. At the same time many Goldonian roles fit into categories inherited largely from Neapolitan comic opera.

The list of characters at the beginning of many of the librettos divides the roles into two categories.[29] Two characters are labeled "parti serie": a woman and a man, usually noble and usually romantically involved. The rest of the cast comes under the heading "parti buffe." Goldoni used this bipartite division as late as 1766, near the end of his busiest and most important period of libretto writing: the cast list of *La cameriera spiritosa* (Milan, 1766) contains two parti serie and six parti buffe.

On rare occasions he explicitly refined this categorization of roles by dividing the parti buffe into two categories. Keeping the term *parti buffe* for the unambiguously comic characters (who included almost all members of the lowest levels of society), he assigned to the category of *parti di mezzo carattere* no more than two characters (often middle class) in whom serious and comic qualities are combined or in whom the more extreme elements of the comic and serious characters are avoided. The cast list of *Il conte Caramella* (Venice, 1751) contains an early example of this tripartite categorization: it labels two roles "seri," three "buffi," and two "mezzi caratteri."

The cast lists in librettos printed for the original productions of Fischietti's *Il mercato di Malmantile* and Piccinni's *La buona figliuola* make no mention of parti serie, buffe,

27. Scarlatti's *Gli stravaganti* survives in full score: A-Wn, Mus. Hs. 17850.

28. The information presented here on the numbers of arias and ensembles in Gassmann's operas is derived largely from Donath, "Gassmann," 92–129.

29. Unless otherwise indicated, I refer here to Goldoni's librettos as they appear in Ortolani's edition of the complete works, which generally follows the first edition of each libretto, i.e., the edition published in conjunction with the first production.

or di mezzo carattere. Yet the tripartite division of roles that these terms represent is clearly evident in both works. Despite the infrequency with which Goldoni used all three terms in a single libretto, they provide us with a useful terminological framework in which to examine characterization in both the words and the music of Goldonian opera as performed in Vienna during the 1760s.[30]

The comedy in Goldoni's librettos depends largely on the parti buffe, the overtly comic roles. (The term *parti buffe* will henceforth be used in its narrow sense: as one of three categories rather than two, coexisting with the parti di mezzo carattere but not including them.) The parti buffe are the most numerous roles in Goldoni's operas. They include old men, servants and chambermaids, peasants and shopgirls, innkeepers, rich merchants, and impoverished noblemen.

Goldoni's buffi generally feel, speak, and act according to the conventions of seventeenth- and eighteenth-century comedy, French as well as Italian. Lampridio, the governor of Malmantile, is one of many old men who fall in love with much younger women. Goldoni's young women of middle and lower class like to flirt, and Lampridio's daughter Brigida is no exception; she sets her sights on Count della Rocca and tries, unsuccessfully, to charm him. The peasant men typically woo peasant women, who are interested in a man of higher social status. In *Il mercato* the peasant Berto loves the peasant girl Lena, who is temporarily distracted by Lampridio. In *La buona figliuola* the peasant Mengotto loves Cecchina (both of them unaware that she is of noble birth); Cecchina loves Marchese della Conchiglia.

Goldoni, like Molière, often exploited for humorous effect the conflict in many of his buffi between susceptibility to sexual charms and desire to retain independence and money (and, in the case of older men attracted to young women, fear of being cuckolded). Comic characters, trying to resolve this conflict, spend much of their time making generalizations about the opposite sex.[31] It is hard to find a Goldoni libretto in which a buffo does not sing an aria praising or vilifying women as a group (sometimes doing both in one aria); arias sung by women about all men or all husbands are also common, as are arias in which women commiserate with one another or defend their sex against criticism by men. *I bagni d'Albano* (Venice, 1753), which contains four arias about women—"È di donna un bel costume," "Chi una donna vuol pretendere," "Voi altre femmine," and "Povere femmine"—is by no means unusual.

Goldoni found much humor in foreign languages and Italian dialects. Several foreigners speak comically faulty Italian, while Italians sometimes try to speak a foreign language. Tagliaferro, the German soldier in *La buona figliuola,* tells of the loss of his commanding officer's young daughter, who turns out to be Cecchina:

30. For another discussion of Goldonian character types see Rabin, "Mozart," 44–60.

31. Osthoff, "Die Opera buffa," 684.

Je recordar mi stato
In fostro marchesato,
Quando per gherra star Tateschi Italia.
Qua recordar che picchla figliola
Per marcia afer perduta,
E mai più picchlina afer veduta.

[I remember I vas in your marquisate ven de Chermans ver in Italy because of de var. I remember dass de leetle daughter vas lost und de leetle vun vas never again seen.]

Marianna, the German servant in *La conversazione,* one of Goldoni's most relentlessly multilingual librettos, speaks similarly. First performed in Venice in 1758, Scolari's setting of *La conversazione* reached Vienna in 1763. It includes not only German but French, English, Latin, and Turkish; not only standard Italian but Venetian, Bolognese, Neapolitan, and Calabrese dialects. Giacinto, an affected traveler, shows off his knowledge of foreign languages by singing a song in French, "Visage adorable." Lucrezia sings a song in Bolognese; later in the opera she announces, in pseudo-Turkish, that she will attend a masked ball disguised as a Turk: "Salamalecch, stara sultana."[32] Arias in foreign language and in dialect invited composers to write exotic-sounding music: from graceful French airs to noisy Turkish marches. The musical diversity encouraged by this *plurilinguismo* was an important component of Goldonian opera buffa.[33]

Librettos of the second half of the eighteenth century often refer to singers who specialized in the portrayal of comic male characters as "buffi caricati," caricature comics. This term (which seems particularly apt in light of Sonnenfels's parallel between Carattoli's gestures and Hogarth's comic drawings) will be adopted here as well. In several librettos Goldoni assigned to a buffo caricato an aria in which he faces a dilemma (often having to do with a younger woman) and comically wavers between the contradictory advice of imaginary voices. Uberto's aria "Son imbrogliato io già" in *La serva padrona* is an early example of the "aria of indecision." In *Il mercato* Lampridio, enamored of the peasant girl Lena, hesitates to marry her because he knows that his am-

32. "Salamelecch, stara sultana" was not Goldoni's only pseudo-Turkish aria. In *Lo speziale* (first performed in Venice, 1755, with music by Fischietti and Vincenzo Pallavicino) Volpino sings a similar text, which gave Haydn, in his setting of the libretto, opportunity to write a fine aria in the "Turkish" style. See Wolfgang Osthoff, "Comicità alla turca, musica classica, opera nazionale: Osservazioni sulla 'Entführung aus dem Serail,'" in *Opera & libretto,* ed. Gianfranco Folena, Maria Teresa Muraro, and Giovanni Morelli (Florence, 1990–93), 2:160–65.

33. On Goldoni's plurilinguismo see Gianfranco Folena, "Goldoni librettista comico," in Muraro, *Venezia,* 2:28; Osthoff, "Die Opera buffa," 691–93; and Daniela Goldin, *La vera fenice: Librettisti e libretti fra Sette e Ottocento* (Turin, 1985), 25–27.

bitious, class-conscious daughter Brigida will not approve. He expresses his indecision in an aria:

Pensieri a capitolo,
　Che abbiamo da far?
　La carica, il titolo
　Mi fanno pensar.
　Mi dice l'Amore:
　"Contenta il tuo core";
　L'Onore mi dice:
　"Non fare, non lice."
　Che abbiamo da far?
　Nel cor poverello
　Campana, martello
　Sentire mi par,
　Che dicano, che parlino,
　Che gridino, che ciarlino:
　"Oh, questa sì ch'è buona,
　Oh, questa sì ch'è bella!"
　La cara villanella
　Contento vuò sposar.

[A chapter-full of thoughts, but what are we to do? My office, my title make me think. Love says to me: "Satisfy your heart"; Honor says to me: "Do not do it; it is not right." What are we to do? In my poor little heart I seem to hear a bell, a hammer saying, speaking, shouting, chattering: "Of course she is good; of course she is pretty!" I am satisfied: I want to marry the dear peasant girl.]

Buffi caricati sing many catalogue arias: arias with lists of places, people, things, or even—as in the aria just quoted—verbs.[34] Near the beginning of *Il mercato* Rubiccone, a charlatan who sells patent medicines, boasts of his many cures in "Noi sottoscritti facciamo fede":

A Boboli ha guarito
　Un etico spedito;
　A Siena ha risanato
　Un povero stroppiato;
　A Pisa ad un idropico
　Donò la sanità.

34. On catalogue arias see Goldin, *La vera fenice*, 23–25, 149–63; Stefan Kunze, "Elementi veneziani nella librettistica di Lorenzo da Ponte," in Muraro, *Venezia*, 2:286–87; and John Platoff, "Catalogue Arias and the 'Catalogue Aria,'" in Sadie, 296–311.

[In Boboli he cured a consumptive at death's door; in Siena he healed a poor cripple; in Pisa he gave health to a man with dropsy.]

Goldoni also found comedy in numbers. His buffi caricati like to count things, as when Fabrizio, in *L'Arcadia in Brenta,* tries to add up all the money he has spent:

Quattrocento bei ducati . . .
  Poverini, sono andati.
  Sessantotto bei zecchini . . .
Sono andati, poverini.
  Trenta doppie . . . oh che animale!
  Cento scudi . . . oh bestiale!
  Quanto fanno? Io non lo so.

[Four hundred pretty ducats, poor things, have disappeared. Sixty-eight pretty *zecchini* have disappeared, poor things. Thirty dubloons . . . what an idiot! One hundred *scudi* . . . how dreadful! How much does it add up to? I do not know.]

Parti Buffe: Melodic Style and Aria Forms

The melodies sung by parti buffe, both male and female, tend to progress in short phrases, usually two measures in length, each phrase containing one line of verse.[35] A single rhythmic idea typically predominates through several phrases. The opening melody of Lampridio's "Pensieri a capitolo" can serve as an example (ex. 3.1).

EXAMPLE 3.1 Fischietti, *Il mercato di Malmantile,* act 2, "Pensieri a capitolo," mm. 16–27 (F-Pn, D.4140–42; facsimile, New York, 1983)

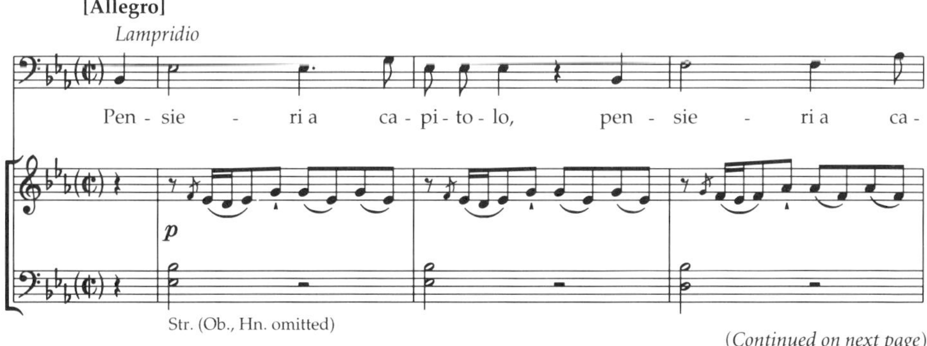

(Continued on next page)

35. For a useful discussion of the rhythmic organization of opera buffa melodies and the relationship of that organization to the poetic text see James Webster, "The Analysis of Mozart's Arias," in *Mozart Studies,* ed. Cliff Eisen (Oxford, 1991), 130–40. Although Webster's essay is primarily concerned with Mozart's later operas, much of his discussion is applicable to Mozart's earlier operas and to those of his contemporaries and immediate predecessors.

EXAMPLE 3.1 (*continued*)

Lampridio's aria also illustrates features that are common in the musical portrayal of male parti buffe in particular. Lampridio is a bass. Fischietti and Piccinni assigned most of their buffo-caricato roles to basses and baritones. Among the purely comic male roles in *Il mercato* and *La buona figliuola* only one, that of Fischietti's Berto, is notated in tenor clef (for Francesco Baglioni, who sang both bass and tenor roles). For their buffi caricati Fischietti and Piccinni wrote melodies that often double the bass line, especially at cadences, as is the case in "Pensieri a capitolo." The opening tune shares with many comic bass arias duple meter and dotted rhythms, which together give it a marchlike quality.

Also characteristic of the music sung by parti buffe (and especially male parti buffe) is patter, a good example of which is to be found in Rubiccone's catalogue aria in act 1 of *Il mercato.* Not a purely comic character, Rubiccone has some very expressive and lyrical music elsewhere in the opera, but this is certainly one of his comic moments. Fischietti arranged Rubiccone's patter, like much patter in Goldonian opera buffa, so that one line of text corresponds to one measure of music instead of the normal two measures, thus contributing to the sense of manic activity associated with this style of singing (ex. 3.2).

The opening theme of Tagliaferro's brilliant aria in praise of the soldier's life, "Star trombette, star tamburi" is a fine example of the masculine buffo style, with its duple meter, disjunct vocal line that sometimes doubles the bass, short phrases, and the

EXAMPLE 3.2 Fischietti, *Il mercato di Malmantile,* act 1, "Noi sottoscritti facciamo fede," mm. 47–60

(Continued on next page)

EXAMPLE 3.2 (*continued*)

And let us truthfully declare and attest that the great doctor, the surgeon, cured many sick people and, persecuted by slanderous pharmacists and physicians, was expelled as an impostor.

repetition of a rhythmic idea in several successive phrases (ex. 3.3).[36] This melody represents another exception to the normal relation between poetic line and musical measure, by which the two most strongly accented syllables in the line coincide with downbeats[37] (in "Pensieri a capitolo," for example, the second syllables of *pensieri* and *capitolo* fall on downbeats). Piccinni could have made a conventional melody by placing the first two notes before the bar line, producing an attractive gavotte rhythm and allowing the second syllables of *trombette* and *tamburi* to coincide with the beginnings of measures. The odd metrical displacement conveys an amusing clumsiness that suits Tagliaferro perfectly: the metrical irregularity corresponds to the grammatical irregularity of his Italian. Rhythmic oddity continues in the following measures as Tagliaferro

EXAMPLE 3.3 Piccinni, *La buona figliuola,* act 2, "Star trombette," mm. 22–28 (MS score in I-Fc; facsimile, New York, 1983)

(*Continued on next page*)

36. Tagliaferro's character and music reflect a fascination with things military that was characteristic of opera buffa during the second half of the eighteenth century; see Osthoff, "Die Opera buffa," 689.

37. Webster, "The Analysis of Mozart's Arias," 134–35.

EXAMPLE 3.3 (*continued*)

There be trumpets, there be drums, there be guitars and flageolets, there be great quantities of instruments.

suddenly accelerates the rate of text declamation to a patterlike one line per measure to suggest the idea of "quantità" and to call attention to the tongue twister "star strumenti."

For female parti buffe Fischietti and Piccinni wrote music that tends to be somewhat lighter and even more repetitious in its use of short rhythmic motives. Paoluccia's "Che superbia maledetta" in *La buona figliuola* begins with a cheerful melody in triple meter that is unmistakably comic and at the same time quite different from the pompous, marchlike melodies characteristic of buffi caricati (ex. 3.4). Goldoni's switch from ottonari to senari for the poem's last seven lines caused Piccinni to introduce a new rhythmic idea. Triplets dominate a melody in which Paoluccia declaims one line per measure, vividly communicating energy and charm.

EXAMPLE 3.4 Piccinni, *La buona figliuola*, act 1, "Che superbia maledetta," mm. 19–24

What outrageous pride one sees everywhere!

Also characteristic of female comic roles are gentle melodies in triple meter that convey some of the elegance of the minuet. Lena's aria "Son chi son, mi maraviglio," begins with such a melody (ex. 3.5). Minuet arias frequently make use of four-measure phrases,

EXAMPLE 3.5 Fischietti, *Il mercato di Malmantile,* act 1, "Son chi son, mi maraviglio," mm. 21–26

I am who I am; "You amaze me" is something that no one will be able to say of me

thus representing an exception to the predominance of two-measure phrases in the music of parti buffe, female as well as male.

Until the end of the 1740s the da-capo aria dominated opera buffa as completely as opera seria. All but one of the twenty-seven arias in Latilla's *La finta cameriera* use da-capo form. Librettists collaborated with composers in the production of da-capo arias by furnishing two-stanza aria texts, the first stanza to be set as the A section, the second as the B section. Goldoni's early librettos (those he wrote up to 1743, before retiring temporarily from the stage) share the predilection for da-capo arias; but later, during the period in which he worked with Galuppi, he helped composers move toward a variety of more flexible forms.

Most aria texts in *Il mercato* and *La buona figliuola* depart from the eight-line, two-stanza poems common in eighteenth-century serious opera and in opera buffa of the 1730s and 1740s. They usually have more than eight lines, the last of which makes a strong concluding statement. This encouraged composers to write arias in which the end of the music coincides with the end of the poem (unlike da-capo arias, which end with the last line of the first stanza). Some aria texts feature a change of poetic meter. "Pensieri a capitolo," quoted above, is a typically Goldonian comic aria text, with its eighteen lines, its change of meter (from senari to settenari), its catalogue of verbs, and its conclusive final lines.

Fischietti and Piccinni responded to Goldoni's new style of aria text with a group of closely related aria forms probably derived from the first part (that is, the A section) of the da-capo aria. Because these forms resemble, in some respects, those used in the same period by composers of instrumental music, it makes sense to borrow from instrumental music terminology for analyzing them. The two most common aria forms in *Il mercato* and *La buona figliuola* will thus be referred to here as sonata form and binary form.[38] Arias in both forms begin (usually after an orchestral introduction) with an exposition: a melody in the tonic followed by a modulation to the dominant, then further melodic material in the new key. A shift of meter, tempo, or both frequently occurs before or after the modulation to the dominant, representing an important difference between sonata and binary forms in arias and those in instrumental music. The exposition ends with repeated cadences in the dominant that usually coincide with the end of the aria text.[39]

After the exposition, arias continue in a number of different ways, but most present the text again from the beginning. A return to the tonic key either coincides with the beginning of the text or occurs shortly before or after. In sonata form the return of the tonic coincides with the return of the aria's opening melody; this is the beginning of the recapitulation. In binary form, the opening melody returns in a key other than the tonic or does not return at all. Most if not all the music presented earlier in the dominant returns in the tonic before the end of the aria.

If the exposition contains a change of tempo or meter, so normally does the recapitulation. This gives many Goldonian arias the form A-B-A′-B′, in which A and A′ share the same tempo and meter. Sections A and B together consist entirely or mostly of the exposition, sections A′ and B′ entirely or mostly of the recapitulation. Such two-tempo or two-meter arias are most unpredictable at the point where B ends and A′ begins. A development, if there is one, can occur either at the end of B or at the beginning of A′.

"Pensieri a capitolo," as set to music by Fischietti, can serve as an example of a sonata-form aria with an A-B-A′-B′ plan (see table 3.1). It begins with music in cut time, without tempo indication but presumably Allegro. After an orchestral introduc-

38. In using this terminology I follow Mary Hunter, "Haydn's Aria Forms: A Study of the Arias in the Italian Operas Written at Eszterháza, 1766–1783" (Ph.D. diss., Cornell University, 1982). Hunter's exemplary analysis can usefully be applied to Goldonian comic operas of the 1750s and 1760s because Haydn's earliest opera buffa arias derive their forms largely from Goldonian opera. See Hunter for further clarification and justification of the use of sonata-form terminology in the analysis of arias.

39. On the vocal exposition see Hunter, "Haydn's Aria Forms," 147–92.

TABLE 3.1 Fischietti, *Il mercato di Malmantile,* Act 2, "Pensieri a capitolo"

	EXPOSITION		DEVELOPMENT	RECAPITULATION	
	A	B	B (CONT.)	A′	B′
Measure numbers	16–52	53–80	81–94	95–118	119–140
Text (by lines)	1–12	13–18	6–8, 15–16	1–12	13–18
Poetic meter	Senari	Settenari	Senari, settenari	Senari	Settenari
Key (I = E♭ major)	I–V	V	V–V/I	I–V/I	I
Tempo	[Allegro]	Non tanto allegro		[Allegro]	Non tanto allegro
Meter	¢	2/4		¢	2/4

tion the exposition begins: Lampridio goes through all eighteen lines of the poem. His opening melody (see ex. 3.1) is solidly in the tonic, E♭ major. This is the A section, which continues with a modulation to the dominant, B♭.

Goldoni's shift from senari to settenari (at the line "Che dicano, che parlino") and the simultaneous beginning of the list of verbs caused Fischietti to change meter (2/4), tempo (Non tanto allegro), and rhythm (a string of eighth notes). He differentiated this material by orchestration as well, withholding the horns that play an important role in the opening section. This is the B section. Fischietti emphasized the last two lines of text, in which Lampridio announces his decision to marry Lena, with repeated cadences in the dominant. The orchestra reaffirms the end of the exposition with seven measures of cadential material. The B section continues with a brief development: fourteen measures in which Lampridio repeats several lines from the middle of the poem over a B♭ pedal.

A return to the tonic coincides with simultaneous returns to the beginning of the text, Lampridio's opening melody, and cut time. This is the beginning of the A′ section and also of the recapitulation. The aria ends with the B′ section: the passage in 2/4 meter, now in E♭. An orchestral passage similar to the one that announced the end of the exposition brings the aria to a conclusion that is satisfying from a musical point of view. But it is not very dramatic, because the second half of the aria is redundant. When setting texts like this one in which a change of mental state occurs or a decision is made, composers who followed Fischietti increasingly avoided sonata form in favor of through-composed form. Such arias frequently begin with an exposition but continue without a recapitulation, and they often save the last part of the text for the end of the aria.

A few da-capo arias, or arias with forms closely related to the da-capo form, remain in *Il mercato* and *La buona figliuola;* but these are limited exclusively to the parti serie. For the rest of the cast Fischietti and Piccinni explored various permutations of the plan exemplified by "Pensieri a capitolo." They found many ways to manipulate this plan for comic and dramatic effect. For example, an unexpected modulation in the exposition of "Star trombette" contributes to the amusing portrait of the German soldier that Piccinni wrote for Carattoli. After the opening melody (see ex. 3.3) Tagliaferro seems to lose his tonal direction. He modulates to the dominant, G, but then moves to A minor and from there back to the tonic, repeating the aria's opening melody to different words. Tagliaferro not only speaks like a foreigner; his music sounds as if it were composed by someone who does not understand the basic principles of sonata form.

In many midcentury opere buffe, ensembles are few; with the important exception of finales, interaction between characters occurs mostly in simple recitative. But one can see signs, especially in the way librettists and composers treated the parti buffe, of an eagerness to expand the role of orchestrally accompanied numbers in depicting the interaction of characters. One such sign is the presence in both *Il mercato* and *La buona figliuola* of pairs of short, simple songs (called *canzoni* in some sources, *cavate* or *cavatine* in others) separated by simple recitative, in which one character responds to another by singing the same music with different words. Near the beginning of act 2 of Fischietti's opera Lena sings the canzone "Ho venduto la gallina"; after some dialogue in simple recitative, Berto responds with the same music in "Ho venduto tutte l'ova." In *La buona figliuola* Cecchina's "Ogni amatore" follows and answers Mengotto's "Quel che d'amore."

These song pairs are limited to parti buffe, with the apparent exception of Cecchina, a gentle and sincere young woman unaware of her noble origins. But this is not really an exception: Cecchina, believing herself to be Mengotto's social equal, can act and sing accordingly.

Parti Buffe in Vienna

Composers of opera buffa active in Vienna during the second half of the 1760s must have known intimately the music of *Il mercato, La buona figliuola,* and other Goldonian operas performed in Vienna. Arias that Giuseppe Scarlatti, Gassmann, and Mozart wrote for their parti buffe have much in common, in structure and melodic style, with those of Fischietti, Piccinni, and other Italians.

Scarlatti's *Gli stravaganti* is particularly well endowed with buffi caricati: the Frenchman Cariglion, the pedant Mortaletto, and the henpecked husband Fastidio (created by Carattoli). In the trio "Sotto sopra la casa," Cariglion's opening melody, with its fast tempo, dotted rhythms, duple meter, and repetition of rhythmic patterns in several successive phrases, typifies those sung by Viennese as well as Italian buffi caricati. Scarlatti took advantage of Carattoli's histrionic ability in Fastidio's aria "Ho tanta collera."

The many gaps in the melody required Carattoli to act out his suffocating anger as well as to express it in song.

The five comic operas that Gassmann wrote between 1766 and 1770 are full of amusing parti buffe. The ridiculous traveler Gandolfo (created by Giuseppe Pinetti), the chambermaid Livietta (Rosa Baglioni), and Don Fabrizio (Carattoli) enliven *Il viaggiatore ridicolo.* In a catalogue aria Gandolfo boasts of noblewomen that he knows in the various cities and countries, much as Leporello would later recount Don Giovanni's exploits (Da Ponte remembered Goldoni's rhyme "Baronesse / Principesse"):

A Lion la Contessa la Cra,
A Paris la Marchesa la Gru,
A Madrid la Duchessa del Bos,
In Inghilterra Miledi la Stos,
In Germania ho le mie Baronesse,
In Italia le mie Principesse,
E conosco le femmine ancor
Nel Serraglio del Turco Signor.

[In Lyon the Countess la Cra, in Paris the Marquise la Gru, in Madrid the Duchess de Bos, in England Milady la Stos; in Germany I have my baronesses, in Italy my princesses. And I even know the women in the harem of the Turkish sultan.]

Fabrizio introduces himself as a typical buffo caricato in his first aria, "Son padron in casa mia." Gassmann conveyed Fabrizio's anger and impatience by having him enter without an orchestral introduction and by compressing the declamation of text to one line per measure. The dotted rhythms and repetition of short motives in the Presto are as characteristic of Gassmann's buffi caricati as of Fischietti's and Piccinni's. In act 2 Livietta sings a minuet aria, "Se al mondo fossevi," as graceful and "feminine" as the one sung by Lena in act 1 of *Il mercato.*

In *La contessina* (based on an early libretto by Goldoni, greatly expanded and altered by Coltellini), the fathers Pancrazio and Baccellone belong to the same musico-dramatic tradition as Lampridio and Tagliaferro.[40] Despite the French-sounding lower appoggiaturas in Pancrazio's first aria, "Anderò da Baccellone," this is clearly music for a buffo caricato; so is Baccellone's "Per esempio, quando viene."

Following a straightforward sonata form without changes of tempo, Pancrazio goes through the text of "Anderò da Baccellone" twice, first modulating to the dominant and then, after a five-measure development, staying in the tonic; the aria concludes with a substantial coda that comically exploits the aria's last word, "canterò."

40. *La contessina,* ed. Robert Haas, vols. 42–44 of *DTÖ* (Graz, 1960), with extensive introduction. See also Strohm, *Die italienische Oper,* 278–90; and Heartz, *Viennese School,* 418–20.

In "Per esempio" Gassmann responded to a text in which Baccellone asks his daughter a series of questions with a through-composed aria. The poem begins with ottonari, which Baccellone declaims at the regular rate of one line per two measures of music. The lively interplay of accompanimental parts is typical of Gassmann. A little motive in the violas depicts the countess's shaking her head in response to Baccellone's question (ex. 3.6). When the text switches to very short quinari, the tempo accelerates to Più allegro and the declamation of text shifts first to one line per measure and then, in a flurry of eighth-note triplets, to two lines per measure. This would have been a relatively conventional exposition if Gassmann had written the Più allegro in the dominant, but he wrote it in the tonic. Instead of setting the text twice, moving first to the dominant

EXAMPLE 3.6 Gassmann, *La contessina*, act 1, "Per esempio," mm. 15–29 (*DTÖ*, vols. 42–44)

(*Continued on next page*)

EXAMPLE 3.6 (*continued*)

For example, when he comes, if I should go halfway down the stairs? (*The countess gestures in the negative*) That would be too much, you are right, it is not proper, I know that myself.

and then to the tonic, he set it only once. Through-composed arias like this one have the obvious advantage over arias in sonata or binary form of being able to depict more realistically a changing dramatic situation.

Mozart's *La finta semplice* has several arias in which parti buffe make generalizations about women, men, and marriage. The servant Simone and the rich landowner Cassandro both claim that they have no interest in marriage. Simone sings "Troppo briga a prender moglie" [To take a wife is too much bother]; the rich landowner agrees: "Non mi vo' matrimoniar" [I do not want to wed]. Beautiful and clever Rosina, like many of Goldoni's heroines, can charm any man, but she also likes to keep men at arm's length. She sets out to cause Cassandro and his foolish brother Polidoro to fall in love with her, and of course they do. Cassandro recounts his dilemma in an aria of indecision in which he compares himself to a dog eager to grab a bone but fearful of a beating.

Mozart's arias for buffi caricati share with those of Fischietti and Piccinni a preference for sonata and binary form, moderate or fast tempos, with text normally declaimed at a rate of two measures of music per line of text, duple meter, march rhythms, disjunct vocal lines, many short phrases (often a series of short phrases with the same rhythmic organization), and patter. Simone's "Troppo briga" and Cassandro's "Ubriaco non son io" depict both characters as buffi caricati; "Troppo briga" begins with a melody much like one that Gassmann was to give Baccellone two years later in "Per esempio, quando viene."

The music that Mozart wrote for Ninetta shares with the music of many opera buffa maids and peasant girls a tendency toward triple and compound meter, vocal lines featuring long chains of eighth notes, and insistent repetition of short rhythmic motives. Ninetta's sonata-form aria "Sono in amore, voglio marito" is one of her two arias that Mozart labeled Tempo di minuetto; both belong to the tradition of minuet-like arias for female parti buffe to which Gassmann also contributed. (Mozart exploited this tra-

EXAMPLE 3.7 Mozart, *La finta semplice,* act 3, "Sono in amore," mm. 87–92 (*NMA*)

Heaven help him who teases or mistreats me: I jump at his eyes like a cat

dition again, much later in his career, when he wrote a beautiful minuet aria for Marcellina to sing in *Figaro,* "Il capro e la capretta.") Shifting in both the exposition and the recapitulation from 3/4 to 3/8, Ninetta sings a pert melody (ex. 3.7) that resembles—in its six-measure length, its reiterated V-I harmony, and its zig-zag contour Paoluccia's melody quoted in example 3.4.

Parti Serie, the Dal-Segno Aria, and the Parody of Serious Opera

One of the most characteristic features of eighteenth-century opera buffa is its incorporation of opera seria gestures, language, and character types. Such "representations of opera seria in opera buffa" communicated to eighteenth-century audiences a wide spectrum of meanings, from outright parody to the sincere expression of heroism, nobility, and suffering.[41]

41. Mary Hunter, "Some Representations of *Opera Seria* in *Opera Buffa,*" *COJ* 3 (1991): 89–108; Bruce Alan Brown, "*Le pazzie d'Orlando, Orlando Paladino,* and the Uses of Parody," *Italica* 64 (1987): 583–605; Caryl Clark, "Intertextual Play and Haydn's *La fedeltà premiata,*" *Current Musicology* 51 (1993): 59–81.

A pair of parti serie represents the upper crust of Italian society in many of Goldoni's librettos. In *Il mercato* Goldoni conveyed the elite social status of Count della Rocca and his fiancée, Marchesa Giacinta, and in *La buona figliuola* that of Cavaliere Armidoro and his fiancée, Marchesa Lucinda, by excluding them from the comic finales. The librettist and those who set his words to music seem to have intended these characters to be interpreted and enjoyed on two different levels. The parti serie are amusing parodies of Metastasian depictions of nobility. Yet Goldoni delineated these parodies with a respect and an admiration that remind us of his own early ambition to win success as a writer of drammi per musica. Eighteenth-century audiences may well have laughed at these noble lovers, with their pretensions, snobbery, and vindictiveness. But they must have also admired the parti serie, delighting in the beauty of their language and the brilliant virtuosity with which they conveyed their high-flown feelings in music.

In Armidoro we can see how parti serie can serve as a source of both comedy and pathos in an opera that was described, in one libretto, as a "dramma serio-buffo."[42] When he learns that the marchese, his future brother-in-law, loves the lowly Cecchina, Armidoro threatens to call off his wedding to the marchese's sister. The old Metastasian conflict between love and honor takes on a slightly ridiculous quality in this recitative, as Armidoro declares that he will die if the marchese, by marrying Cecchina, forces him to renounce the marchesa:

> So che vi adoro,
> So che mi costerebbe,
> Il perdervi, la vita; ma non deggio,
> Ad onta dell'amor che mi consiglia,
> Il decoro tradir di mia famiglia.
> Deh, procurate in tempo
> Impedir che ciò segua. Idolo mio,
> Che sarebbe di me, se mai perdessi
> D'un sì bel core il prezioso acquisto?
> Ah, il pensarvi m'uccide. Ah, non resisto.
>
> [I know that I adore you, I know that losing you would cost me my life; but despite the love that guides me, I must not betray my family's honor. Alas, I beg of you, try to stop that from happening. My darling, what would become of me if I were ever to fail in the precious acquisition of so lovely a heart? Ah, just to think of it kills me. Ah, I can bear it no longer.]

We have to take Armidoro seriously because of the style of his speech and music. Goldoni gave his parti serie the language of opera seria, elegant and free from colloqui-

42. The libretto printed for the production of *La buona figliuola* in Reggio (Fiera, 1763) gave it the title *La baronessa riconosciuta* and described it as a "dramma serio-buffo per musica" (Sartori nos. 3821–22).

alisms; their arias are usually in the two-stanza form normal in Metastasio's operas. Armidoro's first aria is typical of Goldoni's noble style:

Della sposa il bel sembiante
  Favellar mi sento al core.
  Ma la gloria, ma l'onore
  Son costretto a consigliar.
Che l'amor nel seno amante
  Può languire e venir meno,
  Ma l'onor nel nostro seno
  Colla vita ha da durar.

[I hear the lovely visage of my betrothed speaking to my heart, but I am forced to heed glory and honor. Though love may languish and decrease in a lover's breast, yet honor must endure in our breast as long as life itself.]

In writing for parti serie Fischietti and Piccinni turned to musical forms and styles associated with opera seria. They assigned the roles of Count della Rocca and Armidoro to *musici,* the castrated male singers whose normal operatic roles were those of the young romantic heroes in opera seria. (The word *castrato*—"castrated sheep," hence "mutton"—had jocular, derogatory implications when applied to singers. *Musico,* a dignified euphemism frequently encountered in eighteenth-century operatic writing, is preferable.) Fischietti and Piccinni often used the da-capo and dal-segno form when writing for parti serie, most of whose arias are in the common time favored in opera seria, with broad melodies over busy accompaniments. The spaciousness of these melodies usually results from the lines of poetry being set to three or four measures of music instead of the two measures normal in music sung by buffi. Such melodies frequently take the form a-b-b′, with the first line of text set to phrase a and the second line set to phrase b and then repeated as phrase b′. Phrases b and b′ usually share some melodic material, but b′ ends more conclusively than b.[43] Later in the aria the nobleman or woman who sings it usually gives several displays of coloratura.

Armidoro's "Della sposa il bel sembiante," a dal-segno aria, exemplifies all these features (ex. 3.8). Piccinni set the first line of text to four measures of music (phrase a, consisting of two periods of two measures each), the second line to two measures (phrase b, two periods of one measure each), and then repeated the second line of text to three measures of music (phrase b′, which begins with the same rhythm and melodic profile as phrase b). In another dal-segno aria, Marchesa Giacinta's beautiful "Non v'è costante al mondo," dramatic ascending scales seem to reflect the indignation aroused in her by her fiancé's flirting with Brigida (ex. 3.9). Again the first line of text is set to four mea-

43. The predominance of a-b-b′ melodies in midcentury opera seria is documented by Eric Weimer, *Opera Seria and the Evolution of Classical Style, 1755–1772* (Ann Arbor, Mich., 1984); see esp. 18–20.

EXAMPLE 3.8 Piccinni, *La buona figliuola,* act 1, "Della sposa il bel sembiante," mm. 23–32

sures of music. Fischietti repeated the second line of text in the normal manner, but, as if to show that the Marchesa is too excited to sing a conventional a-b-b′ melody, there is little trace of a melodic parallel between the second and third phrases. With its exuberant leaps and syncopations, Fischietti's music vividly demonstrates the brilliance that parti serie contributed to midcentury opera buffa.

Parti serie of the kind exemplified by Armidoro and Giacinta are not common in operas written during the 1760s in Vienna, where operatic managers, composers, or audiences may have been reluctant to accept parti serie. When *La buona figliuola* was per-

EXAMPLE 3.9 Fischietti, *Il mercato di Malmantile,* act 1, "Non v'è costante al mondo," mm. 24–34

There is no one more constant in the world, there is no greater fidelity.

formed in 1764, the role of Armidoro was omitted, leaving some awkward gaps in the plot.[44] Whoever decided which librettos were to be set to music in Vienna seems to have preferred librettos lacking pure parti serie. Several of Gassmann's Viennese comic op-

44. Sartori no. 4191. I am grateful to Federico Pirani for confirming the absence of Armidoro from the libretto for the Viennese production of 1764.

eras contain no parti serie. Their absence from *L'amore artigiano* is acknowledged in the libretto for the first production, which identifies the singers not by the name of the character they sang, but by the category to which each belonged. The list includes two prime buffe (one of them Clementina Baglioni), a seconda buffa, two primi mezzi caratteri (one of them Caribaldi), one primo buffo caricato (Carattoli) and one secondo buffo; but no parti serie, male or female.[45] In bringing *La contessina* up to date for Gassmann in 1770 Coltellini added many ensembles and three finales but did not add parti serie, apparently not deemed necessary or even desirable in Vienna.

La finta semplice likewise lacks clear-cut parti serie, both in the original version of the libretto (Venice, 1764) and as revised for Mozart. The roles that come closest are those of Baron Fracasso, a military officer, and Giacinta, the woman he loves, sister of Don Cassandro. Giacinta's absence from the second finale and all but the last moments of the first strongly suggests that Goldoni conceived of her role as a parte seria. But her language is often less than noble. Her first aria is clearly comic in tone and poetic structure (twelve short senari). These words are worthy of a clever servant girl, not a baron's fiancée:

Marito io vorrei,
  Ma senza fatica.
  Averlo, se comoda;
  Lasciarlo, se intrica

[I'd like a husband, but without the bother; to have him when it's convenient, to leave him when he causes trouble.]

Fracasso (certainly not a noble name) and Giacinta fraternize with the other characters much more freely than do the noble lovers in *Il mercato* and *La buona figliuola,* taking part, for example, in the opera's opening ensemble along with two servants.

In their music for roles most closely resembling parti serie Gassmann and Mozart blurred the distinction between these characters and others with some serious qualities. One way in which they did so was to avoid the use of sopranos (male or female) in male roles. The roles of Prince Lindoro in *Le pescatrici* and of Leonzio in *Il filosofo innamorato* (both settings of adaptations of librettos by Goldoni, and both first performed in 1771) are among the few adult male roles in Viennese opera buffa written for sopranos. Gassmann may have strayed from normal Viennese practice for the sake of the musico Giu-

45. Sartori no. 1541. Of *L'amore artigiano* Heartz (*Viennese School,* 413) writes: "None of the characters can be called seria."

seppe Millico, who sang in Vienna from fall 1770 to the end of October 1771 and probably portrayed Lindoro and Lenzio.

Viennese composers of opera buffa wrote few da-capo or dal-segno arias, and this too contributed to lessening the difference between parti serie and other characters. *Le pescatrici* contains what is apparently the only dal-segno aria in Gassmann's Viennese opere buffe.[46] Eurilda lives among the fisherfolk, unaware that she is a princess; but the dal-segno form of her first aria identifies her as a parte seria: the woman to whom the soprano Prince Lindoro will eventually give his heart.

Mozart seems to have been more interested in the dal-segno form than Gassmann. *La finta semplice,* despite the absence of characters with all the qualities of a parte seria, contains two dal-segno arias, both sung by Fracasso: "Guarda la donna in viso" (in act 1) and "Nelle guerre d'amore" (in act 3).

The long orchestral introduction of "Nelle guerre d'amore" is consistent with the noble, serious implications of the dal-segno form. Yet Fracasso's opening melody, despite its a-b-b′ shape, lacks the long-breathed lyricism of the parti serie of Fischietti and Piccinni. Instead of unfolding in a leisurely succession of three- and four-measure phrases, the melody squeezes phrases b and b′ into four measures, without even a short rest between them, and hastily modulates to the dominant. Mozart probably wanted to portray Fracasso as a noble lover. At the same time, perhaps in recognition of Viennese taste, he did not completely divorce him from the musical world of the parti buffe.

The lack of parti serie in many Viennese opere buffe adumbrated their decline in Italy as well. Distinctions between parti serie and other characters with some of the same qualities broke down during the 1760s and 1770s, to the point where the label *parte seria* no longer made much sense and fell out of common use.[47]

Goldoni's parti serie often come close to parodying Metastasian serious opera, and sometimes Goldoni surely intended parody. But he rarely mocked opera seria wholeheartedly, so as to leave no room for the expression of pathos. The most blatant kind of operatic parody involved quoting passages from Metastasio's librettos or other well-known serious operas, either with enough words changed to make the text funny or in a context so different from the original that the text sounded ridiculous. Such parodies seem to be relatively rare in Goldoni's librettos. A conversation in *Il mondo alla roversa* (act 2, sc. 10) that Goldoni based closely on one in Metastasio's *La clemenza di Tito* (act 1, sc. 11) simultaneously makes fun and conveys the majesty of Metastasian drama.[48] One quatrain of the aria "È la fede degli amanti" (*Demetrio*) reappears in Goldoni's *La scuola*

46. Donath, "Gassmann," 79, 112–15.

47. The process by which the parti serie were integrated into the main plot and lost some of their most distinctive features is examined in detail in Henze-Döhring, *Opera seria, Opera buffa und Mozarts Don Giovanni.*

48. Marinelli, "Goldoni," 139.

moderna (1748),[49] but this quotation is without comic alterations or obvious parodistic intent.

In *Il mercato di Malmantile* Goldoni's quotation of classic authors serves a dramatic purpose: to emphasize Brigida's learnedness. She sprinkles her speeches with a line from Tasso here and one from Petrarch there, and hides two lines (not particularly famous ones) from Metastasio's *Didone abbandonata* in her cavatina "Perfida belva ircana." Angry that the count has lost interest in her, Brigida scolds him:

> Perfida belva ircana
> Stolida mente insana,
> Non, che trattar non sai.
> Se lo provaste mai,
> Ditelo voi per me.
>
> [Perfidious Hyrcanian beast, foolish and mad; no, you do not know how to behave. If you have ever felt this way, tell him about it for me.]

Brigida borrowed the last two lines from Dido's aria "Non ha ragione, ingrato."[50] The words do not make much sense here, with their sudden use of the second person plural (*voi*) after the second person singular in the previous line; by not quoting Metastasio's previous line, "Anime innamorate," Brigida leaves us with no way of knowing to whom she is addressing these lines. She thus reveals the shallowness of the learning she so proudly displays.

In the librettos of some other dramatists of the second half of the century, especially those working in Naples, parody of opera seria is much easier to identify than in those of Goldoni. Gennaro Astarita's *Tra i due litiganti il terzo gode* (Naples, 1766) makes fun of the last lines of *Didone abbandonata,* famous for its tragic ending, with Dido alone on stage singing a recitative. By replacing a few words, Astarita's librettist turned one of the most pathetic speeches in eighteenth-century opera (and one of the most familiar to eighteenth-century audiences) into a hilarious one-liner.[51]

Composers occasionally followed their librettists into the literal quotation of opera seria. In Pietro Guglielmi's *Il ratto della sposa* (Venice, 1765), one comic character shows another how to feign musical sophistication by singing a Metastasian aria. He chooses for this purpose a classic: "Vo solcando un mar crudele" from Leonardo Vinci's setting of Metastasio's *Artaserse,* and quotes it—music as well as words—in the middle of a buffo aria, "Figurati in quel sito."[52]

49. Heartz, *Mozart's Operas,* 229–30.

50. These quotations are pointed out by Ortolani in his annotations to *Il mercato di Malmantile,* in Goldoni, 11:1313–14.

51. Osthoff, "Die Opera buffa," 700.

52. Hunter, "Some Representations of *Opera Seria* in *Opera Buffa,*" 91–92.

Metastasian dramma per musica was not the only kind of serious opera that opera buffa audiences enjoyed seeing parodied. After the success of Gluck's *Orfeo ed Euridice* in 1762 and its subsequent performance in Naples, London, and Paris, it was only a matter of time before it became the object of friendly ridicule. Paisiello's *Socrate immaginario* (Naples, 1775) is one of several opere buffe of the 1770s and 1780s that make fun of Gluck's underworld scene.[53] By transferring the role of Orpheus to the comic character Don Tammaro, Paisiello made any reference to Gluck's opera potentially comic. Don Tammaro sings a cavatina, "Calimera, calispera" (which means "Good day, good evening" in modern Greek),[54] to music originally played by Orpheus on his harp. In the chorus that follows, Paisiello's use of triple meter, his emphasis on the text's quinari sdruccioli ("Chi tra quest'orride / caverne orribili . . .") by reiteration of the rhythmic pattern ♩ ♩ ♩ | ♩. ♪ ♩, his unison textures and descending chromatic sequence all remind us of Gluck, in a context in which Gluck's underworld scene can only sound comic.

Ghost scenes, in which a character in a serious opera, usually a woman, imagines that she sees the ghost of her lover or husband, whom she believes dead, and describes or addresses it, contributed horror and pathos to many eighteenth-century operas; they were especially common in post-Metastasian serious opera.[55] Not surprisingly, ghost scenes served as an object of parody in opera buffa. In Sacchini's *La contadina in corte* Berto (whose portrayal in Vienna by Poggi won Sonnenfels's praise) thinks he is about to be executed. He expresses his fear with a litany of opera seria images, including ghosts; but a reference to chattering teeth makes clear that this is parody:

Qual freddo, qual terrore . . . è notte, è giorno?
Solo mi veggo intorno ombre e spaventi.
Battonsi insieme i denti . . . oimè chi viene . . .
Strepito di catene . . . ove m'ascondo?
Ahi remedio non c'è, non c'è più mondo.

[What a chill, what terror . . . Is it night or day? Alone, I see ghosts and fears surround me. My teeth are chattering. Oh dear, who is coming? The sound of chains . . . where can I hide? Ah, there is no escape, I'm finished.]

Librettists and composers active in Vienna during the 1760s do not seem to have regarded the parody of serious opera as an essential element of opera buffa. Gassmann's almost exclusive dependence on Goldoni's librettos before 1772 kept him from setting to music the Metastasian parodies indulged in by other librettists. The presence in Vi-

53. For fuller discussions of Paisiello's Gluckian parody (with musical examples) see Wolfgang Osthoff, "Mozarts Cavatinen und ihre Tradition," in *Helmuth Osthoff zu seinem siebzigsten Geburtstag*, ed. Wilhelm Stauder (Tutzing, 1969), 171–73, and "Die Opera buffa," 702–4.

54. My thanks to Michel Noiray for pointing this out.

55. On ghost scenes see Hansell, "Opera and Ballet," 289–303.

EXAMPLE 3.10 Gassmann, *L'opera seria,* act 2, "Pallide ombre," mm. 33–40 (A-Wn, Mus. Hs. 17775; facsimile, New York, 1982)

Pallid shadows of my poor lover

enna of Metastasio and Calzabigi, moreover, may have discouraged him from amusing his audience at their expense.

It was only in collaboration with one of these masters of serious opera that Gassmann made fun of the other. Calzabigi's *L'opera seria,* performed in 1769 with Gassmann's music, is an amusing parody of Metastasian opera and of all those involved in its production: impresarios, librettists, composers, and singers.[56] In the course of three acts Calzabigi and Gassmann followed the opera *Oranzebe* from inception to performance. Among the conventions of opera seria that they derided was the ghost scene. Composers often set such scenes in the key of E♭, with melodies that featured long notes and big leaps.[57] Gassmann wrote "Pallide ombre" in E♭; he exaggerated both the long notes and the leaps to the point of parody. Audiences expected serious characters to sing phrases of three or four measures, but a six-measure phrase was ridiculous (ex. 3.10).

Parti di Mezzo Carattere

Some of Goldoni's characters display the strong, passionate emotions of noble lovers but lack the stiffness and exaggerated theatricality of the parti serie. Such parti di mezzo carattere tend to be more deeply involved in the plot than parti serie, taking part in finales from which the parti serie are usually excluded; at the same time they distance themselves from the more exaggerated antics of the parti buffe.

La buona figliuola contains good examples of mezzo-carattere roles: the Marchese and Cecchina. As a nobleman the Marchese shares some qualities with the parti serie; he is on their social level and can interact with them as an equal. But during his many dealings with the peasantry and servants he takes on some of their buffo qualities. Although he loves Cecchina, at the beginning of the opera the apparent difference in their social status keeps him from marrying her. When his sister asks him if he plans to do so, the Marchese answers curtly: "Questo non so." In the first finale the Marchese al-

56. A manuscript copy of *L'opera seria* (A-Wn, Mus. Hs. 17775) has been published in facsimile (New York, 1982).

57. On E♭ as *Ombra-Tonart* see Osthoff, "Mozarts Cavatinen," 157–77, passim.

lows himself to be turned against Cecchina by his servants Sandrina and Paoluccia, who claim that Cecchina is running off with Mengotto. The Marchese can be an ardent lover; but he can also be shrill and compulsive, susceptible to the claims of jealousy and class snobbery.

The beauty and Metastasian purity of the language that Goldoni gave to Cecchina depicts her, already in the first scene, as a gentle, virtuous, and noble young woman, in spite of the fact that she is describing her activities as gardener:

Ah, non potea la sorte,
In mezzo al caso mio duro e funesto,
Esercizio miglior darmi di questo!
Povera sventurata!
Non so di chi sia nata:
Questo è il tristo pensier che mi tormenta;
Pur, tra le piante e i fiori,
Trovo il solo piacer che mi contenta.
Godo colle mie mani
Un germoglio troncar dall'arboscello
E mirarlo cresciuto arbor novello.
Godo io stessa innestar sul prun selvaggio,
In dolce primavera,
Or le pesche succose ed or le pera.

[Fate could not have given me, amid my cruel and dismal lot, a better activity than this! Poor, unhappy girl! I do not know who my parents were: this is the sad thought that torments me; yet, among the plants and flowers, I find the only pleasure that gladdens me. I enjoy cutting a shoot off a sapling with my own hands, and watching it grow into a new tree. In sweet springtime I enjoy grafting onto the wild plum now the juicy peaches, and now the pears.]

The strength and attractiveness of Cecchina's character is related to its mezzo-carattere quality. Although she believes herself a commoner, her innate nobility keeps her from forming close bonds with parti buffe. We take Cecchina completely seriously, pitying her because of her misfortune and rejoicing with her when she finds happiness in the arms of the man she loves.

Musical portrayals of parti di mezzo carattere often use the binary and sonata forms characteristic of parti buffe, but their music tends to be more lyrical. Cecchina's music has the gentleness and sincerity appropriate to a mezzo-carattere role. Most of it is in moderate or slow tempo. Her aria at the beginning of the opera, "Che piacer, che bel diletto," is in sonata form without development. In its combination of triple meter and moderately slow tempo it recalls the minuet songs frequently sung by Goldoni's peasant girls and serving maids (ex. 3.11). And yet the melody itself, reaching up to expressive appoggiaturas, reminds one of Gluck's "Che farò senza Euridice," composed two

EXAMPLE 3.11 Piccinni, *La buona figliuola,* act 1, "Che piacer, che bel diletto," mm. 26–48

What pleasure, what delight to see at daybreak the jasmine and the rose compete in beauty!

years later. Here, as in the lament "Una povera ragazza" and in "Vieni al mio seno," Cecchina communicates to the audience the complexity of her character, the depth and sincerity of her feelings.

"Che piacer" is a cavatina, a relatively short aria, usually in a slow or moderate tempo, that is not followed by the departure of the character who sings it. In comic operas composed throughout the rest of the eighteenth century (including several of Salieri's) an important female character, usually noble, introduces herself with a cavatina, often placed later in the opera than Cecchina's. This tradition culminated in "Porgi Amor," sung by the countess on her first entrance in Mozart's *Figaro.*[58]

"Vieni al mio seno," sung by Cecchina as she falls asleep, is perhaps the finest of her arias, and certainly one of the score's musical high points. Piccinni's prominent use of flutes (which he called for in only one other place in the opera), together with muted violins and pizzicato cellos and basses, enhances the aria's sweetness. The simple harmonic language gives unexpected power to the sudden move to the parallel minor just before the end of the aria.

Fischietti and Piccinni made Rubiccone and the Marchese tenors, thus distinguishing them from male parti serie (sopranos) and male parti buffe (mostly basses). Rubiccone shows off the comic side of his character in the catalogue aria "Noi sottoscritti facciamo fede," with its long stretches of patter (see ex. 3.2). He reveals a more serious, romantic side in "Mia signora, a voi m'inchino," addressed to Brigida and her father Lampridio (ex. 3.12). Parallel thirds and cadences in which the bass descends from the

EXAMPLE 3.12 Fischietti, *Il mercato di Malmantile,* act 1, "Mia signora, a voi m'inchino," mm. 1–4

My lady, I bow to you.

58. Mary Hunter, "Rousseau, the Countess, and the Female Domain," in *Mozart Studies 2,* ed. Cliff Eisen (Oxford, 1997), 1–26, has documented the tradition of entrance arias to which "Che piacer" belongs. These arias mark the first appearance on stage of a woman who typically represents the sentimental focus of the plot.

second scale degree to the fifth (a formula beloved by the young Haydn) give this gentle melody a galant character. Its a-b-b form is similar to the noble a-b-b′ form; but instead of each phrase corresponding to a line of text, as is normal with this kind of melody, Rubiccone breaks up a single line of poetry into three musical phrases, none of which is longer than two measures. Trying to sound noble, Rubiccone gives away his status as a commoner by his inability to sing an a-b-b′ melody with at least one phrase of three or more measures.

Composers in Vienna too put some qualities of parti serie in their music for mezzo-carattere roles. In Scarlatti's *Gli stravaganti* the amorous Alessio reveals his nobility of character in "Con queste che mi dite," with its conjunct melody, elegant syncopations, expressive appoggiaturas, and a-b-b′ melodic structure. Rosina and Giannino, the mezzo-carattere lovers in Gassmann's *L'amore artigiano,* sing coloratura that one might expect in a love duet in an opera seria.[59] In *La notte critica* Leandro expresses his passion in the dignified and tender accents of a noble lover; his tune, with its sighing chromatic appoggiaturas, anticipates those that Mozart wrote much later for Ilia and Tamino (ex. 3.13). Leandro's a-b-b′ melody derives elegance from the extension of the phrase b′ to three measures. But Leandro is no parte seria: he sings this noble music in a comic context, instructing his servant Carlotto to tell Marinetta, the maid of his beloved, to pass on his amorous message. On finding that Carlotto has disappeared Leandro switches abruptly to the parlante style of a parte buffa.[60]

EXAMPLE 3.13 Gassmann, *La notte critica,* act 1, "Tu dirai a Marinetta," mm. 3–9 (A-Wn, Mus. Hs. 18080)

You will tell Marinetta what torment I feel in my heart.

59. Donath, "Gassmann," 99; for more on Gassmann's music for Giannino, see Heartz, *Viennese School,* 416–17.

60. For further discussion of this aria, with a longer musical extract that includes accompaniment, see Edward J. Dent, *Mozart's Operas,* 2d ed. (London, 1947), 20–23; and (quoting Dent's musical example) Allanbrook, *Rhythmic Gesture,* 25–27. Although Allanbrook claims that Dent's discussion misses the point, her own suggestion that Gassmann's orchestral accompaniment (eighth-note triplets in parallel thirds, dolce) "is simultaneously choreographing Carlotto's motions" seems a little far-fetched.

Rosina, the title character in *La finta semplice*, is in some ways a descendant of Piccinni's sentimental heroine Cecchina, but, as often in Viennese opera, the distinctions between character types are less clearly drawn than in *La buona figliuola*. On the one hand Rosina is much more involved in comic intrigue than Cecchina and lacks some of her sincerity and sensibility. On the other hand Rosina's music sometimes takes on exalted qualities of opera seria almost completely absent from Cecchina's music. The beautiful aria "Senti l'eco" conveys Rosina's youthful sweetness and her comic cleverness as it moves from passages that remind one of Cecchina's music to passages that sound more like Paoluccia's. At the same time it alludes to Rosina's nobility with coloratura of a kind that one might expect in a dal-segno aria.

Distribution of Keys

Large-scale tonal planning in Mozart's opere buffe of the 1780s has been subjected to much scholarly discussion and debate, but tonal planning in Goldonian opera has been studied little.[61] Fischietti, Piccinni, and their contemporaries worked within a relatively limited tonal spectrum, setting most of their arias and ensembles in major keys with fewer than four sharps or flats: E♭, B♭, F, C, G, D, and A. In deciding which of these keys to use in a particular aria or ensemble they must have considered many factors including, at least in some cases, tonal relations between numbers.

Several eighteenth-century musical theorists classified keys according to their expressive associations.[62] Some of these theorists derived their classifications from observation of composers' choices of key and uses of particular keys. Francesco Galeazzi, in his *Elementi teorico-pratici di musica*, published between 1791 and 1796, clearly did so: he distinguished often between keys in common use and those used rarely or never. His classification is particularly relevant to Italian opera since he, as an Italian (one of the few to address this issue in print), probably knew more Italian operas than most theorists who wrote about key characteristics. His discussion, moreover, is explicitly concerned with vocal music:

> it is certain that the wise composer begins with the choice of key in order to support the character of the words. This is neither an abstract nor an inconsequential matter. It is true that a clever artist knows how to express any affect in any key, and knows how to write a cheerful composition in the key of E♭ and a pathetic one in D. But he will certainly have to confess that

61. For a useful summary of the principal issues, references to the literature, and some sensible conclusions see John Platoff, "Myths and Realities about Tonal Planning in Mozart's Operas," *COJ* 8 (1996): 3–15. Among the few studies of tonal planning in pre-Mozartian opera buffa one of the most valuable is the analysis of the tonal organization of Paisiello's *La frascatana* in Hansell, "Opera and Ballet," 364–404 passim.

62. For a compilation and discussion of the characteristics assigned to keys before 1850 see Rita Steblin, *A History of Key Characteristics in the Eighteenth and Early Nineteenth Centuries* (Ann Arbor, Mich., 1983).

> doing so presupposes great skill, long experience, and the best judgment in the choice of chords and in the arrangement and disposition of the parts. It is therefore undeniable that all the keys of modern music, although they have the same proportions and intervals, nevertheless have different characters, which is of importance for the composer to know intimately.[63]

Galeazzi's classification of keys shows how clearly and strongly he perceived the differences between the sound and expressive characteristics of different keys. A major, for example, is "perfectly harmonious, expressive, tender, playful, bright, and cheerful." E♭, on the other hand, is "heroic, extremely majestic, grave, and serious." As composers distributed a limited number of keys through a three-act opera, characterizations similar to Galeazzi's presumably played some role in their decisions.

The use of particular instruments sometimes limited a composer's choice of key and thereby contributed to the expressive connotations of particular keys. When they used trumpets (which they did quite rarely in comic opera; *Il mercato di Malmantile* is one of many opere buffe that do not call for trumpets), midcentury composers usually wrote for trumpets crooked in C or D. Two numbers in *La buona figliuola* with trumpets in D (the overture and the finale of act 3) are both in D major.[64] Another uses trumpets in C (Tagliaferro's "Star trombette") and is in C major, like its descendant "Non più andrai," Mozart's evocation of the military life. It can surely be no accident that Galeazzi, even without mentioning instrumentation, associated both C and D major with loudness:

> C [major] is a grandiose key, military, apt for the expression of great events, serious, majestic and loud.
>
> D [major] is the most cheerful and the gayest key that music has; it is loud to an extreme degree and apt for the expression of celebrations, weddings, rejoicing, jubilations, exultations and encomia.

Eighteenth-century composers may have considered certain keys to be especially suitable to certain types of voices. A great number of bass arias in opere buffe of the second half of the eighteenth century are in D major. An association between basses and the key of D is hinted at in *La buona figliuola,* two of whose three arias in D are sung by the bass Mengotto. (Here Piccinni departed from the normal practice of writing every

63. Francesco Galeazzi, *Elementi teorico-pratici di musica,* 2 vols. (Rome, 1791–96), 2:293–95. Quoted in the original and in translation (used here, with some minor changes) in Steblin, *A History of Key Characteristics,* 110–12, 358.

64. Tagliaferro's aria in B♭, "Ah come tutte," calls for trumpets in D, but the notation of the trumpet part, with no key signature, seems to be intended for trumpets in B♭.

aria for a singer in a different key.) On the other hand, basses rarely sang arias in A major (there are no bass arias in A, for example, in *Il mercato* or *La buona figliuola*), while sopranos sang them frequently. Of four arias in A in *La buona figliuola,* three are sung by sopranos. Galeazzi associated cheerfulness with both D and A major, but he distinguished between them by describing D as loud and A as harmonious and expressive. That distinction may well reflect the practice of composers like Piccinni: comic basses are likely to be louder and less expressive than sopranos.

Composers of opera seria often associated E♭ with darkness, sleep, or ghosts, which helps to explain why Galeazzi perceived music in this key as "grave and serious." Piccinni too regarded E♭ as having especially expressive qualities. The only number in E♭ in *La buona figliuola* is Cecchina's sleep aria, "Vieni al mio seno," near the end of act 2. Piccinni deliberately withheld the key until this moment so that its warm, soft colors would contribute all that they could to this touching scene. (The move to the parallel minor makes sense in light of Galeazzi's comment about E♭ minor: "it is an extremely melancholy key, and induces sleep.")

But E♭ could also be used in comic situations. In many arias of indecision a buffo caricato imagines he hears honor or love speaking to him, almost as if he were hearing ghosts. Perhaps that is why composers very frequently chose E♭ for such arias. Already in 1733 Pergolesi set Uberto's "Son imbrogliato io già" in E♭; Lampridio's "Pensieri a capitolo" was by no means the last aria of indecision in E♭, as we shall see.

Fischietti, Piccinni, and their contemporaries seem to have given a good deal of thought to the tonal relations between numbers, despite the frequent separation even of adjacent numbers by long stretches of simple recitative. They cannot have expected many listeners to notice the tonal relation between two numbers separated by five minutes of tonally fluctuating recitative. Yet their sensitivity to the musical and extramusical associations of particular keys normally kept them, for example, from writing adjacent arias in the same key. And occasional patterns of tonal relations suggest that composers thought carefully about these relations even if they did not expect many listeners to hear them. The tour around the circle of fifths at the beginning of act 2 of *La buona figliuola* (the marchese's "Dov'è Cecchina" in B♭, Mengotto's "Ah Cecchina" in F, Tagliaferro's "Star trombette" in C, and Armidoro's "Cara, s'è ver" in G) cannot be accidental, in spite of the recitative that separates all four numbers.

The tonal planning of composers working in Vienna is in many ways close to that of Fischietti and Piccinni. Scarlatti, Gassmann, and Mozart set most of their vocal numbers in the same seven major keys to which Fischietti and Piccinni normally limited themselves. They generally avoided the same key in adjacent numbers and in two arias for the same character.

Gassmann sometimes saved E♭ for a particularly important moment relatively late in the opera; this was clearly the case in his first Viennese opera buffa. The first number in

EXAMPLE 3.14 Giuseppe Scarlatti, *Gli stravaganti,* act 2, "Ho tanta collera," mm. 36–41 (A-Wn, Mus. Hs. 17850)

I am surrounded by so many bosses, so many guardians, so many doctors who want to rein me in like an ass.

E♭ in *Il viaggiatore ridicolo,* Fabrizio's "Quanti son gl'anni," is near the end of act 2. Fabrizio wants to marry, but he hesitates because he thinks he may be too old. By saving E♭ for this aria Gassmann took full advantage of the association between E♭ and the aria of indecision and helped to establish that association in the minds of Viennese audiences and composers. Act 1 of *La contessina* likewise has no numbers in E♭, the first number in that key being the third piece in act 2, Pancrazio's aria of indecision "La faccio o non la faccio."

The distribution of keys in *La finta semplice* suggests that Mozart, like Piccinni, associated A major with sopranos and D major with basses. Mozart limited his use of A major to two arias for sopranos, and he assigned two of three arias in D to the bass Simone.

Mozart was not the first composer working in Vienna to bring a buffo caricato together with what Galeazzi called "the most cheerful and the gayest key," D major. In Scarlatti's *Gli stravaganti* Carattoli (in the role of Fastidio) sang "Ho tanta collera" in D. The aria's concluding Allegrissimo depended largely on his reiteration of D-major triads in the octave between the D below middle C and the D above (ex. 3.14). In another Viennese comic aria in D, Gassmann's "Son padron in casa mia" (in *Il viaggiatore ridicolo*), Carattoli sang exactly the same notes. This octave must have corresponded to the most powerful part of his range, and probably that of many buffi caricati, to judge by the large number of arias written in D major for comic basses and baritones throughout the second half of the eighteenth century in Vienna as well as in Italy.

Musical Continuity in Viennese Opera Buffa

Certain features of opere buffe written in Vienna during the second half of the 1760s attest to an interest on the part of composers in developing musical continuity within the

EXAMPLE 3.15 Gassmann, *La contessina*, act 1, "Si è risposto a quelle lettere?" mm. 58–61

framework—essential to Goldonian opera buffa—of the alternation of orchestrally accompanied numbers and simple recitative.

In several operas Gassmann ended ensembles or arias with transitions (usually played by strings in octaves) that inhibit applause and lead directly into the following recitative by way of an open cadence (usually V^6 of the key a whole step above that of the previous number's tonic). He was especially fond of connecting by this means an opera's introduzione to its first simple recitative. The first vocal pieces of *Il viaggiatore ridicolo, L'amore artigiano,* and *La contessina* (ex. 3.15) close with transitions, as do the first two vocal numbers of *L'opera seria.*[65] Also in *La contessina,* Lindoro's aria "Con quel sospiro," addressed to the countess, concludes very beautifully and expressively with a transition to the following recitative, as Lindoro's passionate pleading breaks through the aria's conventional ending. There are no such links in *Il mercato* or *La buona figliuola.* Gassmann probably borrowed the technique from Viennese serious opera of the earlier 1760s, of which it was a characteristic feature. Several numbers in Hasse's *Il trionfo di Clelia,* for example, end with transitions to the following number or to recitative.

Hasse had also enlivened much of the simple recitative in *Il trionfo di Clelia* with actively moving, melodic bass lines. Viennese composers of opera buffa inserted similar melodic material, often reflecting action on stage, into the accompaniment of simple recitative. These melodic figures enhance dramatic continuity by weakening the otherwise very clear-cut distinction between orchestrally accompanied numbers and simple recitative, in which the accompaniment is normally (as in *Il mercato* and *La buona figliuola*) completely nonmelodic. In act 2 of *Gli stravaganti* a repeated motive in the bass depicts Alessio's indecision. The buffo caricato Pandolfo sneaks around suspiciously near the beginning of *La notte critica,* accompanied by a snakelike line in the bass (ex. 3.16). In act 2 of *La finta semplice* a quarrel between Fracasso and Cassandro leads one to challenge the other to a duel; the accompaniment, with rapid scales, depicts Fracasso's drawing his sword (ex. 3.17). The action on stage and the music anticipate the following duet, which begins with Cassandro taking up the challenge by unsheathing his own sword to the sound of rapid scales in the orchestra similar to those heard earlier in the accompaniment of the recitative.

65. Heartz, *Viennese School,* 414, calls attention to the end of the introduzione to *L'amore artigiano:* "one amazing anticipation of the greatest *Introduzione* of all, in Mozart's *Don Giovanni,* when the piece dissolves on an unresolved $V^{6/3}$ in the strings (the same $G^{6/3}$ in fact!) giving way to simple recitative."

EXAMPLE 3.16 Gassmann, *La notte critica,* act 1, sc. 4, simple recitative, mm. 1–10

I think I heard . . . Who goes there? I fear that someone . . . Thank goodness! Nobody's there . . . Oh poor Pandolfo!

EXAMPLE 3.17 Mozart, *La finta semplice,* act 2, sc. 8, simple recitative, mm. 56–8

I? I have the heart of a lion, a tiger, an elephant . . .

Instrumentation

Near the end of *Il mercato* Lampridio sings (first in recitative, then in an aria) of his musical plans for his wedding with Lena. The aria is one of several in eighteenth-century opera buffa that feature a catalogue of musical instruments.[66]

E andremo alla città,
E faremo le nozze in allegria,
E voglio, Lena mia,
Che si balli, si canti, e che si suoni.
Voglio per la mia sposa
Invitare un'orchestra strepitosa.
Si ha da ballare, si ha da cantar,
Tutti i strumenti si han da suonar.
Voglio i violini, voglio i violoni,
Il violoncello vuò che si suoni,
Voglio il fagotto con l'oboè.
(*Dopo il suono di questi strumenti si sentono i corni di caccia*)
Questi strumenti non fan per me.
Viole e violini fan giubilar:
Tutta l'orchestra si ha da suonar.

[[Recitative:] And we will go to the city and we will celebrate our wedding joyfully; and, my dear Lena, I want people to dance, sing and play music; I want to invite a noisy orchestra for my bride. [Aria:] There must be dancing; there must be singing; and all the instruments must play. I want violins, I want double basses; I want the cello to play; I want the bassoon and the oboe. (*After these instruments have played the horns are heard.*) These instruments do not please me at all. Violas and violins cause merriment; the whole orchestra must play.]

Lampridio's idea of a noisy orchestra reflects the composition of the typical mid-century opera buffa ensemble in Italy. In addition to strings, his orchestra has only oboes, bassoons, and horns (the last he rejects because of their associations with cuckoldry); it lacks flutes, trumpets, and timpani.

Two kinds of orchestration, strings alone and strings with pairs of horns and oboes, account for most of the orchestral accompaniments in *Il mercato* and *La buona figliuola,* insofar as the instruments are notated.[67] Of thirty-three numbers in Fischietti's opera,

66. On *Instrumentenarien* see Osthoff, "Die Opera buffa," 685. Fischietti's aria is quoted and briefly discussed in Engländer, "Domenico Fischietti," 402–3.

67. Eighteenth-century performance practice allowed for a good deal of ad libitum playing by instruments not specifically called for in the score. The discussion here is generally limited to notated instrumentation, but one should keep in mind the possibility, for instance, that in many eighteenth-century orches-

twenty (almost two-thirds) are scored for strings along. Seven have pairs of oboes and horns; two have flutes and horns. The score of "Si ha da ballare" has cues for bassoons to play the bass line in response to the mention of bassoons in the text, but Fischietti wrote no separate parts for them. They probably reinforced the bass elsewhere in the opera. By far the most colorfully scored number in *La buona figliuola* is Tagliaferro's "Star trombette," where the military instruments mentioned in the text prompted Piccinni to call for trumpets and flageolets (but with no timpani in his orchestra he had to use string tremolos to depict *tamburi*).

Viennese opera buffa during the second half of the 1760s tended toward richer orchestration and texture. Having grown used to colorful instrumental effects in the works composed and performed in Vienna during Durazzo's tenure, audiences may have appreciated similar displays in opera buffa. At the same time, however, the impresarios had strong financial motivation to avoid engaging extra musicians. This helps explain why the exploration of orchestral color characteristic of Gassmann's operas is generally restricted to the instruments played by full-time members of the Burgtheater orchestra (as far as we know its roster during the impresarial decade): oboes, flutes, bassoons, horns, and strings. Even one of the most modestly orchestrated of Gassmann's operas, *La contessina* (which lacks parts for flutes), is distinctly Viennese in its elaborate writing for bassoons and its paucity of numbers using strings alone: only three vocal numbers of twenty-nine.

Several of Gassmann's overtures are colorfully scored. In *L'amore artigiano* the oboes and horns are far more prominent than in the overtures to *Il mercato* and *La buona figliuola:* short oboe duets in the second-theme area of the first movement and dialogues between oboes and horns in the second and third movements. (Italian overtures, in contrast, typically score the slow movement for strings alone.) The overture to *L'opera seria* calls for trumpets as well as horns, and flutes and oboes are displayed prominently in first movement's development. Gassmann's use of trumpets in C in an overture in F, not only in the fast movements but also in the B♭-major slow movement, demonstrates his interested in exploring new combinations of instrumental sonority and key.[68]

Gassmann frequently used instrumental solos in arias to depict character and emotional state. In *La notte critica* he emphasized Pandolfo's buffo qualities with a bassoon solo in his first aria. He accompanied the love-struck nobleman Leonzio in *Il filosofo innamorato* with a solo oboe and two English horns,[69] an ensemble whose possibilities Mozart had exploited with great success three years earlier in Rosina's "Senti l'eco." The

---

tras (probably less frequently during the second half of the century than the first half) oboes doubled violin parts in arias scored for strings alone.

68. This is one of several examples of Gassmann's use of brass tuned in keys other than the tonic. The overture to *Achille in Sciro* (Venice, 1766), in D major, has trumpets in D but horns in A, which play a solo in the second-theme area.

69. Donath, "Gassmann," 116.

appearance of English horns in the Viennese pasticcio *Orfeo* (1750) and, more recently, in Hasse's *Alcide al bivio,* Gluck's *Orfeo,* and Traetta's *Ifigenia in Tauride* must have contributed to the favor in which composers in and near Vienna (Haydn even more strongly than Mozart and Gassmann) held the instrument during the later 1760s and the early 1770s. A short French horn solo in the fast concluding part of "D'una parte amor mi dice," sung by the passionate young Giannino in *L'amore artigiano,* has been interpreted as a portrayal of "the lover's bounding heart (cf. the horns at the end of Fiordiligi's 'Per pietà' in *Così fan tutte*)."[70]

Gassmann occasionally brought a solo woodwind together with a coloratura soprano in concerto-like display, a technique that his student Salieri was to exploit much more frequently. In the ghost-aria parody "Pallide ombre" (*L'opera seria*) Stonatrilla warbles in comic dialogue with a bassoon. Concertante arias seem to have been rare in Italian comic opera of the 1750s and 1760s. *La buona figliuola* and *Il mercato* have none.

Mutes allowed Gassmann to achieve unusual and expressive sonorities without requiring the impresario to hire extra musicians. He called for muted oboes at least twice. In *L'amore artigiano* Giannino expresses his love for Rosina, whose father wants her to marry someone else, in "Occhietti cari del mio tesoro"; muted oboes help to convey Giannino's wistfulness and melancholy.[71] In the finale of act 1 of *La notte critica* (in the "dark" key of E♭) a single muted oboe contributes to an atmosphere of mystery and suspense as the characters wander about in a garden at night.

That same finale ends with an orchestral effect of great originality. Instead of the normal raucous conclusion (the *strepitosissimo* described by Da Ponte) the finale has a quiet ending. As the sounds of turmoil and confusion disappear into the night, the instruments of the orchestra become silent: first the winds and brass, then one group of strings after another, until finally only the cellos and double basses sustain the tonic, pianissimo.

Giovanni Gastone Boccherini, Salieri's first literary collaborator, celebrated the richness of Viennese operatic orchestration in one of the earliest operas that they produced together, *L'amore innocente.* The ambitious peasant girl Guidalba, looking forward to her wedding with a wealthy shepherd, imitates Goldoni's Lampridio in thinking of wedding music. In "Non vo' già che vi suonino" she names first all the rustic instruments that she does not want to be played at her wedding and then the sophisticated, urban instruments that she wants to hear:

Non vo' già che vi suonino
  Pive, sampogne, o pifferi,
  Chitarre o calascioni,
  Tamburi, lire, o cembali,

70. Heartz, *Viennese School,* 416.

71. Janet K. Page, "'To Soften the Sound of the Hoboy': The Muted Oboe in the 18th and Early 19th Centuries," *EM* 21 (1993): 69–71 and ex. 7.

Ne sveglie, ne buffoni,
Ribeche o dabbuddà.
Ci voglio violini,
Arpe, oboè, salteri,
Viole e violoncelli,
E flauti traversieri,
Fagotti e contrabassi,
E le spinette e i cimbali,
E le trombette e i corni,
E tutti gli strumenti
Che s'usano in città.

[I do not want to hear shepherd's pipes, bagpipes, or flageolets; guitars or lutes; tambourines, hurdy-gurdies, or cymbals; no more reveilles played by clowns on rebecs or dabbuddàs. I want violins, harps, oboes, hammer dulcimers, violas and cellos and flutes, bassoons and double basses, and spinets and harpsichords and trumpets and horns, and all the instruments that are used in the city.] [72]

Guidalba comes close to Lampridio's phrasing (Goldoni wrote "Voglio i violini," Boccherini "Ci voglio violini"). But the differences between the instruments that Lampridio hopes will be played at his wedding and those that Guidalba hopes will be played at hers are more interesting. In addition to all the instruments mentioned (or, in the case of horns, left unmentioned) by Lampridio, Guidalba mentions violas, harps, dulcimers, flutes, spinets, harpsichords, and trumpets. If Lampridio's list reflects the prevailing orchestral timbres of midcentury opera buffa in Italy, Guidalba's reflects the more colorful sonorities favored by Viennese composers. (Since *L'amore innocente* takes place in the Tyrol, one would have good reason to identify the *città* in Guidalba's aria as Vienna.) Even the harp and the dulcimer had a place in Viennese opera of the 1760s: Gluck used the harp in *Orfeo* and the dulcimer in *Le Cadi dupé*. [73]

72. The first six lines of the aria require some explanation. The names of the instruments in the first line are to some extent interchangeable: all are wind instruments with pastoral connotations. The *calascione* (more frequently spelled *colascione*) is not an ordinary lute but a two- or three-string Neapolitan lute played by wandering minstrels. *Tamburi* can mean "drums" or "tambourines"; the latter seemed better in this context. For the same reason I have preferred "hurdy-gurdies" to "lyres" in translating *lire* and "cymbals" to "harpsichords" in translating *cembali* (which can also mean "pianos," but probably not here). The next line is puzzling. The *Cambridge Italian Dictionary* suggests, as one of several translations of *sveglia*, "reveille, an obsolete wind instrument," but the *Oxford English Dictionary*, 2d ed., has no such definition under "reveille." Since no musical instrument was apparently known under the name *buffone*, Guidalba might be referring back to the beginning of the opera, where her father Cestone (certainly a *buffone*, a clown) plays reveille (*sveglia*), i.e., he wakes up Guidalba with his rebec. I have freely translated the line to convey this meaning. The *dabbuddà* is a stringed instrument of Arabic origin.

73. Salieri did not take full advantage of this opportunity to display the Viennese operatic orchestra in all its finery. He called for an orchestra only slightly larger than the one used by Fischietti in Lampridio's aria (in addition to Fischietti's orchestra he required flutes and supplied a written-out part for cembalo). Horns

The beautiful and expressive music for woodwinds and brass in the operas that Salieri, Martín y Soler, and Mozart wrote during the 1780s had its roots in the Viennese taste for a rich palette of instrumental color, a taste already reflected in the opere buffe written during the late 1760s by Gassmann and Mozart.

Opéra-Comique and Viennese Opera Buffa

French opera, particularly opéra-comique, strongly influenced Viennese music during the period in which Durazzo supervised theatrical life in the Habsburg capital. This influence did not end with his resignation in 1764 and the departure of the French troupe he had assembled, nor with the departure of another French company that arrived in 1768 and performed in Vienna until 1772. French musical culture, like French culture in general, was a characteristic feature of Viennese life throughout much of the second half of the century. Just as members of the Habsburg family corresponded in French, just as the opera-loving bureaucrat Zinzendorf kept his diary in French, so the upper classes of Viennese society that supported its operatic life knew and loved opéra-comique, even when it was not being performed in the court theaters.

Opéra-comique contributed to Viennese opera buffa, helping to differentiate it from opera buffa originating in Italy. (Here we must keep in mind, however, that opéra-comique itself was strongly influenced by Italian comic opera.) The *vaudeville final*, an ensemble concluding many opéras-comiques, found its way into several Viennese opere buffe.[74] (Gluck had already used the vaudeville final in *Orfeo.*) Gassmann's *L'opera seria* ends with a typical vaudeville, "Noi giuriamo per que' numi," in which each of the opera's main characters sings a short solo, and after each solo the rest of the characters join in with a recurring refrain. A similar ensemble, "Per star bene, e far tempone," brings his next opera, *La contessina*, to a close; here pairs of characters, rather than individuals, sing the solo sections. This vaudeville is not part of Goldoni's original libretto but was added by Coltellini in deference to Viennese taste, which is also reflected in Gassmann's music: gavotte rhythms give it distinctly French flavor.

Gassmann used characters who sing in French, such as the comic servants Girò in *L'amore artigiano* and Gazzetta in *La contessina.* Although French-speaking characters appear in several of Goldoni's librettos, Viennese audiences may have viewed such French

---

represent both trumpets and horns, the cembalo represents both *spinetti* and *cimbali*, and violins represent both violins and (played col legno) hammer dulcimers.

Guidalba's aria outlasted the rest of *L'amore innocente.* It is missing from the autograph score (the description above is based on a copy of the opera that includes "Non vo' già": D-Dlb, MS 3796). In its place in the autograph is a note in Salieri's hand: "Guidalba's aria follows; it was later placed in the opera *La cifra*, but transposed down a third." The later version, as it appears in *La cifra*, will be discussed in the context of that opera.

74. Herbert Schneider, "Vaudeville-Finali in Haydns Opern und ihre Vorgeschichte," in Badura-Skoda, 302–9.

interpolations with special favor. The poet (probably Coltellini) who revised Goldoni's *L'amore artigiano* for Gassmann replaced the servant Fabrizio with Girò, a French hairdresser, who sings arias in French—"A Paris tout est beau, tout est charmant"—and in a mixture of French and Italian.[75] Goldoni's original libretto *La contessina* contains no French verses for Gazzetta, whose French song in the third act of Gassmann's setting, "A vos pieds, charmante reine," was added by Coltellini, like the vaudeville with which the opera ends. Gassmann's songs for Girò and Gazzetta, redolent of opéra-comique, are products of a specifically Viennese branch of French musical culture.

75. Goldin, *La vera fenice,* 25; Heartz, *Viennese School,* 414–15.

4

CONSTRUCTING *LE DONNE LETTERATE*

Salieri's training and apprenticeship under Gassmann, which brought him into contact with all levels of personnel at the court theaters; his cordial relations with Metastasio and Gluck; and especially the favor in which Joseph II held him all made it inevitable that he should eventually write operas for the court theaters. The first of many such opportunities arrived when his most important supporters, Gassmann and the emperor, were not in Vienna. That he capitalized on this opportunity without the help of his mentor and his patron says something important about his ability to cultivate useful relations with a wide variety of influential people, an ability that would stay with him throughout his career.

Le donne letterate, Salieri's first publicly performed opera, came into being near the end of 1769, while Joseph was in Italy and Gassmann was preparing an opera seria to be performed during the emperor's visit to Rome. Salieri, nineteen years old, had been in Vienna less than four years. In genre, form, and style *Le donne* represents Viennese opera of the late 1760s: a product of Salieri's education under Gassmann, whose approach to opera buffa was shaped by the librettos of Goldoni and their settings by Piccinni, Fischietti, and their contemporaries. But *Le donne* also has many features typical of the operas that Salieri would write later. In this first opera we can see Salieri not only as a product of his time and place, but also as an individual who would himself help shape Viennese opera during the next thirty years.

Salieri's account of the composition, performance and reception of *Le donne letterate* is one of the most useful and attractive reminiscences that Mosel preserved in the composer's own narrative. It tells us much about how Salieri dealt with his librettist, planned the composition of his opera, and put himself in a position to benefit from the goodwill of powerful figures in the operatic establishment. Without ever applying pressure on the librettist Boccherini and his protector Calzabigi, on the composers Gluck and Scarlatti, or on the impresario (unnamed by Salieri, but probably Affligio, who had refused to bring Mozart's *La finta semplice* to production less than two years earlier), Salieri brought about the performance of his opera.

Daniel Heartz has called attention to Salieri's account as an important source of information about how Mozart, fifteen years later, might have planned and executed the composition of *Figaro*.[1] The reminiscence is especially useful as an indication of how Salieri himself went about these tasks, in 1770 and later, and provides us with a framework for discussion of his first opera buffa.

Untested Collaborator and New Libretto

Salieri's participation in the production of *Le donne letterate* began with a proposal by Boccherini:

> Gaston Boccherini, a dancer in the Viennese opera theater who passionately loved poetry, had written, with Calzabigi's help . . . , an Italian comic opera entitled *Le donne letterate,* which he intended for Gassmann. Calzabigi advised him to entrust it to me instead, since I, a beginner in composition as he was a beginner in poetry, would more easily come to an understanding with him.
>
> So Boccherini came to me one morning and, after greeting me, asked me without further preliminaries: "Would you like to set to music a comic opera libretto that I have prepared?" I calmly answered: "Why not?" And then he told me with complete honesty the plan he had, and how Calzabigi had advised him. "Ah ha," I said to myself, "so they think you are already able to write an opera! Courage! We cannot let this opportunity slip away!"[2]

Salieri's spontaneous decision to collaborate with Boccherini, without reading the libretto first, is attributable in part to his youth and inexperience; but it also anticipates the adult composer's casual attitude toward the quality of his librettos and the talent and experience of his poets. Throughout his career he showed little discrimination in choosing librettos and literary collaborators. There is no evidence in his actions or statements of the fastidiousness that Mozart, as eager in 1783 to prove his abilities as a composer of opera buffa as Salieri was in 1769, displayed in a letter to his father of 7 May 1783: "I have looked through at least a hundred libretti and more, but I have hardly found a single one that satisfies me; that is to say, so many alterations would have to be made here and there, that even if a poet would undertake to make them, it would be easier for him to write a completely new text—which indeed it is always best to do."[3]

1. Heartz, *Mozart's Operas,* 139; the relevant passages are reprinted in Mosel's German translation on pp. 154–55. See also Heartz, *Viennese School,* 425–27.

2. Mosel, 30–31.

3. Mozart to his father, 7 May 1783, in *MBA,* 3:268.

Nor did Salieri demonstrate a preference for librettists with a record of theatrical success. Boccherini was one of several poets with whom Salieri collaborated who had little or no experience in the composition of librettos.

That Salieri's first opera used a newly written libretto rather than one previously set to music anticipates another important aspect of his career. Almost all of his operas are the first and only settings of their librettos. He followed Mozart's precept that "it is always best" to work with "a completely new text" more closely than Mozart himself, whose early Italian operas (with two exceptions, *Lucia Silla* and *Ascanio in Alba*) used texts that had been set before, as did his last, *La clemenza di Tito.*

Salieri's habit of setting new texts robbed him of an opportunity important to the musical development of Haydn and Mozart: that of learning from earlier settings of the same libretto. Some of Haydn's operas reveal how much he profited from the skills of his Italian contemporaries when working with librettos that had previously been set by Anfossi and Cimarosa.[4] In composing *La finta giardiniera* Mozart may have similarly benefited from Anfossi's setting of the same text.[5] Salieri rarely, if ever, took advantage of this practical form of musical education.

Salieri's preference for new librettos helps explain why, despite the importance of Goldoni's texts in Viennese opere buffe of the late 1760s and early 1770s and in Gassmann's operas in particular, Gassmann's student set only one libretto by Goldoni (*La calamita de' cuori*) during the early years of his career. By the time Salieri began composing operas Goldoni had moved to Paris and, with few exceptions, had stopped writing librettos. Salieri's avoidance of texts previously set to music effectively eliminated Goldoni's librettos from consideration. Later, in 1779, offered a commission to set to music a new libretto by Goldoni, he accepted it, collaborating with Giacomo Rust on the first setting of *Il talismano.*

Boccherini's Commedia per Musica

Salieri's first steps toward the composition of *Le donne* were to acquaint himself with the text, to discuss the distribution of roles among members of the impresario's opera troupe, and to make arrangements for possible changes in the libretto: "So I asked the

4. See Reinhard Strohm, "Zur Metrik in Haydns und Anfossis 'La vera costanza,'" in Badura-Skoda, 279–95; Friedrich Lippmann, "Haydns 'La fedeltà premiata' und Cimarosa's 'L'infedeltà fedele,'" *Haydn-Studien* 5 (1982): 1–15; and Heartz, *Viennese School,* 395–98.

5. Abert, *Mozart,* 1:386, concludes from similarities between Anfossi's *La finta giardiniera* and Mozart's later setting of the same libretto that Mozart must have known Anfossi's score; but Volker Mattern (*Das dramma giocoso "La finta giardiniera": Ein Vergleich der Vertonungen von Pasquale Anfossi und Wolfgang Amadeus Mozart* [Laaber, 1989]) disagrees. Heartz, *Viennese School,* 598–99, sides with Mattern; but Michael Robinson, "Mozart and the Opera Buffa Tradition," 16–22, makes a convincing case for the influence of Anfossi's opera on Mozart's.

poet with great impatience to share with me the plot of his opera and to read the poem out loud to me. He did both; and after we had distributed the roles according to the skills of the opera troupe that was then in residence, Boccherini said: 'Now I will leave you, and in the meantime make your annotations, and if you desire changes here and there in consideration of the musical effect, we will make them together when I return.'"[6]

The libretto's title page refers to the work as a "commedia per musica," a term used chiefly in Naples (*commeddeja pe mmuseca*); elsewhere in Italy the term *dramma giocoso per musica,* popularized by Goldoni, was by far the most common designation for full-length comic librettos during the second half of the eighteenth century. Boccherini (probably following his mentor Calzabigi, who called his only comic libretto, *L'opera seria,* a commedia per musica) evidently preferred the Neapolitan term: he used it for almost all his comic librettos. But this does not mean that he rejected Goldoni's approach to opera buffa.

Boccherini's title is a translation of *Les Femmes savantes,* and he borrowed some of his characters and situations, directly or indirectly, from Molière's play of 1672. The reference to Molière is, paradoxically, one indication of Goldoni's influence: Goldoni's oeuvre shares many characters and dramatic situations with Molière's. Donna Artemia and her sister Donna Elvira, the "learned women" of the title, descend from Molière's Philaminte and her sister-in-law Bélise, probably by way of the many intellectual women in Goldoni's plays and librettos.[7] Enthusiastic dilettantes, Artemia and Elvira write poetry, read Latin, search for planets with a telescope, and organize literary salons and scientific *accademie.* In their intellectual activities Boccherini found the same kind of charm and comedy that Pietro Longhi conveyed in his painting *The Geography Lesson* (fig. 4.1), in which two pretty young women study with a tutor who is clearly more interested in anatomy than geography.

Artemia's niece Corilla and Don Prudenzio love one another, and neither shares the learned interests of Artemia and Elvira. The lovers correspond in part to Molière's Henriette (Philaminte's daughter) and her beloved Clitandre. Artemia wants Corilla to marry the most learned man she can find; Philaminte has similar plans for her daughter. Artemia arranges an academic competition between Don Vertigine, a "poeta effeminato e ridicolo" similar to Molière's Trissotin, and Don Trimetro, a doctor who resembles Molière's Vadius.

Although Artemia's husband Don Baggeo, a foolish old Neapolitan, corresponds to Molière's Chrysale, Philaminte's husband, in one important respect they differ. Chrysale has no interest in joining his wife and sister in their intellectual activities. Baggeo, in contrast, having been persuaded by his *donne letterate* to join in their quest for knowl-

6. Mosel, 31.

7. See Pamela D. Stewart, "Le *femmes savantes* nelle commedie del Goldoni," *Yearbook of Italian Studies* 7 (1988): 19–42.

FIGURE 4.1
Pietro Longhi, *The Geography Lesson.* Museo Civico, Padua.

edge, studies arithmetic with a tutor (Don Filberto) and writes a libretto for an opera seria (he calls it a *tragico dramma*), making amusing attempts to find someone willing to listen to him read his work in progress. (Did Boccherini, the dancer who tried to make a literary reputation by publishing a dramma tragico per musica, use Baggeo to make fun of himself?) Baggeo's doctoral examination, reminiscent of the one in Molière's *Le Malade imaginaire,* is the main event of act 3.

All eight of Boccherini's characters belong to the middle class. The interaction between nobility, bourgeoisie, and lower classes that Goldoni used so effectively in many of his librettos is absent. *Le donne* has no parti serie. Boccherini gave several characters—Artemia, Corilla, Prudenzio, Vertigine—short aria texts in the exalted style, but none of these roles is entirely serious. They all include some comic elements and all take part in the finales.

Boccherini gave his parti buffe—Baggeo, Filberto, Trimetro, and Elvira—relatively long, humorous aria texts full of colorful imagery of the kind best projected by specialists in comic roles. These include a fine example of the Goldonian catalogue aria, Filberto's "Sa tutto il greco," which consists mostly of a list of the academic subjects that his pupil Baggeo has supposedly mastered. Boccherini followed Goldoni and Coltellini here in using foreign languages for comic effect. The aria's humor is enhanced by the fact, well known to the audience, that Baggeo really knows very little about anything:

Sa tutto il greco
  Dall'Alfa all'Omega;
  Tutto il francese
  D'un bout all'autre;
  Tutto il latino
  Tamquam Propertius;
  Sa la grammatica,
  L'umanità.
Sa la rettorica,
  Sa la poetica,
  Sa l'aritmetica,
  Sa ben la logica,
  Sa ben la fisica
  E metafisica.
  Filosofia,
  Geografia,
  Cosmografia,
  Idrografia
  Da cima al fondo.
  E fin dell'arte
  Di Raimondo,
  Arcani e regole,
  Enigmi e cabale
  A mente fa.[8]

[He knows all of Greek, from alpha to omega; all of French, *d'un bout à l'autre;* all of Latin, *tamquam Propertius;* he knows grammar and the humanities. He knows rhetoric, literary theory, arithmetic, logic, physics, and metaphysics; philosophy, geography, cosmography, and hydrography from top to bottom; and he has committed to memory Raimondo's art: the secrets, the rules, the riddles, the Cabala.][9]

8. Boccherini's "Sa tutto il greco" turned up later in Giovanni Bertati's libretto *Calandrano* (Venice, 1771), now in the first person: "So tutto il greco." Goldin, *La vera fenice,* 151–52, attributes the aria to Bertati.

9. "Raimondo" may be Raimundo, bishop of Toledo (d. 1152), under whose patronage scholars translated into Latin important scientific and philosophical texts by Arabic and Jewish scholars, included *Fons vitae* by the Jewish poet and philosopher Ibn Gabirol, which inspired the Cabalists (Jewish mystics and occultists) of the Middle Ages (hence "Enigmi e cabale").

Another of Filberto's arias, "Quattro via cinque sedici?" shows Boccherini exploiting a different Goldonian technique: deriving comedy from the combination of singing and numbers. Filberto's attempt to teach Baggeo arithmetic recalls Foresto's attempt, in Goldoni's *L'Arcadia in Brenta,* to figure out how much money he has lost.

The idea that intellectual activity is less suited to women than to men is as important a source of comedy in *Le donne* as in some of Goldoni's librettos. Lampridio's daughter Brigida (in *Il mercato di Malmantile*), eager to show off her knowledge "of law, medicine, or mathematics," is a forerunner of Elvira and Artemia. Goldoni had made fun of amateur astronomers in *Il mondo della luna;* Boccherini, by making one of his learned ladies a stargazer, brought together two sources of Goldonian comedy. Eighteenth-century audiences must have laughed as Elvira sang of her astronomical ambitions in an aria that culminates in a list of male astronomers:

Voglio tutti de' pianeti
  I satelliti scoprire:
  I lor cerchi definire,
  I diametri fissar.
E le stelle che risplendono
  Nubilose nella Lattea
  Tutte voglio numerar.
Così al par del Galileo,
  Del Keplero, dell'Eugenio
  Io mi voglio immortalar.

[I want to discover all the satellites of the planets, to define their orbits, to determine their diameters. And I want to count all the stars that shine like a cloud in the Milky Way. Thus I want to make myself immortal, like Galileo, Kepler, and Huygens.]

Artemia's first aria, "Tre città rinomate," with its catalogues of famous Latin authors and the cities in which they were born, is similarly comic: she boasts of the fame that she and her sister will earn for their native city, Naples. But Artemia's role is not a simple parte buffa. The majesty of serious opera pervades the text of her second aria:

Astrea nel cor mi siede
  Regina degli affetti.
  So giudicar gli oggetti
  Come richiede onor.

[Astrea, queen of the emotions, resides in my heart; I judge objects as honor demands.][10]

10. Artemia's learned allusion to Astrea, ancient goddess of justice, might have reminded Viennese audiences of a scene in *Il mercato di Malmantile.* When Lampridio, as governor of Malmantile, serves as judge, he calls upon his highly educated daughter to help. Brigida refers to Astrea; after she has explained to Lampridio who Astrea is, Rubiccone praises Brigida by saying that Astrea resides in her heart: "La dea giustis-

Corilla's position between the comic and serious spheres is clear from her first appearance. Alone, she reveals herself to the audience as a cheerful, irreverent young woman who speaks the language of opera buffa:

Pur troppo il mio tutore è rimbambito:
Quel vecchio scimunito
Per compiacer la moglie
Imparò l'A. B. C. di cinquant'anni;
E gonfio di superbia letteraria
Sino di compor drammi or si dà l'aria!
Ma gettiam nel giardino il mio viglietto,
Che se del mio diletto
Giungo ad essere sposa,
Addio casa, addio libri, addio rettorica.
Sarà la mia teorica,
La mia scienza, e la mia filosofia,
Amar consorte, figli, e d'economia.

[Alas, my guardian is senile; that foolish old man learned the ABCs in his fifties to please his wife; and full of literary arrogance he gives himself airs, to the point of writing librettos! But let's throw my note into the garden, for if I succeed in becoming the wife of my beloved, farewell house, farewell books, farewell rhetoric. My theory, my science, and my philosophy will be to love my husband and children and to keep house.]

But this recitative is followed by an aria text with the style, vocabulary and elegant brevity of opera seria:

Una volta che si senta
    Risanar d'amor la piaga,
    Non sarà quell'alma vaga
    D'altra scienza che d'amor.

[Once one feels love's wound being healed, that will be the charming spirit of no other science than love.]

Prudenzio, the man whom Corilla loves, shows himself a mezzo-carattere part in his first aria, which begins seriously enough—

sima / Siede nel vostro cor" (act 2, sc. 16). Boccherini's aria text as a whole was probably inspired by one in Goldoni's *Il mondo della luna,* in which Flaminia, a parte seria, praises Reason rather than Justice: "Ragion nell'alma siede, / Regina dei pensieri."

So che mi ama il mio tesoro
  Come anch'io l'amo, e l'adoro,
  Che in due cori è un sol desir.

[I know that my darling loves me as I love and adore her, that in two hearts there is but one desire.]

—but continues in comic style as he thinks of the family of would-be intellectuals blocking his way to his beloved; he reiterates some of the same inelegant, comic words that Corilla used in the recitative quoted above:

E un rivale scimunito,
  Un marito rimbambito,
  E due femmine scapate,
  Impazzate, indiavolate
  Hanno a farmi intisichir?

[And a foolish rival, a senile husband, and two reckless women who are mad, possessed, are going to make me weak?]

Boccherini laid out his drama in the three acts that Viennese audiences had come to expect, with the third act shorter than the first two. The libretto contains sixteen arias and ten ensembles: one duet, two trios, three choruses (one of which, a short exclamation, is sung three times), an introduzione and three finales. In providing Salieri with the opportunity to write so many ensembles, Boccherini departed from examples set by Goldoni and Gassmann. None of Gassmann's operas composed before 1770 has more than eight ensembles. Boccherini's aria-to-ensemble ratio of roughly 3:2 is a little larger than that in Gassmann's *La contessina,* first performed a few months after Salieri's opera. The eleven ensembles in *La contessina* represented the largest number that Gassmann had yet written, while the ten in *Le donne* constituted the starting point for Salieri, whose comic operas, with some important exceptions, became increasingly dominated by ensembles.

Goldoni called for a duet for the newly reconciled mezzo-carattere lovers in the penultimate scene of many of his librettos. Boccherini, in contrast, placed his only duet in act 2; he wrote it for two men, Baggeo and Vertigine; and he made its contents comic rather than romantic. There was a Viennese precedent for this departure from Goldonian practice. *La finta semplice* has only one duet (the text for which was added by Coltellini), and it too is a comic piece sung by two men in the second act.

Singers

That Boccherini and Salieri discussed casting so early in their collaboration points to the crucial role that singers played in the composition of opera during the eighteenth century. Boccherini surely had particular members of the Viennese opera buffa troupe in mind when he shaped the roles in *Le donne letterate.* Although Salieri claimed that he collaborated with his poet in assigning the roles to particular singers, more likely he simply reviewed decisions already made by Boccherini.

Boccherini and Salieri assigned all three male parti buffe—Filberto, Baggeo, and Trimetro—to basses and the two male mezzo-carattere roles—Vertigine and Prudenzio—to tenors. They gave the sole female parte buffa—Elvira—to a contralto and the two female mezzo-carattere roles—Artemia and Corilla—to high coloratura sopranos. The resulting distribution of roles is well balanced, with a satisfying variety of vocal types.

Although eighteenth-century librettos normally list the cast of the production for which they were published, that of *Le donne letterate,* like many Viennese librettos from the second half of the century, names no performers. In Vienna, with its resident opera troupes, works often stayed in the repertory for several months, during which members of the cast might have to be replaced. An edition of the libretto in which no performers were listed could be used during the entire run of an opera, regardless of changes in the cast. The absence of cast lists in many Viennese librettos means that we can establish with certainty the complete casts of relatively few Viennese operas of the second half of the eighteenth century.[11]

Of the cast for whom Boccherini and Salieri wrote *Le donne* we know (from Mosel) only that Clementina Baglioni sang Artemia and that Caribaldi, Carattoli, and Poggi sang in the opera. That Caribaldi created the role of Vertigine follows from Mosel's statement that Salieri wrote an aria in B♭ for Caribaldi in act 1; the only such aria is Vertigine's "Spargerò foglie di rose." Carattoli and Poggi sang two of the opera's three comic bass roles. Since Carattoli specialized in the portrayal of ridiculous old men, he probably created the role of Baggeo, "quel vecchio scimunito."

Tonal Plan

After reading the libretto several times Salieri began the compositional process by working out the distribution of keys throughout the opera. In doing so he followed Gassmann's example:

> When I was alone I locked myself in, and with burning cheeks—which was normal for me, whenever I undertook a project with pleasure and love—I read the poem through again,

11. Other evidence—payment records, diary entries, and so forth—is sometimes useful, but rarely allows us to reconstruct an entire cast.

found it certainly well suited to music; and, after I had read the aria and ensemble texts a third time, I first of all determined, as I had seen my teacher do, the key appropriate to the character of each number. Since it was already noon, and I consequently could not hope to begin composing before lunch, I used the remaining hour to read through the libretto again. I was already beginning to think of the melody in several places when Madame Gassmann (for my teacher was married by then) had me called to the dinner table. My opera libretto never left my head during the entire meal, and I have never been able to remember what I ate that noon.[12]

In chapter 3 we considered some aspects of the tonal organization of opere buffe composed during the 1750s and 1760s. It was presumably some combination of those factors that Salieri took into account in developing the tonal plan of *Le donne.*

One decision that Salieri must have made very early was to set both the introduzione and the finale of the first act in the same key, on the grounds that they begin with the same text. In the introduzione Artemia writes a poem about the burning of the Capitoline Library in Rome, a fire that destroyed much of the literary heritage of antiquity; in the finale she recites her completed verses (which contain one minor change from her earlier draft, in which the third word was *onoranti*):

Degne e onorate lacrime
    Versiam, che è giusto piangere
    La deplorabil perdita
    Di ciascheduna età.

[Let us shed worthy and honored tears, for it is right to mourn the deplorable loss of every age.]

Artemia's somber subject and the seriousness with which she addresses it encouraged Salieri to chose the key of E♭ major for both numbers. Composers used E♭ quite sparingly in comic operas during the 1750s and 1760s and often saved it for a moment of particular pathos and dramatic importance or, alternatively, for a comic aria of indecision. Salieri's decision to cast both introduzione and first finale in E♭ was adventurous.[13]

Salieri set the finale of act 2 in B♭. The finale of act 3 begins in D major and ends in G. Although finales normally begin and end in the same key, there may have been a tradition in the 1760s that allowed for the finale of a third act to begin and end in different keys. *La finta semplice* ends with a finale whose tonal plan is the reverse of Salieri's: it begins in G and ends in D.

Having decided on a symmetrical tonal frame for act 1 and chosen the keys with

12. Mosel, 31–32.
13. Haydn was later to deploy E♭ exactly the same way in the first act of *Il mondo della luna* (1777).

which his subsequent acts end, Salieri followed Gassmann and his Italian contemporaries by filling the intervening tonal space almost exclusively with numbers in the major mode and in keys with no more than three flats or sharps. Like Piccinni (in *La buona figliuola*) and Mozart (in *La finta semplice*) he occasionally had recourse to patterns of tonal relationships between adjacent numbers. From the E♭ introduzione Salieri moved forward in the circle of fifths, as Piccinni had done in act 2 of *La buona figliuola:* a short instrumental reprise of the introduzione (B♭), Elvira's aria "Voglio tutti de' pianeti" (F), Artemia's "Tre città" (C), and Filberto's "Quattro via cinque" (G). The rest of the act exploits third relations: Baggeo's aria "Andiam dunque" (C) is followed by Corilla's "Una volta" (A); Trimetro's "Ma un uom di lettere" (G) is followed by Vertigine's "Spargerò foglie di rose" (B♭); and Prudenzio's "So che mi ama" (C) is followed, after some accompanied recitative, by the finale (E♭). Since every one of these numbers is separated from adjacent numbers by recitative, it doubtful that Salieri expected his audience to perceive these tonal relations. He probably used them mostly as a convenient way to insure tonal variety while limiting himself to a relatively small number of keys.

In choosing keys Salieri did not simply create abstract patterns; he took into account the requirements of individual singers, voice types, and "the character of each number." Piccinni (in *La buona figliuola*) and Mozart (in *La finta semplice*) treated A major as if they considered it especially suited to sopranos. So did Salieri. Corilla's "Una volta" is the only aria in the opera in A. Some of Salieri's predecessors associated D major with basses; so apparently did he. The only aria in D is Filberto's big catalogue aria, "Sa tutto il greco."

Sometimes Salieri had to mediate between conflicting tonal claims. An anecdote that Mosel recorded not only emphasizes the importance of tonal planning for Salieri but also sheds light on the activities and personalities of the Viennese opera buffa troupe, and it shows how well "the greatest musical diplomat," in spite of occasional disagreements, got along with the singers. Caribaldi, who had little formal musical training, wanted an aria in E♭:

> The year before [Caribaldi arrived in Vienna, i.e., 1766] he had sung to great applause in several theaters an aria that happened to be in E♭, and from this he had got it into his head that this key was the most suitable for his voice; and he was strengthened in this caprice by the fact that in the first opera in which he sang in Vienna, Kapellmeister Gassmann's *L'Amore artigiano* [1767], he had made a great impression in an aria that was likewise written in E♭.[14]
>
> Unfortunately, in Salieri's new opera there was no aria composed in this key. He brought to Caribaldi only an aria in the second act that ends with a trio [the cavatina "Donne sapienti e vaghe" in F major, followed by accompanied recitative and an "aria a tre" in C major, "Arde

14. Heartz, *Viennese School*, 416, describes Caribaldi's aria in E♭ in *L'amore artigiano*, "D'una parte amor mi dice," as "the opera's grandest and most beautiful piece."

l'alma, avvampa il core"] and let him think that the aria in the first act ["Spargerò foglie di rose"] was not yet ready. "Which you will surely write in E♭?" said Caribaldi. "That goes without saying," replied Salieri with some embarrassment, since the aria was already finished, and it was in B♭; and there was no time to write another.[15]

Salieri's explanation does not ring true. Like most eighteenth-century opera composers, he probably could have written an aria in a matter of hours. There was a much better reason not to give Caribaldi an aria in E♭ near the end of act 1. Salieri had already chosen E♭ as the act's framing key; use of the same tonality in Caribaldi's aria might have weakened the effect of the simultaneous return, at the beginning of the finale, of the introduzione's music and key.

Salieri realized, even as a beginner, how important it was for singers to be fully and enthusiastically committed to the performance of his opera:

Full of apprehension that Caribaldi, if he were not pleased with his aria, could sing the entire opera with reluctance, Salieri asked Domenico Poggi, another singer of the company, a good musician and friend of Caribaldi, whom he called Signor E-la-fa [Signor E-flat], for advice in this matter. Poggi looked through the aria, found it good, and advised Salieri to tell the copyist to place three flats in the vocal part, since this was the only thing that Caribaldi understood, and the thing that he would see as soon as he received his vocal part, and would consequently believe that it was in his favorite key. Poggi promised to help carry on the little deception in the hope that here was an opportunity to cure his friend of his delusion.

So two days before the performance of the opera Salieri took the aria, which was still missing from the score, to the singer, and he noticed that Caribaldi's eyes immediately sought out the blessed three flats. Salieri sang the aria for him, and the singer, delighted with the composition and gifted with an extraordinary memory, learned it by heart the same day.

Luckily for Salieri, the aria was one of the pieces that received the most applause. But on the second evening, when the orchestra and singers assembled on the stage before the performance, [Giuseppe] Trani, director of the orchestra [i.e., concertmaster], said to Caribaldi: "Well, my friend, now you will no longer imagine that the key of E♭ is the only good one for you, after you won such roars of applause with an aria in B♭." "You are joking," replied the singer. "In my part there are three flats at the beginning; hence the aria is in E♭." "Ha, ha!" answered Trani. "Three flats for B♭!" Caribaldi turned his back on him and asked Poggi if his aria was really written in B♭. Poggi, who wanted to continue the joke, answered him: "Are there not three flats written at the beginning?" "Exactly," said Caribaldi. "Well, if that's the case, and since the aria is in a major key, it must be in E♭." "It is in B♭," said the famous Carattoli, who was also a member of the company. "No, in E♭," Poggi insisted.

In the meantime Trani had taken the score out of the orchestra, to persuade Caribaldi that his aria was provided with only two flats. He finally understood the joke that had been played

15. Mosel, 37–38. The anecdote is discussed in Heartz, *Viennese School*, 427–28.

on him, and when Salieri, who knew nothing of what had just happened, came on stage, Caribaldi pulled off the wig that he was wearing as part of his costume and, threatening with comic fury to throw it at Salieri, shouted "Ha! you rascally little composer!" Salieri, who immediately guessed what it was about, fell upon one knee and began an aria that Caribaldi had sung in another opera a short time before, imitating the singer in song and action:

Eccomi a' piedi tuoi;
Mira bell'idol mio
Un reo d'innanzi a te.

[Here I am at your feet; look, my fair beloved, a guilty man before you.]

All of those present laughed; Caribaldi, putting his wig back on, laughed too, and was, as Poggi had predicted, by means of this trick cured forever of this passion for the key of E♭.[16]

Eighteenth-century composers often waited to write the overture until the rest of the opera was finished, and Salieri may have done so in *Le donne.* His choice of G major for the overture is unusual. D major was by far the most common key for overtures in the second half of the eighteenth century. (A catalogue of Anfossi's sinfonie, most if not all of which are overtures to operas and oratorios, lists fifty-three works in D out of a total of sixty-seven, and only one sinfonia in G.)[17] Salieri's opera ends in G, but that in itself was not sufficient reason to set the overture in G; many operas by Salieri and his contemporaries begin and end in different keys. A more important factor was the easily perceptible tonal relation between the overture and introduzione in E♭. Salieri's preference for third and fifth relations and his avoidance of half steps between the keys of adjacent numbers may have discouraged him from writing his overture in D and left him with the choice between G, B♭, and C. Had he used trumpets in his overture he would have probably set it in the key of C. With trumpets absent from the entire opera, however, it was perhaps his decision to end the work in G that led him to prefer G over C and B♭ as the key of his overture.

Action Ensembles: Introduzione and the Finale of Act 1

With the distribution of keys decided, Salieri next focused his attention on the longest, most complicated numbers: the finales and the introduzione. He started with the introduzione:

After lunch I took a midday nap, with a book in hand, as was my custom from childhood; then my daily walk along the walls around the city, and then I returned to my apartment, full

16. Mosel, 38–39.

17. Joyce L. Johnson, "Pasquale Anfossi, 1727–1797" (thematic catalogue of *sinfonie*), in *The Symphony, 1720–1840,* ed. Barry S. Brook, *Reference Volume* (New York, 1986), 15–22.

of secret pride at the confidence shown in me. I asked the maid (as I had in the morning) to send away any guests on the pretext that I was not at home. The good old woman, to whom the self-important expression of her normally so jovial young gentleman and his repeated instruction may have seemed strange, looked at me with astonishment and could not contain a half-hidden smile. But I said to myself: "Let the poor fool smile, and we will think how to do ourselves honor."

As soon as I was alone, I felt an irresistible urge to set to music the opera's introduzione. I tried to imagine as vividly as possible the personalities of the characters and the situations in which they found themselves, and suddenly I found a motive in the orchestra that seemed to me to carry and unify the piece's vocal line, which was fragmentary on account of the text. I now imagined myself in the parterre, hearing my ideas being performed; I tried them again, and when I was satisfied with them, I continued further. So, in half an hour, a sketch of the introduzione was down on paper. Who was happier than I![18]

The introduzione presents Artemia and Elvira together with Artemia's husband Baggeo. Each is preoccupied with some intellectual activity. Artemia writes her lament on the destruction of the Capitoline Library; Baggeo, nearly asleep, works on arithmetic (Boccherini incorporated elements of the Goldonian "number aria" into the introduzione, just as Da Ponte would do at the beginning of Mozart's *Figaro*); and Elvira reads a Latin poem and comments on its style and moral strength.

Despite Salieri's claim that he "tried to imagine as vividly as possible the personalities of the characters and the situations in which they found themselves," this introduzione has little differentiation of character: Artemia, Baggeo, and Elvira sing in the same declamatory style (exx. 4.1, 4.2, and 4.3). Only when Baggeo, unable to multiply four by five, loses his temper does the music respond to his feelings, modulating from C minor to G minor and increasing the rhythmic activity of the vocal line; then, as the music returns to C minor, its plodding rhythm shows Baggeo growing sleepy (ex. 4.4).

An orchestral motive (*eine Bewegung des Orchesters*) occurred to Salieri as a means of unifying the introduzione, bridging the gaps that are a necessary part of dialogue (including the particular kind of "dialogue" found here, where the characters do not actually speak to one another) but that might easily lead to musical incoherence. Second violins and violas in unison play Salieri's Bewegung, an undulating series of eighth notes slurred in groups of four. The dark sound of the violins' low register, reinforced by the violas, gives the motive a solemn quality that suits Artemia's poem (ex. 4.5).

Salieri described how he approached the composition of the first-act finale:

It was six in the evening and darkness had fallen; I called for a light. Tonight, I decided, you will not go to bed before twelve. Your imagination is alight, this fire must be made use of. I read the first finale, which began, as far as the words were concerned, much like the intro-

18. Mosel, 32.

EXAMPLE 4.1 Salieri, *Le donne letterate,* act 1, introduzione, mm. 7–11 (A-Wn, Mus. Hs. 17833)

Let us shed worthy and respectful tears, for it is right to mourn

EXAMPLE 4.2 *Le donne letterate,* act 1, introduzione, mm. 23–29

Four times five make sixteen . . . no . . . no . . . four times five make thirty.

EXAMPLE 4.3 *Le donne letterate,* act 1, introduzione, mm. 39–42

[Latin] Happy he who was able to look upon the pure source of goodness.

EXAMPLE 4.4 *Le donne letterate,* act 1, introduzione, mm. 32–37

To the devil with counting and arithmetic. I am very sleepy indeed.

EXAMPLE 4.5 *Le donne letterate,* act 1, introduzione, mm. 1–8

(*Continued on next page*)

EXAMPLE 4.5 *(continued)*

> duzione. I read it again, and made a plan of meters and keys suitable to the whole, devoting three hours to this work without writing a note.[19]

The text from which he worked, reproduced here from the libretto printed for the first production of *Le donne,* can give us some idea of how, sitting alone in his room, Salieri developed his "plan of meters and keys" (fig. 4.2).

The finale begins with three quatrains plus three couplets of settenari sdruccioli. The first of these quatrains consists of the beginning of Artemia's poem on the destruction of the Capitoline Library. In the second quatrain (beginning "Ah quel lamento flebile") Baggeo reacts to the first four lines of Artemia's poem and Filberto and Trimetro tell him to let her continue. She resumes her recitation in the third quatrain (beginning "Vestasi a bruno Apolline"). In the three couplets that follow she is interrupted by Vertigine and Baggeo with expressions of sadness ("Ahi, ahi") followed by requests from other characters for silence. By the end of Artemia's poem everyone except Artemia and Filberto is weeping or laughing.

Seven more settenari sdruccioli follow (beginning "Ma perché di qua ridono?"), all of which form rhyming couplets except the line "Senza rispetto a Socrate." Various characters explain their reactions to Artemia's poem. She tries to bring the discussion to an end ("Finite il pianto e il riso!") and at the same time switches to a new verse type: the versi sciolti normally used for recitative. Trimetro helps her change the subject by announcing, in another line of blank verse that forms a couplet with Artemia's line, that he will improvise an *ottava.*

An ottava, or ottava rima—a poem of eight endecasillabi in the rhyme scheme *abababcc,* the last rhyming couplet containing a sententious summing-up or conclusion—was not a normal element in eighteenth-century operatic poetry. Goldoni

19. Mosel, 32–33.

Sì ſtellato è il ſuol di fiori.
Queſti han lievi, e frali odori.
Quelle han fiamme eterne, e belle!

Tri. Brava.
Cor. Brava da ſenno.
Bag. In queſti quattro verſi
V'è fiſica, e morale.
Elv. E' tutta forza dell' aſtronomia.
Fil. A Cicerona.
Art. Ho ſcritta una Elegia
Sull' incendio funeſto
Della gran libraria Capitolina,
Nel qual cento, e più libri
Di Livio ſi perdero. Oh Dio! Non mai
Da' Saggi, e Letterati
Libri abbaſtanza pianti, e ſoſpirati.

FINALE.

Degne, e onorate lacrime
(legge, e recita.)
Verſiam, che è giuſto il piangere
La deplorabil perdita
Di ciaſcheduna Età.
Bag. A quel lamento flebile
Mi ſento il cor commovere.
Fil. Non ſtate ad interromperla. (à Bag.)
Tri. Laſciatela finir. (à Bag.)
Art. Veſtaſi à bruno Apolline
E le canore Vergini
Mai gli occhj aſciutti laſcino.
Elv. Mi ſento intenerir!
Art. Gemere, o Cigni Delfici.
Ver. Ahi, Ahi.

Cor.

Cor. Laſciate dir. (à Vert.)
Art. Piangete, o dotti Hiſtorici.
Bag. Ahi, Ahi.
State a ſentir. (à Bag.)
Art. Il danno irreparabile
Neſſun riſarcirà.
Bag. Elv. Ver. e parte del Coro. } Ahi, Ahi. (piangono.)
Tri. Cor. Pru. e parte del Coro } Ah, Ah, Ah. (ridono.)
Fil. Ma perche di quà ridono,
Mentre che di quà piangono?
Art. Queſto è un ſeguir Democrito.
Elv. Queſto è imitare Eraclito.
Fil. Senza riſpetto à Socrate?
Pru. Voi mi ſforzate à ridere.
Bag. Voi m' inducete à piangere.
Art. Finite il Pianto, e il riſo.
Tri. Via, ſentite un' ottava all' improviſo.
Canto del tuo ſplendor vaſta Ignoranza,
Che benche oziosa, e vil, ſprezzata, e vana;
Nel Mondo con orgoglio, e con baldanza
Fai guerra alla Sapienza, e Virtù ſana.
Trionfi, e Tiranneggi, e per uſanza
Hai varia ſede in ogni mente umana;
Ma il maggior Trono, e la maggior tua gloria
Vertigino l'ha in capo per memoria.
Ver. Bugiardo. Aſinaccio. (à Trim. s'alzano
Tri. A me? Petulante! (à Ver.

Pru. e Bag. a 2. Tacete.
Fil. Riguardo.
Ver. Voi ſiete un' pedante. (à Filb.)
Fil. Tri. Pru. Bag. a 4. } Che termini uſate?
Ver. Pedante, e Aſinaccio
Gli approva il Boccaccio.
E approva che ſubito
Con ſchiaſſi, e labbrate
Vi rompa il moſtaccio.
Fil. Tri. Pru. Bag. a 4. } Ti faccio tacer. (minacciando Ver.)
Art. ed Elv. a 2. Riſpetto. Coſpetto! (contro tutti.)
Così non ſi premia
Di dotta Accademia
L' onore, e il piacer.
Cor. e Pru. a 2. Ogn' alma s'infiamma! (uno all' altra.)
Bag. Vo' dire il mio Dramma.
Art. Via zitto Vecchiaccio. (à Bag.)
Bag. Oh povero Omero!
Fil. Voi ſiete uno zero. (à Vert.)
Ver. Gaglioſſo. (à Fil.)
Sgraziato. (à Tri.)
Tutti, e Coro. Ti rompo il moſtaccio
(minacciandoſi uno coll' altro.)
Ti faccio tacer.
Ver. Ma voi che ne dite
Fioretti del prato?
Elv. E voi che inſulte
O Stelle del Ciel?

Cor.

Cor. Prudenzio partite.
Pru. Partite Corilla.
Art. ed Elv. a 2. Il petto m'accende
Già l'ira, e il diſpetto.
Bag. Almeno il duetto
Sentite dell' Opera.
Elv. Non odo.
Art. Son ſorda.
Ver. S' annuvola il giorno.
Pru. e Cor. a 2. Col nembo, col turbine
Il tuono s' accorda.
Tri. Fil. a 2. Già l'aria d' intorno
Lampeggia sfavilla.
Tutti, e Coro. Frà Scilla, e Cariddi
Non freme di queſta
Tempeſta
Più nera,
Più fiera,
E crudel. (partono ſcompigliati.)
Bag. Che rabbia! Che bile!
Mi ſento morire:
Vo' farlo ſentire
Se caſca anco il Ciel.

Fine dell' Atto primo.

B 5 AT-

FIGURE 4.2 *Le donne letterate,* finale of act 1 in the libretto printed for the first production, Vienna, 1770.

employed it only rarely, sometimes in situations like this one, in which a character recites a poem or sings a song (a *canzone* rather than an aria).[20]

Trimetro's ottava is a mock-heroic poem in praise of ignorance: "Canto del tuo splendor, vasta Ignoranza." Not until the last two lines do we find out that the ignorance in question is that of Vertigine, Trimetro's rival for Corilla's hand.

Enraged, Vertigine returns the insult; the quarrel reminds one of the argument between the pedants Trissotin and Vadius in the third act of *Les Femmes savantes.* The meter changes to senari, whose brevity reflects the sudden intensification of emotion. These short lines continue until the end of the finale (near the end they are broken up into pairs of three-syllable lines). The quarrel builds to two climaxes, as all the characters twice join together to demand silence ("Ti faccio tacer"). After the first of these climaxes Artemia and Elvira join the argument, pleading for calm ("Rispetto! Cospetto!"). The second is followed by a sudden change of atmosphere as the poet Vertigine turns to the poetic imagery of flowers ("Ma voi che ne dite / Fioretti del prato?"). Baggeo pleads in vain for a chance to read his libretto, and all join together, finally, to describe to the audience the storm of emotions that swirls around them.

Salieri mentioned meter and key (in that order) as the musical elements he considered in planning his musical setting of this text. He presumably considered tempo along with meter. He followed the changes of poetic meter in Boccherini's poetry, assigning different musical meters and tempos to Boccherini's various poetic forms (see table 4.1). The tonal content of the finale, also shown in table 4.1, was influenced, above all, by Salieri's decision to begin it with the same music as the introduzione. Since he had already sketched the introduzione in E♭, he began the finale in E♭ as well. And because finales normally begin and end in the same key, it seemed natural to conclude the finale—and the act—in E♭.

Having decided to begin the finale with the same music as that of the introduzione, Salieri chose duple meter and the tempo Andante for the whole of Artemia's poem along with the other characters' reactions. At the conclusion of her poem, Salieri responded to the more loosely organized series of settenari sdruccioli with a shift of meter and tempo: triple meter, Allegro ("Ma perché di qua ridono?").

After establishing the tonic at the beginning of a piece of music in the major mode, eighteenth-century composers almost always moved to the dominant; Salieri was no exception. He set the Allegro in B♭.

The endecasillabi of Trimetro's poem in praise of ignorance are ideally suited to compound meter. (Mozart and Martín y Soler would later set several aria texts with

20. On Goldoni's ottave and the use of similar poetic forms by Da Ponte see Wolfgang Osthoff, "Gli endecasillabi villotistici in *Don Giovanni* e *Nozze di Figaro,*" in Muraro, *Venezia,* 2:311; and Maria Antonella Balsano, "L'ottava di *Così fan tutte,*" in *Liedstudien: Wolfgang Osthoff zum 60. Geburtstag,* ed. Martin Just and Reinhard Wiesend (Tutzing, 1989), 279–91.

TABLE 4.1 *Le donne letterate,* Finale of Act 1

FIRST LINE OF TEXT	VERSE TYPE	METER	TEMPO	KEY
Degne e onorate lacrime	18 settenari sdruccioli and tronchi in 3 quatrains + 3 couplets	¢	[Andante]	E♭
Ma perché di qua ridono?	7 settenari sdruccioli in 3 couplets + 1 extra line	3/4	Allegro	B♭
Finite il pianto e il riso!	1 verso sciolto (settenario)			
Via, sentite un'ottava all'improvviso	1 verso sciolto (endecasillabo)		Recitativo	
Canto del tuo splendor, vasta Ignoranza	8 endecasillabi (ottava)	6/8	Andante	g
Bugiardo! Asinaccio!	11 senari in 2 quatrains + 3 extra lines	3/4	Allegro	B♭
Rispetto! Cospetto!	12 senari in 3 quatrains			E♭–c
Ma voi che ne dite	2 senari (1/2 quatrain)		Più adagio	A♭
E voi che influite	2 senari (1/2 quatrain) + 20 senari in 5 quatrains		Più allegro	A♭–E♭

endecasillabi to music in compound meter, including "Deh vieni, non tardar, o gioia bella" in *Figaro,* "Deh vieni alla finestra, o mio tesoro" in *Don Giovanni,* and "Non farmi più languire, o vita mia" in *Una cosa rara.*) Salieri's choice of G minor (relative minor of the preceding Allegro's B♭) for his setting of the ottava enhanced the finale's musical variety and drew the audience's attention to Trimetro's improvisation.

The argument between Trimetro and Vertigine that follows, with its short senari and its sudden increase in energy and excitement, prompted Salieri to return to the tempo, meter, and key of the passage before Trimetro's poem. Since Artemia began the finale singing in E♭, it is fitting that her return to the dialogue coincides with the reestablishment of the tonic. A shift to the minor mode conveys the animosity of Trimetro and Vertigine. G minor, already exploited in Trimetro's ottava, would have been of less effect than the new key, C minor, with which this part of the finale ends.

Boccherini continued with senari through the end of the finale, and Salieri maintained triple meter. But he changed tempo in accordance with the contents of the poetry. When, after the second tutti climax, Vertigine addresses the flowers, Salieri momentarily slowed the tempo from Allegro to Più adagio. He reinforced the effect of this sudden break in the action by modulating to A♭ major, moving from the relative minor of E♭ to its subdominant. This peaceful moment delays for only a few seconds the return to the fast tempo and the finale's hectic conclusion. Just as the slowing down enhances the effect of the fast tempo when it returns, so the appearance of a fresh new key (yet one closely related to the tonic) enlivens Salieri's emphasis on E♭ as the finale comes to a close.

Having planned his deployment of meter and key in the finale of act 1 "without writing a note," Salieri could not resist the temptation to put music on paper:

> I felt tired, and my cheeks burned. So I paced back and forth in my room, and soon I was drawn back to my writing desk, where I began the first draft [of the finale], and when midnight came, I had made such progress that I went to bed in a state of great joy.
>
> My head had been too full of music and poetry the whole day for me not to dream of them as well. Indeed, I heard in my dream a strange harmony, but so distant and so confused that it gave me more pain than pleasure, and I finally awoke. It was four in the morning, and all my efforts to go back to sleep were in vain. So I lit a candle and looked through everything that I had sketched with a pencil the day before, continued the sketch further, and had come to the halfway point of the first finale when the clock struck eight and, to my surprise, my poet entered the room.
>
> He could not believe that I had sketched the whole introduzione and half of the first finale. I played him at the keyboard what I had written; he was extraordinarily pleased with it; he embraced me and seemed no less delighted than I was myself.[21]

Salieri and his poet had good reason to be pleased. The music planned and sketched that night has what a finale needs: musical and dramatic variety within a structure strong enough to make that variety comprehensible; contrast, conflict, and excitement held in check by musical logic.

The finale begins with a shortened version of the orchestral passage from the beginning of the introduzione, reestablishing immediately the mood of Artemia's mournful poem. Her melody (like her poem) is close enough to what she sang in the introduzione for us to make the association, but not so close that we lose interest (ex. 4.6). From this placid opening the music grows more complex and energetic as Artemia's listeners react to her poem with tears or laughter.

When Filberto interrupts, asking for an explanation, the music parallels his sudden emergence as the most outspoken character: the new tune that he sings sharply articulates the changes in meter, tempo, and key that Salieri planned earlier. The end of his

21. Mosel, 33.

EXAMPLE 4.6 *Le donne letterate,* act 1, finale, mm. 1–7

question coincides nicely with an open cadence. Further discussion ensues, cut off finally by Artemia and Trimetro with their versi sciolti.

Finales normally avoided large amounts of recitative, but Da Ponte, in his description quoted in chapter 3, wrongly claimed that they lacked it altogether. Boccherini's versi sciolti gave Salieri opportunity to introduce a short orchestrally accompanied recitative that serves as a transition between the fast triple-meter passage in B♭ and Trimetro's ottava in G minor. But the beginning of the recitative does not coincide with the beginning of the versi sciolti. Salieri set Artemia's line "Finite il pianto e il riso!" within the triple-meter Allegro; only when Trimetro says "Via, sentite un'ottava all'improvviso" does Salieri switch to recitative style and label the music as such. This lack of synchronization between a new verse type and a new musical style makes dramatic sense. Artemia tries but fails to bring the discussion to an end; Trimetro, by announcing his intention to improvise an ottava, actually succeeds in silencing his companions (ex. 4.7).

For Trimetro's ottava Salieri wrote a melody evoking the *siciliana,* a dance with roots in Sicily and the kingdom of Naples. Siciliane are frequently in the minor mode and usually in compound meter; Salieri probably made his earlier choices of compound meter and minor mode in anticipation of his use of siciliana-like rhythms (ex. 4.8). Many minor-mode siciliane use a particular tonal inflection associated, like the dance

EXAMPLE 4.7 *Le donne letterate,* act 1, finale, mm. 50–56

ARTEMIA: Cease your weeping and laughter! TRIMETRO: Come, come, listen to an ottava that I will improvise.

itself, with southern Italy: the Neapolitan sixth chord. Salieri seasoned the final cadence of Trimetro's ottava with a dash of Neapolitan harmony. *Le donne* takes place in Naples; Salieri's use of the meter, rhythm, harmony, and melodic style of the siciliana is one of his few contributions to the opera's local color.

The quarrel between Trimetro and Vertigine begins suddenly, as quick B♭-major scales followed by emphatic chords coincide with the return to the major mode, triple meter, and fast tempo (ex. 4.9). The thirty-second-note scales with which Salieri depicted Vertigine's reaction to insult resemble those used by Mozart two years earlier to depict Cassandro's similar reaction in *La finta semplice* (see ex. 3.17); one can imagine Trimetro and Vertigine reaching for their swords. The level of energy established here is maintained through the rest of the finale, except for one moment of repose before the last climax. A hectic cadence to C minor is followed by the entrance of Vertigine, singing a melody in A♭, Più adagio, whose lyricism beautifully parallels the tonal gesture that Salieri planned earlier. The melody is just as fresh and attractive as the new key that underpins it (ex. 4.10).

EXAMPLE 4.8 *Le donne letterate,* act 1, finale, mm. 57–68

I sing of your splendor, vast Ignorance, who, although idle and despised and vain, makes war throughout the world proudly and confidently against wisdom and sound virtue.

EXAMPLE 4.9 *Le donne letterate*, act 1, finale, mm. 82–88

VERTIGINE: Liar! ass! TRIMETRO: Are you speaking to me with such insolence?

EXAMPLE 4.10 *Le donne letterate*, act 1, finale, mm. 126–131

But you, flowers of the meadow, what do you say of all this?

Arias and Ensembles

With Boccherini's encouragement, Salieri continued to compose: "In short, after I had continued my work with the same enthusiasm, within four weeks a good two-thirds of the opera was written out in full score and orchestrated."[22]

Salieri portrayed his characters with the comic musical language that he learned from Gassmann and his Italian colleagues. Like the arias of his predecessors and teacher Salieri's are mostly in sonata and binary form, with the text declaimed twice. Salieri was especially partial to binary form. Many of the arias in *Le donne* present the opening melody only once: the "double return" characteristic of sonata form (that is, the simultaneous return of the tonic key and the first theme) is rare in Salieri's first opera.

The moderate-to-fast tempo, duple meter, dotted rhythms, and disjunct melody appropriate to male parti buffe in particular can be found in several arias in *Le donne.* Baggeo's first aria, "Andiam dunque a terminarlo," in which he looks forward to finishing his libretto, makes good use of all these elements. The aria's text is in ottonari throughout; Salieri responded to this poetic uniformity with a single tempo and meter and binary form. The opening melody, with its a-b-b′ structure—the second phrase gaining nobility from its three-measure length—alludes to the exalted style of opera seria, perhaps in connection with the serious subject of Baggeo's libretto; but in this context such reference to the serious style could only enhance the aria's comedy (ex. 4.11). A cascade of sixteenth notes punctuates the tune by depicting the descent of divine inspiration. After the modulation to the dominant Salieri exploited a comic device often placed by composers at this point in the exposition: patter. Baggeo, boasting of the speed with which he can write a libretto, repeats himself as quickly as possible.

Filberto's catalogue aria in act 2, "Sa tutto il greco," is another fine comic piece: a setting of a list (quoted above) of the subjects that Baggeo has supposedly mastered. Although the text consists entirely of quinari, it falls into two parts. In the first six lines Filberto introduces Baggeo's accomplishments at a leisurely rate of one subject per two lines of text, which gives him opportunity to sprinkle his narrative with Greek, French, and Latin. Most of the verses are versi piani. ("Dall'Alfa all'Omega" is a quinario sdrucciolo, though Salieri, in his setting, treated it as a senario piano by accenting the second syllable of Omega.) Then Filberto shifts to a rapid-fire catalogue of subjects, one per line, beginning a long series of versi sdruccioli. Salieri nicely emphasized this change of poetic style by moving from a Maestoso dominated by dotted rhythms and two-measure phrases in the tonic, D major, to a Presto in 6/8 that begins in the dominant.

This is one of several arias in *Le donne* that change tempo. But Salieri, in keeping with his tendency to avoid recapitulation of an aria's opening melody, rarely changed

22. Mosel, 33.

EXAMPLE 4.11 *Le donne letterate*, act 1, "Andiam dunque a terminarlo," mm. 4–11

Let us then finish it, while Apollo inspires my heart.

tempo more than once. "Sa tutto il greco" begins, like many Goldonian arias, with an exposition in the form A-B (A: Maestoso, B: Presto). Although Filberto repeats the text thereafter, he never returns to the opening theme or to its tempo. We thus hear the second part of the exposition and everything that comes after it as one big B section. The aria takes on a two-part, through-composed form instead of the A-B-A′-B′ form so common in opera buffa of the 1750s and 1760s.

The melody of the opening Maestoso (ex. 4.12) recalls one of the most brilliant of midcentury arias for comic bass, "Star trombette" in *La buona figliuola* (see ex. 3.3). In Piccinni's aria the opening phrase is repeated exactly; Salieri gave new comic life to an old melodic idea by transposing the opening phrase up a step when he repeated it. The French words in Boccherini's text caused Salieri to make an amusing allusion to the ornaments of French vocal music, which may have reminded Viennese audiences of musical Gallicisms in Gassmann's *L'amore artigiano.*

Boccherini and Salieri made a brief but effective parody of serious opera in their duet for Baggeo and Vertigine in act 2. As Vertigine begs Baggeo to intervene with Corilla

EXAMPLE 4.12 *Le donne letterate,* act 2, "Sa tutto il greco," mm. 1–7

on his behalf, Baggeo talks of nothing but his libretto. He even recites a passage of which he is particularly proud: a ghost scene. Salieri's teacher had recently parodied a ghost scene in *L'opera seria* by making exaggerated use of the long notes and wide leaps that were standard elements of such scenes in opera seria (see ex. 3.10). Salieri did likewise, beginning his parody with a grotesque seven-measure phrase that depicts a descent into the underworld by means of a descending chromatic scale (ex. 4.13). That a bass should sing such a scene is itself a source of comedy, not only because women were normally the protagonists in ghost scenes but also because roles for basses hardly existed in opera seria. Salieri enhanced the comedy by emphasizing Baggeo's low notes. The word *lunghe* (in reference to the claws of the monster encountered by the ghost in the underworld) appears only once in Boccherini's poetry. It was evidently the composer's idea to have Baggeo sing it three times, as if to call attention to his play on words (*l'unghie . . . lunghe*—long claws).

Salieri's musical depiction of his learned women, like Boccherini's literary and Longhi's visual depictions, depends heavily on the assumption that intellectual activity is inherently masculine. Much of their music has a "masculine" quality, as if written for a comic bass and then transposed up an octave or two. In Elvira's first aria, "Voglio tutti de' pianeti," she expresses her ambition to discover unknown planets (text quoted

EXAMPLE 4.13 *Le donne letterate,* act 2, "Credo che onori la mia tragedia," mm. 39–55

Let the ghost descend to dark Erebus, down to the smoking, boiling ink, amid the claws of the monster who has long ones.

above) with a perky opening melody that is patently comic (ex. 4.14). Elvira's vocal line, sometimes accompanied by the orchestra in octaves, doubles the bass at cadences (ex. 4.15). As in "Andiam dunque a terminarlo," Salieri responded to a text in ottonari throughout with music in a single tempo and binary form. This aria establishes Elvira, right at the beginning of the opera, as a parte buffa.

Artemia too has a masculine tendency to double the bass at cadences. In the orchestral introduction of her first aria, "Tre città rinomate," two horns play a marchlike mel-

EXAMPLE 4.14 *Le donne letterate,* act 1, "Voglio tutti de' pianeti," mm. 10–13

EXAMPLE 4.15 *Le donne letterate,* act 1, "Voglio tutti de' pianeti," mm. 92–102

ody, revealing Artemia, even before she sings, to be strong and assertive (ex. 4.16). One might guess from the combination of two-measure phrases, duple meter, moderate tempo, dotted rhythms, and noisy orchestra, that the singer was a foolish old man or an angry servant. Yet this music is neither consistently comic nor consistently masculine. As Artemia nears the end of the aria, dotted rhythms in the orchestra recall the comic style of the opening melody; but coloratura, high notes, great leaps, and the long cadential trill convey nobility and demand admiration, not laughter (ex. 4.17). In shifting back

EXAMPLE 4.16 *Le donne letterate,* act 1, "Tre città rinomate," mm. 1–6

EXAMPLE 4.17 *Le donne letterate,* act 1, "Tre città rinomate," mm. 87–98

Artemia

fan - no al mon - do su - per - - -

(*p*)

Str.

- bo co - sì, fan - no al mon - do su - per - bo co -

fp *f*

+Ob., Bn., Hn.

- sì, su - per - - - bo co - sì

pp

Str. alone

~Thus they make the world proud

and forth between comic and serious styles Artemia's music reflects the singer for whom it was written: Clementina Baglioni, an experienced performer of both comic and serious opera.

Corilla, a purely "feminine" character, has no interest in scholarship. Her first aria, "Una volta che si senta" (text quoted above) has none of the masculine swagger of "Tre città rinomate." It begins with a melody whose chromaticism hints at strong, sincere feelings within (ex. 4.18). The spacious four-measure phrases are noble, and a little old-fashioned: the opening octave leap up and quick scalar descent that follows are reminiscent of an aria in Pergolesi's *L'Olimpiade* (1735).[23] Corilla's coloratura, as heroic as Artemia's, reaches up to E above high C before the final cadence.

EXAMPLE 4.18 *Le donne letterate,* act 1, "Una volta che si senta," mm. 16–23

Artemia and Corilla were among several high coloratura soprano roles written by Salieri during the 1770s and early 1780s. He was particularly fond of this kind of singing and encouraged its development in his students. Two of the most successful, Catarina Cavalieri and Therese Gassmann (his teacher's younger daughter), became high colora-

23. "Mentre dormi," quoted in Hellmuth Christian Wolff, "Italian Opera 1700–1750," in *NOHM,* 5:124–25.

tura sopranos; the latter specialized in the portrayal of the Queen of the Night when *Die Zauberflöte* reached the court theaters at the beginning of the nineteenth century.

Prudenzio, Corilla's beloved, sings music that clearly conveys his mezzo-carattere status. His first aria, "So che mi ama il mio tesoro" (text quoted above), begins with a lyrical melody that suits the serious but tender words (ex. 4.19). The moderately slow tempo and touch of chromaticism, like that in the melody sung by Corilla at the beginning of "Una volta che si senta," contributes to its tenderness. Its phrase structure, a-b-b, hints at nobility, while two-measure phrases keep Prudenzio from sounding too serious. (In *Il mercato di Malmantile* Fischietti had characterized Rubiccone with the same melodic style and phrase structure; see ex. 3.12). But when Prudenzio thinks of the foolish people who stand in the way of his marriage to Corilla, he suddenly switches to the comic style of a buffo caricato. Duple meter, fast tempo, dotted rhythms, and disjunct melody all help to convey the comedy in Boccherini's text.

EXAMPLE 4.19 *Le donne letterate,* act 1, "So che mi ama il mio tesoro," mm. 4–9

Vertigine's music has much the same combination of tenderness and comedy as Prudenzio's. The lyrical melody with which his aria "Donne sapienti e vaghe" begins shares with the beginning of Prudenzio's "So che mi ama" slow tempo, yearning chromaticism, and graceful triplets and syncopations. Vertigine can also excite laughter, as in his

EXAMPLE 4.20 *Le donne letterate,* act 2, "Credo che onori la mia tragedia," mm. 13–18

But what does it cost you to give me an answer: are you willing to give me Corilla's hand, or have you already promised it to another?

duet with Baggeo. The old man wants to read his libretto to Vertigine, who wants only help in winning Corilla. Vertigine expresses his impatience (ex. 4.20) with a *parlando* melodic line, repetition, and rhythm similar to those with which Piccinni and Mozart portrayed Paoluccia (see ex. 3.4) and Ninetta (see ex. 3.7). Was this Salieri's way of conveying Vertigine's effeminacy?

Continuity

Composers in Vienna during the late 1760s contributed to the musical momentum of their opere buffe by breaking down the distinctions between recitative and aria, adding melodic elements to the accompaniment of simple recitative and providing some orchestrally accompanied numbers with transitions that inhibit applause by leading straight into the following recitative. Salieri used the same techniques in *Le donne letterate.*

Several times in simple recitative Salieri depicted an action on stage by means of a melodic line in the accompaniment. In act 1, scene 3, Filberto maneuvers Baggeo and

Corilla into positions where he can give Baggeo an arithmetic lesson and at the same time help Corilla write a love letter to Prudenzio. A motive in the bass accompanies Filberto as he leads Corilla to a table; another accompanies him as he checks the accuracy of Baggeo's calculation.

Gassmann frequently linked the introduzione to the following recitative by means of a transition passage leading to an open cadence. His student did the same here. After a final full cadence to tonic E♭, the continuous eighth notes described by Salieri as a unifying motive continue, with the violins doubled by cellos and basses, to an open cadence (ex. 4.21). He joined a series of three numbers in act 2 with similar transitions. In doing so, he reinforced a tonal pattern that connects these numbers: each is a fifth higher than the preceding one. Trimetro's aria "Mi fa da ridere," in B♭ major, ends with a transition that leads to an open cadence, followed by the instruction "segue subito." Vertigine enters to sing his aria "Donne sapienti e vaghe" (F major), which closes with a bridge linking it to a long and elaborate orchestrally accompanied recitative. This recitative in turn leads eventually to the trio "Arde l'alma, avvampa il core" (C major). The pattern of tonal relations between these numbers and transitions that link them work together to produce a scene complex in which the action moves forward much more fluidly than is normal in Goldonian opera buffa.

EXAMPLE 4.21 *Le donne letterate,* act 1, introduzione, mm. 63–67

Orchestration

Salieri referred to orchestration only in passing in his account of the composition of *Le donne,* which suggests that this was not a part of the creative process in which he took great interest. And indeed, with a few remarkable exceptions, not much in Salieri's use of the orchestra in this opera can be called imaginative or adventurous. The basic instrumental ensemble in *Le donne* consists of strings with pairs of oboes, bassoons, and horns. Like *La finta semplice* and *La contessina,* the opera has no parts for trumpets or timpani; their absence reflects the lack of full-time performers on these instruments on the permanent rosters of the Burgtheater and Kärntnertortheater during much if not all of the impresarial decade. Salieri showed no interest in *Le donne* (or in his other early operas) in Gassmann's typically Viennese use of the English horn to expand the orchestra's timbral possibilities without engaging extra musicians.

The Burgtheater orchestra did include flutes (during the years in which we know the orchestra's players, 1771 and later), and Salieri made use of them in *Le donne letterate.* He saved them for special occasions, however, as Piccinni had done in *La buona figliuola.* Flutes accompany both of Vertigine's arias. The gentle, sweet sound of flutes and muted strings in "Donne sapienti" helps depict Vertigine as the "poeta effeminato" envisioned by Boccherini and at the same time encourages listeners to take his emotions seriously, just as they do when Piccinni's Cecchina falls asleep to the sound of flutes and muted strings. (One thinks also of Mozart's characterization of Belmonte in *Die Entführung aus dem Serail:* "You hear the whispering and the sighing—which I have indicated by the first violins with mutes and a flute playing in unison.")[24]

Salieri used the orchestra most colorfully in bravura arias for his two coloratura sopranos. We have already seen how horns contribute to the depiction of Artemia in the boastful "Tre città rinomate." In Corilla's "Una volta che si senta" the singer participates in a dialogue with oboe and bassoon. Artemia's "Astrea nel cor mi siede," has even more elaborate concertante solo parts for flute, oboe, and bassoon. This big aria (173 measures in common time) begins with a thirty-five-measure orchestral introduction in which the solo woodwinds play concerto-like passagework. Its concluding tutti is preceded by a cadenza for the three woodwind soloists and the singer: the first of several written-out vocal-instrumental cadenzas in Salieri's early operas (ex. 4.22). This is a serious showpiece, but Salieri did not want us to take it completely seriously. Immediately after Artemia leaves the stage Trimetro, who witnessed her performance, says: "Oh che donna ridicola!"

EXAMPLE 4.22 *Le donne letterate,* act 2, "Astrea nel cor mi siede," mm. 157–168 (cadenza)

(*Continued on next page*)

24. Mozart to his father, 26 September 1781, in *MBA,* 3:163.

EXAMPLE 4.22 (*continued*)

Salieri's love of coloratura arias with concertante winds may have been inspired by Gassmann, who had explored concertante effects in such arias as "Pallide ombre" (the ghost aria in *L'opera seria,* for soprano and bassoon). The particular combination of flute, oboe, and bassoon looks to the future: to soprano arias featuring these instruments by Salieri ("Vedo l'amiche insigne" in the cantata *La sconfitta di Borea* of 1775, later reused by Salieri in at least two operas)[25] and Mozart ("Et incarnatus est" in the C-Minor Mass); both these arias contain written-out cadenzas.

The oboe that "Una volta" and "Astrea nel cor" share already occupied in 1770 a special place in Salieri's orchestral palette as his favorite concertante instrument. Almost all

25. Della Croce/Blanchetti, 530–31.

of his early operas have an important concertante part for oboe in combination with a soprano and sometimes with other solo instruments. Salieri's oboe solos are not limited to opera. As a young man he wrote concertos for oboe, violin, and cello (1770) and for flute and oboe (1774; a work frequently recorded).

This proliferation of oboe solos may have had something to do with the Burgtheater's principal oboist for most if not all of the first half of the 1770s. Vittorino Colombazzo had served the duke of Württemberg (1767) and had briefly earned a high salary in Haydn's orchestra at Eszterháza (1768).[26] By 1770 he was in Vienna, performing as soloist before the court.[27] Almanacs, orchestral rosters and payment records document his presence in the Burgtheater orchestra from 1771 to the end of the impresarial decade.[28] He was the third-best-paid player in the Burgtheater orchestra, with an annual salary of 450 Gulden between 1773 and 1775. He deserved his salary, as one of only three Burgtheater players described as "sehr gut" in an evaluation made in 1773 (see fig. 2.6). One of Salieri's few compatriots among the orchestral players, Colombazzo probably inspired and played some of Salieri's elaborate oboe solos.

The concertante effects in the bravura arias of Artemia and Corilla stand in stark contrast to the relatively plain orchestration of the rest of *Le donne.* This combination of simple, straightforward orchestration through most of the opera and an occasional concerto-like use of wind instruments is typical of Salieri's early operas, distinguishing them from those of Gassmann, whose orchestration was more consistently adventurous and colorful.

Production, Rehearsals, and Performance

Salieri had not yet finished the composition of *Le donne letterate* when the opportunity arose for him to present his opera in the court theaters:

> The impresario had just brought to the stage an opera that did not please the public and felt it necessary to replace it quickly with another work. Boccherini, without telling me anything, had whispered to Calzabigi that I had already made good progress with my opera. The latter, a friend of the impresario, wanted to hear a small rehearsal of what I had composed in his apartment. He invited me and, without guessing the reason, I went there with my poet and with the completed numbers. I was a little surprised to find the impresario and the

26. H. C. Robbins Landon, *Haydn: Chronicle and Works,* 5 vols. (Bloomington, Ind., 1976–80), 2:70.

27. HKA, Hofzahlamtsbuch no. 387 (recording payments related to theater and music during 1770), fol. 9v, records payment to Colombazzo for performance of concertos at "two court table services" ("2. Hof Taffel Diensten"), banquets that featured music as well as food.

28. Possibly the earliest surviving orchestral roster in which Colombazzo appears records the orchestra's personnel in 1771 (*Genaue Nachrichten,* 126–28).

Kapellmeisters Gluck and Scarlatti, but I thought they were there only out of curiosity and was delighted by their presence. I sang and played what I had finished; Gluck and Scarlatti sang with me in the ensembles. Gluck, who had always liked me and encouraged me, showed himself pleased with my work from the very beginning; Scarlatti, who from time to time pointed out small mistakes in composition, praised every number as a whole, and at the end both masters said to the impresario that if I could soon fill in what was missing, the opera could be rehearsed and performed without delay, for (in Gluck's words) the work had "what it takes to please the public."

Who can imagine the joyful surprise that this statement gave me, through which I immediately saw the object of the rehearsal. Full of confidence—"superbo di me stesso" [proud of myself: the beginning of an aria in Metastasio's *L'Olimpiade*]—I promised my judges to show the greatest diligence until the opera reached the stage.[29]

Personal connections were as important in Vienna as anywhere else when it came to the production of an opera. In the case of *Le donne letterate* Boccherini was the crucial link: a protégé of Calzabigi, who was a friend of the impresario, who respected the judgment of Gluck and Scarlatti as well as Calzabigi. Gluck's opinion was especially important because from 1769 to 1770 he belonged to a committee of investors that backed Affligio and, when Affligio abandoned the management of the theaters in 1770, took over his responsibilities.[30]

Salieri's account of preparations for the performance contains information about the role of the composer and librettist in an operatic production:

I wrote night and day, I ran to the rehearsals, I went through the vocal parts with the singers, I corrected the copies, together with the poet I took care of the scenery and costumes, and put such uninterrupted strain on both mind and body that if study, toil, and sweat did not throw me on a sickbed, I can only believe that happiness served me as an antidote.[31]

Some of these activities—running the rehearsals, for example—had already been assigned to Salieri as part of his apprenticeship under Gassmann. The contract that Boccherini concluded with the theater management in January 1772 makes it clear that he, as house librettist, was expected to supervise the preparation of scenery and costumes. That he should be doing so two years earlier in connection with the production of one of his own librettos is not surprising. What is remarkable is Salieri's claim (admittedly vague) that he too was involved in scenery and costumes, suggesting that a

29. Mosel, 33–34.
30. Zechmeister, 397.
31. Mosel, 34.

composer's responsibilities went well beyond composition, musical preparation, and conducting.

As the premiere approached, Salieri grew nervous and excited:

> On the day before the first performance of the opera was the dress rehearsal; in the evening of the same day I went to the theater with my heart pounding, to hear my work announced: "Tomorrow the Italian opera troupe will have the honor to perform a new opera entitled *Le donne letterate,* poem by Herr Gaston Boccherini, music by Herr Anton Salieri, the first work of both." Several members of the audience applauded, which gave me sweet comfort and seemed to be a good omen. The following morning, as soon as I could think that the playbills had been posted at street-corners, I went out to see my name in print for the first time, which gave me great pleasure. Not content to see it once, as if afraid that it might have been left out of the other playbills, I ran through the whole city to read it everywhere.[32]

The premiere presumably took place during Carnival 1770, that is, near the end of the theatrical year 1769; but the exact date is unknown. Nor do we know if the performance took place in the Burgtheater or the Kärntnertortheater.[33]

It was customary in the eighteenth century for the composer of an opera to direct the first three performances from the keyboard, and this custom was carefully followed in Vienna. Mozart led the first three performances—and only the first three—of *Figaro* and *Don Giovanni* (the first Viennese production of 1788) from the keyboard.[34] Salieri acted in the role of composer of *Le donne* when he directed the opera's premiere. His description of his walk to the keyboard and his acknowledgment of the audience's applause is a valuable record of how the performance of an opera began on opening night in the court theaters during the second half of the eighteenth century:

> In vain would I attempt to describe the joyful restlessness that I felt that day as the hour of performance approached; but when it arrived joy turned to fear, my face began to burn, and it blushed scarlet; and thus I went with uncertain steps to the *Clavier.* When I entered the orchestra there was applause, which brought my courage back. I greeted the audience, sat down with a certain ease at the *Spinett,* and the opera began.[35]

Also valuable is Salieri's account of what he did when the opera was over:

> After the end of the performance, and after I had joyfully embraced my poet, I hastened to mingle with the audience as it left the theater, in order to overhear the various opinions of

32. Mosel, 35.

33. Rudolph Angermüller, "Salieri, Antonio," in *NG,* places the premiere in the Burgtheater on 10 January 1770, but I have not found confirmation of place or date.

34. Weigl, "Selbstbiographien," 54, 56.

35. Mosel, 35.

> listeners. One said: "The opera is not bad." Another "I liked it very much." (I could have kissed him.) A third: "It is no small accomplishment for a pair of beginners." A fourth: "As for me, I found it very dull." At these words, I turned down another street, fearing that I might hear an even harsher opinion than this last. At that moment, however, I heard further eulogies of both poet and composer; and satisfied, in my modest way, with these, I reached my apartment, excited and tired, but full of confidence and happiness.[36]

Although the day-to-day schedule of operatic performances in Vienna during 1770 and 1771 is unknown, *Le donne* was sufficiently popular, it seems, to have been still in the repertory in 1771. An almanac that describes the state of Viennese theater in 1771 includes *Le donne* in a list of comic operas performed that year.[37] But Salieri's first opera buffa seems to have been revived only once, in Prague in 1773.[38]

36. Mosel, 35–36.
37. *Theatralkalender von Wien, für das Jahr 1772* (Vienna, [1772]), 91.
38. Sartori no. 8298.

5

YOUTHFUL EXPLORATION AND EXPERIMENT

The modest success of *Le donne letterate* opened doors for its librettist and composer. Boccherini wrote several more librettos for Salieri and Gassmann between 1770 and 1773. He joined the impresario's staff as house poet after Coltellini's departure in 1772. Salieri, while continuing to act as Gassmann's assistant, now shared with him the role of house composer.

The first three years of Salieri's career as an operatic composer were also the most prolific. Between 1770 and 1772 he produced seven operas. His pace slowed after 1772; he wrote only three works during the last three years of the impresarial decade. Although Boccherini continued to serve as house poet until early in 1775, after 1772 Salieri did not collaborate with him as intensively as before. He worked with other poets on two of the operas that he wrote between 1773 and 1775. To the third, *La calamita de' cuori,* Boccherini may have contributed as arranger and stage director; but several other poets may also have been involved.

Having demonstrated with *Le donne letterate* his ability to write and produce a three-act Goldonian opera buffa, Salieri was eager to show what he could do in other kinds of opera. During the early 1770s he explored a wide variety of operatic genres.

Three of the early operas are short comic works, in two parts; their librettos (in chronological order) describe themselves as *pastorale per musica, divertimento teatrale,* and *dramma giocoso per musica.* In the first and third, *L'amore innocente* and *Il barone di Rocca Antica,* Salieri experimented with an operatic genre closely related to Goldonian opera buffa: the Roman intermezzo. In the second, *Don Chisciotte alle nozze di Gamace,* he integrated ballet and opera buffa.

La secchia rapita and *La finta scema* are full-length, three-act comedies, thoroughly Goldonian in form; but their content has little in common with that of Goldoni's comic librettos. Boccherini and Salieri based *La secchia rapita* (*The Rape of the Bucket*) on a mock-epic poem of the same name by the late Renaissance poet Alessandro Tassoni, who called his work a "poema eroicomico." Following his source, Boccherini called his libretto a "dramma eroicomico." He and Salieri translated Tassoni's parody of literary classics such as Homer and Ariosto into operatic parody by making fun of the conventions of opera seria and of famous aria texts by Metastasio. In *La finta scema* De Gamerra and Salieri introduced unexpected violence and pathos into an opera remarkable for its traces of pre-Romantic color.[1]

Salieri wrote only one purely serious opera for the impresarios. *Armida,* on a text by Coltellini, pays tribute to the tradition of French-inspired serious opera cultivated so successfully in Vienna during the 1760s.

Of the nine operas that Salieri wrote for the impresarios after *Le donne letterate,* only three—*La fiera di Venezia, La locandiera,* and *La calamita de' cuori*—closely follow the conventions of full-length Goldonian opera buffa. These works will be discussed in chapter 6; the present chapter examines three early operas that differ in their form or content (or both) from Goldonian opera.

An Experiment in the Combination of Opera Buffa and Ballet: *Don Chisciotte alle nozze di Gamace*

"Opera buffa, entremêlé de danses": with this bilingual phrase Prince Khevenhüller described succinctly and accurately *Don Chisciotte alle nozze di Gamace,* which Salieri, in collaboration with the dancer-poet Boccherini and the great dancer-choreographer Jean-Georges Noverre, presented on the stage of the Kärntnertortheater during Carnival 1771. They combined in a single drama two characteristic but seemingly unreconcilable types of Viennese musical drama. Goldonian opera buffa, with its arias and occasional ensembles separated by simple recitative, is here fused with French-inspired spectacle, with its fluidly constructed scene complexes featuring chorus and ballet.

Since the circumstances of the first and apparently only production of *Don Chisciotte* have never been clarified, and since these circumstances help to explain the nature of the work, it will be useful to consider them in some detail. According to Mosel, Salieri wrote *Don Chisciotte* in 1770, but after *L'amore innocente.* The libretto for the first production is dated 1770. But Salieri's list of his own compositions, compiled in 1818, assigns the opera to 1771.[2] Both Mosel and Salieri were right. Composed in 1770, *Don Chisciotte* was first performed during a ball in the Kärntnertortheater during Carnival 1771, and probably on 6 January 1771.

1. On *La secchia rapita* see Della Croce/Blanchetti, 119–21, 427–29; on *La finta scema,* Della Croce/Blanchetti, 136–38, 435–39.

2. Mosel, 205.

Joseph II was at the Kärntnertor that evening. He wrote the next day to his brother Leopold, grand duke of Tuscany: "to the ball in the German Theater. They presented Don Quichotte, embellished with songs and dances, and there was an incredible crowd."[3] Count Zinzendorf, also in attendance, wrote in his diary: "to the German Theater, where they presented a grand ballet consisting of the story of Dom Quixotte mixed up with pranks and gaity; the stage was crowded."[4] The descriptions of both Joseph and Zinzendorf suggest that they were attending the production for the first time.

That the theatrical entertainment they witnessed was Salieri's *Don Chisciotte* is confirmed by Khevenhüller, who at the end of Carnival 1771 wrote in his diary of the dances that had taken place during Carnival. Having mentioned the balls in the large and small Redoutensäle, he turned to those in the Kärntnertortheater: "The balls in the playhouse at the Kärntner-Thor were likewise continued on the same footing as previous years, and occasionally accompanied by new grand ballets and, a couple of times, by an opera buffa intermixed with dances called *Dom Quichotte aux noces de gamace;* at these balls too the court appeared several times."[5]

The court theaters' professional dancers may have performed quite frequently during Carnival balls. Zinzendorf went to a ball in the large Redoutensaal during Carnival 1772 with the intention not of dancing but of seeing one of Noverre's ballets, which, like Salieri's *Don Chisciotte,* had to do with a wedding: "to the large Redoutensaal to see the ballet *Les Noces chinoises.* The scenery very pretty, but the room badly lit."[6] A year later, during Carnival 1773, Zinzendorf witnessed a performance of Noverre's *Agamemnon* during a ball in the Kärntnertortheater; the performance included a "contredanse of male and female warriors who descended to the parterre"[7] to dance among the masqueraders in the auditorium.[8]

More than twenty years later, on 25 May 1795, a masked ball at the Kärntnertor again included a performance by professional dancers. A notice on the playbill announcing the ball warned spectators to stay off the stage during the performance of a fandango by Salvatore and Maria Medina Viganò.[9] The ball began at nine in the evening and con-

3. au ball du Theatre allemand l'on a donné don quichotte, orné de chants et de danses, et il y avoit un monde etonnant (Joseph to Leopold, 7 January 1771, HHStA, Sb, Kart. 7).

4. au Théatre allemand ou l'on donna un grand Ballet fesant un mélange de l'histoire de Dom Quixotte de polissoneries, de gayeté, un monde sur la scene (Zinzendorf, 6 January 1771).

5. Khevenhüller, 7:60 (12 February 1771).

6. a la grande Sale de la Redoute pour voir le Ballet des *Noces Chinoises.* La decoration assez jolie, mais la sale mal éclairée (Zinzendorf, 16 February 1772).

7. au Théatre allemand . . . [illegible] le Ballet d'Agamemnon, et un Contredanse de guerrier et de guerrière qui descendoient au Parterre (Zinzendorf, 17 February 1773).

8. From another account of the same evening (in the *Theatralalmanach von Wien, für das Jahr 1774* [Vienna, [1774]], 132–33) we learn that the ball also featured the performance, by Noverre's daughter, of a concerto on the *Flügel* (a harpsichord or grand piano).

9. *Theaterzettel,* 25 May 1795, A-Wth.

tinued until five in the morning. The fandango, which took place at midnight, served not only to entertain the revelers but also to give them a chance to rest after three hours of dancing.

The dances in Salieri's *Don Chisciotte,* as choreographed by Noverre, included a fandango, which can be considered an ancestor of the one danced by the Viganò in the same theater a quarter of a century later. Both dances served the same function: professional theatrical entertainment during a long night of Carnival merrymaking.

Boccherini based his divertimento teatrale very loosely on Cervantes's account, in part 2 of *Don Quixote,* chapters 19–21, of preparations for the wedding of the rich peasant Camacho to the beautiful Quiteria. (The episode had provided Telemann with the plot of his comic opera-serenade *Don Quichotte auf der Hochzeit des Camacho* and would later serve Mendelssohn as the basis for his opera *Die Hochzeit des Camacho.*) As Cervantes told the story, Basilio, who loves Quiteria, interrupts the wedding by pretending to stab himself. Apparently about to die, he asks Quiteria to marry him so that he will die happy. Camacho allows the wedding to take place on condition that Quiteria marry him as soon as Basilio dies. Basilio and Quiteria wed; and Basilio immediately reveals his deception. Despite Camacho's protestations the strength of Basilio's love for Quiteria persuades those, including Don Quixote, who have witnessed the wedding to confirm its legitimacy.

Boccherini changed the story completely by leaving Basilio out, thus creating a drama in which little happens except a series of dances and songs in celebration of the expected wedding, enlivened by the buffo antics of Don Quixote and Sancho Panza.

A manuscript score in the Austrian National Library lists the divertimento's many vocal roles and the singers who created them, making this one of only three operas among those that Salieri wrote between 1770 and 1776 of which we know the entire original cast.[10] It did not include Carattoli, Poggi, or the Baglioni sisters, because they had left for Italy around the beginning of the theatrical year 1770 and did not return to Vienna until the beginning of the theatrical year 1771. They were consequently absent from Vienna during Carnival 1771.

Don Chisciotte is in two parts. Buffo scenes generally alternate with dances and choruses. The divertimento begins with an impressive sequence of dances, choruses, ensembles, and solo song. Boccherini describes the scene: "Countryside with cooking fires and tables where several cooks are working. View of Gamace's house in the distance. Other rustic dwellings on one side; trees and shrubs on the other. Gamace and Chitteria surrounded by peasant men and women who dance and sing."[11] The chorus-dance

10. The cast list, in A-Wn, Mus. Hs. 17835, is quoted in Angermüller, *Leben,* 1:87.

11. Campagna con fuochi, e tavole ove lavorano diversi Cuochi. Veduta della Casa di Gamace in Lontano. Altri rustici Alberghi da un lato; Alberi, e Cespugli dall'altro. Gamace, e Chitteria in mezzo a' Contadini e Contadine che ballano, e cantano.

"Mille ignudi amoretti vezzosi," in the form of a vaudeville, presents a choral refrain in alternation with a single melody sung in turn by several soloists. The movement is French not only in form but in melody. The choral theme has the rhythmic features of a gavotte; Noverre probably choreographed it as such. Dance pervades Salieri's score, which begins (after the overture) with a thirteen-measure orchestral introduction labeled "ballo"; the short duet for Gamace and Chitteria that follows "Mille ignudi" is labeled Tempo di minuet.

Don Quixote (bass, the role created by Vincenzo Schiettini) and Sancho (tenor, Antonio Boscoli) arrive on the scene as this chorus-dance is ending. The peasants quickly see that the eccentric knight errant and his gluttonous servant will give them much amusement. Don Quixote rises immediately to their bait and at the same time announces himself as a buffo caricato in his first aria, "Ah taci, m'offende," which makes use of the devices—duple meter, dotted rhythms, vocal line doubling the bass, and moderately fast tempo—that Viennese audiences had by 1771 come to expect of buffi caricati.

When the wedding party bids farewell to Don Quixote near the end of the divertimento, Lena (soprano, Gabriella Tagliaferri) adopts the mock-heroic, buffo tone of Don Quixote's music in "Quando avrai purgato l'Africa," in which she tells of his future exploits. Lena's naming all four continents makes this a catalogue aria, which an audience familiar with Goldoni's librettos must have recognized immediately as comic in intent. Yet the music is full of heroism: long trills, big leaps, a high D. The opening melody features noble three-measure phrases in a-b-b′ form; but its odd repeated notes, exaggerated emphasis on the sdrucciolo rhythms of "Africa" and "indomite," and staccato sixteenth notes depicting the rushing of wild beasts undercut the heroism (ex. 5.1). Lena and her friends are making fun of Don Quixote up to the end.

Sancho's eagerness to partake of the feast leads Gamace (tenor, Francesco Bussani) and his companions to think of ways to prolong their dancing and singing. Boccherini carefully indicated the distribution of the dances by having his characters announce them. Gamace commands, "Proseguisca il Ballo" [Let the dance begin]; later he says, "Lasciam prima ballare anche un fandango" [Let us first also dance a fandango]. Sancho, having eaten, turns his attention to the attractive Giocondina, to whom he says, "Balliamo il minuetto." Later Don Quixote says, "Dunque si balli."

Gamace's "Proseguisca il Ballo" is followed, in Salieri's score, by a suite of instrumental dances in a wide variety of meters, tempos, and keys: 6/8, Allegro, G major; 3/4, Menuetto, C major (with trio); 2/4, Spiritoso, F major (with trio in F minor); 2/4, Sbalzante ("leaping"), B♭ major; 2/4, Allegretto spiritoso, G major; 3/4, Cantabile, C major; 6/8, Giga, C major (with trio in C minor). All the dances are in binary form with repeats, the first half eight measures long and the second half eight or twelve measures long. To this semi-independent ballet, the opera's main dance sequence, the singers must have acted as spectators. The action on stage thus reflected the action at

EXAMPLE 5.1 *Don Chisciotte alle nozze di Gamace,* pt. 2, "Quando avrai purgato l'Africa," mm. 5–13 (A-Wn, Mus. Hs. 17835)

When you have rid Africa of untamed wild beasts

the Kärntnertor itself, where a group of merrymakers (the social dancers in the parterre and the spectators in the boxes) watched the professional dancers and singers perform.

A buffo interlude follows. Sancho cannot keep his mind on the dancing; he says to himself:

> Il ballo è lungo, l'appetito è grande
> E l'odor della carne
> Al cor mi va.
>
> [The ballet is long, my appetite is big, and the aroma of roast meat goes straight to my heart.]

Gamace teases the famished Sancho by calling for another dance, a fandango, for which Salieri provided music that has none of the exotic color that we expect of this dance (ex. 5.2).[12]

12. On the fandango in eighteenth-century ballet see Monika Woitas, "'. . . Bewegungen von unvergleichlicher Sinnlichkeit . . .': Auf den Spuren des berühmt-berüchtigten Fandango," in *De editione musices:*

EXAMPLE 5.2 *Don Chisciotte alle nozze di Gamace*, pt. 1, fandango, mm. 1–8

Just when Sancho imagines, at the end of the fandango, that he will be able to eat, a series of songs begins. Chitteria (soprano, Teresa Eberardi) accompanies herself on a guitar (pizzicato strings) as she sings a strophic song, "Servi del nume arcier." Later Rosa (soprano, Clementina Chiavacci) sings "Non m'inganni o lusinghiero," which serves, in an interesting combination of opera and ballet, as the accompaniment to a dance. Boccherini's text includes instructions for a pantomime to be performed by Alfeo, described in the libretto as one of two "peasants who dance" (fig. 5.1). These instructions also guided Salieri in composing the number. The following translation of Boccherini's stage directions is interspersed with a description of Salieri's music.

> While she [i.e., Rosa] tunes [a guitar] Alfeo dances around her amorously. [Six measures of pizzicato arpeggiation accompany Rosa's tuning and Alfeo's dance.] Alfeo continues to express to Rosa his tender feelings.

The aria begins in B♭ major, with an Andante grazioso in 3/4 time; the music supports the pantomime with one of Salieri's favorite instrumental devices, an elaborate oboe solo, this one particularly tender and expressive. The accent on the second beat in measures 5–6 gives this music the character of a sarabande, whose Spanish origins and connotations of dignity and nobility made it an ideal accompaniment to Alfeo's courtship (ex. 5.3).

Festschrift Gerhard Croll zum 65. Geburtstag, ed. Wolfgang Gratzer and Andrea Lindmayr (Laaber, 1992), 203–18.

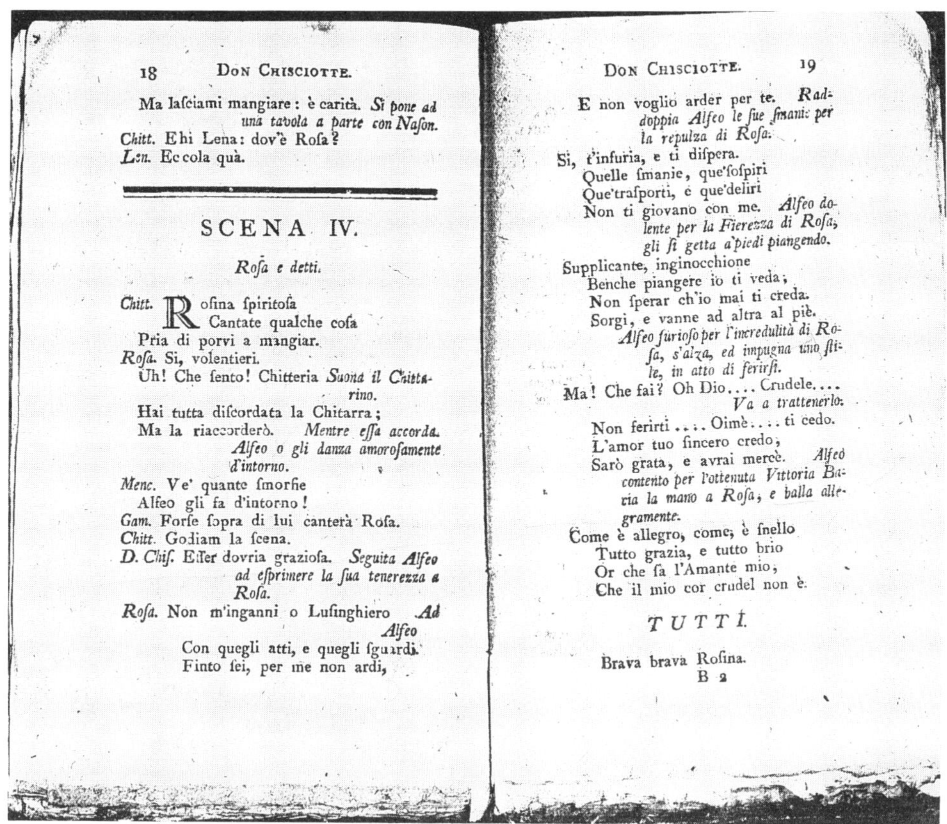

18 DON CHISCIOTTE.

Ma lafciami mangiare: è carità. *Si pone ad una tavola a parte con Nafon.*
Chitt. Ehi Lena: dov'è Rofa?
Len. Eccola quà.

SCENA IV.

Rofa e detti.

Chitt. Rofina fpiritofa
Cantate qualche cofa
Pria di porvi a mangiar.
Rofa. Si, volentieri.
Uh! Che fento! Chitteria *Suona il Chittarino.*
Hai tutta difcordata la Chitarra;
Ma la riaccorderò. *Mentre effa accorda. Alfeo o gli danza amorofamente d'intorno.*
Menc. Ve' quante fmorfie
Alfeo gli fa d'intorno!
Gam. Forfe fopra di lui canterà Rofa.
Chitt. Godiam la fcena.
D. Chif. Effer dovria graziofa. *Seguita Alfeo ad efprimere la fua tenerezza a Rofa.*
Rofa. Non m'inganni o Lufinghiero *Ad Alfeo*
Con quegli atti, e quegli fguardi.
Finto fei, per me non ardi,

DON CHISCIOTTE. 19

E non voglio arder per te. *Raddoppia Alfeo le fue fmanie per la repulza di Rofa.*
Si, t'infuria, e ti difpera.
Quelle fmanie, que'fofpiri
Que'trafporti, e que'deliri
Non ti giovano con me. *Alfeo dolente per la Fierezza di Rofa, gli fi getta a'piedi piangendo.*
Supplicante, inginocchione
Benche piangere io ti veda;
Non fperar ch'io mai ti creda.
Sorgi, e vanne ad altra al piè.
Alfeo furiofo per l'incredulità di Rofa, s'alza, ed impugna uno ftile, in atto di ferirfi.
Ma! Che fai? Oh Dio.... Crudele....
Va a trattenerlo.
Non ferirti.... Oimè.... ti cedo.
L'amor tuo fincero credo,
Sarò grata, e avrai mercè. *Alfeo contento per l'ottenuta Vittoria Bacia la mano a Rofa, e balla allegramente.*
Come è allegro, come, è fnello
Tutto grazia, e tutto brio
Or che fa l'Amante mio,
Che il mio cor crudel non è.

TUTTI.

Brava brava Rofina.
B 2

FIGURE 5.1 *Don Chisciotte alle nozze di Gamace,* beginning of scene 4 in the libretto printed for the first production, Vienna, 1771.

To the accompaniment of pizzicato strings, Rosa sings her aria

> to Alfeo. Rejected by Rosa, Alfeo intensifies his expression of madness. [Six-measure oboe solo modulates to V of V; the aria continues in F major.] Mournful because of Rosa's harshness, Alfeo falls to his knees weeping. [Eight-measure oboe solo; then Rosa returns to B♭ and the aria's opening vocal melody.] Alfeo, driven to distraction by Rosa's refusal to believe him, rises and takes hold of a dagger, about to stab himself. [Eight-measure orchestral passage moving from E♭ major to C minor.] She restrains him. Alfeo, happy to have won the victory, kisses Rosa's hand and dances joyfully.

Alfeo's joyful dance at the end of the aria is accompanied by music in 6/8, Allegretto: a festive gigue.

Under the influence of this evolving dramatic situation, Salieri broke away from the sonata and binary aria forms that he inherited from Gassmann. "Non m'inganni" is

EXAMPLE 5.3 *Don Chisciotte alle nozze di Gamace,* pt. 2, “Non m’inganni o lusinghiero,” mm. 1–12

through composed. The Andante grazioso begins with a straightforward exposition and continues with a development and recapitulation. But the recapitulation, interrupted by Alfeo’s threat to kill himself, is never resumed. The Allegretto in 6/8 is no mere coda: in keeping with the transformation of the relationship between Rosa and Alfeo, the Allegretto is as important dramatically, choreographically, and musically as the Andante grazioso.

The beautiful oboe solo in Rosa’s aria is exceptional in a score in which Salieri seems to have been less interested than Gassmann in variety and originality of instrumentation. Even when Boccherini expressly called for unusual sonorities (a march accompanied by *vari strumenti burleschi*), Salieri responded with a conventional combination of

EXAMPLE 5.4 *Don Chisciotte alle nozze di Gamace,* overture, first movement, mm. 1–16

oboes, horns, and strings. He may have been limited in his instrumental choices by the size and composition of an orchestra whose primary function was the performance of dance music for Carnival balls.

Salieri announced in his overture the important role that dance would play in *Don Chisciotte.* In the normal three-movement form, it begins with material so charming and memorable (ex. 5.4) that Salieri, more than twenty years later, reused it as the opening theme of the overture to *Il mondo alla rovescia* (first performed in 1795). His use of a minuet for the second movement (ex. 5.5)—one of the first of many delightful minuet tunes, vocal as well as instrumental, in his early operas—nicely anticipates the dancing later in the opera. The overture's tonal plan also looks forward to the dancing to come. The minuet is in the same key as the first and third movements, which gives

EXAMPLE 5.5 *Don Chisciotte alle nozze di Gamace,* overture, second movement, mm. 1–8

the overture the flavor of Viennese ballet music of the 1750s and 1760s. Unlike operatic overtures, these ballet scores often feature—in the manner of a suite—two or more adjacent numbers in the same key.[13]

The experiment represented by *Don Chisciotte* did not please. Mosel wrote: "This opera received very little applause, according to Salieri's own statement."[14] It is not known to have been revived in Vienna or elsewhere. The dramatic possibilities suggested by the idea of "opera buffa, entremêlé de danses" were not taken up by Salieri in later works, nor were they developed by other Viennese composers. Ballet and opera buffa remained distinct creative enterprises, with rare exceptions such as the wedding scene in Mozart's *Figaro.*[15]

"The New Sort of Drama": *Armida*

Armida is the first of Salieri's operas to whose premiere we can assign a specific date with certainty. Joseph II wrote to his brother Leopold in Florence on 3 June 1771: "Yesterday a new opera, *Armida,* was performed for the first time. The music is by Salieri, Gasman's student. It was very successful; I will send it to you."[16]

In *Armida* Salieri collaborated for the only time with Coltellini, the impresarios' house poet from 1766 to 1772. Salieri's setting of Coltellini's libretto may not, however, have been the first. A version of *Armida* somewhat different from the one Salieri set to

13. On the tonal organization of Viennese ballet scores of the 1750s and 1760s see Brown, *Gluck,* 165–88 passim and 300–343 passim.

14. Mosel, 43.

15. By "ballet" I mean the performance of professional dancers, not the dancing often required of singers in opera buffa (as in *Don Giovanni* and Martín y Soler's *Una cosa rara*).

16. Joseph to Leopold, 3 June 1771, HHStA, Sb, Kart. 7; quoted in Rice, "Emperor," 74.

music was published in Vienna in 1766 with a title page declaring that the libretto was "to be performed with music by Giuseppe Scarlatti."[17] The libretto says nothing about when or where it was to be performed; and nothing further is known of Scarlatti's opera (assuming that he did indeed set *Armida* to music). No score is known to exist and there is no evidence (besides the libretto) of a performance.

Why did Salieri set Coltellini's libretto to music in 1771? The impresarios (including Kohary, who ran the court theaters from 1770 to 1772) were firmly committed to opera buffa and limited the Italian repertory to comic opera during most of the decade in which they were in charge. The singers they assembled, with few exceptions, specialized in opera buffa. Yet *Armida* is a serious opera, and with its important choral element, ballets, and demands for spectacular scenery, it must have been an expensive opera to produce—not the kind that Kohary would have been eager to underwrite, especially coming from the pen of a twenty-one-year-old musician with no experience as a composer of serious opera.[18]

Between 1767 and 1770 the impresarios had presented several lavish serious operas, including Gluck's *Alceste* and *Paride ed Elena,* Hasse's *Partenope,* and Gassmann's *Amore e Psiche.* But most of these celebrated special occasions at court, such as weddings; and most had the court's financial support. No such occasion can explain the production of *Armida,* nor does documentary evidence link the court to this opera.

One possible connection between the court and *Armida* has to do with the cast. Salieri wrote the principal roles for Catharina Schindler and (probably) the male soprano Giuseppe Millico, specialists in serious opera who sang in Vienna from 1770 until the end of October 1771. (Millico presumably created the soprano role of Rinaldo; he is the only male soprano known to have taken part in opera in Vienna during 1771.)[19] Millico sang Orfeo in Gluck's *Orfeo ed Euridice* during May 1770 ("with well-deserved applause on account of his voice and his acting," according to Khevenhüller)[20] and Admeto (originally a tenor part) in a revival of *Alceste* during fall 1770; he and Schindler created the title roles in *Paride ed Elena* in November 1770, and they continued to perform Gluck's opera during 1771.[21]

The enthusiastic report about the premiere of *Paride* in the official *Wienerisches Diarium* (which did not even mention the titles of most operas performed in Vienna) and

17. Sartori no. 2680.

18. Except for his student opera *La vestale* (1768).

19. Della Croce/Blanchetti, 419.

20. Khevenhüller, 7:22 (13 May 1770).

21. *Genaue Nachrichten,* 75–76, says that Schindler created the role of Armida. She arrived in Vienna sometime before 6 September 1770, when she sang in a revival of Hasse's *Piramo e Tisbe* at Laxenburg, delighting listeners with her "beautiful appearance and pleasing voice" (Khevenhüller, 7:41). That Schindler and Millico sang in Vienna until the end of October 1771 and that *Paride ed Elena* remained in their repertory during 1771 we know from *Genaue Nachrichten,* 73, 75.

the dedication of the libretto to Archduke Leopold, grand duke of Tuscany (who was visiting Vienna when the opera was performed) suggest that the court played an important (but as yet unknown) role in the production of *Paride.* Certainly it is difficult to understand why Kohary engaged two specialists in opera seria (including one of Italy's leading musici) unless the court encouraged him, perhaps by means of a subsidy, to do so. The continued presence in Vienna of Schindler and Millico, in turn, encouraged Salieri to write a Gluckian serious opera.

An earlier opera based on the story of Armida and Rinaldo, as told by Tasso in *Gerusalemme liberata,* had important associations with the Habsburg court and with Emperor Joseph II. The performance of Traetta's *Armida* in 1761 celebrated Joseph's wedding to Isabella of Bourbon-Parma and the alliance between the Habsburg and Bourbon dynasties that this wedding represented. Traetta's opera, on a libretto derived from Jean-Baptiste Lully's *Armide* (1686), brought Italian song together with the dances, choruses and spectacular scenic effects of tragédie lyrique; this amalgam served as a potent symbol of the dynastic alliance.[22] Under Durazzo's supervision, these same elements became characteristic features of Italian serious opera as cultivated in Vienna during the 1760s. If Traetta's *Armida* represented one of the first steps in the development of French-inspired Italian serious opera in Vienna, Salieri's *Armida* represented a continuation of that tradition into the 1770s.

That Salieri collaborated with Coltellini rather than Boccherini to produce *Armida* is indicative of the opera's place in an operatic tradition established by Durazzo and artists assembled by him. Calzabigi considered Coltellini his artistic successor. Writing to Prince Kaunitz in 1767, Calzabigi alluded to his own innovations and to Coltellini's role in perpetuating them: "things are rather different in the new sort of drama—if not invented by me, then at least carried out for the first time in Orfeo, then in Alceste, and continued by Sig. Coltellini."[23]

Coltellini had contributed to "the new sort of drama" while Calzabigi was still active in Vienna, both during Durazzo's regime (Traetta's *Ifigenia in Tauride,* 1763) and under the impresarios (*Amore e Psiche*). But he did little to further the state of Viennese serious opera thereafter. *Armida* seems to have been the only serious libretto by Coltellini performed in the court theaters between 1767 and the poet's departure in late 1771 or early 1772.

Like Traetta, Salieri used Tasso's story as an opportunity to combine the dramatic and musical devices of French and Italian opera. He successfully exploited the melodic richness of Italian opera within the dramatic framework of tragédie lyrique; in doing so, he

22. Daniel Heartz, "Traetta in Vienna: *Armida* (1761) and *Ifigenia in Tauride* (1763)," *Studies in Music from the University of Western Ontario* 7 (1982): 65–88; Heartz, *Viennese School,* 174–79; and Brown, *Gluck,* 279–80.

23. Quoted in translation in Brown, *Gluck,* 431.

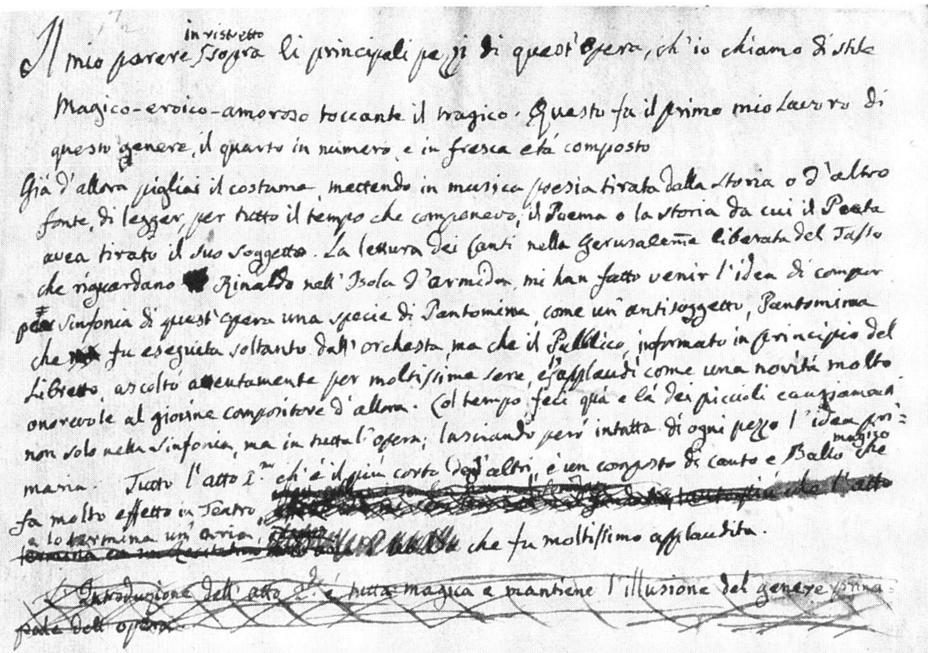

Il mio parere in ristretto sopra li principali pezzi di quest'opera, ch'io chiamo di stile magico-eroico-amoroso toccante il tragico. Questo fu il primo mio lavoro di questo genere, il quarto in numero, e in fresca età composto

Già d'allora pigliai il costume, mettendo in musica poesia tirata dalla storia o d'altro fonte, di legger, per tutto il tempo che componevo, il Poema o la storia da cui il Poeta avea tirato il suo soggetto. La lettura dei Canti nella Gerusalemme liberata del Tasso che riguardano Rinaldo nell'Isola d'Armida, mi han fatto venir l'idea di compor per sinfonia di quest'opera una specie di Pantomima, come un antisoggetto, Pantomima che fu eseguita soltanto dall'orchestra, ma che il Pubblico, informato in principio del Libretto, ascoltò attentamente per moltissime sere, e applaudì come una novità molto onorevole al giovine compositore d'allora. Col tempo feci quà e là dei piccoli cangiamenti non solo nella sinfonia, ma in tutta l'opera; lasciando però intatta di ogni pezzo l'idea primaria. Tutto l'atto 1.mo ch'è il più corto degli altri, è un composto di canto e Ballo magico che fa molto effetto in Teatro, e lo termina un'aria, che fu moltissimo applaudita.

~~L'Introduzione dell'atto 2.do è tutta magica e mantiene l'illusione del genere principale dell'opera.~~

FIGURE 5.2 The first of three pages of annotations in Salieri's hand in the autograph score of *Armida*, 1771. Musiksammlung, Österreichische Nationalbibliothek, Vienna.

not only recalled the success of Traetta's *Armida* but anticipated many aspects of Gluck's *Armide* (Paris, 1777).

Coltellini called *Armida* a dramma per musica, but the libretto has little in common with those to which eighteenth-century librettists normally attached this generic designation. Like Metastasio's drammi per musica, Coltellini's has three acts, but they are much shorter than Metastasio's acts, which typically have between ten and fifteen scenes (a scene change being defined by the arrival or departure of one or more characters). Act 1 has only three scenes; act 2, five; act 3, six. In length Coltellini's libretto closely resembles the short *azione teatrale* that Giannambrogio Migliavacca and Durazzo had prepared for Traetta. *Armida* has only four characters rather than the six or seven normal in Metastasio's librettos: Armida (soprano), her confidante Ismene (soprano), Rinaldo (soprano), and his friend Ubaldo (baritone; Salieri used both tenor and bass clefs in notating the role).

The autograph score of *Armida* is the earliest with extensive annotations in Salieri's hand (fig. 5.2). Having developed, in his late years, an almost obsessive interest in the problems of operatic genre and style (terms which he generally used interchangeably), Salieri placed *Armida* "in the magico-heroico-lyrical style, touching the tragic." He went on to describe an aspect of his compositional technique that seems to be recorded nowhere else:

> Already then [i.e., at an early age], when I set to music a poem derived from history or from another source, I had adopted the custom of reading, during the whole period of composition, the poem or the history from which the poet derived his subject. My reading of the cantos of *Gerusalemme liberata* of Tasso concerning Rinaldo on the island of Armida gave me the idea of composing, as the overture to this opera, a kind of pantomime as prelude, a pantomime executed by the orchestra alone, but which the public, informed beforehand by the libretto, listened to attentively for many evenings, and applauded as a novelty that did great honor to the young composer.

The overture is one of many by Salieri in which he followed the precept stated by Calzabigi and Gluck in their preface to *Alceste* (published two years earlier) "that the overture ought to apprise the spectators of the nature of the action that is to be represented." With the help of an explanatory note in the libretto for the first production we can follow the overture as action-filled program music (or pantomime, as Salieri called it) that sets the stage for the drama to come. The note, which ends with a disarming expression of uncertainty, may well be by Salieri himself:

> Gentle, generous spectator,
> In the sinfonia of this opera, an attempt has been made to express with music what happened in the drama immediately before the beginning of the action; namely the arrival of Ubaldo on Armida's island, amid the dense dark fog that surrounds it, the guardian monsters that hurl themselves at him from above in an attempt to frighten him; the horrible shrieks and the confusion in which they are put to flight by Ubaldo as he simply reveals the magic shield; the difficulty of the painful ascent up the mountain's rugged cliff; and the rapid passage at the peak to a delightful, peaceful serenity.
>
> If the music really has the power to represent to your imagination all these images, the young composer's courage will be strengthened by well-deserved praise; but if the effect does not correspond to the plan, accept his good intention, forgive him because of the difficulty of the enterprise, and put this sinfonia together with all those that mean nothing whatsoever.[24]

The overture begins with a slow introduction in C minor for strings alone. Sinuous lines in imitation (which, however, avoid even a hint of counterpoint by the use of a "countersubject" consisting mostly of a single sustained note), pianissimo, depict the fog that surrounds Armida's island (ex. 5.6). At the same time, this music anticipates (in tonality, tempo, and melodic material) the beginning of act 3, in which Armida and her handmaidens cast a magic spell in a dungeon.

Tempo, dynamics, mode, and orchestration change simultaneously to depict the attacking monsters. An orchestra of oboes, horns, bassoons, trombones, and strings plays an Allegro in C major, beginning fortissimo. Salieri's use of trombones, in imitation of

24. For the original see Swenson, 42.

EXAMPLE 5.6 *Armida,* overture, first movement, mm. 1–15 (A-Wn, Mus. Hs. 17837)

Gluck's trombones in *Orfeo* and *Alceste,* signaled right at the beginning of the opera that with this work he intended to contribute to the tradition of innovative Viennese drama to which *Orfeo* and *Alceste* belonged. Later in the overture the tempo changes to Allegro assai for a passage that, according to Salieri's autograph, depicts the monsters fleeing in terror before Ubaldo's magic shield. The movement ends with an open cadence, followed by a lyrical Andantino grazioso, also in C, that announces Ubaldo's discovery of the "deliziosa tranquilla serenità" of Armida's island.

The serenity conveyed by Salieri at the end of the overture is represented visually in the opera's opening scene, described by Coltellini as a "pleasant park that opens onto several shady avenues, at the end of which one sees in the distance the magnificent entrance of Armida's enchanted palace. In the middle of the great park, on the flowery bank of a large lake, tables are richly set, and pretty young women play, combining with a joyful dance the following chorus."[25]

The beautiful young women who inhabit the island dance and sing of the transience of youthful beauty ("Sparso di pure brine"). Salieri's music, a minuet-like Andantino

25. Parco delizioso, che s'apre in vari Viali ombrosi, in fondo a' quali si vede in lontananza il magnifico ingresso dell'incantato Palazzo d'Armida. In mezzo al gran Parco, alle fiorite sponde d'uno spazioso lago sono imbandite delle riche mense e stanno scherzando leggiadre donzelle, intrecciando a una lieta danza il seguente. CORO.

grazioso, maintains the mood established by the Andantino grazioso at the end of the overture. The chorus, in F, includes an episode in B♭ for two soloists. The choral dance is interrupted by Ismene, who warns (in simple recitative) of Ubaldo's approach and urges her companions to defend Armida's palace. They respond by asking, in chorus, who could have penetrated the darkness and scattered the monsters that surround the island. In fashioning his choral text from outraged questions about a man who has dared to enter a forbidden place and casting his poetry in quinari (including several quinari sdruccioli), Coltellini bowed to his predecessor Calzabigi and to the underworld scene in *Orfeo*. Calzabigi wrote:

Chi mai dell'Erebo
   Fralle caligini
   Sull'orme d'Ercole
   E di Piritoo
   Conduce il piè?
D'orror l'ingombrino
   Le fiere Eumenidi,
   E lo spaventino
   Gli urli di Cerbero
   Se un dio non è!

[Who has ventured into the fog of the underworld, in the footsteps of Hercules and of Pirithous? Let the fierce Eumenides block his way with their horror and let the roars of Cerebus fill him with fear, unless he is a god!]

Coltellini:

Ah fralla nera
   Densa caligine
   La riva inospita
   Chi mai scuoprì?
Ah fralla schiera
   De' mostri orribili
   Qual Dio, qual Demone
   La via s'aprì?

[Who has discovered the unwelcoming path through the black, thick fog? What god, what demon has opened the way through the band of horrible monsters?]

As if to avoid sounding too much like Gluck, Salieri made his setting in duple meter instead of Gluck's triple (which the poetry clearly invites). He chose the key of E♭, whose associations with darkness and ghosts were discussed in chapter 3. The chorus ends with a transition to an accompanied recitative for Ismene; the recitative in turn is followed by a reprise of the chorus with which the opera begins. But the young women cannot complete the chorus; on Ubaldo's arrival, they stop in midphrase.

This brief description of the opera's overture and opening scenes suggests the dramatic and musical fluidity of the opera as a whole. Salieri bridged gaps between one vocal number and another and between vocal numbers and recitative by means of transitions leading to open cadences. Accompanied recitative alternates freely with simple recitative. As in *Le donne letterate,* fifth relations between adjacent numbers enhance the score's sense of momentum: the overture (C minor–C major)–chorus (F)–episode for two soloists (B♭)–chorus (E♭).[26] Elsewhere in the opera Salieri exploited third relations, as, for example, in Rinaldo's scena in act 2, where a cavatina in G is followed, after accompanied recitative, by an aria in E♭.

Choruses consisting of Armida's young female courtiers, of monsters or demons, and of magicians (*incantatori*) play an important role in the opera. Their singing often accompanies dance, choreographed in the first production by Noverre.[27]

Coltellini demanded a wide variety of impressive scenic effects and described them in detail in his libretto. His description of the "pleasant park" with which act 1 begins has been quoted above. Later in the act, when Ubaldo rejects the young women's welcome, Ismene calls on monsters to punish him. Suddenly the scene changes: "The stage darkens and is transformed into a frightful place in which demons appear in various threatening groups to scare Ubaldo." The knight manages to defend himself with his magic shield; "The monsters having fled, the stage returns to its original brightness."

In act 2 poet and composer turned their attention from the supernatural and the marvelous to the emotions of their principal characters. Scenery, dance, and chorus play less important roles here. Dancers appear only once, when Rinaldo goes to sleep at the end of "Vieni a me sull'ali d'oro."

Act 3 begins in a "subterranean chamber used for magic spells, with altar and tripod. Armida's courtiers, wearing black veils, are celebrating a sacrifice to the infernal gods with a slow and solemn dance around the altar. Armida, seated on the tripod and holding a magic wand in her hand, takes part [in the ceremony], rising with a troubled expression at the end of the following chorus."[28] This image inspired in Salieri an Adagio

26. In moving from C major to E♭ at the beginning of his opera Salieri came close to duplicating the organization of Gassmann's *L'opera seria,* in which vocal numbers in B♭ and E♭ follow an overture in F; Salieri reversed the tonal organization of the opening scenes of *Le donne letterate,* whose introduzione in E♭ is followed by a short instrumental passage in B♭, then arias in F, C, and G.

27. The libretto mentions no choreographer, but the dances are attributed to Noverre in *Theatralkalender von Wien, für das Jahr 1772,* 90.

28. Spazioso sotterraneo a uso d'incanti con Ara e Tripode. Le seguaci d'Armida cinte di nere bende stanno amministrando con una danza grave e solenne intorno all'ara un Sacrifizio agli Dei infernali. Armida assisa sul tripode, e tenendo in mano la magica verga vi assiste, alzandosi crucciosa al finir del seguente. CORO.

FIGURE 5.3 *Armida,* beginning of act 3 in the autograph score.

con un poco di moto in C minor, the same tempo and key as the overture. (He later changed the tempo to Andante sostenuto.) Instruments (including trombones) used in their low register, a prominent diminished seventh chord, and a chromatically descending bass all contribute to a dark and sinister tonal picture (fig. 5.3). Salieri described this number in his annotations as "un pezzo di musica tutto magico."

The opera ends with the destruction of Armida's palace, which, however, is heard more than seen: "One hears thunder and lightning; the stage is engulfed in darkness. . . . One hears in the distance the sound of the destruction of the island. . . . Armida climbs into a chariot pulled by winged dragons, and around her, on black flaming clouds, her courtiers in various groups repeat [the last two lines of Armida's aria] in chorus."[29] According to Salieri's annotations, the music that accompanies these scenic effects "is of an infernal effect, and therefore *ad locum,* and worthy of the finale of an opera that belongs almost in its entirety to the diabolical genre."

Of Catharina Schindler, the first Armida, we read in a theatrical almanac: "Mademoiselle Leitnerinn, otherwise known under the name Schindlerinn, a Viennese, was

29. Si sentono fulmini e tuoni e s'ingombra di tenebre la scena. . . . Si sente in lontananza lo strepito della rovina dell'Isola. . . . Monta Armida sopra un carro tirato da' Dragoni alati, e intorno ad essa in vari gruppi sulle nere infuocate nubi le sue seguaci, che replicano in Coro.

EXAMPLE 5.7 *Armida,* act 2, "Tremo, bell'idol mio," mm. 1–8

I tremble, my darling, but my fear is no torment.

assigned [during 1771] to the first roles of the opera seria. She has a beautiful appearance, and a pleasant, pure, bright voice in the higher notes. We would like it if she were somewhat stronger in the middle range. But she compensates for this with her lively and expressive acting, the likes of which one cannot find on the Italian stage. Hardly had she appeared on the stage when she already won applause."[30]

Armida's first aria, "Tremo, bell'idol mio," made full use of Schindler's strengths. A simple accompaniment (strings alone) focused attention on a beautiful melody that, especially in the initial three-measure phrase, reminds one of Gluck (ex. 5.7). Coloratura ascending to high D exploited Schindler's "pleasant, pure, bright voice in the higher notes." Her "lively and expressive acting" must have come to the fore in her final scene,

30. Mademoiselle Leitnerinn, sonst unter dem Namen Schindlerinn bekannt, eine Wienerinn, war zu den ersten Rollen der *Opera seria* aufgenommen. Sie hat eine schöne Gestalt, und eine überaus angenehme, reine und helllautende Stimme in den höhern Tönen. Wir wünchten daß sie etwas stärker in den mittlern Tönen wäre. Doch dies ersetzt sie durch das lebhafteste und ausdruckvolleste Spiel, dergleichen man auf dem italiänischen Theater nicht kennet. Kaum erschien sie auf dem Theater, so hatte sie schon allgemeinen Beyfall. Sie befindet sich itzt in Prag (*Theatralkalender von Wien, für das Jahr 1772,* 84).

a long accompanied recitative and aria, "Io con voi la nera face," in which Armida, abandoned by Rinaldo, expresses her passion, confusion, and anger.

Giuseppe Millico, the male soprano who probably created the role of Rinaldo, was "an outstanding singer," according to a critic who witnessed his performances in Vienna: "His voice is quite strong and pleasant. He knows how to hide its few imperfections with such artistry and acting that one can consider him the best singer of Italy. His greatest strength lies especially in the type of singing that requires expression. There he knows how to give the strongest emphasis to each emotion."[31]

Rinaldo's scena in act 2 gave Millico ample opportunity to display his vocal and dramatic art. Coltellini's poetry is pervaded by the intense emotion that Millico could convey so vividly. After a passionate accompanied recitative Rinaldo expresses his love for Armida in a cavatina in G, "Lungi da te, ben mio," cast in the rhythmic accents of a slow, noble minuet (ex. 5.8). Rinaldo's repetition of "ben mio" nicely echoes Armida's repetition of "idol mio" at the beginning of her aria "Tremo, bell'idol mio." The

EXAMPLE 5.8 *Armida,* act 2, "Lungi da te, ben mio," mm. 9–22

(*Continued on next page*)

31. Herr Millico, erster Diskantist, ist ein vortreflicher Sänger. Seine Stimme ist ziemlich stark und angenehm. Er weis einige Unvollkommenheiten derselben mit so vieler Kunst und Spiel zu verbergen, daß man ihn immer für den ersten Sänger Italiens halten kann. Seine größte Stärke hat er besonders in der Gattung des Gesanges, welche Ausdruck fodert. Da weis er der Empfindung den stärksten Nachdruck zu geben (*Theatralkalender von Wien, für das Jahr 1772,* 83).

EXAMPLE 5.8 (*continued*)

If I cannot live away from you, my love, light of my eyes, life of my heart

cavatina ends with a transition from G major to the dominant of A minor. More accompanied recitative follows, then the scena's climax, the lovely aria "Vieni a me sull'ali d'oro," whose slow tempo allows us to relish the sweet clash (on the second syllable of "Vieni") of leading tone D against tonic harmony (ex. 5.9). Salieri called attention to the

EXAMPLE 5.9 *Armida,* act 2, "Vieni a me sull'ali d'oro," mm. 18–27

(*Continued on next page*)

EXAMPLE 5.9 (*continued*)

Come to me on golden wings, alluring dream of love

importance of this aria by beginning it with a seventeen-measure orchestral introduction featuring a solo oboe. Rinaldo goes to sleep as the aria ends (like Cecchina, in *La buona figliuola,* at the end of another sleep aria in E♭, "Vieni al mio seno"). According to Coltellini's stage directions, "to the sound of sweet instrumental music, charming spirits representing various pleasures appear from different places, dancing around Rinaldo." It was probably in reference to the oboe solo that Salieri wrote in his annotations: "Rinaldo's entire *scena a solo,* and particularly the aria 'Vieni a me sull'ali d'oro,' has always made a good effect, especially through the instrumentation."

The role of Ubaldo may have been created by the buffo caricato Francesco Bussani, who sang both tenor and bass roles in comic operas and had experience in Viennese serious opera; he sang the role of high priest in the revival of Gluck's *Alceste* in 1770[32] and created that of Gamace in Salieri's *Don Chisciotte* a few months later. If Salieri wrote Ubaldo for the versatile Bussani, this would explain why he apparently could not decide whether to make Ubaldo a tenor or a bass. The first of Ubaldo's arias, "Finta larva, d'Abisso frall'ombra," with a long text, fast tempo, and disjunct melodic line that often doubles the bass, sounds as if it were intended for a buffo caricato rather than a character in a serious opera. Ubaldo's participation in the trio in act 3, "Strappami il cuor dal seno," transforms that number from a passionate duet for two noble lovers into something more akin to an opera buffa finale, with rapid dialogue and many changes of tempo.

Armida was well received in Vienna. One critic wrote: "The music is an effort by a young student of Herr Gaßmann, Herr Anton Salieri, and it turned out very well. This opera was exceptionally successful. Mlle. Schindler distinguished herself in the role of Armida, which she acted ravishingly."[33] Joseph II, quoted earlier, reported the success

32. Sartori no. 593.

33. Armide, ein neues Drama von Herrn Coltelini, Dichter des Theaters. Die Musik ist ein Versuch eines jungen Schülers des Herrn Gaßmann, Hrn. Anton Salieri, und ist sehr gut ausgefallen. Dieses Singspiel gefiel außerordentlich. Madlle. Schindler that sich in der Rolle der Armide, die sie zum Entzücken spielte, besonders hervor (*Genaue Nachrichten,* 75–76).

of *Armida* to his brother Leopold. Zinzendorf also attended the premiere; he wrote in his diary: "to the opera *Armide;* it is beautiful, not only the spectacle but also the scenery and music."[34] When he saw the opera again two weeks later he had something more insightful to say: "the opera *Armide,* which is beautiful, but there are some passages of opera buffa."[35] This comment, which shows that Zinzendorf, and doubtless others in the audience, were sensitive to the stylistic diversity of Italian opera, probably referred to Ubaldo's arias and to the finale-like trio in which he takes part.

Of further performances of *Armida* in Vienna we know nothing, but it is unlikely to have been performed after the departure of Schindler and Millico at the end of October 1771. Salieri's first serious opera seems never to have been revived in Vienna.

Armida enjoyed a much happier fate in northern Germany, where it won much critical praise and received several productions during the 1770s and 1780s. A performance of excerpts in Hamburg in 1776 delighted Heinrich von Gerstenberg, the distinguished poet and critic, and an enthusiastic music lover. He wrote to his wife Sophia of Salieri's music: "divine! I shed tears ten times; it was too strong for me."[36] Inviting a singer to perform at his house, Gerstenberg put Salieri in exalted company: "bring your best music with you—Gluck, Salieri, Händel—whatever you want."[37] Also in Hamburg the musical journalist Carl Friedrich Cramer heard *Armida* at about this time.[38] He later became Salieri's principal advocate in Germany, publishing a German translation of the libretto of *Armida* and a keyboard-vocal score of the opera (Leipzig, 1783). Cramer's enthusiastic support of Salieri's music, inspired primarily by *Armida,* did much to enhance the composer's reputation in German-speaking cities other than Vienna.

A Roman Intermezzo in Vienna: *Il barone di Rocca Antica*

Visiting Rome during Carnival 1784, Mary Berry, a young Englishwoman, found a distinctively Roman form of comic opera: "In the evening, the Teatro della Valle, where there is an Italian comedy of three acts, and an intermezzo in music, that is to say, an opera buffa between the acts; the music was some of the prettiest of the kind I ever heard."[39]

34. a l'opera d'*Armide,* il est beau, tant pour le Spectacle que pour la decoration et la musique (Zinzendorf, 2 June 1771).

35. On donna l'opera d'*Armide* dont la musique est belle, il y a cependant quelques passages d'opera buffa (Zinzendorf, 17 June 1771).

36. Letter dated 15 April 1776, in Klopstock, *Briefe 1776–1782,* 1:383.

37. Gerstenberg to Klopstock and Johanna Elisabeth von Winthem (the singer), 8 May 1776, in Klopstock, *Briefe 1776–1782,* 1:25.

38. Cramer mentioned the opera in a letter of 4 May 1776, in Klopstock, *Briefe 1776–1782,* 1:383.

39. Theresa Lewis, ed., *Extracts from the Journals and Correspondence of Miss Berry from the Years 1783 to 1852,* 2d ed., 3 vols. (London, 1866), 1:72.

Although the Teatro Valle specialized in the performance of spoken plays, it contributed to the history of opera by presenting, from the early 1740s, comic operas in two parts as entertainment during intermissions. Each part of the opera was known as an intermezzo; the complete work was referred to in the plural: *intermezzi per musica.* (Here, to avoid confusion, the genre and each pair of intermezzi will be referred to in the singular.) In function Roman intermezzi differed little from *La serva padrona* and other Neapolitan intermezzi (which, however, were usually performed between the acts of serious operas rather than plays) and from the Venetian intermezzi written by Goldoni during the 1730s. But in other respects they had more in common with full-length Goldonian comic operas.

The Neapolitan intermezzo flourished during the 1720s and 1730s; the Roman intermezzo during the second half of the century.[40] Instead of the two or three singing characters typical of intermezzi produced in Naples and Venice, most Roman intermezzi had four or five, permitting a greater variety of characterization and more possibilities for ensembles. Roman intermezzi were usually divided into scenes, like full-length drammi giocosi per musica; Neapolitan and Venetian intermezzi, in contrast, usually lacked this organization.[41]

Roman intermezzi differed from Goldonian opere buffe in having two parts instead of three acts. Their casts did not allow for the full spectrum of character types explored by Goldoni in his seven-role operas. Yet Roman intermezzi were strongly subject to the influence of Goldoni's opere buffe. Several, indeed, consist of settings of Goldoni's librettos or those of his contemporaries reduced from three acts to two parts and with several characters (most commonly the parti serie) eliminated.[42] Others betray Goldonian influence in their use of introduzioni and finales and in their plots and characters.

The reduced vocal forces required by Roman intermezzi made them extremely popular with impresarios who found it difficult or expensive to assemble enough singers for a Goldonian opera buffa. The brevity of these works may have endeared them to performers and audiences alike, especially outside Italy. Sacchini's *La contadina in corte* (1765) and other Roman intermezzi spread through Europe with amazing speed.

Viennese impresarios and audiences shared a special fondness for Roman intermezzi—although they did not use the term *intermezzo* often, preferring *operetta gio-*

40. Weiss, "Carlo Goldoni, Librettist," 104, calls into question statements by Goldoni and Burney about the demise of the intermezzo during the 1730s, but the important differences between the Neapolitan and Venetian intermezzi on the one hand and their Roman successor on the other help to explain the views of Goldoni and Burney. The Roman intermezzo continued to flourish into the 1780s. See Federico Pirani, "*I due baroni di Rocca Azzurra:* Un intermezzo romano nella Vienna di Mozart," in *Mozart e i musicisti italiani del suo tempo,* ed. Annalisa Bini (Lucca, 1994), 89–112.

41. Weiss, "Carlo Goldoni, Librettist," 142–43.

42. For a study of one such transformation, see Michael Robinson, "Three Versions of Goldoni's *Il filosofo di campagna,*" in Muraro, *Venezia,* 2:75–85.

cosa. La contadina in corte was one of the first comic operas that Salieri could see and hear after arriving in Vienna in 1766. In the years that followed he heard and probably directed rehearsals and performances of many Roman intermezzi, including Piccinni's *Il barone di Torreforte* (1765; Vienna, 1769) and *Lo sposo burlato* (1769; Vienna, 1770), Sacchini's *L'isola d'amore* (1766; Vienna, 1769), and Sarti's *La giardiniera brillante* (1768; Vienna, 1769).[43]

We might expect Salieri to have tried his hand at this particular subgenre of opera buffa, and indeed he did. Although the libretto printed for the first production of *Il barone di Rocca Antica* calls itself a dramma giocoso per musica, it is in fact an intermezzo, by the Roman poet Giuseppe Petrosellini. Under the generic designation "Intermezzi per musica a quattro voci," the libretto was first set to music by Carlo Franchi and performed in the Teatro Valle during Carnival 1771.[44] Salieri, or whoever chose the libretto for him, clearly went straight to the genre's Roman source.[45]

First performed on 12 May 1772,[46] Salieri's *Barone* had been in the repertory almost four months when Charles Burney witnessed a performance in the Kärntnertortheater on 1 September 1772:

> At half an hour past six this evening, I went to the comic opera of *Il barone.* The music, composed by Signor Salieri, a scholar of M. Gasman. I did not receive much pleasure from the overture, or the two first airs; the music was languid, and the singing but indifferent. There were only four characters in the piece, and the principal woman did not appear till the third scene; but then she gave a glow to every thing around her; it was one of the Baglioni, of Bologna, whom I had heard both at Milan and Florence, during my tour through Italy.[47]

Burney's comment that "there were only four characters in the piece" suggests that, misled by the printed libretto's generic designation, he expected a six- or seven-character dramma giocoso per musica, not a Roman intermezzo in which a cast of four was quite normal.

Il barone enjoyed more success in Vienna than Burney's comments might suggest. A theatrical almanac referred to the composer in terms that reflected his growing reputa-

43. Zechmeister; Sartori.

44. Sartori no. 3782.

45. *Il barone* was not Salieri's first intermezzo. On the title page of the libretto of *L'amore innocente* (1770) the librettist Boccherini called his drama a "pastorale per musica"; in the autograph score (the earliest of Salieri's many extant operatic autographs) the composer referred to the opera variously as "operetta" and "pastorale." The term "operetta" hints at the genre of *L'amore innocente,* whose brevity, relatively few characters (four), lack of parti serie, and two-part structure all place it within the tradition of the Roman intermezzo. On *L'amore innocente* see Mosel, 41–42, and Della Croce/Blanchetti, 102–3, 412–14.

46. The date of the premiere, but not the location, is given in *Theatralalmanach von Wien, für das Jahr 1773* (Vienna, 1773), 161.

47. Burney, *Germany,* 84.

tion: "The music [is] by Herr Salieri, and is worthy of this great composer. . . . [The opera] won general applause and held its own."[48] *Il barone* was performed eighteen times between May and November 1772 and three times during Carnival 1773. It left the repertory at the end of Carnival and was apparently never revived thereafter.

Petrosellini's libretto, like many others that formed the basis for Roman intermezzi, was the product of Goldonian influence as well as of specifically Roman traditions. Both parts end with long finales. The opera's penultimate number, as in many of Goldoni's librettos, is a love duet. The cast consists of two pairs of estranged lovers: Barone Arsura (tenor; the name means "heat" or "dryness"), an impoverished nobleman "of eccentric character," has abandoned Beatrice (soprano), a wealthy young woman who, disguised as a lowborn fortune-teller, comes in search of the baron. The farmer Giocondo (bass) has promised to marry the peasant girl Lenina (soprano), but now refuses to do so.

Of the original cast we know (from Burney) only that one of the Baglioni sisters created the role of Beatrice. Whether Clementina, Costanza, or Rosa sang Beatrice we do not know, but to judge from Burney's description of her singing (quoted at greater length in chap. 2) it was probably Clementina.

The baron and Beatrice are parti di mezzo carattere. In his first aria, "Vieni, vieni o mio tesoro," the baron reveals the comic side of his personality by means of a jolly, disjunct tune; the coloratura that he sings in a later aria, "Tu che ferita sei" helps to depict his nobility. Beatrice's personality, similarly complex, wavers between rustic charm and noble heroism. She conveys the former in "Rondinella pellegrina," with its pastoral melody in compound meter (ex. 5.10). When she later reveals her true identity, her aria "Più non sono l'indovina" projects nobility through its combination of tempo (Andante maestoso), meter (duple), and vocal register (the melodic line ascends twice to high C, sustained for a full measure). The opening melody's heroic leap up a major

EXAMPLE 5.10 *Il barone di Rocca Antica*, pt. 1, "Rondinella pellegrina," mm. 12–15 (A-Wn 16511)

Wandering swallow fly, fly across the sea

48. Die Musik von Hrn. Salieri, welche dieses großen Tonkünstlers würdig ist, und die Worte vom Hrn. Abbate Pedroselini. Es gefiel allgemein und erhielt sich (*Theatralalmanach von Wien, für das Jahr 1773*, 161).

EXAMPLE 5.11 *Il barone di Rocca Antica,* pt. 2, "Più non sono l'indovina," mm. 9–24

I am no longer a fortune-teller, I am no longer a wanderer. I am a lady and a noblewoman, and I was born to command.

tenth at the words "son signora e sono nobile" and the extension of the phrase to three measures immediately identify Beatrice as a noblewoman (ex. 5.11).

Burney noticed Beatrice's absence at the beginning of the opera and the dramatic effect of her entrance. The late appearance of an important female character, usually a noblewoman, was to be a characteristic feature of opera buffa during the rest of the eighteenth century. "Rondinella pellegrina" is a good example of the cavatina sung by many prime donne on their first entrance. It shares this introductory function with "Che piacer," sung by Cecchina at the beginning *La buona figliuola,* but differs significantly from Cecchina's cavatina in being placed later in the first act.

Salieri's use several times of transitions leading into and out of Beatrice's arias enriches his portrayal. Transitions at the ends of arias and ensembles (of the kind illustrated in exx. 3.15 and 4.21) are not rare in Salieri's early operas; but here he seems to have associated them with Beatrice in particular, perhaps as a way of focusing the audience's attention on her. Her delayed entrance is accompanied by an unusual transition from simple recitative to aria. The cadence at the end of the recitative in which Giocondo admires the unknown woman is apparently leading to A major, but it leads instead to F and directly to Beatrice's cavatina. The shift of a third contributes to the effect that Burney felt at her entrance: "she gave a glow to every thing around her" (ex. 5.12). The aria ends with another transition: a more normal unison passage for the strings ending on the dominant of G minor (that is, tonicizing the second degree of F major, the aria's key). Beatrice's more heroic aria in part 2, "Più non sono l'indovina," is also in F, and it too ends with a transition (which emerges as an extension of the aria's principal melody) leading to the dominant of G minor (ex. 5.13).

EXAMPLE 5.12 *Il barone di Rocca Antica,* pt. 1, sc. 3, simple recitative, mm. 18–22 and "Rondinella pellegrina," mm. 1–3

But who might she be? A pilgrim? An astrologer? Heavens! What a lovely, refined manner! What a charming appearance!

EXAMPLE 5.13 *Il barone di Rocca Antica,* pt. 2, "Più non sono l'indovina," mm. 61–64 (transition to simple recitative)

By setting two of Giocondo's arias in D major, Salieri made sure that Viennese audiences would recognize him as a parte buffa (cf. the pairs of D-major arias for Mengotto in *La buona figliuola* and Simone in *La finta semplice*). Giocondo's third aria, "Voglio che sappia tirar lo schioppo," is in a much more unusual key: E major. Like Tagliaferro's "Star trombette," this comic evocation of military life refers in the text to trumpets and drums. But Salieri may not have had access to these instruments during May 1772: he scored the aria for oboes, horns, and strings. He must have known early, before determining "the key appropriate to the character of each number," that he would not use trumpets and drums in *Il barone;* otherwise he would not have written the aria in E, a key normally treated in the eighteenth century as inaccessible to these instruments.

Salieri established Lenina as a parte buffa near the beginning of the opera. Her first aria, "Che mal ti fece," is labeled Tempo di minuetto. This graceful minuet aria, like many of those that Salieri, following Gassmann and his Italian contemporaries, wrote for his early female parti buffe, is dominated by four-measure phrases.

EXAMPLE 5.14 *Il barone di Rocca Antica,* pt. 1, finale, mm. 131–39

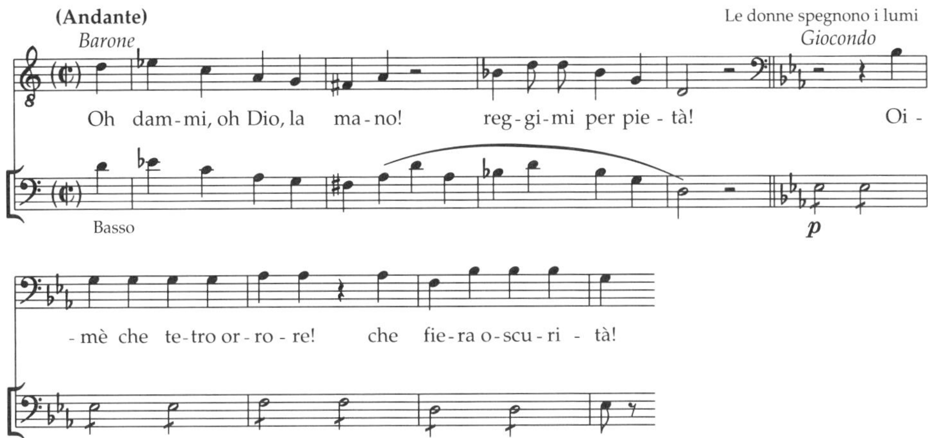

BARON: For God's sake, give me your hand, please help me! (*The women put out the lights*) GIOCONDO: What shadowy horror! What wild darkness!

Salieri's early finales (such the first finale of *Le donne letterate,* discussed in chap. 4) are largely limited, in their main tonal areas, to tonic, dominant, subdominant, and their relative minors. Some (for example, that of the second part of *Il barone*) have simpler tonal plans.[49] During the 1770s and 1780s, however, Salieri and his contemporaries exploited with increasing frequency third relations other than that of major to relative minor. The first finale of *Il barone,* in C major, contains an early example of the dramatic possibilities of the expanding tonal realm: a sudden and dramatic move to the flat mediant, E♭.

The modulation to E♭ is facilitated by an intermediate move to the minor mode. After the expected modulation from tonic to dominant, G major, Beatrice and Lenina pretend to be ghosts; the fear that they arouse in the baron and Giocondo is represented by a shift to the parallel minor, G minor. The baron cries out for help, ending his plea on the pitch D, harmonized as the dominant of G minor. The women extinguish the lights as the bass suddenly moves up a half step from D to E♭. The new key helps dramatize Giocondo's words: "What shadowy horror! What wild darkness!" (ex. 5.14). Later in his career Salieri became especially fond of such modulations by means of sudden bass movements up a half step, and not only in finales.

49. Salieri's dependence on tonic, dominant, and subdominant in his early finales is typical of the time. The finale of the first act of Paisiello's *La frascatana* (1774), based on the tonal plan I–V–I–IV–V–I, shows how the best composers could use very few closely related keys as the tonal basis for long and dramatically effective finales; see Hansell, "Opera and Ballet," 549–60.

6

THREE GOLDONIAN COMEDIES

Despite Goldoni's obvious influence on Salieri's early comic operas, the composer did not set any librettos by the Venetian dramatist during his first three years of operatic composition. In 1773 and 1774, however, Goldoni's work came to dominate the operatic output of Salieri, who set to music a libretto based on the play *La locandiera* and a lightly revised version of the libretto *La calamita de' cuori.* These were preceded in 1772 by *La fiera di Venezia,* which represents the composer's return to an operatic genre, the three-act Goldonian opera buffa, to which he had given little attention since the completion of *Le donne letterate* two years earlier.

La fiera di Venezia

For the Carnival of 1772 Salieri, in collaboration with Boccherini, produced an opera that was by far the most widely performed of his early Viennese works. First performed on 29 January 1772, *La fiera di Venezia* is set in the city from which Salieri had come to Vienna six years earlier.[1] The opera takes place during the carnival-like fair with which the Venetians celebrated the Feast of the Ascension (see fig. 1.1). As Belfusto explains in a catalogue aria, "In primis: qua si spacciano," one could find goods from all over the world at the Ascension fair:

> Vi si contrattan anco
> Con paroline tenere

1. We know the date of the premiere of *La fiera* from the *Theatralalmanach von Wien, für das Jahr 1773,* 154; but that source does not tell us if the performance took place in the Burgtheater or the Kärntnertortheater.

Trine, vezzetti, e gioie,
Cristalli, armi, e coralli,
Stoffe, zendali, e maschere,
E merci d'ogni genere,
Che fabbricansi qua.
Dal lido poi d'America,
Dal lido d'Asia ed Africa,
Di Russia e d'Alemagna,
Di Napoli e di Spagna,
Di Francia e d'Inghilterra,
Di Persia e di Turchia
Vien tanta mercanzia,
Che di Venezia il traffico
Al non plus ultra è già.

[Here they bargain politely over the price of lace, of necklaces, of jewelry, of crystals, arms, corals, fabrics, silks, and masks, and goods of every sort manufactured here. Then from the shores of America, from the shores of Asia and Africa, of Russia and Germany, of Naples and Spain, of France and England, of Persia and Turkey, so much merchandise arrives that trading in Venice has reached its ne plus ultra.]

The Ascension fair had special meaning for Salieri. It was during the fair that he met Gassmann, in Venice to oversee the production of *Achille in Sciro;* that meeting led to Gassmann's decision to bring Salieri to Vienna.

Boccherini's commedia per musica contains descriptions of scenery unusually detailed for an opera buffa.[2] He evidently had in mind a series of Canaletto-like *vedute* alternating with interior scenes of the kind that Pietro Longhi depicted with such charm. Reading these descriptions, we can imagine the city in which Salieri met Gassmann, alive with the commercial activity and carnivalesque festivity of the fair:

A Venetian piazza with booths full of rich and diverse merchandise, with the stores of the hatmaker, silversmith, wigmaker, braid seller, clothier, greengrocer, and pastry seller clearly visible.

A room in Rasoio's inn reserved for [Marchesa] Calloandra. Table and mirror on one side, a harpsichord and chairs on the other. . . .

View of the famous Rialto Bridge and the edge of the Grand Canal. . . .

Narrow streets or alleys crossed by narrow canals, and little bridges that one crosses on the way to the masked ball; streetlamps that light the way for the masqueraders.

A magnificent room furnished and illuminated for the ball; orchestra with musicians, and through several doors one can see places to take refreshment and to gamble. . . .

2. Della Croce/Blanchetti, 423.

> A pleasant place on the Riva della Zueca [Giudecca], next to the Black Ox Inn, with dining tables under a leafy arbor from which grow brightly colored roses; but the flowery greenery and the charming vases do not obstruct the view of the placid lagoon, and one can see on the other side the magnificent sight of the city of Venice, and despite the distance one can make out the piazza in which the fair takes place. The closest buildings are the customs houses. And near the Lido is a felucca.[3]

This visual background has a musical counterpart in the several choruses throughout the opera representing different parts of Venetian society during fair time: choruses of merchants and salesmen; of servants, cooks, and scullery boys; of masqueraders; and of gondoliers, boatmen, and sailors.

Against these backgrounds *La fiera* follows characters of various classes whose odd names, in some cases, tell us something of their personality. Duke Ostrogoto (tenor; the name means "Ostrogoth," i.e., barbarian) and his fiancée, Marchesa Calloandra (coloratura soprano), represent the aristocracy. Stingy old Grifagno (baritone—Salieri wrote part of the role in tenor clef, part in bass clef; the name means "predatory"), his charming daughter Falsirena (coloratura soprano; "false siren"), and her jealous lover Belfusto (tenor; "nice hunk") represent the bourgeoisie. The innkeeper Rasoio (bass; "razor") and his sweetheart, the shopkeeper Cristallina (soprano; "crystal clear"), represent the lower classes. The breakdown of the normal code of conduct during the Ascension fair allows these characters to mingle, with amusing results that come to a climax in the elaborate masked ball at the end of act 2.

Boccherini's title, which echoes that of Goldoni's *La fiera di Sinigaglia,* is by no means the only part of his libretto that reminds us of Goldoni. The characters resemble those of *Il mercato di Malmantile.* The duke, engaged to the marchesa but enamored of the commoner Falsirena, resembles Conte della Rocca, engaged to Marchesa Giacinta but happy to flirt with Brigida. Falsirena, like Brigida, is a beautiful, clever young woman with a stupid old father; Grifagno resembles Lampridio. Marchesa Calloandra reacts to Ostrogoto's attraction to Falsirena just as Marchesa Giacinta reacts to Rocca's dalliance with Brigida; Calloandra's jealousy and aristocratic outrage gave Salieri the same opportunity to write brilliant coloratura that Fischietti took advantage of in writing for Giacinta. Cristallina and Rasoio are urban relatives of the peasants Lena and Berto.

The opera opens on a crowded Venetian piazza, with merchants hawking their wares:

> Chi compra? Chi spende?
> Qui tutto si vende,
> A prezzo onestissimo
> Qui tutto si da.

3. *La fiera di Venezia* (Vienna, 1772), 3–4.

[Who buys? Who spends? Everything is for sale here; everything here is at a most reasonable price.]

This is a typically Goldonian scene, vividly evoking the everyday life of contemporary Italy: reminiscent of the "piazza rustica" in which the action of *Il mercato di Malmantile* begins. Goldoni's peasants advertize their produce:

Chi vuol capponi, chi vuol galline?
Chi vuol comprare le ricottine?
Chi vuol dell'ova si accosti qua.

[Who wants capons? Who wants hens? Who wants to buy little ricottas? Whoever wants eggs should come here.]

Later they join in a terzet:

Io vendo roba buona
Di meglio non si da.

[I sell good stuff: there is none better.]

In Salieri's autograph of *La fiera* we can see that two of Boccherini's lines—

È roba buonissima
Ch'eguale non ha

[This is the best stuff: it has no equal.]

—were set to music by Salieri but subsequently crossed out and omitted from the libretto; had they been left in, the scene would have resembled Goldoni's even more closely.

The opening scene continues to unfold in simple recitative, as Falsirena and the duke trick her father Grifagno into thinking that all the merchandise for sale at the fair is ridiculously cheap. Delighted to hear that a new suit, a sword, a wig, a hat, and a coat cost only two *soldi* each, Grifagno tries everything on. Salieri had occasionally departed in *Le donne letterate* from the normal nonmelodic accompaniment of simple recitative to comment on or to depict action on stage. He did the same here, using the accompaniment to depict Grifagno's actions as he tries each item and then pays for them all (ex. 6.1). One might expect Grifagno, like Goldoni's misers, to count his money; he does so in an aria that begins with a recitation of numbers: "Sette, e un otto, e cinque dodici."

La fiera revolves around a beautiful, lively young woman. Falsirena displays that intriguing, exasperating mixture—typical of Goldoni's leading ladies—of virtue and sexual playfulness. Although she remains faithful to her lover, Belfusto, she enjoys flirting

EXAMPLE 6.1 *La fiera di Venezia,* act 1, sc. 1, simple recitative, mm. 22–31 (A-Wn, Mus. Hs. 1048)

GRIFAGNO: Hey, tailor, bring me that suit. TAILOR: At your service. GRIFAGNO: Let's try it on. Silversmith, bring that sword here. SILVERSMITH: Here it is. GRIFAGNO: Hairdresser . . .

with the duke and arousing the jealousy of both Belfusto and the marchesa. Falsirena takes advantage of masks and other disguises to pass herself off first as an opera singer (she sings an elaborate, mock-serious aria, "Rabbia, bile, affanno, e stizza"),[4] then as the wife of a French merchant, then as a German baroness.

Venice was a cosmopolitan city, especially at fair time; *La fiera* and Falsirena in particular reflect that cosmopolitanism with the Goldonian technique of mixing languages. In her French disguise Falsirena sings a chanson, "L'Amour est un dieu cauteleux." In her role as German baroness she takes part in a trio in which German and Italian are sung simultaneously, "So wie bei den deutschen Tänzen."[5] The same cosmopolitanism that shaped Falsirena's character and music also shaped the Venetian Salieri, one of the very few eighteenth-century composers who wrote operas in all three of Falsirena's lan-

4. The aria is quoted and discussed in Hunter, "Some Representations of *Opera Seria* in *Opera Buffa,*" 99–100.

5. Salieri's French song is quoted and discussed in Osthoff, "Die Opera buffa," 691–92. On "So wie bei den deutschen Tänzen" see Heartz, *Viennese School,* 429–30.

guages. (Gluck, in contrast, wrote no operas in German; Mozart and Haydn no operas in French.)

Rasoio brings the duke a note from the marchesa informing him of her unexpected arrival at Rasoio's inn, the very place to which the duke hoped to bring Falsirena. The news throws him into confusion, but Rasoio insists that he is too busy with other customers to help. The innkeeper launches into a catalogue of all the different kinds of visitors in Venice during the Ascension fair:

Per dovere, per rispetto
Venni pronto col biglietto.
Io son muto, son discreto,
Ma l'avviso con segreto
Della brutta novità . . .
Lei risolva, dia rimedio,
Io farò quel che vorrà.
OSTR. Senti . . . va . . .
RAS. Compatirà.
Or son troppo affaccendato:
Ho foresti, viandanti,
Vagabondi, bettolanti,
E schiavoni, e dalmatini,
Turchi, greci, e pellegrini.
Quando è Fiera all'osteria
Viene gente in quantità.
OSTR. Sì, lo so . . . basta . . . dirai . . .
RAS. (Oh cospetto! V'è de' guai.)
Se la sbrogli a suo capriccio.
(Sarà questo un bel pasticcio,
Un bel caso in verità.)

[Duty and respect led me to deliver the letter promptly. I am mute, I am discreet; but the news with the secret of the ugly new development—you resolve it, you fix it; I will do what you want. OSTROGOTO: Listen . . . go . . . RASOIO: Excuse me, I am too busy now. I have guests, travelers, wanderers, drinking patrons, and Slovenes and Dalmatians, Turks, Greeks, and pilgrims. At fair time crowds of people come to my inn. OSTROGOTO: Yes I know . . . enough . . . you will say . . . RASOIO: (Heavens! He's a pain.) Extricate yourself as you see fit. (This will be a pretty mess, a pretty case indeed.)]

Salieri's setting of "Per dovere" perfectly captures the witty Goldonian spirit of the poetry with clever use of devices that he had gotten to know in the music of Gassmann and his Italian contemporaries. But one important element of the aria does not depend on Goldonian precedent. Ostrogoto interrupts Rasoio several times, and the innkeeper responds to these interruptions. Rasoio interacts with another character while the musical focus remains on him. Ostrogoto serves here as a so-called *pertichino* (literally, "bit-player"). Arias with pertichino (or more than one), quite rare in the 1770s, became more common in the 1780s and 1790s. Salieri, who was to make much use of pertichini in his later operas, handled Ostrogoto's interruptions with skill, using them to enhance the aria's comedy and dramatic interest without turning it into a full-fledged ensemble.

Although Boccherini's poem is in ottonari throughout, Salieri derived a plan of contrasting musical sections, A-B-A′-B′-C, from the poem's changing content and style and integrated these sections into sonata form. He responded to Rasoio's plain, matter-of-fact declaration at the beginning of the aria with a buffo-caricato melody in duple meter, with dotted rhythms and the normal rate of text declamation: two measures per line of poetry (this is the A section; ex. 6.2). The melody begins and ends in the tonic, B♭. For the innkeeper's recitation of his guest list Salieri modulated to the dominant, shifted to patter, and accelerated the text declamation to one measure per line (the B section). The tronco line "Viene gente in quantità" encouraged Salieri to end the exposition before going through the complete text. This meant that Rasoio's final quatrain could serve, after an abbreviated recapitulation, as the text for a coda.

"Per dovere" begins with a motive identical to one that Gassmann had used in "Per esempio," a comic aria in *La contessina* (at the words "Dite bene"; see ex. 3.6). The melodic parallel highlights an important difference between Salieri and his teacher. Gassmann, who tended to think contrapuntally, transferred Baccellone's motive to the orchestra, creating a brief canon between the vocal line and the second violin. (It was probably similar passages that caused Burney, after hearing Gassmann's *I rovinati,* to write: "the instrumental parts were judiciously and ingeniously worked.")[6] Salieri, despite his study of Fux's *Gradus ad Parnassum* under Gassmann's guidance, thought more homophonically than his teacher. Instead of having the voice and orchestra share the same melodic material, he assigned a pert thirty-second-note motive to the orchestra, which effectively fills in the gaps in Rasoio's melody without leaving even a hint of polyphony.[7]

Within conventional melodic material and form Salieri found both comedy and drama. The opening melody moves suddenly to the parallel minor at Rasoio's reference to the marchesa's note as "brutta novità." This phrase is stated twice, both times ending with an open cadence and a melodic line encompassing a dissonant interval, the "ugly" diminished fourth (D♭-A), waiting to be resolved. The tonal resolution (coinciding with the return to the major mode) comes in the following phrase, as Rasoio tells the duke that he, Ostrogoto, must resolve the problem presented by the letter.

6. Burney, *Germany,* 116.

7. Heartz, *Viennese School,* 419, attributes some of Gassmann's polyphony to his wish to satisfy the emperor's "predilections for counterpoint," but that leaves one wondering why Salieri, who wanted to please Joseph as much as Gassmann did, consistently avoided polyphony in his operas.

EXAMPLE 6.2 *La fiera di Venezia,* act 1, "Per dovere, per rispetto," mm. 3–18

While the duke prepares to entertain two women simultaneously in different parts of Venice, Belfusto expresses his annoyance at Falsirena's flirting in an aria that, like many comic arias in Goldoni's librettos, berates all women. "Oh donne, donne a dirvela" is an unusual example of a comic-bass aria in A major. Salieri may have chosen this key because it allowed him to use high-pitched horns in A, which contribute to an effect that he saved for late in the aria. When Belfusto, declaiming the aria's text a second time (in the recapitulation), reaches the line "Ma quel di sempre fingere" [But your constant deception] he lets his imagination get the best of him. He stops singing, and the horns in A, bright and clear, tell us unmistakably that he is thinking about being cuckolded. The effect anticipates Mozart's use of horns in another aria against women: Figaro's "Aprite un po' quegl'occhi."

Belfusto's aria in A is followed, without intervening recitative, by Marchesa Calloandra's first appearance, in the F-major cavatina "Col Zeffiro e col rio." By delaying the appearance of a major female character, having her sing an entrance cavatina, and coordinating her entrance with a shift of a third, Boccherini and Salieri created much the same effect as that of Beatrice's entrance in *Il barone di Rocca Antica.* The marchesa is close to a Goldonian parte seria, but even she, in keeping with the Viennese tendency to blur the distinction between parti serie and other characters, is integrated fully into the drama; for example, she takes part in all three finales. Salieri's characterization of the marchesa does, however, involve seria gestures, such as the a-b-c-c′ melody at the beginning of "Col Zeffiro" (an extension of the a-b-b′ phrase structure) and coloratura.

The high point of the marchesa's role is her bravura aria "Vi sono sposa e amante," with concertante parts for flute and oboe, that she sings near the end of the opera. The solo winds have nothing directly to do with the fidelity of which the marchesa boasts, but their exuberance and brilliance are in keeping with her exultant state. After a forty-measure orchestral introduction in which flute and oboe play passagework as elaborate as anything in Salieri's concerto for these instruments (in the same key of C), the marchesa enters heroically, rising quickly to G and—an illustration of her constancy—sustaining it for four measures as the oboe plays figuration below (ex. 6.3). The spaciousness of the sonata form in which the aria is laid out also brings the concerto to mind. Unlike most of Salieri's early arias this one has an extensive development section, eighteen measures long.

Salieri's instrumental display is typical of Viennese opera of the impresarial decade: beautiful and dramatic effects that did not require the impresario to hire extra musicians. It is also typical of Salieri. Like Artemia's "Astrea nel cor" in *Le donne letterate,* "Vi sono sposa e amante" culminates in a long cadenza for the soloists, vocal and instrumental (horns as well as oboe and flute).

In his overture, all of whose movements reappear in the opera itself, Salieri painted musical pictures of Venetian life during fair time that complement the colorful *vedute* imagined by Boccherini in his descriptions of scenery. The overture opens with a

EXAMPLE 6.3 *La fiera di Venezia,* act 3, "Vi sono sposa e amante," mm. 53–69

∼I am your wife and lover; may you too be faithful, and I will always adore you more than myself.

EXAMPLE 6.4 *La fiera di Venezia,* overture, first movement, mm. 1–8

vigorous movement that later becomes the orchestral accompaniment to the chorus of merchants with which the drama begins. The excitement of the fair finds expression in Salieri's music, with its very fast tempo and raucous double-stops in the violins. The opening three-measure phrase, forte, is more noise than melody, consisting almost entirely of two notes repeated in alternation over tonic harmony. This phrase is followed by a more conventional, lyrical idea, piano (ex. 6.4). The impression of hectic activity becomes even more pronounced when Salieri uses his opening material, broken into smaller units, in his modulation toward the dominant.

Just as Boccherini's libretto echoes those of Goldoni, so Salieri's music echoes that with which Italian composers of the 1750s and 1760s brought Goldoni's librettos to life. The beginning of the overture recalls equally noisy music in the same key near the beginning of Fischietti's overture to *Il mercato di Malmantile.* With this musical parallel Salieri nicely prepared audiences for the Goldonian character of the opening scene.

The fair was also a time of gallantry, of sophisticated lovemaking and lavish entertainment; these are alluded to in the second movement of the overture, which anticipates the masked ball at the end of act 2 by presenting the first of its two courtly minuets. The overture's third movement consists of the forlana danced in the ballroom scene by Belfusto and Falsirena. Called for and danced by middle-class characters disguised as gondoliers, this music represents the middle and lower classes of Venetian society as clearly as the minuet represents the aristocracy. It thus serves well, socially as well as musically, as a way of leading the listener from the refined sounds of the minuet back to the noise and activity of the first movement, which returns, as the curtain rises, transformed into a chorus of merchants.

Salieri set overture and introduzione in the same key, following a procedure whose effectiveness had been demonstrated by his predecessors Fischietti (in *Il mercato*), Gassmann (in *L'amore artigiano* and *La contessina*), and Mozart (in *La finta semplice*). He did this in an effort to bring these pieces together into a single musico-dramatic unit.

The overture's first movement ends with an open cadence that marks the end of the development section, leaving listeners with a sense of incompleteness. On its return after the third movement (which also ends with an open cadence) the music of the first movement, now beginning pianissimo, sounds like the recapitulation promised but not delivered earlier in the overture. The recapitulatory function of this movement is confirmed when the first movement's second theme, originally in the dominant, is presented in the tonic. But then the chorus enters, redefining the movement as the opera's first vocal number. The sense of overlapping functions continues until the end of the introduzione, whose final cadential flourish is derived from the overture's opening gesture. The introduzione's being in the same key as the overture allows us to hear this cadence as the end of the overture as well as the end of the introduzione. The overture comes to its much-delayed completion; meanwhile, the opera is already well under way.

After attending one of the first performances of *La fiera* in the Burgtheater, on 2 February 1772, Zinzendorf wrote in his diary: "*La fiera di Venezia* bored me. There is nothing there except very pretty music."[8] Others found Salieri's opera more satisfying. According to a contemporary theatrical almanac, *La fiera* was "outstandingly set to music and delighted its audience. This opera received the loudest applause of the public, which cannot grow tired of it." The same almanac later reported: "This opera attracted large audiences for a long time on account of its excellent music and variety of theatrical effects."[9]

The impresario revived *La fiera* during November 1772, and during the subsequent Carnival it was performed eleven times, with the last two evenings of Carnival devoted to performances of Salieri's celebration of the Venetian fair.[10] By this time the opera had developed an association with Carnival that the theatrical management exploited again the following year. Carnival 1774 also ended with a performance of *La fiera*.

Within a few years of its first performance *La fiera* had spread throughout northern Europe, with performances in Mannheim, Bonn, Warsaw, and Dresden before 1776. Many further performances followed in Germany and in a few cities elsewhere: Turin,

8. au Théatre françois. *La fiera di Venezia* m'ennuya, il n'y a rien qu'une tres belle musique (Zinzendorf, 2 February 1772).

9. Den 29. [January 1772] zum erstenmale: *La fiera di Venezia*, die Worte von dem arkadischen Dichter Boccherini, und die Musik von dem Herrn Salieri, welche vortreflich gesetzt ist, und die Zuschauer entzückte. Dieses Singspiel erhielt den vollkommensten Beyfall des Publikums, welches sich nicht satt daran sehen konnte. . . . Dieses Singspiel hatte wegen der vortreflichen Musik und seines abwechselnden Schauspiels lange Zeit starken Zulauf (*Theatralalmanach von Wien, für das Jahr 1773*, 154, 157).

10. *Almanach des Theaters in Wien*.

Florence, Milan, Copenhagen, Budapest, St. Petersburg, and Moscow. *La fiera* was revived in Vienna for ten performances during 1785 and 1786.[11]

One of the few productions of the opera in Italy was in Habsburg-dominated Florence during May 1779. Salieri, on his way from Rome to Milan, supervised a dress rehearsal of the opera, whose important choral element gave rise to a temporary misunderstanding. Mosel's anecdote shows why Salieri's frequent use of chorus in opera buffa might have discouraged Italian impresarios from staging his works: "The rehearsal was in the evening; the hour in which it was to begin had struck; singers and orchestra were ready, but no chorister was yet to be seen. 'Why are they late?' asked Salieri. 'Because the shops are not yet closed' was the answer. In Italy in those days choristers were for the most part shop assistants who, without understanding anything about music, learned their parts by ear and sang to the audience's complete satisfaction."[12] A reference to this production in the *Gazzetta toscana* mentioned the opera's Ascension setting, pointed out that the Ascension fair was taking place in Venice just as the opera was being performed in Florence, and praised the scenery as well suited to the occasion and place represented in the opera.[13]

Leopold Mozart wrote of a performance of *La fiera* in Munich in 1785: "Salieri's *La fiera di Venezia,* which offended me: indeed, as far as the music is concerned, it is full of worn-out commonplace ideas, old fashioned, its harmony unnatural and empty; only the finales are still tolerable; the subject of the work, as usual, is stupid Italian childishness, past all human understanding."[14] Leopold's criticism of Salieri's thirteen-year-old opera may reflect hostility toward his son's rival in Vienna, the evolution of musical style between 1772 and 1785, and the quality of the performance he witnessed in Munich as much as or more than real weaknesses in Salieri's score.

La locandiera

Having begun his career by setting to music the first comic librettos of the dancer-turned-poet Boccherini, Salieri continued his association with inexperienced librettists by setting the first libretto by the singer-turned-poet Poggi, who derived *La locandiera* from Goldoni's play of that title.

Salieri's *La locandiera,* first performed in the Kärntnertortheater on 8 June 1773, was well received, according to an almanac: "Both [words and music] received loud and de-

11. Sartori; Angermüller, *Leben,* 2:34–36.

12. Mosel, 65.

13. *Gt,* 1779, p. 78 (article dated 15 May); quoted in Robert Lamar Weaver and Norma Wright Weaver, *A Chronology of Music in the Florentine Theater 1751–1800* (Warren, Mich., 1993), 421.

14. Leopold Mozart to his daughter, 28 November 1785, in *MBA,* 3:459.

served applause. . . . Several scenes gave most delightful pleasure."[15] The opera was "sehr approbiret," according to Khevenhüller.[16] Zinzendorf, who saw the opera for the first time on 26 September 1773, wrote in his diary: "lovely music; the duet, the next-to-last number, was charming."[17] The court theaters presented *La locandiera* thirty-four times during the theatrical year 1773. Box-office receipts for one of the later performances, which was followed on the same evening by Noverre's great tragic ballet *Les Horaces,* record a respectable take of 411 Gulden, 41 Kreuzer (fig. 6.1). The large number of performances probably reflects both the opera's popularity and the fact that, with a small orchestra, relatively undemanding vocal parts, and no chorus, it was cheaper and easier to present than many other Viennese operas.

Poggi, who also sang the role of the servant Fabrizio, introduced his characters in a sonnet at the beginning of the libretto printed for the first production, in which he interpolated the names of the characters and of the singers who created them. The poem hints at the richness of characterization and the cleverness of plot that make Goldoni's *La locandiera* one of his finest plays.

Vi presento, Signori, una ragazza	
Etrusca di nazione, e locandiera	
Che ha spirto sollevato, ed ha maniera	
Rara per lusingar; ma non è pazza . . .	*Mirandolina Locandiera*
	La Sig. Costanza Baglioni
Un cavaliere strano, che strapazza	
Il sesso feminin con brusca cera;	
Ma quando in esso Amor alza bandiera	
Resta sconfitto e quasi quasi impazza . . .	*Il Cavalier di Ripafratta*
	Il Sig. Dom. Guardassoni
Un conte ricco tutto splendidezza . . .	*Il Conte d'Albafiorita*
	Il Sig. Fran. Guerrieri
Un povero geloso che singhiozza . . .	*Fabbrizio Cameriere della locanda*
	Il Sig. Dom. Poggi
Una servetta tutta compitezza . . .	*Lena Serva*
	La Sig. Rosa Baglioni
Un ridicol marchese che si strozza	
Da tanto predicar la sua grandezza;	
Ma che colla miseria sempre cozza . . .	*Il Marchese di Forlipopoli*
	Il Sig. Virginio Bondicchi

15. Beydes fand allgemeinen verdienten Beyfall. . . . Verschiedene Scenen machten gar ein entzückendes Vergnügen (*Theatralalmanach von Wien, für das Jahr 1774,* 144–45).

16. Khevenhüller, 7:176 (15 July 1773).

17. Au Theatre. On donna la *Locandiera.* belle musique, l'avant dernier duo est charmant (Zinzendorf, 26 September 1773).

Nro. 224

Theatre près de la Cour.

Jeudi	27	Janvier	1774

La Locandiera = gli Orazzi, ed i Curiazzi

Gallerie.	Billets.	126	à 1. fl. 25. kr.	178 | 30
Parterre.	detto	210	à - 24. kr.	84 | —
3me. Etage.	detto.	59	a - 40. kr	39 | 20
4me. Etage.	detto.	98	à - 20. kr.	32 | 40
Officiers de la Garn.	detto.	1	à - 45. kr.	— | 45
			En Caiſſe.	335 - 13
pour la petite Poste, et à la Garde.				4 - 6
			Reſte.	331 - 7
Loges au Rez-de-chauſſeé.		5	á 4. fl. 14. kr.	21 | 10
detto au 1re. Etage.		—	á 4. fl. 14. kr.	— | —
detto au 2de. Etage.		2	à 4. fl. 14. kr.	8 | 28
detto au 3me. Etage.		7	à 3. fl. - -	21 | —
Chaiſſes fermeés.		17	à 1. fl. 42. kr.	28 | 54
Confiturier.		—	—	1 | —
			Somme	
			De plus	
Pour le jeu.				— | —
Abonnements.				— | —
			Total.	411 - 41

Pour la Commedie, & Ballets.

Comparſes. 72 -	Menuſiers. —	Maneuvres. 10 —

Officier de la Garde.	Commiſſaire.
Mr. de Pirzel dans julaÿ	Mr. de Spaun

Commiſſaire du feu Groÿ.

Reodint Brabbeé

ORSZÁGO... P. szekció 262

Jean Ligeri Caissier

Gorropek Controleur.

FIGURE 6.1 Box-office receipts for a performance of *La locandiera* in the Burgtheater on 27 January 1774. Keglevich papers. (Courtesy of National Archives of Hungary, Budapest.)

[Gentlemen, let me introduce a girl, Etruscan [i.e., Tuscan] by birth, an innkeeper who is high-spirited and has an unusual talent for enticement, but she is no fool . . . a strange cavalier who mistreats the female sex with angry looks, but when Love raises his banner in him, he is defeated and almost goes mad . . . a rich count, all generosity . . . and a poor jealous man who sobs . . . a well-mannered maidservant . . . a comical marquis who strains his voice to extol his own greatness, but is always impoverished.]

Poggi's introductions reveal the most important change he made in Goldoni's plot: he omitted the two traveling actresses and the several scenes in which they take part. Another change, and one that is not entirely successful, is the addition of the role of the maid Lena, whom Poggi introduced presumably because he wanted to have more than one female role. But Poggi, having invented Lena, did not invent much of interest for her to do or say.

The action of Salieri's opera, like that of Goldoni's play, revolves around Mirandolina, the charming innkeeper who fends off amorous noblemen, teases her faithful servant and suitor Fabrizio, and teaches the misogynist Cavaliere di Ripafratta a lesson about love that he will never forget. The opera has no parti serie. All six characters take part in all three finales, with the exception of Lena, absent from the finale of act 1. Poggi and Salieri made parti buffe out of Fabrizio, the marchese (both basses), the count (tenor), and Lena (soprano). Mirandolina and the cavaliere resemble a pair of Goldonian parti di mezzo carattere except that, unlike most mezzo-carattere pairs, they do not end up engaged to be married.

The music that Salieri wrote for his parti buffe has much in common with music written for comic characters by Gassmann and his Italian contemporaries. Lena's gentle aria near the beginning of the score, labeled Tempo di minuetto, is in the tradition of minuet arias assigned to female parti buffe by Fischietti, Gassmann, Mozart, and Salieri himself. Doubtless Rosa Baglioni sang many minuet arias in her career; but few could have featured more charming tunes than this one (ex. 6.5). Fabrizio's aria "Tutti dicon che la moglie" exemplifies, in its long text, Goldonian comic generalization about the opposite sex; but instead of attacking women, like Belfusto in "Oh donne, donne a dirvela" in *La fiera di Venezia,* Fabrizio defends them (more specifically, wives) against such attacks, thus anticipating Don Alfonso's "Tutti accusan le donne" in *Così fan tutte:*

Tutti dicon che la moglie
  È una brutta malatia;
  Ma però come la sia,
  Non mi so capacitar.
Molti dicon: ella è un fuoco
  Che l'uom strugge a poco a poco;
  Ma poi giusto questi tali

Fanno cento memoriali
Per potersi a una tal fiamma
Un tantino riscaldar. . . .

[Everybody says that a wife is a dread disease; but I cannot understand how this could be. Many say: she is a fire that burns a man little by little; but these same men try a hundred times to warm themselves a bit at such a flame.]

In his through-composed setting, Salieri developed each of Poggi's comic metaphors, beginning with the wife as fire that slowly consumes her husband, which he cleverly depicted with syncopations and suspensions in descending sequence (ex. 6.6).

EXAMPLE 6.5 *La locandiera,* act 1, "Dall'amor com' ognun dice," mm. 9–16 (A-Wn, Mus. Hs. 16179)

It is true, as everyone says, that jealousy is born of love

EXAMPLE 6.6 *La locandiera,* act 1, "Tutti dicon che la moglie," mm. 21–25

Many say: she is a fire that destroys a man little by little

Also characteristic of Goldonian parti buffe is the pair of short songs—canzoni—that Poggi and Salieri assigned to Fabrizio and Mirandolina and that serve, like the pairs of canzoni in *Il mercato di Malmantile* and *La buona figliuola,* as a musical conversation between these characters. In act 2, scene 4, according to Poggi's stage directions, Fabrizio "enters singing." He begins the conversation with an ultimatum to Mirandolina, whose presence on stage he pretends not to notice: she must choose between him and other men. He frames his statement in the form of an ottava, the poem of eight endecasillabi that Boccherini and Salieri used in the first finale of *Le donne letterate.*

Salieri's setting (like that of the ottava in *Le donne,* ex. 4.8) is in 6/8 meter and has the sound of a folk song, with three-measure phrases that end on weak beats and a simple chordal accompaniment (ex. 6.7). Salieri set the first four lines and the last four to the same melody in the same key; this strophic form contributes to the aria's folklike effect. After some simple recitative Mirandolina responds by improvising her own ottava to the same music, transposed from D major to E♭.

Mirandolina and Fabrizio sing the opera's only love duet. In keeping with the character of their relationship, "Presto spicciatevi" is comic. The innkeeper and her servant

EXAMPLE 6.7 *La locandiera,* act 2, "Padrona bella," mm. 10–21

(Continued on next page)

EXAMPLE 6.7 *(continued)*

~Mistress fair, so as to suffer no longer and for my own good I want it so: I want to love you as much as I can, but I do not want to love you in company.

flirt in much the same style as Susanna and the count in Mozart's *Figaro* ("Crudel, perché finora"): Mirandolina teases Fabrizio with repeated questions, to the last of which he says "yes" when he should say "no" (ex. 6.8).[18] One can understand how this duet charmed Zinzendorf.

From Mirandolina's being paired with Fabrizio, unambiguously a parte buffa, one might assume that she too is a parte buffa; and much of her music is indeed comic. "Figliuola del capriccio," for example, is a cheerful buffo aria with some playful sexual innuendo. Fabrizio, trying to guess the skill of which she is proudest, whispers an an-

EXAMPLE 6.8 *La locandiera,* act 3, "Presto spicciatevi," mm. 126–35

(Continued on next page)

18. Della Croce/Blanchetti, 432; Leopold Kantner, "Antonio Salieri rivale o modello di Mozart?" in *Mozart e i musicisti italiani del suo tempo,* ed. Annalisa Bini (Lucca, 1994), 9–19.

EXAMPLE 6.8 *(continued)*

⁓MIRANDOLINA: But will you be faithful? FABRIZIO: Mistress, yes. MIRANDOLINA: Will you be constant? FABRIZIO: Mistress, yes. MIRANDOLINA: And loving? FABRIZIO: Mistress, yes. MIRANDOLINA: Will you be jealous? FABRIZIO: Mistress, yes. MIRANDOLINA: Will you be jealous? FABRIZIO: Mistress, no.

swer in her ear (ex. 6.9). The violas represent his whispering with a motive similar to one that Gassmann had assigned to the violas in *La contessina* to represent communication between characters on stage that is unheard by the audience: the countess's shaking her head ("Per esempio," ex. 3.6). But Mirandolina's personality has a more serious side. Poggi and Salieri depicted her colorfully in "Arrogante, chi credi ch'io sia?" which she sings when Fabrizio accuses her of being unfaithful:

Arrogante, chi credi ch'io sia?
Son ragazza onorata e modesta;
Se ti gira, ti frulla la testa,
Presto vanne lontano di qui.

EXAMPLE 6.9 *La locandiera,* act 1, "Figliuola del capriccio," mm. 41–46

(Continued on next page)

EXAMPLE 6.9 *La locandiera,* act 1, "Figliuola del capriccio," mm. 41–46

~I have it . . . I have it . . . you guess . . . (*Fabrizio whispers in her ear*) No . . .

The opening melody, first presented by horns and oboes, fortissimo, in unison with the violins, also fortissimo, is a march tune of the kind normally sung by male parti buffe (ex. 6.10). Both melody and orchestration—as well as the assigning of such music to a female character—recall "Tre città rinomate," Artemia's boastful aria in *Le donne letterate* (see ex. 4.16). But later the melodramatic words "mi divora la rabbia" in-

EXAMPLE 6.10 *La locandiera,* act 2, "Arrogante, chi credi ch'io sia?" mm. 1–6

EXAMPLE 6.11 *La locandiera*, act 2, "Arrogante, chi credi ch'io sia?" mm. 71–74

spired Salieri to a Gluckian evocation of horror: a shift to the minor mode, sudden pianissimo, dissonant suspensions, and tremolos over a dominant pedal (ex. 6.11). Just as suddenly, when he reached Mirandolina's comic last line, Salieri turned to a cheerful gavotte, with the vocal line lightly accompanied by strings alone, as befits a female parte buffa more than a male one (ex. 6.12).

The aria's last three words had an important effect on its form. "Ti basti così" demands strong musical closure; Salieri responded by accentuating the end of the expo-

EXAMPLE 6.12 *La locandiera*, act 2, "Arrogante, chi credi ch'io sia?" mm. 93–100

sition with a series of strong cadences. The only way that he could top those cadences later in the aria was with a coda, and indeed "Arrogante" ends with an impressive coda of twenty-six measures.

The cavaliere, like Mirandolina, expresses the passion and anger of an opera seria hero but also exploits the conventions of the buffo caricato. Mirandolina's attempt to charm him into falling in love succeeds, and he expresses his confusion in an aria of indecision, "Son confuso, sto perplesso," in which he imagines that he is hearing the contradictory advice of Love and Honor. His indecision is conveyed tonally by a series of unexpected modulations. The exposition moves from I to V, but instead of staying in V, modulation continues back to I and on to vi and IV. This turn to the subdominant, E♭, is dramatically significant because it coincides with the cavaliere's imagining that Honor is addressing him: "Sconsigliato bada a te" [Heedless man, be careful]. (In Pergolesi's *La serva padrona* Uberto imagined that he heard similar advice: "Uberto, pensa a te.") The association between the key of E♭ and the aria of indecision was evidently so strong that Salieri needed only to modulate unexpectedly to E♭ to exploit that association.

One of the cavaliere's finest moments is his scene at the beginning of act 2, when, alone on stage, he expresses his feelings of uncertainty and confusion.[19] The scena consists of a lyrical passage, Larghetto, "Vo pensando e ripensando," followed by accompanied recitative, and then a return to the Primo tempo but with new musical material. The scena is the opera's first number in E♭. This is yet another example of Salieri, like Gassmann and his Italian contemporaries, saving that key for an important moment relatively far from the beginning of an opera. Listeners do not need perfect pitch to recognize the key. The opening chords, to which the violins, playing double-stops, contribute the resonant sound of the open G string, have the warm, solemn sonority characteristic of E♭ (ex. 6.13).

In the cavaliere's elegant opening melody, the meandering coloratura and the surprising tonicization of E♭ after the modulation to the dominant both nicely reflect the cavaliere's uncertainty. The predominance of two-measure phrases reminds one that the cavaliere is a parte di mezzo carattere (not a parte seria), while the coloratura conveys his nobility as well as his wavering mental state.

The coloratura, transferred to the orchestra, becomes the main feature of the accompaniment in the recitative, in which the cavaliere wistfully thinks of the peace that he enjoyed before he met Mirandolina. The return to the Primo tempo coincides with a fleeting reference to C minor; syncopations, dissonant suspensions, and a lyrical three-measure phrase in the vocal line coincide with a lovely modulation back to E♭, as the

19. The cavaliere's scena is the object of more detailed discussion in James Webster, "Understanding Opera Buffa: Analysis = Interpretation," in *Opera Buffa in Mozart's Vienna,* ed. Mary Hunter and James Webster (Cambridge, 1997), 340–77.

EXAMPLE 6.13 *La locandiera,* act 2, "Vo pensando e ripensando," mm. 11–23

↝I keep thinking and rethinking, between yes and no. What should I do, I ask myself, but cannot decide.

cavaliere begs Love to stay hidden deep in his heart (ex. 6.14). The deceptive cadence in E♭ and subsequent tonicization of B♭ were later to appear in a solemn tenor aria in Salieri's *La passione di Gesù Cristo* (1777; ex. 6.15), the parallel suggesting that Salieri wanted audiences to take the cavaliere's feelings completely seriously.

This beautiful scena was inspired in part by the musical and dramatic talents of the

EXAMPLE 6.14 *La locandiera,* act 2, "Vo pensando e ripensando, mm. 77–87

(*Continued on next page*)

singer for whom it was written, Domenico Guardasoni, who sang both tenor and bass roles in Vienna during 1772 and 1773. (His lower register may well have encouraged Salieri to write several important low notes in the passage quoted in ex. 6.14.) In the early 1780s he gave up his career as a singer and became impresario of the Italian opera troupe in Prague. In this capacity he commissioned and oversaw the production of Mozart's *Don Giovanni* and (after failing to persuade Salieri to compose an opera for the coronation of Leopold II in 1791) *La clemenza di Tito.*

Salieri's characters interact in three entertaining finales that demonstrate the skill with which the twenty-three-year-old composer handled this most challenging of opera buffa techniques. All three finales are full of dialogue rapidly declaimed over repeated orchestral figures—the "Bewegung des Orchesters" of which Salieri wrote in his ac-

EXAMPLE 6.14 (*continued*)

(*Continued on next page*)

count of the composition of *Le donne letterate.* Limiting himself to the tonic and a few closely related keys (with none of the sudden shifts up or down a third that would become so common by the end of the decade), Salieri laid out his finales in simple, easily followed tonal plans.

Among the best moments in these finales are the climactic tutti passages, in which Salieri could indulge his fondness for choral writing in an opera without choruses by massing his soloists in homophonic blocks of sound. The finale of act 1 ends with a drinking song, "Sì, sì, beviamo," in the form of a vaudeville. The previous section, 3/8 Allegro, leads into the vaudeville, 3/4 Allegro, without a break—a fine, dramatic effect. Rushing violin figuration in sixteenth notes gives the beautiful tutti that follows something of the effect of festive Viennese church music (ex. 6.16).

The orchestra in *La locandiera* is the smallest that Salieri used in any of his operas: it

EXAMPLE 6.14 (*continued*)

But if you, Love, are the reason for my suffering, hide yourself in my heart, and do not let yourself be seen.

consists of oboes, bassoons, horns, and strings—the same orchestra that Gassmann had used in *La contessina.* Compared to Salieri's previous opera, *La secchia rapita, La locandiera* sounds bare. Salieri achieved some interesting orchestrational effects nevertheless. The passage in example 6.14 is quoted in full score to show how expressive and colorful Salieri's orchestration can be even when it uses a small orchestra. The instruments enter gradually, starting with first violins, violas, and horns, all piano, accompanying the cavaliere, who sings sotto voce. Bassoons, cellos, and basses enter next, then second violins. Turbulent syncopations shift suddenly from piano to pianissimo at the word "nasconditi." Salieri saved the oboes for the descending sequence at the words "e non ti palesar" where oboe II, sustaining E♭, adds harmonic as well as timbral piquancy. There is colorful writing for horns in the overture's first movement (in sonata-rondo form). The rondo theme, with attractive open fifths, is played three times: on its first

EXAMPLE 6.15 *La passione di Gesù Cristo,* pt. 1, "Tu nel duol felice sei," mm. 57–60 (vocal score, ed. Rudolf Kelber [Stuttgart, 1993])

(Cantabile)
Pietro
su le lab - bra di co - le - i che nel se - no un Dio por - tò.
p

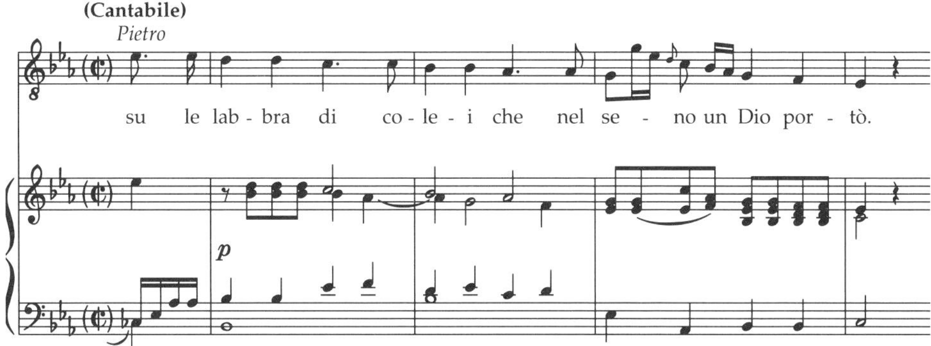

~On the lips of the woman who carried a god in her womb

EXAMPLE 6.16 *La locandiera,* act 1, finale, mm. 189–200

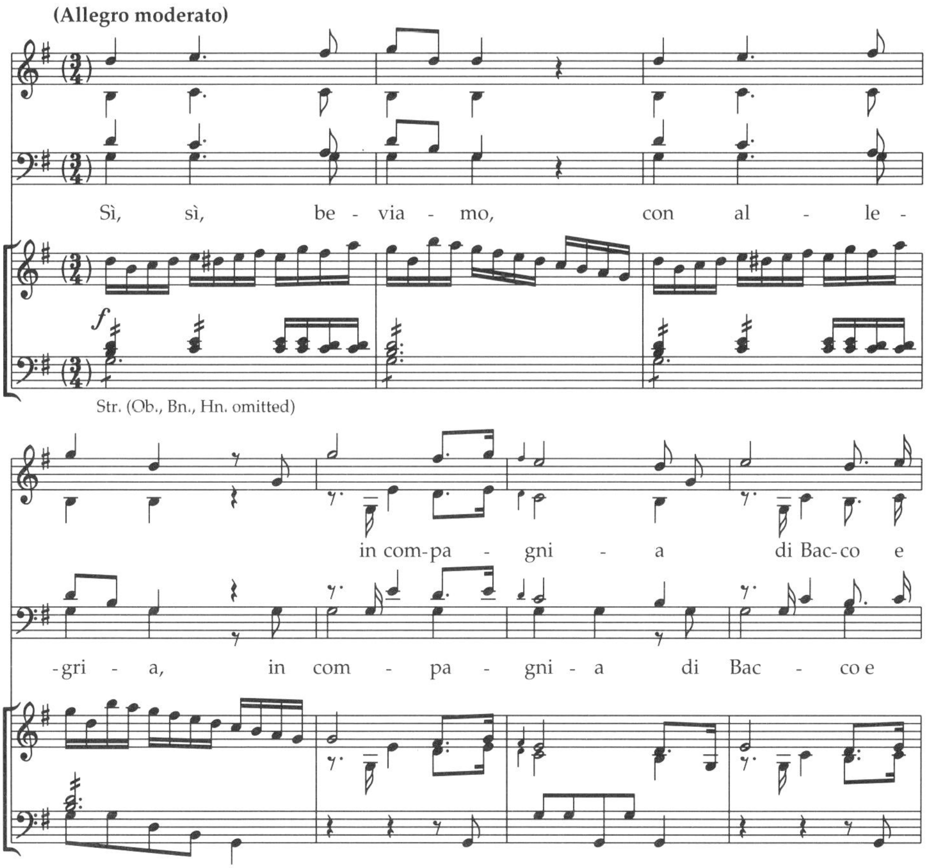
(Allegro moderato)
Sì, sì, be - via - mo, con al - le -
f
Str. (Ob., Bn., Hn. omitted)
in com-pa - gni - a di Bac-co e
-gri - a, in com - pa - gni - a di Bac - co e

(*Continued on next page*)

EXAMPLE 6.16 (*continued*)

~Yes, let us drink with joy, full of passion, in the company of Bacchus and Venus.

EXAMPLE 6.17 *La locandiera,* overture, first movement, 1–13

two appearances by horns alternating with strings (ex. 6.17); on its final appearance by full orchestra.

Salieri made good use of a device that Gassmann had also used in his comic operas: muting an instrument that was rarely muted in the eighteenth century, in this case the horn. In the count's aria "Io quand'ero ragazzo innocente" (an example, very unusual in Salieri's early comic operas, of a vocal rondo) the orchestra is arranged in two ensembles that play in alternation. One consists of muted horns, second violins and violas (both divisi, con sordini), and bass; the other consists of the same instruments as the first ensemble (but the horns without mutes), together with oboes, bassoons, and first violins (divisi, without mutes). The one ensemble sounds like a distant echo of the other.

La calamita de' cuori

More than a year separated the premiere of *La locandiera* from that of Salieri's next opera. *La calamita de' cuori* (the accent frequently added to the word *calamita*—which means magnet, not calamity—is spurious) was first performed in the Kärntnertortheater on 11 October 1774. The gap may have something to do with the many important events that occurred in Salieri's life during 1774: Gassmann's death, Salieri's appointment to the position of Kammer-Kompositor, and his courtship of Therese Helferstorfer, whom he married on 10 October 1774, the day before the premiere of *La calamita de' cuori.*

First set to music by Galuppi and performed in Venice during Carnival 1753, Goldoni's *La calamita de' cuori* takes its title from its principal character, called "the magnet of hearts" because, like Falsirena and Mirandolina, she can charm any man. Beautiful Bellarosa (high coloratura soprano) attracts, flirts with, and rejects ardent Armidoro (tenor), boastful and violent Saracca (bass), and stingy Pignone (bass), causing Armidoro and Saracca to abandon and then, at the end of the opera, to return to their original partners, Albina and Belinda (sopranos). Bellarosa finally settles for the charming Giacinto (tenor).

The action takes place in Palermo (according to Goldoni's original libretto, but there is no indication of geographical setting in the libretto printed for the first production of Salieri's opera). The historical period to which the action belongs is not clear. The first scene of act 1, set in a "temple dedicated to Love, with a statue of Cupid and burning altar" before which Bellarosa's admirers bow in supplication, suggests Greek or Roman antiquity. But the ballroom in act 2, where Goldoni called for minuets to be played and danced, is redolent of the eighteenth century. In the finale of act 1, when various characters try to guess where Bellarosa was born, the towns they mention are not Greco-Roman but Italian.

Like the many librettos by Goldoni that Gassmann set to music in Vienna during the impresarial decade, *La calamita* had to be revised before Salieri set it to music; but the revision, which involved the replacement of several aria texts but left Goldoni's blank verse almost completely intact, was a relatively light one. A puzzling note in a contemporary theatrical almanac attributes the revision to several authors: "The Marquis of xxx, Abbé Casti, Domenikus Poggi, Herr Pocherini, and Herr Salieri were supposed to have improved and patched up the poetry of Goldoni's opera; but the book was still unable to please."[20] Why such a minor revision required so many hands is unknown. If Giambattista Casti really worked with Salieri in the preparation of *La calamita,* it marks

20. *Historisch-Kritische Theaterchronik* 11 (29 October 1774): 166–67; quoted in Angermüller, *Leben,* 2:41.

the beginning of a collaboration that would, during the 1780s and early 1790s, produce four operas.

The lack of thorough revision of a libretto first performed in 1752 resulted in an opera that by the standards of 1774 is rather old fashioned, with fewer ensembles and much shorter, simpler finales than in many operas written during the 1770s, including some of Salieri's. *La calamita* is unusual among Salieri's comedies in having characters who are clearly recognizable as parti serie. The absence of Armidoro and Albina from the finales helps to preserve their dignity and nobility, which they express in elegant arias. Armidoro's "Sperar il caro porto" is completely serious in its words (a two-quatrain poem, the opening line of which recalls that of "Sperai vicino il lido" in Metastasio's *Demofoonte*) and its music (an opening melody with three- and four-measure phrases in a-b-b′ form and, later in the aria, coloratura). In his annotations Salieri explained how a serious aria could enhance a comic opera: "The aria 'Sperar il caro porto' . . . is rather serious and well suited to the role, the character being rather serious or at least not comic; moreover this number is dedicated to the voice, and to vocal agility, which results in a contrast of effect in the context of numbers in parlante style."

Courtship and gallantry pervade the libretto of *La calamita,* and Salieri's music conveys these qualities. The introduzione, in which Bellarosa's admirers ask Cupid to help them gain her hand, is an Andantino in triple meter. Parallel thirds, expressive appoggiaturas, the graceful triplet on the downbeat of measure 2—all these features of the *style galant* help to announce the opera's character (ex. 6.18); Armidoro's serenade in act 2 and the minuets in the ballroom scene contribute further to this important element of the drama.

Salieri's distribution of keys in *La calamita* is much the same as that of his earlier op-

EXAMPLE 6.18 *La calamita de' cuori,* act 1, introduzione, mm. 1–10 (A-Wn, Mus. Hs. 16508)

eras and those of his teacher. His choice of D major for Saracca's aria "Tagliar braccia? Bagatelle" and Pignone's "Zitto, che non si senta" and A major for Albina's arias "Son fuori di me" and "Dolce rimedio del core" reflect the tendency of opera buffa composers in the 1750s and 1760s to use D for bass arias and A for soprano arias. His avoidance of E♭ until Armidoro's "Sperar il caro porto" in the ninth scene of act 1 is consistent with the careful handling of that key that one finds in many earlier opere buffe. The appearance of E♭ here (as in the cavaliere's scena at the beginning of act 2 of *La locandiera*) helps audiences notice the "contrast of effect" that Salieri intended this number to produce.

La calamita is one of three richly orchestrated comic operas (the others being *La fiera di Venezia* and *La secchia rapita*) that alternate in Salieri's early output with less colorful scores (*Il barone di Rocca Antica, La locandiera,* and *La finta scema*). Salieri displayed his big orchestra in the overture, which he scored for trumpets, horns, flutes, oboes, bassoons, and strings. In combining rich orchestration, one-movement form, and the key of C Salieri recaptured some of brilliance of his overture to *La secchia rapita.* Of the overture to *La calamita* he wrote in his autograph: "The sinfonia has the merit of at least not being contrary to the genre of the opera."

Even more elaborately scored is the scene in act 2 in which Armidoro serenades Bellarosa. Goldoni's stage directions (which are reproduced word for word in the libretto printed for the production of Salieri's opera) call for a "spacious place in which one sees a moving platform, illuminated, with instrumental musicians and singers who are to perform the serenade organized by Armidoro. On one side Bellarosa's house, with a practicable balcony. At the appearance of the platform one hears a merry sinfonia, during which Bellarosa appears on the balcony."[21]

Salieri, who ignored Boccherini's request for onstage musicians in the ballroom scene in *La fiera di Venezia,* followed Goldoni's instructions more closely. He scored the sinfonia and the serenade that follows for two orchestras: a pit orchestra of oboes, trumpets, and strings and a stage orchestra of flutes, bassoons, horns, and strings (for the beginning of the serenade as laid out in Salieri's autograph score see fig. 6.2). These ensembles accompany Goldoni's beautiful love poetry—

Bell'aure che liete
D'intorno spirate,
La fiamma svelate
Che m'arde nel cor.

[Lovely breezes that happily blow about me, reveal the flame that burns in my heart.]

21. Notte. Luogo spazioso, in cui vedesi una macchina illuminata, con suonatori e musici, per eseguire la serenata ordinata da Armidoro; da un lato la casa di Bellarosa con terrazzino praticabile. All'apparir della macchina s'ode un'allegra sinfonia, e frattanto sul terrazzina comparisce BELLAROSA (Goldoni, *La calamita de' cuori,* act 2, sc. 6).

FIGURE 6.2 *La calamita de' cuori,* act 2, beginning of the sinfonia for two orchestras. Autograph. Musiksammlung, Österreichische Nationalbibliothek, Vienna.

—with solos for some of the instruments on stage: flute (accompanied by pizzicato strings), cello, and bassoon. Salieri's sinfonia and serenade for two orchestras may have reminded his patron Joseph II of a scene in Hasse's *Alcide al bivio* in which an onstage band of flutes, oboes, English horns, bassoons, and horns is accompanied in the pit by oboes, flutes, and muted strings.

One of the most unusual instrumental effects in this scene is Salieri's use of trumpets crooked in B♭. Viennese composers of the 1770s and 1780s called for trumpets in B♭ much more rarely than trumpets in C or D, which have a higher, more brilliant sound. Mozart, for example, used trumpets in B♭ in none of the operas that he wrote between *Lucio Silla* and *Così fan tutte.*[22] (On the other hand, he called quite frequently for trumpets in E♭, which Salieri rarely if ever used.) Salieri seems to have liked the mellow sonority of trumpets in B♭, for he used them often from 1774 on. They help to give not only *La calamita* but also *Europa riconosciuta, Semiramide, Il ricco d'un giorno,* and several of the operas that followed a sound that we may be able to recognize, in the context of Viennese opera, as distinctively Salierian.

All that was needed to produce a trumpet in B♭ was a crook especially designed for this purpose. Salieri may have had two such crooks made in preparation for the production of *La calamita de' cuori.* In the Keglevich papers is a receipt, signed by Salieri, for 9 Gulden, of which 6 were "for the rental of a violone [i.e., double bass] which served for the performance of the second orchestra of the serenade" (presumably the onstage orchestra that participated in the sinfonia preceding Armidoro's serenade and that accompanied the serenade itself) and 3 were "for 2 trumpet pieces [*pezzi di tromba*] ordered expressly for the above opera" (fig. 6.3). Since the opera contains no pieces of trumpet music to which the receipt might refer, these "trumpet pieces" were almost certainly the crooks that allowed two trumpeters to take part in the sinfonia and serenade in B♭.[23]

The rich orchestration of *La calamita* and its use of chorus added to the cost of the production, which is documented more fully than that of Salieri's other early operas. Several receipts record payments to Anton Ignaz Ulbrich, "k. k. Hofmusicus," for performance of the choruses. The impresarios had no regular chorus in their opera buffa troupe; when they needed one, Ulbrich served as choral director, organizing, rehearsing, and paying the chorus with money that he received from the theater management.[24] His bills for services rendered during October 1774, the month in which *La calamita* was first performed, and the following month are preserved in the Keglevich

22. On the rarity of trumpets in B♭ in Viennese instrumental music before 1790 see Landon, *Haydn,* 3:531–32.

23. MOL, P 421 (Keglevich Cs.) V/15, fol. 213. I am grateful to Bruce Alan Brown for his interpretation of this document.

24. Ulbrich had prepared the chorus for court theater productions since Durazzo's administration; see Brown, *Gluck,* 91.

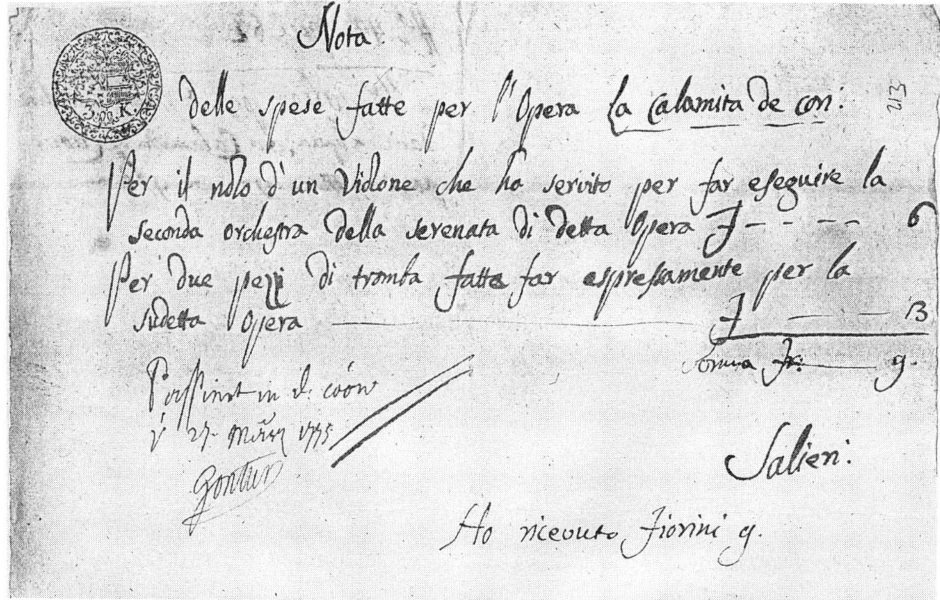

Nota

delle spese fatte per l'Opera La calamita de cori:

Per il nolo d'un Violone che ha servito per far eseguire la seconda orchestra della serenata di detta Opera f. – – – 6

Per due pezzi di tromba fatta far espressamente per la sudetta Opera f. – – 3

Somma f. 9.

Salieri:

Ho ricevuto fiorini 9.

FIGURE 6.3 Receipt signed by Salieri for 9 Gulden, expense incurred in preparation for *La calamita de' cuori.* Keglevich papers. (Courtesy of National Archives of Hungary, Budapest.)

papers.[25] The chorus consisted of twenty singers: ten women and ten men. It attended two rehearsals, on 7 and 10 October, for which it received 40 Gulden in payment (1 Gulden per singer for each rehearsal—of which Ulbrich presumably kept some portion for himself). For its participation in the premiere on 11 October and subsequent performances (six during October, six more in November) the chorus received 35 Gulden per performance: 20 Gulden for the women (2 Gulden each) and 15 Gulden for the men (1 Gulden, 30 Kreuzer each).[26]

The dress rehearsal for *La calamita* took place on 10 October 1774, Salieri's wedding day. The level of hectic activity, like that preceding the premiere of Salieri's *Le donne letterate* four years earlier, seems to have risen to the point where distinctions between composer/music director and poet/stage director (presumably Boccherini) were ignored. The *Historisch-Kritische Theaterchronik* reported: "An unusual circumstance is to be noted, that during the last rehearsal the music director supervised the scenery and the acting on stage, while the theatrical poet was in the orchestra distributing the music."[27]

25. MOL, P 421 (Keglevich Cs.) V/17, fol. 410 (October 1774); V/16, fol. 304 (November 1774).

26. Ulbrich's chorus was paid at the same rate for rehearsals and performances of Tobias Philipp von Gebler's *Thamos König in Ägypten* (the choruses in which may have been those composed for this play by Mozart), performed in Vienna in April 1774; see Edge, "Mozart's Viennese Orchestras," 68–71. It is not clear why the women received more than the men. Edge suggests that the men were paid less because "they had less to do" in the choruses of *Thamos,* but such an explanation cannot be applied to *La calamita de' cuori,* in which male and female choristers participated equally.

27. *Historisch-Kritische Theaterchronik* 11 (29 October 1774): 166–67; quoted in Angermüller, *Leben,* 2:41.

La calamita aroused considerable interest among Viennese opera lovers. According to a record of box-office receipts for the first performance, the theater management sold 855 seats and forty-seven boxes, for a take of 639 Gulden, 23 Kreuzer.[28] Without knowing how many people sat in each box we cannot know how many people witnessed the premiere of Salieri's opera; but the unusually large take suggests that this was a large audience, especially for an Italian opera (operas tended to attract smaller audiences than German plays). The audience was divided in its opinion, according to the journal cited above: "Of the music some connoisseurs and music lovers wish to assert that it is artful, beautiful, harmonious, and does great honor to Herr Salieri. The plot is too childish, others asserted, and the music, while beautiful, is too serious for the book."

Favorable opinion prevailed, at least in the short term. A document in the Keglevich papers records the daily receipts for all performances between 1 October and 22 October 1774 (fig. 6.4). It shows that *La calamita,* performed three more times during this period, earned more income than any spectacle except Noverre's *Les Horaces.*

The Ballroom Scenes in *La calamita de' cuori* and *La fiera di Venezia*

Many of Goldoni's librettos contain ballroom scenes, which reflect the function of opera buffa, especially in Venice, as entertainment during Carnival and the Ascension fair. With choruses in praise of wine and descriptions of scenery that call for rooms brightly lit and festively decorated, Goldoni's opere buffe convey a sense of celebration and revelry. Specifically reminiscent of Carnival are the many disguises that Goldoni's characters take on. The balls themselves, with masks, dance music, and dancing on stage, contributed to the carnival-like atmosphere of Goldoni's librettos and of the festive seasons for which many of them were originally intended.

Although Goldoni normally placed his ballroom scene at the end of an act, he did not fully integrate the ball into the finale with which the act often ends. The finale that coincides with a ballroom scene does not typically depict the activity of the ball in all its complexity. Goldoni's finales are primarily ensembles of conversation: of verbal rather than physical interaction. Many of them are witty, often very dramatic and exciting dialogues in which there is very little physical activity, and the poet needed to supply few if any stage directions.[29] The dancing, the mingling, the entrances and exits characteristic

28. MOL, P 421 (Keglevich Cs.) V/19, fol. 297.

29. In the first-act finale of *La buona figliuola,* for example, the action is largely limited to the arrival on stage of each character: the scene begins with Sandrina and Paoluccia; Cecchina arrives at the beginning of the finale, then Mengotto, then finally the marchese. Aside from these arrivals, the drama comes almost entirely from the contrast of different personalities and the rapidly changing mental states of Mengotto and the marchese, both of whom are turned against Cecchina by Sandrina and Paoluccia. In the first-act finale of *La calamita de' cuori* Bellarosa announces she will give her hand to whoever guesses her native city. For the game that follows Goldoni provided no stage directions. None is needed; the finale requires no physical action but only witty verbal interaction among the characters.

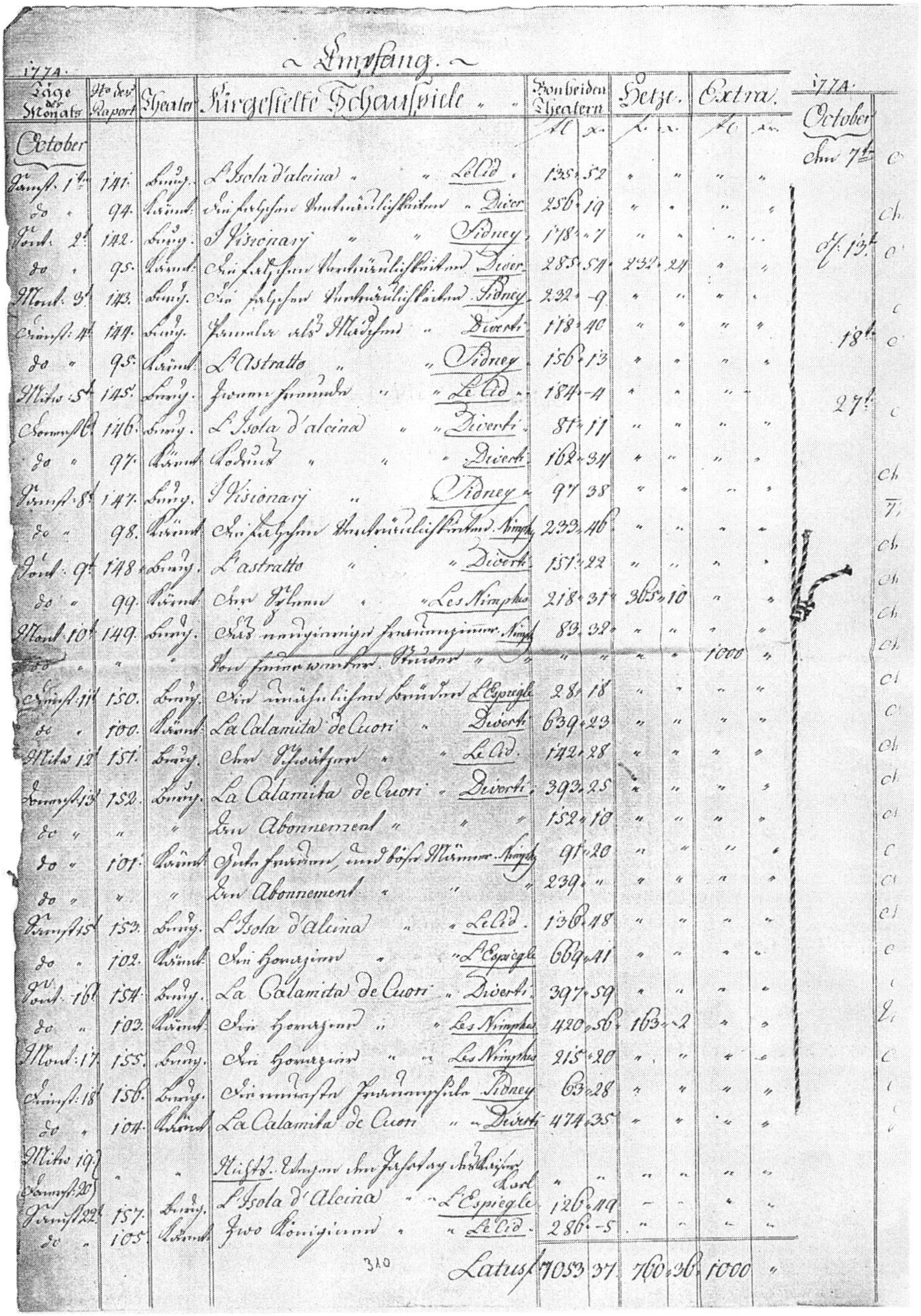

FIGURE 6.4 Record of daily income, 1–22 October 1774, showing that *La calamita de' cuori* brought in more money than any spectacle except Noverre's ballet *Les Horaces.* Keglevich papers. (Courtesy of National Archives of Hungary, Budapest.)

of a ball are to some extent incompatible with the conversational Goldonian finale.

By placing the ball at the end of act 3, which normally lacks a fully developed finale, Goldoni avoided the problem of integrating the ball into the finale. *La conversazione* (of which Giuseppe Scolari's setting, first performed in Venice in 1758, reached Vienna in 1763) ends with a ball. Stage directions for the *scena ultima* call for a "Salone illuminato per la festa di ballo." During several previous scenes various characters look forward to the ball, discussing their costumes and, in a duet, learning how to dance the minuet. The scena ultima begins with dance, according to Goldoni's stage directions: "Various minuets are danced, and other dances if desired; after which the opera is concluded with the following CORO." The ensemble that follows begins "And here our *conversazione* [i.e., party] will end for this evening." The dancing and the ensemble are completely separate; Goldoni made no attempt to integrate the action of the ball within the opera's last vocal number. The dancing serves as a nonverbal interlude between dialogue in recitative and the final ensemble.

La calamita de' cuori has a ballroom scene in act 2, which ends with a finale. But the finale, both in its original version as set by Galuppi and in its Viennese revision as set by Salieri, is typical of Goldoni's finales in that it consists mostly of conversation. The act culminates in a "Sala illuminata e magnificamente adornata per Festa di ballo." As the curtain rises, we see two dancers finishing a minuet. After the dance the guests converse in blank verse, with Belinda expressing her jealousy because Bellarosa is always asked to dance. Another minuet is played and danced. Dialogue in blank verse then resumes. Belinda threatens to leave if she is not asked to dance; the other characters defend Bellarosa. The finale begins: Bellarosa and Belinda quarrel while the others try to keep them apart. Goldoni made no reference to the ball in stage directions or dialogue in the finale. The argument has brought the dancing to an end before the finale even begins.

Following his normal practice, Goldoni excluded the parti serie Armidoro and Albina from the finale, and with them the dignity and pathos that their presence might have brought to it.

The ballroom scene is one of several dramatic situations in Salieri's *Calamita* that would probably have been treated differently if Goldoni's libretto had undergone more thorough revision. Instead of bringing the ball to musical life by expanding the finale and incorporating the dancing into it, Salieri let the ball be acted out in simple recitative. In doing so he followed the revised libretto, in which Goldoni's blank verse was largely preserved rather than recast into a poetic form suitable for a finale. He composed minuets to accompany the dancing referred to by Goldoni in his stage directions; in his score he wrote specifically that the minuets are "ballabili." But they are followed by simple recitative. The orchestra remains silent until the beginning of the finale, which follows Goldoni in omitting Armidoro and Albina and in lacking any reference to the ball. The result is a ball and a finale that are completely distinct and a finale from which the spirit of dance, and indeed physical action of any kind, is largely absent.

The ballroom scene in Salieri's *Calamita* looks to a Goldonian past; that in *La fiera di Venezia* to a Da Pontian and Mozartian future. Salieri and Boccherini (himself a dancer) integrated the ball into the finale much more fully than Goldoni's librettos allowed. The ballroom scene in *La fiera* resembles—and may well have served as a model for—the "gran festa di ballo" with which Mozart and Da Ponte brought the first act of *Don Giovanni* to its extraordinary conclusion.[30]

The Marchesa Calloandra, full of noble jealousy, hopes to observe and expose her wayward fiancé, Duke Ostrogoto, at a masked ball at the end of act 2. Falsirena and Belfusto use the ball as an opportunity to make fun of both the duke and the marchesa, and also of Falsirena's moneygrubbing father, Grifagno.

Boccherini described the setting of his ballroom scene in Goldonian terms as "Magnifica sala illuminata per il Ballo." The entire scene, as it appears in the libretto printed for the first production, is reproduced as figure 6.5. Boccherini and Salieri began their ball and their finale simultaneously, coordinating new scenery, the entrance of orchestra and chorus, and shortly thereafter, the beginning of the dancing itself. Like many of Goldoni's successors, Boccherini saw the drawbacks of keeping the drama's most noble characters out of the finale. The marchesa and the duke, whom Goldoni might have banished by means of exit arias shortly before the beginning of the finale, play crucial roles in Salieri's ballroom scene.

The scene begins with a short but brilliant chorus, "Allegre, allegre, signore maschere" (3/4, Allegro maestoso, D major), accompanied by a large orchestra of oboes, bassoons, flutes, horns, trumpets, timpani, and strings, which immediately establishes an atmosphere of celebration. Goldoni often specified what dances were to be performed in his ballroom scenes; Boccherini did so here. In response to his instructions that masqueraders "dance several minuets," Salieri wrote several beautiful dances. The first minuet, in A, is as perfect an expression of eighteenth-century musical elegance as the minuet that Mozart wrote for his operatic masked ball fifteen years later (ex. 6.19); Salieri wrote at the beginning of this minuet in his autograph: "Si balla." After the chorus is repeated, a second minuet, in G, is played (ex. 6.20). Mozart used this dance tune as the theme for keyboard variations, K. 173c.

Salieri repeated the G-major minuet and alternated between it and two dances, also in triple meter and binary form, one in C major and one in G minor. These dances, unlabeled in the score, will be referred to here as trios. The minuet and its trios have their own distinctive orchestrations: the minuet has a solo oboe, the trio in C pairs of oboes and horns, and the trio in G minor a pair of flutes. We hear the minuet five times and

30. The ballroom scene in *La fiera* is discussed briefly in Heartz, *Viennese School,* 430–32. Points of similarity and difference between it and the ballroom finale in *Don Giovanni* will be discussed in chap. 14.

each trio twice. But the layout of dances, including internal repetition or lack thereof, is not very systematic, as can be seen in the following plan:

La fiera di Venezia, Finale of Act 2, Measures 78–285: Layout of Minuet in G and Trios in C and G Minor

Measure numbers include all repeats, whether they are written out in the score or not. Source: A-Wn, Mus. Hs. 1048.

Measure 78:
Minuet in G, both halves repeated, 32 measures
Measure 110:
Minuet in G, no repeats, 16 measures
Measure 126:
Trio in C, no repeats, 16 measures
Measure 142:
Minuet in G, second half repeated, 24 measures
Measure 166:
Trio in G minor, both halves repeated, 32 measures
Measure 198:
Trio in G minor, first half repeated, 24 measures
Measure 222:
Minuet in G, no repeats, 16 measures
Measure 238:
Trio in C, no repeats, 16 measures
Measure 254:
Minuet in G (variation with triplets), no repeats, 16 measures
Measure 270:
Trio in G minor, no repeats, 16 measures

This music accompanies the dancing and serves as the musical background to the intrigues of the masked ball. As the minuet in G is played for the first time, Falsirena and the duke flirt. The names with which they address one another, Adonis and Venus, may be references to their costumes.[31] They presumably dance the minuet together, although Boccherini did not specify this in his libretto. Grifagno asks his daughter Falsirena for money on the pretext that he wants to gamble; then he proceeds to pocket the money. In their depiction of the masked ball, Boccherini and Salieri projected the same complex interaction of dance, erotic play, intrigue encouraged by masks, and the excitement of gambling perceptible in Longhi's painting of a Venetian masked ball (fig. 6.6).

31. A ballroom scene in Boccherini's *La casa di campagna,* as set to music by Gassmann, is preceded by a discussion of costumes to be worn during the ball. Fiorilla intends to disguise herself as Venus: "Io di Venere vorrei / Comparir nella sembianza."

52 *La Fiera, di Venezia,*

SCENA XIII.

Magnifica sala illuminata per il Ballo, Orchestra con suonatori. Luogo da mangiare, e luogo da giocare alla Bassetta.

CORO di Maschere alla Veneziana, che seggono intorno, poi FALSIRENA con OSTROGOTO, GRIFAGNO, CALLOANDRA con RASOJO, BELFUSTO, indi CRISTALLINA, tutti in Maschera.

Coro di Maschere. Allegre, allegre,
Signore Maschere,
In Festa, e in giubilo
Qui s'ha da star.
Fra giochi, e balli
Bagordi, e Musica
Sempre all'amore,
Qui s'ha da far. *(ballano alcuni Minuetti, poi replicasi il detto Coro.)*

Falſ. Mio caro Adone.
Oſtr. Mia bella Venere.
Falſ. } *Oſtr.* } Seguiam l'esempio
Di giubilar.
Grif. Fra tanti spassi, *(a Falsirena)*
Figlia Carissima,
Un par di carte
Vorrei tentar,
Ma...

Falſ. Già capisco. *(a Grifagno)*
Duca carissimo;
Vizioso è il Padre,
Vorria giocar.
Ma, .
Oſtr. Già capisco.
Queste son Doppie. *(Dà denaro a Falsirena, e Falsirena lo dà a Grifagno.)*
Grif. (Oh non son pazzo
Di arrischiar. *(va a finger di giocare)*
Raſ. Ecco là il Duca,
Che per sua Maschera *(alla Marchesa, colla quale si ferma in disparte)*
L'astuta Donna
Fà passeggiar.
Cal. Zitto, Rasojo:
E qui fermiamoci,
Ciò che succede
Ad osservar.
Falſ. Mio caro Adone.
Oſtr. Mia bella Venere *(passeggiando)*
Falſ. } *Oſtr.* } Seguiam l'esempio
Di giubilar.
Belf. Oh maledetta:
Con quel suo fingere *(da se stando in disparte)*
Il fiato, e l'anima
Mi fà cascar.

D 3 Grif.

54 *La Fiera di Venezia,*

Grif. Tutte son' ite
Sopra d'un paroli; *(torna a Falsirena)*
Ne di rifarmi
Posso sperar.
Falſ. Che cosa dite? *(a Grif. forte)*
Grif. Non c'è più doppie.
Oſtr. E l'hai perdute?
Grif. Senza fiatar.
Oſtr. Vien quà, vo' darti
Da ricattarle. *(lo trae in disparte)*
Belf. Adesso il tempo *(piano a Falsirena)*
Saria d'andar.
Falſ. Sì: già son teco;
Ma tosto in Maschera
Da Gondolieri *(a Belfusto, e parte seco)*
S'ha da tornar.
Call. Or che si scosta
La scaltra Femmina:
Rasojo, avanti
Lasciami andar. *(s'avanza sola)*
Oſtr. Con più giudizio
Avverti, giocale;
E sopra all'asso *(a Grifagno, dandogli denaro)*
L'hai da puntar.
Grif. Io la ringrazio
Con tutta l'anima.
(Ma non son pazzo
D'arrischiar. *(torna a finger di giocare)*
Call. Mio caro Adone. *(al Duca)*

Oſtr.

Comedia per Musica. 55

Oſtr. Mia bella venere. *(da il braccio alla Marchesa credendola Falsir.)*
Call. } *Oſtr.* } Seguiam l'esempio
Di Giubilar.
Raſ. (Oh Cristallina)
Quà veggo in maschera;
E seco in pace
Vorrei tornar.)
La riverisco. *(a Cristallina)*
Criſt. Non ha più macchina?
Raſ. Se del suo braccio
Mi vuol degnar.
Mi farà grazia.
M'è onar grandissimo
Criſt. } *Raſ.* } *Criſt.* } Con lei Signor e / a
Di passeggiar. *(s'accompagnano)*
Falſ. Bel Momoletto
Belf. Mia cara Momola.
Falſ. } *Belf.* } Allegramente *(tornano travestiti*
Vegnimo a star *alla Barcaruola)*
Call. Mio caro Adone.
Oſtr. Mia bella Venere. *(passeggiando insieme)*
Call. } *Oſtr.* } Seguiam l'esempio
Di giubilar.
Grif. Digli, che ancora
Perduti ho gl'ultimi. *(a Call. credendola Falſ. e tirandogli la veste)*
(Io qualcos' altro
Vorrei cavar)
Call. (Che vuol quest' Uomo?

D 4 Mi

FIGURE 6.5 *La fiera di Venezia,* act 2, finale in the libretto printed for the first production, Vienna, Carnival 1772.

Mi ſtrappa l'abito)
Ahi pizzicotto!
Laſciami ſtar. *Grif. la ſtuzzica, e pizzica, ed ella gli dà uno ſchiaffo)*

Grif. Un ſchiaffo al Padre? *(con ſtrepito)*

Falſ. } Queſto xe un ſpaſſo,
Belſ. } Che il cuor m'alletta,
La Furlanetta
Voggio ballar. *(ballano la Furlana)*

Grif. Un ſchiaffo al Padre?
Corpo del Diavolo.. *(minaccioſo)*

Raſ. Si fermi:
Criſt. Aſcolti. *(trattenendo Grifagno)*

Oſtr. Laſciam gridare. *(a Calloandra)*
Tuo Padre a' Sordi:
Laſciam ballare
Queſti balordi;
Ed a godercene
Andiamo a cena,
Mia Falſirena
Dea del mio cor.

Call. Ah riconoſcimi *(ſi cava la Maſchera)*
O Traditor.

Oſtr. Che mai veggo!

Grif. E' Calloandra!
E mia Figlia dove ſta?

Oſtr. Che mi avvenne?

Tutti, e il Coro. Che avverrà?

Oſtr. e Grif. Son reſtato qual Uomo, che ſogna,
E non vede che immagini ſtrane!
Con-

Confuſione, rimorſo, e vergogna
Muto, muto tremare mi fà

Call. Spoſo ingrato, ſpergiuro, infedele *(a Oſtrogoto)*
A una Dama par mia tanto ſcherno?
A una Spoſa mercè sì crudele?
Ah la rabbia morire mi fa *(sviene)*

Falſ. Ohe! Saldi! Sviene.

Criſt. Coſpetto! Ehi gente?

Coro. Che coſa è ſtato? *(corrono tutte, e portono da ſedere)*

Oſtr. Non sò che farmi.

Falſ. Xe convulſioni.
Non ſarà niente.

Belſ. Comanda Gondola? *(e Oſtrogoto)*

Falſ. Vorla battelo?

Criſt. Ci vuol dell' acqua. *(parte)*

Grif. Ci vuole aceto. *(parte)*

Raſ. Ci vuole un Spirito, *(parte)*

Oſtr. Perdo il Cervello.

Falſ. Ghe vuole un Miedego.

Belſ. Ghe vuol Barbier.

Falſ. Nol ſtaga a crederghe
A mio Mariò.

Belſ. Nol ſtaga a crederghe.
A mia Mujer.

Falſ. Ghe vuole un Miedego.

Belſ. Ghe vuole barbier.

Oſtr. Via Boja, o Diavolo
Fate venir,

Falſ. } *a due* Da Commar Momola
Belſ. } Da Compar Momolo

Falſ.

Falſ. Belſ. Mi i vo' ſervir. *(partono poi tor.)*

Raſ. Ecco uno Spirito;

Criſt. Quì pronta è l'acqua.

Raſ. Sotto il bel naſo
L'appoggerò.

Criſt. Nel viſo pallido
La Spruzzerò.

Grif. Con queſto aceto
Meglio io farò.

Raſ. Voi ſtate cheto,
Che ſiete un Aſino.

Grif. A me dell' Aſino!
Come! Coſpetto!

Raſ. Se mi ci metto:

Grif. } E calci, e pugni.
Raſ. } Ti renderò. *(s' attac. a pugni)*

Coro. Orſù finitela
d' Uomini Siori Smargiaſſi;
O ſe ſia luogo
Da dare ſchiaffi.
Chiamando i Zaffi
V' integnerò.

Oſtr. Naſce ſcompiglio
Sopra ſcompiglio:
Son diſperato
Non ho conſiglio....

Criſt. Già rinviene.

Call. Ahi fier tormento!

Falſ. Vorla aſeo?

Belſ. Vorla triaca?

Raſ. Vuol Cordiale?

Grif. Vuol ſalaſſo?

Call.

Call. Io vorrei, che Santanaſſo *(s'alza con ſdegno)*
Vi portaſſe tutti via.

Tutti, e Coro Non sò più dov'io mi ſia,
Non sò più quel che mi fò!

Tutti fuori che. Di due Donne innamorate

Falſ. e Call. Rabbia impegno, e geloſia.

Falſ. D'una afflitta innamorata
Sdegno, picca, e geloſia.

Call. D'una Furba intereſſata
L'imprudenza, e la pazzia.

Tutti Oh che imbrogli; che diſordini,
Che ſcompigli cagionò! *(partono)*

ATTO TERZO.

SCENA I.

Camera nella Locanda.

RASOJO, ed OSTROGOTO.

Raſ. Eccelenza tant' è: più la Marcheſa
Non vuol ſaper di nozze:
Non vuol più rivederla, ed ha riſolto
Di tornare a Vicenza.

Oſtr. Faccia pure.
Io non poſſo penſar che a Falſirena;
Ma

EXAMPLE 6.19 *La fiera di Venezia,* act 2, finale, mm. 28–59

As the orchestra plays the C-major trio for the first time, the marchesa, disguised as Falsirena, enters, accompanied by the innkeeper Rasoio, who points out for her the duke and Falsirena. Later Grifagno returns, saying he has lost all the money at the gaming table and asking for more. The trio in G minor, performed for the first time, mirrors his mournful plea. Falsirena and Belfusto whisper to one another, planning to leave together unobserved.

When Falsirena leaves, the marchesa takes her place at the duke's side and begins to flirt with him, repeating Falsirena's endearment ("Mio caro Adone"; by this time the orchestra has returned to the minuet in G). The duke responds, unwittingly giving his arm to his own fiancée. Rasoio in the meantime converses with the object of his affections, the shopgirl Cristallina.

Falsirena and Belfusto soon return, dressed as gondoliers and speaking in Venetian

EXAMPLE 6.20 *La fiera di Venezia,* act 2, finale, mm. 78–89

FALSIRENA: My dear Adonis. OSTROGOTO: My lovely Venus. TOGETHER: Let us follow their example, and celebrate.

dialect. Again to the sound of the G-minor trio Grifagno asks for money. He approaches the duke and the marchesa, whom he too believes to be Falsirena, and gives her a paternal pinch. Angered by Grifagno's familiarity, the marchesa slaps him. The slap occurs in measure 285 of the finale, the first measure of example 6.21. Up until the slap, the G-major minuet and its trios have been played continuously for 208 measures. Suddenly the dance music stops on a fermata. Grifagno, stunned, says only "Un schiaffo al padre?" Another fermata follows. What would have been an awkward moment of silence is avoided by Falsirena and Belfusto, who, still speaking in Venetian dialect, announce that they want to dance a forlana (ex. 6.21).

FIGURE 6.6 Pietro Longhi, *The Ballroom.* (Courtesy of Fondazione Quirini Stampalia, Venice.)

The forlana is a lively dance in compound meter, with music not unlike that of the gigue, that was long associated with Venice. In his *Dictionnaire de musique* Rousseau stated that the forlana was popular with gondoliers. According to Daniel Gottlob Türk's *Klavierschule* of 1789 the forlana is "a dance in 6/4 or more commonly in 6/8 meter which is much in use among the common people of Venice. The rather fast tempo

EXAMPLE 6.21 *La fiera di Venezia,* act 2, finale, mm. 285–318

(Continued on next page)

EXAMPLE 6.21 (*continued*)

(*Continued on next page*)

EXAMPLE 6.21 *(continued)*

GRIFAGNO: You slap your father? Your father? FALSIRENA, BELFUSTO: This is a joke that delights my heart; I want to dance a little forlana. GRIFAGNO: You slap your father? What the devil, you slap your father? RASOIO TO GRIFAGNO: Stop . . . CRISTALLINA TO GRIFAGNO: Listen . . . OSTROGOTO TO CALLOANDRA: Let your father shout to the deaf; let these fools dance, and let us go enjoy ourselves at dinner, my Falsirena, goddess of my heart. CALLOANDRA TO OSTROGOTO: Know who I am, traitor! OSTROGOTO: What do I see? GRIFAGNO: Is it Calloandra? And where is my daughter? OSTROGOTO: What has happened? ALL: What will happen? OSTROGOTO, GRIFAGNO: I am like the man who dreams and sees nothing but strange images!

FIGURE 6.7 Pietro Longhi, *The Forlana.* (Courtesy of Museo Ca' Rezzonico, Venice.)

requires a somewhat light execution."[32] Longhi's painting of a lower-class couple dancing the forlana in a simple tavern nicely captures the dance's gestures as well as its social connotations (fig. 6.7).

32. Daniel Gottlob Türk, *School of Clavier Playing,* trans. Raymond H. Haggh (Lincoln, Nebr. 1982), 394. On the history of the forlana see Paul Nettl, "Forlana," in *Musik in Geschichte und Gegenwart,* ed. Friedrich Blume (Kassel, 1949–86), with extensive bibliography and several musical examples.

EXAMPLE 6.22 Fischietti, *Il mercato di Malmantile,* act 3, "Se voi mi amate," mm. 187–90

Salieri accompanied the dancing of Falsirena and Belfusto with vigorous, loud music in fast tempo, with lean texture (usually just two parts), strong downbeats, big melodic leaps, and fiery passagework in the violins, all of which may have reminded Viennese audiences of a forlana that suddenly appears near the end of *Il mercato di Malmantile,* in the trio "Se voi mi amate." In response to Berto's mention of "la furlanetta" (the diminutive, as in Salieri's ballroom scene), Fischietti wrote music much like that which accompanies Salieri's forlana (ex. 6.22).

The introduction by Boccherini and Salieri of this second dance is a departure from Goldonian practice. In stage directions for his ballroom scenes Goldoni usually mentioned only one dance by name—typically the minuet. Occasionally he left open the possibility of other dances, as in *La conversazione:* "Various minuets are danced, and other dances if desired." Boccherini and Salieri went further, specifying a second dance and making it as important a part of their ballroom scene as the minuet. The switch from minuet to forlana and the extreme musical contrast between them signals a change of focus from the noble characters to the middle-class ones.

With Falsirena and Belfusto now occupying the center of attention, the duke tries to coax away the woman he thinks is Falsirena by inviting her to dinner. The marchesa has heard enough. She reveals her identity, denouncing the duke as a traitor, as the whole orchestra unites with her in an accusatory unison. The duke and Grifagno express their astonishment, followed by everyone on stage, including a chorus that has been silent since near the beginning of the finale, and the forlana comes to a sudden halt at the words "Che avverrà?" [What is going to happen?]. The interrupted passage in A major is so similar to the A-major cadence in Fischietti's forlana (see ex. 6.22) that we can imagine easily how Salieri's dance would have continued had it not been interrupted.

A switch from compound to duple meter and a brief excursion to E minor together tell us that the dancing is over. Astonishment, recrimination, and confusion are expressed at length, first in this Andante con moto (at the end of which Calloandra faints), then in an Allegro assai in triple meter. A Presto in 2/4 brings to an end a finale that, for all its dependence on Goldonian precedent, shows Boccherini and Salieri moving confidently into new dramatic and musical territory.

7

JOSEPH II AND THE END OF THE IMPRESARIAL DECADE

The Emperor visited the theater very constantly, especially the Italian opera, in which he took great pleasure," according to a report of Joseph's musical activities published shortly after his death.[1] Although the leasing of the court theaters limited his influence on opera, it did not keep him out of the theaters or discourage him from furthering the operatic ambitions of his favorite musicians, as he did by engaging Salieri as Kammer-Kompositor in 1774. With his reorganization of the court theaters in 1776 he served notice that he, not his aged mother, court officials appointed by her, or impresarios, would be in charge of the theaters, and that henceforth he would supervise them closely.

Joseph as Operagoer and Promoter of Salieri's Operas

Although Joseph followed Salieri's career as an opera composer from the beginning, he was probably unable to take much pleasure in the success of Salieri's first opera, *Le donne letterate.* The emperor's only child, seven-year-old Maria Theresa, died of smallpox on 23 January 1770, leaving him heartbroken.[2] We do not know exactly when *Le donne letterate* was first performed, but it was probably within a few weeks of little Maria Theresa's death. By the time Joseph was ready to hear Salieri's opera, the theaters were closed for Lent. He had the opera performed in his private chamber concert, a performance in which he, together with Gassmann and Salieri, probably took part: "The monarch, who was always graciously disposed toward our Salieri, noted with great sat-

1. "Auszug eines Schreibens aus Wien," in Angermüller, *Leben,* 3:55.
2. Derek Beales, *Joseph II,* vol. 1, *In the Shadow of Maria Theresa, 1741–1780* (Cambridge, 1987), 201.

isfaction that the teacher not only found no important mistakes in the musical composition but also was exceptionally pleased with the setting of every single number, with the musical ideas, with the character of the music in general, and with the relation of the music to the opera's subject matter in particular."[3]

In letters to his younger brother Leopold, grand duke of Tuscany and from 1790 his successor as emperor, we can follow Joseph's theatergoing and get some idea of his operatic tastes. The letters are inconsistent in the attention they give to opera. During some periods they refer to it often; at other times rarely or not at all. He seems to have followed Viennese opera particularly closely during 1771 and 1772, just as Salieri's career was getting started. His remarks on opera during this period reveal a special interest in the music of his protégés Gassmann and Salieri: he seldom mentioned other composers.

On 1 August 1771 Joseph wrote of the first performance of Paisiello's *Don Chisciotte della Mancia,* with several arias by Gassmann: "*Don Quichotte* was finally performed for the first time yesterday. The music is rather pretty, and there are many jokes, so crowded together one after another that by the end they become boring. Gasman had to add several arias."[4] At the bottom of the page Joseph, lapsing into Italian, added: "Ecco il libreto dell opera buffa."

"We have a new opera buffa, called *Il tutore e la pupilla,* which I do not like at all," Joseph wrote a week later of a pasticcio.[5] And on 25 September he wrote of an unnamed opera by Gassmann that must have been *Le pescatrici:* "I wanted to enclose the score of the new opera buffa, which has been very successful and of which the music is by Gasman and the libretto is rather pretty. As for the latter, here are two copies. The score is not yet copied and I will send it to you on another occasion."[6] At the end of the letter he added: "Il spartito e arrivato . . . and here is a new German play."

3. Mosel, 41.

4. Don quichotte a enfin paru hier pour la premiere fois, la musique est assés jolie, et il y a une quantité de boufoneries, si entossés les unes sur les autres, qui a la fin enuyent Gasman y a du mettre plusieurs airs (Joseph to Leopold, 1 August 1771, HHStA, Sb, Kart. 7). This is new evidence of the exact date of the premiere; cf. Zechmeister, 525.

5. nous avons une nouvelle opera buffa, nomé il tutore è la Pupilla, qui ne me plait point (Joseph to Leopold, 8 August 1771, HHStA, Sb, Kart. 7). This is new evidence for the approximate date of the premiere; cf. Zechmeister, 525.

6. je comptois y joindre le spartito de la nouvelle opera buffa qui a trés bien reussie et dont la musique est de Gasman et le libretto est assés jolie pour de ce dernier, en voilla deux exemplaires. le spartito, n'est pas encore copié et je vous l'enverai, par une autre occasion (Joseph to Leopold, 25 September 1771, HHStA, Sb, Kart. 7). This is new evidence for the approximate date of the premiere of *Le pescatrici;* cf. Zechmeister, 525. Joseph's approval of Goldoni's libretto is of interest in light of Daniel Heartz's suggestion that *Le pescatrici* served as a source of the plot of Da Ponte's *Così fan tutte* (*Mozart's Operas,* 230–32). The story that Joseph suggested the plot of *Così fan tutte* to Da Ponte is rendered more plausible by the emperor's fondness for Goldoni's libretto.

Joseph mentioned many of Salieri's operas to his brother—a good indication of his fondness for the composer and his music. On 6 January 1771 he witnessed a performance (probably the first) of *Don Chisciotte alle nozze di Gamace.* Although this work, according to Salieri himself, failed to please the public, there is no hint of failure in the emperor's letter to Leopold, quoted in chapter 5. The success of Salieri's next opera, *Armida,* caused Joseph, in a letter also quoted in chapter 5, to promise to send his brother a score. He kept his promise, reminding Leopold who Salieri was and urging his brother to try *Armida:* "You will receive by way of the diligence that is leaving today a package addressed to you containing the opera *Armida* that is being given here and that has been successful. It is by Salieri, this young man, Gasman's student. It merits your trying it sometime."[7] Exactly what Joseph meant by "try" (eprouviez) is not clear. Perhaps he had in mind the kind of chamber-music group that gathered around him in Vienna, which included in its repertory excerpts from serious operas; or perhaps he hoped that Leopold would have *Armida* staged in Florence.

By early 1772 Joseph may have felt that he had laid the groundwork for a more aggressive attempt to promote Salieri's interests. He asked his brother for help in finding an opportunity for Salieri to write an opera for one of the theaters of Florence (fig. 7.1):

> *a propos,* I have been asked to make you a proposition. Gasman's student Salieri, this young man whom you know and whose scores are very successful, would like to find a theater in Italy where he could write an opera, buffa or seria, to make himself better known. Would there be an occasion in Florence this spring to commission one from him? I believe that it would please. If you find the means, have him contacted directly, because I do not want to get involved in this intrigue.[8]

Typical of Joseph: initiating a project and then distancing himself from it. He should have learned from the controversy surrounding Mozart's *La finta semplice* what trouble he could cause himself by getting involved in an operatic project to which he was not fully committed. Leopold, perhaps sensing his brother's ambivalence, politely avoided any promises by return of post:

> As for what you mentioned concerning Salieri, Gasman's student, I will find out more, but our theatrical impresarios in Florence, who do not like to spend money, much prefer to give the

7. Joseph to Leopold, 4 July 1771, HHStA, Sb, Kart. 7; quoted in Rice, "Emperor," 74. Leopold thanked Joseph for the score in a letter dated 12 July 1771: "Tres cher frere j'ai reçu votre tres chere lettre du 4 de ce mois de meme que l'opera d'Armide que je compte eprouver et dont je vous fais bien mes remercimens" (HHStA, Sb, Kart. 7).

8. Joseph to Leopold, 9 January 1772, HHStA, Sb, Kart. 7; quoted in Rice, "Emperor," 74. The letter is published, with spelling and punctuation corrected and modernized, in *Maria Theresia und Joseph II: Ihre Correspondenz sammt Briefen Joseph's an seinen Brüder Leopold,* ed. Alfred von Arneth, 3 vols. (Vienna, 1867–68), 1:359–60, and, following Arneth's text, in Angermüller, *Leben,* 2:31–32.

> public opere buffe that are already known, changing a few arias that the musicians bring with them, rather than to make new ones. As for opere serie, these are given only during Carnival, and it is always a pasticcio; and this year the impresario wanted to have a new score for the second opera, and offered a young Florentine composer 12 sequins for the entire score. That is only to give you an idea of the generosity of our impresarios.[9]

Joseph seems to have made no further propositions of this kind, but he continued to keep Leopold posted on Salieri's work. A letter from Leopold to the emperor dated 13 February 1772 refers to an opera buffa promised by Joseph in a letter, dated 1 February, that seems not to have survived: "I thank you in advance for the music of the opera buffa that you are kind enough to promise me and which I expect one of these days."[10] To judge by the date of Joseph's missing letter, the opera in question was *La fiera di Venezia,* first performed on 29 January. On 26 October 1772 the emperor told Leopold of his intention to send "Salieri's new opera," which must have been *La secchia rapita,* first performed on 21 October.[11]

Joseph's epistolary support of Gassmann and Salieri paid off in the frequency with which their works were performed in Tuscany.[12] Productions of *L'opera seria* (Florence, 1771) and *I rovinati* (the grand-ducal villa of Poggio a Caiano, 1773) were apparently the only productions of these operas in Italy. At least two of Salieri's early Viennese operas were performed in Florence: *La locandiera* in July 1775 (the only known Italian production) and *La fiera di Venezia* in May 1779 (second known Italian production). These performances may have been based on scores sent by Joseph to Leopold.

During his Italian tour of 1778–80, Salieri visited Florence and supervised rehearsals of *La fiera di Venezia.*[13] He met Grand Duke Leopold and talked with him about the problems of engaging singers for Joseph's Singspiel troupe in Vienna.[14] Thanks to the emperor's letters and the many scores he had sent from Vienna, Leopold was quite familiar with the twenty-nine-year-old composer and his works.

The Decline of the Viennese Opera Buffa Company

The temptation for Joseph to get involved in the management of the court theaters must have increased during the decade of the impresarios. When, in 1774, he offered Salieri a

9. Leopold to Joseph, 21 January 1772, HHStA, Sb, Kart. 7; quoted in Rice, "Emperor," 74–75; and Weaver and Weaver, *A Chronology of Music in the Florentine Theater,* 39–40.

10. Je vous faits d'avance bien remercimens de la musique de l'opera buffa que vous voulés bien me promettre et que j'attends un de ces jours (Leopold to Joseph, 13 February 1772, HHStA, Sb, Kart. 7).

11. par Wiltscheck qui va partir je vous enverai quelques papiers et la musique de la nouvelle opera de Salieri (Joseph to Leopold, 26 October 1772, HHStA, Sb, Kart. 7).

12. The productions mentioned in this paragraph are documented in Sartori.

13. Mosel, 65.

14. Leopold mentioned his meeting with Salieri in a letter to Joseph of 18 April 1779, quoted in chap. 9.

Très chere frere. voilà le Courier assuré, et je
ne puis vous rien mander de positive le Prince
Kaunitz fait un travaill, duquell l'on ne sait
jamais rien, jusqu'à ce qu'il soit achevé
je crois, qu'il s'agira, d'un traité de partage
mais cella n'est point sure encore.
si je puis avoir de lui, copie de la reponse
Russe je vous l'enverrai par cette occasion
S: M: l'Imperatrice, ayant un gros rhume
auquell se joignit un peu de fievre, a été
incomodé une couple de jours, et elle dut
se faire saigner, ce qui la soulagea, et mo-
yenant un peu de Regime tout se remettra
dans peu. elle n'a pas été alitté une jour
née, et se trouve aujourdhui si bien, qu'
elle regimbe deja aux loix de la faculté,
en ne voulant plus boire les decoctions
ordonnés. vous avés été a florence je ne doute
pas, que vous y aurés trouvé vos enfans
en bonne santé. a propos, je suis chargé
a vous faire une proposition l'ecolier de
Gasman Salieri ce jeun homme que vous
conaissés et dont les musiques reussissent
trés bien desireroit de trouver un Theatre
en Italie ou il pourait ecrire une Opera
buffa ou Serea pour se faire conoitre est
ce que au Printemps a florence il n'y au.

FIGURE 7.1 Autograph letter dated 9 January 1772 from Joseph II to his brother Leopold, grand duke of Tuscany, asking if there was an opportunity for Salieri to compose an opera for Florence. Haus-, Hof-, und Staatsarchiv, Vienna.

roit pas occasion de lui en faire ecrire une je crois, qu'ón en seroit content. si vous en trouvés le moyen, faite que ón s'ádresse a lui, car je ne veux pas etre melé de ce tripot adieu chere frere je vous embrasse de bon coeur etant pour la vie J

ce 9 Janvier 1772

mes respects a votre chere Epouse.

massive raise in pay on condition that he direct the Italian opera and "continue to do so if His Majesty brings the opera under his own management," he may already have made up his mind eventually to take over from the impresarios.

The court in the meantime was pushed in different directions. On the one hand Prince Kaunitz led a party of nobles that supported the performance of French plays and opéras-comiques, protesting in 1772 the impresario's decision to dismiss a French troupe.[15] Since the nobility's financial support of the court theaters, through subscriptions, was essential to the impresarios' financial survival, its preferences carried much weight. On the other hand intellectuals like Sonnenfels (who, despite his father's ennoblement in 1746, still represented middle-class ideals foreign to most of the Viennese nobility) wanted to see the court theaters transformed into a "national theater" dedicated to the performance of spoken drama in German.

Financial limitations made it difficult for the impresarios to present opera of the highest quality. Mosel recorded an anecdote about the Burgtheater's *Spinett* (evidently a harpsichord because he referred specifically to quills) that tells us something of the conditions under which the company had to work. Years of use had rendered the instrument almost unplayable; but the impresario, out of what Mosel called "misplaced thriftiness," had refused to replace it.

> One morning, when Salieri had once again tortured himself horribly at a rehearsal, he stayed behind to correct some wrong notes in the score. As he waited for the copyist, he was overcome by the urge finally to put some limit on the avarice or the negligence of the theatrical impresario. He opened up the Spinett completely, put a chair next to it, climbed on the chair, and jumped into the Spinett. Those who know the mechanism of such an instrument can imagine the effect of his action! Having completed his work he closed the Spinett quickly and continued to correct the score. The copyist arrived; Salieri calmly spoke with him about the changes being made; the copyist took the score and they left the rehearsal room together.

When the destruction came to light, no one suspected Salieri of being the perpetrator. "Yet he was not completely at ease until he heard his teacher say: 'Be that as it may! Thank heavens the impresario has finally been forced to have a new instrument made.' And so it happened."[16]

15. Kaunitz's activities on behalf of the French troupe are documented in great detail in letters (mostly copies) preserved in HHStA, St.K. Interiora, Kart. 86 (alt 108), fols. 202 ff.; see also Khevenhüller, 7:113 and 8:72–73; Michtner, 21; and Franz A. J. Szabo, *Kaunitz and Enlightened Absolutism, 1753–1780* (Cambridge, 1994), 205–8.

16. Mosel, 27–29. As so often happened during Salieri's life, reality imitated art. Goldoni's libretto *La bella verità*, set to music by Piccinni in 1762, is a parody of the opera buffa business. Petronilla, who specializes in parti serie, accompanies herself at the cembalo as she sings an old-fashioned Metastasian metaphor aria. But the impresario who engaged her must have given as little attention to the harpsichord as those in Vienna. The instrument's state of disrepair keeps her from finishing: "Fra le tempeste ancora / Tenta il nocchiero ardito / Di ritrovare il lito, / Di superare il mar. / E del nemico fato . . . / Ma il cembalo è scordato: (*s'alza*) / La mano—tocca invano / I tasti—che son guasti / E non si può sonar."

Calzabigi, writing to a friend in Italy in May 1771, looked back on *Paride ed Elena* as "his last work for the theater." He explained: "Theatrical affairs here have been reduced to such strenuous parsimony that it is necessary to banish forever spending on opera seria."[17] Calzabigi was too pessimistic—Salieri's *Armida* came to the stage only a month later—but *Armida* seems to have been the last serious opera produced by the impresarios.

The impresarial decade began with the hiring of several very fine singers; but as financial conditions worsened, later impresarios were forced to hire ones with less skill and experience. Carattoli died in Vienna in 1772. The contracts of Costanza and Rosa Baglioni expired at the end of the theatrical year 1774; those of several other singers may have expired at the same time, because not only Costanza and Rosa but also Clementina Baglioni and her husband Poggi were absent from Vienna during the theatrical year 1775, replaced by singers about whom—with one exception—we know very little. Khevenhüller noticed a change for the worse when he attended the opera on 29 April 1775. He had praise for only one newcomer:

> This evening one of the new opere buffe, *La frascatana*, was finally performed. Several new singers performed: Caterina Consiglio, known as La Ciecatella [the little blind girl] because she squints very noticeably; Signor Marchetti, one of the best buffi I have ever heard; Signora Anna Paganelli Bernucci and Signora Anna Santori [Marianna Santoro], both of whom look better than they sing, and Signor Novi Seni [probably Giovanni Battista Seni], a weak tenor. The music by Signor Giovanni Paisiello, a Neapolitan, was nevertheless applauded with uncommon enthusiasm.[18]

Only one of these singers, the comic bass Baldassare Marchetti, had enjoyed a substantial career in Italy before coming to Vienna. He had sung leading buffo roles in northern Italy since the 1760s, creating that of Fabrizio in Paisiello's very successful comedy *La frascatana* (Venice, fall 1774) shortly before joining the Viennese troupe; he sang the same role in Vienna. His career culminated in a long engagement in St. Petersburg (1779–85), where he created the role of Basilio in Paisiello's *Il barbiere di Siviglia* (1782).

Paisiello's music and Marchetti's portrayal of Fabrizio made *La frascatana* a success in Vienna despite the mediocrity of the rest of the cast; but Salieri's *La finta scema*, first performed by a very similar cast in the Burgtheater on 9 September 1775, was not so fortunate. In concluding his annotations to the autograph score, Salieri blamed the singers for the opera's lack of success: "From everything that I have said of this opera, one might believe that in spite of some of the voices of the troupe, the opera nevertheless

17. Calzabigi to Paolo Frisi, in "Dagli archivi milanesi: Lettere di Ranieri de Calzabigi e di Antonia Bernasconi," ed. Mariangela Donà, *Am* 14 (1974): 292–93.

18. Khevenhüller, 7:75.

met with great success. Perhaps it would have been so; but the hoarse, indistinct voices were precisely those of the three leading roles; so I have to say that this music was esteemed more than it was applauded."[19]

Joseph's Nationaltheater and the *Schauspielfreiheit*

Even before the premiere of *La finta scema* the emperor had begun to lose patience with the impresario Keglevich and the entire system in which he was operating. "La troupe de l'opera buffa est détestable," he wrote to Leopold on 20 July 1775.[20] On the same day he had sent a memorandum to Khevenhüller, who, as Obersthofmeister, had nominal authority over the impresario, expressing his displeasure with the quality of all aspects of the theatrical operation and threatening drastic action if improvements were not made:

> Dear Prince Khevenhüller!
> Since the mismanagement that the theatrical administration has allowed itself in the decline of every kind of spectacle violates all the contracts signed by it and exceeds the authority granted to it, and I am not disposed to tolerate this disorder for long, and especially since the entire public is unhappy about the current situation, you will inform it [i.e., the theatrical administration] by decree, through the normal channels, that it must immediately make arrangements to put the opera buffa, the ballets, and also the German troupe on a more advantageous footing, or at least give a strongly binding assurance, and present in three months' time the correspondence and the arrangements made for this purpose, by which one can be certain that all three of these spectacles will unfailingly be set on an entirely new footing, and especially that the truly substandard ballets in the German Theater will be completely changed and improved and that the almost worthless singers of the opera buffa will be replaced with the best from Italy; if not, the provisions of the contract will be considered void, and from 1 November, without further compensation for the costs of scenery and costumes belonging to it, the whole management will end, and the spectacles well be run on an entirely different basis.[21]

Keglevich, aware that his job was threatened, responded by listing the singers that he planned to engage for the theatrical year 1776. The list included some who had proved their abilities in Vienna—Poggi and Marchetti among the men, Clementina Baglioni among the women—but it also included several who had been recently criticized by

19. Salieri's annotations to the autograph of *La finta scema* are transcribed in Angermüller, *Leben,* 3:7–10, and Angermüller, *Fatti,* 108–10.

20. HHStA, Sb, Kart. 7.

21. Quoted in Franz Hadamowsky, *Die Josefinische Theaterreform und das Spieljahr 1776/77 des Burgtheaters* (Vienna, 1978), 3.

Khevenhüller: Seni, Consiglio, and Santoro. These singers (three of whom Salieri blamed for the failure of *La finta scema*) were hardly "the best from Italy." And yet Keglevich warned that hiring this troupe, together with everything else necessary to improve the quality of opera buffa, would cost more than had been spent the previous year, implying that he might need a subsidy from the court if he were to follow through on his intended improvements.[22]

Keglevich's response did not satisfy Joseph, who was unimpressed by the impresario's plans or unwilling to foot the bill. Or perhaps he had already decided to run the Burgtheater himself. He initiated the legal maneuvering necessary to dissolve the contract by which Keglevich was running the theaters. At the end of the theatrical year 1775 (that is, at the end of Carnival 1776), Joseph finally dismissed Keglevich, bringing an end to the impresarial decade and inaugurating a new epoch in the history of Viennese theater.[23]

The theatrical reorganization that Joseph undertook during the spring of 1776 bears features characteristic of his reforms in general. The changes that he made were, typically, sudden and drastic. Dissolving the contract with Count Kohary, in whose name Keglevich had managed the theaters since 1772, the emperor brought all aspects of the theater management under the direct supervision of the court. He hired as court employees the troupe of actors that had performed plays in German under the impresarios. For the performance of overtures and entr'acte music he assembled a small orchestra consisting largely of former members of the impresario's two theater orchestras and made these players court employees.[24] He did not engage the opera buffa and ballet troupes that had been assembled by Keglevich, leaving them, together with most of the orchestral musicians who had been employed by the impresarios, suddenly without work. Following the advice of Sonnenfels and his partisans, and imitating the example set by the founding of the Nationaltheater in Hamburg in 1767, Joseph commanded that the Burgtheater be henceforth called "das teutsche National Theater."

Joseph's founding of the Nationaltheater was consistent with three of the most important aims of his political reforms, all related to the ultimate goal of transforming the

22. Zechmeister, 95–96.

23. On Joseph's theatrical reform see Franz Hadamowsky, "Die Schauspielfreiheit, die 'Erhebung des Burgtheaters zum Hoftheater' und seine 'Begründung als Nationaltheater' im Jahr 1776," *Maske und Kothurn* 22 (1976): 5–19; Hadamowsky, *Theaterreform;* and Beales, *Joseph II,* 1:230–36. The reorganization is discussed in the context of the larger German "national theater" movement in Roland Krebs, *L'Idée de "Théâtre National" dans l'Allemagne des Lumières: Théorie et réalisations* (Wiesbaden, 1985). On the role played by Sonnenfels see, in addition to Krebs, Ernst Wangermann, *The Austrian Achievement, 1700–1800* (London, 1973), 121–24, which considers Sonnenfels "the chief protagonist of bourgeois culture in Austria"; and Robert A. Kann, *A Study in Austrian Intellectual History* (New York, 1960), 208–24.

24. Joseph's orchestra consisted at first (April 1776) of only eighteen players: four first violins (including orchestra director Melchior Jäger), four second violins, two violas, two cellos, two double basses, two oboes, and two horns (HHStA, GH, Rechnungsbuch 1776; transcribed in Hadamowsky, *Theaterreform,* 104–5).

Habsburg monarchy into a modern state that could match France, Britain, and Prussia in military and economic power. To increase the efficiency of government he initiated a program of Germanization, increasing the use of German in many parts of his polyglot empire, in schools, churches, and government business. The establishment of a theater for the performance of German spoken drama was a powerful symbol of the preeminence of German. At the same time it allowed the court to save money, another important goal for the emperor. Spoken drama was somewhat cheaper to produce than opera and ballet (and a theatrical program without opera and ballet was naturally cheaper than a program with them). Spoken drama, furthermore, normally attracted larger audiences than opera.[25] Finally, the theatrical reorganization represented a short-lived victory for the monarchy in a long struggle that lay at the heart of the Theresian-Josephinian reforms: the monarchy's efforts to bring the nobility under the authority of the central government, to hasten and complete the transition from a feudal to a modern state. Since the nobility had made plain its preference for French plays and Italian opera, the transformation of the Burgtheater into the Nationaltheater must have been regarded as blow to the nobility's prestige and a slight but symbolically important shift in the balance of power.

Another important aspect of Joseph's reorganization was his institution of so-called *Schauspielfreiheit,* a policy that opened the court theaters, when they were not being used by the court and its German troupe, to whoever wanted to use them for concerts, plays, or operas. At the same time Joseph lifted some of the restrictions that had severely limited theatrical activity outside the court theaters. The suburban theaters that began to thrive in the 1780s—the Theater auf der Wieden, the Leopoldstädter Theater, and others—had their roots in the Schauspielfreiheit of 1776.

The Effect of Joseph's Reorganization on Viennese Opera Buffa and on Salieri

Joseph's cancellation of the contract by which impresarios had presented opera buffa in the court theaters did not bring an end to the performance of opera buffa in Vienna. In spite of having been called "detestable" by the emperor, the troupe that performed in 1775 reconstituted itself shortly after the beginning of the theatrical year 1776. Under Poggi's leadership the troupe took advantage of the Schauspielfreiheit to present a full repertory of works during the theatrical years 1776 and 1777. They performed in both court theaters, using the Nationaltheater on evenings when the German actors did not

25. Box-office reports in the Keglevich papers (MOL, Keglevich Cs., P 421, V/15–22) show that audiences for German plays were generally larger than those for Italian operas during the years covered by these documents, late 1772 to early 1776.

perform. Opera buffa thus continued to occupy an important place in the repertory of the Burgtheater, despite its change of name.

A theatrical almanac published in 1777 reports the number of times that particular operas were given by the Italian troupe during the theatrical year 1776. It is valuable as one the few sources of information about operatic repertory in the Kärntnertortheater.[26] The opera buffa troupe presented Galuppi's *Il marchese villano* sixteen times in the Nationaltheater and eight times at the Kärntnertor. Other popular operas were Anfossi's *L'avaro* (thirteen performances in the Nationaltheater, four at the Kärntnertor), Paisiello's *La frascatana* (sixteen performances in the Nationaltheater, nine at the Kärntnertor), and Gassmann's *L'amore artigiano* (six performances in the Nationaltheater, eight at the Kärntnertor).

An anonymous partisan of the German company, describing the events of 1776, was glad to report that it withstood the competition of the opera buffa troupe: "As excellent as this Italian opera was, it did no harm to the Nationaltheater; indeed the Italian troupe encouraged the acceptance of the Nationaltheater instead of hindering it. It has always been the fate of Italian opera in Vienna to be loved and attended only by a small number of music lovers and connoisseurs, and, to be honest, as much as we ourselves love the Italian opera, we are also happy that in the principal city of Germany an Italian theater is accorded only one percent of the value of a German theater."[27]

Joseph did not forget Salieri. On 23 March 1776 he gave Khevenhüller detailed instructions concerning the management of the Nationaltheater. The memorandum mentions only one musician by name: "the composer Salieri is to be assigned a yearly salary of 200 ducats."[28] This salary, paid by the court theater, presumably represented the extra 200 ducats that Salieri had received annually from the court since 1774 in addition to his regular salary (as chamber musician) of 100 ducats. Joseph did not tell Khevenhüller what a composer of Italian opera was to do in a theatrical program devoted entirely to German spoken drama. As if uncertain about Salieri's function, the accountant who entered Salieri's salary into the theatrical payment records described it, together with the salary paid to the ballet composer Starzer, as "payments to extra per-

26. *Taschenbuch des Wiener Theaters* (Vienna, 1777), 94–95. Since we know from Hadamowsky, *Hoftheater,* vol. 1, the schedule of performances in the Burgtheater during 1776–77, we can deduce the number of performances of an opera at the Kärntnertor by subtracting the number of Burgtheater performances from the total number of performances (as supplied by the *Taschenbuch*).

27. So vortrefflich nun übrigens diese Italienische Oper war, so that sie doch dem Nationaltheater keinen Eintrag, ja sie war seiner Aufnahme vielmehr behülflich als nachtheilig—es ist in Wien von jeher das Schicksal der welschen Opern gewesen nur von der kleinen Zahl der Musik Liebhaber, und Kenner geliebt, und besucht zu werden—und aufrichtig, so sehr wir selbst Liebhaber der italienischen Oper sind, so sind wir doch sehr zufrieden, daß in der Hauptstadt Deutchlands ein welsches Spektakel nur den hundertsten Theil so viel gilt, als ein deutsches (*Taschenbuch des Wiener Theaters,* 72).

28. The document is quoted in Hadamowsky, *Theaterreform,* 16–17.

sonnel" and described Salieri—in terms only an experienced bureaucrat could have invented—as "former music director to the former theatrical administration of Johann Count Kohary."[29]

Daliso e Delmita

Joseph said nothing to Khevenhüller about Salieri's duties, perhaps, because he expected Salieri to work outside the official purview of the Nationaltheater and its German troupe. In accordance with conditions to which Salieri agreed when Joseph added 200 ducats to his court salary in 1774, he continued to act as music director to the opera buffa troupe after Joseph's dismissal of the last impresario. In this capacity he conducted rehearsals and performances; he composed replacement arias and, in collaboration with De Gamerra, one opera.

Daliso e Delmita was completed, according to a note in Salieri's autograph, on 3 June 1776; it was first performed in the Nationaltheater on 29 July 1776. (It may have been performed earlier in the Kärntnertortheater, but the daily repertory of that theater after Carnival 1776 is unknown.) The two editions of the libretto published for the first production of *Daliso e Delmita* both describe Salieri as "Maestro di musica all'attual servizio di S. M. I. Imperatore, e dei Cesarei Teatri" and De Gamerra as "Poeta de' Cesarei Teatri."

Daliso is a difficult work to categorize, as it was, apparently, for its librettist. In one edition of the libretto De Gamerra called *Daliso* an azione pastorale; in the other, a dramma per musica. A contemporary almanac referred to *Daliso* as a serious opera.[30] Mosel called it an opera seria; but later, in his translation of Salieri's list of his own works (drawn up in 1818), it appears under the rubric "Im ländlichen Style" (in the rustic style) along with five comic operas.[31]

The pastoral content of *Daliso* is certainly not as important as that of *L'amore innocente,* as one might guess from the fact that none of its four principal characters is a real shepherd or shepherdess. Unlike *L'amore innocente,* and despite its original cast, which consisted entirely of opera buffa singers, *Daliso* is a serious opera. Set in ancient Greece, *Daliso* derives its plot from Greek mythology: the decree by Minos, king of Crete, that Athens every year send several of its young men and women to be sacrificed to the Minotaur. The action takes place in the country, and shepherds (male and female) play an important role, but only in the opera's many choruses and dances.

29. "Besoldungen der extra angewiesenen Partheyen. . . . Salieri, gewesten Maestro, bey der fürgewest Johann Graf Koharischen theatral Pachtung jährlich 853. f. 20 kr." Financial records for the theatrical year 1776 are published in Hadamowsky, *Theaterreform,* 93–116.

30. *Taschenbuch des Wiener Theaters,* 85.

31. Mosel, 61, 205.

Astidimante, a retired Athenian soldier (bass, the role created by Poggi), lives in the countryside near Athens with his daughters Delmita and Eurilla (sopranos, Clementina Baglioni and Madame Morigi) and with Daliso (tenor, Guglielmo Jermoli), who believes himself to be Astidimante's son but is really the son of another Athenian soldier. Daliso and Delmita love one another, assuming their love to be fraternal, not romantic. De Gamerra made little of one potential source of dramatic interest by having Astidimante reveal to Delmita near the beginning of the opera that Daliso is not his son; the lovers never have a chance to think that their relations are incestuous.

Delmita is chosen by lot to be one of the Minotaur's victims. Much of the opera depicts the parting of the lovers and expressions of grief from Delmita's father and sister and from a chorus and corps de ballet consisting of shepherds. Sorrow suddenly turns to joy when news arrives that the Athenian hero Theseus has killed the Minotaur.

The simple plot derived from Greek mythology, the lack of comic roles, the small number of characters, and the importance of chorus and ballet all help to place *Daliso,* despite its pastoral setting, in the tradition of Viennese serious opera with chorus and dance cultivated by Gluck during the 1760s and continued by Salieri in *Armida.*[32]

Why did Salieri return to Gluckian serious opera in 1776? One of the two editions of the libretto suggests an answer. Its title page describes the opera as having been "performed in the Imperial Theater for the arrival of the Royal Sovereign of Tuscany during the summer of 1776."[33] Grand Duke Leopold of Tuscany (who visited Vienna during summer 1776, arriving on 13 July)[34] had earlier signaled interest in Italian serious opera as cultivated by Gluck and Calzabigi by accepting dedications of the score of *Alceste* (published in 1769) and, on a visit to Vienna in 1770, the libretto of *Paride ed Elena.* On that occasion Leopold had requested a performance of *Alceste.*[35] Salieri and De Gamerra, aware of the grand duke's tastes, may have intended *Daliso* as a bid for his patronage.

In *Daliso* Salieri returned to the rich orchestration of *La secchia rapita, La calamita de' cuori,* and, more significantly, Gluck's *Paride ed Elena.* The overture is in the same key as that of Gluck's last Viennese opera, C major, and requires the same orchestra. Salieri's use of horns in F rather than in C reflects Gassmann's tendency, when using trumpets and horns together, to choose horns tuned to a key other than the tonic. He took full advantage of his large orchestra, combining big chords in the first violins, reinforced by the brass, woodwinds, cellos, and basses, with tremolos in the second vio-

32. Heartz (*Viennese School,* 234) does not take *Daliso* (or Naumann's *Armida,* performed by the same troupe in 1777) into account when he says that after Salieri's *Armida* "no more *opere serie* were performed in either of the court theaters."

33. Sartori no. 7055.

34. Khevenhüller, 8:150.

35. Calzabigi to Paolo Frisi, Vienna, 11 October 1770, in Calzabigi, "Dagli archivi milanesi," 290–91.

EXAMPLE 7.1 *Daliso e Delmita,* overture, mm. 13–16 (A-Wn, Mus. Hs. 16189)

lins and violas (ex. 7.1). A somewhat smaller orchestra echoes this massive sonority and triadic ascent in the duet for Delmita and Daliso at the end of act 1, "Dal braccio mio trafitto" (also in C), giving this act a pleasing symmetry. The overture's orchestra returns complete at the end of the opera, accompanying a festive vaudeville for soloists, chorus, and dancers.

In that final number and elsewhere in *Daliso* Salieri used his large orchestra to enhance De Gamerra's most impressive scenic tableaux, often in response to cues that the poet, as in *La finta scema,* provided in his libretto. The opera begins with a wrestling competition announced, in De Gamerra's words, by "a resounding of martial instruments." Salieri provided a fanfare in C for trumpets in C, horns in F, and timpani. The contest itself, presumably in pantomime, is accompanied by an orchestral *lotta* (battle) in A minor, played by an orchestra of trumpets and timpani, horns, oboes, and strings. (Salieri used A minor very seldom, apparently agreeing with Galeazzi that this key "is of little practical use except to depict carnage, massacres and funeral laments.")[36] The same orchestra accompanies the following choral celebration of Daliso's victory. Later in act 1 shepherds pray to Venus in the choral dance "Dolce dea, cura di Giove." De Gamerra had in mind a "tenera amabilissima sinfonia," which Salieri provided by way of an orchestra of flutes (including an elaborate solo), oboes, horns, trumpets, and strings.

36. Quoted in Steblin, *A History of Key Characteristics,* 110–12 and 358.

EXAMPLE 7.2 *Daliso e Delmita,* act 2, "L'affanno d'amore," mm. 34–47

There could be no harsher fate, no more painful torment, no more horrendous moment.

Writing for opera buffa singers, Salieri had trouble avoiding the melodic styles of opera buffa. The bass Astidimante (like Ubaldo in *Armida*) occasionally sounds like a buffo caricato, as for example in his aria "Nacqui anch'io fra le pompe," with its dotted rhythms, repetition of a rhythmic idea in successive phrases, and disjunct melody that sometimes doubles the bass. But in the trio near the end of the opera, "L'affanno d'amore," Salieri managed, while using these same elements of buffo-caricato style, to communicate Astidimante's sadness by means of the minor mode and diminished seventh intervals in the melody (ex. 7.2). Salieri discouraged Viennese audiences from associating Astidimante with comic opera, despite the singer's being well known to them as a buffo caricato, by beginning his first aria, "Per trapassarmi l'anima" (which he sings just after hearing that Delmita must be sacrificed to the Minotaur), with a short but harmonically eventful introduction in G minor. Horns in E♭, silent in measure 1, nicely highlight the Neapolitan harmony in measure 2 (ex. 7.3).

EXAMPLE 7.3 *Daliso e Delmita,* act 1, "Per trapassarmi l'anima," mm. 1–6

Just as effective is Salieri's use, in his musical characterization of Daliso, of the musical style with which he conveyed the tender and sincere emotions of mezzo-carattere roles in his previous comic operas. When, in the duet "Dal braccio mio trafitto," Delmita refuses to believe Daliso's declaration of love, Daliso falls on his knees, the tempo changes from Allegro assai to Larghetto and the meter from duple to triple, and he sings a sweet melody that Salieri might have written for an ardent young lover in an opera buffa (ex. 7.4). This beautiful moment of amorous supplication in the middle of a duet prefigures both dramatically and musically a moment in the middle of a duet written fourteen years later. In *Così fan tutte* Ferrando resorts to a sensuous melody in triple meter, Larghetto ("Volgi a me pietoso il ciglio"), to complete his seduction of Fiordiligi in the duet "Fra gli amplessi."

EXAMPLE 7.4 *Daliso e Delmita*, act 1, "Dal braccio mio trafitto," mm. 81–92

If you do not soften your look, you will see me die at your feet.

Salieri also adopted the forms and styles of serious opera (both Gluckian music drama and opera seria as cultivated in Italy during the 1770s). Daliso's big aria in act 2, "Nel lasciarti, oh Dio! mi sento," is a rondò in one tempo (to be distinguished from the two-tempo rondò, common during the 1780s and 1790s), often reserved in opere serie of the 1770s for the soprano hero to sing at a crucial moment late in the drama.[37] The popularity of the single-tempo rondò was surely inspired in part by the most famous of such arias, Gluck's "Che farò senza Euridice," whose eight-syllable lines, moderately slow tempo, and simple, major-mode melody with gavotte rhythms that returns twice after intervening episodes (A-B-A-C-A) are typical of the rondò. "Care luci del mio bene," the rondò that Paisiello wrote for the soprano Ferdinando Tenducci to sing in *Andromeda* (Milan, 1774), contains all the same features;[38] so does Salieri's "Nel lasciarti." Both "Care luci" and "Nel lasciarti" differ from "Che farò" in ending with codas

37. On the single-tempo rondò of the 1770s see Hansell, "Opera and Ballet," 467–78.

38. Paisiello's rondò is transcribed and analyzed in Hansell, "Opera and Ballet," 472–78, 989–96.

EXAMPLE 7.5 *Daliso e Delmita,* act 2, "Nel lasciarti, oh Dio! mi sento," mm. 1–7

In leaving you, oh God, I feel my soul turn to ice.

in which the singer leaps repeatedly to an expressive high note. (Gluck brought "Che farò" up to date in the Paris version of *Orfeo* by adding such a coda.) Salieri tried in "Nel lasciarti" to create a melody as touching and memorable as those invented by Gluck and Paisiello; he came quite close to succeeding (ex. 7.5). Salieri's coda, with its gavotte rhythm and passionate leaps up to G, is heartfelt (ex. 7.6).

EXAMPLE 7.6 *Daliso e Delmita,* act 2, "Nel lasciarti, oh Dio! mi sento," mm. 86–97

Salieri and De Gamerra called several times for offstage singing, both solo and choral. In the love duet, after Daliso has convinced Delmita that he loves her and a short canon depicts their embrace, Astidamante interrupts their reconciliation by singing, offstage and in minor, of the daughter he is about to lose. Salieri used an offstage chorus in two very different ways near the end of the opera. As the shepherds mourn Delmita's fate in the D-minor choral dance "Ah Delmita or che t'affretta," their phrases are echoed by a group of shepherds in the distance. A tragic march in C minor follows, then the trio in B♭ for Delmita, her lover, and her father, with more expressions of grief and farewell. Suddenly a chorus in the distance announces, in D major, that Theseus has killed the Minotaur, establishing from afar the key and the mood of the opera's final triumphant vaudeville-dance (which the chorus sings on stage).

Daliso was given only five times, twice in the Burgtheater and three times in the Kärntnertortheater.[39] Mosel blamed its failure on some unfortunate incidents that oc-

39. *Taschenbuch des Wiener Theaters,* 94–95; Hadamowsky, *Hoftheater,* 1:25.

curred during performances of the opera. His account is valuable for the glimpses that it allows us into operatic production in Vienna. It suggests that audiences were able and willing to follow the words of an Italian opera. And it tells us something about the relation between singers and audience during a performance.

> The first scene presents a rural amphitheater in which people are assembled to watch young shepherds wrestling. After the dress rehearsal, when everything went well, the scene designer had the idea, without telling the poet or the composer a word about it, to paint spectators into the ranks of the amphitheater, among the trees with which the entire stage was embellished. In other circumstances this would have produced a useful illusion of extras representing the people. But when the contest ended, and after the victor [i.e., Daliso] was crowned, everyone left the stage except the community's chief, who stayed behind with his two daughters, to whom he wants to reveal a secret, and begins with the words "Or che siam soli, o figlie . . . " [Now that we are alone, oh daughters . . .]. The audience, who saw all the painted figures among the shrubbery, not only began to laugh, but laughed louder and louder as they noticed that the singers, who could not guess why the audience was laughing, looked around for some explanation for this interruption, but were unable to find one.
>
> Such accidents rarely happen alone. In the second act Daliso, Delmita's beloved, appeared on stage in armor, with visor down, ready to do battle with the monster to whom Delmita, according to the country's law, must be sacrificed. Daliso wants to reveal his identity to Delmita, who flees in terror, with these words: "Non fuggir, non temer, son'io Daliso." [Flee not, fear not: it is I, Daliso.] At this point he was supposed to open his visor, but he was not able to do so, and at each fruitless attempt the audience laughed louder.
>
> At the end, after the monster was slain, the city of Athens, illuminated, was supposed to be visible in the distance. But the signal was given too late, and when the audience heard one of the characters on stage say
>
> . . . Vedete come allo splendor
> Di mille faci e mille
> Festaggia Atene . . .
>
> [See how Athens celebrates in the splendor of thousands of torches]
>
> without seeing any of it, laughter rang out a third time; and it grew to its loudest when the illumination first began to appear at the same moment as the curtain fell.
>
> So everything conspired to turn this opera seria into an opera buffa. At the end Salieri himself laughed too, especially since he had never expected much of this opera, which he set to music only after repeated, urgent requests and which was sung by members of the comic opera troupe.[40]

40. Mosel, 60–61.

The Tonkünstler-Sozietät and *La passione di Gesù Cristo*

The failure of *Daliso* may have discouraged Salieri and De Gamerra from further collaboration. Henceforth the independent opera buffa troupe performed few new works, depending almost entirely on operas previously performed in Vienna or elsewhere. As music director of the Italian troupe Salieri had to compose individual numbers for insertion in operas performed by the troupe, but he directed most of his compositional energy elsewhere.

In 1776 he became a member of the Tonkünstler-Sozietät, an organization of professional musicians founded by Gassmann in 1772 to raise money for the support of musicians' widows and orphans. Membership in the society completed his process of integration into Viennese musical life. The process had begun with his "adoption" by Gassmann and his arrival in Vienna in 1766; it had continued with his education in Vienna, his acquaintance with Gluck and Metastasio, his achievement of a position at court, the successful production of his operas at the court theaters, and his marriage into a Viennese family. By granting him admission to the Tonkünstler-Sozietät, Salieri's peers recognized him as a Viennese musician.

Near the end of Lent and Advent the Tonkünstler-Sozietät presented large concerts, usually featuring an Italian oratorio.[41] The finest Viennese musicians provided music for these concerts. Gassmann set Metastasio's *Betulia liberata* in 1772; Dittersdorf presented *Esther* in 1773; Haydn wrote *Il ritorno di Tobia* (to a libretto by Boccherini) for performance during Lent 1775. Virtuosos both vocal and instrumental contributed their talents to the worthy cause. The concerts typically included at least one concerto in addition to the oratorio.

To perform their oratorios the Tonkünstler-Sozietät customarily amassed large performing forces. Dittersdorf mentioned in his memoirs that Gassmann's *Betulia liberata* was performed by an orchestra of two hundred.[42] This figure probably includes chorus and vocal soloists as well as instrumentalists, but the Tonkünstler orchestras were still extremely large ensembles for Vienna.

With his setting of Metastasio's *La passione di Gesù Cristo,* performed by the Tonkünstler-Sozietät near the end of Advent 1777, Salieri sought to match the achievements of Gassmann, Dittersdorf, and Haydn. The oratorio consists of two parts, both of which conclude with grand choruses that end with fugues.[43] But neither choral music nor polyphony is typical of the work as a whole. After an overture that represents, according to a note in the autograph, "Peter's remorse and despair," Metastasio's meditation

41. The following paragraphs are adapted from Rice, "Vienna," 146–47.

42. Dittersdorf, *Lebensbeschreibung,* 197–98.

43. The following remarks are based on a piano-vocal score of *La passione di Gesù Cristo,* ed. Rudolf Kelber (Stuttgart, 1993).

on the passion of Christ unfolds in a succession of recitatives and arias. The aria texts share with those of Metastasio's serious operas short poems in two stanzas, several containing similes of the kind also common in opera seria. Joseph's "Torbido mar che freme" is a storm aria; Mary Magdalen's "Ai passi erranti" compares Christian believers to sailors without a helmsman and to sheep without a shepherd. Salieri responded with music much in the spirit of opera seria: most arias begin with long orchestral introductions, and several include dramatic flights of coloratura, the most brilliant of which he saved until near the end of the oratorio, when Mary Magdalen philosophizes ecstatically in "Ai passi erranti."

Uncharacteristic of opera seria is Salieri's emphasis on the minor mode. In no less than three arias he combined the minor mode and fast tempo to depict his characters' grief. He gave expression to his love of concertante effects with big solos for oboe (in the overture) and bassoon (in Peter's aria "Se a librarsi in mezzo all'onde").

A less attractive feature of Salieri's musical style is more apparent in *La passione* than in earlier works: an excessive dependence on one melodic formula mars not only this oratorio but vocal solos in many of his later operas. Mary Magdalen's first aria exemplifies the pattern. The vocal line begins with two phrases of two measures each in a antecedent-consequent relation. The second phrase reaches its high point at the second degree of the scale and then, in dotted rhythms, descends a seventh to the third scale degree as the harmony moves from V^7 to I (ex. 7.7). Peter's aria "Tu nel duol felice sei" begins with a melody that follows the same plan (ex. 7.8). Melodies of this type were part of the common musical language.[44] But Salieri, who continued to exploit these and

EXAMPLE 7.7 *La passione di Gesù Cristo,* pt. 1, "Vorrei dirti il mio dolore," mm. 1–4

I would like to tell you of my sadness

EXAMPLE 7.8 *La passione di Gesù Cristo,* pt. 1, "Tu nel duol felice sei," mm. 11–14

You are lucky in grief, you who will have the name of son

44. For examples of its use by Luigi Boccherini and Mozart see Heartz, *Viennese School,* 560, 599.

similar melodic patterns (such as one with a descent from the fourth scale degree instead of the second) throughout the rest of his career, made them a characteristic feature of his own style. What sounded fresh and beautiful in 1777 must have sounded somewhat stale in 1795 and 1800, when Rosmino (in *Palmira regina di Persia*) and Nicanore (in *Cesare in Farmacusa*) sang similar melodies (exx. 7.9 and 7.10). Such a mannerism invited parody. Mozart borrowed Salieri's favorite melodic formula for Elvira's first aria in *Don Giovanni*, "Ah chi mi dice mai." He probably wanted his listeners (who knew Salieri's music well, whether they lived in Prague or Vienna) to perceive Elvira's tune, and hence Elvira herself, as a bit stiff and old fashioned.

EXAMPLE 7.9 *Palmira regina di Persia,* act 1, "Signor, che giungi," mm. 26–29 (A-Wn, Mus. Hs. 16183)

You must dispel our miserable misfortune

EXAMPLE 7.10 *Cesare in Farmacusa,* act 1, "Ai coraggiosi, ai forti," mm. 9–12 (A-Wn, Mus. Hs. 16513)

Fate is finally under the control of the brave and the strong.

La passione was the most important work that Salieri completed during the two years in which he wrote no operas. Under a German rendering of the title, it won praise in an anonymous letter in doggerel verse, written from Vienna during Advent 1777. The poem provides a pleasing glimpse of life in Vienna during that time of year. Here is part of it, loosely translated:

> 'Tis Advent time, and though it snows all day,
> One cannot see a single horse-drawn sleigh.
> Because the theaters are all shut down,
> One cannot even find a comic clown
> To rock the crowd with laughter's jolly note.
> An oratorio, *Des Heilands Tod*

Of Metastasio, is sung; what's more,
Salieri has contributed the score.
Whoever hears this score and does not melt,
His heart most certainly has never felt.
Imagine this: joined with the heavenly song,
An orchestra one hundred sixty strong.[45]

45. Wir haben starken Schnee / Jedoch es ist Advent, / Deswegen auch kein Schlitten rennt. / Die Schauspielhäuser sind geschlossen, / Nun machen keine komische Possen / Der Lacher grosse Menge froh; / Das Oratorium von Metastasio: / *Des Heilands Tod* genannt, wird uns izt aufgeführet, / Und Salieri hat die Musik componiret; / Wer da nicht schmelzen will, der muss ganz fühllos seyn, / Man bilde sich nur einmal ein, / Zum Accompagnement der himmlischen Accenten / Sind hundert sechzig Instrumenten (*Konstanzisches Wochenblatt,* 12 January 1778; photocopy, Stadtarchiv, Konstanz).

8

ITALY, 1778–80

Joseph's theatrical reorganization of 1776, despite the epochal importance that historians have attributed to it, did not in fact have much immediate impact on the operatic repertory in Vienna. In 1778, however, Joseph took actions that radically changed Viennese opera. He initiated and oversaw an expansion of the German troupe, incorporating singers who were to perform opera in German, and at the same time he denied further access to the Nationaltheater to the independent opera buffa company resident in the Kärntnertortheater. The Singspiel troupe made its debut on 17 February 1778, with the public premiere of Umlauf's *Die Bergknappen;* the opera buffa troupe made its last appearance in the Nationaltheater (a performance of Vincenzo Righini's *La vedova scaltra*) on 2 March. It disbanded during Lent.

From 1778 to 1781 the performance of opere buffe in Italian (as opposed to those in German translation given by Joseph's troupe) was limited to the occasional productions of traveling troupes at the Kärntnertor. Although our knowledge of their repertory is incomplete, we do know from surviving librettos that the impresario Giuseppe Bustelli presented several operas in 1779 and 1780.[1] Despite these performances the period of five years in which Joseph's Singspiel troupe was active was a dark age for Italian opera in Vienna. It can be no accident that Salieri, after the failure of *Daliso e Delmita* in 1776, wrote no opera for Vienna until 1781, and no Italian opera for that city until 1784. Nor was it by chance that he left Vienna in April 1778, shortly after the dispersal of the opera

1. Sartori records performances in 1779 of Traetta's *Il cavaliere errante nell'isola incantata,* Johann Gottlieb Naumann's *Le nozze disturbate,* Felice Alessandri's *La sposa persiana,* Anfossi's *Lo sposo disperato,* and Giuseppe Gazzaniga's *La vendemmia,* and in 1780 of Anfossi's *La forza delle donne* and Salieri's *La scuola de' gelosi.*

buffa troupe, and that he spent much of the next seven years away from Vienna, fulfilling commissions in Milan, Venice, Rome, Munich, and Paris.

Joseph's cancellation of arrangements whereby an opera buffa troupe under Salieri's musical direction had performed regularly in both theaters left the twenty-eight-year-old composer with little operatic work to do in Vienna. Looking to Italy, he began a tour that lasted exactly two years, from April 1778 to April 1780. In 1772 he had been unable, despite Joseph's help, to win commissions to compose operas in Italy, but six years later he had better luck. Between 1778 and 1780 he composed four operas, one serious and three comic, for theaters in three of Italy's leading operatic centers and collaborated with another musician in the composition of a fifth opera.

Salieri's departure from Vienna did not represent a break with the emperor. He left with Joseph's permission and probably with his encouragement. A year later, at Salieri's request, Joseph extended the leave of absence another year.[2] It was clear to both composer and patron that Salieri would return to Vienna and to his prestigious post in the imperial *Kammermusik.*

The Italian tour had important effects on Viennese opera during the 1780s and 1790s. When Joseph replaced Singspiel with opera buffa in 1783, Salieri helped him choose singers for the new company with advice based on what he had seen and heard in Italy.[3] The Italian troupe included a singer who had created roles in two operas written by Salieri in Italy, Francesco Bussani. A production of one of the Italian operas, *La scuola de' gelosi,* inaugurated the troupe. Two others, *Il talismano* and *La dama pastorella,* formed the basis for operas that he presented as new works in the late 1780s. The Italian journey also left its mark on music that Salieri wrote during the 1790s and later. In 1795 he produced an opera that he had begun, but left unfinished, in Italy in 1779; he reused the overture to *Europa riconosciuta* and part of an aria from *La dama pastorella* in operas that he wrote twenty years later. His very last opera, the Singspiel *Die Neger,* contains echoes of the Italian journey, according to Mosel: "The march of the black men that appears in the first finale (which is also the main theme of the overture) was invented by Salieri when, as a young man, he traveled on foot from Rome, and preserved by him in his memory with special fondness until the opportunity for him to use it arrived."[4]

Salieri began his Italian tour with an elaborate serious opera, *Europa riconosciuta,* performed in celebration of the opening of Teatro alla Scala in Milan. After supervising its production in August 1778, he went to Venice, where he composed, in collaboration with the poet Caterino Mazzolà, a comic opera for the Teatro San Moisè: *La scuola de' gelosi.*[5] He completed it on 15 October 1778, according to a note on the first page of his

2. Mosel, 62, 68. 3. Mosel, 75. 4. Mosel, 165.

5. The librettist of *La scuola de' gelosi,* unnamed in the libretto printed for the first production, is identified as Mazzolà in Mosel, 63.

autograph score. The first performance is often dated 27 December 1778 in secondary sources, a date consistent with the title page of the earliest surviving printed libretto, according to which the opera was "to be performed during Carnival 1779." A manuscript copy of the opera bears an inscription confirming that it was "rappresentata in Venizia [*sic*] nel Teatro Giustiniani in S. Moisé il carnavale del anno 1779."[6] Carnival 1779 began on 26 December 1778, but of course not all Carnival operas were first performed at the beginning of Carnival.

A composer in eighteenth-century Italy normally supervised rehearsals of his opera and led the first three performances. But *La scuola* may have been performed without Salieri's participation; by late December he was probably in Rome, completing his next opera.

According to the libretto for the first production of *La partenza inaspettata,* this two-part intermezzo was performed in the Teatro Valle in Rome during Carnival 1779. Salieri inscribed the autograph score "In Roma li 22 dec. 779," thereby adding another element of doubt to the chronology of his tour.[7] He must have meant 1778; otherwise *La partenza inaspettata* could not have been performed during Carnival 1779. It is unlikely that the libretto was misdated, because Salieri was undoubtedly in Rome early in 1779; Grand Duke Leopold in Florence wrote to his brother Joseph on 18 April 1779, in a letter quoted at greater length in chapter 9, that Salieri had "come from Rome on his way to Milan."

Salieri returned to Milan in spring or summer 1779 in anticipation of the opening of another theater, the Teatro alla Cannobiana. He intended to help celebrate the inauguration with productions of *La fiera di Venezia* and a new opera, *Il talismano,* on a libretto sent by Goldoni from Paris. A third opera, to be composed by Giacomo Rust, was originally planned to complete the opening season. But delays in the opening of the theater and in the arrival of Goldoni's libretto caused the performance of Rust's opera to be canceled. On Salieri's suggestion, Rust collaborated with him on *Il talismano* by composing the second and third acts.[8] Nine years later, in Vienna, Salieri returned to his partial setting of *Il talismano* and in collaboration with Da Ponte presented a setting of a revised version of Goldoni's complete libretto.

From Milan Salieri went to Venice, where he resumed collaboration with Mazzolà on a second comic opera, *L'isola capricciosa.* He had already begun composition when news arrived that the impresario who had engaged him had died and that his successor

6. Della Croce/Blanchetti, 443.

7. Della Croce/Blanchetti assigns the premiere to Carnival 1779; Swenson, 77, and Angermüller, *Leben,* 2:53, follow the dating of Salieri's autograph by placing the first performance of *La partenza inaspettata* in Carnival 1780. This date conflicts with Mosel's testimony, with the evidence presented here that Salieri was indeed in Rome during early 1779, and with the libretto (Rome, 1779), whose title page refers to a production "Nel Carnevale dell'Anno 1779."

8. Mosel, 65–66.

had canceled Salieri's contract.[9] The commission went instead to Rust, whose *L'isola capricciosa* was performed in Venice during Carnival 1780.[10] Salieri always waited patiently for an opportunity to use music that for one reason or another had not been performed, and to reuse in Vienna music that was not well known there. It was not until 1795 that he presented in the Viennese court theaters, under the title *Il mondo alla rovescia,* the opera that he had begun to compose in 1779.

Having returned to Rome, Salieri followed up the apparent success of *La partenza inaspettata* with another two-part intermezzo. *La dama pastorella* was first performed at the beginning of Carnival 1780 (that is, near the end of December 1779) between the acts of an improvised comedy, *Il chiacchierone imprudente.*[11]

Europa riconosciuta

Lombardy, an Austrian province, was governed from Milan by Archduke Ferdinand, one of Joseph's younger brothers. In August 1778 a great new theater opened in Milan under the auspices of the monarchy and its archducal representative: the Regio Teatro alla Scala. Ferdinand probably helped to decide who was to write the inaugural operas, and Joseph probably exerted influence on his brother. According to a contemporary account Gluck was asked in 1777 to compose an opera seria for Milan.[12] Whether this commission was related to the forthcoming inauguration of La Scala is unknown, but in any case Gluck, busy with his Parisian operas, turned down the offer. Salieri and Michele Mortellari received the prestigious commissions to write the operas that celebrated the opening of La Scala during summer 1778.

Salieri and Mortellari collaborated in Milan with the innovative theatrical poet Mattia Verazi, who, like Salieri, had found more success north of the Alps than in Italy.[13] Verazi had served as theatrical poet at the court of Stuttgart since 1755, producing there and in Mannheim a series of adventurous serious operas in Italian, in collaboration with Jommelli, Traetta, Francesco de Maio, and J. C. Bach. He incorporated ballet and pantomime into several operas; he experimented with the use in serious opera of the multisectional ensemble finale that was at this time limited almost exclusively to comic

9. Mosel, 66–67.

10. Sartori no. 13785.

11. *Diario ordinario,* 1 January 1780, quoted in Swenson, 78.

12. Report dated Milan, 8 July 1777, in *Musikalisch-kritische Bibliothek,* ed. Johann Nikolaus Forkel, 391; quoted in Swenson, 65.

13. The following paragraph is based on Marita McClymonds, "Mattia Verazi and the Opera at Mannheim, Stuttgart, and Ludwigsburg," *Studies in Music from the University of Western Ontario* 7 (1982): 99–136, "Verazi, Mattia," in *NGDO,* and "Transforming Opera Seria: Verazi's Innovations and Their Impact on Opera in Italy," in *Opera and the Enlightenment,* ed. Thomas Bauman and Marita McClymonds (Cambridge, 1995), 119–32.

opera (as in Bach's *Temistocle,* 1772); he inserted numerous footnotes into his librettos specifying actions, gestures, and musical events (as in Traetta's *Sofonisba,* 1762). Although it is not always clear whether these notes are prescriptive (instructions to be followed by scenographer, composer, singers, and so forth) or descriptive (merely putting in print what the scenographer, composer, and singers have decided for themselves), they suggest that Verazi exerted an unusual amount of control over many aspects of operatic creation and production.

Verazi found in Salieri another collaborator willing and able to bring his innovations to dramatic life. Their contribution to the inaugural festivities, *Europa riconosciuta,* was conceived and produced with a lavishness that suited the occasion.[14] It brought together several of Italy's leading singers. It was unusual, indeed, in having two pairs of leading roles, requiring the engagement of two prime donne and two primi uomini (both musici). The libretto printed for the first production makes a special point of saying that Maria Balducci and Fransziska Danzi Lebrun "both have parts that are exactly equal"; it says the same about the two leading men, soprano Gasparo Pacchierotti and contralto Giovanni Rubinelli. A large number of choruses, a military band that appears on stage and many extras increased the splendor and the cost of the opera, as did the large number of sets, designed by the Galliari brothers of Turin. Ignoring many of the conventions of Metastasian serious opera, Verazi and Salieri gave an important role to the chorus, which often interacts musically with one or more soloists. They presented in action ensembles scenes that would have been set as recitative in more traditional operas. The opera is cast in two acts instead of the normal Metastasian three, and both acts end with finales in which both chorus and soloists take part.

Europa is full of dramatic and violent events. After a shipwreck Europa, princess of Tyre (soprano; the role was created by Balducci), her husband Asterio, King of Crete (soprano, Pacchierotti), and their small son are captured by the evil Egisto (tenor, Antonio Prati). Egisto wants to marry Semele, a princess hoping to occupy the throne of Tyre (soprano, Danzi Lebrun), but she refuses him because she is in love with the Phoenecian prince Isseo (contralto, Rubinelli). A sacrificial ceremony about to claim Asterio's life is interrupted by a battle in which Isseo slays Egisto, a deed that according to Metastasian precept should have been described rather than shown on stage, as here. Europa's generous decision to cede the throne of Tyre to Semele and Isseo brings the opera to a joyful conclusion.

The overture, like that of De Maio's setting of Verazi's *Ifigenia in Tauride* (1764), de-

14. The following discussion benefited greatly from Marita McClymonds, "Verazi's Controversial *Drammi in Azione* as Realized in the Music of Salieri, Anfossi, Alessandri and Mortellari for the Opening of La Scala, 1778–1779," a forthcoming study the typescript of which McClymonds kindly shared with me.

EXAMPLE 8.1 *Europa riconosciuta*, overture, mm. 1–10 (A-Wn, Mus. Hs. 17836)

picts a violent storm that results in a shipwreck.[15] Verazi helped listeners interpret Salieri's overture and what follows with detailed stage directions.

Salieri's overture in D major is suitably stormy, exploiting many of the same conventions for the musical depiction of storms that Gluck used so effectively in the overture to *Iphigénie en Tauride:* tremolos, syncopations, a full orchestra including trumpets, and sudden alterations of piano and forte. Gluck's storm music, which had earlier served as the overture to *L'Ile de Merlin* (1757), was probably well known to Salieri, as was the music that Gassmann had written to accompany a "terrible storm with lightning, thunder, rain, and wind" at the beginning of act 2 of *La casa di campagna* (1773). Salieri's score indicates the timing of lightning and thunder. After an opening measure of silence, during which lightning flashes, the orchestra enters on a unison D, fortissimo: a long string tremolo reinforced by trumpets, horns, and bassoons (ex. 8.1). The music depicts the gradually clearing sky by means of a thirty-five-measure prolongation of dominant harmony, bringing the overture to a gentle conclusion with softly arpeggiated A-major chords. Salieri must have been fond of this storm overture. Twenty-two years later he wrote another opera that begins with a storm at sea, *Cesare in Farmacusa,* taking advantage of the fact that *Europa* was unknown in Vienna to reuse its overture.

A reference in Verazi's first footnote to an oboe solo "which takes the place of the overture's Andante" means that a Milanese audience (and perhaps also Verazi) still recognized in 1778 the three-movement form (fast-slow-fast) as normal for an overture.

15. On the tradition of storm overtures in eighteenth-century opera see Julie E. Cumming, "Gluck's Iphigenia Operas: Sources and Strategies," in Bauman and McClymonds, *Opera and the Enlightenment,* 217–40.

Verazi and Salieri made use of the audience's expectation that a slow movement would follow the initial fast movement by casting the overture in one movement and placing a cavatina for Asterio directly after it. Just as the opera's action (in the form of the storm itself, represented on stage with the curtain up) begins with the overture, so the overture (in the form of what at first seems to be its expected second movement) infiltrates the action. Salieri had experimented with a similar dovetailing of overture and dramatic action six years earlier in *La fiera di Venezia,* where the opera's opening chorus can be heard as the overture's fourth and final movement.

Salieri assigned to Asterio's melancholy cavatina, "Sposa, figlio," the very unusual tempo indication "Andantino patetico." With its dialogue of sighing strings and the solo oboe to which the footnote in the libretto refers, this aria touchingly conveys the shipwrecked family's sadness.

The beginning of *Europa* impressed the Milanese, one of whom, Pietro Verri, wrote to his brother in Rome:

> Do you know how the drama begins? While you are waiting for it to start, you hear thunder, then a flash of lightning, and this is the signal for the orchestra to begin the overture. As the curtain rises you see a storm at sea, lightning, laments of those on shore, blasts of wind, foundering ships; and the overture imitates the rain, the wind, the bellowing of the waves, the cries of those whose ships are going down. Little by little the calm returns, the sky lightens, the actors disembark from a ship, and the chorus and a few soloists begin the action.[16]

The prominence of the solo oboe in "Sposa, figlio" and elsewhere in *Europa* is surely related to the presence in Milan of Fransziska Danzi Lebrun's husband, the great oboe virtuoso Ludwig August Lebrun. The couple traveled together frequently between 1778 and 1790, sometimes performing in the same opera. That Salieri wrote the concertante oboe parts in *Europa* for Ludwig August Lebrun is suggested strongly by the fact that the opera's most extravagant oboe solo is in an aria sung by Danzi Lebrun.

The musico Pacchierotti was famous for the expressivity of his singing and acting. Salieri gave him several opportunities besides "Sposa, figlio" to display that expressivity, none more remarkable than the G-minor aria in act 2, "Del morir l'angoscie adesso," which he sings as he prepares for death. After a long and emotionally intense dialogue between Asterio and Europa, set by Salieri as accompanied recitative, "Del morir" begins with a plaintive melody in G minor that echoes a melodic fragment heard earlier in the accompanied recitative (ex. 8.2). Asterio enters, moving surprisingly from the fifth degree to the sixth, and then leaping down a minor seventh: a most unconventional melody. A modulation from G minor to its relative major, B♭, is momentarily darkened by a diminished seventh chord (the D♭ introduced here plays a more

16. Pietro Verri to Alessandro Verri, 5 August 1778, quoted in McClymonds, "Mattia Verazi and the Opera at Mannheim," 135.

EXAMPLE 8.2 *Europa riconosciuta*, act 2, "Del morir l'angoscie adesso," mm. 1–17

Now I feel all the anguish of death in your presence. Woe is me! Ah, this embrace will be my last.

prominent role later in the aria). Having established B♭ major, the melody reaches its climax, ascending by yearning half steps to G before subsiding in a lovely cadence.

Throughout the opera opportunities for great singers to display their brilliant virtuosity alternate with displays by poet and composer of their inventiveness and eagerness to undermine convention. One finds both innovation and vocal virtuosity in the duet for Egisto and Semele near the beginning of the opera, "Va coll'aura scherzando talora," which is perhaps better called a double aria than a duet. It begins as if it were an aria for Semele, with a long passage for her alone. Egisto responds with another long passage, the beginning of which coincides with the end of Semele's line: this half measure is the only place in the number in which Semele and Egisto sing together. After Egisto's solo Semele sings virtuoso passagework of a kind that one would expect in a bravura aria, not a duet. Her cadence in the tonic seems to promise the end of the number, but instead it is followed by another passage for Egisto, who brings this double aria to a close. Semele wants to have nothing to do with Egisto; her avoidance of him is expressed musically by the absence of simultaneous singing in "Va coll'aura."

To the number that follows it is equally difficult to assign a generic term. The Marcia, as it is called in Salieri's score, certainly sounds like a march: maestoso, duple meter, an orchestra consisting of trumpets, horns, oboes, bassoons, and strings. But it begins to sound like an aria when Isseo enters singing "Le spoglie guerriere." Finally a chorus of soldiers enters, transforming the number yet again but maintaining the musical momentum established earlier. Verazi wrote in a footnote: "The same musical idea serves for the chorus as for Isseo's cavatina."[17]

The libretto describes the parts of the two prime donne as "exactly equal"; Salieri took this description seriously in his writing for the two high coloratura sopranos, both of whom must have been astonishing virtuosos. Benedetto Frizzi, an opera lover who heard both Balducci and Danzi Lebrun, remembered Balducci as "excellent in the upper register and in coloratura."[18] Of Danzi Lebrun he wrote: "The adagio was not her specialty, but her aria di bravura could not have been better. The most perfect trill, the most distinct coloratura, the most intricate cadenzas of every kind, leaps of every interval: she executed all of these with ease and perfection."[19] In addition to innovative numbers in which they interacted with other soloists and with the chorus, both Danzi Lebrun and Balducci received more conventional vehicles for the display of the virtuosity that Frizzi remembered. "Ah lo sento il suo tormento," sung by Balducci as Europa, and "Quando più irato freme," sung by Danzi Lebrun as Semele, are both brilliant showpieces. Both Europa and Semele have to sing extraordinary coloratura in very

17. Serve per il coro lo stesso motivo musicale della cavatina d'Isseo (act 1, sc. 6).

18. Benedetto Frizzi, *Dissertazione di biografia musicale* (n.p, n.d.), 72; "Benedetto Frizzi on Singers, Composers and Opera in Late Eighteenth-Century Italy," ed. John A. Rice, *Studi musicali* 23 (1994): 374.

19. Frizzi, *Dissertazione,* 77–78; Frizzi, "Singers," 376.

high register. Semele ascends to Queen of the Night F. Europa, after touching high D several times, ascends to high F♯; hers is quite possibly the highest vocal line in any of Salieri's operas.

But the ornate oboe solo in Semele's aria, probably written for Ludwig Lebrun, makes this the more memorable of the bravura arias. "Quando più irato freme," in which Semele, near the end of the opera, expresses joy at her sudden good fortune, begins with a fifty-seven-measure orchestral introduction that sounds more like an oboe concerto than an aria and that pauses, even before Semele sings, for the oboist to play a cadenza. The oboe concerto then becomes a double concerto for soprano and oboe.

The concerto-like sonata form of Semele's aria resembles closely the structure of the many concertante arias in Salieri's early comic operas, through which he learned how to combine the soprano voice and one or more instrumental soloists (including oboe) in virtuoso display. In composing "Quando più irato freme" he built on that experience, but he also used the solo instrument to express the meaning of the text. Semele likens her former struggles to a storm at sea. The oboe is silent as she depicts the tempest with a declamatory melody full of awkward leaps. But when she sings of the ray of hope that can shine even in the darkest storm, she does so with a lyrical, conjunct tune. The oboe joins her as a symbol of hope, playing in thirds and sixths: Semele is no longer alone. The word "balenar" (to flash) gave Salieri a perfect opportunity for sparkling coloratura, of which he took full advantage; he borrowed part of the vocal line (measures 84–85) from "Ai passi erranti," a bravura aria in *La passione di Gesù Cristo* (ex. 8.3).

Danzi Lebrun must have had a good messa di voce in her upper register, able to sustain high C for two and a half measures as the oboist played passagework. Having played

EXAMPLE 8.3 *Europa riconosciuta*, act 2, "Quando più irato freme," mm. 58–87

(*Continued on next page*)

EXAMPLE 8.3 (*continued*)

⁓When the sea roars more angrily, when it threatens deadly destruction, a ray of friendly hope may shine again amid the tempests.

a cadenza by himself, the oboist played another with the soprano as the aria reached its conclusion. Salieri composed neither of these cadenzas, unlike those that he inserted in concertante arias in some of his early Viennese comedies, probably because he felt that the Lebruns could improvise their own.

Frizzi witnessed the performance by Danzi Lebrun and her husband of this or a similar aria: "Her fortunate marriage to the celebrated oboist Monsieur Le Brune was the finishing touch in the making of this couple into the image of musical enchantment. I heard twice, in Milan and in Mantua, arias *a due* with obbligato oboe, with continuous alternation of every kind, with canons perfectly suited to that amazing voice and to that inimitable master, which aroused in me, and in every sensitive listener, sincere admiration and delightfully tender feelings."[20]

Burney too heard Danzi Lebrun and her husband. Before and after her participation in Salieri's *Europa* she sang in London, where Burney admired her technical virtuosity but complained that her singing lacked expression. His memory of the Lebruns' performance corresponds perfectly to the interaction of oboe and soprano in "Quando più irato freme" and suggests that they brought the aria back to London with them: "In the summer of 1778 she went into Italy and sung at Milan with Pacchierotti, Rubinelli, and the Balducci; and during this journey it was imagined that she would have improved her style of singing; but travelling with her husband, an excellent performer on the hautbois, she seems to have listened to nothing else; and at her return to London she copied the tone of his instrument so exactly, that when he accompanied her in divisions of thirds and sixths, it was impossible to discover who was uppermost."[21]

First performed on 3 August 1778, *Europa* drew mixed reactions from its Milanese audience, whose attention was attracted mainly by Verazi's libretto. Many were repelled by its innovations; a few found them the most attractive aspect of the opera.[22] Pietro Verri seems to have been quite overwhelmed by the production and unable to decide if he liked it or not. He mixed enthusiastic praise for Verazi with comments suggesting that the poet had not completely won him over:

> Signor Verazi . . . is a man not of poetry, nor of letters, but of the theater. He has an imagination and experience developed outside Italy. He puts on the airs of a genius, and with this title he beats and abuses all our theatrical heroes, by which he gives the impression of having

20. Frizzi, *Dissertazione*, 78; Frizzi, "Singers," 376.

21. Burney, *A General History of Music*, 2:886. That Pacchierotti or the Lebruns brought part or all of *Europa* to London is suggested also by the appearance of Salieri's duet "Ah se gli affetti miei" (*Europa*, act 1) in the pasticcio *Il soldano generoso* (London, 1779). See Curtis Price, Judith Milhous, and Robert D. Hume, *Italian Opera in Late Eighteenth-Century London*, vol. 1, *The King's Theatre, Haymarket, 1778–1791* (Oxford, 1995), 229–30.

22. On Milanese reaction to *Europa* see Hansell, "Opera and Ballet," 268–74.

> finally put a decent operatic production on the stage. The choristers are actors instead of statues; the extras do their duty; the scenes are changed without the carpenters being visible to you as they carry the columns and boxes of candles. Everything is organized. The actors do not abuse the recitative. The work has neither head nor tail, but the spectacle pleases because it is varied.[23]

The uniqueness of the circumstances surrounding the creation of *Europa* produced an opera that was difficult to perform under different circumstances. That it was apparently never revived can be attributed, at least in part, to the expensiveness and impracticality of assembling a cast that could perform the leading roles, a chorus able to handle the challenging choral parts, and an oboist able to play the concerto-like accompaniment to Semele's bravura aria.

La scuola de' gelosi

Like many late-eighteenth-century opere buffe created in the spirit of Goldoni, *La scuola de' gelosi* presents characters from three distinct social classes. Count Bandiera (tenor) and his countess (soprano) represent the nobility; the grain dealer Blasio (bass) and his wife Ernestina (soprano), the bourgeoisie; Blasio's servant Lumaca (tenor) and the chambermaid Carlotta (soprano), the working class. The lieutenant (tenor), a cousin of Blasio and a friend of the count, serves as a link between the nobility and the middle class and the chief instigator of the plot.

The absence of Goldonian parti serie from Mazzolà's libretto is a product of a transformation by Goldoni's successors of his tripartite categorization of roles by which parti serie in their purest form largely disappeared and the term *parte di mezzo carattere* became associated with male characters only, and especially the romantic lead. The count is a parte di mezzo carattere, not a parte seria. He is more deeply involved in the plot than the parti serie in many of Goldoni's librettos: he has an important role in the finales. His aria texts are not limited to the form and style of opera seria arias.

The count finds Ernestina attractive. His attempts to seduce her inflame the jealousy of the countess and Blasio, who is so angry that he tries, unsuccessfully, to lock his wife up. The countess's jealousy is mixed with class snobbery of a kind that Goldoni delighted in deriding: it irks her especially that her husband courts "a plebeian, the wife of a merchant."

The countess makes the late appearance that one expects of the female character of highest social rank in an opera buffa. Like the marchesa in *La fiera di Venezia* and the

23. Pietro Verri to Alessandro Verri, 5 August 1778, quoted in McClymonds, *Niccolò Jommelli*, 392. My translation of Verri's ambiguous prose differs considerably from McClymonds's (p. 208).

countess in Mozart's *Figaro,* she introduces herself with a cavatina in slow tempo ("Ah, non è ver") in which she complains of the coldness of the man she loves. Also like those other noblewomen, she later disguises herself in an effort to observe her wayward man and to confront him. In the finale of act 1 she dresses up as a gypsy fortune-teller and reads her husband's palm. She later reveals her identity, much to the count's surprise and embarrassment.

Women who pretend or believe themselves to be fortune-tellers appear with some frequency in opere buffe. Salieri had already depicted, in *Il barone di Rocca Antica,* a rich woman disguised as a fortune-teller. Carolina, the gypsy palm reader in Goldoni's *Il talismano,* turns out to be no gypsy; but she proves her palm-reading abilities during the opera. Salieri and his librettists depicted in these operas and in *La scuola de' gelosi* theatrical versions of the palm reader painted by Pietro Longhi in 1752 (fig. 8.1).

The lieutenant, the teacher of the school to which the title alludes, advises Blasio and the countess to make their spouses jealous. The lieutenant is a man of experience; his role in the opera is analogous to that of Don Alfonso in *Così fan tutte,* whose subtitle, *La scuola degli amanti,* may have been understood by Viennese audiences as a reference to Salieri's opera. Like Alfonso, the lieutenant conveys some of his knowledge of women in the form of a musical motto. The lieutenant's adage, "He who wishes to find fidelity in a woman should leave her mistress of her liberty," appears at the beginning of his aria "Chi vuol nella femmina" (ex. 8.4), again at the end of that aria, and a third time, quoted by Lumaca, in the finale of act 2, always accompanied by two high horns in G (whose connotations of cuckoldry amusingly contradict the motto).

EXAMPLE 8.4 *La scuola de' gelosi,* act 2, "Chi vuol nella femmina," mm. 1–8 (A-Wn, Mus. Hs. 17845)

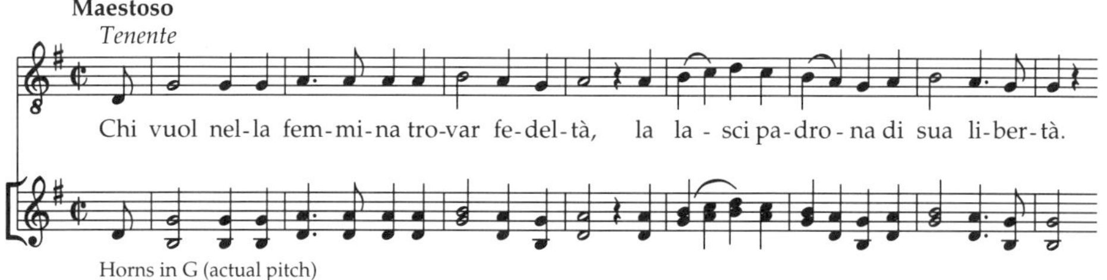

He who wishes to find fidelity in a woman should leave her mistress of her liberty.

Following the lieutenant's advice Blasio leaves a woman's portrait for Ernestina to find; the lieutenant writes the countess a love letter for the count to discover. The jealousy thus aroused restores the equilibrium of the social and sexual status quo.

FIGURE 8.1 Pietro Longhi, *The Fortune-Teller.* (Courtesy of Museo Ca' Rezzonico, Venice.)

There is much in *La scuola,* besides plot and characters, that reminds one of Goldoni. Goldonian aria types abound, especially comic arias in which a male character discusses women: Lumaca's "Una donna che affetto non sente," the lieutenant's "Oggidì le donne nascono," and "Chi vuol nella femmina." The count's "A me par che il mondo sia" is both an aria about women and a catalogue aria, listing the many kinds of women who distract him from his wife:

A me par che il mondo sia
Di ragazze d'ogni sorte
Una vasta galleria.
Chi si muove sussiegata,
Chi par Dido sulla scena.
Sulle braccia ripiegata
Ivi un'altra si dimena:
Quella è grave, questa è snella,
Bianca è l'una, l'altra bruna.
In passeggio piano piano
Miro questa, miro quella.
Esser parmi il gran Sultano,
Crescer sento il cor nel petto,
Ed a tutte il fazzoletto
Io vorrei poter gettar.

[The world seems to me to be a vast gallery of girls of every sort. One moves with dignity; another looks like Dido on the stage. There yet another walks about in agitation, her arms folded. That one is serious, this one lighthearted. One is blond, another dark. As I go for a drive I admire this one, that one. I think of myself as the great sultan: I feel my heart swelling in my breast, and to every girl I would like to toss my handkerchief.]

The count's climactic reference to "the great sultan" reminds one of the catalogue of women in Goldoni's *Il viaggiatore ridicolo,* in which Gandolfo boasts: "E conosco le femmine ancor / Nel Serraglio del Turco Signor."

This text, partly because of its being intended for a buffo di mezzo carattere rather than a buffo caricato, is not nearly so amusing as Leporello's catalogue of women seduced by Don Giovanni. Salieri wrote elegant and charming music in D major, but Mazzolà's poem did not inspire him to attempt the kind of delightful tone painting that Mozart achieved in his D-major setting of Da Ponte's text. The amorous count goes through his women with disappointingly little musical characterization (ex. 8.5). Salieri completely ignored the musical possibilities offered by the juxtapositions of *grave* and *snella* and of *bianca* and *bruna,* falling back instead on his favorite melodic formula: the descent from the second degree to the third in the second of a pair of phrases (at mm. 30–31). The orchestral flourish that punctuates the opening melody (at mm. 18–19) must have sounded old-fashioned in 1779. Piccinni had used much the same music for the same purpose almost twenty years earlier (see ex. 3.8, mm. 31–32).

La scuola differs from Goldoni's librettos in having only two acts. Roman intermezzi were traditionally in two parts, but they were also shorter than regular opere buffe. This is a full-length comic opera whose two acts anticipate the structure of many opere buffe of the 1780s in Vienna as well as Italy.

EXAMPLE 8.5 *La scuola de' gelosi,* act 1, "A me par che il mondo sia," mm. 13–31

(Continued on next page)

EXAMPLE 8.5 (*continued*)

Both acts contain long, complex finales and other important ensembles. Act 1 begins with a fully developed introduzione for three characters. Act 2 includes a long quintet, "Ah! la rabbia mi divora," whose conversational style and sectional structure (Andante con moto, predominantly piano, followed by Allegro assai, predominantly fortissimo) give it the character of a finale. The number of surviving copies (in print and manuscript) of individual numbers from *La scuola* shows that its ensembles were particularly popular among late-eighteenth-century music lovers. The quintet and the duet "Quel visino è da ritratto" both circulated widely in manuscript, and both were printed in Venice shortly after the first performance.[24]

The vividness of characterization in "Ah! la rabbia mi divora," its clever incorporation of a singing lesson (with solfège syllables) within a scene of emotional confusion, and the sheer musical energy conveyed by its climactic Allegro assai all help to explain its success. Blasio puts the lieutenant's motto into practice: he tries to make Ernestina jealous by pretending to be happy, and completely unconcerned about her behavior; but his own jealousy is not far below the surface. The quintet begins with Blasio expressing his rage in comic asides, accompanied by a lively and witty dialogue in the orchestra (ex. 8.6). In *La locandiera* Mirandolina sings almost exactly the same words as Blasio ("Mi divora la rabbia"); but because she makes no attempt to hide her anger, Salieri's musical treatment of her words is completely different from his setting of Blasio's "la rabbia mi divora" (see ex. 6.11). The trick works; as Ernestina expresses her belief that Blasio has a mistress the orchestra conveys her nervousness with tremolos. Meanwhile the lieutenant urges the countess to hide her jealousy by pretending to enjoy a singing lesson with him. While the lieutenant and the countess vocalize, the count and Ernestina express their jealousy and Blasio murmurs with ill-disguised rage. The emotional conflicts within and between characters explode in the Allegro assai (ex. 8.7), where the music communicates excitement by means of speed, sudden alternations of loud and soft, repetition of short motives, and lean textures (with the whole orchestra and all five soloists often in a single, unharmonized line). This scurrying movement brings to a

24. Angermüller, *Leben*, 1:164–67; *RISM* S 560 and 567.

EXAMPLE 8.6 *La scuola de' gelosi,* act 2, "Ah! la rabbia mi divora," mm. 8–11

Ah, anger devours me

EXAMPLE 8.7 *La scuola de' gelosi,* act 2, "Ah! la rabbia mi divora," mm. 103–33

(Continued on next page)

EXAMPLE 8.7 (*continued*)

(*Continued on next page*)

EXAMPLE 8.7 (*continued*)

What tumult in my breast! I can no longer . . . I'm in a rage . . . Anger . . . love . . . fear . . . disdain . . . are tearing at my heart.

lively conclusion a number singled out for praise when *La scuola* was performed in London in 1786.[25]

In the first comic opera that Salieri wrote for an Italian theater, he adapted his compositional procedures to the expectations of Italian performers and audiences and abandoned some of the features that made his earlier operas specifically Viennese. The orchestra consists of oboes, flutes (used very rarely), bassoons, horns, and strings. The festive sounds of trumpets and drums, so much a part of *La secchia rapita, La calamita de' cuori,* and *Daliso e Delmita,* are absent. So, for the most part, is the concertante use of winds characteristic of the early opere buffe. Salieri had followed Gassmann in writing important, independent parts for bassoons in his early operas, even those like *La locandiera* that in other respects are quite plainly orchestrated. But in *La scuola,* in keep-

25. *Morning Post and Daily Advertiser,* 15 March 1786.

ing with Italian practice, he left the bassoons' part, with few exceptions, unnotated and limited to reinforcing the bass.

The transitions that lead listeners, in several of Salieri's early opere buffe, directly from the end of an orchestrally accompanied number into the following recitative are completely absent from *La scuola.* So are the lively, melodic bass lines with which Salieri sometimes accompanied simple recitative in his earlier comic operas.

At the same time as he acknowledged Italian taste and operatic conditions, Salieri managed to infuse *La scuola* with his own musical individuality as shaped by Viennese taste. Two horns alone as the accompaniment for the lieutenant's adage on feminine fidelity betray a Viennese fondness for wind and brass color. Salieri's tendency, amply demonstrated in his early operas, to exploit his prima donna's highest notes and her ability to sing coloratura is evident here as well. The countess's cavatina "Ah non è ver" ascends to high C; so does her bravura aria "Gelosia, dispetto e sdegno," written in much the same heroic style as the bravura arias for Artemia in *Le donne letterate* and Marchesa Calloandra in *La fiera di Venezia,* but without concertante winds. The happy ending is celebrated, as in several Viennese operas of the 1760s and 1770s, with a vaudeville in gavotte rhythms.

Salieri seems to have felt that the simple orchestration and textures of *La scuola* might not please the Viennese as much as the Venetians. At some time (or times) after the first production he substantially revised the autograph score. Some of his revisions can, by means of comparisons between scores and librettos, be connected with the production of *La scuola* with which Joseph's opera buffa troupe was inaugurated in 1783. Other revisions cannot be attributed to any particular production, but may well have been made with a Viennese audience in mind. One such change is in the orchestral accompaniment to the introduzione, the beginning of which is scored for strings alone in a presentation score that represents an early state of the opera.[26] Salieri later increased the timbral and textural complexity of this accompaniment by introducing horns, whose repeated eighth notes enhance the music's momentum (ex. 8.8).

La scuola was probably the most frequently and widely performed of Salieri's operas, and the only one that won popularity in Italy.[27] Bologna, Monza, Padua, Prato, and Varese saw it within a year of its first production. While maintaining its popularity in Italy during most of the following decade, *La scuola* became an international success through performances in Eszterháza, Vienna, Dresden, Prague, London, Paris, St. Petersburg, and elsewhere. Audiences throughout Europe seem to have agreed with the *Morning Post and Daily Advertiser,* which announced, when *La scuola* was performed in London in 1786: "The whole together is a masterly composition, and does great honour to Salieri, whose reputation as a composer must rise infinitely in the musical world, from this very pleasing specimen of his abilities."[28]

26. A-Wn, Mus. Hs. 17845.

27. Sartori nos. 21348–82; Angermüller, *Leben,* 2:50–53.

28. *Morning Post and Daily Advertiser,* 15 March 1786.

EXAMPLE 8.8 *La scuola de' gelosi*, act 1, introduzione, later (Viennese?) version, mm. 1–6 (A-Wn, Mus. Hs. 16615)

Hush! . . . I think I hear someone . . .

Return to Vienna

Mosel related in some detail the circumstances that led to Salieri's return to Vienna in April 1780. The story begins with a commission that probably reached the composer while he was writing or rehearsing *La dama pastorella* during fall 1779:

> In Rome Salieri received an invitation to Naples, to write an opera seria for the famous Teatro San Carlo. . . . In order to accept this invitation he needed a third leave of absence from the emperor. Salieri, fearing to appear presumptuous, was long undecided about whether to make this request or not. But since this was a matter of extending his leave only three months, and because, moreover, he had received this invitation at the king's command (as is customary at that great theater), and through the imperial ambassador Count Lamberg, he took courage and sent his request to Vienna, to Count (later Prince) Rosenberg, imperial-royal high chamberlain and superintendent of the Court Theater, who had secured a leave for him the previous year, and went to Naples to await the answer and immediately to begin his new opera.[29]

29. Mosel, 67–68.

Having been "presented at court by the ambassador and received by Their Majesties with uncommon grace," Salieri began setting to music the libretto assigned to him, Metastasio's *Semiramide.* But he did not finish it. Mosel's account depicts Salieri's skill as a courtier: his sensitivity to the feelings of his imperial patron and his ability to distinguish between the long-term benefits of personal relations (especially those with Joseph) and the short-term benefits to be derived from the composition of a single opera. Faced with the choice between these benefits, Salieri quickly chose the first.

The request for an extension of his leave of absence that Salieri had sent from Rome

> was composed in the most respectful language, the reasons for the request laid out in the clearest manner, and there was no reason to doubt that, if the monarch had read it, he would have granted it. But Count Rosenberg, as he himself later admitted, forgot the petition in his desk, and communicated Salieri's request to the emperor in person, and in a few words, without mentioning the important circumstances that gave rise to the request. Salieri later received the following answer: "In response to your petition, submitted to His Majesty, for permission to stay still longer in Italy, His Majesty has charged me with writing to you that you can stay there as long as you like, and think proper; indeed, that if you find it better for you there than here, you can stay there forever. I regret that I am unable to send you pleasanter news and remain etc."[30]

Rosenberg's sarcasm brought Salieri, who had depended on Joseph's goodwill during his entire career, to a state of crisis:

> One can imagine the surprise and shock that Rosenberg's answer caused him. Count Lamberg, to whom he immediately hastened for advice, tried to calm him with the hope that if the queen, the emperor's sister, wished to intercede on his behalf, events would soon take a more favorable course. At that moment Salieri decided to beg His Majesty to reconsider, but when he came home he suddenly saw the whole situation in an entirely different light. He knew the emperor's way of thinking. The emperor was gracious with everyone, and especially with his servants; nevertheless he did not like to be forced to say yes when he had already said no. Full of fear that such favor, having been refused a second time, could easily turn to disfavor, he returned to Count Lamberg with the urgent request that he release him from his contractual obligations in Naples, and immediately began his journey to Vienna. Before he entered the carriage he wrote to Count Rosenberg, begging forgiveness for his arrogance and notifying him that he was on the point of leaving Naples.
>
> At midday on 8 April 1780 he returned to the bosom of his joyful family: the same day as that on which, two years earlier, he had begun his journey to Italy.[31]

30. Mosel, 68–69.
31. Mosel, 69.

Mosel recorded nothing of the journey except (quoting Salieri) that the composer traveled day and night. He carried a letter of introduction addressed to Padre Martini in Bologna by the composer Giuseppe Gazzaniga.[32] The letter, dated 18 March 1780, mentions that Salieri planned to leave Naples that very evening. If he did so, his trip to Vienna by way of Bologna took exactly three weeks.

The same sensitivity and diplomatic skill that had persuaded "the Talleyrand of music" to leave Naples also guided his behavior in Vienna.

> After first seeking out Count Rosenberg, whom he did not find at home, he went to court to demonstrate his submission: not in the emperor's chamber, where he, as chamber composer, could have gone, but instead in the corridor (the so-called *Controlorgang*) in which the monarch was accustomed every day at three o'clock in the afternoon to hear petitioners and to receive their written requests. There, where about twenty supplicants, mostly people from the country, awaited the emperor, Salieri stood a little apart from the others, not without fear that he would be received coldly by his master.
>
> At three o'clock the emperor returned from a drive, walked, as usual, through the corridor, listened to the petitioners, whom he addressed with the expression and tone of an affectionate father. He suddenly noticed Salieri and immediately approached him with these words: "Look who's here, Salieri! Welcome! I didn't expect you so soon. Have you had a good trip?" "A very good trip, Your Majesty," answered Salieri fearfully, "although I thought it necessary to travel day and night to correct my error, for which I most humbly beg forgiveness, so that I might all the sooner return to my duties at court." "It was not necessary," answered the monarch graciously, "to hurry things so, but it is good to see you again. Go upstairs; we want to try some excerpts from your new operas that were sent to me from Italy."
>
> These kind words calmed and cheered Salieri so much that he immediately forgot all the hardship that his unprepared journey had caused him. As he entered the antechamber he found already assembled several of the older members of the court chapel, whose faces expressed happiness all the more heartfelt, the rumor having circulated that Salieri had fallen from the emperor's favor.[33]

Mosel's account of Salieri's conversation with Joseph during the emperor's dinner shows the composer to have been a perceptive observer of Joseph's personality and behavior:

> Half an hour later the emperor entered . . . , sat down at a table in the music-room, where he was accustomed to eat alone, and summoned Salieri to converse with him during the meal (which never lasted much longer than a quarter of an hour). He asked if Salieri had found his family in good health, inquired about his travels, about the compositions that he had finished

32. Quoted in Angermüller, *Leben*, 3:12.

33. Mosel, 69–70.

in Italy, and so forth. Salieri spoke, and in the course of his narrative he naturally had to come to the Neapolitan episode. When, with some nervousness, he confessed that he had traveled from Rome to Naples without permission, in expectation of receiving it, the emperor looked at him with a sudden movement of the head (such movements were characteristic of him). Salieri stopped, and a small pause followed during which it seemed to him that the monarch, unaware that the project had gone so far, was momentarily sorry not to have granted Salieri's request. But he said nothing about it; instead, changing the subject, he asked: "Where did you find the best orchestra?" Salieri now realized that Naples should be discussed no further, and spoke accordingly.

At the end of the meal the regular musicians who waited in the antechamber were admitted, and several vocal numbers from the operas *Europa riconosciuta* and *La scuola de' gelosi* were performed from the score.[34]

34. Mosel, 70–71.

9

JOSEPH'S SINGSPIEL TROUPE AND *DER RAUCHFANGKEHRER*

Joseph's formation of a Singspiel company in 1778 represented a reversal of one aspect of his reorganization of 1776, since it brought a resident operatic troupe back into the Burgtheater. Yet the performance of German opera was consistent with the idea that the court theater should serve as a center for the promotion of German language and culture (although it is true, as we will see, that many of the operas presented by Joseph's troupe were German only in language). It was also consistent with Joseph's goal of saving money. Most German operas of the 1770s were spoken plays with songs that generally required less virtuosity from their performers than Italian operas; the German singer-actors who performed them were easier to find and cheaper to employ than Italian opera singers.

German opera of the kind presented by Joseph's troupe was not new to Vienna. Taking advantage of the Schauspielfreiheit decreed in 1776, the impresario Johann Böhm had presented a series of opéras-comiques in German translation in the Kärntnertortheater from April to June 1776. The most popular of Böhm's productions (to judge from the number of performances) were Grétry's *L'Ami de la maison* and François-André Danican Philidor's *Le Jardinier et son seigneur*. The small size and poor quality of the company led to failure in Vienna, but another impresario soon followed Böhm's lead. Johann Christian Wäser's troupe performed more operas in German at the Kärntnertor during the following months, included Singspiele by Johann Adam Hiller, opéras-comiques (German versions of Pierre-Alexandre Monsigny's *Le Déserteur* and Gluck's *La Rencontre imprévue*), and an opera buffa (a German version of Guglielmi's *La sposa fedele*).[1] The performances by Böhm and Wäser in 1776 may have inspired Joseph when,

1. On the little-known visits of the Böhm and Wäser troupes to Vienna see *Taschenbuch des Wiener Theaters*, 64–70, 74–84.

less than two years later, he founded a German opera company whose repertory strongly resembled those of the troupes that visited Vienna in 1776.

The Viennese playwright Tobias Philipp von Gebler, in a letter to his friend Friedrich Nicolai in Berlin, wrote with enthusiastic expectation of the inauguration of Joseph's Singspiel troupe. The letter nicely captures the contradictory qualities of Joseph's project. By mentioning only Italian and French composers, Gebler belied his statement that "no foreign plays will be performed in the court theater":

> you may have heard that our truly German emperor is now establishing a German opera for the performance of both serious and comic works. The singers must be real virtuosos, and no Lieder singers; and the operas constituted along the lines that we are familiar with from those of Piccini, Anfossi, Paisiello, and, to some extent, Gretri as well. The first rehearsals will begin during the next few weeks, with a small piece entitled *Die Bergknappen*. Mlle. Cavalieri, a singer whose organ is extraordinary, with high notes and low notes together with a strong chest, will take the principal role. There are only four *parti cantanti*, and one character with a speaking part. . . . After Easter no foreign plays will be performed in the court theater; Italians and Frenchmen will be restricted to the theater at the Kärntnertor.[2]

The Company and Its Repertory

The organization of the German opera troupe in 1778 marks the beginning of Joseph's activity as opera director. Normally the Musikgraf, or someone under his authority, managed the theaters in the absence of an impresario. The Musikgraf was in turn under the supervision of the Obersthofmeister, who answered to the sovereign. In other words, a layer of bureaucracy separated the emperor from the day-to-day management of the theaters. Joseph began cutting through this layer by not replacing Count Sporck as Musikgraf when he transferred him to another position in 1775. In 1778 he took control of the theaters from the Obersthofmeister and placed it in the hands of his trusted advisor, *Oberstkämmerer* (High Chamberlain) Count Franz Xaver Rosenberg-Orsini (fig. 9.1). He did not intend to let Rosenberg run the theaters, however, but to use him as a means through which to run the theaters himself.

Joseph assembled the troupe, to some extent an ongoing process. Singspiel, which traditionally contained a considerable amount of spoken dialogue, allowed for much diversity in the attention given to music. The emperor's decision to inaugurate the troupe with a one-act opera by Ignaz Umlauf, who had written only one opera of minor importance, suggests that his musical aims were not very high at the beginning. But his efforts over the next two years to hire some of Europe's best singers show that his ambitions concerning the sophistication and lavishness of the company's musical com-

2. Gebler to Nicolai, 9 February 1778, in *Aus dem Josephinischen Wien: Geblers und Nicolais Briefwechsel während der Jahre 1771–1786*, ed. Richard Maria Werner (Berlin, 1888), 92.

FIGURE 9.1
Count (later Prince) Franz Xaver Rosenberg-Orsini, 1783. Engraving by Jacob Adam after a painting or drawing by C. Vinazer. (Photo courtesy of Bildarchiv der Österreichischen Nationalbibliothek, Vienna.)

ponent developed significantly during these years. These ambitions are reflected in the increasing amounts that he spent on the troupe. Total expenditures for the Nationaltheater (including actors, singers, and orchestra) rose from 94,029 Gulden in 1778 to 106,394 in 1779 to 110,146 in 1780.[3]

3. HHStA, OMeA, SR, Kart. 369, contains a chart documenting the court's theatrical expenses and income from 1776 to 1788.

We can follow Joseph's efforts to build up the Singspiel company in a letter that Rosenberg wrote to Salieri during the composer's leave of absence in Italy and in correspondence between the emperor and his brother Leopold in Florence. Joseph used both Salieri and Leopold to help in tracking down and evaluating singers. In looking to Italy, he sought German singers with experience in the performance of opera seria: singers, in other words, who could sing and act in German and at the same time could bring to his troupe the pathos and vocal brilliance of Italian serious opera.

Rosenberg's letter mentions only two singers, the tenors Valentin Adamberger and Giacomo David (whom Joseph and Rosenberg mistakenly believed to be German), both leading performers of opera seria:

> Most esteemed Sig. Salieri,
>
> His Majesty the Emperor orders me to commission you to make inquiries about the merit of two German singers, one named Valentino Ademberg, the other David. It is assumed that both have sung with applause in several theaters of Italy. H. M. believes that, being German, they will be suitable for the Nationaltheater in which *burlette con arie* are being performed. You will be kind enough to make inquiries, and to learn if, and on what conditions, they would be willing to be engaged here, and to favor me with this information; in the meantime I remain, with great esteem,
>
> Your true servant
> Count Rosenberg
> Vienna 15 Feb. 1779[4]

In a letter that has apparently not survived, but probably written in early March 1779, Joseph expressed to Grand Duke Leopold interest in engaging Elisabeth Teyber, born in Vienna but famous in Italy as an opera seria soprano; her younger sister Therese Teyber was already singing in Vienna.[5] That Joseph had a place for such a singer in a troupe that already included Catarina Cavalieri shows that he wanted his company to have not only capacity for vocal virtuosity (which Cavalieri certainly had) but also experience in the performance of opera seria in Italy (which she lacked); and both, as in Adamberger's case, had to be combined with an ability to sing in German. Leopold an-

4. Stimat.^{mo} Sr Salieri

Sua Maestà l'Imperatore m'impone d'incaricarLa d'informarsi del merito di due Tenoristi di nazione tedeschi chiamati l'uno Valentino Ademberg, e l'altro David. Si suppone ch'essi abbino cantato in varj Teatri d'Italia con applauso. Essendo di nazione tedeschi, crede S. M. che potranno convenire pel Teatro Nazionale in cui si rappresentano delle burlette con arie. Ella si compiacerà di ricercarne, e di procurare di sapere, se, ed a che condizioni vorebbero impegnarsi, ed indi favorirmene l'avviso mentre mi dico con molta stima

Suo vero Servitore
Il Conte di Rosenberg
Vienna 15 Feb.^{o} 1779

(This letter, in the Goethe- und Schiller-Archiv, Weimar, is cited but not quoted in Swenson, 73.)

5. Elisabeth Teyber had already sung briefly in Joseph's Singspiel troupe in 1778; see Michtner, 52–53, 452.

swered: "I will not fail to investigate in accordance with your orders and to inform you where La Teüberin is; but I doubt that she would wish to agree to sing at the opera buffa."[6]

Two weeks later Joseph wrote, in answer to a letter from Leopold that is apparently not extant: "Dearest brother, I received your dear letter, and thank you for the news. 50 sequins a month for la Teüberin, to enjoy only her appearance, without hearing her sing, is an exorbitant price for her ugliness." He went on to report that the soprano Marianne Lange (née Schindler) had died and that Cavalieri was sick: "The opera is going badly: La Lang is dead; La Cavalieri is out of the fray with an illness of the chest; the new woman singer speaks German with an Italian accent; her voice is weak, she sings through the nose and she is ugly: those are my little problems. We have been led to hope for a better soprano from Venice, who is now in the house of la Durazzo [probably Giacomo Durazzo's wife]; her name is Romani, I believe."[7] The emperor's "new woman singer" was Teresa Bellomo, a soprano of little importance who had performed previously in Graz. She made her Viennese debut on 6 April, two days before Joseph wrote his letter, in a German version of Sacchini's *Il finto pazzo per amore.* She lasted in Vienna less than a year. Joseph's criticism of her for speaking German "with an Italian accent" helps to explain why he preferred to engage German singers, yet—demonstrating the paradoxical nature of his enterprise—he went on in the next sentence to mention the possible engagement of yet another singer in Italy.

The correspondence continued with a letter from Leopold in which he referred to Joseph's interest in Teyber and the tenors Adamberger and David and his use of Salieri as adviser and agent. When Leopold and Salieri met, the emperor's troupe was a subject of conversation: "one cannot consider her [i.e., Teyber] further because, from what is being said, she is married and she no longer performs on the stage. I talked about that with Salieri, who was here yesterday with me and who has come from Rome on his way to Milan. He has seen the tenor David; he likes him, but he is not German and does not know the language. As for Valentino Adamberg, who is of course German, he has not been able to find him yet. I told him that he was in England, but he doubts that he would want to sing in the buffo."[8]

6. Je ne manqueray pas de m'informer selon vos ordres et de vous rendre compte où se trouve la Teüberin, mais je doubte qu'elle veuille accepter de chanter à l'opera buffa (Leopold to Joseph, 26 March 1779, HHStA, Sb, Kart. 7).

7. Trés chere frere, j'ai reçu votre chere lettre, et vous rends graces, de vos nouvelles, pour la Teüberin 50 Sequins le mois, pour ne jouir que de sa vue, sans l'entendre chanter, est un prix exorbitant pour sa laideur. . . . l'opera va mal la lang morte est la Cavalieri est hors de combat d'un mal de poitrine la nouvelle chanteuse parle l'allemand avec un accent italien, la voix faible, elle chante du nez et est laide voila des petits inconveniens. on nous en fait esperer une meilleure de venise, qui est dans la maison de la Durazzo, et s'appelle je crois Romani (Joseph to Leopold, 8 April 1779, HHStA, Sb, Kart. 7).

8. on ne peut plus penser à Elle puisqu'Elle est à ce que l'on dit mariée et qu'Elle ne joue plus sur le Théatre, j'ay parlé de cela avec Salieri qui a été hier ches moy et qui vient de Rome et passe à Milan, il a vu le

Adamberger, like Teyber, was among the handful of eighteenth-century German singers who had devoted their careers to opera seria. Leopold seems to have been able to accomplish something toward bringing him to Vienna. Adamberger sang in two opere serie in Florence during spring 1780.[9] It was probably then that Leopold interceded with the singer on Joseph's behalf, although exactly what the grand duke did is not clear from his letter of 23 April 1780: "You will have seen by my previous letters that the business with the tenor Adamberger is settled, and I am only too happy to have been able to contribute to your service."[10]

Adamberger made his Viennese operatic debut four months later, on 21 August 1780.[11] In singing Graf Asdrubal in a German version of Anfossi's *L'incognita perseguitata* he laid to rest Salieri's doubts as to his willingness "to sing in the buffo." He spent the rest of his career in Vienna, singing not only in Joseph's Singspiel troupe (in which he specialized in the portrayal of "gentle and passionate lovers"[12] and created, among other roles, that of Belmonte in Mozart's *Die Entführung aus dem Serail*) but also in the opera buffa troupe that succeeded it.[13]

Joseph was directly involved in the hiring of another important member of the German opera troupe, the bass Ludwig Fischer. Writing to Rosenberg from Linz on 25 October 1779, he instructed him to engage Fischer for one year.[14] Fischer made his Viennese debut on 13 June 1780 in Ignaz von Beecke's setting of Goethe's *Claudine von Villa Bella.* He went on to create several important roles, including those of Herr von Bär in Salieri's *Der Rauchfangkehrer* and Osmin in *Die Entführung,* delighting the Viennese with his skillful acting and rich low register.

Many of the operas in which Fischer and his colleagues sang were opere buffe and opéras-comiques in German translation, which dominated the repertory not only because so many of them were performed, but also because they tended to be performed more often than the operas composed by local composers, despite the fact that several of these Viennese operas were themselves settings of opéra-comique librettos.

Not all opéras-comiques and opere buffe were successful, and not all operas newly composed by Viennese musicians were failures; but generally speaking the Viennese

---

tenore David, il luy plait, mais il n'est et ne sçait point l'allemand, pour valentino adamberg qui est allemand surement il n'a pas encore pu le découvrir, je luy ay dit qu'il étoit en angleterre, mais il doute qu'il veuille chanter in Buffo (Leopold to Joseph, 18 April 1779, HHStA, Sb, Kart. 7).

9. Sartori nos. 1625, 3083.

10. Vous aurez vû par mes lettres précedentes que l'affaire du Tenore Adamberger est arrangée et je suis trop aise d'avoir pû contribuer à vous servir (Leopold to Joseph, 23 April 1780, HHStA, Sb, Kart. 7).

11. Michtner, 87–89.

12. "Er singt den Tenor, erste junge sanfte und feurige Liebhaber sind seine Rollen" (*Allgemeiner Theater Allmanach von Jahr 1782* [Vienna, [1782]], 124).

13. On Adamberger see Thomas Bauman, "Mozart's Belmonte," *EM* 19 (1991): 557–63.

14. "Fischer se peut engager pour une année" (Memorandum from Joseph to Rosenberg, Linz, 25 October 1779, Klagenfurt, Kärntner Landesarchiv, Rosenberg papers).

FIGURE 9.2 Catarina Cavalieri, silhouette by Hieronymus Löschenkohl, published in 1786. Wiener Stadtbibliothek.

public preferred the former. Although Umlauf's *Die Bergknappen* was well received and performed often (thirty-one times during the life of Joseph's troupe), the next opera, Carlo d'Ordonez's *Diesmal hat der Mann den Willen,* had a different fortune. When Count Zinzendorf attended the premiere he recognized the libretto as a reworking of an opéra-comique text that had been set by Monsigny (although he mistakenly attributed it to Grétry): *Le Maître en droit* had been performed by Vienna's French troupe in the Burgtheater in 1763. Zinzendorf may have had Monsigny's music in mind when he criticized Ordonez's as "trop difficile, trop peu chantante."[15] The opera was withdrawn after seven performances. The first opéra-comique with French music offered by the troupe, Monsigny's *Rose et Colas,* evidently pleased the Viennese: it was performed twenty-one times over four years. Grétry's *L'Ami de la maison* was equally popular. Umlauf could not consistently match the charm of Monsigny and Grétry: his second opera for the troupe, *Die Apotheke,* was performed only six times. Nor could other Viennese composers compete with consistent success against opéras-comiques and opere buffe.

Catarina Cavalieri

As principal soprano of Joseph's company, Cavalieri personified its contradictions (fig. 9.2). A native of Vienna, she signed her name Cavalier as late as 1775; yet she Italian-

15. Zinzendorf, 22 April 1778; quoted in Michtner, 361 n. 7.

EXAMPLE 9.1 Salieri, *La finta scema,* act 3, "Se spiegar potessi appieno," mm. 69–85

Some tender pity

ized it before singing in the Singspiel troupe. And she continued to cultivate the Italianate virtuoso style in which Salieri had trained her and for which Joseph II applauded and paid her.

Under Salieri's tutelage Cavalieri learned to sing the high coloratura that he liked to write for his opera buffa heroines. She made one of her earliest operatic appearances in the minor role of Vanesia in Salieri's *La finta scema* of 1775. In her biggest aria, "Se spiegar potessi appieno," she showed what she had learned from Salieri. "Se spiegar," in C major, is an elaborate vocal display: neither words nor music has much to do with Vanesia's character. After a thirty-four-measure orchestral introduction Vanesia enters with an elegant melody in a-b-b′ form; later, as she sings glittering coloratura that eventually reaches high D, the violins interject a lustful chromatic surge (ex. 9.1).[16] Cavalieri's performance did not disappoint his teacher, who remembered it fondly. He wrote of this aria in the autograph: "It was sung marvelously by a most beautiful voice, and pleased greatly."

The importance of "Se spiegar" lies less in what it contributed to *La finta scema* than in its being one of the first of many brilliant arias, several of them in C, that Cavalieri

16. On the erotic connotations of the "upward striving chromatic surge" see Heartz, *Mozart's Operas,* 210–15.

inspired Viennese composers (not only Salieri but Mozart, Umlauf, and others) to write for her. On the basis of that music a scholar has described her singing as "essentially athletic, her coloratura tending to elaborate more or less routine scales or triplet figures in extended sequences. Whereas [Aloysia] Lange can reach almost casually into the third octave and remain aloft, Cavalieri has an earnestness about her upper range, which she attains with scales that push upward powerfully and terminate with a final quick high note. Her approach is proclamatory; her texts are often syllabically declaimed in minims which yield to pairs of quavers."[17] Much of that description could be applied with equal validity to music written by Salieri for several other sopranos, such as Clementina Baglioni, in his early operas. This leads one to suspect that part of Cavalieri's vocal profile can be ascribed to Salieri's teaching, a suspicion strengthened by the fact that another of his students, Therese Gassmann, later made a specialty of performing a bravura aria that Salieri had written for Cavalieri.[18] "Se spiegar" shows that Cavalieri's vocal profile was already fully formed in 1775, at the very beginning of her public career. Other composers adopted aspects of Salieri's vocal style when they wrote for his student.

"Se spiegar" documents Cavalieri's vocal personality as shaped and exploited by Salieri; it also hints at a change in the relations between teacher and student. Written less than a year after his own marriage, the aria reads like a love letter, alluding to a passion that must remain unexpressed (except by the violins' wordless commentary):

Se spiegar potessi appieno
    Quel ardor, che l'alma accende,
    Vi farei destar nel seno
    Qualche tenera pietà.

[If I could explain fully the desire that burns in my heart, you would feel in your breast some tender pity.]

Cavalieri went on to play a leading role in Viennese opera during next decade and a half, taking part in the original productions of many important operas in both German and Italian. Salieri eventually found words or actions to express "Quel ardor, che l'alma accende." At some time unknown to us he apparently exchanged the role of Cavalieri's teacher for that of her lover.[19]

17. Patricia Lewy Gidwitz, "'Ich bin die erste Sängerin': Vocal Profiles of Two Mozart Sopranos," *EM* 19 (1991): 566–68.

18. "Vedo l'amiche insigne" in the cantata *La sconfitta di Borea* (1774 or 1775); see Della Croce/Blanchetti, 530–31.

19. That Salieri and Cavalieri were lovers was suggested by Da Ponte (136), who blamed the enmity that developed between Salieri and him during 1789 on rivalry between two singers, Cavalieri and Adriana Ferrarese, the former supported by Salieri, the latter by Da Ponte. The poet says that he loved Ferrarese and implies that Salieri loved Cavalieri. In his account of his audience with Emperor Leopold II in Trieste in 1791 Da Ponte quoted the emperor as referring to Cavalieri as Salieri's "bella" (150). Mozart, in his last surviving

Two Operas by Umlauf

Among operas composed by Viennese musicians especially for Joseph's troupe, two of Umlauf's won repeated applause. The inaugural opera *Die Bergknappen* (*The Miners*) and *Die pücefarbnen Schuhe, oder Die schöne Schusterin* (*The Purple Shoes, or The Pretty Shoemaker's Daughter*, 1779) can serve as examples of Viennese Singspiel during the second half of 1770s: the kind of works that Salieri had in mind when he wrote his only contribution to Joseph's Singspiel repertory, *Der Rauchfangkehrer.* Like many of the operas written for the emperor's company, Umlauf's borrow freely from several operatic traditions. The libretto of *Die Bergknappen* is an original work, by the Viennese actor-playwright Paul Weidmann. That of *Die pücefarbnen Schuhe* is more typical of the works performed by Joseph's troupe in that it is based on a foreign model: Gottlieb Stephanie the younger (who later collaborated with Mozart on *Die Entführung*) derived the libretto from an opéra-comique, *Les Souliers mordorés,* performed in Paris in 1776 with music by Alessandro Fridzeri. *Die Bergknappen* and *Die pücefarbnen Schuhe* are spoken plays with musical numbers interspersed, resembling in this respect both opéra-comique and north German opera (itself strongly influenced by opéra-comique).[20]

Reminiscent of opera buffa are the extensive ensembles in both operas. The overture to *Die Bergknappen* (which ends, like the overtures to Gassmann's *La contessina* and Salieri's *La secchia rapita,* with an open cadence) is followed by a duet in the same key that Viennese audiences may have recognized as an introduzione. The trio "Erinn're dich stets meiner Schwüre" in *Die Bergknappen* (fig. 9.3) resembles an opera buffa aria in its form, A-B-A′-B′: the A section in slow duple meter and the B section in fast 6/8. Act 1 of *Die pücefarbnen Schuhe* ends with a finale, although it lacks some of the conversational quality of many Italian finales. Ensembles for two or three men, conspicuously rare in Goldoni's librettos, were characteristic of Viennese opera buffa in the late 1760s and early 1770s (there are duets for men in Mozart's *La finta semplice* and Salieri's *Le donne letterate;* trios in Gassmann's *L'opera seria* and *La contessina* and in Salieri's *La fiera di Venezia*).[21] The trio for men "Madam, madam, madam!" in *Die pücefarbnen Schuhe* belongs to this tradition.

The overtures to both operas are in one movement, reflecting the increasing use of one-movement overtures in Vienna and Italy during the middle and late 1770s. The overture to *Die Bergknappen,* in C major, begins with a slow introduction labeled Maestoso. Comic-opera overtures with slow introductions were rare in the 1770s; but

letter (14 October 1791, *MBA,* 4: 161–63), wrote to his wife that Cavalieri had accompanied Salieri to a performance of *Die Zauberflöte.*

20. On *Die Bergknappen* see the very detailed and useful introduction to the edition by Robert Maria Haas (*DTÖ,* vol. 36), which covers the Singspiel troupe and its entire locally composed repertory; on *Die pücefarbnen Schuhe* see Thomas Bauman's introduction to the facsimile (New York, 1986).

21. Heartz, *Viennese School,* 419, 429.

FIGURE 9.3 Catarina Cavalieri (as Sophie), Joseph Martin Ruprecht (as Fritz), and Franz Fuchs (as Walcher) in the trio "Erinn're dich stets meiner Schwüre" in Umlauf's *Die Bergknappen*. Engraving by Carl Schütz. (Courtesy of Historisches Museum der Stadt Wien.)

Salieri's one-movement overture to *La secchia rapita,* also in C, with its grandiose and memorable slow introduction, could have served Umlauf as a model.

Both operas end with vaudevilles of the kind used often in opéras-comiques. The gavotte rhythms of Umlauf's vaudevilles also suggest the influence of French opera; but since vaudevilles with gavotte rhythms were not uncommon in Viennese comic operas of the 1770s, it is impossible to attribute Umlauf's to the influence of any particular type of opera.

Characteristic of both opéra-comique and north German opera are the short, simple songs in both operas. Sophie's "Hoffnung, Labsal aller Müden," near the end of *Die Bergknappen,* is typical of the Lieder that, along with spoken dialogue, constitute the major difference between Umlauf's Singspiele and opere buffe. Like many of these songs, Sophie's has no changes of tempo and features a clear A-B-A′ form.

Several of Umlauf's arias belong to aria types traditional in opera buffa in general and in Viennese opera buffa in particular. The bass Walcher in *Die Bergknappen* reminds one of a buffo caricato. His aria "Mein Herz fängt an zu sagen," with a disjunct vocal line in D major, is comic music in the Italian style. The baron's first aria in *Die pücefarbnen Schuhe,* "Ein herrliches Vergnügen," exemplifies the Goldonian comic aria that exploits the effects of various musical instruments. In its evocation of the trumpet it echos "Star trombette" in *La buona figliuola* (with which it shares the key of C major), but this aria is about the joys of sleigh-riding, not military life.[22] Like many arias sung by buffi caricati since the mid-eighteenth century, it features a long, colorful text:

Ein herrliches Vergnügen,
  Auf Schnee und Eis,
  So scharenweis,
In Schlitten hinzufliegen.
Da zieht ein Chormusik voran,
  Ein and'res schließt sich hinten an,
Man hört Trompeten, Pauken schallen,
Die Knechte mit den Peitschen knallen . . .

[What a splendid pleasure to dash in sleighs over snow and ice in orderly formation. A band of musicians is at the front, another follows behind. One hears the trumpets and drums resound and the servants crack the whip.]

Umlauf responded to this text with many of the same musical elements found in arias written for buffi caricati by Salieri, Gassmann, and their Italian contemporaries: duple meter, fast tempo, dotted rhythms, and a disjunct vocal line doubled by the orchestra in unison and octaves (ex. 9.2). Umlauf's illustration of musical instruments mentioned in the text is charming in its simplicity (ex. 9.3).

Typical of Viennese opera buffa in particular is the absence from both of Umlauf's operas of completely serious roles that could be considered the equivalent of parti serie. But that did not keep Umlauf from incorporating the vocal display associated with parti serie into music that he wrote for a female character who is not entirely serious: Sophie, the heroine of *Die Bergknappen,* created by Cavalieri. Sophie's coloratura aria "Wenn mir der Himmel lacht" displays the strengths of young Cavalieri's powerful and agile voice. Like many arias written for her, it features firm, marchlike rhythms and brilliant coloratura ascending to high D. The vocal coloratura in "Wenn mir der Himmel lacht" shares its figuration with an elaborate solo oboe part.

The opéras-comiques performed in Vienna contain occasional vocal showpieces of great brilliance (such as "Je romps la chaîne qui m'engage" in Grétry's *L'Amant jaloux,* in the Burgtheater repertory from 1780). And concertante arias are not completely absent from opéra-comique; Grétry's *Zémire et Azor,* for example, has a big "Air de la

22. Sleigh rides were important social events for the Viennese court and high nobility. The trumpets and drums mentioned and heard in Umlauf's aria seem to have been a normal part of sleigh rides, as when Emperor Joseph himself led thirty sleighs carrying much of the Viennese nobility through the city's streets on 26 January 1775; the procession was preceded by a sleigh carrying a drummer and ten trumpeters (*WZ,* 28 January 1775, Anhang).

EXAMPLE 9.2 Umlauf, *Die pücefarbnen Schuhe,* act 1, "Ein herrliches Vergnügen," mm. 9–19 (A-Wn, Mus. Hs. 16481; facsimile, New York, 1988)

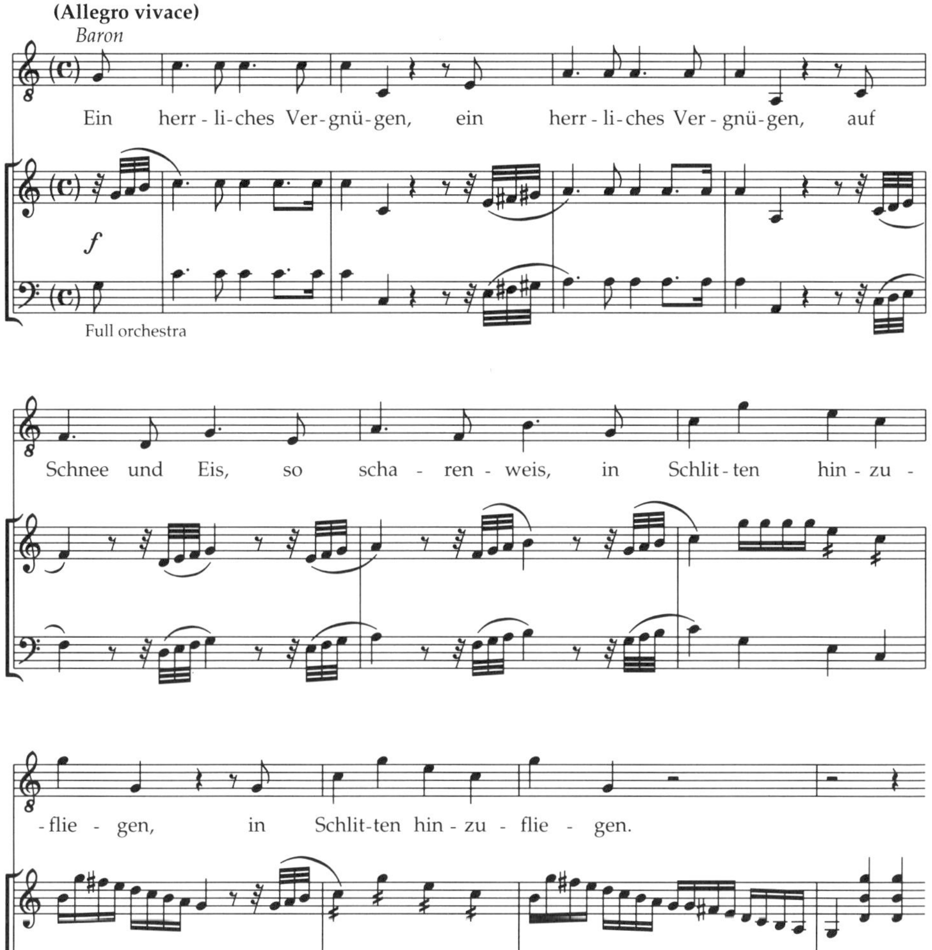
(Allegro vivace)
Baron
Ein herr - li-ches Ver-gnü-gen, ein herr - li-ches Ver - gnü-gen, auf
f
Full orchestra
Schnee und Eis, so scha - ren - weis, in Schlit-ten hin - zu -
- flie - gen, in Schlit-ten hin - zu - flie - gen.

EXAMPLE 9.3 Umlauf, *Die pücefarbnen Schuhe,* act 1, "Ein herrliches Vergnügen," mm. 36–43

Tr.
Man hört Trom - pe - ten,
Timp.
Pau - ken schal - len

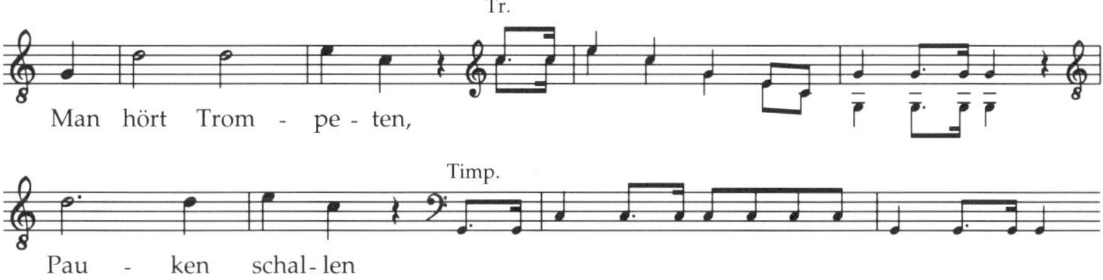

EXAMPLE 9.4 Umlauf, *Die pücefarbnen Schuhe,* act 2, "Ohne Überzeugung schliessen," mm. 1–14

To reach a decision without conviction often weighs heavily on one's conscience; so trust not appearance if you want to be fair.

fauvette" (warbler song) for soprano and solo flute. But "Wenn mir der Himmel lacht" belongs to a specifically Viennese tradition: that of the heroic aria for soprano and one or more solo instruments including oboe, cultivated above all by Salieri in his opere buffe of the early 1770s.[23]

Like many composers of opera buffa during the third quarter of the eighteenth century in Vienna as well as in Italy, Umlauf withheld the key of E♭ until relatively late in both operas so as to enhance its effect when it finally appeared. Its sound in Lehne's aria "Ohne Überzeugung schließen" (the third number in act 2 of *Die pücefarbnen Schuhe* and the opera's only number in E♭) contributes as much to that aria as the tender gavotte melody, the folklike naiveté of the cadence, and the horn solo that echoes the vocal line (ex. 9.4)[24]. The first appearance of E♭ in *Die Bergknappen,* simultaneously with the opera's first sustained Adagio, helps Fritz, Sophie's lover, convey his passion in the aria "O Traumgott, wieg' meine Sophie." Umlauf took advantage here of the association between E♭ and sleep that had been reinforced by sleep arias in such diverse operas as *La buona figliuola* and Salieri's *Armida.*

23. "Wenn mir der Himmel lacht" was the first of many bravura arias, many of them with one or more solo instruments, written for Cavalieri by Viennese composers of German opera. Patricia Lewy Gidwitz ("Vocal Profiles of Four Mozart Sopranos" [Ph.D. diss., University of California, Berkeley, 1991], 52–53) discusses an aria in Franz Asplmayr's *Die Kinder der Natur,* "So gut, wie er mir scheine," in which Cavalieri performed a cadenza together with a solo violin. In *Frühling und Liebe* Maximilian Ulbrich wrote an aria for Cavalieri, "Singt, ihr süssen Philomelen," that features brilliant coloratura and elaborate solos for flute, oboe and bassoon.

24. This horn solo was probably written for the virtuoso Joseph Leutgeb, for whom Mozart wrote his horn concertos; Leutgeb was one of the Burgtheater's two horn players from 1779 to 1782 (Edge, "Mozart's Viennese Orchestras," 71).

Der Rauchfangkehrer

On his return to Vienna on 8 April 1780, Salieri rejoined Joseph's private musical group. Although the first concert in which he took part, that same day, was devoted to the performance of excerpts from two of the operas written during his Italian trip, it is clear from Mosel's account that Joseph had German opera on his mind:

> After the concert was over, Salieri was instructed to attend, the same evening, the "National Singspiel," to use the name given by the emperor to the German opera troupe he had established at his own expense shortly before Salieri's departure for Italy and had continued to support. "You must then tell me," the monarch added, "if the opera troupe and the whole organization has made progress during your absence."

Mosel does not mention what opera Salieri heard, but we know that Grétry's *Lucile* received its eighth performance that evening in the Nationaltheater.[25]

Mosel's narrative continues:

> when he [Salieri] was next present at the chamber concert, the emperor asked him as soon as he saw him, "Well, what do you think of our National Singspiel?" Salieri, who was in fact delighted with what he had heard and seen, answered that he found this musical theater wonderfully perfect in every respect.
>
> "Now you must compose a German opera," said the emperor. Salieri suggested that one of the five operas that he had written in Italy be translated into German. "No translation" replied the emperor, smiling. "An original Singspiel!" "Your Majesty," answered Salieri, "I would not know how to begin composing an opera in German; I speak it so badly . . . " "Well," the emperor interrupted, still smiling, "then this work will serve as an exercise in the language. Tomorrow morning I will direct Count Rosenberg to have a German libretto prepared for you."[26]

The death of Joseph's mother Maria Theresa on 29 November 1780 was followed by the closing of the theaters for two months, delaying the production that resulted from Joseph's command. Salieri's first German opera, *Der Rauchfangkehrer* (*The Chimney Sweep*), reached the stage of the Burgtheater about a year after Joseph commissioned it, on 30 April 1781. Salieri's librettist was Leopold von Auenbrugger, a Viennese physician of some distinction whose acquaintance with the composer went back at least as far as 1774, when he served as a witness at Salieri's wedding.

Der Rauchfangkehrer derives much of its humor and dramatic interest from the interaction of social classes. Volpino ("Little Fox"), an Italian chimney sweep and musi-

25. Michtner, 463; Hadamowsky, *Hoftheater*, 1:79.

26. Mosel, 72.

cian, is engaged to Lisel, a cook in the house of the young widow Frau von Habicht ("Hawk"). The middle-class Frau von Habicht and her stepdaughter Nannette are the objects of amorous advances by the petty noblemen Herr von Bär and Herr von Wolf. Volpino puts into action an elaborate trick that he hopes will result in a dowry for him and Lisel. With his musical skills he charms both widow and stepdaughter into falling in love with him. Then to Bär and Wolf he proposes a deal by which he will reject the two women in exchange for a handsome dowry. The little fox outsmarts the bear and the wolf. After a suitable amount of confusion and misunderstanding, Volpino's plan is successful, and the opera ends with all the principal characters happily anticipating marriage.

In spite of the German text *Der Rauchfangkehrer* is in many ways more Italian than German: both libretto and music remind one more of opera buffa than of north-German Singspiel or opéra-comique. In its length it represents an expansion of the Viennese Singspiel as cultivated by Umlauf, whose *Die Bergknappen* has one act and *Die pücefarbnen Schuhe* two. Salieri's opera has three full acts, like most opere buffe written before 1780, with thirty-two numbers (*Die pücefarbnen Schuhe* has twenty-one). Both acts 1 and 2 end with finales.

Auenbrugger provided Salieri with aria texts to which he could respond with all the musical devices of opera buffa. The catalogue aria that in Goldoni's skillful hands became a standard aria type makes its appearance here as "Bei meiner Seel'," sung by Fischer in the role of Bär. The long text with short lines, with its incorporation of foreign words and musical terminology, invited musical commentary from Salieri as irresistibly as Boccherini's catalogue of musical instruments "Non vo' già che vi suonino" (in *L'amore innocente*) had a decade earlier.

Bei meiner Seel', dies wäre viel,
Kein Sänger singt all's, was er will;
Er hat sein Ziel.
In dem lobt man nur,
Passagen, Bravour,
Im tönenden Gesang,
Hat jener den Rang,
Der zwickt den Falset,
Und wird sehr erhebt.
Man staunt bei dem Mann,
Die Tiefe des Ton.
Wo bleibt das *Crescendo?*
Wie klingt das *Calando?*
Die schmelzende Bindung,
Die schmachtende Schwindung?

Wie sind die Gruppetten,
Tenuten, Falseten?
Das *Liscio Staccato?*
Das *Tempo rubato,*
Dann das Sincopiren,
Und and're Manieren?
Kurz: das Portament;
Das Trillern am end'?
Bei meiner Seel', das wäre viel!
Kein Sänger singt all's, was er will,
Er hat sein Ziel.

[Upon my soul, that would be too much! No singer sings everything that he would like: he has his limits. In this singer one praises only passaggi, bravura; that one has earned his rank by the beauty of his cantabile. This one squeaks the falsetto and is highly exalted; that one excites admiration for the depth of his tone. Where is the crescendo? How does the calando sound? The languishing legato, the yearning diminuendo? How are the gruppetti, the tenuti, the falsetti? The liscio [simple] staccato, the tempo rubato? Then the syncopation and the other devices? In short, the portamento, and the trill at the end? Upon my soul, that would be too much! No singer sings everything that he would like: he has his limits.]

Salieri's setting incorporated many of the musical elements that his audience would have expected from an Italian aria for comic bass. But the aria conveys, perhaps under the inspiration of the singer who first performed it, an attractive sense of individuality. Salieri managed to imbue even his conventional marchlike opening melody in D major with a melodic distinctiveness rare in arias written for buffi caricati (ex. 9.5). He responded to words written especially for Fischer ("Die Tiefe des Ton") with music written for him: low F♯ sustained over four and a half measures, reinforced by horn, cellos, and bassoons on the same pitch and double basses an octave lower (ex. 9.6).

Another comic aria whose ancestry in opera buffa Viennese audiences may well have recognized is Bär's "Zwei tausend Gulden Kapital." The question that Bär repeatedly asks himself—"Herr Bär, was wirst du tun?"—identifies this as an aria of indecision. By setting it in E♭, Salieri acknowledged a tradition of arias of indecision in this key that went back to the 1730s.

The anonymous author of *Meine Empfindungen im Theater,* a commentary of Viennese theater published in 1781, probably had "Bei meiner Seel'" and "Zwei tausend Gulden Kapital" in mind when discussing Fischer's performance: "His excellent singing, his voice's infinite low register, which remains pleasing and pure down to the lowest notes, and his pleasant, light upper register, his artistry and style make him one of the greatest singers; but his acting makes him also a good actor, as long as one gives him roles that suit his rather fat body and his mature appearance. He played Herr von

EXAMPLE 9.5 Salieri, *Der Rauchfangkehrer,* act 1, "Bei meiner Seel'," mm. 1–19 (A-Wn, Mus. Hs. 16611; facsimile, New York, 1986)

(Continued on next page)

EXAMPLE 9.5 (*continued*)

EXAMPLE 9.6 *Der Rauchfangkehrer,* act 1, "Bei meiner Seel'," mm. 106–13

Bär excellently; and in many intelligently acted moments he helped the unintelligent libretto."[27]

Auenbrugger and Salieri introduced Habicht and Nannette with a device characteristic of Goldonian opera buffa, in which it was normally limited to parti buffe. Volpino, at the keyboard, accompanies Habicht in a performance of the first stanza of a German song, which they read from a printed anthology. In the spoken dialogue that follows, Nannette tells Volpino: "You will now accompany me in the second strophe of the same song." This procedure might have reminded Viennese audiences of similar pairs of numbers in *La buona figliuola, Il mercato di Malmantile,* and Salieri's *La locandiera.* The

27. Herr Fischer war Herr von Bär—sein vortreflicher Gesang, die unendliche Tiefe seiner Stimme, die angenehm und rein bis in den letzten Ton bleibt, und seine leichte angenehme Höhe, seine Kunst und Weise machen ihn zu einem der größten Sänger; aber sein Spiel macht ihn auch zum guten Schauspieler, wenn man ihm nur solche Rollen zutheilet, die seinem etwas fetten Körper und gesetzten Ansehen anpassen. Den Herrn von Bär hat er recht vortreflich gespielt, und durch manche raisonnirte Stelle dem unraisonnirten Gedichte nachgeholfen (*Meine Empfindungen im Theater,* Erster Quartal [Vienna, 1781], 193).

delicate melody with gavotte rhythms to which Habicht and Nannette sing the "German song" is accompanied by an attractive mixture of bowed and plucked strings that represents Volpino's keyboard playing.

Like Umlauf (and following his own earlier practice in opera buffa) Salieri wrote no parti serie; but that did not keep him from indulging in all the extravagant virtuosity associated with that kind of role. He wrote brilliant coloratura arias for both his leading ladies, saving the most dramatic vocal display for his protégée Cavalieri in the role of Nannette.

Nannette's "Wenn dem Adler das Gefieder" (the text develops the zoological imagery already evident in the names of some of the characters) is a worthy successor to the bravura arias sung by Cavalieri in *La finta scema* and *Die Bergknappen*, both of which are in the same key of C major. The heavy orchestration (trumpets and drums, oboes, bassoons, and strings) and impressive length of the orchestral introduction (twenty-eight measures) announce the importance of this aria even before Nannette begins to sing. The vocal line, with its marchlike dotted rhythms and fiery coloratura reaching repeatedly up to high C and once to high D, is typical of those written for Cavalieri.[28] This is the kind of music in which she excelled: a display of musical brilliance that required little in the way of acting.

The author of *Meine Empfindungen im Theater* described Cavalieri's performance in *Der Rauchfangkehrer* with enough detail for us to visualize her rendition of "Wenn dem Adler":

> Cavalieri . . . who has earned a reputation among connoisseurs as one of the leading singers and who delights the ears even of those who know nothing of music, played Fräulein [Nannette]. Her acting gets better every day and one notices how much more trouble she takes when she performs together with others whose acting has attained greater energy, more exactness, and greater skill. In speaking she is still not natural enough: she still emphasizes the last syllable of words too much and shortens the last word of the sentence so much that she becomes difficult to understand. Her use of the arms is still a little too stiff; they are bent forward too much and not relaxed enough. And yet she already is capable of great expression. She has a fine sense of decorum in her bearing and her countenance, and she will soon satisfy us as an actress as much as she delights us with her voice.[29]

28. Gidwitz, "Vocal Profiles of Four Mozart Sopranos," 57–58, discusses "Wenn dem Adler" briefly in the context of other music written for Cavalieri by Salieri and other Viennese composers.

29. Demoiselle Cavalieri, die den Ruhm der Kenner als eine der ersten Sängerinnen für sich hat, und durch ihren schönen Gesang auch das Ohr des Nichtkenners vergnüget, spielte das Fräulein—Ihr Spiel wird täglich besser, und man bemerket, wie viel mehr Mühe sie sich giebt, wenn sie neben anderen spielet, deren Spiel höheren Schwung, mehrere Richtigkeit und sichere Festigkeit erhalten hat.—Im Sprechen hat sie noch zu wenig Natur, stoßt die Endsylben noch zu viel, und verkürzet die letzten Worte der Rede meist so sehr, daß sie dadurch unverständlich wird. Ihr Armspiel ist noch ein wenig zu steif, zu viel hervogebogen und nicht gelößt genug—aber doch hat sie schon sehr vielen Ausdruck in ihrer Gebärde und Mine, hat einen

A year after the first performance of *Der Rauchfangkehrer* Mozart exploited Cavalieri's virtuosity on an even grander scale in *Die Entführung.* "Martern aller Arten," over twice as long as "Wenn dem Adler," was Mozart's emphatic answer to the C-major showpieces that Umlauf, Salieri, and other Viennese composers wrote for her between 1775 and 1782 and his enthusiastic contribution to the Viennese tradition of concertante arias for coloratura soprano that Salieri had fostered since the early 1770s. Mozart simultaneously paid tribute to and parodied Salieri's concertante effects, he surpassed the orchestral splendor of "Wenn dem Adler,"and he showed off Cavalieri's "agile throat" (as he put it in reference to another aria)[30] even more brilliantly than her teacher had.[31]

Salieri probably intended the title role in *Der Rauchfangkehrer* as something of a self-portrait. Volpino is not only a chimney sweep but an Italian musician residing in a German-speaking capital city (a Viennese audience would have thought of Vienna itself); he speaks faulty German and insists, at every chance he gets, on singing in Italian and having his music students sing in Italian. This results in the inclusion in *Der Rauchfangkehrer* of no less than four arias in Italian, two sung by Volpino and one by each of his students (a fifth aria begins with an Italian phrase). One, perhaps two Italian arias might have been justified by the precedent of occasional arias in foreign languages in Goldoni's librettos and those of his followers, such as Boccherini's *La fiera di Venezia* and De Gamerra's *La finta scema.*[32] But four arias in Italian amounted to an impudent and witty subversion of the idea of German opera. Keeping in mind Salieri's initial response to Joseph's commission, it is tempting to think that he expressed, in the guise of sly Volpino, what he as an Italian musician thought of German opera in the Burgtheater and of his assignment to write a Singspiel. Instead of serving, as Joseph smilingly put it, "as an exercise in the [German] language," the composition of *Der Rauchfangkehrer* served Salieri as an exercise in the ingenious incorporation of Italian language and musical style into a supposedly German opera.

Salieri needed a fine comic actor to bring off this self-parody. He found one in Gottfried Heinrich Schmidt, of whom the author of *Meine Empfindungen im Theater* wrote: "The poet owes him thanks for having taken this role, for through his good, fine acting (in which he did not however descend to vulgar buffoonery, but at the same time let no comic opportunity slip away unused) the book's tediousness and absurdities were made bearable."[33]

---

schönen Anstand, und bald wird sie uns auch als Schauspielerin eben so genug thun, als sie uns durch ihre Stimme entzückt (*Empfindungen,* 191–92).

30. Mozart to his father, 26 September 1781, in *MBA,* 3:163.

31. On "Martern aller Arten" see Thomas Bauman, *W. A. Mozart: Die Entführung aus dem Serail* (Cambridge, 1987), 77–82.

32. "En enfant timide," in act 2 of *La finta scema.*

33. Herr Schmid spielte den Volpino; und der Dichter darf ihm Dank wissen, diese Rolle übernommen zu haben; denn durch sein gutes und schönes Spiel, in dem er nicht bis zum niedrigen Lustigmacher herab-

Volpino claims that he studied in Italy with the great musico Carlo Broschi, also known as Farinelli. Broschi was a close friend of Metastasio; this helps explain why Volpino knows Metastasio's poetry. So did Salieri and many members of his audience in the Burgtheater, who probably recognized as settings of Metastasio's verse the Italian songs that Volpino assigns to his students. "Se più felice oggetto" (sung by Frau von Habicht, with phrases sung by Volpino correcting her faulty pronunciation) is from the first act of *Attilio Regolo;* the recitative "Basta, vincesti: eccoti il foglio" and aria "Ah non lasciarmi, no" (sung by Nannette) are from the second act of *Didone abbandonata.*[34] The quotation of "Ah non lasciarmi, no" in a comic opera may have reminded some members of the audience of an opera buffa. Paisiello's *Le due contesse* (first performed in Rome in 1776 and later the same year, probably under Salieri's direction, in Vienna) parodies Dido's plea by having Livietta, a maidservant, quote from it in the middle of a comic aria.[35]

Salieri occasionally made fun, in his Italian arias, of the bel-canto style associated with Metastasian opera seria, as when he had Volpino, in "Augelletti che intorno cantate" (yet more birds!), sing a roulade up to high D. By switching from tenor to soprano clef Salieri asked Volpino, like Bär in "Bei meiner Seel'," to sing falsetto. (Salieri, who called for falsetto quite frequently throughout his career,[36] obviously liked this comic technique, one that Haydn also exploited often but that Mozart, in contrast, seems to have consistently avoided.)

"Augelletti" may be primarily parodistic in intent; but elsewhere, and nowhere more obviously than in "Ah non lasciarmi, no," Salieri reveled with apparent sincerity in the vocal beauty encouraged by Metastasio's mellifluous verse (ex. 9.7). To depict Volpino's keyboard accompaniment Salieri combined strings played pizzicato and coll'arco, just as he did with the pair of Lieder sung earlier by Habicht and Nannette.

Salieri set the five lines of blank verse preceding this aria as simple recitative, in which Volpino teaches Nannette (as Metastasio taught Salieri and Salieri must have taught Cavalieri) the proper declamation of Metastasio's poetry. When Nannette mispronounces the *g* in "foglio," Volpino corrects her. Salieri provided no music for Volpino, who either repeated Nannette's notes or recited the words without music (ex. 9.8).

Salieri began *Der Rauchfangkehrer* with a one-movement overture whose relatively thin texture and orchestration may reflect his two years in Italy. It lacks flute, bassoon,

---

fällt, aber auch keine komische Gelegenheit vorbeyschlüpfen läßt, ohne sie zu benützen, ist vieles von dem Langweiligen, Abgeschmackten des Buches erträglich geworden (*Empfindungen*, 192–93).

34. Volkmar Braunbehrens, *Maligned Master: The Real Story of Antonio Salieri* (New York, 1992), 75, seems to have been first to recognize Metastastio's poetry in *Der Rauchfangkehrer.*

35. "Sapete che dicea," in act 2 of *Le due contesse;* see Hunter, "Some Representations of *Opera Seria* in *Opera Buffa,*" 92–95.

36. Among the operas in which Salieri required falsetto are *L'amore innocente, La finta scema, Il ricco d'un giorno, Prima la musica e poi le parole, Il talismano,* and *Falstaff.*

EXAMPLE 9.7 *Der Rauchfangkehrer,* act 3, "Ah non lasciarmi, no," mm. 1–6

Ah, do not leave me, no, my beloved; whom will I be able to trust?

and timpani parts, while the trumpets merely double the horns. With this small orchestra he made effective use of textural and dynamic contrast, limiting the texture to octaves until the entrance of oboes and horns at measure 9 and withholding the full ensemble until the forte assai at measure 13 (ex. 9.9). The overture is missing from the autograph score. Its absence probably has something to do with Salieri's reuse of most of it as the overture to a later opera, *La cifra.*

EXAMPLE 9.8 *Der Rauchfangkehrer,* act 3, simple recitative before "Ah non lasciarmi, no," mm. 1–7

Enough, you have won; here is the paper.

EXAMPLE 9.9 *Der Rauchfangkehrer,* overture, mm. 1–14 (A-Wn, Mus. Hs. 16518)

Der Rauchfangkehrer was moderately successful in Vienna, performed nine times during the rest of 1781 and three more times during 1782.[37] It achieved this number of performances despite unanimous criticism of the libretto, which seems to have touched a raw aesthetic nerve when read by critics who wanted to judge it as spoken drama or its aria texts as poetry. The comments of one anonymous Viennese critic are typical: "Never were reason, taste, and the art of poetry more wickedly desecrated than in this opera. It is wretched from beginning to end, miserable, and nonsensical, and one must pity the excellent Salieri that he had to expend his fine talent on such worthlessness."[38]

The last performance of *Der Rauchfangkehrer* in the Burgtheater took place on 5 July 1782, less than two weeks before the premiere of *Die Entführung,* Mozart's first opera for the Viennese court theaters since the ill-fated *La finta semplice* of 1768. Mozart had arrived in Vienna in March 1781, a few weeks before the premiere of *Der Rauchfangkehrer.* He must have known Salieri's opera well, and he must have hoped to outdo it. There can be little doubt that the success of *Die Entführung* contributed to the final abandonment of *Der Rauchfangkehrer* by the Viennese court theaters.

Although never revived in the court theaters, *Der Rauchfangkehrer* was taken up by the suburban theaters as they gained strength in the 1780s. The Theater in der Leopoldstadt presented Salieri's opera several times in 1785 and the Theater auf der Landstrasse revived it again in 1790.[39]

Salieri's opera enjoyed considerable success on German stages for several years. The libretto continued to be the object of disdain, as in the remarks appended to an anonymous arrangement of the libretto prepared for the production of *Der Rauchfangkehrer* in Berlin in 1783. In describing the aria texts as wretched (*elenden*), the editor used a word that had been applied to the entire libretto by the Viennese critic quoted above. Unable to believe it to be an original German work, he suggested that "its origins lie in the ruins of an Italian opera buffa."[40]

In 1783 Leopold Mozart asked his son to send him a copy of Salieri's score, probably in anticipation of a production in Salzburg. When Wolfgang responded in a letter of 10 December 1783 he described the opera (again probably referring to the libretto rather than the music) using one of the same words, *elendes,* that had occurred to critics in Vi-

37. But Bauman's characterization of *Der Rauchfangkehrer* (in his introduction to the facsimile of the autograph score) as "the hit of the [1781] season" is something of an exaggeration. Paisiello's *Die eingebildeten Philosophen* (*I filosofi immaginari*), which came to the stage a month after Salieri's opera, was performed thirteen times in 1781 and eleven times in 1782, clearly surpassing *Der Rauchfangkehrer* in popularity.

38. Nie ist Menschenvernunft, Geschmak und Dichtkunst ärger entweiht worden, als in dieser Oper. Sie ist vom Anfange bis zu Ende elend, jämmerlich und unsinnig, und man mus den vortreflichen Salieri beklagen, daß er sein schönes Talent an solchem Wust hat verwenden müssen (*Allgemeiner Theater Allmanach von Jahr 1782,* 57).

39. Angermuller, Leben, 2: 60–61.

40. Quoted in Angermüller, *Leben,* 2:59–60 n. 1.

enna and Berlin: "I'm writing in the greatest hurry to tell you that I have already bought *Der Rauchfangkehrer* for 6 ducats and have it at home. . . . To judge from your letter, you think that *Der Rauchfangkehrer* is an Italian opera. No, it is German and, on top of that, a wretched original play, the author of which is Herr Doctor Auernbrucker of Vienna. You will remember that I told you about it, that Herr Fischer parodied it publicly in the theater."[41] Mozart's last sentence may refer to a letter that is now lost, or perhaps to conversations that took place during his recent visit to Salzburg (July–October 1783). In view of the Italianate qualities of *Der Rauchfangkehrer,* the liberal use of the Italian language within it, the fact that its composer had written no German operas before, and the Viennese practice of making Singspiele by translating opere buffe into German, it would not be surprising if Leopold, like the anonymous editor in Berlin, assumed that *Der Rauchfangkehrer* was originally an opera buffa.

41. Mozart to his father, 10 December 1783, in *MBA,* 3:296. Bauman argues (in his introduction to *Der Rauchfangkehrer,* n. 6): "The context makes it clear that Mozart refers only to the text, not the opera as a whole, as Michtner would have it (*Das alte Burgtheater,* p. 100). Mozart certainly would not have spent six ducats for the score and then have it sent to Leopold had he considered Salieri's music 'wretched.'"

10

LES DANAÏDES

Grand Duke Paul Petrovich, heir apparent to the Russian throne, and his wife Sophia Dorothea visited Vienna during November and December 1781 as part of a tour of western Europe. Four months earlier Prince Kaunitz had emphasized to Joseph II the importance of the visit as an opportunity to impress the grand duke and duchess with "the power of this monarchy," as he put it in a letter of 22 July 1781: "To this end it seems to me that, as with all occasions of this importance, *chi più spende, meno spende;* that both for this reason and to make their stay in Vienna as pleasant as possible, it would be most useful to present the court and the city with as much brilliance as possible. The first of these things can only be done by Your Majesty's calling from Italy, for example, three or four of the best voices to give a magnificent Italian serious opera, as well as the best possible ballet troupe with the younger Vestris and Mlle. Hennel."[1] With these suggestions, which conspicuously ignored Joseph's Singspiel troupe, the minister of state not only revealed his own theatrical tastes but also implied that the German troupe and the composers associated with it could not present a new opera grand enough for the occasion.

Joseph rejected the idea of opera seria and in doing so made his opinion of the genre clear: "In regard to serious opera from Italy, it is too late to arrange something good; and anyway, it is such a boring spectacle that I do not think I will ever use it."[2] On the same day he wrote to Count Rosenberg of his intention to display his German operatic and theatrical troupes during the royal visit.[3] But he showed no more confidence in his

1. Kaunitz to Joseph, 22 July 1781, in *Joseph II., Leopold II. und Kaunitz: Ihr Briefwechsel,* ed. Adolf Beer (Vienna, 1873), 92.

2. Joseph to Kaunitz, Versailles, 31 July 1781, in *Joseph II., Leopold II. und Kaunitz: Ihr Briefwechsel,* 101.

3. Joseph to Rosenberg, 31 July 1781, HHStA, OKäA 1781, no. 146 (not in *Joseph II*).

composers of German opera than Kaunitz. He ordered Rosenberg to prepare a production of Gluck's *Iphigénie en Tauride,* which was indeed performed (by the German troupe in translation) during the royal visit, along with three other operas by Gluck: *Alceste* and *Orfeo ed Euridice,* both in the original Italian, and a German version of *La Rencontre imprévue.* He had not forgotten the effectiveness of Gluckian spectacle as a symbol of the power, wealth, and good taste of the Habsburg court. Although Mozart hoped *Die Entführung aus dem Serail* might be performed before the grand duke and duchess, its production (and consequently its composition) was postponed in favor of a celebration of Gluck's achievement.

The disagreement between Joseph and Kaunitz, the failure of the German troupe and the composers associated with it to present a new German opera on this important occasion, and the decision to perform both *Alceste* and *Orfeo* in Italian all suggest that Viennese opera at the beginning of the 1780s was affected by a lack of confidence in German opera as a genre to which the prestige of the monarchy could be safely entrusted.

Joseph's theatrical reorganization had not rid Vienna of its taste for Italian opera, and the performance of opere buffe in German translation did not satisfactorily replace the real thing sung by Italian singers. Popular support for the Singspiel troupe was weak. Umlauf's *Welches ist die beste Nation?* failed miserably (it received just two performances in December 1782); so did a German version of Gassmann's *La notte critica,* which likewise lasted only two performances. Mozart's *Entführung,* when finally performed in July 1782, brought enthusiastic crowds into the theater. "The people, if I can say so, are really crazy about this opera," he wrote to his father on 27 July.[4] But the German troupe could not survive on one work or on the work of one composer. That is probably why Mozart was not asked to write another German opera for the Burgtheater. In late 1782, as he enjoyed the success of *Die Entführung,* he had already turned his attention to another operatic genre. Plans for the formation of an Italian opera buffa troupe and for the disbanding of the German opera troupe were under way, and Mozart looked forward to the forthcoming transformation of the repertory: "I want to write an Italian opera," he wrote his father on 21 December 1782. "I have already made an arrangement to receive, on approval, the newest opera buffa librettos from Italy. . . . Italian singers will arrive here at Easter."[5]

A step toward the return of an Italian troupe to the Burgtheater had been taken earlier in 1782, with the performance of two opere buffe in Italian by the German troupe. Sacchini's Roman intermezzo *La contadina in corte* returned to the stage on 19 April; Salieri's *La locandiera* was revived on 12 November. But old opere buffe performed by German singers did not please the Viennese: both were dropped from the repertory after a few performances.

4. *MBA,* 3:214–16; see also Mozart's letters of 20 July and 21 December (*MBA,* 3:212–13, 243–45).

5. *MBA,* 3:243–45 (21 December 1782).

One of the purposes of these performances was probably to find out how many members of the Singspiel company could be kept on as members of the future opera buffa troupe. To replace the German singers who were not able to make the transition to Italian opera, Joseph entered into correspondence with several members of the Austrian diplomatic corps in Italy concerning the engagement of Italian singers for his opera buffa troupe.[6]

Although the emperor, like Mozart, looked to the future, late in 1782 Salieri had little time to think about the return of opera buffa to the Burgtheater. He helped Joseph choose the singers for the new troupe; he probably recommended the engagement of Da Ponte, the friend of a friend, as house poet; but his compositional energy was directed elsewhere. Already in 1781 he had responded to the apparent lack of operatic consensus in Vienna by looking away from the capital, much as he responded to the founding of the German opera troupe in 1778. He accepted a commission from the electoral court in Munich to supply an opera seria, *Semiramide,* for Carnival 1782.[7] It was probably later in 1782 (but in any case before February 1783) that he set to music a French libretto that Gluck had begun to set but then, old and infirm, passed on to Salieri. *Les Danaïdes,* his first French opera, reached the stage of the Opéra in April 1784.

Joseph's opera buffa troupe made its debut in April 1783 with a performance of *La scuola de' gelosi.* That Salieri revived a four-year-old opera to mark this festive occasion instead of composing a new one reflects his preoccupation, during the two years that preceded the debut of the opera buffa company, with the composition of opera seria for Munich and tragédie lyrique for Paris.

Origins

The progress of Salieri's career reflected the power of the Habsburg family and especially that of Joseph II. Having established his reputation under Joseph's protection in Vienna, he gained a foothold in his native land by winning a commission to write the inaugural opera for La Scala, Milan, a city governed by Joseph's brother Ferdinand. The emperor's sister Marie Antoinette exercised considerable influence over the production of opera in Paris, and her support contributed to the success of Salieri's first French opera. In dedicating the printed score of *Les Danaïdes* to the queen, Salieri alluded to the chain of influence that led to its performance: "It is to the honor and the priceless advantage of being in the service of His Majesty the Emperor that I owe the protection with which Your Majesty has wished to honor me, and it is to this glorious protection that the music of *Les Danaïdes* owes its principal success."[8] Exactly what Marie An-

6. Michtner, 132.
7. On *Semiramide* see Della Croce/Blanchetti, 163–64, 453–56.
8. Dedicatory letter in the engraved full score of *Les Danaïdes* (Paris, ca. 1784; facsimile, Bologna, [1969]).

toinette's "protection" amounted to (beyond the obvious favor of accepting Salieri's dedication) is unknown. But Joseph's role in the production of *Les Danaïdes* is well documented in a series of letters that he wrote to Count Mercy-Argenteau, the Austrian ambassador in Paris, during 1783 and 1784. These hitherto unpublished letters reveal, perhaps more clearly than anywhere else, the strength of Joseph's fondness for Salieri and of his confidence in Salieri's abilities.[9]

After the successful production of *Iphigénie en Tauride* and the failure of his last opera, *Echo et Narcisse,* first performed four months apart in 1779, Gluck returned to Vienna for the last time. Old age, illness, and disappointment at the reception of *Echo et Narcisse* together discouraged him from further operatic projects. In reaction to the offer of a libretto from Paris at the end of 1779 Gluck wrote bitterly: "you doubtless do not know that henceforth I will write no more operas and that I have ended my career. My age and the disgust I experienced recently in Paris in connection with my opera *Narcisse* have robbed me for ever of any desire to write others."[10]

But a project initiated earlier brought Gluck once again to the forefront of theatrical debate in Paris, this time as Salieri's mentor and somewhat reluctant promoter. On 21 August 1784, four months after the premiere of *Les Danaïdes,* the *Mercure de France* published a letter from Ranieri de' Calzabigi in which Gluck's former collaborator claimed authorship of the libretto set by Salieri: "It was in 1778, and after the great success of my Orpheus and my Alceste upon your stage, that M. Gluck . . . induced me, with great promises, to write a new drama for him. . . . I had once spoken to him about a Hypermnestra; he urged me so earnestly to write it, that I decided to comply; he received that poor Hypermnestra in Paris, where he was, in the month of November of that year; he was enthusiastic about it; he sent word that he would have it translated in order to give it to the stage; and that was all he let me know about it."[11]

Gluck entrusted Calzabigi's *Ipermestra, o Le Danaidi* to François Louis Du Roullet, librettist of *Iphigénie en Tauride,* and Ludwig Theodor Tschudi, librettist of *Echo et Narcisse.* (This was not Du Roullet's first project involving a libretto by Calzabigi; he had translated *Alceste* for the Parisian production of 1776.) Du Roullet and Tschudi not only translated but substantially revised *Ipermestra.* Preoccupied with preparations for *Iphigénie* and *Echo,* Gluck left *Les Danaïdes* unset.[12]

9. The letters are cited but not quoted in Michtner, 178, 394 n. 28.

10. Gluck to Nicolas Gersin, Vienna, 30 November 1779, in *Ecrits de musiciens,* ed. Jacques-Gabriel Prod'homme (Paris, 1912), 428; in English translation (used here, with some changes) in *The Collected Correspondence and Papers of Christoph Willibald Gluck,* ed. Hedwig and E. H. Mueller von Asow (New York, 1962), 165; another translation in Patricia Howard, *Gluck: An Eighteenth-Century Portrait in Letters and Documents* (Oxford, 1995), 208.

11. Ranieri de' Calzabigi, *Scritti teatrali e letterari,* ed. Anna Laura Bellina, 2 vols. (Rome, 1994), 1:257–67; quoted in translation (used here) in Alfred Einstein, *Gluck,* trans. Eric Blom (New York, 1972), 177.

12. Bruno Brizi, "Uno spunto polemico Calzabigiano: *Ipermestra o Le Danaidi,*" in *La figura e l'opera di Ranieri de' Calzabigi,* ed. Federico Marri (Florence, 1989), 119–45.

Neither Gluck nor the directors of the Opéra forgot *Les Danaïdes.* By 1782 Gluck had apparently warmed to the idea of returning to Paris. On 19 August 1782 the directors met to consider his proposal that he set *Les Danaïdes* to music and travel to Paris to supervise the production.[13]

The young composer Joseph Martin Kraus was in Vienna during the following winter and spring. He met Gluck and learned something of the genesis of *Les Danaïdes.* His comments deserve special attention because they are among the very few by someone with no vested interest in the matter:

> [Gluck's] right hand also lacks its former flexibility. This was the reason that *Salieri* was able to copy his *Les Danaïdes* on paper for him, but every so often it became such an obsession that his doctor feared for a resurgence of apoplexy; he has given up on the opera and Salieri has been called to Paris to set it in his stead. Gluck thinks that the music would be too close to his own ideas, which Salieri often had the opportunity to hear, for it to be Salieri's own, yet he did not have full trust in this young man's ability for him to let the music be passed off under his [Gluck's] name.[14]

In January 1783 Gluck informed the directors of the Opéra that his health would not allow him to come to Paris and offered to send Salieri in his place. That offer did not in itself mean that Salieri had written the music; but Gluck, in stating his willingness to accept a fee much smaller than the one originally agreed to, seems to have been hinting at Salieri's authorship. Such a hint would be consistent with what Kraus perceived as Gluck's lack of confidence in Salieri's ability to write music that he would be willing to put his name to.

The minutes of the directors' meeting of 20 January 1783 show that they read between the lines of Gluck's letter and guessed that Salieri had composed much if not all of *Les Danaïdes:*

> An extract of a letter from M. le chevalier Gluck, sent to the committee by M. le Bailli Du Roullet, was read. This letter contains news that the poor health of M. Gluck could well keep him from making a trip to Paris. He therefore proposes that in the event that M. De Sallieri arrives here alone with the score of *Les Danaides,* the 20,000# [livres] that he demanded for this work would be reduced to 12,000 for the words and the music.
>
> On the basis of this letter's contents, the committee could not but believe that M. Salieri is the author of the music of *Les Danaides,* although it can be presumed that M. Gluck has

13. Angermüller, *Leben,* 3:238–39.

14. Joseph Martin Kraus, draft of a letter dated 15 April 1783, in "The Travel Diary of Joseph Martin Kraus," ed. and trans. Bertil van Boer, *JM* 8 (1990): 288; another translation in Howard, *Gluck,* 234.

> guided this composer in a career in which he has made himself immortal, and that this presumption encourages a favorable opinion of the work.[15]

The directors went on to recommend that Gluck's offer be refused.

Salieri, in the meantime, minimized Gluck's role in his unofficial comments about the opera. In a letter of 25 February 1783 to his admirer Carl Friedrich Cramer he implied that he had written all of *Les Danaïdes,* stating that he had recently completed the score "under his [i.e., Gluck's] direction" ("sotto la sua direzione").[16]

Shortly thereafter Joseph, probably having learned from Salieri that the directors of the Opéra were reluctant to accept *Les Danaïdes,* joined an effort to persuade them to do so. On 31 March 1783, just a few weeks before the inauguration of his opera buffa troupe, Joseph had tragédie lyrique on his mind. He wrote to Count Mercy in Paris:

> P.S. The composer Salieri has just written an opera entitled L'Hypermnestre ou les Danaïdes, and he did so almost under the *dictée* of Gluck. The little of it that I have heard on the keyboard seemed very good to me. Since Gluck will probably not be in a state to go to Paris himself, I ask you, my dear Count, to tell me if Salieri would do well to go there, and if you think that his work might be accepted there and performed, because, being employed by me and at the theater here, he would not want to make this journey in a state of incertitude and to stay in Paris for no reason.[17]

Joseph's letter corroborates Salieri's statement to Cramer that the opera was complete, more than a year before its first performance, and his implication that he was the sole author. At the same time it capitalizes on Gluck's reputation without being specific about what his contribution was. The phrase "presque sous la dictée de Gluck" is ambiguous by intention. *Dictée* can mean dictation or inspiration. Without telling an outright lie, Joseph managed to allude vaguely to the changing nature of Salieri's role, as described by Kraus: having started by writing Gluck's music down, Salieri continued by writing his own music under Gluck's inspiration.

In response to Joseph's letter Count Mercy wrote to the directors, turning the emperor's vague assertions into facts. The minutes of the directors' meeting of 14 April re-

15. "Compte que le Comité rend au Ministre de ce qui s'est passé en son assemblée extraordinaire du Lundi 20 Janvier 1783," in Adolphe Jullien, *La Cour et l'opéra sous Louis XVI: Marie Antoinette et Sacchini, Salieri, Favart et Gluck* (Paris, 1878), 167–68, and Angermüller, *Leben,* 3:239–40.

16. Salieri to Carl Friedrich Cramer, 25 February 1783, in Angermüller, *Leben,* 3:18, and Angermüller, *Fatti,* 115–17.

17. P. S. Le Compositeur Salieri vient d'ecrire un Opera intitulé l'Hypermnestre ou les Danaïdes et cela presque sous la dictée de Gluck. Le peu que j'en ai entendu sur le Clavecin m'a paru assés bien. Comme Gluck ne sera probablement pas en etat de se rendre Lui même à Paris, je vous prie, mon cher Comte, de me dire un mot, si Salieri feroit bien de s'y rendre et si vous croyés que sa piece pourroit y etre reçue et representée, parcequ'étant employé chés moi et au theatre d'ici, il ne voudroit pas faire ce voyage dans l'incertitude et s'arreter inutilement à Paris (Joseph to Count Mercy, 31 March 1783, HHStA, HP, Bd. 27, no. 289).

cord Mercy's assurance that the first two acts of *Les Danaïdes* were by Gluck and that the third act was "made under the *dictée* of that famous composer" by Salieri.[18] The directors may have been led to doubt the truthfulness of the ambassador's statement (assuming it was reported correctly in the minutes) by his erroneous partition of the opera into three acts. But they let the production go forward.

Gluck's feelings about the whole affair were mixed, in Kraus's view, and his motives were not entirely altruistic. But he too went along with the deception. Mosel, not unexpectedly, put the collaboration in a warmer light. An anecdote passed on by Salieri himself allows us a charming glimpse of the two composers working together at the keyboard:

> In 1784 Salieri, "under Gluck's direction [*Leitung*]" (as he himself writes), wrote his first French opera, *Les Danaïdes.* When he was finished with it and sang it at the keyboard in Gluck's company, they came across a passage in an aria that did not please the composer, without his being able to say why this was so. Gluck looked through the score of this aria, then had Salieri sing it, and then, after he had listened attentively, he said to him: "You are right, my dear friend, the whole aria is good, but this passage with which you are dissatisfied displeases me too; but I cannot find the problem. Sing the aria a second time . . . a third time. . . ." When Salieri came to the problematic passage this last time, Gluck shouted suddenly, interrupting him: "Now I have it! This passage smells of music!" And indeed they found that this idea had been introduced more for its artistic effect than for other necessary reasons.[19]

Salieri probably traveled from Vienna to Paris in December 1783, carrying a letter from Joseph to Count Mercy dated 30 November 1783. He could not have hoped for a stronger testimonial from his sovereign and patron. Eleven years earlier Joseph had introduced Salieri to his brother Leopold as "this young man, Gasman's student." The thirty-three-year-old Salieri was still "this young man" for Joseph; but now he was "a student of Gluck" and—a remarkable claim—the only musician capable of taking Gluck's place as Vienna's leading operatic composer:

> My dear Count de Mercy,
> The bearer of this letter is Salieri, my Kapellmeister, who is going to Paris to perform an opera that he has composed under the *dictée* of Gluck. I ask you to give him all the support and help that he will need for the success of his work. I address to you a letter to this effect to the Queen that you will give to Salieri, obtaining for him the occasion and the means to be able to present it to her himself.
>
> I believe that if there is no cabal this young man, who has already written some very good Italian scores and who is moreover a student of Gluck, by whom he is highly esteemed, will alone be capable of replacing him one day, now that he is out of the fray.

18. "Raport que le Comité fait au Ministre de ce qui s'est passé en son Assemblée du Lundi 14 avril 1783," in Jullien, *La Cour et l'opéra,* 169–70, and Angermüller, *Leben,* 3:241.

19. Mosel, 79–80.

Farewell, my dear Count, and rest assured that my respect for you will always remain as great as my friendship.[20]

The fiction that Gluck composed a large part of *Les Danaïdes* was maintained, for the public, until the opera came to performance in April 1784. The title page of the libretto printed for the premiere attributes the music to Gluck and Salieri.

On the same day as *Les Danaïdes* reached the stage, Gluck wrote to Du Roullet that Salieri was its sole composer; his declaration was duly published in the Parisian press.[21] Gluck's letter could be interpreted as confirmation of Kraus's statement that "he did not have full trust in this young man's ability for him to let the music be passed off under his [Gluck's] name." Salieri may have feared as much. He quickly responded with a letter of his own that puts the best possible construction on Gluck's statement:

The declaration of M. le Chevalier Gluck that I just read in your journal is a new favor received by me from this great man, whose friendship allows me to reflect a ray of his glory. It is true that I alone wrote the music of *Les Danaïdes,* but I wrote it entirely under his direction [*direction,* not *dictée*], led by his wisdom and enlightened by his genius.

The merit of musical ideas is too common and too unimportant by itself for one to be able to take pride in it. It is the use to which one puts such ideas, their applicability to the words, their dramatic sense, that represents their value and gives them real merit; and everything good in this regard in *Les Danaïdes* I owe to the author of *Iphigénie.*[22]

Thus, even after Gluck himself claimed that Salieri had written the whole opera, Salieri cleverly continued to invoke Gluck's name, putting himself in a position in which he was able to claim credit for the success of *Les Danaïdes* while gaining prestige from being associated with Gluck. Meanwhile, Gluck's compositional role, earlier exaggerated to the point where two-thirds of the opera was attributed to him, was now quickly for-

20. Mon cher Comte de Mercy, le porteur de la presente est Salieri, mon maitre de Chapelle, qui se rend à Paris pour y faire executer un Opera qu'il a composé sous la dictée de Gluck. Je vous prie de Lui prêter tout l'appuy et les secours dont il pourroit avoir besoin pour le Succés de son ouvrage; Je vous address aussi à cet effet une Lettre à la Reine que vous remettrés à Salieri, en lui procurant l'occasion et les moyens afin de pouvoir la presenter lui-même.

Je crois que s'il n'y a pas de cabale, ce jeune homme qui a deja fait de très bonnes musiques Italiennes et qui d'ailleurs est un Eleve de Gluck dont il est fort estimé, sera seul capable de le remplacer un jour, étant mis hors de combat. Adieu, mon cher Comte, croyés que je serai toujours avec autant d'estime que d'amitié (Joseph to Count Mercy, HHStA, HP, Bd. 27, no. 955).

21. Swenson, 102; and, in English translation, Howard, *Gluck,* 237.

22. *Journal de Paris,* 18 May 1784; quoted in Jullien, *La Cour et l'opéra,* 183–84, Angermüller, *Leben,* 3:273–74, and, in English translation, Howard, *Gluck,* 237.

gotten by everyone, with Salieri's encouragement. He did not want anyone to know what Kraus knew: that he had begun *Les Danaïdes* not as composer but as Gluck's amanuensis.

Libretto

The angry letter sent by Calzabigi to the *Mercure de France* claiming authorship of the libretto of *Les Danaïdes* and criticizing the changes that Du Roullet and Tschudi introduced into his *Ipermestra* was incited, in part, by a misleading notice included in the libretto by Du Roullet: "A manuscript by M. de Calzabigi, author of the Italian Orphée and Alceste, was passed on to us, from which we helped ourselves a great deal. We borrowed several ideas from the ballet of the Danaides by the celebrated M. Noverre . . . to these we added our own, and out of all of these we formed our plan."[23]

Calzabigi noticed that this statement carefully avoided giving readers the impression that he was the libretto's principal author. He also claimed that Du Roullet's acknowledgment of Noverre served to obscure his own role. Noverre's *Hypermnestre, ou Les Danaïdes* was first performed in Stuttgart on 11 February 1764, with music by Jean-Joseph Rodolphe.[24] As represented by a scenario published in 1764, Noverre's ballet had very little in common with the libretto set by Salieri almost twenty years later.[25]

The problem of assessing the relationship between Calzabigi's *Ipermestra* and the libretto of *Les Danaïdes* is complicated by the fact that *Ipermestra* is itself thoroughly French in many ways. It has five acts, not the three acts normal in Italian serious operas through most of the eighteenth century. *Les Danaïdes* also has five acts, but its authors had no need of Calzabigi's guidance here, since most tragédies lyriques were in five acts. *Ipermestra* calls for spectacular scenic effects, choral music, and dance. So does *Les Danaïdes,* not only because it is based on Calzabigi's libretto but also because these were elements that audiences expected in tragédie lyrique.

The gruesome story of Danaus and his fifty daughters, the Danaids who give the opera its title, had served Aeschylus as the subject of a trilogy of which only one play survived the end of Greco-Roman antiquity.[26] Danaus swears an oath of friendship to the fifty sons of Egyptus, his brother and archenemy. Egyptus is dead; the eldest of his sons, Lyncée, now leads the family. As part of the treaty of friendship, Lyncée and his

23. Swenson, 102.

24. Personal communication (26 November 1987) from Kathleen Hansell, to whom I am grateful for much information about Noverre's ballet—scenario and music—and its surviving scores.

25. Brizi, "Uno spunto polemico," 135–37. It is of course possible that later versions of Noverre's *Ipermestra* differed from the version he presented in Stuttgart in 1764.

26. The surviving play, *The Suppliant Women,* was originally followed by *The Sons of Egyptus* and *The Danaids.*

brothers are engaged to be married to the Danaids; Lyncée himself will wed his beloved Hypermnestre, the eldest of the Danaids. In his aria "Jouissez du destin propice" Danaus urges the young couples to enjoy the pleasures of marriage because, he adds darkly, such pleasures could be cut off at any time by death:

Jouissez du destin propice
Dont l'amour flatte vos désirs.
Sans bruit souvent la Mort se glisse,
Et vous frappe au sein des plaisirs.

[Rejoice in the happy destiny with which Love has granted your desires. Often without a sound Death steals in and strikes you in the lap of pleasure.]

Lyncée and Hypermnestre sing of their love for one another in the duet "Oublions tous ces jours de peine."

Act 2 is set in a dungeon consecrated to Nemesis, the goddess of vengeance. Danaus reveals to his daughters that he arranged the reconciliation with the sons of Egyptus as a deception, part of his plan to avenge the wrongs committed against him by Egyptus. He commands his daughters to kill their husbands on their wedding night. All except Hypermnestre swear an oath to Nemesis ("Divinité de sang avide"), promising that their wedding beds will serve as tombs for the sons of Egyptus. When all the Danaids except Hypermnestre have left, Danaus confronts her, demanding that she too promise to kill her husband. He refers to the prediction of an oracle: that if his vengeance is not complete, one of his nephews will kill him. Left alone, Hypermnestre faces her dilemma. There is only one way out: in the aria "Foudre céleste je t'appelle" she asks the gods to strike her dead.

Amid the dancing and singing in celebration of the wedding, Hypermnestre comes close to telling Lyncée of her father's intentions. She pleads with Danaus for mercy, but without success. Hypermnestre meets Lyncée again, this time in private; she tells him that they must separate, without telling him why. Suddenly the cries of Lyncée's brothers are heard off stage as the Danaids attack them. Lyncée flees.

When, at the beginning of act 5, Hypermnestre tells her father that she saved Lyncée, Danaus is outraged. The Danaids enter with bloody swords; Danaus orders them to find Lyncée and kill him. Lyncée attacks the palace with an army, slaughtering the Danaids. Danaus is about to kill Hypermnestre when he himself is killed by one of Lyncée's brothers. The palace is destroyed, the ruins engulfed in flames. A change of scene reveals the Danaids imprisoned in the underworld with Danaus chained to a rock, his entrails devoured by a vulture; a chorus of furies promises that their torments will never cease.

Following Calzabigi, Du Roullet and Tschudi arranged the action so that the public ceremonies and great events of acts 1, 3, and 5 alternate with the shorter acts 2 and 4, in which individual characters—Hypermnestre, Lyncée, and Danaus—interact with one another privately. The chorus has a place in every act (in the fourth we hear it only from offstage) but its role is most important in the "public" acts 1 (where it celebrates the reconciliation of Danaus and the sons of Egyptus), 3 (where it celebrates the mass wedding), and 5 (where the Danaids celebrate their bloody crime and later cry out in agony from the depths of the underworld). Dancing is limited to the three "public" acts.

Music

Salieri's music enters fully into the spirit and style of tragédie lyrique, with its fluid alternation of orchestrally accompanied recitative, arias, choruses, and ballets. It combines the nobility and simplicity of Gluck's melodies and the monumentality of his choruses with the warmth and lyricism of the Italian masters of tragédie lyrique Piccinni and Sacchini.[27]

Some of the most Gluckian passages are to be found in Lyncée's two arias. "A peine aux autels d'Hyménée" (in act 4) features an elegant, plaintive melody reminiscent of "J'ai perdu mon Eurydice," but with Salieri's characteristic descent from the second degree to the third at the end of the second phrase (ex. 10.1). Equally fine is Lyncée's first aria, "Rends-moi ton coeur." As the opening melody reaches up to a climactic high A before descending to a cadence (ex. 10.2), it sounds much like another passage in C major, also reaching up to A, in "Je chérirai, jusqu'au trépas," sung by the hero Ali in

EXAMPLE 10.1 *Les Danaïdes,* act 4, "A peine aux autels d'Hyménée," mm. 9–12 (engraved full score, Paris, *ca.* 1784; facsimile, Bologna, 1969)

No sooner had I reached Hymen's altar than his vows fulfilled my desires.

27. For an incisive but almost unremittingly hostile analysis of the opera see Julian Rushton, "Music and Drama at the Académie Royale de Musique (Paris), 1774–1789" (doctoral diss., Oxford University, 1970), 274–82.

EXAMPLE 10.2 *Les Danaïdes,* act 3, "Rends-moi ton coeur," mm. 1–8

Give me your heart, confide in me; give me those blessings that I have lost.

Gluck's *La Rencontre imprévue* (ex. 10.3). Salieri's aria, like Gluck's, is in a simple A-B-A form. Counterpoint is so rare in Salieri's operatic music that a very small amount of imitation in the B section adds significantly to the beauty of this passage (ex. 10.4).

The intense emotions expressed by the leading characters encouraged Salieri to look for striking harmonic gestures, such as sudden harmonic shifts from tonic to flat sixth at climactic moments. Near the end of the duet for Hypermnestre and Lyncée in act 4, the words "quelle est ta barbarie extrême!" are brought to life stunningly by a violent move from D major (the tonic), fortissimo, to B♭ major, also fortissimo, and by dissonance both harmonic (on the downbeat of m. 60) and melodic (Lyncée's leap from D up to G♯), before an augmented sixth chord leads back to the tonic (ex. 10.5). A similar harmonic surprise adds to the dramatic effect of Hypermnestre's aria at the end of act 2, "Foudre céleste." The closing material is solidly in the tonic, C major; but as Hypermnestre cries out "Viens" in the hope that a thunderbolt will strike her dead, an A♭-major chord, fortissimo, followed by an A♭-major scale tumbling down two octaves, depicts the thunderbolt (ex. 10.6).

The music accompanying the wedding festivities in act 3 shows Salieri expertly employing the conventions of French ballet and choral music. One of the best of these

EXAMPLE 10.3 Gluck, *La Rencontre imprévue,* act 1, "Je chérirai, jusqu'au trépas," mm. 19–22 (*Sämtliche Werke,* 4:7)

No beauty would make me unfaithful.

EXAMPLE 10.4 Salieri, *Les Danaïdes,* act 3, "Rends-moi ton coeur," mm. 11–18

All our wishes, satisfied beforehand, were anticipated each by the other; before breaking silence we understood each other's expressions.

EXAMPLE 10.5 *Les Danaïdes*, act 4, "Hélas! que ne puis-je te suivre," mm. 55–63

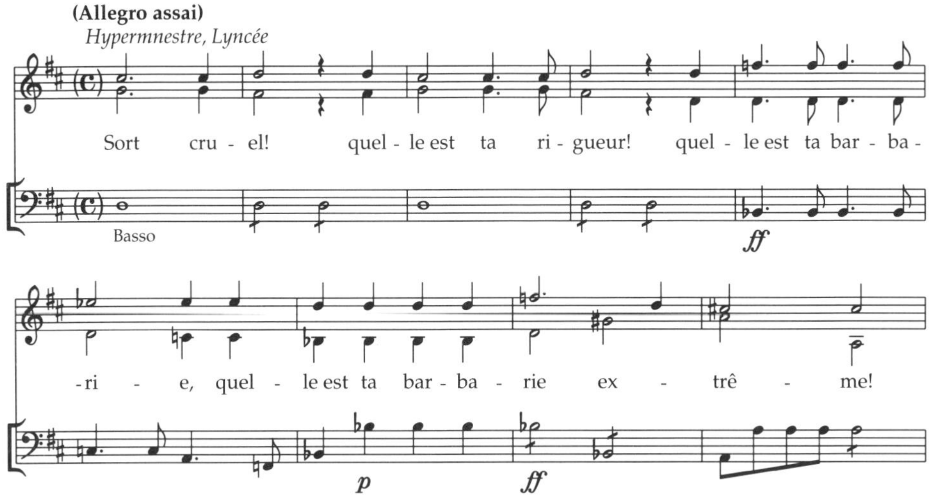

Cruel fate! How harsh you are! How outrageous your barbarity!

EXAMPLE 10.6 *Les Danaïdes*, act 2, "Foudre céleste, je t'appelle," mm. 70–78

Why does it delay in crushing me? Come! Put an end to my misfortunes; come and crush me!

numbers is the male chorus "Descends dans le sein d'Amphitrite," in which the sons of Egyptus ask night to pass slowly so that they might fully enjoy nuptial bliss. A strikingly deployed deceptive cadence enhances the sensuousness of their prayer (ex. 10.7).

EXAMPLE 10.7 *Les Danaïdes,* act 3, "Descends dans le sein d'Amphitrite," mm. 2–7

Descend to the breast of Amphitrite; hide your fires, jealous star!

Salieri did full justice to the libretto's horror and violence, nowhere more skillfully than in his music for the final underworld scene. He brought together the minor mode, an orchestra that includes trombones as well as trumpets and horns, syncopations, offbeat sforzandos, tremolos, and diminished seventh harmony to produce an overwhelming evocation of demonic terror.

The orchestra of the Opéra was bigger and included more kinds of instruments than any of the orchestras for which Salieri had written his earlier operas. Salieri had at his disposal instruments—trombones, trumpets, timpani, and clarinets—that had been available to him only sporadically in the past, and never all of them together. He did not have to use all these instruments. The operas that Sacchini presented at the Opéra during the 1780s rarely require more than flutes, oboes, bassoons, horns, and strings. *Renaud* (1783) uses neither clarinets nor trombones. *Oedipe à Colone* (1786) does not even require trumpets.[28] Salieri's taking full advantage of the orchestral forces available in Paris reflects Gluck's influence and perhaps also Piccinni's, whose French operas are as richly orchestrated as Gluck's.

Salieri did not handle all the instruments in his big orchestra with equal imagination. His use of clarinets is largely limited to doubling the oboes, which results in a sonority that, while attractive in itself, soon grows tiresome. It may have been in reference to this doubling that the *Mercure de France* criticized Salieri's orchestration: "We also think that the composer makes too frequent use of wind instruments, the effect of which is very interesting when they are adapted to the characters and to the emotions which are proper to them; but they necessarily weaken this effect when they are applied to every-

28. According to the full scores of *Renaud* and *Oedipe* published in Paris shortly after the first performances of these operas.

thing and when they are mixed indistingishably with other instruments. This abuse becomes more common every day: an abuse that deprives theatrical music of a rich source of beautiful effects, and that must be attributed to the progress of instrumental music."[29]

Salieri's writing for timpani shows him exploring their dramatic potential, which he was to exploit further in Paris and Vienna. The effect of the A♭ chord near the end of Hypermnestre's aria in C, "Foudre céleste" (see ex. 10.6), is enhanced by a drumroll on C, the timpani having been silent through the aria until this moment. Salieri used timpani very differently, but with equally dramatic effect, earlier in the same act. The stormy chorus of Danaids in D minor, "Oui, qu'aux flambeaux des Euménides," combines a continuous torrent of sixteenth notes in the strings (in octaves) with an almost equally continuous drumroll (sixteen beats to the measure).[30]

Frances Crewe, an Englishwoman visiting Paris in the mid-1780s, wrote of the Opéra: "They have a very full Orchestra here, and a new Instrument in it which, I think, is called *un Trombeau*—It has a mixed sound of Drum and Trumpet and produced great effect."[31] She meant the trombone, "new" perhaps in the sense that she had not heard one in Italian opera in England. Her description of its sound is naive but not unperceptive. Salieri used trombones in *Les Danaïdes* for the first time in an opera since *Europa riconosciuta* six years earlier. They serve as an audible counterpart to the opera's dark, violent color, almost always in conjunction with the minor mode (as in the slow introduction to the overture, the dungeon scene at the beginning of act 2 that is foreshadowed by the slow introduction, and the underworld scene in act 5). Trombones contribute their somber tones to the orchestral unison—B♭ sustained for three measures, building from pianissimo to fortissimo—that announces, near the end of act 4, that the Danaids have begun murdering their new husbands. The trombones reappear in the brilliant chorus in act 5 in which the Danaids celebrate the accomplishment of their crime.

Perhaps more vividly than anywhere else in the opera, this chorus, "Gloire, gloire, Evan, Evoé!" shows why *Les Danaïdes* could be successfully revived in Paris as late as the 1820s. It is music of which Berlioz or Weber might have been proud. Stage directions in the printed score describe the ghastly scene: "The enraged Danaids enter from all sides, their hair disheveled; they are half covered with the skins of tigers, etc. Some hold a thyrsus in one hand, a bloody dagger in the other. Others carry drums on which they beat with their daggers. Others carry burning torches."[32]

29. *Mercure de France,* 22 May 1784; quoted in Angermüller, *Leben,* 3:265–69.

30. The effect is much like one achieved by Sacchini in act 1, sc. 4, of *Renaud,* where a drumroll notated as repeated sixteenth notes accompanies strings playing a tremolo also notated as repeated sixteenth notes.

31. Quoted in Black, *The British Abroad,* 257.

32. Engraved score, p. 224.

Salieri scored the chorus for full orchestra, including trumpets, timpani, and trombones. The syncopated half note in all the parts in measure 3 is reinforced by an isolated chord played fortissimo by the three trombones (fig. 10.1). Throughout the chorus Salieri used the trombones this way, their sudden bursts of sound contributing to the chorus's extraordinary vitality.

But the strangest passage in the chorus (in the form of a rondo, A-B-A′-C-A″, in which A is sung by the chorus and B and C by Plancippe, one of the Danaids) has no trombones or trumpets. In section C Plancippe sings:

A ton pouvoir Panthée insulte,
Sa famille venge son culte,
Elle a détruit ses nombreux combattants,
Sous le tirse ils tombent sans vie;
Et la ménade assouvie
S'endort sur leurs corps palpitants!

[Panthea insults your power; her family avenges her cult; she has destroyed her many soldiers; under the thyrsus they fall lifeless and the satiated maenad falls asleep on their palpitating bodies.]

Salieri's setting of these horrific words starts in B minor, with music whose energy reflects that of the poem; but at the last two lines of text he modulates from B minor to G major in a quiet passage in which the bassoons, reinforcing the violas, highlight a beautiful inner line. The juxtaposition of lyrical music and the poetry's bloody image makes this one of the opera's most striking moments (ex. 10.8).

A review of *Les Danaïdes* in the *Mercure de France,* written before the publication of Gluck's announcement that Salieri was the sole composer, found Gluck's influence in Salieri's overture, which the reviewer praised for its anticipation of elements of the drama:

The overture seemed to us to be of fine inspiration. The beginning is noble and serious. It is followed by a movement with a fast tempo and gay melody, which conveys an idea of the festivities. This movement is interrupted with other passages whose strong emotions and pathetic accents bring us back to dark and tragic thoughts. These different characters are contrasted and mixed artistically, and sustained with fine orchestration; but perhaps the first serious passage is not sufficiently developed and its expression is effaced too soon by the gay movement that follows it. In general one recognizes in it the authentic spirit of that compositional genius of which M. Gluck gave the first model to our theater, in the sublime overture of *Iphigénie en Aulide.* That of *Les Danaïdes,* without being able to be compared with that one, is certainly above those insignificant symphonies which do not express anything, do not announce anything. Such works, cast in the common mold of the sonata, are all composed of

FIGURE 10.1 *Les Danaïdes,* act 5, beginning of the chorus "Gloire, gloire, Evan, Evoé!" ("Trom: in G" is an engraver's error; these are trumpets in C). Full score (Paris, ca. 1784).

EXAMPLE 10.8 *Les Danaïdes,* act 5, "Gloire, gloire, Evan, Evoé!" mm. 76–86

three or four movements of different character and tempo, without unity just as they are without meaning, and yet skillful composers call them overtures.[33]

Salieri's slow introduction in D minor, orchestrated with trombones, an initial fortissimo followed immediately by a decrescendo (ex. 10.9), should have reminded Parisian audiences of the beginning not of *Iphigénie en Aulide* but of *Alceste,* likewise in D minor and with trombones; in its Parisian version the overture begins Lentement and forte, followed by a decrescendo.

EXAMPLE 10.9 *Les Danaïdes,* overture, mm. 1–8

(*Continued on next page*)

33. *Mercure de France,* 22 May 1784; quoted in Angermüller, *Leben,* 3:265.

EXAMPLE 10.9 (*continued*)

Undoubtedly inspired by Gluck, Salieri's overture also looks to the future. The slow introduction, with its syncopations and slow harmonic rhythm, anticipates the slow introduction of Mozart's overture to *Don Giovanni,* not least in its reference to a dramatic moment in the opera, the opening of act 2. Even closer to *Don Giovanni* is a passage later in the overture, where a gentle, major-mode melody (to reappear at the end of the joyful wedding festivities in act 3) is followed by a savage fortissimo diminished seventh chord (almost exactly the same sonority that announces the appearance of the stone guest near the end of Mozart's opera) and a wild, tonally unstable Presto.[34]

Reception

Joseph II, eager to learn of public reaction to his protégé's opera, wrote to Count Mercy on 2 April 1784, several weeks before the premiere: "when you know how Salieri's opera went, I ask you to tell me about it, since I have an interest in this young man."[35] Finally the emperor received good news, to which he responded with great satisfaction on 18 June: "I am delighted that Salieri has found favor with his opera. In the letters that he writes here he expresses infinite gratitude for the kindnesses that you have done him. It is extraordinary that since the secret has been revealed, and everyone knows that this opera is completely by him, it wins even more approval. That shows that the public is well disposed toward this first attempt, and looks with favor on a composer's goodwill."[36]

By the time Gluck claimed that Salieri was the sole composer of *Les Danaïdes,* his name had helped to win critics and audiences over. Not that Gluck by himself could as-

34. Martin Cooper quotes this passage in "Opera in France," in *NOHM,* 7:242.

35. et quand vous saurés comment l'Opera de Salieri aura reussi, je vous prie de m'en instruire, m'interessant à ce jeune homme (HHStA, HP, Bd. 31, no. 172).

36. Je suis charmé que Salieri ait bien rencontré avec son Opera. Dans les lettres qu'il a écrites ici, il se loue infiniment des bontés que vous avés eues pour lui. Il est singulier que depuis que le sécret est devoilé, et qu'on sait que cette piece est toute entiere de lui, elle trouve plus d'approbation. Cela fait voir que le public est indulgent pour ce premier Essai en faveur de la bonne volonté du Compositeur (HHStA, HP, Bd. 31, no. 429).

sure success; witness the recent failure of his own *Echo et Narcisse.* Joseph's influence at the highest levels of government and the strengths of *Les Danaïdes* itself both contributed to the opera's success.

Les Danaïdes inspired strong reactions from its audience, both positive and negative. That the production was a fine one seems to have been agreed by all. According to the *Journal de Paris,* "Few works present such a rich and imposing mis-en-scène. The large variety of characters, the number of scene changes and their picturesque quality, the beautiful working of the stage machinery, the brilliant costumes, and the choice of incidents of every kind all contributed to the success of the first performance."[37]

William Bennett, an Englishman in Paris in 1785, attended a performance of Salieri's opera. He left a valuable description of its sound and appearance, with details recorded nowhere else:

> . . . to the Opera of the Danaides. The music loud and noisy in the French taste, and the singers screamed past all power of simile to represent. The scenery was very good, no people understanding the *jeu de theatre* or tricks of the stage, so well as the French. We had in the dark scenes not above one light, and in the bright ones above twenty large chandeliers, so as to make a wonderful contrast, nor was there the least error or blunder in changing the scenes, except once when a candle pulled up too hastily, was very near to setting fire to a whole grove of trees. The stage being deeper than ours, was filled sometimes with fifty persons, a great advantage to the Chorus's and bustling parts. . . . Our Opera ended with a representation of Hell, in which the fifty Danaides were hauled and pulled about as if the Devils had been going to ravish them. Several of them in the violence of the French action being literally thrown flat upon their backs; and they were all at last buried in such a shower of fire, that I wonder the Playhouse was not burned to the ground. We paid somewhat more than 6 shillings each for our places, and were on the whole well entertained.[38]

The libretto won praise but also much criticism. Some found it poorly crafted. "Une autre monstruosité nouvelle" is how François Métra described *Les Danaïdes* (the first monstrosity being Beaumarchais's *Le Mariage de Figaro,* performed a few days earlier): "a thousand improbable events, a thousand unnecessary effects, a thousand tedious places that slow down the action and dampen the audience's enthusiasm."[39] But the opera's final scene, he admitted, was "truly beautiful and magnificent." For Jean-François La Harpe (a devoted *Piccinniste* who could not be expected to find anything to admire in an opera composed under Gluck's direction) *Les Danaïdes* violated common sense and good taste, starting from the improbability that any man could have "at one time

37. *Journal de Paris,* 27 April 1784; quoted in Angermüller, *Leben,* 3:249–52.

38. Quoted in Black, *The British Abroad,* 255–56.

39. François Métra, *Correspondance secrète, politique et littéraire* (London, 1787–90), 12 May 1784; quoted in Angermüller, *Leben,* 3:271–72.

fifty daughters of marriageable age and fifty nephews as sons-in-law."[40] The *Journal de Paris,* on the other hand, praised the librettists for having taken advantage of the story's opportunities for festivity (in acts 1 and 3), so as to counteract the story's horror and violence.[41]

Salieri's music also drew contradictory opinions. La Harpe described Salieri's recitative as if it had been composed by Gluck: "shrill, monotonous, and crude." He found the opera as a whole "lacking in melody, except for some ballet tunes, and lacking in musical effects, except for the chorus in the second act, the oath of the Danaids."[42] In contrast the *Mercure de France,* a semiofficial organ of the French government, published a long and generally favorable review of the music—not unexpected in view of the royal patronage that Salieri enjoyed. It found much to praise in Salieri's overture (in a passage quoted above), arias, and choruses, and criticized only his recitative and (in a passage also quoted above) his orchestration.

The *Mercure de France* concluded its review with the following note: "P.S. Since this article was delivered to the printer, we have seen in the *Journal de Paris* a letter of M. Gluck declaring that the music of *Les Danaïdes* is entirely by Salieri. . . . This declaration cannot but do honor to the already well-known talents of M. Salieri. The great and true beauties so abundant in this opera and the evidence that they present of his very exact knowledge of our theater must give us the greatest hopes for the productions that we have the right to expect from him."[43]

This reviewer was not the only one looking to the future with hope. Salieri too looked forward to writing more operas in Paris. His name stood alone on the title page of the full score published in Paris shortly after the premiere. But in his dedicatory letter to Marie Antoinette he could not resist yet another reference to Gluck, this time in connection with a hint about further patronage: "I wrote it [the music] under the eyes and under the direction of the famous Chevalier Gluck, this sublime genius, the creator of dramatic music, which he raised to the highest possible level of perfection. I hope, with the advice of this great man, to be able to compose some other work more worthy of the enlightened taste of Your Majesty and of the favor that Your Majesty wishes to bestow in accepting the dedication of the music of *Les Danaïdes.*"[44]

Salieri did not hope in vain. By the time he returned to Vienna he had agreed to compose two more operas for Paris. During the next four years he divided his time about equally between Vienna and Paris.

The traditions of French opera influenced not only the operas that Salieri wrote in

40. Jean-François La Harpe, *Correspondance littéraire* (Paris, 1801–7), 4:234; quoted in Angermüller, *Leben,* 3:274.

41. *Journal de Paris,* 27 April 1784; quoted in Angermüller, *Leben,* 3:251.

42. La Harpe, *Correspondance littéraire,* 4:237; quoted in Angermüller, *Leben,* 3:275.

43. *Mercure de France,* 22 May 1784; quoted in Angermüller, *Leben,* 3:268–69.

44. Preface to the engraved score.

Paris but also those that he wrote in Vienna. In this respect his career differed from Gluck's, whose Parisian operas were his last: the culmination of a career as musical dramatist in Italy, London, Vienna, and Paris. Salieri wrote his Parisian operas exactly midway through his thirty-year career as an opera composer, and while he was still actively involved in Viennese opera. Like Gluck he brought with him to Paris the experience of operatic composition in Italy and Vienna; unlike Gluck, he made good use of his experience as a composer of French opera in the Viennese operas that followed.

Les Danaïdes was performed at the Opéra 127 times, winning applause into the 1820s.[45] Berlioz, who arrived in Paris in 1821 with the intention of studying medicine, remembered a performance of Salieri's opera as having initiated the mental process that led to his decision to devote his life to music (a process that culminated at a performance of Gluck's *Iphigénie en Tauride*). He wrote in his *Memoires:*

> I was about to become a student like so many others, destined to increase by one the disastrous number of bad doctors when, one evening, I went to the Opéra. They were performing Salieri's *Les Danaïdes.* The splendor and brilliance of the spectacle; the sheer weight and richness of sound of the orchestra and choruses; the pathos of Mme. Branchu [in the role of Hypermnestre], her extraordinary voice; the rugged grandeur of Dérivis [as Danaus]; Hypermnestre's aria in which I detected, imitated by Salieri, all the features that I had attributed in my imagination to Gluck's style on the basis of excerpts from his *Orphée* that I had found in my father's library; and finally the astonishing bacchanal and the ballet music, so melancholy in its voluptuousness, that Spontini had added to his old compatriot's score disturbed me and thrilled me to an extent which I will not attempt to describe. I was like a young man born to be a sailor who, having seen only the little boats on the lakes of his native mountains, found himself suddenly transported to a three-deck ship on the high seas.
>
> As will easily be believed, I hardly slept the night following this performance, and the anatomy lesson the next day felt the effects of my insomnia. I sang the aria of Danaus "Jouissez du destin propice" while I cut into the skull of my cadaver. And when Robert, tired of hearing me murmur the melody "Descends dans le sein d'Amphitrite" instead of reading Bichat's chapter on aponeuroses, shouted: "Let us concentrate on our business! We are not working! In three days our cadaver will be spoiled! It cost eighteen francs! Be reasonable!" I answered with the hymn to Nemesis, "Divinité de sang avide!" and the scalpel fell from his hand.[46]

45. Alfred Loewenberg, *Annals of Opera, 1597–1940,* 3d ed. (Totowa, N.J., 1978), col. 410.

46. Hector Berlioz, *Mémoires,* ed. Pierre Citron (Paris, 1991), 57–58.

11

JOSEPH'S ITALIAN TROUPE AND THE RENEWAL OF VIENNESE OPERA BUFFA

Salieri returned to Vienna in late spring or summer 1784, after the successful production of *Les Danaïdes.* In July he wrote to his German admirer Cramer of his intention to write two more operas for Paris, declaring his preference for French opera over Italian: "The Parisian public generally enjoys and seeks the truth in music. I, who hate my art when it lacks truth, therefore feel myself inclined, strongly inclined, to exert all my powers to make myself worthy of its applause, and therefore believe and hope that I am unlikely to write any more Italian operas."[1]

This reformist talk, with its high-flown Gluckian invocation of musical truth and its denigration of Italian opera, sounds a little false coming from Salieri, who had devoted most of his career to Italian opera, had already begun an opera buffa that would soon reach the stage (*Il ricco d'un giorno*), and would write two more before returning to Paris. A consummate courtier committed to the service of Joseph II, Salieri must have suspected in 1784 that there would be plenty of opera buffa in his future.

Although several numbers from *Les Danaïdes* were performed in a Burgtheater concert during February 1788,[2] Salieri probably had no intention of staging the opera in Vienna during the 1780s. The libretto's violence and horror, and the score's emphasis on the minor mode, its free-flowing alternation of arioso, aria, accompanied recitative, and chorus, its extensive ballet music, its orchestra enriched with trombones, were calcu-

1. Salieri to Cramer, 20 July 1784, in Angermüller, *Leben,* 3:28–31, and Angermüller, *Fatti,* 119–21.
2. Morrow, *Concert Life,* 271.

lated for their effect at the Opéra, not the Burgtheater. Yet Salieri's admiration for French opera was real, and so was his affinity for its musical and dramatic techniques. He could not return to the composition of opera buffa without the experience of *Les Danaïdes* influencing his work. Instead of rejecting Italian comic opera in favor of tragédie lyrique, he brought the genres closer together by incorporating aspects of French serious opera into some of the Italian operas that he composed after *Les Danaïdes.* In doing so, he contributed much to the distinctive character of Viennese Italian opera in the 1780s.

The inauguration of Joseph's opera buffa troupe in April 1783 marked the displacement of German opera by Italian in the Burgtheater and the return of opera buffa to a status equal to that of German spoken drama. The emperor assembled a company of comic singers second to none; he seems for once to have spared no expense. Already present in Vienna were two experienced composers of Italian opera, Salieri and Mozart. Another talented operatic composer, the Spaniard Martín y Soler, soon joined them. Joseph naturally preferred (on a personal level) Salieri, whom he had known for seventeen years and whose career he had watched over from its beginning. The emperor reinstated Salieri in the position of operatic music director that he had occupied from Gassmann's death in 1774 to the inauguration of the Singspiel troupe in 1778. But Joseph had the musical sophistication to appreciate the newcomers and the generosity to support them with commissions.[3] Two inexperienced but clever librettists, Da Ponte and Giambattista Casti, inspired Joseph's composers.

True to his character, the emperor maintained control over the whole complex enterprise, as his letters to Count Rosenberg, his high chamberlain and opera director, show clearly.[4] In his *Reminiscences* the tenor Michael Kelly, one of the original members of the troupe, remembered his employer fondly: "As the theatre was in the palace, the Emperor often honoured the rehearsals with his presence, and discoursed familiarly with the performers. He spoke Italian like a Tuscan, and was affable and condescending. He came almost every night to the opera. . . . He was passionately fond of music, and a most excellent and accurate judge of it."[5]

Joseph was hardly a perfect manager. Within a few weeks of the debut of the company that he had gone to such trouble to assemble he authorized Rosenberg to dismiss it, complaining that three singers were costing him as much as one hundred soldiers.[6] He changed his mind, of course, and the troupe stayed. But his indecisiveness, impatience, impulsiveness, and above all his reluctance to spend money meant that the future was never certain.

3. The success of Martín's first Viennese opera, *Il burbero di buon cuore* (1786), allowed him temporarily to take Salieri's place as "the composer most favored by Joseph" (Da Ponte, 107).

4. Many of Joseph's letters to Rosenberg are published in *Joseph II.*

5. Kelly, *Reminiscences,* 103.

6. Joseph to Rosenberg, 25 June 1783, in *Joseph II,* 33–34.

Virgin Muses: Da Ponte and Casti

Before his troupe could perform Joseph needed to find an Italian poet capable of fulfilling the manifold responsibilities of house librettist. A Venetian poet happened to be in Vienna in 1782; to him Joseph entrusted the job of librettist to the opera buffa troupe.

Da Ponte's early years resembled Salieri's in some respects. Born in 1749, one year before Salieri, in Ceneda, a small city on the Venetian terraferma (today Vittorio Veneto), Da Ponte fell in love with literature as passionately as Salieri with music. In his father's tiny collection of books he discovered some volumes of Metastasio, "whose verses produced in my soul the sensation of music itself."[7] Like many young Italians of modest means but substantial literary talent and ambition, Da Ponte found in the priesthood a way to financial independence and social acceptance. He immersed himself in the classics of Italian literature while taking his religious studies seriously enough to qualify for ordination as a celebrant priest in 1773.

Abate Da Ponte, like Salieri, moved from the Venetian mainland to Venice itself before finding professional success on the Viennese stage. But while Salieri spent only a few months in Venice (1766), Da Ponte spent much of his early adulthood there and in the nearby cities of Treviso and Padua. Priestly duties were the last thing he had in mind when he arrived in Venice, eager to taste the city's pleasures. He did so with the same lack of discretion that later made his life difficult in Vienna. Within a few years he had made so many enemies that the government used his relations with a married woman as a pretext for banishment.

Da Ponte went north, first to Austrian Gorizia, northeast of Trieste, and then, in 1781, to Dresden. There Mazzolà, one of his Venetian friends, had just been appointed poet to the court theater. Da Ponte assisted him, thus adding some practical theatrical experience to the good literary taste that his boyhood reading of Metastasio's librettos had inculcated in him. Mazzolà's friendship was of crucial importance not only because it provided Da Ponte with access to the craft of theatrical poetry and its ancillary activities but also because Mazzolà, having collaborated with Salieri in Venice (on *La scuola de' gelosi* and the aborted *L'isola capricciosa*), was in a position to recommend Da Ponte to Salieri's protection.

From Dresden Da Ponte went to Vienna, bearing a letter from Mazzolà to Salieri:

> My friend Salieri,
> My dearest Da Ponte will deliver these few lines to you. Do for him all that you would do for me. His heart and his talents deserve everything. He is, moreover, *pars animae dimidiumque meae* [part and half of my soul].
>
> Your
> Mazzolà[8]

7. Da Ponte, 12.

8. Da Ponte, 91. The Latin is a misquotation of Horace, *Odes* I, 3, a prayer for the safe journey of the poet Virgil to Greece.

Da Ponte quoted this letter in his *Memorie* and continued:

> Salieri was in those days one of the most famous composers of music, the emperor's favorite, an intimate friend of Mazzolà, cultivated, learned despite being a music director, and a great lover of literati. This letter, which I did not forget to bring him when I arrived in Vienna, produced in time excellent results for me, and was the real beginning of the favor that Joseph II showed me."[9]

Da Ponte arrived in Vienna shortly before the inauguration of Joseph's troupe, a circumstance that the poet took advantage of skillfully:

> Remembering Mazzolà's suggestion, it occurred to me that I might become Caesar's poet. . . . I went to Salieri . . . and he not only encouraged me to apply for the position, but offered to speak personally to the theater director and to the sovereign himself, by whom he was especially loved.
>
> He managed the affair so well that I went to Caesar for the first time not to ask for a favor, but to thank him for one. . . . Eager to know everything, he asked me many questions about my country, my studies, and the reasons that I had come to Vienna. I answered everything briefly, which seemed to satisfy him very much. Finally he asked me how many dramas I had written, to which I answered frankly, "None, Sire." "Good, good!" he replied, smiling. "We will have a virgin muse."
>
> It is easy to guess the state in which I left that ruler. My heart was full of a thousand grateful feelings of joy, of respect, of admiration. That was, without a doubt, the sweetest and most delightful moment of my life. My happiness increased when Salieri, after having spoken with the emperor, told me that I had had the good fortune to please him. . . .
>
> A few days later the company of singers called by the sovereign from every part of Italy arrived in Vienna. It was truly splendid.[10]

Da Ponte thus became Joseph's theatrical poet, successor to Coltellini, Boccherini, and De Gamerra; but despite his use of the phrase "Caesar's poet" he did not fill the position of court poet—*poeta cesareo*—left vacant by Metastasio's death. Nor did his appointment preclude the activity of other poets in the Burgtheater, of whom the most important had, like him, very little experience in the theater before writing a libretto for Vienna.

Twenty-five years older than Da Ponte, Casti was born in 1724 in Acquapendente, a village just south of the border between the Papal States and Tuscany.[11] An enthusiastic

9. Da Ponte, 91.

10. Da Ponte, 93–95.

11. The following account is based largely on Herman van den Bergh, *Giambattista Casti (1724–1803): L'Homme et l'oeuvre* (Amsterdam, 1951); and Gabriele Muresu, *Le occasioni di un libertino (G. B. Casti)* (Messina, 1973).

and untiring traveler during his old age, he led a surprisingly sedentary and uneventful youth devoted to study for the priesthood and writing of poetry in Montefiascone (near Acquapendente) and Rome. It was not until he passed the age of forty that he began to gain the celebrity that followed him for the rest of his long life. That celebrity had as much to do with his friends as with his talents and poetic achievements. With brilliant conversation, lively recitation of verse, and amusing letters he impressed and won over powerful and faithful patrons.

In Florence during the 1760s Casti earned the friendship and patronage of Count Rosenberg, then adviser to young Grand Duke Leopold and later Joseph's theater director in Vienna. Presumably on Rosenberg's urging Leopold granted Casti, despite his having published very little, the honorary title of court poet. Rosenberg introduced him to Joseph II and Count Joseph Kaunitz (youngest son of the chancellor of state), who joined his admirers.

The friendship of such men greatly increased the ease and pleasure of travel in eighteenth-century Europe. Casti began a series of tours that brought him to Vienna and Berlin (1772–73), St. Petersburg, Stockholm, and Copenhagen (1776–79), and Madrid and Lisbon (1780–81). His travels and his associations with rulers and noblemen encouraged in him a bent toward political verse. His visit to St. Petersburg inspired the long *Poema tartaro,* which made fun of the court of Catherine the Great, clearly identifiable under a thin allegorical disguise.

Casti returned to Vienna in 1783, shortly after the inauguration of Joseph's opera buffa troupe. He hoped to replace Metastasio as court poet, but he does not seem to have wanted to write librettos or to take part in the other activities required of a full-time theatrical poet; he did not want to replace Da Ponte. He received a warm welcome from the emperor but no position, despite Rosenberg's continued support. Da Ponte enjoyed recounting a conversation between Rosenberg and Joseph: "'Casti,' the count added, 'and I too hope that Your Majesty will deign to honor him with the precious title of *poeta cesareo.*' 'Dear Count,' replied Caesar, 'I have no need of poets, and for the theater Da Ponte will suffice.'"[12]

During an earlier visit to Vienna Casti may have contributed to the reworking of Goldoni's *La calamita de' cuori* for Salieri's setting, first performed in 1774. In an account quoted in chapter 6 a contemporary periodical attributed the revision to several poets, including "Abbé Casti." In St. Petersburg in 1778 he produced what seems to have been his first libretto. *Lo sposo burlato,* with music by Paisiello, is largely a pasticcio: an assemblage of numbers from Paisiello's earlier operas held together by a tenuous plot.[13]

12. Da Ponte, 116.

13. On *Lo sposo burlato* see Michael F. Robinson, *Giovanni Paisiello: A Thematic Catalogue of His Works* (Stuyvesant, N.Y., 1991), 1:226–29; and Gabriele Muresu, *La parola cantata: Studi sul melodramma italiano del Settecento* (Rome, 1982), 79–88.

Otherwise Casti had little to do with opera before 1784, when Paisiello, having served the Russian court for several years, stopped in Vienna on his way back to Italy. Joseph commissioned him to write an opera buffa, and Paisiello persuaded the sixty-year-old Casti to collaborate with him.

After the successful premiere of *Il re Teodoro in Venezia* Paisiello resumed his journey to Italy, but Casti stayed in Vienna for another two years, a thorn in Da Ponte's side. His appetite for theatrical activity whetted, he turned to a new musical collaborator, Salieri, with whom he produced two operas during 1785 and early 1786.

Singers

In assembling his opera buffa company Joseph called on the services of several singers already in Vienna. Because of his own earlier decisions the Singspiel troupe included several German singers who had experience in Italian opera. Some of them moved directly to the opera buffa troupe in 1783. They were joined by opera buffa specialists: singers whom Joseph coaxed away from engagements in Italy's leading theaters and who brought with them to Vienna familiarity with the newest and most successful Italian operas.

Two of the sopranos who sang in Joseph's troupe during its early years were familiar to Viennese audiences from the Singspiel troupe: Catarina Cavalieri and Aloysia Lange. Among the newcomers one soprano, Nancy Storace, emerged quickly as a favorite (fig. 11.1*a*).

Trained in London by the distinguished musico Venanzio Rauzzini, Storace was only twelve years old in 1777 when she appeared in London as Cupid in an opera seria, Rauzzini's *Le ali d'amore.*[14] With her mother and her brother Stephen, a keyboard player and budding composer, she went to Italy shortly thereafter. Although some of her earliest roles in Italy were in opera seria,[15] she found greater success on the comic stage, to which, as an actress, she was better suited. According to the English opera lover Richard, Earl of Mount Edgcumbe, who witnessed her later career in London and knew nothing of her early roles in opera seria: "She had a harshness in her countenance, a clumsiness of figure, a coarseness to her voice, and vulgarity of manner, that totally unfitted her to the serious opera, which she never attempted."[16] But her exceptional virtuosity, her background in opera seria, and her ability and willingness to put both at the service of comic as well as dramatic effect may have contributed to her sudden rise to prominence in the world of opera buffa.

14. Sartori nos. 904, 905.

15. Storace sang Febe and Ebe in Francesco Bianchi's *Castor e Polluce* (Florence, 1779; Sartori no. 5204) and the prima-donna role of Emirena in Anfossi's *Adriano in Siria* (Treviso, 1780; Sartori no. 443).

16. Richard, Earl of Mount Edgcumbe, *Musical Reminiscences of an Old Amateur,* 2d ed. (London, 1827), 64.

A

B

C

D

FIGURE 11.1 Silhouettes by Hieronymus Löschenkohl of members of Joseph's opera buffa troupe, 1786. *A*, Nancy Storace; *B*, Vincenzo Calvesi; *C*, Francesco Benucci; *D*, Francesco Bussani. Wiener Stadtbibliothek.

These qualities helped Storace win a place in Joseph's troupe, which maintained the Viennese tradition of favoring singers who had experience in the performance of opera seria in Italy. She delighted the Viennese with her vivacious charm and her figure, which was at this time handsomer than Mount Edgcumbe remembered it; but perhaps just as important was her ability to play with the interaction between buffa and seria in such operas as Sarti's *Fra i due litiganti il terzo gode.* Here, in a role written for her, she electrified audiences with a dramatic scena the size and weight of those written for the greatest musici. She created the role of Dorina in Milan in 1782; she brought it with her the following year to Vienna, where *Fra i due litiganti* became one of the most popular operas of the decade. She went on to make such roles her specialty.[17]

"La Storace has expressive features, a plump figure, beautiful eyes, beautiful skin, and the petulance of a child," wrote Zinzendorf.[18] At a performance of *Fra i due litiganti* he carefully and admiringly inspected her body from the darkness of his box: "La Storace played her part like an angel. Her beautiful eyes, her white neck, her lovely throat, her fresh mouth make a charming effect. Sarti's music is delightful."[19] "La Storace se surpassa"; "La Storace joua comme un ange": Zinzendorf kept repeating himself as he wrote again and again of her performance in *Il re Teodoro in Venezia* in 1784.[20]

During a tour of Italy from December 1783 to March 1784 (coinciding, not by accident, with the Carnival season) Joseph heard many singers, carefully considering which might be suitable for his troupe. He reported his observations to Rosenberg in a series of letters that vividly document his operatic taste and style of management. The most important of his acquisitions, and the one to which he gave most thought, was that of Celeste Coltellini (fig. 11.2).

A comic soprano with strong Viennese connections, Coltellini was a daughter of the librettist Marco Coltellini. Like Storace she studied with a celebrated musico: Giovanni Manzuoli. She made her first public appearances in 1773 while still a "piccola fanciulletta."[21] During the rest of the 1770s she sang frequently in concerts in Florence. But it was in Naples during the early 1780s that she joined the ranks of the leading opera buffa sopranos. Norbert Hadrava, secretary to the Austrian ambassador in Naples and one of Joseph's chief operatic agents in Italy, summed up her strengths and limitations shortly before Joseph's visit to Naples: "Coltellini is an excellent comic singer. She sings with purity yet with feeling. Her voice comes from the chest. Although she has much knowledge of music, she is not very successful with embellishments and cadenzas. Her comic

17. For a detailed and illuminating study of Storace's voice and stage personality as revealed by the music written for her, see Gidwitz, "Vocal Profiles of Four Mozart Sopranos," 103–205.

18. Zinzendorf, 1 July 1783, quoted in Michtner, 385.

19. Zinzendorf, 28 May 1783, quoted in Michtner, 387–88.

20. Michtner, 393.

21. *Gt,* 1773, p. 98, quoted in Weaver and Weaver, *A Chronology of Music in the Florentine Theater,* 315.

FIGURE 11.2 Celeste Coltellini. Engraving by G. Stuppi. (Courtesy of Civica Raccolta Stampe "A. Bertarelli," Castello Sforzesco, Milan.)

acting enhances the value of her singing, for she performs all her roles with truth and naturalness."[22]

On 31 December 1783 Joseph wrote to Rosenberg from Caserta, the royal residence near Naples: "La Coltellini . . . has much less voice than la Storacci, and a less agreeable

22. Coltellini ist eine vortrefliche comische Sängerin singt rein mit Gefühl, Ihre Stimme kömt von der Brust ob zwar sie viele Kenntnisse zu der Musick hat; dennoch ist sie nicht sehr glücklich in Veränderungen und Cadenzen. Ihr comisches Spiel erhebt Ihre Verdienste im Singen noch mehr, denn sie stellt alle Rollen

one. Her acting is exaggerated, but one cannot deny that she plays a wide variety of characters into which she can enter very quickly."[23]

Hadrava may have helped Joseph see Coltellini's strengths more clearly. Two weeks later the emperor announced that he had already begun negotiations to bring her to Vienna: "after having seen la Coltellini more closely and at greater leisure, I cannot deny that she is an actress of the first order and although her voice and her singing are not comparable to that of la Storacci, she cannot but please those who look at her. I had her approached as to whether she would want to come to Vienna, and she had me assured of her great desire to do so, and under exactly the same conditions as la Storacci. Her engagement in Naples is for another year, after which she is determined to come to Vienna with her mother and sister."[24]

Joseph liked musical rivalry, as he had demonstrated in 1781 by pitting Mozart and Clementi together in pianistic competition.[25] His continued references to Storace in letters concerning Coltellini's engagement suggest that he looked forward to enjoying a rivalry between the two prime donne. A letter of 20 February shows that he also concerned himself with the arrangement of repertory according to the wishes of his new recruit: "There is no longer any doubt that la Coltellini will come to our theater. I am assured moreover that Benucci has no objection to singing with la Coltellini and to staying with her even if la Storacci were to be engaged elsewhere, all the more so because he is a friend of la Coltellini and because she wants very much to sing with him. The opera in which la Coltellini wants to make her debut in Vienna is entitled *Il matrimonio inaspettato,* of which Baron Swieten has had a copy for two years; you could ask him for it in order to have it copied."[26]

Coltellini arrived in Vienna as planned. She made her first appearance at the beginning of the theatrical year 1785, and in the opera mentioned by Joseph, Paisiello's *Il matrimonio inaspettato* (under the title *La contadina di spirito*).[27] The Viennese applauded warmly, and Joseph wrote happily to his brother Leopold: "Yesterday la Coltellini made her debut here and she had a complete success."[28] Storace stayed in Vienna, whose opera lovers could witness the rivalry that Joseph had staged so astutely.

Storace and Coltellini at first avoided a possible confrontation by singing in different

---

mit Wahrheit und Natur vor (Norbert Hadrava to Johann Paul Schulthesius, 30 August 1783, from a collection of letters by Hadrava in A-Wn, MS 8979).

23. Joseph to Rosenberg, Caserta, 31 December 1783, in *Joseph II,* 38–39.

24. Joseph to Rosenberg, 16 January 1784, in *Joseph II,* 41–42.

25. See Mozart's letter to his father, 16 January 1782, in *MBA,* 3:191–93.

26. Joseph to Rosenberg, Milan, 20 February 1784, in *Joseph II,* 47.

27. Michtner, 185–86. *Il matrimonio inaspettato* was first performed in St. Petersburg in 1779.

28. Joseph to Leopold, 7 April 1785, in *Joseph II. und Leopold von Toscana: Ihr Briefwechsel von 1781 bis 1790,* ed. Alfred von Arneth, 2 vols. (Vienna, 1872), 1:281–82.

operas: the former in *Gli sposi malcontenti* by her brother Stephen, the latter in *La contadina di spirito* and Cimarosa's *Il pittor parigino.*[29] It was up to Salieri, probably at Joseph's urging, to bring the two rivals together. He did so first in *La grotta di Trofonio,* which, by making Ofelia (Storace) and Dori (Coltellini) twin sisters, comically emphasized the differences in their stage personalities and voices. A few months later Salieri brought Storace and Coltellini together again. In *Prima la musica e poi le parole* the rival sopranos played themselves: a seria star (Storace) and a prima buffa (Coltellini) forced to sing together in the same opera. Coltellini sang in Vienna only a year,[30] but that was long enough to leave a distinctive impression on Salieri's operatic oeuvre.

Valentin Adamberger had contributed to the growing musical sophistication of Joseph's Singspiel troupe after his arrival in Vienna in 1780. His bilingualism allowed him easily to move from *Liebhaberrollen* in Singspiel to the mezzo-carattere roles in opera buffa. Praised by Gebler for combining "great artistry with a splendid voice,"[31] Adamberger contributed the same qualities to his performance in such operas as Anfossi's *Il curioso indiscreto.* But Joseph seems to have been dissatisfied with Adamberger in opera buffa, perhaps because of his colorless acting ("Adamberger is a statue," wrote Zinzendorf of his portrayal of Belmonte).[32] Adamberger does not seem to have appeared in many opere buffe. In 1784 he was largely displaced as the leading mezzo carattere by Giuseppe Viganoni, who sang only briefly in Vienna, and in 1785 by Vincenzo Calvesi. Adamberger spent his later years as the court chapel's leading tenor.

Calvesi (fig. 11.1*b*) sang in comic operas in Italy during the late 1770s and early 1780s. In Rome during Carnival 1779 Salieri had the opportunity to hear Calvesi, who appeared in two opere buffe at the Teatro delle Dame while Salieri's *La partenza inaspettata* was being performed at the Teatro Valle.[33] Calvesi sang with success the role of the count in *La scuola de' gelosi.* Zinzendorf heard him in Trieste during Carnival 1780 and admired his performance in Salieri's opera: "The mezzo carattere Calvesi enchanted everyone in the aria 'A me par che il mondo sia' [see ex. 8.5] . . . and in the duo . . . 'Quel visino è da ritratto.' . . . Calvesi has a silvery tenor voice, and he enunciates with astonishing clarity."[34]

"Well, the Italian opera buffa has started again here and is very popular," wrote Mozart to his father on 7 May 1783, a few days after the inauguration of Joseph's troupe.

29. Michtner, 185–90.

30. She returned for a brief engagement in 1788.

31. Gebler to Friedrich Nicolai, 31 October 1780, in *Aus dem Josephinischen Wien: Geblers und Nicolais Briefwechsel,* 104.

32. Zinzendorf, 30 July 1782, quoted in *MDL,* 180.

33. Sartori nos. 13340, 14733.

34. Zinzendorf, 26 December 1779, quoted in Carlo L. Curiel, *Il Teatro S. Pietro di Trieste 1690–1801* (Milan, 1937), 129.

"The buffo is particularly good. His name is Benucci."[35] A comic bass of exceptional ability as an actor as well as a singer, Francesco Benucci (fig. 11.1*c*) contributed much to Viennese musical life during his twelve years as a member of the Viennese opera buffa troupe, from its inception in 1783 until 1795 (with only a few short engagements elsewhere during this period). He created roles in operas by all the leading composers of comic opera in Vienna, including Mozart, who wrote for him the roles of Figaro and Guilelmo.

In one of his earliest appearances (Livorno, 1768) Benucci sang Tritemio in *Il filosofo di campagna.*[36] That he began his career in an opera by Galuppi and Goldoni and in a role created by Carattoli is emblematic of his place in the history of opera buffa. He took up the tradition of the buffo caricato to which Goldoni, in collaboration with such composers as Galuppi and such singers as Carattoli, had contributed so much in the late 1740s and 1750s; he maintained and developed that tradition for a new generation of operatic audiences, many of whom had never seen Carattoli perform. Later in his career Benucci occasionally sang roles that Carattoli had made famous—his portrayal of Piccinni's Tagliaferro in London in 1788 won praise[37]—but more often he inspired compositional followers of Piccinni and Galuppi, such as Salieri, Mozart, Martín, and Cimarosa, to write comic music of great brilliance.

A discussion of Viennese opera published in 1793 applauded Benucci for his "exceptionally round, beautiful, full bass voice" and his "unaffected, excellent acting." In the critics' praise one can sense the same German antipathy to buffo-caricato antics that led Sonnenfels to censure Carattoli in the 1760s: "He has a rare habit that few Italian singers share: *he never exaggerates.* Even when he brings his acting to the highest extremes, he maintains propriety and secure limits, which hold him back from absurd, vulgar comedy."[38]

Longevity and adaptability are words that come to mind when one scans the career of Francesco Bussani (fig. 11.1*d*). Born in Rome in the 1730s or early 1740s, he was one of several comic male singers of the period (Francesco Baglioni was another) who sang both bass and tenor (or high baritone) roles. After singing in Rome in 1762 and 1763, he began a hectic schedule of appearances that made his abilities as a buffo caricato and mezzo carattere known in Venice, Milan, Bologna, Florence, and Turin before the end of the decade.

From 1770 to about 1772 Bussani sang in Vienna; it was probably there that Salieri heard him for the first time. He portrayed not only comic characters (such as Gamace—a tenor—in Salieri's *Don Chisciotte*) but also serious ones (such as the high priest—a

35. Mozart to his father, 7 May 1783, in *MBA,* 3:267–69.

36. Sartori no. 10376.

37. Petty, *Italian Opera in London,* 269.

38. "Italienische Theatermusik in Wien," *BmZ* (1793): 138–39; in Rice, "Emperor," 442.

baritone—in a revival of Gluck's *Alceste,* 1770).[39] He went on contribute to Viennese opera during three decades in the course of a career that touched Salieri's several times.

After his first Viennese engagement Bussani returned to Italy, where he created tenor roles in two of the operas that Salieri wrote during his Italian tour of 1778–80: Armidoro in *La partenza inaspettata* and Lindoro in *Il talismano.* Presumably on Salieri's recommendation Bussani, by now a veteran buffo, returned to Vienna in 1783 as one of the original members of Joseph's comic troupe. The operatic management tended to assign him the parts of fathers and other old men, such as Aristone in *La grotta di Trofonio* and Don Alfonso in *Così fan tutte* ("Ho i crini già grigi" are Alfonso's first words). Bussani's ability to sing tenor as well as bass helps explain why Mozart assigned to him the tenor (or high baritone) role of Pulcherio in his projected setting of *Lo sposo deluso.*[40]

The Burgtheater Orchestra

The orchestra that accompanied Joseph's Italian troupe was essentially the same as the one that had accompanied the Singspiel troupe. Quite similar in size and composition to the orchestras that the impresarios had maintained during the first half of the 1770s, the Burgtheater orchestra represented an important element of continuity between opera buffa of the impresarial decade and opera buffa as reestablished by Joseph. During 1773 the orchestra of the Burgtheater had consisted of thirty-two players (see chap. 2); a decade later, during the theatrical year 1783–84, it had grown to thirty-three: six first violins, six seconds, four violas, three cellos, four double basses, and pairs of flutes, oboes, clarinets, bassoons, and horns.[41] It differed from the Burgtheater orchestra of a decade earlier in having two fewer violins, one more double bass, and two clarinets.

The clarinets had only recently become regular members of the orchestra: Joseph had authorized the hiring of the brothers Anton and Johann Stadler in 1782.[42] A pair of trumpeters finally joined the orchestra in 1785. With the addition of a timpanist in 1788 the Burgtheater's permanent ensemble reached the size and composition that it maintained, except for minor changes in the size of the string section, for the rest of Salieri's career as an opera composer.

The Burgtheater orchestra of 1783–84 included several players who had been members of the orchestra ten years earlier. Most remarkable in this respect—considering the disruptions that occurred during the intervening decade, especially Joseph's reorganization of the court theaters in 1776—was the cello section, which consisted of the

39. Zechmeister, 285.

40. The *Wiener Musik- und Theater-Allmanach auf das Jahr 1786* [Vienna, 1786], 60, refers to Bussani as *Tenorist.*

41. HHStA, GH, Rechnungsbuch 1783. For a more detailed discussion of the evolution of the Burgtheater orchestra from the mid 1770s to the late 1780s see Edge, "Mozart's Viennese Orchestras."

42. Joseph to Rosenberg, 8 February 1782, in *Joseph II,* 27–30.

same three players (Joseph Weigl the elder, Joseph Orsler, and Joseph Pacher) who had played in 1773–74.

It was probably in reference to the Burgtheater orchestra that a Swiss visitor to Vienna, Johann Kaspar Riesbeck, wrote this account, published in 1783:

> The number of real virtuosi [in Vienna] is small; but as far as orchestral musicians are concerned, one could hardly hear anything in the world more beautiful. I have already heard about thirty to forty instruments play together; and they all produce a tone so correct, pure and clear that one might believe one were hearing a single, supernaturally powerful instrument. One stroke of the bow brings all the violins to life, one breath all the wind instruments. An Englishman next to whom I sat thought it amazing that through an entire opera one could hear, I won't say not a single dissonance, but none of those things that normally occur in a large orchestra, such as a too hasty entrance, a note held too long, or an instrument bowed or blown too loud. He was enchanted by the purity and correctness of the harmony; and yet he had just come from Italy.[43]

The orchestra that accompanied Joseph's opera buffa troupe was a thoroughly seasoned ensemble, accustomed to and capable of playing the rich orchestral accompaniments that Gassmann and Salieri had written during the first half of the 1770s and that Salieri, Mozart, and Martín would write in the 1780s.

Repertory

Joseph's troupe made its debut on 22 April 1783 in an opera by its music director. *La scuola de' gelosi* had already been heard in Vienna. A traveling company had presented it at the Kärntnertor in 1780. Salieri wrote several new arias for the cast of the inaugural production of 1783, which included Storace (the countess), Cavalieri (Ernestina), Benucci (Blasio), and Bussani (the count).[44] Thus revised, *La scuola* effectively displayed the talent assembled by Joseph, especially that of Storace, who had sung the countess in a revival of the opera in Venice just a few months before joining the Viennese troupe.[45]

Zinzendorf had heard *La scuola* in Trieste in 1780. When he witnessed the Viennese company's first performance he focused his attention on new singers rather than on a score that—except for Salieri's replacement arias—was familiar to him: "La scuola de' gelosi. Mlle. Storace, l'inglesina ['the little English girl'—the Italian nickname acknowledges both her English birth and her Italian training and experience] has a pretty,

43. Johann Kaspar Riesbeck, *Briefe eines reisenden Franzosen über Deutschland an seinen Bruder zu Paris*, ed. Wolfgang Gerlach (Stuttgart, 1967), 139; quoted in English translations (from which I have borrowed some turns of phrase) in Landon, *Haydn,* 2:214, and Neal Zaslaw, *Mozart's Symphonies: Context, Performance Practice, Reception* (Oxford, 1989), 100.

44. On Salieri's revisions see Gidwitz, "Vocal Profiles of Four Mozart Sopranos," 64–65, 114–27.

45. Sartori no. 21368.

voluptuous figure, a beautiful neck; she looks good dressed as a gypsy [in the finale of act 1 the countess disguises herself as a gypsy fortune-teller]. The buffo Venucci [*sic*] very good; the romantic lead Bussani less so. The audience very happy."[46]

Joseph, who knew *La scuola* from having performed excerpts from it with his chamber musicians in 1780, probably chose it to inaugurate his troupe. His control over repertory was one of the most important ways in which he shaped Viennese opera during the 1780s. In writing to Count Ludwig Cobenzl, his ambassador in St. Petersburg, in February 1783, he alluded to three different aspects of his repertorial planning: he made decisions about genre, composers, and specific works. "It remains for me to thank you for the opera of Paisello [*Il barbiere di Siviglia*], which I ask you to charge to me in your accounts. I hope to have it performed after Easter by a new troupe of Italian comic singers that I have had engaged and that ought to be good. You will also do me the pleasure of buying all the works in this genre (and not serious) composed by Paisello whenever they appear."[47] A year later Joseph named another opera by Paisiello, *Il matrimonio inaspettato,* as the one in which Coltellini, more than a year after that, was to make her Viennese debut.

Joseph's repertory mixed comic operas written especially for his troupe, works imported from abroad (including several performed in Vienna during the 1770s), and a single older Viennese opera: Salieri's *La fiera di Venezia.* During 1783 and 1784 the troupe, many of whose members had arrived recently from Italy, concentrated on imported works, especially those that one or more members had sung successfully before coming north to Vienna. Da Ponte spent more time arranging librettos than writing new ones. Salieri's *Scuola,* Cimarosa's *L'italiana in Londra,* and Sarti's *Fra i due litiganti* and *Le gelosie villane* were among the operas most often performed. The popularity of *Il barbiere di Siviglia,* performed in St. Petersburg in 1782 and in Vienna the following year, paved the way for the acclaim with which Paisiello was greeted on his arrival in Vienna in 1784 and for the repeated applause earned by the opera that he wrote for the troupe, *Il re Teodoro a Venezia.*

Although composers wrote operas for Joseph's company with increasing frequency in the years that followed, works continued to be imported in great quantities. The Italian troupe presented sixty-two operas in the Burgtheater between April 1783 and Joseph's death in February 1790. Only twenty-three of these (37 percent) were written especially for Vienna. But imported operas dominated the repertory much less than this might suggest, because operas written for the troupe tended to be performed more often than imported operas. If one considers only operas performed in the Burgtheater more than twenty times, the importance of works written outside of Vienna greatly

46. Zinzendorf, 22 April 1783, quoted in Michtner, 150.

47. Joseph to Count Cobenzl, 24 February 1783, in *Joseph II. und Graf Cobenzl: Ihr Briefwechsel,* ed. Adolf Beer and Joseph von Fiedler, 2 vols. (Vienna, 1901), 1:370.

diminishes. This group of popular favorites contains fourteen operas, fully half of which were written for the troupe: *Figaro, Il re Teodoro,* Martín's *Una cosa rara* and *L'arbore di Diana,* Salieri's *La grotta di Trofonio* and *Axur,* and Stephen Storace's *Gli sposi malcontenti.*[48]

An Inauspicious Beginning to a Fruitful Collaboration

Inspired by the successful debut of Joseph's troupe, Mozart looked for an opportunity to demonstrate his abilities as a composer of opera buffa. "Our poet here is now a certain Abbate Da Ponte," he wrote to his father on 7 May 1783. "He has an enormous amount to do in revising pieces for the theater and he has to write *per obbligo* an entirely new opera for Salieri, which will take him two months."[49] This "entirely new opera" was Da Ponte's first libretto, *Il ricco d'un giorno.*[50] Salieri interrupted work on the opera at the end of the year, when he traveled to Paris for rehearsals and production of *Les Danaïdes,* and resumed it on his return to Vienna later in 1784.

In his *Memorie* Da Ponte recounted his struggles with the libretto of *Il ricco d'un giorno:*

> Since my first production was to be set to music by Salieri (who was, to tell the truth, a most cultivated and intelligent man), I proposed to him a number of plans, a number of subjects, leaving him to choose. Unfortunately he liked the one that was perhaps least susceptible to a beautiful and theatrically effective setting, namely *Il ricco d'un giorno.* I set courageously to work; but very soon I realized how much more difficult it is to accomplish a project than to conceive it. . . .
>
> Finally, for better or for worse, I finished most of the first act. Only the finale was lacking. [Here follows Da Ponte's witty description of a typical finale, part of which is quoted in chap. 3.]
>
> After this picture, it will not be hard to imagine the difficulty in which I found myself in composing my first finale. Ten times I was on the point of burning what I had done, and going to offer my resignation.

Da Ponte nevertheless gave the libretto to Salieri, who was quoted by the poet as having said: "It is well written, but we must see it on the stage. There are some very good

48. This paragraph is based on the calendar of Burgtheater performances in Michtner.

49. Mozart to his father, 7 May 1783, in *MBA,* 3:267–69.

50. For more detailed discussion of the libretto of *Il ricco d'un giorno* see Rabin, "Mozart," 106–16, Della Croce/Blanchetti, 191–93, Lorenzo della Chà, *Lorenzo da Ponte: I libretti d'opera viennesi, 1783–1791* (Parma, 1999, forthcoming), and, on the music, Della Croce/Blanchetti, 457–63, and John Platoff, "Musical and Dramatic Structure in the Opera Buffa Finale," *JM* 7 (1989): 197–200.

arias and scenes that I like very much. But I will need you to make some small changes, more for the musical effect than for anything else."[51]

Salieri's words are strikingly similar to what he remembered Boccherini saying about the first product of their collaboration, *Le donne letterate.* After the poet had read his libretto to the composer, he gave him the manuscript and said: "if you desire changes here and there in consideration of the musical effect, we will make them together when I return."[52]

Salieri made no mention of any changes that he required Boccherini to make in *Le donne letterate.* His youth and inexperience may have discouraged him from taking an active role in the shaping of the libretto. But the seasoned operatic composer of 1784 seems to have been as undemanding of his librettist as the young beginner of 1770.

Only one piece of evidence to the contrary might tempt us to attribute to Salieri the kind of musico-dramatic assertiveness with which Mozart helped to shape the librettos of *Idomeneo* and *Die Entführung* (and probably the librettos of the operas that he wrote after these): Da Ponte's account of what happened next.

> I left him as happy as a paladin, and . . . began to hope that my drama might not be as bad as I had judged at first. But what did these "small changes" consist of? Of mutilating or lengthening most of the scenes; of introducing new duets, terzets, quartets, etc.; of changing meters halfway through arias; of mixing in choruses (to be sung by Germans!); of deleting almost all the recitatives, and consequently all of the opera's plot and interest, if there was any. When the drama went on stage I doubt whether there remained a hundred verses of my original.[53]

Da Ponte exaggerated here, as often. He did not delete "almost all the recitative." The opera as Salieri composed it contains the usual dialogue in blank verse. It contains rather fewer ensembles than one might expect from Da Ponte's use of the plural in enumerating them: one duet, one trio, one quintet, one sextet, one introduzione, two finales, and a short homophonic ensemble at the end of the opera.

There is no better way to earn the respect and admiration of writers than to praise their work. The happiness that Da Ponte felt on hearing Salieri praise his libretto gave rise to friendship. The poet remembered the composer as one "whom I loved and esteemed both out of gratitude and by inclination, with whom I passed many learnedly happy hours, and who for six continuous years . . . was more than a friend: he was my brother."[54] Da Ponte was not alone in his admiration. Many of the librettists with whom Salieri worked expressed similar feelings of friendship and respect. De Gamerra

51. Da Ponte, 96–97.
52. Mosel, 31. 53. Da Ponte, 97.
54. Da Ponte, 136.

went beyond epistolary formula when he declared himself "forever your most affectionate true friend,"[55] while Boccherini addressed Salieri as "Carissimo amico" in a letter of 1781.[56] Verazi's expression of friendship also seems sincere: "Give me your news: remember that if on your return to Vienna you need me and my pen, I will always be at your disposal. Once a friend, always a friend. Imitate me, and do not cease to love me."[57] Beaumarchais, after collaborating with Salieri on *Tarare,* dedicated the libretto to the composer and declared himself "honored to be your poet, your servant, and your friend."[58]

Some of these protestations of friendship surely arose from the librettists' recognition that Salieri, as music director of Joseph's opera buffa troupe, was in a perfect position to help them find work in Vienna (although Beaumarchais could have had no such motivation). But Salieri's generally favorable reception of Da Ponte's first libretto—a work with which the poet himself was thoroughly dissatisfied—suggests another reason why librettists liked Salieri so much: his willingness to accept, to praise intelligently, and to set to music what these poets handed him.

"Una Musica Interamente Francese"?

For his friendly relations with librettists Salieri paid a high price: several of his operas are weakened by poor librettos, among them *Il ricco d'un giorno* (about whose quality the poet was more astute than the composer). *Il ricco* did not please when finally performed in the Burgtheater on 6 December 1784. Zinzendorf enjoyed its visual evocation of Venice and noticed its wealth of choruses, but he found the libretto or music unoriginal: "Il ricco d'un giorno, stolen from everywhere; beautiful scenery. An illuminated gondola [in the serenade scene in act 2]. Many choruses."[59] After six performances the opera was dropped from the repertory, never to return.

The libretto was subject to much ridicule, which Da Ponte attributed to the machinations of Casti's partisans, but even the singers and Salieri (who should, of course,

55. senza fine Tuo Aff.^{mo} amico vero (De Gamerra to Salieri, Livorno, 21 April 1778, Weimar, Goethe- und Schiller-Archiv).

56. Boccherini to Salieri, 16 May 1781, Vienna, Nationalbibliothek, Handschriftsammlung; in Angermüller, *Leben,* 3:13–14.

57. Datemi vostre nuove: pensate che se di ritorno a Vienna avete bisogno di me, e della mia penna, io sarò sempre alla vostra disposizione. Una volta amico, so esserlo sempre. Imitatemi, e non cessate di amarmi (Verazi to Salieri, Mannheim, 4 November 1779, Weimar, Goethe- und Schiller-Archiv).

58. Pierre-Augustin Caron de Beaumarchais, *Oeuvres,* ed. Pierre Larthomas and Jacqueline Larthomas (Paris, 1988), 495.

59. Zinzendorf, 8 December 1784, quoted in Michtner, 394. Zinzendorf made the same charge of plagiarism against Mozart, describing the music of *Die Entführung* as "pillée de differentes autres" (30 July 1782, quoted in *MDL,* 180).

have spoken up much earlier) could not remain silent: "The singers themselves, and at their head, Salieri, said frightful things. They did not know, they said, how they had ever been able to declaim such wretched words; or how the composer had been able to set them to music; and Salieri—a sensible man, however, and no fool—solemnly swore he would rather allow his fingers to be cut off than set another verse of mine to music."[60]

While acknowledging his libretto's weakness, Da Ponte blamed the failure of *Il ricco* partly on what he perceived as the influence of French opera, and of *Les Danaïdes* in particular, on the music: "Salieri, having returned from Paris with his ears full of Gluck, of Lais [François Lays, tenor at the Opéra], of Danaids, of the shrieks of the possessed, wrote a score that was entirely French, and the beautiful popular melodies of which he had been so fertile he had drowned in the Seine."[61]

Da Ponte exaggerated the extent of French influence on *Il ricco* (some of which in any case Salieri probably wrote before he went to Paris to produce *Les Danaïdes*); nor had Salieri ever enjoyed a reputation as a prolific composer of "beautiful popular melodies." But certain aspects of *Il ricco* may well owe something to Salieri's experience in the composition and performance of *Les Danaïdes* (which Salieri had completed by February 1783, probably before beginning *Il ricco*).

Il ricco is a Goldonian farce about money and love set against a background of Venetian revelry. Da Ponte paid tribute to Goldoni not only in the characters, the plot, and the setting, but also in the form of his libretto, which follows Goldoni's three-act plan, old fashioned by 1784. The Venetians Da Ponte and Salieri may have hoped to repeat the success of *La fiera di Venezia,* with which *Il ricco* shares many Goldonian features besides its Venetian setting.[62]

Two brothers, Giacinto (tenor) and Strettonio (bass), have inherited a fortune. Giacinto, a spendthrift who loves the beautiful Emilia (soprano), looks forward to a life of ostentatious luxury in his brilliant catalogue aria "Barca alla riva io voglio" (ex. 11.1). Strettonio, a miser, plans to hold on to his money and add to it as much of his brother's as he can get. Giacinto's servant, the wily Mascherone (bass), promises to help him spend his money, but Mascherone and his fiancée Lauretta plan a deception by which Giacinto's inheritance will become a generous dowry.

Emilia sings of her love for Giacinto and looks forward to their wedding, but Strettonio emerges as a rival for Emilia's hand. He declares his love to her in an aria, "Già tutto intesi, o cara," in which he uses falsetto to imitate the sound of her voice. Strettonio's quick alternation between natural voice and falsetto is amusing. Competing for

60. Da Ponte, 100–101.

61. Da Ponte, 100.

62. The Venetian setting is actually more characteristic of Goldoni's spoken plays than of his librettos, "whose settings are either indeterminate or foreign to Venice, for the most part" (Weiss, "Carlo Goldoni, Librettist," 129).

EXAMPLE 11.1 *Il ricco d'un giorno,* act 1, "Barca alla riva io voglio," mm. 9–26 (A-Wn, Mus. Hs. 16609)

I want a boat at the quay-side, carriages in the country, barbary horses in the stables sent all the way from Spain. I want cooks and servants, bodyguards and gondoliers, pages, lackeys, footmen who can address me in at least four languages.

Emilia's favor, the brothers sing serenades from gondolas floating beneath her window. Mascherone's deceit is eventually uncovered, and Giacinto prevails against his stingy brother's claims on Emilia. Having lost all his money in one day, Giacinto consoles himself with the hand of his beloved.

The orchestration of *Il ricco* betrays the influence of Paris more clearly than any other element of the opera. It is considerably heavier and richer than that of Salieri's previous comic operas. Salieri made frequent use of trumpets in *Il ricco,* which is also probably the first of his Viennese operas to use clarinets.[63]

The overture announces the brilliance of orchestration that characterizes the opera as a whole. Its opening idea, declaimed fortissimo by full orchestra, will reappear as the main theme of Giacinto's "Barca alla riva io voglio." The large orchestra that accompanies that aria, with dotted rhythms in the melody and accompaniment in busy triplets, expresses the exuberance of a newly rich man eager to spend his money. In foreshadowing "Barca alla riva," the overture helps us hear the opera's rich orchestration as an expression of the wealth that the title character will so rapidly lose (ex. 11.2). The over-

63. There is some doubt about when Salieri first used clarinets in an opera. The autograph scores of some early operas (e.g., *Armida*) have clarinet parts, but comparisons between these autographs and early copies in which clarinets are absent suggest that some if not all these clarinet parts were added at some time after the operas were first performed.

EXAMPLE 11.2 *Il ricco d'un giorno,* overture, mm. 1–14

ture ends with a coda that deploys treble and bass in contrary motion and then inverts the parts (ex. 11.3): the same technique that Mozart, seven years later, used at the end of the equally festive overture to *La clemenza di Tito.*

The frequent sound of trumpets in *Il ricco* is typical of Salieri's opere buffe of the 1780s but differentiates this opera from Mozart's, which use trumpets more sparingly.

EXAMPLE 11.3 *Il ricco d'un giorno,* overture, mm. 161–69

They contribute not only color (as, for example, in the overture), but also incisive rhythms, and sometimes even help to clarify the structure of a number, as in the case of Giacinto's boastful aria "Rendiam coi tratti illustri." At the beginning of this through-composed aria, trumpets amplify the galloping accompaniment (ex. 11.4). The opening melody never returns, and yet the trumpets and their distinctive rhythmic motive do return near the end of the aria, greatly enhancing its musical coherence.

EXAMPLE 11.4 *Il ricco d'un giorno,* act 2, "Rendiam coi tratti illustri," mm. 1–4

(*Continued on next page*)

EXAMPLE 11.4 (*continued*)

Salieri continued in *Il ricco* to demonstrate his liking for the unusual sound of trumpets crooked in B♭, which appear several times in the opera, nowhere more strikingly than in passages in which they reinforce the opera's emphasis on the minor mode. In the finales of both acts 1 and 2 passages in G minor are accompanied by an orchestra that includes trumpets in B♭.[64] In the second of these passages, marked Allegro disperato, Strettonio angrily announces that he has lost money gambling and calls, like Hypermnestre in "Foudre céleste," on heaven to strike him dead (ex. 11.5). Trumpets in B♭ add somber brilliance to the sextet "Volgi, volgi o bella dea" and to the chorus "Grazie, grazie ognuno renda." Salieri extended his use of trumpets to instruments tuned in A, even rarer than trumpets in B♭, in Giacinto's A-major aria "Tenero ha il cor la femmina."[65] Salieri's use of low-pitched trumpets in B♭ and A, so striking in light of Mozart's avoidance of these instruments, may be related in some way to his avoidance of high-pitched trumpets in E♭, which Mozart used quite frequently.[66]

Salieri's clarinet parts are not as interesting as his trumpet parts; here too one can draw a parallel between *Il ricco* and *Les Danaïdes.* In both operas Salieri largely limited his clarinets to doubling the oboes.

In *Il ricco* Salieri all but abandoned a practice in which he had frequently indulged

64. Salieri had experimented with the use of trumpets in B♭ in music in G minor already in *La passione di Gesù Cristo* of 1776, where they contribute to the horror of Joseph's aria "All'idea de' tuoi perigli." Mozart, when he finally admitted B♭ trumpets into his opera buffa orchestra in *Così fan tutte,* used them in the context of G minor in the finale of act 1; like Salieri he had them repeat octave Ds. See Bruce Alan Brown, *W. A. Mozart: Così fan tutte* (Cambridge, 1995), 151.

65. H. C. Robbins Landon commented on the rarity of trumpets in A in connection with Haydn's use of them, apparently for the first time, in a chorus composed during his first visit to London, "Su, cantiamo." Landon suggested that Haydn intended the use of trumpets in low A (sounding a minor third lower than written) rather than high A. "If so, we have the first known use in music of low A trumpets" (Landon, *Haydn,* 3:356–57). Salieri, whose trumpets parts are probably also meant to be played by trumpets in low A, seems to have anticipated Haydn by six years.

66. Salieri's preference for low trumpets is revealed in a comparison of the overture to *Il ricco* and the aria "Barca alla riva io voglio," which begin with the same music. The overture in D uses trumpets in D; but the aria in E♭ uses trumpets in B♭, as if Salieri felt that the more obvious trumpets in E♭ were somehow unsuitable (too high?).

EXAMPLE 11.5 *Il ricco d'un giorno,* act 2, finale, mm. 252–60

Destroy me, floods; strike me with lightning, elements; and give up in despair with me, all you furies of Erebus.

in his early operas, but which he had avoided in *Les Danaïdes:* that of combining one or more wind instruments, including oboe, with a high coloratura soprano in concertante display. Only in Emilia's aria "Sento da un lato il padre" can one see evidence of his earlier fascination with concertante writing; but here the bassoon and flute solos—not nearly as complex as some of the wind solos from the 1770s—have a relevance to the text that the concertante parts in the early operas sometimes lack. As Emilia wrestles with the conflicting calls of filial duty and romantic love, the bassoon symbolizes her father and the flute her love for Giacinto.

Da Ponte, unaware that Salieri's fondness for choruses in comic opera extended back to his first such opera, quite reasonably attributed Salieri's demands for choruses in *Il ricco* to the composer's recent experience in Paris. But the elaborate choral component of *Les Danaïdes* could only have reinforced Salieri's predilection for operatic choral music.

Also reminiscent of *Les Danaïdes* is the frequent sound of the minor mode in *Il ricco.* The G-minor passages in the finales have already been mentioned. In Mascherone's "Se una notte essendo in letto" Salieri called attention to the line "Di paura il cor mi batte" (my heart pounds with fear) by having Mascherone sing in D minor while the whole orchestra (including trumpets) depicts his heart with offbeat repeated notes. As Lauretta describes a nightmare in her scena "Dopo pranzo addormentata," the horror of the lines

Non udia che pianti e gridi,
Urli, smanie, tonfi e stridi

[I heard nothing but weeping and crying, howling, raging, crashing, and shrieking]

is emphasized by a turn to E minor, string tremolos, offbeat accents, and diminished seventh chords clashing with a tonic pedal. The word "pietà" suggested a brief respite from the minor mode. Salieri's move to A minor and D minor at "Vedo il diavol" coincides with the arrival of a faster tempo and an accompaniment of scales in octaves that depict the devil's footsteps (ex. 11.6). Although Da Ponte blamed Salieri for introducing the "stridi de' spiritati" into his score, some of the blame (if blame is required) ought to go to the "stridi" in Da Ponte's text.

The Two-Tempo Rondò in Comic Opera

During the 1770s the rondò, an aria in a single slow or moderate tempo that usually took the form A-B-A-C-A (as in "Nel lasciarti, oh Dio! mi sento" in *Daliso e Delmita*), achieved a role of great importance in serious opera, where the *primo uomo* laid claim to it as his primary vehicle for the display of virtuosity, improvisatory brilliance, and ability to move an audience to tears. By 1779 the rondò had evolved into a two-tempo

EXAMPLE 11.6 *Il ricco d'un giorno,* act 2, "Dopo pranzo addormentata," mm. 19–36

(*Continued on next page*)

EXAMPLE 11.6 (*continued*)

I heard nothing but weeping and crying, howling, raging, crashing, and shrieking, and a voice not unknown to me that seemed to plead for mercy. While my head was immersed in a flood of confused ideas, I see the devil who carries you here and there through the valleys

aria, whose form and melodic style quickly became just as standardized.[67] Soon thereafter the leading female singers of opera buffa expropriated the rondò, through which, at a climactic moment late in the opera, they expressed the drama's most intense pathos. Joseph's establishment of an opera buffa troupe with Salieri as its music director forced the composer to recognize and respond to a recently established convention: that of placing a rondò for the prima donna immediately before the finale of the second act of an opera buffa.[68]

67. Daniel Heartz, "Mozart and His Italian Contemporaries: 'La clemenza di Tito,'" *Mozart-Jahrbuch* (1978–79), 275–93 (esp. 281–84); Helga Lühning, "Die Rondo-Arie im späten 18. Jahrhundert: Dramatischer Gehalt und musikalischer Bau," *Hamburger Jahrbuch für Musikwissenschaft* 5 (1981): 219–46. For a discussion of rondò form as exemplified by a typical early two-tempo aria (Sarti's "Mia speranza io pur vorrei," 1779), see John A. Rice, "Sense, Sensibility, and Opera Seria: An Epistolary Debate," *Studi musicali* 15 (1986): 101–38.

68. John Platoff, "How Original Was Mozart? Evidence from *Opera Buffa*," *EM* 20 (1992): 106; and Richard Armbruster, "Salieri, Mozart und die Wiener Fassung des *Giulio Sabino* von Giuseppe Sarti: Opera seria und 'Rondò-Mode' an der italienischen Oper Josephs II.," *Studien zur Musikwissenschaft*, 45 (1996):

Salieri's revision of *La scuola de' gelosi* for performance in Vienna in 1783 reflects the two-tempo rondò's new role in comic opera. As performed in Venice in 1779 *La scuola* contained no rondò; but when Nancy Storace sang the countess in Vienna, her role culminated, just before the second-act finale, in "Ah sia già de' miei sospiri," a two-tempo rondò that closely follows the parameters—both literary and musical—of the aria type.

The text of "Ah sia già" (probably by Da Ponte, who, as house poet, was responsible for textual adjustments of operas performed in the Burgtheater) is typical of the two-tempo rondò in consisting of twelve ottonari in three quatrains. The poetry expresses amorous despair of a rather conventional, impersonal character:

Ah sia già de' miei sospiri
  Sazio il fato e sazio il ciel.
  Abbastanza a suoi martiri
  Mi serbò destin crudel.
Fra gli orror d'avversa sorte
  Dovrei sempre i dì passar?
  Il tormento della morte
  Men terribile mi par.
Torna, torna amato sposo
  Al desio del primo amor,
  E bei giorni di riposo
  Sien compenso al mio dolor.

[Ah, may fate and heaven be satiated with my sighs; destiny has preserved me long enough for its tortures. Must I always pass my days among the horrors of adverse fortune? Death's torment seems less terrible to me. Come back, come back, beloved husband, to the pleasures of first love; and let fine days of peace compensate me for my suffering.]

Salieri's setting of these words consists of two parts, the first in slow tempo and the second faster (see table 11.1). The first quatrain of the text is set as a melody in duple meter in F major (ex. 11.7). This tune has the gentle, dignified character and the gavotte rhythm (at "sazio" and "mi serbò") that had been typical of rondò tunes since Gluck's "Che farò senza Euridice" had helped initiate the vogue for the single-tempo rondò. In the context of such placid music the diminished seventh appoggiatura on the word "crudel" stands out strongly. Melody A is followed by contrasting material in C major, the dominant: a setting of the second quatrain (B). Then melody A returns in the tonic, and slightly extended. The transition that follows, announced by a shift to F minor, is a setting of the second quatrain (somewhat rearranged) and the first two lines of the first

133–66. Among some important departures from this convention is the queen's rondò near the beginning of act 2 of *Una cosa rara.*

TABLE 11.1 *La scuola de' gelosi,* Act 2, "Ah sia già de' miei sospiri" (Rondò Written for the 1783 Version)

	UN POCO ADAGIO				ANDANTE CON MOTO			
	A	B	A′	C	D	E	D	F
Measure	9–18	19–30	31–42	43–54	55–66	67–81	82–93	94–110
Text (by lines)	1–4	5–8	1–4	5–8, 1–2	9–12	11–12, 5–6	9–12	11–12
Key (I = F major)	I	V	I	i–V/i	I	IV–ii–V/I	I	I

EXAMPLE 11.7 *La scuola de' gelosi,* act 2, "Ah sia già de' miei sospiri" (insertion aria for 1783 version), mm. 9–18 (A-Wn, Mus. Hs. 16615)

EXAMPLE 11.8 *La scuola de' gelosi,* act 2, "Ah sia già de' miei sospiri," mm. 55–66

quatrain (C). It ends on an open cadence, followed by the principal melody of the fast section (D) in the tonic, which takes as its text the third and final quatrain (ex. 11.8). Gavotte rhythms again predominate both in melody D and in the contrasting material that follows (E). After a return to melody D the aria ends with closing material (F), a setting of the last two lines of the poem.

Many rondòs follow this plan or very similar ones and present melodies of a similar shape. This standardization facilitated, indeed necessitated, the improvisatory elaboration of melodic lines that audiences expected of great singers. And by allowing the audience to identify the rondò as such during the performance, its conventionality played an important role in the audience's perception of its singer and of the opera in which he or she appeared.

"Ah sia già" shows that Salieri was willing to write a standard two-tempo rondò and capable of doing so. But he also attempted less conventional rondòs. Several times during the decade, perhaps under the influence of the older, single-tempo rondò, he experimented with the idea of a return to the opening slow melody after the fast section. And with increasing frequency he introduced sudden third modulations into his rondòs. "Amor, pietoso Amore," in *Il ricco d'un giorno,* exemplifies both these departures from the norm.

Emilia sings "Amor, pietoso Amore," as expected, just before the finale of act 2, expressing love for Giacinto in language that anticipates that of the countess in *Figaro* ("Porgi Amor qualche ristoro"). Unlike most rondòs "Amor, pietoso Amore" is not an exit aria, and this may have affected Salieri's setting. The text is a twelve-line poem arranged in three quatrains; but Da Ponte's poem is exceptional in that the first two quatrains consist of settenari; only the third quatrain has the normal ottonari:

Amor, pietoso Amore,
    Rendimi alfin al pace,
    Porgi ristoro a un core
    Stanco di tollerar.
Basti il mio lungo pianto
    L'ire a saziar del fato;
    Cessi un amante ingrato
    Di farmi sospirar.
Ah se invano io mi lusingo,
    Se pietà di me non hai,
    Crudo Amor, perché mi fai
    Le tue leggi seguitar?

[Love, merciful Love, give me peace at last; grant relief to a heart that is tired of suffering. May my long complaint be enough to satiate the anger of fate; may an ungrateful lover stop making me sigh. Ah, if I deceive myself in vain, if you, cruel Love, have no mercy on me, why do you make me follow your laws?]

Salieri's setting of this poem, in A major, begins with a conventional structure—a setting of the first two quatrains in slow tempo (Larghetto) and in the form A-B-A′—but with unconventional meter and rhythm. Under the influence of Da Ponte's settenari Salieri chose to set his slow section in triple meter, departing from the duple meter and two-note upbeat figures typical of the rondò (ex. 11.9).

Salieri set the third quatrain to faster music (Allegretto), beginning with a new melody in the tonic A major (section C). His switch to duple meter reflects Da Ponte's switch to ottonari; the text's ending with a question caused Salieri to end his melody with an open cadence. The tonal question is answered unexpectedly: an abrupt modu-

EXAMPLE 11.9 *Il ricco d'un giorno,* act 2, "Amor, pietoso Amore," mm. 5–15

lation brings us to C major and a new melody that represents the episode within the fast section.

The home key of A major and the music of section C return simultaneously, after which one would expect, as closing material, a setting of the last two lines of the poem in the fast tempo; instead, we return to the slow tempo and the last ten measures of section A′ (words as well as music). Salieri sacrificed the excitement and energy that closing material in the fast tempo would have generated, probably in the hope that the unexpected return to the slow melody would vividly convey Emilia's plight. He may also have felt that since Emilia does not leave the stage after singing "Amor, pietoso Amore," a quiet, slow ending would lead effectively to the recitative that follows.

Comedy and Black Magic in *La grotta di Trofonio*

The failure of *Il ricco d'un giorno* made Salieri reluctant to collaborate further with Da Ponte. He turned to Casti, the success of whose libretto for *Il re Teodoro* had made him suddenly Da Ponte's rival. *La grotta di Trofonio,* an *opera comica* in two acts, was performed for the first time in Vienna at the Burgtheater on 12 October 1785. It was probably performed earlier at the imperial villa at Laxenburg, in the countryside a few kilometers south of Vienna. The title page of the earliest surviving libretto reads "da rappresentarsi nell'imperial villeggiatura di Laxembourg, l'anno 1785"; and the *argomento* that follows describes the opera as having been "composed expressly to be performed" at Laxenburg. *La grotta* was the only one of Salieri's Italian operas to be published in full score during his lifetime: one of the few eighteenth-century comic operas in Italian to be accorded this honor.[69]

We have no specific information about the production of *La grotta* at Laxenburg, but we do have, from Kelly, a pleasing description of a visit by the opera company:

> The palace is only a few miles from Vienna, and nothing can be more magnificent; it is surrounded by forests full of all kinds of game; the park, gardens, and grounds, truly beautiful, and in the centre of rich and luxuriant country. The theatre was very pretty, and very well attended; for all had the entrée to it gratis, including the surrounding peasantry.
>
> Italian operas were performed three times, German plays twice, and German operas twice each week. I passed the time here most delightfully. Every performer of the Italian opera had separate apartments allotted to him, and his breakfast was sent thither. There was a magnificent saloon, in which we all met at dinner. The table was plentifully and luxuriantly supplied, with every delicacy of the season; with wines of all descriptions, as well as all kinds of fruits, ices &c.; and every night, after the spectacle, an excellent supper. In the mornings I had nothing to do (there were no rehearsals,) but to amuse myself.[70]

La grotta is a sophisticated *jeu d'esprit:* an elegant, artificial exercise in the depiction of contrasting personalities, probably conceived with the aim of bringing Storace and Coltellini together on the same stage. In its ancient Greek setting and its evocation of magic and pagan philosophy the opera owes something to Paisiello's *Socrate immaginario,* which Casti knew well: he had borrowed heavily from it in creating his pasticcio *Lo sposo burlato* in 1778.

Deep in a forest that might have reminded the imperial family of its sylvan surroundings at Laxenburg is a magic cave. When the magician Trofonio (sung in Vienna by Benucci, who presumably created the role at Laxenburg)[71] summons the spirits of

69. *RISM* S 520.

70. Kelly, *Reminiscences,* 125–26.

71. The original cast of the Viennese production can be deduced from Zinzendorf's diary, as quoted in Michtner, 398.

the cave, all who enter will emerge with their personalities transformed. Trofonio's cave and its transformations of character dominate the opera to such an extent that the normal emotional dynamics of opera buffa—jealousy, infatuation, seduction, concerns about money and social status—are largely absent. Absent too, the wide variety of picturesque and colorful sets that many opere buffe demand.

Trofonio's is black magic: through the cave he exerts power over the demons of the underworld. He boasts near the end of the opera:

> Dell'inferno e del demonio
> Io son l'arbitro e il padron.
>
> [I am judge and master of the underworld and of the devil.]

In his annotations to the autograph score Salieri described *La grotta* as being "di stile magico-buffo."[72] In doing so he suggested a parallel between *La grotta* and a much earlier opera, the French-influenced *Armida,* whose style he described as "magico-eroico-amoroso toccante il tragico." In that opera too "magico" means black magic.

Salieri's conception of the "magico" as stylistic-generic category is clarified by his description of act 3, scene 1, of *Armida* as "tutto magico." This scene (see fig. 5.3) begins with an orchestral passage accompanying a "sacrifice to the infernal gods." Many of its musical features, including slow tempo, minor mode, and the sound of trombones, reappear in the dungeon scene at the beginning of act 2 of *Les Danaïdes.* It is to this conception of the "magico" that Salieri, probably under the more immediate influence of *Les Danaïdes,* returned in *La grotta.*

The sound of French opera is particularly clear at Trofonio's first appearance, about halfway through act 1. Salieri's annotations place this scene, one of the opera's most memorable, within the stile magico and also say something important about the singer for whom he wrote it: "The aria 'Spirti invisibili,' with chorus at the end, is purely magic; and it seems to me that the music has the right character. But for it to have effect the voice that sings it must be of great power, and dark [*tenebrosa*]." "Benucci acquitted himself wonderfully in the sorcerer's invocation," wrote Zinzendorf in his diary after seeing *La grotta* in the Burgtheater.[73] Benucci evidently brought to this role the power and darkness that it demanded.

An orchestral passage, Un poco adagio, proclaims the key of D minor with a stark ascending unison (fig. 11.3). D minor (the key with which the dungeon scene in *Les Danaïdes* begins) is associated with Trofonio's cave not only here but in the finale of act 2,

72. Salieri's annotations to the autograph of *La grotta di Trofonio* are transcribed in Angermüller, *Leben,* 3:32–33; Angermüller, *Fatti,* 110–11; and Swenson, 110–12.

73. Zinzendorf, 12 October 1785, quoted in Michtner, 398.

FIGURE 11.3 *La grotta di Trofonio*, beginning of act 1, sc. 10. Full score (Vienna, ca. 1786).

which begins with a summoning of Trofonio in D minor. A single trumpet enters as the violins play repeated syncopated quarter notes, first piano, then forte, reiterating the dissonance D-E. Trofonio sings his incantation in quinari (mostly quinari sdruccioli) that Viennese audiences had learned from Gluck's *Orfeo* and Salieri's *Armida* to associate with the supernatural and the demonic.

EXAMPLE 11.10 *La grotta di Trofonio,* act 1, "Spirti invisibili," mm. 133–38 (engraved full score, Vienna, ca. 1786; facsimile, Bologna, 1984)

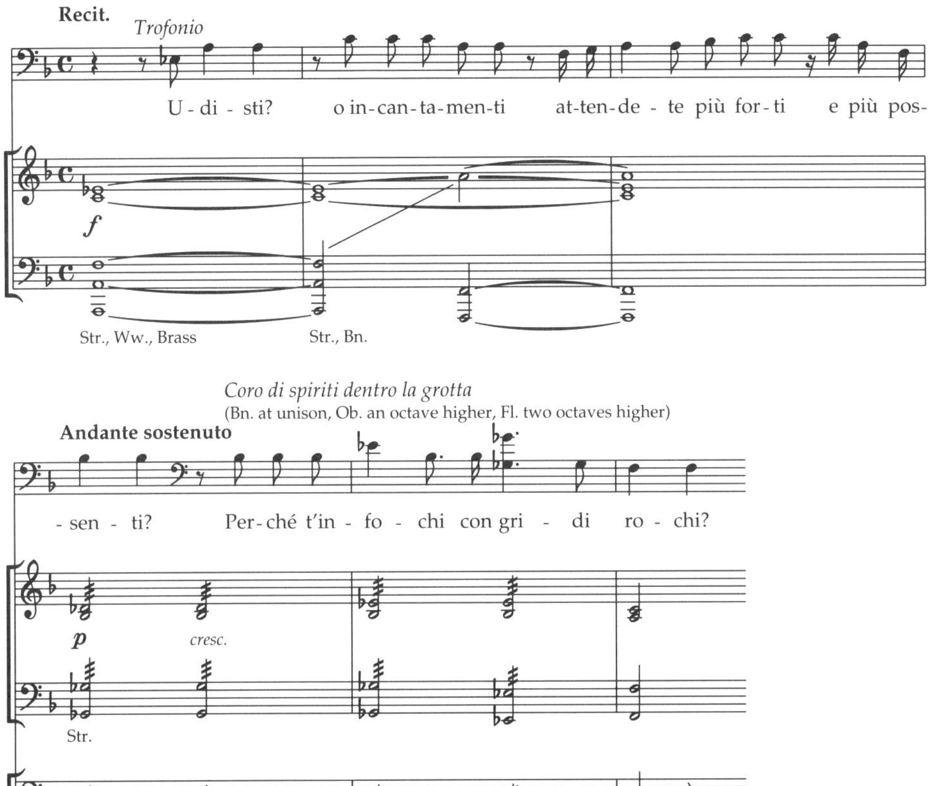

TROFONIO: Did you hear? Or do you await stronger and more powerful incantations? CHORUS OF SPIRITS WITHIN THE CAVE: Why do you work yourself up with raucous shouts?

The incantation ends with a short recitative whose tonal destination is apparently B♭; but the dominant of B♭ is followed instead by the flat sixth, G♭, which is immediately reinterpreted as the third degree of E♭ minor as the chorus of unseen spirits responds to Trofonio in unison. The tonal surprise is reinforced by an instrumental one: the timpanist, inactive since the beginning of the scene, plays a drumroll on G♭, then a single note on a drum tuned in C (ex. 11.10). The idea of tuning the timpani a tritone apart was original, perhaps unprecedented. The "diabolus in musica" contributes its sinister sound to the magic spell. The timpanist had to retune his instruments quickly, unless he had another pair of drums available: only sixteen measures separate the passage requiring timpani in C and G♭ from a passage requiring timpani in D and A. Salieri had already experimented with an unusual number of timpani (three in *La secchia rapita*) and with delaying their entrance until a particularly crucial moment in a number (Hypermnestre's "Foudre céleste"). With the tritone tuning in *La grotta* he continued his expansion of the timpani's operatic role.[74]

To call attention to this dark and mysterious scene Salieri quoted its orchestral introduction at the beginning of the overture, transposed from D minor to C minor.[75] The idea of beginning a comic opera with a slow introduction was not entirely new. Many Viennese listeners were familiar with the slow introduction in C major to the overture to Umlauf's *Die Bergknappen;* some may have remembered the majestic slow introduction, also in C, with which the overture to Salieri's *La secchia rapita* begins. But precedents for a comic opera that begins with a slow introduction in the minor mode are hard to find. *Les Danaïdes,* with its slow introduction in D minor anticipating the scene in act 2 in which Danaus tells his daughters of his deadly plot, was surely in Salieri's mind. The slow introduction gives way (as in *Les Danaïdes*) to a cheerful Allegro in the major; but the introduction's minor mode, slow tempo, and dark sonority have had their effect. We know that the darkness of Trofonio's cave is at the heart of this opera, just as violence and death are at the heart of *Les Danaïdes.* (As if in agreement with criticism of the overture to *Les Danaïdes* in the *Mercure de France* that "the first serious passage is not sufficiently developed and its expression is effaced too soon by the gay movement that follows it," Salieri wrote a significantly longer slow introduction in the overture to *La grotta* and gave it a slower tempo than the earlier introduction.)

The twin daughters of Aristone (bass, sung in Vienna and probably created by Bussani) have very different personalities.[76] Ofelia (soprano, Storace) is serious; she likes to read, to think about philosophy. Dori (soprano, Coltellini) is lighthearted and playful. Each of the daughters loves a man of similar character: Ofelia the philosophic Artemidoro (tenor, Calvesi), Dori the fun-loving Plistene (baritone, Stefano or Paolo Mandini). Aristone approves of their choices and all look forward to the approaching weddings. Alone, Ofelia sings of her love for Artemidoro in a cavatina, "D'un dolce amor la face," whose long orchestral introduction (ex. 11.11), with elaborate parts for clarinets and bassoons and moderately slow tempo, adumbrates the countess's first appearance, also in a cavatina, at the beginning of act 2 of Mozart's *Figaro.*[77]

74. David Charlton, "Salieri's Timpani," *Musical Times* 112 (1971): 961–62. Salieri's tritone tuning anticipated Beethoven's use, in the introduction to act 2 of *Fidelio,* of timpani in E♭ and A, which help depict the darkness and horror of Florestan's dungeon.

75. The beginning of the overture as it appears in Salieri's autograph is illustrated in Rudolph Angermüller, "Salieri, Antonio," in *NG.*

76. I am grateful to Ronald Rabin for pointing out to me that the sisters are twins (as their father states in act 1, sc. 7).

77. Long orchestral introductions to arias are rare in Mozart's late opere buffe; see Webster, "The Analysis of Mozart's Arias," 124–25. In his annotations to the autograph score of *La grotta* Salieri referred to "D'un dolce amor" as an "aria a rondò," thus calling attention to the lack of a real rondò in this opera. For a more detailed analysis of "D'un dolce amor" see Rabin, "Mozart," 181–88.

EXAMPLE 11.11 *La grotta di Trofonio*, act 1, "D'un dolce amor la face," mm. 1–12

At the same time, "D'un dolce amor" reflects Salieri's experience in Paris. Using the terminology of sonata form one could say that it begins with an exposition (the opening Larghetto moves from I to V), continues with a development in which the tempo shifts to Allegro assai in response to the words "pena ed affanno," and concludes with an abbreviated recapitulation (in which the music of the Larghetto stays in the tonic) and coda. Yet the aria's overall shape is completely different from the sonata-form arias of Salieri's early operas. The strongly contrasting material in the development—not only fast tempo but also minor mode, wide leaps in the vocal line, and the orchestra's tremolo and loud bursts of sound—gives Ofelia's cavatina much the effect of a French operatic air in A-B-A form, of which Salieri wrote several fine examples in *Les Danaïdes* (see table 11.2).

TABLE 11.2 *La grotta di Trofonio,* Act 1, "D'un dolce amor la face"

	A (EXPOSITION)	B (DEVELOPMENT)	A′ (RECAPITULATION)	CODA
Measure numbers	13–32	33–53	54–66	66–77
Text (by lines)	1–6	7–8	1–4	5–8
Key (I = C major)	I–V	iii–vi	I	I
Tempo	Larghetto	Larghetto–Allegro assai	Larghetto	Larghetto

A change of scene reveals a forest. With the music described earlier Trofonio summons the spirits of the cave. Artemidoro, a volume of Plato in hand, wanders thoughtfully through the woods. The orchestra paints a lyrical picture of rural peace, with oboes and flutes playing birdcalls, much as in Gluck's depiction of the Elysian Fields in *Orfeo.* The key of E♭, heard here for the first time in the opera, contributes its mellow sonorities and serious associations to the scene and anticipates the word *ombroso* in Artemidoro's cavatina, "Di questo bosco ombroso." Like Ofelia's "D'un dolce amor," this aria has a tonal plan characteristic of sonata form, but the short exposition and strongly differentiated development (noisy music for the words "di città lo strepito") encourage us to hear it in the form A-B-A.

Artemidoro discovers Trofonio's cave and the magician invites him to enter, an invitation that Artemidoro, always in search of knowledge, eagerly accepts. Plistene, singing happily, arrives; when Trofonio tells him that his friend is in the cave, he enters in search of him.

Artemidoro emerges from another entrance, completely transformed. Full of gaiety, he cares nothing for philosophy and can sing only "Evviva la gioia." His recitative and aria are characterized by "unnatural, forced cheerfulness," wrote Salieri; "and they must be played, sung, and acted accordingly in order to produce a strong effect." Plistene too emerges, surprised by his new personality: he is now as serious as Artemidoro used to be. He sings an accompanied recitative and a gentle, lyrical cavatina, "Viene o maestro e duce," addressed to the volume of Plato that Artemidoro has dropped on the ground. An accompaniment of low wind instruments reflects his new seriousness. Salieri originally called for two bassoons and bass; he later revised this accompaniment for two English horns and bassoon, which appear in the printed score.[78] According to his annotations, "Everything must be performed in a tranquil, almost somber style, but one that goes to the heart, particularly in the cavatina."

78. Mosel, 88–89.

In a garden Ofelia begins the finale of act 1 by singing, in the serious key of E♭, of the pleasure that she feels when she is with Artemidoro ("È un piacer col caro amante"). She is shocked when Artemidoro enters, singing happily. Dori awaits Plistene, who arrives in serious thought and expressing a philosophical sentiment in E♭. Dori assumes that he is joking. Aristone enters, eager to announce wedding plans to his daughters, who tell him that their lovers have suddenly gone mad. The acts ends in a general expression of perplexity.

As act 2 begins Aristone tries to persuade his daughters that they will be able gradually to change their husbands according to their tastes, but they are unconvinced. Plistene and Artemidoro seek out the cave and enter it again. On reemerging they find their original personalities restored. Artemidoro sings a cavatina, "Sognai, o sogno ancor?" that has much in common with an aria that Mozart wrote for the same singer four years later in *Così fan tutte.* Like Ferrando's "Un'aura amorosa," Artemidoro's more modest aria uses the key of A major, important parts for clarinets, bassoons, and horns (Salieri included a flute as well), and muted strings to convey a mood of dreamy lyricism.

Trofonio begins a grand aria rejoicing in his power, "Questo magico abituro." This is the first of three numbers in the printed score whose texts are missing from the libretto printed for the Laxenburg production, and which were probably added to the opera before it was presented in Vienna.[79] Salieri's annotations explain why he added this number, which he described as "only a little energetic piece to break up the delicate things that surround it; it produces a nice *chiaroscuro.*" "Questo magico abituro" gave Benucci an opportunity to display his "Stentorian lungs" (as Kelly put it in reference to Benucci's performance of "Non più andrai")[80] in competition with an orchestra that includes trumpets, horns, flutes, oboes, clarinets, and bassoons. Ofelia and Dori enter, causing Trofonio to break off his aria in the middle of the exposition. He invites the women into the cave ("Venite o donne meco").

This moment is recorded in an engraving on the title page of the printed score, which may represent an actual performance in Laxenburg or Vienna (fig. 11.4). The inscription suggests that this is the Viennese production. Zinzendorf witnessed several performances in the Burgtheater; his comments on the costumes can help us identify the characters and singers in the picture: "The music was charming, the costumes extraordinary. Storace with her philosopher's robe was pretty and Calvesi looked perfectly fine. Coltellini was wonderful in her role. Benucci dressed as an old philosopher."[81]

79. The text of two of these added numbers is present in a copy of the Laxenburg libretto in I-Rsc, which evidently represents a transitional state of the opera, before all the changes documented in the printed score were made.

80. Kelly, *Reminiscences,* 131.

81. Zinzendorf, 12 October 1785, quoted in Michtner, 398.

LA GROTTA
DI
TROFONIO
OPERA COMICA IN DUE ATTI
Rappresentata nel Regio Imperial Teatro di Corte l'anno 1785.
Posta in musica dal' Sig.r
ANTONIO SALIERI
Maestro di Cappella all' attual Servizio di Sua Maestà Cesarea

TROFONIO. *Venite o donne, meco,*
Venite in questo Speco,
Atto II. Scena IX.

VIENNA *presso Artaria Compagni*

FIGURE 11.4 *La grotta di Trofonio,* title page of the full score. (Courtesy of Newberry Library, Chicago.)

Trofonio, on the right (stage left), invites the two women into his cave with a coaxing gesture of both hands. We can recognize the singer, under a fake beard and clothing suitable for "an old philosopher," as Benucci. The costumes of Storace and Coltellini differ mainly in that the woman on the left wears a cloak—similar to Trofonio's—on her right shoulder, while the other woman (whose right side is partly invisible) does not seem to be wearing one. Zinzendorf's comment that "Storace with her philosopher's robe was pretty" encourages us to guess that she is the woman on the left.

The men, learning that Ofelia and Dori have disappeared, sing "Ma perché in ordine," a lively comic trio in which Plistene sends Artemidoro and Aristone off in different directions to look for the women. They agree to meet again where they are, all of them repeating the word "qua" at the end of the trio, first on successive downbeats (ex. 11.12) and then in a more intricate pattern of strong and weak beats. Zinzendorf must have found this repetition amusing, for he cited the trio not by its first words but by its last: "at the end of the tenth scene Casti added a terzetto that is very pretty, 'Qua,

EXAMPLE 11.12 *La grotta di Trofonio,* act 2, "Ma perché in ordine," mm. 154–69

(Continued on next page)

EXAMPLE 11.12 *(continued)*

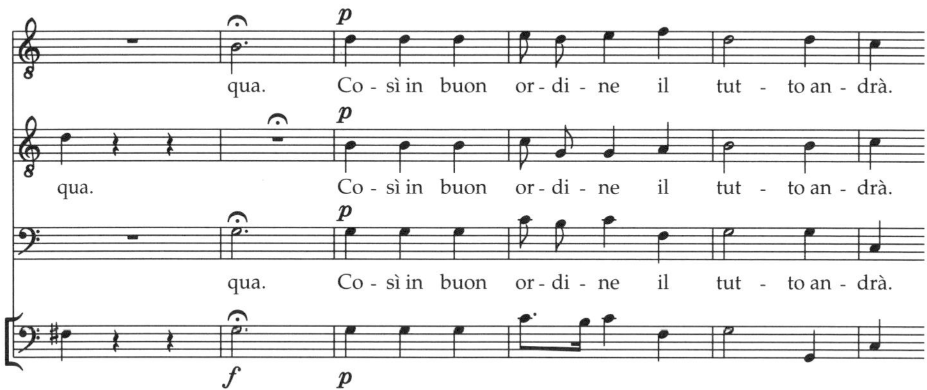

PLISTENE: From the bridge over there . . . ARISTONE: I understand . . . PLISTENE: Toward the hill . . . ARTEMIDORO: I know very well . . . PLISTENE: Turn to the right . . . ARISTONE: And I will return here . . . PLISTENE: By the other road . . . ARTEMIDORO: I will return here . . . ALL: Here, here. Thus will everything proceed in good order.

qua, qua.'"[82] This comment, which presumably means that Casti and Salieri wrote the trio between the productions at Laxenburg and Vienna, helps explain why the text is not in the libretto printed for Laxenburg.[83] Casti and Salieri may have added it in an attempt (successful, to judge from Zinzendorf's reaction) to enliven the opera before presenting it in the Burgtheater.

The women emerge transformed; now it is their lovers' turn to be astonished. The transformation gave Salieri a chance to display Storace's ability to amuse as well as to move an audience. With a delightful melody in triple meter Ofelia expresses her new frivolousness on leaving the cave. Aware of its beauty, Salieri had Storace sing this tune no less than four times.

In his annotations Salieri called Storace's song a "minuetto," leading one to suspect that she danced as well as sang. The later history of "La ra la ra" suggests that this was indeed the case. The minuet-aria took on a life of its own. Giuseppe (or Joseph) Sardi, a Viennese pianist and composer, wrote variations on it.[84] When Storace returned to London in 1787 she brought "La ra la ra" with her. Four years later she created a role in *The Siege of Belgrade,* cobbled together by her brother Stephen from music by several composers, but mostly by Martín y Soler. Storace sang, among other arias, Salieri's

82. Zinzendorf, 12 October 1785, quoted in Michtner, 398.

83. It is, however, in the copy in I-Rsc.

84. Published by Artaria as *Variazioni del minuetto La ra dell'opera La grotta di Trofonio, per cembalo con violino obligato, RISM* S 1070. Scholars, assuming that "Sardi" was a misspelling of "Sarti," have frequently attributed Sardi's piano music to the opera composer Sarti. But Sardi was a musician in his own right; see Richard Armbruster, "Joseph Sardi, Autor der Klaviervariationen KV 460 (454a): Zum Schaffen eines unbekannt gebliebenen Komponisten in Wien zur Zeit Mozarts," *Mozart-Jahrbuch* (1997) 225–48.

FIGURE 11.5 Salieri's "La ra la ra," as sung and danced by Nancy Storace in Stephen Storace's *Siege of Belgrade*, London, 1791.

minuet-aria (fig. 11.5). The libretto tells us that she also danced: "During the Song she dances slowly between Peter, Leopold, and Ghita."[85] Storace's "dancing air" was one of the opera's most popular numbers. According to the *Gazetteer* (4 January 1791), "Storace danced her favourite air with much grace—it was encored." The title page of an English edition of Sardi's variations made no mention of Salieri or Sardi, but took full advantage of Storace's success as a dancer: *The* FAVORITE MINUET, *with* VARIATIONS *for the Piano Forte or Harpsichord as* DANCED *by Sig.ª Storace in the* SIEGE OF BELGRADE.[86]

In the finale of act 2 Aristone calls on Trofonio in an incantation. Trofonio explains that by entering the cave by the other entrance the young people will regain their original personalities. Ofelia enters, singing happily; then Dori. They emerge with their original personalities restored. Salieri signaled the return to normalcy by setting Ofelia's first words in E♭. All express their amazement at the cave's powers in a quiet, homophonic passage whose repeated interruptions of cadences to E♭ by diminished seventh

85. *The siege of Belgrade; a comic opera, in three acts. As it is performed at the Theatres Royal, in London and Dublin* (Dublin, n.d.), 29. I am grateful to Jane Girdham for telling me of this stage direction and for sharing with me her transcriptions of reviews of *The Siege of Belgrade.*

86. London, [1791]; *RISM* S 6895.

EXAMPLE 11.13 *La grotta di Trofonio,* overture, mm. 79–90

chords, forte, anticipate Mozart's similar tonal disruptions, also of cadences to E♭, in the first-act finale of *La clemenza di Tito.*

Salieri made more elaborate and varied use of wind instruments in *La grotta* than in any of his previous operas. Already in the overture the winds are more prominent than we might expect from Salieri: not in concerto-like solo passages but in colorful combinations, with long trills played by flute, oboe, and bassoon (ex. 11.13). These woodwind trills recur in act 2, where the text makes their significance clear. In Dori's pretty aria "Un bocconcin d'amante" the words "che scherzi, che rida, che balli, che canti" are accompanied by a four-measure trill in the flute and first violins.

By freeing the clarinets from the doubling role to which he had generally restricted them in *Les Danaïdes* and *Il ricco d'un giorno* and by bringing them together in ensembles that included bassoons, Salieri produced sonorities that would be characteristic of Viennese opera buffa during the second half of the 1780s. He associated clarinets, like the key of E♭, with the philosophical seriousness of Ofelia and Artemidoro. The clarinets, bassoons, and horns in Ofelia's "D'un dolce amor" and in her solo at the beginning of the first finale are echoed in act 2 in Artemidoro's aria "Sognai, o sogno ancor?" which he sings after he leaves the cave for a second time, with his original seriousness restored.

Salieri's emphasis on winds reflects an interest on the part of Viennese composers and audiences in rich orchestral color that had already been evident in the 1760s and 1770s. Joseph II, himself particularly fond of wind instruments,[87] acknowledged the Viennese love of wind and brass and at the same time stimulated it further by adding clarinets and later trumpets to the permanent roster of the Burgtheater orchestra. His formation in 1782 of a court wind ensemble made up of members of the Burgtheater orchestra may have had the same effect.[88] By making the Burgtheater's clarinetists, oboists, bassoonists, and hornists into his personal wind octet, he enhanced their prestige and probably affected the way in which composers treated them in operas.

Zinzendorf attended the first performance of *La grotta* in the Burgtheater; in his unusually informative comments he praised everything except the plot and the scenery's lack of variety: "the theme is without imagination, without art; there is no scenery: always the garden, always the cave, always transformations."[89]

Despite Zinzendorf's reservations *La grotta* was popular in Vienna. Attending a performance a week after the premiere, he mentioned the numbers that had to be repeated: "The terzetto of the women with the magician was encored, so was 'Trofonio, Trofonio' [the first part of the second-act finale] and the quartet in the first act ['Il diletto che in petto mi sento'] and 'Qua, qua, qua.'"[90] A few days later he concluded that the libretto, even if it made little sense, was pretty, and he praised several numbers in particular: Ofelia's cavatina "D'un dolce amor," her solo at the beginning of the finale of act 1, and a comic duet sung by Dori and Plistene earlier in act 1.[91]

Composers of operas for Joseph's troupe normally received a fee of 100 imperial ducats for each work.[92] The emperor made a few exceptions, most notably when he awarded Paisiello 300 ducats for the composition of *Il re Teodoro in Venezia*. His fond-

87. "Auszug eines Schreibens aus Wien," in Angermüller, *Leben*, 3:58.

88. Georg Triebensee and Johann Went (oboe), Wenceslaus Kautzner and Ignatz Drobney (bassoon), Anton and Johann Stadler (clarinet), and Martin Rupp and Jacob Eisen (horn) were engaged on 1 March 1782, according to an undated list that refers to each musician individually as "Kammer Harmonie Musicus" (HHStA, HMK, Kart. 1).

89. Zinzendorf, 12 October 1784, quoted in Michtner, 398.

90. Zinzendorf, 17 October 1784, quoted in Michtner, 398.

91. Zinzendorf, 24 October 1784, quoted in Michtner, 398.

92. Edge, "Mozart's Fee," 220–24; this paragraph is based on data in Edge's table 1.

ness for Salieri did not persuade him, in the case of *Il ricco d'un giorno,* to give the composer more than the usual fee. It was perhaps in recognition of the popular success of *La grotta* that Joseph gave Salieri 200 ducats for having composed it.

Performed twenty-six times in the Burgtheater before it left the repertory in 1788, in several German cities during the late 1780s, and in Trieste, Prague, Budapest, Copenhagen, and Paris, *La grotta* won international popularity of a kind achieved by none of Salieri's operas since *La scuola de' gelosi.* But the success did not last. Stephen Storace, probably inspired by the success of Salieri's minuet-song in *The Siege of Belgrade,* presented an adaptation of *La grotta* in London later the same year. But "The Cave of Trophonius," wrote Kelly, "did not meet the reception which I think it deserved."[93] Revived in Vienna in 1799, at the same time as several of Mozart's operas were being successfully returned to the stage, *La grotta* lasted only one performance.[94]

The Opera Buffa Troupe as Object of Self-Parody: *Prima la musica e poi le parole*

In 1785 Joseph II reversed two of his earlier decisions concerning Viennese theaters. As one result of his reorganization of 1776 the Kärntnertortheater had been out of the court's direct control. Joseph's troupes—German and Italian, singers and actors—were all based in the Burgtheater (or Nationaltheater). In 1783 Joseph disbanded his Singspiel troupe, so that during the rest of his reign the Burgtheater witnessed an alternation of spoken plays in German and Italian operas. But in 1785 he revived the Singspiel troupe and installed it in the newly refurbished Kärntnertortheater, where it performed until 1788. The German opera company made its debut on 16 October 1785, just four days after *La grotta di Trofonio* received its first public performance in the Burgtheater. The emperor probably hoped to enjoy competition between the troupes. A few months after the Singspiel troupe resumed performances, he conceived of a way to make sure that competition would indeed take place.

During Carnival 1786 Joseph organized a festivity at Schönbrunn in honor of the visiting Prince Albert of Sachsen-Teschen and his wife (Joseph's sister), Archduchess Marie Christine. He commissioned two short operas for the occasion, one to be performed by the Singspiel troupe, the other by the opera buffa troupe. The party took place on 7 February. At one end of the palace's *orangerie* the Italians performed Salieri's *Prima la musica e poi le parole,* a divertimento teatrale in one act, with poetry by Casti; at the other end the Germans presented Mozart's one-act Singspiel *Der Schauspieldirektor.*

93. Kelly, *Reminiscences,* 180. The score of *The Cave of Trophonius* is lost. Although Kelly, who must have known Salieri's opera well, states clearly that Salieri's music was featured in *The Cave of Trophonius,* according to attributions published with the texts of the songs Storace composed most of the music. See Jane Girdham, *English Opera in Late Eighteenth-Century London: Stephen Storace at Drury Lane* (Oxford, 1997), 173.

94. Hadamowsky, *Hoftheater,* 1:55.

The production reflected Joseph's fondness for musical competition on several levels. It set in rivalry Vienna's two leading operatic composers. Each composed a short example of the genre in which he had recently achieved success (Mozart was not yet known in Vienna as a composer of opera buffa). The operas allowed the audience to compare the court opera troupes. Within these troupes, the operas highlighted the rivalry between prime donne: Cavalieri and Lange among the Germans; Coltellini and Storace among the Italians.

Two weeks earlier Casti had looked forward to the evening in a letter to his friend Count Paolo Greppi that carefully omitted any mention of the German troupe: "His Majesty . . . has charged me with producing a spectacle one hour in length. I have already done it and the music too is almost finished. And I hope that it will be found pleasing both in words and music and in the excellence of the actors and singers. The guests will consist of about thirty couples; and after that I hope it will also be given in the city."[95] Casti's hopes were fulfilled. *Prima la musica* did please its audience of merrymakers at Schönbrunn, and together with *Der Schauspieldirektor* it subsequently enjoyed a short run at the Kärntnertor.[96]

Like *Der Schauspieldirektor* and many other eighteenth-century comic operas, *Prima la musica* presents a satirical view of the organization and creation of an opera.[97] More specifically it is a satire of the very people who presented it: the Italian troupe, Casti, Salieri, and their patron the emperor. In function it closely resembled *L'ape musicale,* a pasticcio that Da Ponte assembled in 1789, of which he wrote: "This opera was a very witty and pleasing lampoon [*critica*] of the audience, the impresarios, the singers, the poets, the music director, and finally of me, myself."[98]

A music director (bass, Benucci) and theatrical poet (baritone, Stefano Mandini) argue about preparations for an opera. The music director, following the orders of Count Opizio, insists that the opera must be made ready for performance in four days. When the poet protests that more time is needed, the music director explains that the music is already written; the poet need only write verses to fit the music; it is of little importance that the music express the meaning of the words.

95. Casti to Count Paolo Greppi, 24 January 1786; in Luigi Pistorelli, "I melodrammi giocosi di G. B. Casti," *Rivista musicale italiana* 2 (1895): 52; and, quoting from Pistorelli, in Swenson, 113.

96. On the libretto see Edward Elmgren Swenson, "*Prima la musica e poi le parole:* An Eighteenth-Century Satire," *Am* 9 (1970): 112–29; Josef Heinzelmann, "Prima la musica, poi le parole: Zu Salieri's Wiener Opernparodie," *Österreichische Musikzeitschrift* 28 (1973): 19–28; Muresu, *Le occasioni di un libertino,* 151–61; Lionel Salter, "Footnotes to a Satire: Salieri's 'Prima la musica, poi le parole,'" *MT* 126 (1985): 21–24; Della Croce/Blanchetti, 206–18; and, on the music, Della Croce/Blanchetti, 468–71.

97. Manuela Hager, "Die Opernprobe als Theateraufführung: Eine Studie zum Libretto in Wien des 18. Jahrhunderts," in *Oper als Text: Romanistische Beiträge zur Libretto-Forschung,* ed. Albert Gier (Heidelberg, 1986), 101–24.

98. Da Ponte, 136.

Although Da Ponte thought the theatrical poet was intended as a parody of him, it is more likely that Casti, like Da Ponte in *L'ape musicale,* made fun of himself. The opening duet for poet and composer surely depicts Casti and Salieri trying to come up with an opera for Joseph's party at Schönbrunn. Casti referred to Count Opizio as having engaged famous singers. Joseph, who had engaged Coltellini and many others before her, must have enjoyed hearing the composer jokingly praise Opizio's musical ability:

> Ma il Signor Conte Opizio
> L'altrieri mi parlò d'una famosa
> Insigne virtuosa,
> Almen per quanto ei dice, ed io lo credo,
> Perch'egli (e questo ancor lo so da lui)
> Ha un singolar talento musicale.
>
> [But the day before yesterday Count Opizio told me of a famous, distinguished virtuosa, at least he says as much, and I believe him because (and this too I know because he told me himself) he has exceptional musical talent.]

When the composer and poet discuss the fee that Count Opizio has promised them, the composer says that he would not refuse 100 zecchini. (The zecchino, a Venetian gold coin, had roughly the value of a ducat. Salieri himself wrote "zecchini" when he meant ducats.)[99] Joseph must have taken notice. After the performance he sent instructions to Count Rosenberg about how those who participated in *Prima la musica* and *Der Schauspieldirektor* were to be paid. He directed that Salieri be given 100 ducats, a generous reward for a short work in which Salieri incorporated the music of two other composers.[100]

Eleonora (soprano), a prima donna who specializes in the performance of opera seria, enters. The role of Eleonora was created by Storace, whose contribution to *Prima la musica* cannot be fully understood without reference to an incident that took place in Italy in 1779, when she was trying to make her name as a singer in opera seria. Kelly, a close friend of the Storaces, both Nancy and Stephen, wrote of a memorable performance of Francesco Bianchi's *Castore e Polluce* in Florence in which Storace shared the stage with Luigi Marchesi, one of the greatest male sopranos of the age:

> Bianchi had composed the celebrated cavatina, "Sembiante amabile del mio bel sole," which Marchesi sung with most ravishing taste; in one passage he ran up a voletta of semitone oc-

99. For example, he reported that as a young man he received 50 to 80 zecchini from Joseph II as New Year's presents (Salieri to Count Kueffstein, 20 May 1816; in Angermüller, *Leben,* 3:162–63, and Angermüller, *Fatti,* 185); according to Mosel he received 50–80 ducats (Mosel, 26).

100. The memorandum is reproduced in Rice, "Vienna," 154.

taves [probably a passage in which octave leaps down alternate with upward leaps of a minor ninth or octave leaps up alternate with downward leaps of a major seventh, both of which result in two parallel ascending chromatic scales], the last note of which he gave with such exquisite power and strength, that it was ever after called "La bomba di Marchesi!" Immediately after this song, Storace had to sing one, and was determined to shew the audience that she could bring a bomba into the field also. She attempted it, and executed it, to the admiration and astonishment of the audience, but to the dismay of the poor Marchesi. Campigli, the manager, requested her to discontinue it, but she peremptorily refused, saying, that she had as good a right to shew the power of her bomba as any body else. The contention was brought to a close, by Marchesi's declaring, that if she did not leave the theater, *he* would; and unjust as it was, the manager was obliged to dismiss her, and engage another lady, who was not as ambitious of exhibiting a bomba.[101]

On her arrival in Vienna Storace was quick to exploit her ability to sing in the serious style. In a private concert on 1 July 1783 she sang an aria from Sarti's *Giulio Sabino,* one of the most popular opere serie of the late eighteenth century. Benucci accompanied at the keyboard.[102] Marchesi, although he had not created the title role in Sarti's opera, had sung it; and Storace and Benucci had probably heard his performance.[103] We do not know what aria from *Giulio Sabino* Storace and Benucci performed in Vienna, but very likely it was one of Sabino's.

The Viennese had a chance to hear and see Marchesi himself in the role of Sabino during summer 1785. Invited to Russia by Empress Catherine, Marchesi stopped in Vienna long enough to participate in a special production of *Giulio Sabino* in the Kärntnertortheater. Joseph himself organized the production in consultation with Marchesi and Salieri.[104] Marchesi sang the title role; Cavalieri sang Sabino's wife Epponina; and Adamberger, taking advantage of his experience as an opera seria singer in Italy, sang Tito.[105] Salieri's role in the production included the composition of several new numbers, but his was not the only music added to the score. So many of Sarti's arias and ensembles were replaced by works of other composers that *Giulio Sabino* became a pasticcio.[106]

101. Kelly, *Reminiscences,* 49.

102. Zinzendorf, 1 July 1783. I am grateful to Bruce Alan Brown for this reference.

103. In Florence during fall 1781 Storace and Benucci participated in a series of comic operas at the Teatro degl'Intrepidi while Marchesi sang the title role in *Giulio Sabino* a few blocks away in the Teatro di Via della Pergola; see Weaver and Weaver, *A Chronology of Music in the Florentine Theater,* 466–72. I am grateful to Richard Armbruster for calling my attention to this early performance of *Giulio Sabino* by Marchesi.

104. Joseph to Rosenberg, 23 July 1785, in *Joseph II,* 64–65.

105. Adamberger's participation is recorded in *WZ,* 31 August 1785, quoted in Armbruster, "Salieri, Mozart und die Wiener Fassung des *Giulio Sabino,*" 161.

106. On the Viennese version of *Giulio Sabino* see Armbruster, "Salieri, Mozart und die Wiener Fassung des *Giulio Sabino,*" 136–54.

FIGURE 11.6 Luigi Marchesi and Catarina Cavalieri performing *Giulio Sabino* in the Kärntnertortheater, August 1785. (Courtesy of Civica Raccolta Stampe "A. Bertarelli," Castello Sforzesco, Milan.)

An engraving records this rare production of an opera seria in Vienna: in one of the opera's climactic scenes Sabino bids farewell to his wife and children (fig. 11.6). He does so with music not by Sarti but by Angelo Tarchi. In the score in the Austrian National Library that documents the Viennese production of *Giulio Sabino* Sarti's beautiful aria "Cari figli, un altro amplesso" has been replaced with Tarchi's elaborate rondò, "Cari oggetti del mio core."

Zinzendorf saw *Giulio Sabino* no less than five times within three weeks, never tiring of Marchesi.[107] From his reaction to the first performance, on 4 August, we know that he was already aware of Storace's ability to mimic Marchesi; he incorrectly (perhaps jokingly) called her Marchesi's student: "Marchesini, Italy's leading soprano, enchanted the whole audience with his beautiful voice: soft, sonorous, harmonious, and expres-

107. Harbecke, "Das Tagebuch des Grafen Karl von Zinzendorf," 47.

sive. In the duet Cavalieri obscured Marchesini's voice with her screams. Marchesini has a woman's face, a woman's gestures, which Storace, his student, has imitated very well, a voice beyond that of a woman, with astonishingly flutelike tones."[108]

Joseph too was pleased. Marchesi, continuing his journey to St. Petersburg, carried a letter of recommendation to Count Cobenzl in which the emperor, in spite of his admiration, could not resist making fun of Marchesi's emasculated state. He called the singer "a good child, for it would be doing him too much honor to say that he is a good man, because he lacks such a characteristic feature of the latter. He is not at all difficult or impudent, as these *messieurs* sometimes are."[109]

The Viennese might have expected Storace to respond somehow to Marchesi's performance, and in *Prima la musica* she did. Casti and Salieri gave her the last word, exploiting her virtuosity and her ability to imitate Marchesi to hilarious effect. As poet and music director discuss with Eleonora her experience on the serious stage, the subject of Marchesi and *Giulio Sabino* quickly comes up. The poet and music director join Eleonora in a ridiculous "staging" of scenes from the Viennese version of *Giulio Sabino*, with a good deal of music quoted directly from the pasticcio. The brilliant aria "Là tu vedrai chi sono" and the accompanied recitative that precedes it are by Sarti, not Salieri; written for an opera seria, not an opera buffa; for a male, not a female soprano. That this music occupies a central place in Salieri's *Prima la musica* is a vivid example of how Viennese fondness for opera seria singers, coupled with Joseph's rejection of the genre, contributed to the richness of Viennese comic opera during the 1780s. Salieri turned Tarchi's solemn rondò for Sabino into slapstick parody by having poet and music director take the roles of Sabino's children, to whom he addresses his tearful farewell. Their comic asides completely undercut the aria's pathos, especially when the poet, running to a chair that is supposed to represent Epponina, personifies her by singing falsetto.[110]

Choosing an aria from an obscure setting of Metastasio's *Alessandro nell'Indie*, "Se possono tanto," the poet and music director adapt it to a new dramatic context and to Eleonora's voice and temperament. The music director, at the keyboard, sings his work in progress. (Benucci thus reenacted on stage the accompanimental role he had played in real life during the private concert in 1783 in which Storace had sung an aria from *Giulio Sabino*.) His rendition of Eleonora's melody, which begins with a noble, four-measure phrase, is not only amusing but dramatically crucial. The audience must know this melody and be able to recognize it if it is to understand and enjoy the opera's conclusion (ex. 11.14).

Having patched together an aria for his serious singer, the maestro proceeds to do the same for his comic singer. The melody, as quoted earlier by the music director, be-

108. Zinzendorf, 4 August 1785, quoted in Michtner, 397.

109. Joseph to Count Cobenzl, 18 August 1785, in *Joseph II. und Graf Cobenzl*, 2:51.

110. Armbruster, "Salieri, Mozart und die Wiener Fassung des *Giulio Sabino*," 154.

EXAMPLE 11.14 *Prima la musica e poi le parole,* sc. 3, simple recitative, mm. 42–45 (A-Wn, Mus. Hs. 17814)

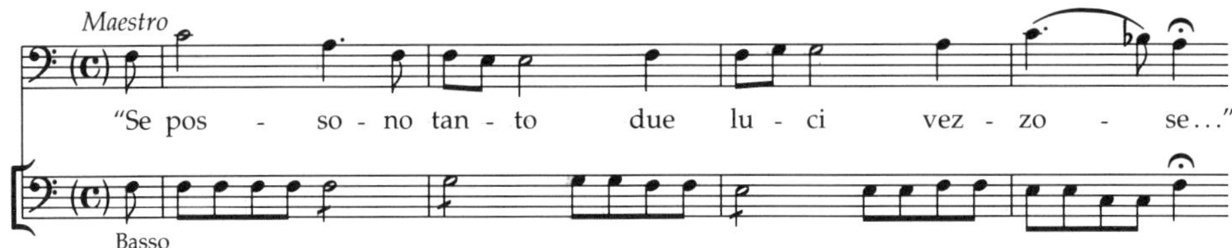

"If two charming eyes can do so much . . ."

EXAMPLE 11.15 *Prima la musica e poi le parole,* sc. 3, simple recitative, mm. 134–37

COMPOSER: "For pity's sake, my mistress, do not be distressed." POET: This could work well.

gins with plebeian, two-measure phrases. The poet interrupts, giving his approval in recitative (ex. 11.15). All that is needed is to change a few words, which he does quickly.

Tonina (soprano, Coltellini), the comic soprano who will sing this aria, finally appears. She looks through a pile of scores, throwing each on the floor as she rejects it. In what must have been intended mostly as a private joke for the composer and for his patron Joseph, Casti alluded to Salieri's first opera by having Tonina throw down the score of *La donna letterata* with the comment

Non lo conosco, ma dal titol solo
Capisco che esser deve
Una gran seccatura.[111]

[I don't know it, but from the title alone I understand that it must be mighty tedious.]

The opera may also contain a musical reference to *Le donne letterate.* As the maestro arranges Eleonora's aria, Salieri accompanied his labors with music in E♭, dominated by

111. Later in the opera Tonina makes another reference to an early opera by Salieri. When the composer introduces Eleonora with the words "Quell' è la donna Eleonora, / Che ora viene di Spagna," Tonina responds: "Fosse anche la Contessa di Culagna, / Non me n'importa un fico." Gherarda, Contessa di Culagna, is a principal character in *La secchia rapita.*

EXAMPLE 11.16 *Prima la musica e poi le parole,* finale, mm. 1–4

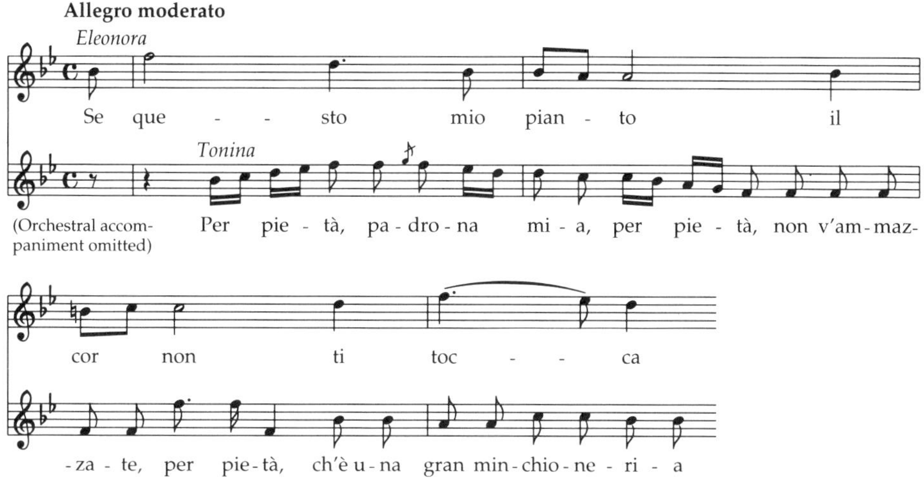

ELEONORA: If my tears do not touch your heart . . . TONINA, *simultaneously:* For pity's sake, my mistress, do not kill yourself, for that would be a silly blunder.

a bass line consisting mostly of arpeggiated quarter notes slurred in groups of four. This music is reminiscent of the introduzione of *Le donne letterate,* also in E♭, where slurred arpeggiated eighth notes accompany the intellectual labors of Artemia, Elvira, and Baggeo (see ex. 4.5). If anybody besides Salieri remembered that music, it may have been the emperor himself, who probably played it when he and his chamber musicians performed *Le donne letterate* during Lent 1770.

Eleonora returns and the two singers quarrel over who is to sing first; thus Storace and Coltellini brought to dramatic life the rivalry between them that had entertained Viennese opera lovers since Coltellini's arrival almost a year earlier. Eleonora and Tonina end up singing simultaneously, Eleonora her aria in the serious style and Tonina hers in the comic. The two songs, by now familiar to the audience, harmonize perfectly (ex. 11.16). The poet and music director join in the ensemble, bringing the opera to a happy end.

More remarkable than the opera's final celebration is the contemplative passage that precedes it ("Si stringa costante / sincera amistà"). This hymnlike praise of harmony, both musical and social, in the midst of a busy finale reminds one of the more exalted slow passage before the final Allegro assai in Mozart's *Figaro* ("Ah tutti contenti / saremo così"), first performed only three months after the premiere of *Prima la musica.* (In poetic organization the two passages are identical: unanimous praise of reconciliation as the last two lines of a long stretch of senari.)

Storace must have dominated the performance of *Prima la musica.* Zinzendorf mentioned little of the opera besides Storace and her seria talents: "la Storace imitated

Marchesi perfectly in singing arias from *Giulio Sabino.*"[112] The *Realzeitung* agreed: "Madame Storace excited universal enthusiasm; she imitated the famous Herr Luigi Marchesi in singing arias from *Giulio Sabino* so skillfully that one imagined one was hearing Marchesi himself."[113]

After its premiere during Joseph's Carnival party, *Prima la musica* was presented in Vienna, in the theater in which *Giulio Sabino* had been performed the previous year. The Italian troupe made three rare appearances at the Kärntnertor, home of the Singspiel troupe, between 11 and 25 February 1786, when the two companies reenacted their Schönbrunn rivalry for the Viennese public.[114] Despite the success with which Storace executed her role, the double bill was soon abandoned, perhaps because of logistical difficulties in bringing the troupes together in one theater. The brevity of *Prima la musica,* its dependence on Storace's particular talents, its allusions to Viennese operatic policies, personalities, and relationships, its references in both text and music to a musico who had recently sung in Vienna and to the opera in which he had performed, all meant that Salieri's opera was not likely to travel well. It does not seem to have been performed (until some twentieth-century revivals) outside of Schönbrunn and Vienna.

112. Zinzendorf, 7 February 1786, quoted in *MDL,* 229–30, and Swenson, 114.
113. *Wiener Realzeitung,* 21 February 1786; quoted in Swenson, 118.
114. Hadamowsky, *Hoftheater,* 1:100, 109.

12

BETWEEN PARIS AND VIENNA: *TARARE* AND *AXUR RE D'ORMUS*

Following the success of *Les Danaïdes* the directors of the Opéra commissioned two more operas from Salieri: *Les Horaces* and *Tarare.* On his return to Vienna he reported to Cramer, once again invoking Gluck's name, that he would compose *Les Horaces* first: "This is the advice of Gluck; and the other requires too much time on account of the peculiar manner in which the subject is treated."[1] Three Italian operas for Joseph's opera buffa troupe caused him to postpone work on his French operas; it was not until 1786 that he returned to Paris to complete them and to supervise rehearsals. *Les Horaces* failed, but the success of *Tarare* was felt as strongly in Vienna as in Paris. It formed the basis for the opera that Salieri, in collaboration with Da Ponte, wrote for Joseph's opera buffa troupe after his return to Vienna. *Axur re d'Ormus* represents most clearly the influence of French serious opera on Viennese Italian opera of the 1780s.

We do not know exactly when Salieri left Vienna on his second and, as it turned out, last trip to Paris. Leopold Mozart, in a letter to his daughter of 28 April 1786, accused him of fomenting cabals against Wolfgang's forthcoming *Figaro.*[2] If there is any truth to the accusation, Salieri was presumably still in Vienna; he probably witnessed the first performance on 1 May. He arrived in Paris sometime before 31 July, when Beaumarchais, with whom he would collaborate on *Tarare,* invited him to discuss their project.[3] But his first concern was *Les Horaces.*

1. Salieri to Cramer, 20 July 1784, in Angermüller, *Leben,* 3:29, and Angermüller, *Fatti,* 119.
2. *MBA,* 3:536.
3. Swenson, 123.

The librettists of tragédie lyrique rarely dared to invite close comparison with great spoken tragedies of the seventeenth century precisely because of the kind of criticism that greeted the attempt by librettist Nicolas-François Guillard to put Corneille's *Horace* on the operatic stage. (Noverre's ballet on the same subject had faced similar comparisons.) And just as Guillard suffered in comparison to Corneille, so Salieri's music suffered in comparison to *Les Danaïdes.* Jokes making fun of the name "Curiaces," the first syllable of which sounds like *cul* (ass), sealed the fate of *Les Horaces.* The opera was withdrawn after a few performances.[4]

The failure of *Les Horaces* annoyed Emperor Joseph, informed of it by his ambassador in Paris. He wrote to Count Mercy: "I am angry about what you wrote me about the failure of Salieri's opera. He can sometimes be a little too mannered in seeking expressivity in music. But what I would never have believed is that the name of the heroes of the work could affect the reception of his composition—namely that of *Curiaces*—, and that people made fun of the first syllable of a proper name that was neither his choice nor that of the poet, but is a name so well known in history. Perhaps he will have more success with Beaumarchais's opera."[5]

The emperor looked forward to Salieri's next French opera with hope. "He is certainly a man of talent, as long as the poet provides him with the means to allow his genius to be appreciated."[6] Beaumarchais—adventurer, playwright, pamphleteer, and musician—did just that.

Beaumarchais as Operatic Reformer

Always drawn to controversy, Beaumarchais used *Tarare* to contribute to the debates about the nature and purpose of opera that had been part of French intellectual life for much of the eighteenth century. In the long polemical preface to the libretto he set himself up as a reformer of opera who sought, like so many before him, to bring to it the

4. On *Les Horaces* see Mosel, 94–98; Jullien, *La Cour et l'opéra,* 201–13; Julian Rushton, "Music and Drama at the Académie Royale de Musique (Paris), 1774–1789," 294–302, and "Salieri's *Les Horaces:* A Study of an Operatic Failure," *Music Review* 37 (1976): 266–82; Angermüller, *Leben,* 2:127–37; and Della Croce/Blanchetti, 218–23 and 478–82.

5. Je suis faché de la chûte que vous me mandés de l'opera de Salieri; il lui est arrivé par fois, d'être un peu trop baroque en cherchant l'expression dans la musique; mais ce que je n'aurais jamais cru, pouvoir nuir à sa composition, c'est le nom des Heros de la pièce, savoir celui de Curiaces, et qu'on eut rélévé en plaisanterie la premiere syllabe d'un nom propre, que n'etoit ni de son choix ni di celui du Poete; mais qui est un nom si connu dans l'Histoire, peut etre, qu'il reussira mieux avec l'opera de Beaumarchais (Joseph to Count Mercy, 2 January 1787, HHStA, HP, Bd. 45, 1787, no. 2).

6. Je vous suis fort obligé de l'intérêt que vous prenés de Salieri pour qu'il lui soit rendu justice de la part des directeurs de l'Opera pour la recompense de ses peines. c'est certainement un homme à talens, pourvuque le Poete lui fournisse les moyens de faire valoir son genie (Joseph to Count Mercy, 7 February 1787, HHStA, HP, Bd. 45, no. 104).

grandeur and dramatic power of Greek tragedy.[7] But the preface is more remarkable for the charm of its language than for the originality of its ideas or the integrity of its argumentation.

Beaumarchais set out to solve a problem whose existence he failed to demonstrate (one of several questionable *donnés* on which his preface depends): that audiences were turning away from French opera. Why does opera not appeal to them as much as one might expect? Because music, which should be limited to its useful function "of embellishing the words," is abused by composers:

> There is too much music in our music for the theater; it is always overloaded with it. And to use the naive remark of a justly famous man, the illustrious Chevalier Gluck, "our opera stinks of music" (*puzza di musica*).[8]

Beaumarchais stated his belief in the supremacy of words over music without any justification:

> The true hierarchy of these arts, it seems to me, ought to proceed as follows in the esteem of spectators: first comes the action or plot, which commands the greatest interest, next the beauty of the poem or the skillful manner of relating the events, then the charm of the music, which is but a novel expression added to the charm of the poetry, and finally the ballet, whose grace and gaiety help to warm some frigid situations. Such, in the order of the pleasure they afford, is the rank occupied by all these arts.

Beaumarchais based his choice of operatic subject on another assumption that was hardly self-evident:

> First of all let us remember that an opera is neither a tragedy nor a comedy but participates in both and can embrace all of the genres.
>
> Accordingly, I shall not choose a subject that is altogether tragic, since the general mood would be so sinister that the festive occasions would seem to drop out of nowhere, thereby killing the interest. Let us also refrain from using purely comic intrigues, from which the passions and grand effects are excluded, so that the music lacks nobility.

7. "Aux Abonnés de l'opéra qui voudraient aimer l'opéra" (preface to *Tarare*), in Beaumarchais, *Oeuvres,* 497–509; in English translation in *The Essence of Opera,* ed. Ulrich Weisstein (New York, 1969), 140–52. The preface is discussed in Edward J. Dent, *The Rise of Romantic Opera* (Cambridge, 1976), 38–39; Thomas Betzwieser, *Exotismus und "Türkenoper" in der französischen Musik des Ancien Régime* (Laaber, 1993), 332–38; and, more briefly, in Thomas Betzwieser, "Exoticism and Politics: Beaumarchais' and Salieri's *Le Couronnement de Tarare* (1790)," *COJ* 6 (1994): 91–112.

8. Beaumarchais presumably learned of Gluck's phrase from Salieri, who had heard Gluck use it in reference to a passage in a draft of *Les Danaïdes* (see chap. 10, "Origins").

He went on to argue against historical and mythological subjects, thus rejecting—without mentioning any of them—most of the subjects treated by librettists and composers of serious opera, Italian as well as French.

> I would think, then, that one must take a setting halfway between the marvelous and the historical. I have also noticed that our very civilized manners are too well established to be theatrically effective. Oriental manners, more varied and less familiar, leave more opportunity to the imagination and appear to be better suited for our purpose.

Beaumarchais freely acknowledged his conceptual debt to Gluck but ignored such equally important sources of inspiration as Francesco Algarotti, Calzabigi, and the librettists with whom Gluck had worked in Paris. In stating that opera should encompass both serious and comic he differed strongly from most theorists of serious opera, but his views are consistent with the integration of serious and comic in opéra-comique and opera buffa (genres he was careful not to mention). Goldoni's librettos, with their sentimental heroines, ardent young lovers, and parti serie, had pushed opera buffa toward a mixed genre; some of his successors, such as De Gamerra and Giovanni Battista Lorenzi, had increased the importance of serious characters and situations in comic opera. "Neither a tragedy nor a comedy": one could say the same of many opéras-comiques of the 1770s and 1780s, including Philidor's *Tom Jones,* Monsigny's *Le déserteur,* and Grétry's *Richard coeur-de-lion.*

Unmentioned in Beaumarchais's promotion of oriental subjects is the long tradition of such subjects in opéra-comique.[9] *Tarare* has much in common with *Les Pèlerins de la Mecque* by Alain-René Lesage (from which Gluck had derived *La rencontre imprévue*) and *Zémire et Azor* by Jean-François Marmontel and Grétry, which represent a subtype of oriental opera in which all or most of the leading characters are oriental, as distinct from Favart's *Soliman second, ou Les Trois Sultanes* and Mozart's *Entführung,* which involve the interaction of European and oriental characters.

Beaumarchais was drawn to oriental subjects partly because they offered a way of commenting indirectly on the political situation in France, but in this too he was far from unique. French politics serve as an underlying theme in *Soliman second.*[10] Roxelane, a spirited Frenchwoman in Soliman's harem, brought down the house during a performance at the Comédie Italienne in 1777, according to Grimm, when she urged the tyrannous sultan to emulate the king of France:

> There is in *Les Trois Sultanes* a verse in the tragic style that was applauded by the respectable parterre of the Opéra-Comique, as it could have been in England in the House of Commons:
>
> Tout citoyen est roi sous un roi citoyen.

9. On this tradition see Betzwieser, *Exotismus und "Türkenoper,"* 201–306.
10. On *Soliman* see Betzwieser, *Exotismus und "Türkenoper,"* 219–26, 252–58.

> What conception must one not form of the wisdom and seriousness of a people who amuse themselves at the comic opera with sentiments and sayings of such power? And these are the people whom one dares to accuse of frivolity![11]

Beaumarchais's originality reveals itself less in the content of his libretto than in the place for which he intended its performance. His preface uses the word "Opéra" as a double-entendre. An attack on the supposed defects of opera in general can also be read as an attack on the Opéra in particular: the venerable Académie Royale de Musique that preserved traditions dating back to Lully, including a rejection of comic characters and situations (Lully had used the term "tragédie en musique" to refer to many of his operas) and a preference for subjects from Greco-Roman mythology and history. But even in challenging the Opéra Beaumarchais was less a pioneer than he wished his readers to believe. Grétry's very successful *La Caravane du Caire* (1784) had already presented on the stage of the Académie Royale de Musique a mixture of serious and comic in an opera based on a nonhistorical, nonmythological, oriental subject.[12] Grétry's effort to open up the Opéra to the influence of other operatic institutions, genres, and traditions helped to prepare the way for Beaumarchais's attempt.

Beaumarchais and Salieri

To put his operatic philosophy (if it can be dignified with this phrase) into practice Beaumarchais needed the cooperation of singers and orchestra, whom he addressed eloquently in his preface:

> Orchestra of our Opéra! Noble participant in the system of Gluck, of Salieri, and of mine! You will express only noise if you stifle the word; emotion is that which it is your glory to express.
>
> Two brief maxims have served, during our rehearsals, as my theory of opera. To our actors, so full of good will, I have proposed but one precept: ENUNCIATE CLEARLY! To the best orchestra in the world I have said only these two words: BE QUIET! Well understood, I added, this will render us worthy of the public's attention.

That the librettist, in his normal role of stage director, should have coached the singers on declamation is to be expected. Beaumarchais was surely not the first librettist to encourage his singers to declaim the text clearly. In exercising control over some of an opera's musical parameters Beaumarchais was simply following in the footsteps

11. Grimm, *Correspondance littéraire,* 11:414, refers to Roxelane's speech in act 2, sc. 3 (*Théâtre de M. Favart* [Paris, 1763], 4:35–36), which includes the lines "Point d'esclaves chez nous; on ne respire en France / Que les plaisirs, la liberté, l'aisance. / Tout citoyen est Roi, sous un Roi citoyen."

12. On *La Caravane du Caire* see Betzwieser, *Exotismus und "Türkenoper,"* 317–32.

of other innovative, energetic, and ambitious librettists with whom Salieri had worked, such as De Gamerra and Verazi.

But not all composers were as willing as Salieri to place the demands of drama, as articulated by the librettist, above those of music. (One wonders how Mozart would have gotten along with Beaumarchais.) The grateful poet wrote of his collaboration with Salieri:

> But what belongs to me even less is the beautiful music by my friend Salieri. This great composer, who brings honor to the school of Gluck, having the style of that great master, had received from Nature a delicate sensibility, a true spirit, a most exceptional talent for dramatic music, and a wealth of ideas that is almost unique. He had the virtue to renounce, in order to please me, a crowd of musical ideas with which his opera sparkled, only because they lengthened scenes and slowed down the action; but the manly, energetic color of the work, its rapid, intrepid tone, will compensate him well for so many sacrifices.
>
> This man of genius, so misunderstood and scorned for his beautiful opera *Les Horaces,* has responded in advance in *Tarare* to the objection that will be made that my poem is not very lyrical. Lyricism was not the object that we sought, but only to make dramatic music. My friend, I said to him, to soften ideas, to make phrases effeminate so as to make them more musical, is the true source of the abuses that have spoiled opera for us. Let us dare to elevate music to the level of a poem that is vigorous and strongly plotted; we will render to it all of its nobility; we will attain perhaps those great effects vaunted so much in the ancient spectacles of the Greeks. These are the ambitious labors that we undertook years ago. I say sincerely that I would never have consented, for any price, to leave my study to work with an ordinary man on a project that has become, thanks to M. Salieri, my evenings' recreation and often a delightful pleasure.
>
> Our discussions, I believe, would have made a very good theory of operatic poetry, for M. Salieri was born a poet, and I am something of a musician. One will perhaps never succeed without the cooperation of all these things.

Beaumarchais's reference to pleasant evenings of discussion about opera remind one of Da Ponte's memory of the "many learnedly happy hours" that he spent in Salieri's company.

In dedicating the libretto to the composer (which librettists very rarely did in the eighteenth century), Beaumarchais expressed again respect and gratitude:

> My friend,
>
> I dedicate my work to you because it has become yours. I only gave it birth; you have raised it to the status of theater.
>
> My greatest merit in this is to have foreseen the opera of *Tarare* in *Les Danaïdes* and *Les Horaces,* despite the prejudice that harmed this last, which is a very beautiful work, but a little severe for Paris.

> You have helped me, my friend, give the French an idea of ancient Greek theater, as I have always imagined it. If our work has success, I will owe it almost entirely to you. And when your modesty makes you say to everyone that you are only my musician, I, for my part, am honored to be your poet, your servant, and your friend.[13]

Has any librettist expressed such admiration, in print, to the composer who set his words to music? Surely not so elegantly as Beaumarchais. Salieri's willingness to set librettos more or less as written helped him to add Beaumarchais to a list of literary friends that already included Boccherini, De Gamerra, Verazi, and Da Ponte.

"Sadak and Kalasrade"

Beaumarchais sent readers curious about the source of his story to "volume 3 of *Les Génies.*" He referred to an English work, *The Tales of the Genii, or The Delightful Lessons of Horam, the Son of Asmar,* first published in 1764. Although described on the title pages of early editions as having been "faithfully translated from the Persian manuscript," *The Tales of the Genii* were in fact written by an Englishman, James Ridley, under the inspiration of *The Arabian Nights.* They enjoyed considerable popularity during the late eighteenth century, to judge from the large number of editions that appeared and the several translations made of them. As La Harpe was quick to discover, Beaumarchais derived *Tarare* from Ridley's tale "Sadak and Kalasrade."[14]

Sadak, a retired Turkish general, lives happily with his wife Kalasrade and their children near the shores of the Bosporus. The sultan Amurath, jealous of Sadak's happiness, has Kalasrade abducted and imprisoned in his harem; when he sees her for the first time he falls in love with her.

Unaware that Kalasrade is in the palace, Sadak asks Amurath for help in finding her. Doubar, the chief eunuch of Amurath's harem, was once saved from certain death by Sadak's father; now, in return, he offers to help Kalasrade escape Amurath's increasingly threatening sexual advances. Following Doubar's advice, Kalasrade promises to give herself to Amurath on condition that he bring her a potion that will enable her to forget Sadak. Amurath agrees to do so, without knowing that the potion can be obtained only on an island in the Indian Ocean. He commands Sadak to bring the potion. Much of Ridley's story is taken up with an account of Sadak's travels.

Sadak returns with the potion of forgetfulness. Curious about its effect, Amurath drinks part of it himself. He falls dead, death being the only sure source of oblivion. Amurath's courtiers acclaim Sadak the new sultan. At first reluctant to accept the throne,

13. Beaumarchais, *Oeuvres,* 495.

14. La Harpe, *Correspondance littéraire,* 5:194. Della Croce/Blanchetti, 229, misleadingly refers to "Sadak and Kalasrade" as "un racconto arabo" without mentioning Ridley.

Sadak finally consents: "The shouts of the faithful rent the air with notes of triumph when Sadak yielded to his people's supplication."

Tarare

Beaumarchais took almost every major element of *Tarare* from Ridley's story. He derived his hero Tarare from Sadak and his heroine Astasie from Kalasrade. The name Tarare (Nonsense) is a joke, probably related to Beaumarchais's belief that an opera should encompass comedy as well as tragedy and also, no doubt, intended to incite curiosity and increase ticket sales. Perhaps under the influence of *Zémire et Azor* Beaumarchais transferred the action from the Bosporus to Hormuz, on the Persian Gulf, where part of Grétry's opera takes place. The sultan Amurath became King Atar of Hormuz. By giving Tarare and Atar names that are partial anagrams, Beaumarchais may have alluded to Metastasio (Tomiri and Mirteo in *Semiramide,* Cleonice and Fenicio in *Demetrio*). Amurath's eunuch Doubar became Atar's eunuch Calpigi. An Italian castrated in childhood to preserve his beautiful treble voice, Calpigi was later captured by pirates and eventually rescued by Tarare.

Beaumarchais omitted Ridley's potion of oblivion. He replaced Sadak's expedition to the Indian Ocean in search of the potion with a military expedition whose events are narrated rather than depicted. Amurath's accidental death became Atar's suicide. Tarare, like Sadak, reluctantly agrees to take the place of the dead tyrant.

The opera begins with a bow to the past: to the prologues with which early French operas often began. The very long prologue (713 measures) depicts a nonbiblical creation of the world by means of allegorical figures, chorus, and dance.[15] After an *ouverture* representing night and its chaotic winds, Nature (soprano) imposes calm and the Spirit of Fire (bass) brings light. They create out of the disparate elements the characters who will take part in the drama. Like two *philosophes* of the French Enlightenment, they discuss the relative importance of innate character and social rank before deciding to make Atar a king and Tarare a common soldier. The drama that follows thus emerges as an experiment about man and society, character and class. Five acts later the allegorical philosophes return, their uncertainty resolved, to hear a chorus declaim grandly in the opera's epilogue its most famous lines:

> Mortel, qui que tu sois,
> Prince, Brame ou Soldat,
> HOMME! ta grandeur sur la terre
> N'appartient point à ton état:
> Elle est toute à ton caractère.

15. On Salieri's prologue see Betzwieser, *Exotismus und "Türkenoper,"* 337–40.

[Mortal, whoever you are, prince, brahmin or soldier, MAN! Your greatness on earth depends not at all on your place in society but entirely on your character.]

Salieri's colorful orchestration contributes much to the prologue. Trombones help to convey the solemn mystery of creation. The effect of the timpani is enhanced, as in *Les Danaïdes* and *La grotta di Trofonio,* by their being delayed; the drums enter only at measure 62. As in the incantation scene in *La grotta,* Salieri experimented with unconventional tuning in the prologue and elsewhere in *Tarare.* Here the timpani play D and B♭. Salieri saved his clarinets until scene 3 of the prologue, where human spirits begin to come to corporeal life. The novelty of the clarinets' sound, accompanied by muted strings, mirrors the words "Quel charme inconnu nous attire."

An Italianate one-movement overture—Salieri called it "Nouvelle Ouverture d'un genre absolument différent de la première"—follows the prologue. Salieri reused this second overture in *Axur.* In his annotations to the autograph score of that opera he described the overture as "a mixture of the barbarous, the heroic, and the mournful, because these three colors dominate the whole opera."[16]

The overture conveys "the barbarous" by means of "Turkish" orchestration: cymbals and bass drum. The Turkish orchestration here and elsewhere in *Tarare* lacks an instrument, the piccolo, commonly used by other composers (such as Gluck in *La Rencontre imprévue* and Mozart in *Die Entführung*) to evoke Middle Eastern settings. Salieri intensely disliked the piccolo. When the Opéra revived *Tarare* in 1818, the aged composer revised the score, sending the revisions to Paris with a long letter that includes some advice on how to perform the opera. He insisted that no piccolo be used: "Above all do not allow the piccolo, music's shame, to be played in my operas, not even in foreign dance airs. This miserable instrument [should be used] only to make a bear dance."[17]

Another element of the overture that sounds Turkish and hence "barbarous" is the opening theme's rhythm, with several long notes followed by much shorter notes, and its insistent repetition of the raised fourth degree of the scale.[18] In both rhythm and

16. Salieri's long and informative annotations to the autograph of *Axur* have been published in Angermüller, *Fatti,* 83–97, and in Bruno Brizi, "Il *Parere* di Salieri sull'*Axur re d'Ormus,*" in *Varietà d'harmonia et d'affetto: Studi in onore di Giovanni Marzi per il suo LXX compleanno,* ed. Antonio Delfino (Lucca, 1995), 221–41 (with useful commentary).

17. Surtout ne permettez pas qu'on joue le *piccolo,* la honte de la musique, dans mes operas, pas mêmes dans les airs de danse etrangeres. [illegible word] ce miserable instrument seulement pour faire danser l'ours (Salieri to Louis-Luc Loiseau de Persuis, director of the Opéra, probably written in September 1818). Excerpts and a photograph of one page are published in catalogue 116, Richard Macnutt Ltd., item no. 251. I am grateful to Daniel Heartz for bringing this letter to my attention.

18. These are among the common features of music *à la Turque* in late eighteenth-century Europe, as summarized in Bauman, *W. A. Mozart: Die Entführung aus dem Serail,* 62–65.

EXAMPLE 12.1 Gluck, *La Rencontre imprévue,* overture, mm. 1–5 (*Sämtliche Werke,* 4:7)

EXAMPLE 12.2 Salieri, *Tarare,* second overture (also overture to *Axur re d'Ormus*) mm. 1–6 (full score, ed. Rudolph Angermüller [Munich, 1978])

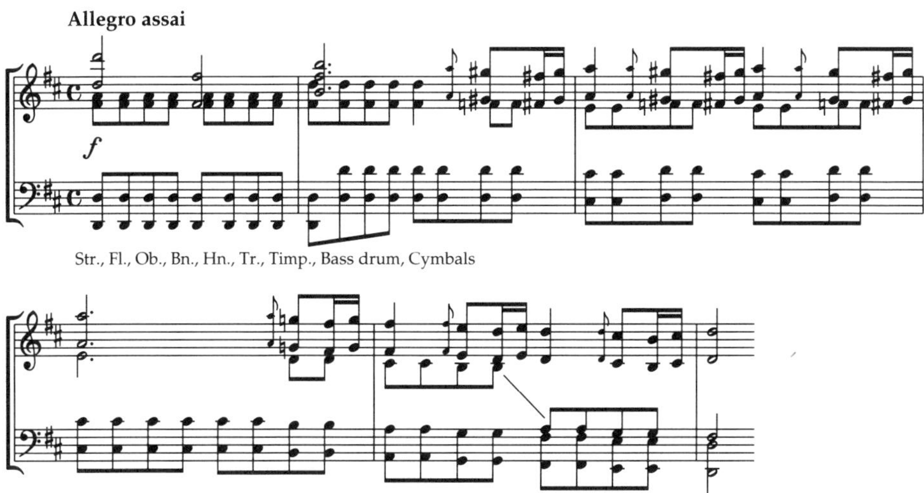

modal inflection Salieri's music echoes the beginning of the overture to *La Rencontre imprévue* (ex. 12.1).[19] Salieri added a "barbarism" not present in Gluck's opening: by harmonizing the raised fourth degree with a diminished seventh chord he introduced a harsh cross-relation between F♯ in the melody and F♮ in the accompaniment (ex. 12.2).

As for the heroic and the mournful, there is some of both in the overture's closing material. March rhythms, scalar flourishes, and pompous cadences sound heroic; but inserted into this passage is a prominent pitch (F♮) and chord (B♭ major) derived from the parallel minor (D minor) that carry with them a hint of the suffering and sorrow that King Atar will inflict during the drama (ex. 12.3). This passage also has "barbarous" connotations. In *Les Danaïdes* (the duet "Hélas! que ne puis-je te suivre") the words "quelle est ta barbarie" had caused Salieri to move from D major to a B♭-major chord

19. Betzwieser, *Exotismus und "Türkenoper,"* 340.

EXAMPLE 12.3 *Tarare*, second overture, mm. 94–98

(see ex. 10.5). Here he made a similar harmonic gesture more potent by introducing parallel fifths (F♯-F♮ over B♮-B♭): a deliberate affront to musical propriety.[20]

King Atar (bass), having made Tarare (tenor) general of his armies after he saved the king's life, is jealous of Tarare because the young man finds happiness in doing his duty and in loving his wife Astasie (soprano). He tells his eunuch Calpigi (*haute-contre:* the part notated in alto clef) that he has ordered Astasie abducted in order to make Tarare unhappy.

Atar and Calpigi converse in orchestrally accompanied recitative that contains occasional short arialike passages (Atar's "Oui, le fils du grand-prêtre," an Allegretto of twenty-two measures, and Calpigi's "Il est vrai, son nom adoré," a Larghetto of seventeen measures). The printed score, published shortly after the premiere, labels most of the recitative "parlé" and most of the arias and arialike passages "chanté." Beaumarchais's insistence on the preeminence of the verbal text may have led him and Salieri to urge, with the word "parlé," their singers toward a kind of *Sprechstimme* in which exactitude of pitch and rhythm is less important than clear and expressive declamation of words.

Atar's general Altamort (bass) announces that he has captured Astasie. After Atar orders a great festivity to celebrate her entry into the harem, slaves perform a choral dance in praise of her beauty, "Dans les plus beaux lieux de l'Asie." Astasie is attended by Spinette (soprano), the opera's most consistently comic character: "a European slave, Calpigi's wife, a Neapolitan singer, *intriguante et coquette.*" Outraged at finding herself

20. My thanks to Bruce Alan Brown for this point.

Atar's prisoner, Astasie calls on the god Brahma for revenge and then faints. When a slave blurts out "the veil of death has covered her eyes," Atar stabs him in full view. The king gives Astasie the name Irza and orders her to be brought to the harem.

Informed by Urson, captain of the guards (bass), of Tarare's unhappiness at his wife's abduction, the king is finally satisfied. Tarare tells the king of his misfortune. Atar offers him a female slave in compensation for his loss, but Tarare can only praise his beloved: "Astasie est une déesse." The sensuous accompaniment of clarinets and bassoons shows what Salieri had learned since he composed *Les Danaïdes* about writing for this combination of instruments. He associated clarinets with Tarare not only here but in the short, lyrical prayer, "Dieu tout puissant," that his hero sings at the end of act 3.[21]

Atar responds to Tarare's lament with a brilliant aria mocking him for his apparent weakness: "Qu'as-tu donc fait de ton mâle courage?" Again Salieri delayed the timpani's entrance in order to dramatize an important moment, in this case a striking modulation from B minor to D major (suddenly replaced with D minor, as in the passage from the second overture quoted above) with offbeat fortissimo blasts at the words "Le fer, le feu, le sang et le carnage." Tarare swears vengeance on the abductor, whoever he is.

Act 2 begins with a long conversation in accompanied recitative ("parlé") between Atar and Arthénée, high priest of Brahma and father of Altamort. A military campaign against the Christians is soon to begin. Atar announces his intention of appointing Altamort to the position of leadership in the army now held by Tarare, who is to be killed. Arthénée warns the king that he will pay with his throne for killing Tarare. Atar sings a big bravura aria in C major with trumpets and drums, "Qu'une grande solennité."

Alone, Tarare prays to Brahma for help. Calpigi, who owes his life to Tarare, tells him where Astasie is. In a brief heroic aria, "J'irai! Oui, j'oserai," the hero vows to rescue his wife.

To the sound of a vigorous and memorable march in A minor (one of several minor keys in *Tarare* that Salieri used very rarely in his operatic oeuvre) Arthénée and the priests of Brahma assemble in their temple, joined by Atar and his court. Trombones add to the ritualistic quality of the music as Arthénée prays to Brahma to inspire the boy Elamir with knowledge of the identity of the next leader of the army. In the annotations to the autograph of *Axur* Salieri drew a picture of the platform on which the boy is to be carried on stage (fig. 12.1). To the amazement of all Elamir announces that the leader should be Tarare (for an illustration of the analogous scene in *Axur*, see plate 1). The priest says that the boy has made a mistake, but the crowd of soldiers and people is convinced that Brahma wants Tarare to be leader. In a short Allegro Tarare summons the soldiers and people to fight with him; they respond with enthusiastic shouts: an inge-

21. Quoted (but without identification of the accompanying instruments) in Cooper, "Opera in France," 246–47.

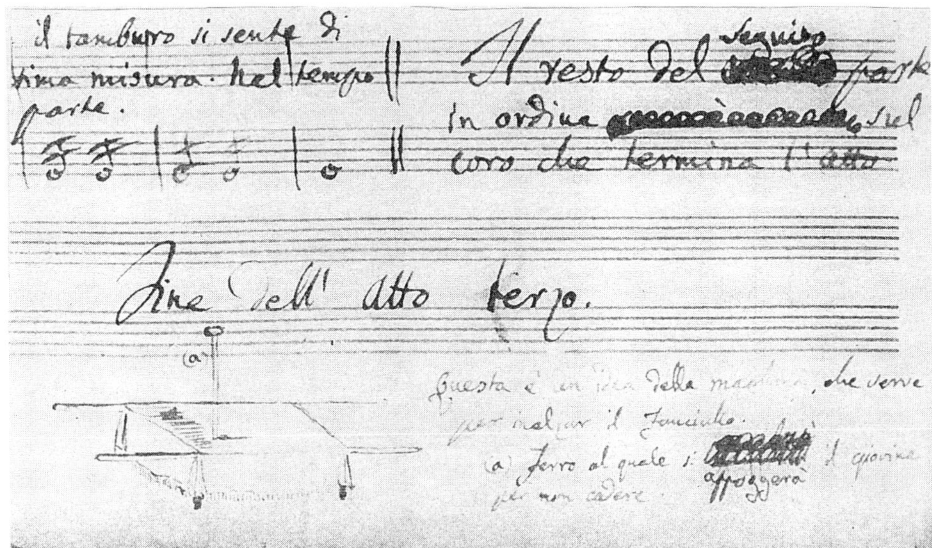

FIGURE 12.1 Instructions by Salieri for the performance of *Axur re d'Ormus:* "This is a sketch of the platform which serves to lift up the boy [Elamir]. (a) iron rod against which the youth will lean so as not to fall." Autograph score. Musiksammlung, Österreichische Nationalbibliothek, Vienna.

nious integration of solo and chorus. Tarare and Altamort confront one another angrily. Tarare arranges to meet Calpigi later that night. In a choral march, massively orchestrated with pairs of flutes, oboes, clarinets, bassoons, horns, trumpets, timpani, bass drum, and strings, the people pray for victory in the impending battle against the infidels.

Near the beginning of act 3 Urson tells of Tarare's victory over Altamort in a great recitative whose accompaniment includes trombones and timpani tuned in G♯ and C, which Salieri used separately to underline single tonal shifts. The trombones help dramatize the moment when Altamort—"his appearance fierce and somber, like specters of night"—meets Tarare in mortal combat (ex. 12.4). A drumroll on C announces the establishment of C major; one on G♯ at the word "s'élance" depicts the charge of Tarare's horse at the battle's climax (ex. 12.5).

Calpigi organizes a festival for Astasie, a "fête européenne": shepherds and shepherdesses, gaily dressed, and peasants with their farming tools perform a series of dances and choruses that represent the largest part of this enormous *divertissement.*[22] Calpigi contributes to the festivities with a strophic romance in which he tells his life story: "Je suis né natif de Ferrare," whose 6/8 meter contributes to its folklike effect; Salieri himself called the tune a "barcarolle." Pizzicato strings represent the mandolin with which Calpigi accompanies himself; he sings the last phrase of each strophe in his

22. The "fête européenne" is analyzed in Betzwieser, *Exotismus und "Türkenoper,"* 343–50.

EXAMPLE 12.4 *Tarare,* act 3, "Tarare le premier arrive au rendezvous," mm. 30–42 (sc. 2, mm. 36–48)

His appearance is fierce and somber, like specters of the night. Measuring his adversary with fiery eyes: "Let us decide the fate of the vanquished." "My law," says Tarare, "is death."

EXAMPLE 12.5 *Tarare,* act 3, "Tarare le premier arrive au rendezvous," mm. 63–65 (sc. 2, mm. 69–71)

His brave steed, feeling the spur that pierces him, charges

native language. The chorus echoes these last phrases. The divertissement comes to a chaotic conclusion when Calpigi, in the middle of his autobiographical narrative, mentions Tarare. Enraged, Atar pulls out his dagger and the crowd disperses. Meanwhile Tarare finds his way into the harem and Calpigi disguises him as an African mute.

Act 4 begins with an elaborate scena in F♯ minor (a key that Salieri had seldom if ever used before as tonic) in which Astasie expresses her desperation and calls for death to end her sorrow. When she hears that Atar will force her to marry one of his slaves, she persuades Spinette to exchange clothes with her so that she might be spared this dishonor. Tarare is caught by Atar's troops before he can find Astasie; Calpigi angrily denounces the king's abuse of power in the aria "Va! l'abus du pouvoir suprême."

The fifth and final act begins with Atar gloating over Tarare's impending execution ("Fantôme vain! Idole populaire") in another unusual key, B minor. The slaves sing a mournful "choeur funèbre" in G minor in which a march played by winds and brass (including trombones), a continuous drumroll, and continuous tremolos in the cellos and double basses contribute to the funereal effect. The expressivity of the diminished seventh chord in measure 3 is enhanced by the clash between F♯ in the cellos and basses and G in the timpani (ex. 12.6). Tarare and Astasie are finally reunited and fall into each

EXAMPLE 12.6 *Tarare*, act 5, choeur funèbre, mm 1–5 (sc. 4, mm. 30–34)

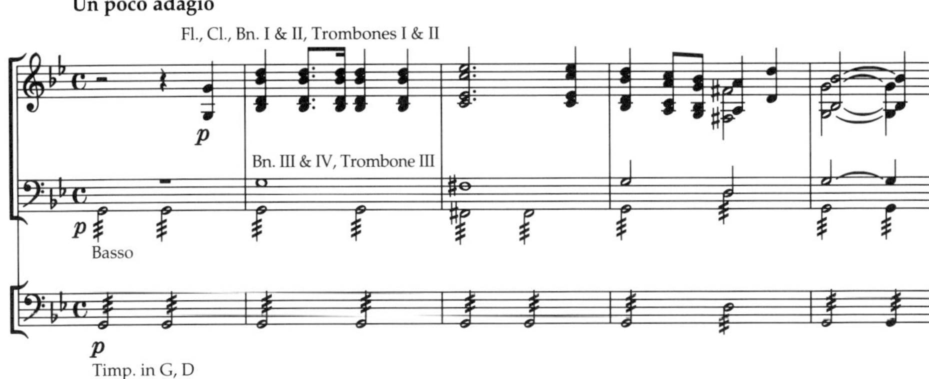

other's arms. A trio for Astasie, Tarare, and Atar, "Le trépas nous attend," is interrupted by slaves crying out for help as Calpigi enters with an army, ready to defend Tarare, to whom they declare allegiance. Atar stabs himself to death. Tarare at first refuses the crown, but the soldiers persuade him to accept it. Arthénée crowns Tarare as the people celebrate with the chorus "Quel plaisir de nos coeurs s'empare!"

Tarare contains much that we associate with tragédie lyrique and its home, the Opéra: the allegorical prologue, five long acts, much use of chorus and ballet, orchestral accompaniment throughout. Yet Beaumarchais and Salieri called their work not tragédie lyrique but simply *opéra.* They presented on the stage of the Académie Royale de Musique a musical drama that mixes tragedy and comedy, exoticism and romance, together with a current of political allegory that appealed strongly to prerevolutionary Parisian audiences. The conflict between Tarare and Atar is a conflict between reason, nature, and virtue on the one hand and violence, selfishness, and hatred on the other. Salieri and Beaumarchais showed the king's overthrow to be completely justified, even though his suicide renders it unnecessary. In doing so they helped lay the ideological and emotional foundation for the revolution that broke out two years later.

Promotion and Reception

Beaumarchais, a skillful and tireless self-promoter, made sure that *Tarare* was talked about all over Paris during the months before it reached the stage.[23] Already in February 1787 the *Mémoires secrets,* a chronicle of Parisian culture published in London during the 1780s, attested to the interest that he had aroused: "People have been talking for some time about Tarare, this opera of Sieur de Beaumarchais that, from the title, one

23. For a detailed account of the promotion, rehearsal, performance, and reception of *Tarare* see Angermüller, *Leben,* 2:138–79.

might judge to be a comedy, but that today was said to be on a heroic subject, a tragedy of the darkest kind. It is a most complicated harem story, resulting in a very long poem."[24]

The *Mémoires secrets* later confirmed what Beaumarchais said in his preface about his role in the production vis-à-vis Salieri's and about how he addressed the orchestra:

> The rehearsals of Tarare continue, and le sieur de Beaumarchais follows them with the greatest care. He wants his opera to be given around mid-June at the latest. Although le sieur Saliery always accompanies him the musician is only his subordinate: he does not say a word; it is le sieur Beaumarchais who makes all the comments, even concerning the music, which he believes must do nothing but enhance and accentuate the poem's manifold beauties. He cries out to the orchestra often: "Pianissimo, gentlemen. I want the words to predominate, I want nothing to be lost."[25]

The premiere on 8 June 1787 was a success for both librettist and musician. So perfectly did Beaumarchais manipulate the pamphleteering and debates that preceded it that they attracted a large audience without arousing passions to the level that might have caused the authorities to close the theater. If La Harpe's account is accurate and his opinions widely shared (as an ardent anti-Gluckist he exaggerated the novelty of *Tarare*), the audience agreed with Beaumarchais's preface and found its arguments supported by the opera and its performance:

> Despite the storms raised on every side against Beaumarchais and the satires, in prose and in verse, that unceasingly rain down upon him, the first performance of *Tarare,* which was expected to be very tumultuous, was very peaceful. The two authors were called out obstinately; but Beaumarchais, more obstinate than the audience, did not want to appear; and so the audience had to be content to see the composer of the music, Salieri, who was certainly not the one who excited most actively the general curiosity. Not that the music did not give one pleasure: it contributed much to the opera's success. It seemed well adapted to the words. Its execution is expressive and rapid, almost as rapid as spoken dialogue, and several very beautiful arias and choruses made one regret that there are not more of them. But the drama is so long that if the musician had wanted to give himself free scope, the spectacle would have lasted until midnight. *Tarare* has thus presented at the Opéra innovations that are truly different. It is the first time that the poem did not submit to the musician; the first time that, on the contrary, the musician submitted himself to the poet's authority. It is the first time that the orchestra was willing to renounce its customary pretensions of dominating the singing on stage and of covering the actors' voices; the first time that one has been able to hear perfectly the words of an opera.[26]

24. *Mémoires secrets* 34 (21 February 1787): 174–75; quoted in Angermüller, *Leben,* 3:313.
25. *Mémoires secrets* 35:83–84; quoted in Angermüller, *Leben,* 3:325.
26. La Harpe, *Correspondance littéraire,* 5:192–93; quoted in Angermüller, *Leben,* 3:332–33.

Tarare returned to the stage in the midst of the French Revolution, subjected to a revision that involved a new scene at the end of the opera. In one of the rare political blunders that Salieri made during his long career at the Habsburg court, he agreed to collaborate with Beaumarchais in a politically charged divertissement, *Le Couronnement de Tarare,* that celebrates Tarare's coronation and his first acts as king.[27] Beaumarchais took advantage of the occasion to emphasize (probably to exaggerate) the role that *Tarare* had played in encouraging the Revolution. In his preface to the 1790 version of the libretto, dated on the first Bastille Day, he reminded revolutionary operagoers of the original *Tarare:* "Citizens! Remember the time when your disquieted thinkers, forced to disguise their ideas, clothed them in allegories, laboriously prepared the field for the Revolution. After various attempts I cast down—at my own risk and peril—this seed of a civic oak upon the scorched earth of the Opéra. . . . The work has reached its completion in *Le Couronnement de Tarare* in the first year of liberty; we offer it to you on its anniversary. 14 July 1790."[28]

But the political content of *Tarare* was acceptable to a surprisingly large variety of political viewpoints, and it outlasted the Revolution. With a total of 131 performances at the Opéra (the last in 1826) *Tarare* matched *Les Danaïdes* in popularity and staying power. But neither opera achieved the kind of classic status of Sacchini's *Oedipe à Colone,* which remained in the repertory until 1844 and reached an astonishing total of 583 performances.

More French Operas to Come?

The success of *Tarare* further strengthened Salieri's reputation in France. His growing prominence attracted the attention of several librettists who hoped that he would be willing to collaborate with them. Had he stayed in Paris he might have written *Bellérophon, Sappho, Les Phéniciennes,* and *La Princesse de Babylone.*[29]

During the late 1780s the essayist and novelist Isabelle de Charrière sought a composer for her libretto *Les Phéniciennes.* She considered several who had written no French operas (Cimarosa, Martín y Soler, Mozart, Sarti), but she seems to have preferred Salieri. Writing to a friend in January 1789, she mentioned that she had received advice on the suitability of Viennese composers for her project from a Monsieur Stahl (probably Philipp Stahl, a Viennese bureaucrat): "In Vienna M. Stahl knows Salieri and

27. Beatrice Didier, "La Représentation de la Révolution à l'Opéra: Le 'Couronnement de Tarare' de Beaumarchais," in *La Révolution française et les processus de socialisation de l'homme moderne* (Paris, 1989), 627–34; Betzwieser, "Exoticism and Politics." Salieri's glorification of the French Revolution in *Le Couronnement* may well have contributed to the coolness with which Emperor Leopold II, who came to the throne in 1790, treated his Hofkapellmeister.

28. Quoted in the original and in translation (used here) in Betzwieser, "Exoticism and Politics," 93.

29. On *Bellérophon* and *Sappho* see Mosel, 125.

thinks that *Les Phéniciennes* would not fare badly in his hands. If we could cause it to end up there I would be very happy. There are certainly some fine pieces in *Tarare,* and he knows French perfectly. As for Mozart, whom he [i.e., Stahl] also knows, he does not find his genius sufficiently regulated by taste and experience."[30] Whether Charrière contacted Salieri we do not know, but her project, in any case, seems to have come to nothing.

Negotations with Désiré Martin, author of *La Princesse de Babylone,* were more fruitful. Salieri began setting Martin's libretto to music in 1788 or 1789, and several of his letters to the librettist survive. The opera on which they collaborated—or rather an Italian version of it, *Palmira regina di Persia*—was to play an important role in the last phase of Salieri's career as a composer of operas.

By the time of Gluck's death, shortly after Salieri's return to Vienna, Salieri had fulfilled the prediction of Joseph II. He had taken Gluck's place as the Viennese operatic master who could be counted upon to provide the Opéra with a steady supply of well-crafted and at the same time controversial new works. He would probably have continued to occupy this position, traveling back and forth between Vienna and Paris, if the French Revolution had not made it impossible for a loyal subject of the Habsburg monarchy and recipient of Habsburg patronage to write operas for the principal opera house of France. When citizens arrested and later put to death Marie Antoinette, sister of Emperors Joseph and Leopold, and the most important of Salieri's Parisian patrons, they also brought to an end his career as a composer of French opera.

The Composition of *Axur re d'Ormus*

Salieri returned to Vienna sometime before 3 August 1787.[31] The most important operatic event that had occurred during his absence (assuming he left Vienna after the first performance of *Figaro*) was the premiere of Martín y Soler's wildly popular *Una cosa rara* on 17 November 1786. Now that Martín, Mozart, and Salieri (with *La grotta di Trofonio*) had all shown themselves capable of competing with the best composers of opera buffa in Italy, they worked simultaneously in 1787 to follow up their earlier success. Casti's departure from Vienna earlier in 1786 had left Da Ponte as Vienna's only Italian librettist; it was to him that all three of these composers turned in 1787.

Probably intrigued by the commotion that *Tarare* had stirred up in Paris, Joseph commissioned Salieri to produce an Italian version for the opera buffa troupe. The composer set to work with Da Ponte on a translation of Beaumarchais's libretto, but they soon re-

30. Isabelle de Charrière to Jean-Pierre de Chambrier d'Oleyres, 13 Jan 1789, in *Oeuvres complètes,* ed. Jean-Daniel Candaux et al. (Amsterdam, 1979–84), 3:126–28.

31. On 3 August 1787 Gluck wrote to J. C. Vogl in Paris, thanking him for a score brought to Vienna by Salieri; see Swenson, 130.

alized that a simple translation would not work. Mosel continued the story in Salieri's own words:

> The music, written for French singing actors, is everywhere too wanting in melodies for Italian acting singers. Moreover, when the poet was satisfied with his verses, the music—to use Gluck's expression—tasted too much of translation; and when, to satisfy my ear, the text was adapted to the existing music, Da Ponte was displeased with his poetry. In my fear that we might both labor in vain, I decided instead to compose new music to the same material. I therefore asked the poet to draft a new plan for the libretto based on the French original but suited to the Italian opera company, and to distribute the vocal numbers in consultation with me, but to write the verse as he wished; I would see to the rest.[32]

Da Ponte's account of the preparation of *Axur,* unlike Salieri's, placed it within the context of operas by Martín and Mozart:

> Martini, Mozzart, and Salieri . . . came . . . at the same time [probably late summer 1787] to ask me for a libretto. I loved and esteemed all three, and from all of them I hoped for compensation for past failures and some enhancement of my theatrical fame. I wondered whether it might not be possible to satisfy them all and write three operas at a time. . . .
>
> I went to the emperor and laid my idea before him. . . . "You will not succeed," he replied. "Perhaps not," I responded, "but I will try. At night I will write for Mozzart, imagining Dante's *Inferno;* during the morning, for Martini, pretending I am studying Petrarch; in the evening, for Salieri, and he will be my Tasso!" He liked my parallels; and as soon as I returned home I went to work. . . .
>
> The first day . . . I wrote the two first scenes of *Don Giovanni,* two more for *L'arbore di Diana,* and more than half the first act of *Tarar,* whose title I changed to *Assur.* I presented those scenes to the three composers the next morning. They could hardly believe that what they were reading with their own eyes was possible. In sixty-three days the first two operas were completely finished and about two-thirds of the last.
>
> *L'arbore di Diana* was the first to be produced [on 1 October 1787]. . . . This opera had been given only once when I was obliged to leave for Prague, where Mozzart's *Don Giovanni* was given for the first time. . . . but before it went on stage I had to hurry back to Vienna, because of a fiery letter I received from Salieri in which he informed me, truly or not, that *Assur* had to be performed immediately for the wedding of [Archduke] Francis, and that the emperor had ordered him to call me home.
>
> So I returned to Vienna, traveling day and night. . . . I sent for Salieri, and went to work. In two days *Assur* was ready. It was performed; and such was its success that I was long in doubt as to which of the three operas was the most perfect, whether in the music or in the words.[33]

32. Mosel, 129.
33. Da Ponte, 127–32.

During much of the composition of *Axur* an illness kept Salieri at home, out of contact with the emperor. This gave rise to an episode amusingly retold by Mosel:

To hasten the performance, he wrote scene by scene, as Da Ponte brought them to him, and for the time being just the vocal lines with the bass, and sent them to the copyist, so that the singers could rehearse them without delay.

The emperor, who had heard that three acts had been thus copied, but unaware of how Salieri had gone about this work (he was under the impression that it involved only the translation of the French libretto and the underlaying of the Italian text in the already existing music) wanted to hear the completed portions during the customary afternoon concert. He arranged for the original manuscript to be retrieved from the copyist and for the normal musicians to be assembled. The musicians soon noticed that the score contained only the vocal parts, the other staffs (with the exception of some ritornellos, or here and there an indication of the accompaniment) being left empty for the instruments. They communicated this observation to the monarch, who answered: "No matter. We have the engraved score of the French opera; the instruments can be played from it, and the rest of you sing with me at the pianoforte from the Italian manuscript."

In the belief that this would do, each sat down at his place. The emperor, sitting at the pianoforte, began to read: "First act, first scene, duet." The others answered: "The French opera begins with a prologue." "They must have left that out of this translation," answered His Majesty. "Find the first scene." "Here," the musicians answered, "it begins with a dialogue in recitative." "In my score," responded the monarch, "the opera begins with a duet, which serves as the introduction, then an aria and then another small duet." "In ours none of that is to be found," was the answer.

Almost two hours were passed in searching and comparing, without finding anything that was completely in agreement, and the result of all this effort was at most the occasional discovery of a similar musical idea, which was mostly written in a different key, and introduced with an entirely different connection to the rest. Finally the monarch exclaimed with a laugh: "It is enough to drive one mad! What in the world have those two been up to?" He ordered the orchestra director Kreibich, who was always present at these concerts: "Go to Salieri and tell him about the nice comedy that we have put on."

Salieri was able to go to court a few days later.

The kind monarch was hardly aware of his presence when he called to him: "I'm glad to see you back in good health. The day before yesterday you almost brought us to despair with your music. But tell me, why have you so completely changed your beautiful French music?" When Salieri explained the reasons that led him to do so, the emperor not only approved fully of his course of action, but also, after he had heard and praised the Italian opera, bestowed on its composer an imperial reward for the effort he had expended on it.[34]

34. Mosel, 129–31.

The "imperial reward" was the unusually large fee, 200 ducats, that Salieri received for *Axur.*[35]

Axur: Dramaturgy and Music

Neither Salieri nor Da Ponte emphasized sufficiently the extent to which the words and music of *Tarare* survive in *Axur.*[36] From Salieri's statement that he asked Da Ponte "to draft a new plan for the libretto based on the French original but suited to the Italian opera company," one might not guess that much of the libretto of *Axur* is a very close translation of *Tarare.* Nor would his statement that he decided "to compose new music to the same material" lead one to suspect that he transferred several numbers from the one opera to the other with only minor changes, and that many other numbers in *Axur* contain melodic, rhythmic, and accompanimental ideas from *Tarare.*

Da Ponte renamed most of Beaumarchais's characters. King Atar became Axur; Tarare became Atar. In giving the hero the name of the original villain Da Ponte may have been developing a point made by Beaumarchais when he gave his two principal characters names whose anagrammatic relation to one another is so clear. In the prologue to *Tarare* Nature and the Spirit of Fire had more or less randomly made Tarare a lowborn soldier and Atar a king; as if repeating their experiment in reverse, Da Ponte made Atar the soldier. He may have borrowed the name Axur from *Zémire et Azor,* which (as mentioned earlier) takes place partly in Hormuz; in writing of *Axur* in his memoirs Da Ponte referred to it as *Assur.*

Among Da Ponte's most important changes was his elimination of two of the most distinctly French elements of *Tarare* (and elements most incompatible with an opera buffa company): the prologue and the divertissement in act 3, both of which required

35. Edge, "Mozart's Fee," 223.

36. The following discussion is based mainly on an early MS copy of *Axur* (A-Wn, Mus. Hs. 17832), which corresponds very closely to the libretto printed for the first production (Vienna, [1788]). This MS presents the opera in its original five-act version, beginning with the duet "Qui dove scherza l'aura." The autograph score (A-Wn, Mus. Hs. 17049) has been subjected to many revisions, including the addition of a new scene at the beginning of the opera and the joining of acts 1 and 2 into a single act; this required the renumbering of the original acts 3, 4, and 5 as acts 2, 3, and 4. All references to acts in the following discussion will use the original numbering as found in the 1788 libretto and Mus. Hs. 17832.

Among several useful analyses of *Axur* are Michael Louis Raynaud, "A Guide to Antonio Salieri's *Axur re d'Ormus*" (master's thesis, University of Houston, 1992); Della Croce/Blanchetti, 241–46 and 486–90; Paolo Gallarati, "'Axur re d'Ormus': Appunti sulla drammaturgia di Salieri," in *Convegno,* 33–39; and Della Chà, *Lorenzo da Ponte.* For a discussion of the evolution of the opera as reflected in early librettos and scores see Bruno Brizi, "Da Ponte e Salieri," and "Libretto e partiture: A proposito dell' 'Axur re d'Ormus' di Lorenzo da Ponte (Salieri) e del 'Telemaco' di Marco Coltellini (Gluck)," in *L'edizione critica tra testo musicale e testo letterario* (Lucca, 1995), 437–42.

dance. He also omitted the epilogue and its politically suspect conclusion. Da Ponte added a new first act, increased the size of several ensembles already present in *Tarare,* and shifted them to the end of acts, where they serve as finales. These changes had the effect of giving *Axur* something of the shape and character of an opera buffa.

Act 1, instead of beginning (as in *Tarare*) with a conversation in recitative between the king and his eunuch, begins with a duet in which Atar and Aspasia (Beaumarchais's Astasie) happily express their love: "Qui dove scherza l'aura." By calling this duet an introduzione in his autograph score Salieri showed that he understood Da Ponte's change as an incorporation of an opera buffa element. The end of this duet, an open cadence that leads to the following recitative, belongs to a Viennese tradition of open cadences at the end of introduzioni that went back to Gassmann's operas of the late 1760s. That the introduzioni of *Una cosa rara* and *Don Giovanni* also end with transitions to recitative suggests that Viennese composers rediscovered this tradition in the mid-1780s.

The very short first act, which is entirely new, goes on to show Aspasia's abduction by Axur's soldiers. Although the abduction scene is not derived from *Tarare* (except insofar as it dramatizes an episode narrated in Beaumarchais's libretto), it nevertheless makes use of musico-dramatic techniques characteristic of French opera. An offstage chorus singing "Ah" on a diminished seventh chord follows the cannon shot that interrupts the second of the two duets sung by Aspasia and Atar (ex. 12.7). Several musical numbers in *Tarare* are interrupted by unexpected events, reflecting Beaumarchais's assertion of the priority of verbal and dramatic interests over purely musical ones. The chorus in *Tarare* often interacts with soloists, just as it does in Da Ponte's abduction

EXAMPLE 12.7 *Axur re d'Ormus,* act 1, "Per te solo amato bene," mm. 43–53 (A-Wn, Mus. Hs. 17832)

(Continued on next page)

EXAMPLE 12.7 *(continued)*

ASPASIA, ATAR: And may heaven and earth learn to rejoice . . . OFFSTAGE CHORUS: Ah! ATAR: What is this cry? CHORUS: Atar! ATAR: Heavens! A terrible fire spreads around our house!

scene. But the specific idea of an offstage choral "Ah" may have come from *Les Danaïdes* rather than *Tarare.* When, at the end of act 4, the Danaids attack their husbands, all we hear from the men is an offstage chorus that ends with "Ah" on a diminished seventh chord.

In his autograph Salieri provided unusually detailed instructions, illustrated with musical examples, on how the abduction scene is to be performed. He indicated exactly where the firing of a cannon interrupts the duet. After Aspasia sings the words "Salvatemi lo sposo eterni dei,"

> she runs, then stops in an attitude of anxiety to look toward the place where Atar will have exited, and from where one will see, from the moment of the first cries of Atar's slaves, the first signs of fire. In the tenth measure of the music that expresses this disorder, Altamor leaves his hiding place, runs on tiptoes behind Aspasia, covers her with a black cloak, abducts her, and carries her, above the ground, behind the stage at the same place from which he appeared.
>
> The blast made backstage to represent the explosion that causes the fire in Atar's house will be arranged so as to be heard on the beats marked here.

(*Continued on next page*)

EXAMPLE (*continued*)

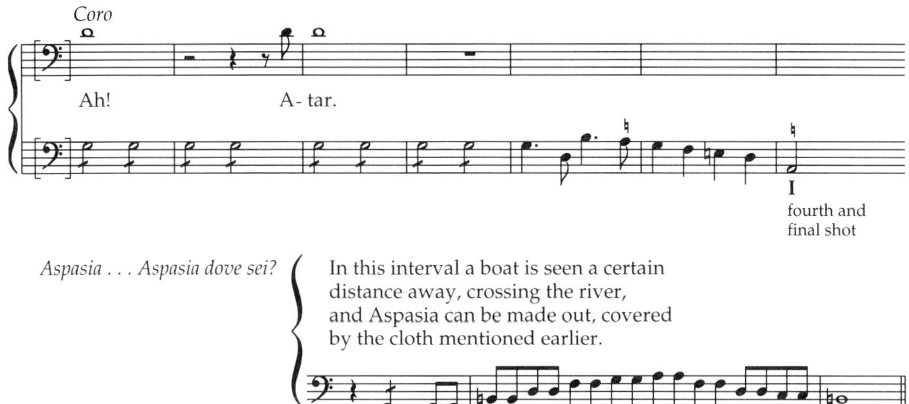

Presentimenti atroci ora v'intendo. Having spoken this verse, in the six measures that follow, the actor must express his desperate indecision, as the music in this place expressly indicates. Then, on the last note, as he remains suspended in an attitude that fits the situation, the signal for the curtain will be given and the act will end.

N.B. The six measures of music that express the above-mentioned pantomime must be played with great force and without strictness of tempo.[37]

Da Ponte replaced Beaumarchais's "fête européenne" with a much shorter commedia dell'arte scene for three characters. He thus preserved the idea of a play within the play as the backdrop against which the chief eunuch begins his autobiographical song. The little comedy (perhaps inspired by the commedia dell'arte scene in Goldoni's *Arcadia in Brenta*) culminates in a three-part canon in Venetian dialect, "All'erta zovenotti." Martín y Soler had composed several roundlike canons in *Una cosa rara.* Viennese audiences must have liked them, because he wrote more in *L'arbore di Diana,* establishing a Viennese tradition of operatic canons to which Salieri, Mozart (in *Così fan tutte*), and later Ferdinando Paer and Beethoven contributed.[38] Salieri took advantage of the commedia dell'arte scene to compose what seems to have been his first extensive operatic canon, a delightful comic number.[39]

Salieri found instrumental music easiest to transfer from *Tarare* to *Axur.* Not only the colorful "Turkish" overture of *Tarare* (see exx. 12.2, 12.3) but also the fine march in A minor and a marchlike instrumental piece in A major in act 3 of *Tarare* reappear in *Axur* (acts 3 and 4, respectively) with only a few differences in orchestrational detail.

37. Transcribed in Brizi, "Il *Parere* di Salieri sull'*Axur re d'Ormus,*" 229.

38. Winton Dean, "Italian Opera," in *NOHM,* 8:401; and Dorothea Link, "The Viennese Operatic Canon and Mozart's *Così fan tutte,*" *Mitteilungen der Internationalen Stiftung Mozarteum* 38 (1990): 111–21.

39. For an excerpt of this canon see John A. Rice, "The Operas of Antonio Salieri as a Reflection of Viennese Opera, 1770–1800," in *Music in Eighteenth-Century Austria,* ed. David Wyn Jones (Cambridge, 1996), 213.

The instrumentally accompanied pantomime that follows the interruption of Biscroma's autobiographical song in act 4 of *Axur* is almost identical to the music in the analogous moment in *Tarare* (act 3).

Salieri transferred only a few vocal numbers without major changes. One of these is the short dialogue between Tarare and chorus in which he urges the people to follow him into battle. "Chi vuol la gloria, alla vittoria vola con me" (*Axur,* act 3) differs from "Qui veut la gloire à la victoire vole avec moi" only in requiring a chorus in four parts (SATB) instead of three (ATB). The final chorus of *Axur,* "Qual piacer la nostr'anima ingombra" differs from the final chorus in *Tarare* (before the epilogue), "Quel plaisir de nos coeurs s'empare!" mainly in key; Salieri transposed this chorus down from D major to C, one of many downward transpositions made in the process of transforming *Tarare* into *Axur.* Even when transposed the sustained high soprano part in this final chorus looks forward to Beethoven's choral writing. Beethovenian too is Salieri's harmony, especially his sudden move to the dominant of the dominant.[40]

In other numbers Salieri used elements of his previous setting but developed them and combined them differently. Biscroma's short song in act 2 of *Axur,* "È ben ver, quel nome amato," begins with the same triadic idea as Calpigi's "Il est vrai, son nom adoré" but then moves in a different direction (exx. 12.8, 12.9). The chorus "Ne' più vaghi sog-

EXAMPLE 12.8 *Tarare,* act 1, "Il est vrai, son nom adoré," mm. 1–6 (sc. 1, mm. 96–101)

It is true: his beloved name is a proverb spoken by everyone with reverence.

EXAMPLE 12.9 *Axur,* act 2, "È ben ver, quel nome amato," mm. 1–4

It is true: that beloved name is the delight of every heart.

40. For an excerpt see Rice, "The Operas of Antonio Salieri," 219.

giorni dell'Asie" (*Axur,* act 2) begins differently from "Dans les plus beaux lieux de l'Asie," but later in the Italian chorus a striking unison passage using the "Turkish" raised fourth is clearly derived from the analogous chorus in *Tarare* (exx. 12.10, 12.11).

EXAMPLE 12.10 *Tarare,* act 1, "Dans les plus beaux lieux de l'Asie," mm. 22–26

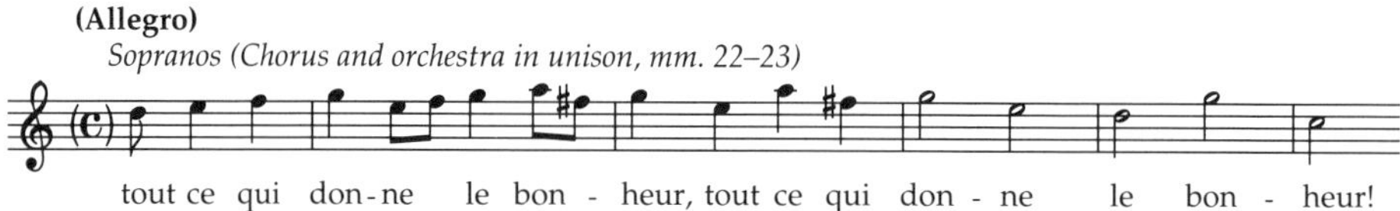

Everything that gives happiness!

EXAMPLE 12.11 *Axur,* act 2, "Ne' più vaghi soggiorni dell'Asia," mm. 23–31

Amid the brilliance of royal grandeur, wealth, and perfect pleasure!

Atar's "Soave luce di Paradiso" (act 2) derives its A-B-A form, a rhythmic idea (a group of four sixteenth notes on the third beat of the measure), and its accompaniment of clarinets, bassoons, and horns from Tarare's "Astasie est une déesse." In the B section the interaction of voice and wind instruments produces music of extraordinary beauty that perfectly matches the words (ex. 12.12).

"Soave luce" is one of many examples of the transfer of orchestrational ideas from *Tarare* to *Axur.* The same Turkish instruments (always without piccolo) sound in both operas. Salieri's colorful use of timpani in *Tarare* is echoed, on a smaller scale, in *Axur.* The great funeral chorus in act 5 of *Tarare* (see ex. 12.6) is reduced in *Axur* to an eight-measure orchestral fragment, but Salieri preserved its most distinctive feature: the constant drumroll and the tremolo in the basses and cellos.[41]

The trombones that contribute to the religious formality of the temple scene in act 3 of *Tarare* reappear in the Salieri's autograph score of *Axur,* but their parts are crossed

41. Della Croce/Blanchetti, 396.

PLATE 1 Costume designs by F. A. Lohrmann for Wojciech Bogusławski's production of *Axur re d'Ormus* in Polish, Warsaw, 1793: Arteneo, high priest of Brahma, and Elamir, a boy through whom Brahma reveals his will, in act 3. (Courtesy of Warsaw University Library.)

PLATE 2 Costume design by F. A. Lohrmann for Wojciech Bogusławski's production of *Axur re d'Ormus* in Polish, Warsaw, 1793: Urson, captain of the guards, about to arrest Atar near the end of act 4. (Courtesy of Warsaw University Library.)

EXAMPLE 12.12 *Axur,* act 2, "Soave luce di Paradiso," mm. 11–23

(Continued on next page)

out. Axur's aria "Idol vano d'un popol codardo," in act 5, uses several elements of Atar's aria "Fantôme vain": the key of B minor, some melodic material, and the tempo Allegro assai. The autograph shows that Salieri originally preserved the French opera's three trombones but later crossed them out and replaced them with two horns in D. A manuscript of *Axur* that probably represents an early version of the opera (earlier than some

EXAMPLE 12.12 *(continued)*

Her glances and gestures seemed to come from heaven; the sweet sound of her dear voice filled my heart with happiness.

of the revisions in the autograph)[42] has no trombone parts, suggesting that Salieri eliminated them very early in the opera's history, probably after the first run of performances. (Because the Burgtheater had no full-time trombonists, their participation in-

42. A-Wn Mus. Hs. 17832.

volved extra expense.) The trombone parts in Mozart's *Don Giovanni* probably suffered the same fate when that opera reached the stage of the Burgtheater later in 1788.[43]

In creating an opera for Joseph's opera buffa troupe, Da Ponte and Salieri gave buffo elements a prominent place; one can see this not only in the incorporation of an introduzione and finales, but also in characterization. Librettist and composer tended to emphasize those aspects of character closest to what is typical of opera buffa. King Axur is more of a caricature than Beaumarchais's King Atar; he is a buffo tyrant, less threatening than Atar. Salieri probably wrote the part for Benucci, who certainly sang it later.[44] In his annotations he described Axur as "a ferocious man, without scruples. He will be dressed *alla turca,* if desired. The costume must be splendid, but with a combination of colors that serves as much as possible to characterize a tyrant."[45]

Biscroma (Beaumarchais's Calpigi), a former musico, was already a source of some humor in *Tarare;* Da Ponte took this humor much further, especially in scenes in which Biscroma interacts with Axur. Salieri described him as "always a buffoon when he speaks to the king, and also when he pleads; but at heart honest and sensible, and, out of gratitude to Atar, very much concerned about his interests."

If Axur and Biscroma have something of the buffo caricato in them, Atar has something of the mezzo carattere. Calvesi probably created the role of Atar, of whom Salieri wrote: "He will be nobly dressed, but without extravagance. His part is a mixture of the heroic and the sensitive. Everything that he sings, whether pathetic or sweet, must always have a foundation of energy so as not to descend to the effeminate, which would greatly weaken this beautiful role."

One way in which Da Ponte and Salieri changed an opera written for singing actors into one for acting singers—and specifically comic singers—was to transform recitative into ensembles. For example, the opening dialogue in recitative for Atar and Calpigi with which act 1 of *Tarare* begins became the duet for Axur and Biscroma, "Non mi seccar, Biscroma," at the beginning of act 2 of *Axur.* For an eighteenth-century audience

43. The account book for the theatrical year 1787–88 records the payment of 21 Gulden to the trombonist Johann Adelmann "and other musicians for extra duty in the opera *Axur, re d'Ormus*" (HHStA, GH, Rechnungsbuch 1787). The document is quoted in Edge, "Mozart's Viennese Orchestras," 77–78, 87, which notes that *Axur* "was performed a total of seven times before the end of the season. . . . the payment to Adelmann of 21 Gulden was obviously intended to compensate three trombonists for seven performances." Edge points out that payment records for the theatrical year 1788–89, when *Don Giovanni* as well as *Axur* was performed, make no mention of payments to trombonists and that the Burgtheater's performance score of *Don Giovanni* has no trombone parts. From this and other evidence he concludes persuasively: "it seems virtually certain that trombones were not used in the Burgtheater in the season 1788/9, either in *Axur* or in *Don Giovanni.*"

44. We do not know the original cast of *Axur* with certainty. Michtner, 244, gives a cast list, but cites no evidence for it. The source for most of his list was probably a copy of the libretto for the first production in A-Wn, in which the singers are identified in pencil by an unknown hand. The role of Axur is attributed to Benucci, that of Atar to Calvesi, and that of Aspasia to Luisa Laschi Mombelli. My thanks to Dorothea Link for sharing with me her research on the original cast.

45. This and the following passages are transcribed in Brizi, "Il *Parere* di Salieri sull'*Axur re d'Ormus,*" 230.

a duet for two men, one of them a eunuch, could hardly have been anything but comic. Salieri emphasized the comedy by traditional means: he chose the buffo-caricato key of D major, duple meter, and disjunct melodic lines that often double the bass. Da Ponte and Salieri treated the dialogue between Calpigi and Atar at the beginning of act 3 of *Tarare* in much the same way: they turned it into another comic duet, "Non borbotto, parlo schietto." One finds the same kind of comic interaction between master and servant in the duet for Don Giovanni and Leporello at the beginning of the second act of Mozart's opera.[46]

Yet *Axur* is no opera buffa. Da Ponte and Salieri preserved much of the spectacle of Beaumarchais's drama. Their extensive use of chorus and their preference for orchestrally accompanied over simple recitative (though simple recitative is not excluded entirely) point to the work's origins at the Opéra and differentiate it from the other operas written for Joseph's company. So do the several numbers in minor mode, including pieces in the unusual keys of A minor and B minor taken directly from *Tarare.* Audiences may have sometimes laughed at Benucci's portrayal of Axur, especially when he interacted with Biscroma; but they also admired the seriousness that Benucci brought to the role. A critic later wrote of him: "I would not have believed that, in spite of being a comedian, he portrays Salieri's Axur in quite a serious style."[47] *Axur* fully deserves the generic categorization that Da Ponte and Salieri gave it: "dramma tragicomico." Mosel alluded to its more serious qualities when he praised it as "the most excellent of all serious Italian operas—even including Mozart's *La clemenza di Tito.*"[48]

Axur as Political Opera: Imperial Wedding, War with Turkey, and Rebellion in the Netherlands

Axur was first performed in the Burgtheater on 8 January 1788, in celebration of the marriage of Archduke Francis, Joseph's nephew and the future emperor. Joseph and his family were present, and free admission insured a full house and contributed to a festive atmosphere.[49] Simultaneously, at the Kärntnertor, the German troupe performed Favart's *Soliman second.* The concurrence of these oriental dramas on such an important occasion could hardly have been accidental. At a time when diplomatic relations between the monarchy and the Ottoman Empire were steadily deteriorating, Joseph must have hoped that unflattering depictions of Middle Eastern despots in *Axur* and *Soliman* would strengthen the public's support for the war against Turkey that he was to declare almost exactly a month later.

46. Della Croce/Blanchetti, 489. Both Axur and Don Giovanni say "Non mi seccar."

47. "Italienische Theatermusik in Wien," 138–39; in Rice, "Emperor," 442.

48. Mosel, 113. Uncomfortable with this statement, he qualified it: "be it well understood, only as a dramatic musical work, not as vocal composition in a larger sense."

49. *WZ,* 9 January 1788.

As in his adaptation of Beaumarchais's *Le Mariage de Figaro,* Da Ponte toned down the political rhetoric of *Tarare* in transforming it into *Axur.*[50] In the last act of *Tarare* the soldiers who enter to rescue their hero are ready to kill the king if he has had Tarare executed. Despite Tarare's plea that they respect the king's person and position, when Atar asks for a show of support ("suis-je encore votre roi?") only a single eunuch comes to his aid; the rest declare Tarare their king. Atar stabs himself, saying to Tarare as he dies:

La mort est moin dure à mes yeux . . .
Que de regner par toi . . . sur un peuple odieux.

[Death is less hard in my eyes . . . than to rule through you . . . over a hateful people.]

Da Ponte altered the scene crucially by eliminating even the ideas of regicide and deposition. The soldiers who rescue Atar have no intention of overthrowing or killing Axur, who never asks if he is still their king. He abdicates of his own free will, throwing his crown to the ground before stabbing himself. Only after his suicide do the people declare Atar their king.

One part of *Tarare* was eliminated by Da Ponte for both political and structural reasons. Calpigi's aria at the end of act 4, in which he angrily berates kings who abuse their power, would have made Viennese censors nervous had they seen it. Da Ponte got rid of an inflammatory political statement and brought *Axur* closer to opera buffa by replacing the aria with a finale that incorporates some text and music from scenes in *Tarare* immediately preceding Calpigi's aria.

Yet Da Ponte left enough politics that operagoers could draw parallels between the opera and real life, and not only in regard to Turkey. Count Ferdinand Trauttmansdorff, Joseph's minister in charge of the Austrian Netherlands, could not resist an allusion to *Axur* when giving the emperor political advice. Having temporarily suppressed a rebellion in 1789, he urged Joseph to treat the rebels leniently. He referred to the end of *Axur,* where Atar commands his soldiers to put down weapons raised against the king, and intercedes on their behalf. Trauttmansdorff saw himself as Atar (whom he mistakenly referred to as "Tarrare"), Joseph as Axur, and the rebellious Belgians as Axur's soldiers: "Today I would like to venture to say, like Tarrare in Axure: 'Or che sono sommessi / Pietà e perdono chiedo per essi' [Now that they have submitted, I ask you to show them mercy and to pardon them]. Your Majesty's sovereignty will be restored with an authority much less constricted than that of all your august predecessors.

50. Jacques Joly, "Riscrittura di melodrammi per Salieri e Cherubini: Tarare/Axur e Demofoonte/Démophoon," in Muraro, *Mozart,* 1:241–72; and Jacques Joly, "Un fol opéra: 'Tarare' de Beaumarchais et Salieri," in *Les Ecrivains français et l'Opéra* (Cologne, 1986), 95–108.

May Your Majesty deign to be once again the father of a nation seduced into an evil it had not dreamed of committing!"[51]

"This Magnificent Work"

Axur was an immediate and lasting success. Joseph's favorite opera[52] found favor with the Viennese public as well. With a hundred performances between 1788 and 1805, it was one of the most often performed operas in the Viennese court theaters during this period.[53] Many performances in Germany, mostly in translation, attest to the opera's popularity. A member of the audience in Frankfurt in 1790 called *Axur* "un opéra tout à fait charmant et plein d'intrigue."[54] The philosopher Friedrich Schleiermacher was delighted by a performance in Berlin in 1798.[55] An enthusiastic—though not entirely positive—review of a production in Berlin in 1791 helps to explain the enduring popularity of *Axur* among German opera lovers:

> The music is full of the most beautiful strokes of genius and fine individual effects. There are numbers and passages in it that surpass everything else that is known of Salieri. . . . But in particular several of the scenes in which Salieri's masterful music strengthens the effect produced by the poet's well-chosen situations made an indescribable impression on the viewer. The temple scenes in the second act may be cited as an example. The effect of this music could only be felt, not described; and one could rightly place it among the best of its kind, if it were not here and there a little too rhapsodic. Occasionally one wishes one could follow a fine idea somewhat further; and even at the moment when that wish arises one is carried forward to something else.[56]

The young E. T. A. Hoffmann, whose warm praise of *Axur* (based on a production in Königsberg in 1795) was quoted in the introduction to this book, was clearly not alone

51. Trauttmansdorff to Joseph, 3 March 1789, in *Geheime Correspondenz Josefs II. mit seinem Minister in den Österreichischen Niederlanden Ferdinand Grafen Trauttmansdorff, 1787–1789,* ed. Hanns Schlitter (Vienna, 1902), 215.

52. "Salieri's *Axur, Rè d'Ormus* war sein Lieblingsoper" ("Auszug eines Schreibens aus Wien," in Angermüller, *Leben,* 3:57).

53. Hadamowsky, *Hoftheater,* 1:13.

54. Count Ludwig von Bentheim-Steinfurt, quoted in Angermüller, *Leben,* 2:200.

55. Schleiermacher to his sister Charlotte, Berlin, 25 July–16 August 1798, in *Briefwechsel 1796–1798,* ed. Andreas Arndt and Wolfgang Virmond (Berlin, 1988), 371.

56. Die Musik ist voll der schönsten Geniezüge, und treflicher einzelner Effekte. Es giebt Sätze und Stellen darinnen, die selbst alles, was man sonst von *Salieri* kennt, zurücklassen. . . . Besonders aber in den Scenen, in welchen die meisterhafte Musik eines *Salieri* die Würkung verstärkte, welche die wohlgewählten Situationen des Dichters hervorbrachten, war der Eindruck unbeschreiblich, den verschiedene derselben auf den Zuschauer machten: worunter als Beispiel vorzüglich die Scenen im Tempel, im zweiten Act, anzuführen sind. Überhaupt machte diese Musik einen Effekt, der sich nur empfinden, nicht beschreiben lässt; und man könnte sie füglich unter die ersten in ihrer Art rechnen, wenn sie nicht hie und da ein wenig

in finding much to admire in Salieri's opera, which won applause not only in Germany but in Prague, Budapest, Moscow, Paris, Lisbon, and Rio de Janeiro.[57]

Axur played an unexpected role in the establishment of a tradition of Polish grand opera. Before the 1790s opera in Polish was mostly limited to spoken plays with music. For more sophisticated operatic entertainment Poles had to depend on visits by Domenico Guardasoni's opera troupe from Prague, which performed several Italian operas in Warsaw, including *Axur,* in 1790. Three years later Wojciech Bogusławski, a singer, playwright, translator, and impresario who is sometimes called the father of Polish theater, assembled a company of Polish singers with the aim of presenting operas in Polish, but matching the musical richness of the Italian operas offered by Guardasoni. For his company's debut Bogusławski prepared an elaborate production of *Axur,* which he remembered vividly in his history of the Polish National Theater.[58]

Bogusławski's production is recorded in costume designs in watercolor by Fryderyk Antonii Lohrmann (title page, plates 1 and 2, and fig. 12.2*a–c*), which represent a valuable source of information about how *Axur* looked in Warsaw's National Theater, and

FIGURE 12.2
Costume designs by F. A. Lohrmann for Wojciech Bogusławski's production of *Axur re d'Ormus* in Polish, Warsaw, 1793. A, Axur; B, Semira (probably Fiammetta); C, Atar. (Courtesy of Warsaw University Library.)

A

(*Continued on next page*)

zu rhapsodisch wäre. Man wünscht zuweilen einen vortreflichen Gedanken etwas länger verfolgen zu können; und in eben dem Augenblick, in welchem dieser Wunsch entsteht, ist man auch schon wieder zu etwas anderm mit fortgerissen (*Musikalisches Wochenblatt* [Berlin], 1791, p. 5).

57. Angermüller, *Leben,* 2:199–204.

58. Wojciech Bogusławski, *Dzieie Teatru Narodowego* (Warsaw, 1820; reprint, Warsaw, 1965), 75. I am grateful to Andrei Grabiec for translating this passage.

FIGURE 12.2 *(continued)*

B

C

how it might have looked as it charmed audiences in the other theaters of central and Eastern Europe, including those of Vienna. Salieri's instructions for Axur's costume—"with a combination of colors that serves . . . to characterize a tyrant"—finds realization in Lohrmann's watercolor. Axur wears a long-sleeved tunic of green, fringed with white or silver; his red breeches are fringed with gold; over a white, short-sleeved vest embroidered with red, he wears a fur-trimmed crimson cape; atop his jewel-studded turban are feathers of black and red. By dressing Atar, in contrast, in an outfit of white and sky blue, Lohrmann left us with an idea of what Salieri might have meant when he wrote that Atar "will be nobly dressed, but without extravagance."

Axur inspired Polish librettists and composers, according to an anonymous article (possibly by Bogusławski himself) that appeared in the *Allgemeine musikalische Zeitung* in 1812. It attributed to Salieri (by way of *Axur*) an important place in the history of Polish opera: "Also in the same year [1793] Salieri's *König Axur* was given for the first time in Polish, with great splendor and real propriety, and in the same form as this magnificent work was written by the composer in Italian (with all the recitatives and continuous accompaniment). . . . From this production one can date Polish grand opera; and thus Salieri has earned special praise from us: he must always be remembered gratefully in the history of musical culture in Poland."[59]

59. "Die Oper der Polen," *AmZ* 14 (1812): cols. 323–31; quoted in Swenson, 230.

13

DA PONTE, FERRARESE, AND HOFKAPELLMEISTER SALIERI

Having declared war on the Ottoman Empire in February 1788, Joseph was absent from Vienna for much of 1788, leading his army against the Turks. During the campaign he fell seriously ill, and this illness affected his management of the opera buffa troupe. In August 1789 Salieri referred to Joseph's poor health in explaining to the French librettist Martin why he had made little progress on *La Princesse de Babylone:* "Add to all this the state of uncertainty in which we have been here in Vienna because of the emperor's long and terrible illness; after eight months he is only now beginning to give us hope, if not of a complete recovery, at least of a partial one that will preserve him for a few years in the love of his subjects." [1]

Shortly before leaving for the front in 1788 Joseph had rewarded Salieri with a position he had long expected, that of Hofkapellmeister, which Joseph Bonno had occupied rather ineffectually since Gassmann's death in 1774. Salieri took his new duties seriously. In return for the salary and prestige that came with his position, he devoted increasing time and energy to the administration of the *Hofkapelle* (the court chapel's musical forces) and to the composition and conducting of church music.

Having depended throughout his career on Joseph's goodwill and found encouragement in the emperor's enthusiastic admiration, Salieri was strongly affected by his patron's prolonged absence and precarious health, and by the uncertain future of Viennese opera. Faced, moreover, with the new responsibilities that came with his promotion, he found it difficult to repeat his earlier operatic success.

During the last two years of Joseph's reign (February 1788–February 1790) Salieri

1. Salieri to Désiré Martin, Vienna, 16 August 1789, in Angermüller, *Leben,* 3:52, and Angermüller, *Fatti,* 127–28.

completed four operas and abandoned another, *La scola degli amanti,* after having just begun to compose it. Of the four complete operas one, *Cublai, gran kan de Tartari,* was never performed. Two of those that reached the stage, *Il talismano* and *La cifra,* were based on earlier works. Only *Il pastor fido* was a setting of a newly written libretto, but even it shared its overture with an earlier opera.

That a composer as well connected as Salieri, at the height of his career, should complete an opera that went unperformed is extraordinary; such a thing had never happened to him before (except in the case of his student work, *La vestale*). The eighteenth-century composer almost always wrote an opera for a specific cast, with the understanding that a production was forthcoming. The failure of *Cublai* to reach performance suggests that Salieri, despite his recent successes, had momentarily lost touch with those who were making decisions in the Burgtheater.[2]

He seems also to have momentarily lost touch with public taste. *Il pastor fido* did not please. Salieri withdrew it after a few performances, revised it, and presented it again; but again it failed.

Salieri as Hofkapellmeister and the Reorganization of the Hofkapelle

It was probably the success of *Axur* that prompted Joseph to take action that finally placed Salieri in the most prestigious and lucrative musical post in Vienna. On 12 February 1788, a little more than a month after the premiere of *Axur* (and only four days after declaring war on Turkey), Joseph directed his Obersthofmeister Prince Starhemberg to arrange for Bonno's retirement at full pay, and he named Salieri to replace Bonno as Hofkapellmeister.[3] Starhemberg's decree concerning Bonno's retirement went into effect on 1 March, on which date, presumably, Salieri became Hofkapellmeister. Court documents are inconsistent on the date of Salieri's promotion. Some give 1 March 1788; others 29 March.[4] Bonno's death shortly thereafter, on 15 April, confirmed the transfer of authority. Salieri, only thirty-eight years old, had reached the pinnacle of Viennese musical life.

Bonno's main responsibility as Hofkapellmeister was church music; but the emperor had let the court chapel's musical staff deteriorate to the point where, at the beginning of 1788, Bonno oversaw only a small chorus and orchestra. This was soon to change. Salieri's promotion was part of a thorough reorganization of the Hofkapelle overseen by Joseph during the winter of 1787–88, the effects of which can be seen by comparing

2. On the libretto of *Cublai* see Muresu, *Le occasioni di un libertino,* 171–80, and Della Croce/Blanchetti, 252–57; on the music, Della Croce/Blanchetti, 490–91.

3. HHStA, OMeA, Prot. 46 (1788–89).

4. According to payment records in HKA, Hofzahlamtsbücher no. 184, fol. 159r, Salieri became Hofkapellmeister on 1 March 1788; but according to no. 185, p. 114, he became Hofkapellmeister on 29 March.

a list of musical personnel at the end of 1787 to a list made up only a few months later.[5] In 1787 Bonno presided over a chorus of sixteen, consisting of one "sopranist" (presumably a musico), eight choirboys, one "altist," three tenors, and three basses; and an orchestra of four "violins" (which presumably included at least one viola), two cellos, two double basses, two organists, and one trombonist. At the end of the list Joseph's chamber musicians have been added in another hand: four string players, the wind octet engaged by Joseph in 1782, and two composers, Mozart and Salieri.

The decree announcing Mozart's appointment in December 1787 refers to the position as that of *Kammermusikus.*[6] In court payment records he is variously referred to as Kammermusicus and Compositor.[7] He was both: as Kammercompositor he belonged to a group of court musicians, mostly instrumentalists, known as the Kammermusici or the Kammermusik. Mozart's post was similar to the one given Salieri in 1774, although it does not seem to have required him to perform in the emperor's chamber-music sessions. For a few months, from December 1787 to Salieri's promotion to the post of Hofkapellmeister in March 1788, the two composers were both among Joseph's Kammermusici. Mozart received a salary (800 Gulden) almost twice as high as that of Salieri (416 Gulden, 40 Kreuzer), who also received an annual salary of 853 Gulden, 20 Kreuzer as music director of the court theaters.

By the end of 1788 Salieri, who continued to receive his theatrical salary, had added to it the Hofkapellmeister's salary of 1,200 Gulden. He presided over a much larger Kapelle than his predecessor. Ignaz Umlauf occupied a newly created (or newly filled) position as Salieri's substitute. The addition of two tenors (including the former opera star Adamberger) and two basses had increased the size of the chorus to twenty (assuming the number of choirboys, not mentioned in the list, remained at eight). The orchestra had been greatly enlarged with the addition of several violins and violas, as well as the incorporation of the oboes and bassoons previously listed as Kammermusici. Salieri's promotion left Mozart as Joseph's only Kammercompositor.

Da Ponte's Rise and Joseph's Withdrawal from the Theater

No person was more closely connected to the development of a distinctive kind of Viennese comic opera during the life of Joseph's Italian troupe than Da Ponte. Having come to Vienna shortly before the arrival of Joseph's Italian singers, he left a year after Joseph's death, his dismissal by Leopold II one of the necessary first steps in the new emperor's transformation of Viennese opera.

5. HHStA, OKäA, Akten 1788, no. 100.

6. *MDL,* 269–71.

7. HKA, Hofzahlamtsbücher no. 184, fol. 159r; no. 185, p. 114; no. 186, p. 128.

Casti's departure from Vienna in May 1786 left Da Ponte without poetic rivals. Salieri, Mozart, and Martín had no choice but to collaborate with him if they wanted to see their operas performed in the Burgtheater. Between 1786 and 1789 Salieri set to music four librettos written or arranged by Da Ponte, but only one by Casti; and his setting of *Cublai* did not come to performance. Da Ponte's prestige was enhanced further by his participation in a successful effort to persuade Joseph to reconsider his decision to dismiss the buffa troupe.

Joseph spent much of the spring and summer of 1788 in Semlin (Serbian Semun, just north of Belgrade), from which he directed military operations against the Turks. Disease spread quickly through the Austrian camp. An attack of influenza kept Joseph confined to his quarters for three days in May. He may never have completely recovered. Writing to his brother Leopold in April 1789, he mentioned "the indisposition that has tormented me for the last nine months." [8] The illness that led eventually to his death in February 1790 thus began in July 1788, the very month in which he announced his intention to disband the opera buffa troupe.

Prolonged absence from Vienna, illness, and war did not keep Joseph from managing the theater, but they did finally kill the pleasure that it had given him. His letters from Semlin reveal a man tired of theatrical intrigues and frivolities and fed up with the enormous expenditures that the theater required. One cannot find a single glimmer of enthusiasm in Joseph's reactions to Rosenberg's theatrical news. The emperor's only well-documented comment about Mozart's operatic music—"The music of Mozard is very difficult for the voice" [9]—is no more negative than his other comments about opera in the letters from Semlin, which together represent a sad conclusion to his active contribution to Viennese opera.

Already in May 1788, reacting to Rosenberg's news that the theatrical year had begun badly, Joseph mentioned the possibility of temporarily discontinuing the production of opera buffa. He insisted on not giving in to the salary demands of Nancy Storace, who had left the troupe at the end of the theatrical year 1786, even if it meant losing a chance to bring her back from London. He ordered Rosenberg to dismiss Celeste Coltellini, who had recently returned to Vienna, at the end of the theatrical year. The letter differs greatly in tone from those that he wrote from Italy about the same singers four years earlier: "The poor success of the opera does not surprise me. Only novelty is valued in Vienna; and if one gave them a year of operatic abstinence, I think that would be the only way to win appreciation for a company much more mediocre than the one that now exists." [10]

8. l'incommodité qui déja depuis 9 mois me tourmente (Joseph to Leopold, 16 April 1789, HHStA, HP, Bd. 5, p. 250).

9. Joseph to Rosenberg, Semlin, 16 May 1788, in *Joseph II*, 75. Joseph's comment must be in reaction to a report by Rosenberg of the Viennese production of *Don Giovanni* (first performance on 7 May 1788).

10. Joseph to Rosenberg, Semlin, 3 May [1788], in *Joseph II*, 74.

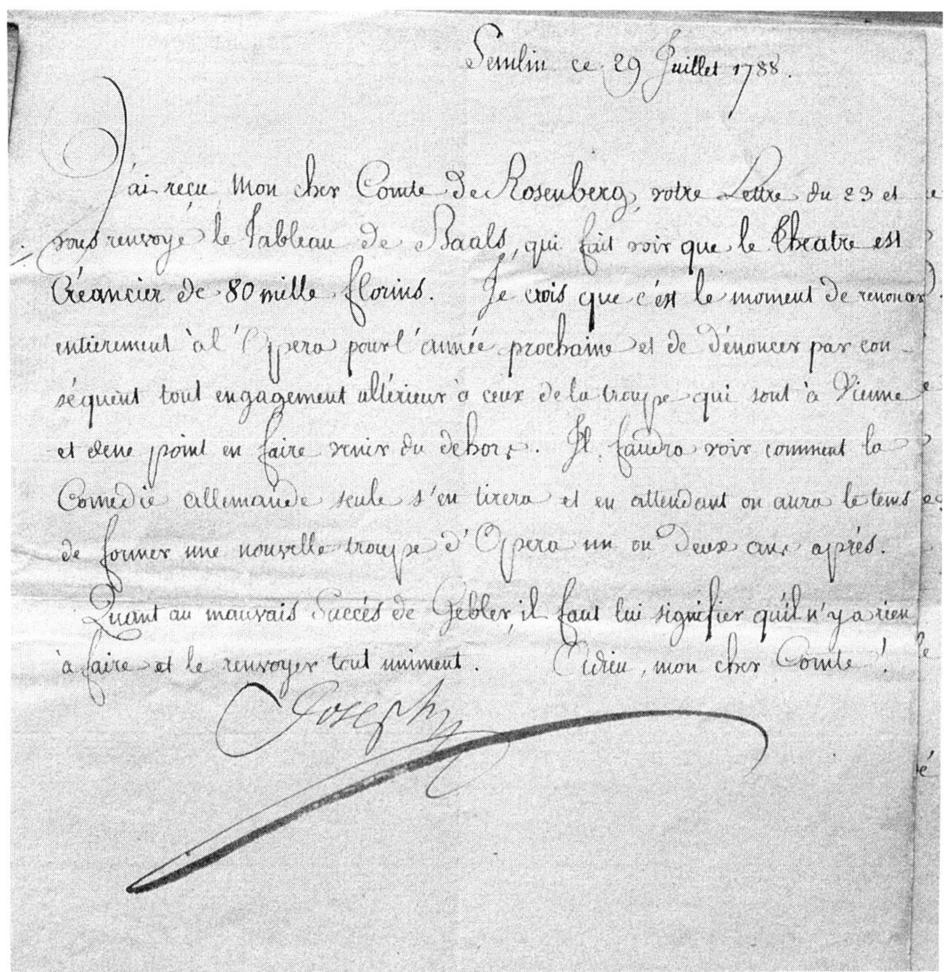

Semlin ce 29 Juillet 1788.

J'ai reçu mon cher Comte de Rosenberg, votre Lettre du 23 et vous renvoye le Tableau de Baals, qui fait voir que le Theatre est Créancier de 80 mille florins. Je crois que c'est le moment de renoncer entierement à l'Opera pour l'année prochaine et de dénoncer par conséquent tout engagement ultérieur à ceux de la troupe qui sont à Vienne et de ne point en faire venir du dehors. Il faudra voir comment la Comédie allemande seule s'en tirera et en attendant on aura le tems de former une nouvelle troupe d'Opera un ou deux ans aprés.

Quant au mauvais Succés de Gebler, il faut lui signifier qu'il n'y a rien à faire et le renvoyer tout uniment. Adieu, mon cher Comte!

Joseph

FIGURE 13.1 Letter from Joseph II to Rosenberg, Semlin, 29 July 1788, announcing his decision to dismiss the opera buffa troupe. Rosenberg papers, Kärntner Landesarchiv, Klagenfurt.

Rosenberg must have mentioned the possibility of engaging the soprano Adriana Ferrarese, because on 14 July the emperor, as pessimistic as always, wrote: "La Ferraresi will surely not please at all."[11] And a week later: "As far as I remember Ferraresi, she has a very weak contralto voice, she knows music very well, but has an ugly appearance."[12] In the same letter he alluded again to the possibility of a dismissal of the whole company, "not knowing if the opera will exist then [1790]."

Finally, on 29 July, Joseph announced his decision to dissolve the troupe, citing a document prepared by the court accountant Daniel Baals (fig. 13.1): "I received, my

11. Joseph to Rosenberg, 14 July 1788, in *Joseph II,* 80.

12. Joseph to Rosenberg, Semlin, 26 July 1788, in *Joseph II,* 81.

dear Count, your letter of the 23rd and send you Baals's table, which shows that the theater is 80,000 Gulden in debt. I believe that this is the time to abandon opera entirely for next year and consequently to cancel all engagements beyond those of the troupe which is now in Vienna and to bring no others from elsewhere. It will be necessary to see how the German theatrical troupe will draw by itself and to wait one or two years before forming a new opera troupe."[13]

Rosenberg passed this letter on to his secretary and assistant opera director, Johann Thorwart, according to Da Ponte's account of what happened next:

> Thorwart, vice-director of the theater and mortal enemy of the Italians, came in great glee to the opera rehearsal and read a letter written from the field to the Count Director, which ordered him peremptorily to say to each of us that at the end of that season His Majesty intended to close the Italian theater.
>
> This news saddened the whole city, all the singers, and at least one hundred other persons—what with musicians, stage lighters, extras, costumers, painters, stage hands, and so on, who derived support for themselves and their families from that establishment. Into my head came the ambitious thought of making the emperor change his mind.[14]

Da Ponte went on to describe his elaborate scheme to save the troupe (and his own job), involving the creation of a permanent fund that would guarantee the opera's financial security.

On Joseph's return to Vienna Da Ponte went to him immediately:

> As soon as he saw me, he led me to his office and asked how the theater was going. "Sire, the theater could not go worse." "What? Why?" "Because we are all in despair at having to leave our adored patron this September." And as I spoke the words some tears fell from my eyes. This he noticed; and with a kindness not to be described in words, he said: "No, you will not lose him!" "But if the theater ceases to exist, how many people, how many families, will perish?"[15]

Da Ponte presented his plan to Joseph, who only glanced at it, according to the librettist, before approving it and reversing his decision to disband the troupe.

Salieri left an account of the episode that makes no mention of Da Ponte. He wrote Martin in Paris that the end of opera buffa had represented for him an opportunity to compose *La Princesse de Babylone:*

13. Joseph to Rosenberg, Semlin, 29 July 1788, in *Joseph II,* 81. My thanks to Dr. Bernd Samobor, librarian of the Haus-, Hof- und Staatsarchiv, for identifying Daniel Baals as an accountant who held various financial positions at the Viennese court from 1769 to 1818.

14. Da Ponte, 132.

15. Da Ponte, 132–33.

> The emperor had ordered that the Italian opera be disbanded for this year [i.e., 1789], which was to have taken effect after last Carnival. [This date conflicts with, and is probably more accurate than, Da Ponte's "September."] I thought I would be able to devote myself entirely to working on your poem; but some time after the emperor's orders, the lords of the court, devotees of this spectacle, succeeded in changing His Majesty's mind, and consequently my plans were foiled, because I must always be in charge of this spectacle, which keeps me extremely busy.[16]

Da Ponte was certainly involved in the effort to persuade Joseph to reverse his decision, even if his role may not have been as prominent as he liked to remember. On 15 January 1789, a little more than a month after Joseph returned from the front, Da Ponte met with Rosenberg about a plan to save the troupe, according to Zinzendorf, who was also present: "Visited the grand chamberlain. The Abbé da Ponte spoke to him about a subscription plan to keep the Italian opera here, to which all the foreign ministers want to subscribe."[17] How Da Ponte's subscription system differed from the one he hoped it would replace (by which the theater was likewise heavily supported by the diplomatic corps) is unclear. His proposal may have served mainly as a pretext for the emperor to change his orders. The opera buffa troupe stayed in Vienna under more or less the same conditions as before, with one important difference: Joseph himself withdrew from active participation. He left the management of the troupe to Rosenberg, who in turn left Da Ponte with a good deal of authority.

The extent to which Da Ponte's librettos dominated the repertory during 1789 reflects his leadership. Eight of his operas were performed, occasionally to the complete exclusion of works by other poets. During the first week of November 1789, for example, Viennese audiences could hear settings of four of Da Ponte's dramas, two by Salieri: *Il pastor fido, Una cosa rara, Figaro,* and *Axur.* During Carnival 1790, which ended early because of Joseph's death, the company gave twenty-three performances, of which twenty-one were settings of librettos by Da Ponte. The repertory, neatly divided among his three principal collaborators, featured two operas by each: *La cifra* and *Axur, Una cosa rara* and *Il burbero di buon cuore, Figaro* and *Così fan tutte* (including the premiere).

"The Lyre of Melpomene and the Reeds of Thalia": Ferrarese in Vienna

A new singer shared the limelight with Da Ponte and his musical collaborators. The soprano Adriana Ferrarese arrived in Vienna in 1788, engaged by Rosenberg despite Joseph's insistence that the Viennese would not like her. Her short period of success

16. Salieri to Martin, 16 August 1789, in Angermüller, *Leben,* 3:51–53, and Angermüller, *Fatti,* 127–28.
17. Zinzendorf, 15 July 1789, quoted in Michtner, 419, and *MDL,* 293.

in Vienna, which coincided with the peak of Da Ponte's prestige, was thus a product of Joseph's resignation from theatrical affairs.

Ferrarese united exceptional virtuosity and a background in opera seria with an ability and willingness to put both at the service of comic as well as dramatic effect. She received training at the Ospedale S. Lazzaro de' Mendicanti in Venice, where she sang Latin oratorios under the name Andreanna Ferrarese. Oratorio at the Mendicanti was used by several prime donne as preparation for a career in opera seria, but Ferrarese evidently had different ideas. In 1784 we find her in Florence, performing in concerts with opera buffa singers.[18] What she sang in these concerts is unknown, but her willingness to sing with buffi hints at the direction that her career was later to take. In the following year she sang opera seria in London and tried her hand at opera buffa as well. In Paisiello's *Il matrimonio inaspettato* (presented under the title *Il marchese Tulipano*) English audiences admired her rendition of the aria "Per salvarti o mio tesoro" (an anonymous aria added to the score for her benefit): "From the nature of its composition it gave this lady an opportunity, which she properly improved, of shewing that her talents are equally conspicuous in the serious and the comic, and that she can with unabated abilities, accompany the lyre of Melpomene, and the reeds of Thalia."[19] She won similar praise for her performance in *La scuola de' gelosi,* in which sang the role of Ernestina, earning much applause and praise for her acting as well as her performance of another inserted aria, the rondò "Partirò dal caro sposo":

> The fairy Warbler, *Ferrarese,* we see every time with fresh pleasure. She gave her part the most lively colouring by her action, and did, as she is wont to do, the greatest justice to the songs allotted to her. We long to see her in the serious, after having had so many occasions of admiring her exertions in the comic parts of the Lyric Drama. We think her fully equal to the task, not only from what we have seen of her in *Eurydice* last season, but from the inexpressible feeling and pathetic manner, in which she delivered the *Aria* in the second act of this evening's performance, which is set to a most melodious music in the serious style.[20]

Ferrarese returned to Florence for the fall season, 1786, and there she excited applause with her portrayals of the great tragic heroines in *Didone abbandonata* (a pasticcio), Tarchi's *Ifigenia in Tauride,* Gluck's *Alceste,* and Alessio Prati's *La vendetta di Nino* (based on Voltaire's tragedy *Sémiramis*).[21]

Within two years Ferrarese settled in Vienna, where she could have little hope of singing roles like Dido and Iphigenia. But her decision to join the Burgtheater's comic troupe is consistent with her success in comic opera in London; and her engagement in

18. *Gt,* 1784, p. 82 (article dated 22 May).
19. *Morning Herald,* 30 January 1786; quoted in Petty, *Italian Opera in London,* 232.
20. *Morning Post and Daily Advertiser,* 28 March 1786.
21. *Gt,* 24 February 1787, p. 31.

Vienna is consistent with Joseph's efforts, starting in the late 1770s, to engage singers with experience in opera seria for his Singspiel and opera buffa troupes.

Ferrarese rose quickly to the rank of prima donna, making her mark not only in new operas but in previously performed Viennese works such as *L'arbore di Diana* (in which she sang Diana), *Figaro* (Susanna), and *Axur* (Aspasia). She and Da Ponte became romantically involved, and their personal closeness paralleled a compatibility in their operatic tastes and skills. About an opera planned with Salieri for performance in 1791, *Il filarmonico,* Da Ponte wrote to the theater management: "According to our plan a woman of Ferrarese's character is absolutely necessary, for the first act will be *buffissimo* and the second, by parody, completely serious."[22] The work was never written, for reasons that will become evident in chapter 15. But the attitude expressed by Da Ponte here informed several of the operas written during Joseph's last year. In his memoirs Da Ponte put Ferrarese at the center of his creative life during 1789—the raison d'être for his last three Viennese librettos: "For her I wrote *Il pastor fido* and *La cifra* with music by Salieri, two dramas that marked no epoch in the annals of his glory, though they had great beauty here and there; and *La scola degli amanti* with music of Mozzart, a drama that holds third place among the sisters born of that most celebrated father of harmony."[23]

Il pastor fido, a Second Dramma Tragicomico

The first of the librettos that Da Ponte wrote for Ferrarese, set to music by Salieri and presented in the Burgtheater on 11 February 1789, was withdrawn after three performances. *Il pastor fido* did not return to the stage until 14 October. Revisions to the opera (for which Salieri was later paid in addition to the normal fee for composing it)[24] presumably took place between the two sets of performances. Two versions of the libretto probably reflect the original and revised versions. One (to which the following discussion refers) presents the opera in four acts, the other in three.[25]

22. The entire document is in Michtner, 441–43.

23. Da Ponte, 135.

24. Salieri received 200 ducats as a fee for *La cifra* and for revisions to *Il pastor fido;* see Edge, "Mozart's Fee," 224.

25. The title page of libretto A (of which there is a copy in D-MHrm) reads: "IL PASTOR FIDO. DRAMMA TRAGICOMICO PER MUSICA IN QUATTRO ATTI DA RAPPRESENTARSI NEL TEATRO DI CORTE L'ANNO 1789. *La poesia è dell'Abate da* PONTE, *Poeta del Teatro Imperiale. La Musica è del Signore Antonio* SALIERI, *Primo Maestro di Cappella all'attual Servigio di S. Maestà Cesarea.* IN VIENNA NELLA IMPER. STAMPERIA DEI SORDI, e MUTI." The title page of libretto B (of which there is copy in I-Rsc) reads: "IL PASTOR FIDO. DRAMMA *TRAGICOMICO PER MUSICA* IN TRE ATTI. DA RAPPRESENTARSI NEL TEATRO DI CORTE L'ANNO 1789. VIENNA." I am very grateful to Federico Pirani for sharing the results of his comparison of the librettos and for sending me a copy of libretto B.

Libretto A represents an earlier version of the opera than libretto B, which was produced cheaply by cutting up libretto A, removing some of its pages, rearranging what was left, and adding, where necessary, a few

Da Ponte's youthful lessons in mathematics and philosophy had not kept him from literary exploration: "While the teacher laboriously explained Euclid or some abstruse treatise of Galileo or Newton, I was furtively reading now Tasso's *Aminta*, now Guarini's *Il pastor fido*, both of which I had almost learned by heart."[26] About eighteen years later Da Ponte collaborated with Salieri on an operatic version of *Il pastor fido*, which Giovanni Battista Guarini had called a "tragicomedia pastorale."

For all its influence on seventeenth- and eighteenth-century Italian literature, including librettos, *Il pastor fido* served as the basis for surprisingly few operas, the most famous being Handel's (1712, revised 1734). The play's mixture of comedy and tragedy may have discouraged eighteenth-century poets from turning it into a libretto, but Da Ponte probably found that mixture appealing. Salieri had already used Tassoni's poema eroicomico *La secchia rapita* as the basis for a dramma eroicomico; in *Axur* he and Da Ponte had shown that Joseph's opera buffa troupe could convey the tragedy as well as the comedy of dramma tragicomico. Da Ponte used the same generic term for his operatic version of *Il pastor fido*, which represented for him and Salieri another opportunity to explore interactions and juxtapositions of serious and comic.

Salieri, as the author of *L'amore innocente, Daliso e Delmita*, and *La dama pastorella*, had much experience in the composition of operas in pastoral settings. Da Ponte too had written pastoral operas, mostly in collaboration with Martín: *Una cosa rara* and *L'arbore di Diana* both contain pastoral elements.[27] Martín's departure from Vienna during fall 1787 encouraged Da Ponte and Salieri to discover their common interest in the pastoral, which they explored not only in *Il pastor fido* but also in *La cifra*.

Da Ponte preserved most of Guarini's important elements of plot. Mirtillo (the title's faithful shepherd, assigned by Salieri, in imitation of opera seria, to a soprano) loves Amarilli (soprano), who has been promised in marriage to Selvaggio (Silvio in Guarini's play, tenor). The original cast is unknown, but the prima-donna role of Amarilli was probably created by Ferrarese.[28] Although she loves Mirtillo, Amarilli hides her feelings from him so as not to be unfaithful to her fiancé. Clever and manipulative Orimba (Guarini's Corisca, soprano) also loves Mirtillo; she plays an elaborate trick by which

---

newly printed pages. Most of the cuts were in the original acts 1 and 2, which were combined into a single act. (The original five-act version of *Axur* was reduced to four by the same means.) The pages preserved from the earlier version contain the original page numbers and the original scene and act numbers, resulting in much confusion. The shoddiness of libretto B, probably produced for the revival of *Il pastor fido* in October 1789, may reflect the lack of effective supervision under which Da Ponte worked during the last months of Joseph's life.

26. Da Ponte, 19.

27. Dorothea Link, "The Da Ponte Operas of Vicente Martín y Soler" (Ph.D. diss., University of Toronto, 1991), and "*L'arbore di Diana:* A Model for *Così fan tutte*," in Sadie, 362–73; Edmund J. Goehring, "Despina, Cupid and the Pastoral Mode of *Così fan tutte*," *COJ* 7 (1995): 107–33.

28. Michtner, 276, states that Luisa Laschi Mombelli created the role of Amarilli, which is possible, but he cites no evidence.

Amarilli is made to appear unfaithful to Selvaggio and is therefore (according to the laws of Arcadia) sentenced to death. Orimba hopes that Mirtillo will fall in love with her after Amarilli dies. But he insists on being killed in Amarilli's place. He is about to die when Orimba confesses her deception. (This part of Da Ponte's libretto replaces Guarini's much more complicated resolution involving the discovery that the priest Montano is Mirtillo's father; in the opera we know from the beginning that they are father and son.) Most of the comedy in Guarini's play and Da Ponte's libretto comes from the relations between Dorinda and Selvaggio. She loves him, but he, interested only in hunting, rejects her. When he accidently wounds her with an arrow, he realizes that he loves her after all. The two pairs of lovers look forward to wedded bliss.

Da Ponte had to cut much in order to transform Guarini's sprawling play into a libretto. He reduced nineteen characters to ten, omitting some (such as Carino, believed to be Mirtillo's father) and combining others (Da Ponte's Corbaccio, a buffo caricato assigned by Salieri to a bass, is a combination of Guarini's Linco and Satiro). He cut many scenes and shortened most of the others. But his recitative preserves hundreds of Guarini's words and phrases, many lines, and several passages of some length, whose versi sciolti made Da Ponte's appropriations easy, except where he felt it necessary to modernize the vocabulary or style. Da Ponte acknowledged his borrowing in a note at the end of the libretto: "Having derived this drama from the famous work of C. [Cavaliere] GUARINI, I have tried to leave as far as possible the author's verses so as not to cheat the public of all those delightful charms of which that work is full."[29]

In turning Guarini's five-act play into a libretto, Da Ponte probably had in mind the libretto he had earlier produced for Mozart from a five-act play by Beaumarchais. Having successfully imitated Paisiello's *Il barbiere di Siviglia* in casting *Le nozze di Figaro* in four acts, he used the same four-act structure in *Il pastor fido.* In *Figaro* he followed Paisiello in ending an act with an aria (Figaro's "Non più andrai") rather than a finale. He and Salieri doubtless hoped to achieve the same kind of success by ending acts 1 and 2 of *Il pastor fido* with arias. In the second of these, "Non son queste, Narcisi ridicoli," the comic bass who portrayed Corbaccio (probably Benucci) sang a text resembling that of "Non più andrai" not only in its use of decasillabi followed by ottonari, but also its language: "Narcisi" recalls the earlier aria's "Narcisetto."[30] Salieri's music has the same marchlike dotted rhythms and two-note upbeats as Mozart's. If Benucci did indeed create the role of Corbaccio, it was perhaps he who inspired Da Ponte and Salieri to attempt another "Non più andrai" (ex. 13.1).

Da Ponte's opening scene is one of the few that he added to Guarini's play. He dramatized an episode narrated but not shown in the play: the famous kissing game in

29. Quoted in Swenson, 146.

30. Da Ponte used *Narcisi* again in another aria that strongly resembles "Non più andrai," and one that we know was intended for Benucci: Mozart's "Rivolgete a lui lo sguardo" (Daniel Heartz, "When Mozart Revises: The Case of Guglielmo in *Così fan tutte*," in Sadie, 355–61).

EXAMPLE 13.1 *Il pastor fido,* act 2, "Non son queste, Narcisi ridicoli," mm. 1–9 (A-Wn, Mus. Hs. 16606)

Vain, ridiculous men, are these not the sweet, eternal chains that cost you an ocean of dangers, that keep your heart bound up?

which Mirtillo, dressed as a girl, steals a kiss from Amarilli's luscious and willing lips. A young man sung by a female soprano and dressed in women's clothes may have reminded Viennese audiences of Cherubino. Mirtillo's request for Orimba's attention as he tries on the clothes during the opening duet—

Guarda un pò che questa gonna
Stretta e corta a me non sia

[See if this gown is not too tight and short]

—and Orimba's response—

Tutto, o caro, fatto sembra
Al tuo dosso ed a tue membra

[My dear, everything seems made for your size and shape]

—remind us of Susanna trying on her wedding hat in the first scene of *Figaro.*

The kissing game is framed by a chorus of nymphs, "Spogliamo compagne," one of many choruses throughout the opera, sung by shepherds, hunters, and priests as well as nymphs. The "choruses" in Guarini's play—more like the commentary in a Greek tragedy than musical choruses in the modern sense—inspired Da Ponte to make *Il pastor fido* a choral drama, but Salieri's fondness for choral music probably played a role as well. Even before the nymphs begin to sing, Salieri's music (ex. 13.2) establishes an unmistakably pastoral atmosphere by means of a combination of tempo (Allegretto),

EXAMPLE 13.2 *Il pastor fido,* act 1, "Spogliamo compagne," mm. 1–8

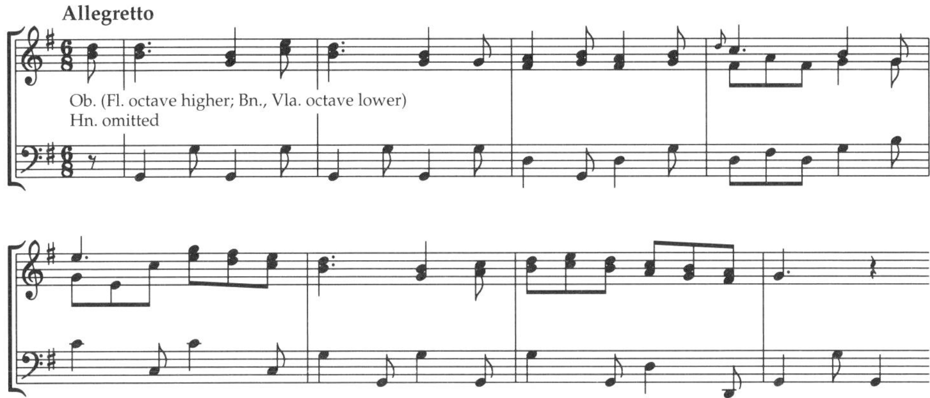

meter (6/8), key (G major), and orchestration (oboes, flutes, bassoons, and strings). Mozart combined many of the same elements in his peasant choruses in *Figaro* and *Don Giovanni.*

Salieri's choruses also convey the tragic side of *Il pastor fido.* In act 4 a chorus of priests, many of whose words Da Ponte took from a chorus in act 5 of Guarini's play, sing a prayer in preparation for the execution of Amarilli. Salieri made his setting a funeral march in D minor, heavily orchestrated with trumpets, horns, clarinets, oboes, bassoons, and strings. The impact of this music is weakened only by Salieri's recourse, in the cadence to the relative major, to a melodic phrase much overused by him: the descent through a dominant seventh chord from the second degree to the third (ex. 13.3).

EXAMPLE 13.3 *Il pastor fido,* act 4, "Figlia di Giove," mm. 10–20

(*Continued on next page*)

EXAMPLE 13.3 (*continued*)

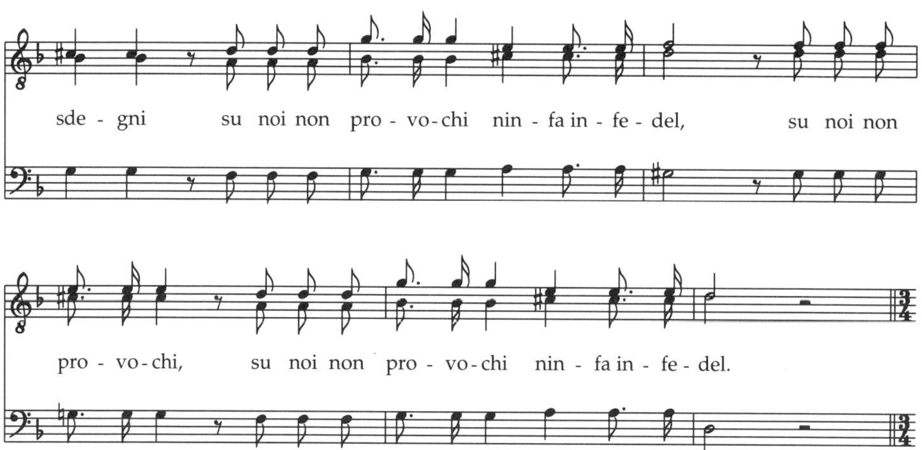

~Jove's daughter, second Phoebus [Diana, as goddess of the moon and Apollo's twin sister, is "second sun"] who shined to earth in the first sky, may the unfaithful nymph not provoke on us the vengeful punishments of your great anger.

Salieri integrated choral music into the opera's dramatic development by means of a device that he used frequently in his early operas and returned to in *Axur:* an orchestral transition that leads away from the drive to the final cadence and toward the dominant or tonic of a new key. The kissing game in act 1 is interrupted by the sound of hunting horns in the distance (horns in D, offstage). The nymphs end their game with another rendition of the chorus "Spogliamo compagne," at the end of which the orchestra moves from G major to E♭, whose arrival is announced by the distinctive sound of the violins' open string G (ex. 13.4). Selvaggio and Corbaccio sing a vigorous hunting

EXAMPLE 13.4 *Il pastor fido,* act 1, "Spogliamo compagne" (reprise), mm. 27–32; "Pastori, su su," m. 1

song, "Pastori su su," to the accompaniment of horns as Selvaggio (according to instructions in Salieri's autograph) "pretends to play the hunting horn." The horns play the same signal, now in E♭, that they had played in D during the previous scene. The appearance of the hunting call in both numbers strengthens the modulatory transition that links them.

With four substantial treble roles, *Il pastor fido* is an opera for sopranos. Amarilli sings an aria, "Deh perdona, amato bene," whose fine craftsmanship and emotional intensity—worthy of Ferrarese—are apparent already in the way the accompanied recitative gives way to aria in a transition played by wind instruments (ex. 13.5). But in

EXAMPLE 13.5 *Il pastor fido*, act 3, recitative "Oh Mirtillo, Mirtillo" and aria "Deh perdona, amato bene," mm. 31–40

... if destiny departs, perfidious Love? Please forgive me, beloved, if I am cruel to you.

the three duets (Mirtillo-Orimba, Amarilli-Orimba, and Mirtillo-Amarilli) one finds Salieri's most remarkable response to his wealth of soprano roles. The love duet for Mirtillo and Amarilli, "E come poss'io vivere," makes expressive use of third relations and changes of tempo. Mirtillo establishes A major with a lovely melody in slow tempo (ex. 13.6), whose hint of the minor mode and surprising augmented second interval at measure 9 (D♯-C♮) call attention to the words "morte" and "gemiti." Amarilli responds by moving to A minor, as if taking the hint in Mirtillo's melody. Suddenly, as the tempo accelerates to Allegro assai, Mirtillo enters in F major: a tonal gesture that colorfully conveys his uncontrollable passion (ex. 13.7).

EXAMPLE 13.6 *Il pastor fido,* act 3, "E come poss'io vivere," mm. 1–12

And how can I live without my beloved, and how can I stop my lamentations without dying?

EXAMPLE 13.7 *Il pastor fido,* act 3, "E come poss'io vivere," mm. 24–29

AMARILLI: . . . who live in sorrow. MIRTILLO: But my torment, my suffering has no parallel.

EXAMPLE 13.8 *Il pastor fido*, act 2, "Dove vai? t'arresta," mm. 65–80

AMARILLI: May heaven reward your pity. ORIMBA: I pity you and him.

The soprano duet and the pastoral style found common ground (as they had in *Una cosa rara* and *L'arbore di Diana*) in the many passages in parallel thirds in Salieri's duets. Particularly pastoral in sound (partly because of its being in G major) is the climax of the duet sung by Orimba and Amarilli in act 2, "Dove vai? t'arresta . . . o Dei!" (ex. 13.8).

Mosel rightly criticized the overture to *Il pastor fido* for its lack of pastoral character.[31] Given Salieri's tendency to write overtures that anticipate the drama in some obvious way, the absence of pastoral music in this overture should alert us to the possibility that he borrowed it from an earlier opera, which in fact he did. As with most of his borrowings, he carefully chose music that few of his listeners knew well, in this case an overture to an opera that had been performed very little, and never in the Burgtheater: *Prima la musica e poi le parole.*[32]

A Return to Goldonian Opera Buffa and to Operas Written in Italy

Having achieved such success, in *Axur*, with a heavily rewritten version of an opera first performed elsewhere, Da Ponte and Salieri may have hoped to achieve the same success with other operas written for cities other than Vienna. In 1788 and 1789 they presented

31. Mosel, 133.
32. Della Croce/Blanchetti, 403, 492.

new versions of operas that Salieri had written during his Italian tour a decade earlier. First they rewrote an opera to which he had contributed only one act of three: he and Giacomo Rust had collaborated on the first setting of Goldoni's late libretto *Il talismano* in Milan in 1779. Then, after the failure of *Il pastor fido,* they revised and expanded one of the intermezzi that Salieri had written for the Teatro Valle in Rome: *La dama pastorella,* to a libretto by Petrosellini, became *La cifra.* Both *Il talismano* and *La cifra* represent a return of librettist and composer, amid the tragicomic innovations of *Axur* and *Il pastor fido,* to Goldonian opera buffa. Da Ponte revised *Il talismano* relatively little, and *La cifra* has almost as much Goldonian flavor as *Il talismano.*

Like many Roman intermezzi, *La dama pastorella* differs from Goldonian opere buffe in having only five characters and in consisting of two parts rather than the three acts typical of Goldoni's librettos. It shares elements of plot with one of the most celebrated Roman intermezzi, Sacchini's *La contadina in corte,* in which a nobleman out hunting falls in love with a country girl. At the same time *La dama* represents Goldonian values and techniques as vividly as the operas of Goldoni himself. It opens with a bucolic scene interrupted with the sound of hunting horns in the distance, a device found in Goldoni's *Buovo d'Antona* as well as in *La contadina in corte.* Goldonian too is the interaction between noble hunters and simple country folk from which Petrosellini derived much of his dramatic interest. Goldoni explored this interaction in *Il re alla caccia,* which he based on Michel-Jean Sedaine's opéra-comique *Le Roi e le fermier,*[33] and which inspired Petrosellini in several ways. Clearly *La cifra,* by way of *La dama pastorella,* had a complex and distinguished ancestry.[34]

Il talismano and *La dama pastorella,* like Goldoni's *La buona figliuola,* are variations on the theme of the virtuous and beautiful young woman brought up by a man of much lower social status than her real father. Carolina grew up among the gypsies; but she is really the daughter of Pancrazio, governor of the rural region in which *Il talismano* takes place. Eurilla, Petrosellini's "noble shepherdess," was raised by shepherds in the Scottish countryside, unaware that she is really Olimpia, daughter of a count. Like Goldoni's Cecchina, both Carolina and Eurilla fall in love with men of higher social rank; not until the women's real identity is revealed can the lovers be united.

Pancrazio's wealthy young nephew Lindoro loves Carolina; Milord Fideling, who appears, incognito, in search of the lost Olimpia and immediately falls in love with Eurilla, awakens in her a consciousness of her noble heritage. (*Il re alla caccia* features a character named Milord Fidelingh, perhaps in misspelled homage to the author of *Tom*

33. Michel Noiray, "Roi et le fermier, Le," *NGDO.*

34. Yet another libretto by Goldoni inspired Petrosellini in the composition of *La dama.* Caryl Clark and Ronald Rabin (personal communication) have discovered, independently of each other, close connections between the librettos of *La dama* and *La cifra* on the one hand and Goldoni's *Le pescatrici* on the other.

Jones.) Fideling expresses his growing passion in his aria "Fra l'orror di queste selve." (Fidelingh sings an aria with an identical first line in *Il re alla caccia.*)

Both Carolina and Eurilla are surrounded by an amusing array of comic characters. Pancrazio, who wants Lindoro to marry his daughter Sandrina so as to get his hands on Lindoro's money, is a classic buffo-caricato role. He introduces himself with an aria, "Padre son e son tutore," whose text parodies a famous aria in Metastasio's *Didone abbandonata,* "Son regina e sono amante."[35] Rusticone, a sly old shepherd, has raised Eurilla in the hope of marrying her himself. His real daughter Lisandra is a silly girl convinced that *she* is of noble birth. As Fideling comes closer to identifying Eurilla, Rusticone's sense of confusion increases: he expresses his conflicting emotions in a comic aria of indecision, "Parliamo basso basso," in which, like so many buffi caricati before him, he addresses himself by name. Both operas have a subsidiary pair of lovers. In *Il talismano,* Sandrina loves Perillo; in *La dama pastorella,* Lisandra loves Fideling's friend Corifeo.

Carolina has learned the art of gypsy palm reading; studying Pancrazio's hand, she tells him that he has not one but two daughters, and both are alive. Cardano, the gypsies' leader, gives Carolina a talisman that allows her to take on the appearance and voice of anyone she wishes. She puts it to good use, allowing Goldoni to revel in the disguises he and his audience loved so much. And Carolina is not the only character who changes identity in *Il talismano.* During the finale of act 1 Pancrazio summons a notary to record the marriage that he intends for Sandrina and Lindoro. Perillo foils Pancrazio's plans by appearing disguised as a notary. (Goldoni had used the convention of the fake notary more cleverly in *Lo speziale,* where not one but two fake notaries appear at a wedding ceremony, both of whom hope to marry the bride.) When Perillo reveals his identity, Pancrazio orders him imprisoned. Carolina uses her talisman to take on the appearance of the guards' commanding officer, thereby rescuing Perillo.

Carolina's talisman comes in handy again in act 2: she appears both as an old woman (the nurse of Pancrazio's long-lost daughter) and as Lindoro's defense lawyer during the trial that takes up all of the finale of act 2. She and Perillo manage to have the trial postponed by distributing snuff, which causes everyone to sneeze in an amusing use of a dramatic device that was a favorite of eighteenth- and early-nineteenth-century comic librettists (Goldoni's *L'Arcadia in Brenta,* as set by Galuppi, and Giuseppe Scarlatti's *Gli stravaganti* feature sneezing ensembles, as does *Il barbiere di Siviglia*).

Cardano proves Carolina's identity by presenting Pancrazio with a box containing documents from which it is clear that she is Pancrazio's firstborn daughter, thought to have died in a shipwreck when she was a baby. Pancrazio's dream of uniting Lindoro's

35. Della Croce/Blanchetti, 446. Salieri had alluded to this line in his most consistently parodistic opera, *La secchia rapita.* In the first-act finale Renoppia sings: "Son guerriera e sono amante."

fortune and his own is realized in the marriage of Carolina and Lindoro, and he therefore blesses the marriage of Sandrina and Perillo.

Part 1 of *La dama pastorella* culminates in a hunt. Fideling and Corifeo, accompanied by a chorus of hunters, wound but do not kill a wild boar. They flee the raging animal. Only Eurilla, armed with bow and arrows, has the courage to stand her ground and to kill the animal. She realizes now that she must be the noble Olimpia; expressions of astonishment and admiration are interrupted by a violent storm, with which the finale comes to a hectic conclusion. (Following his French model, Goldoni had already provided the finale of act 1 of *Il re alla caccia* with a hunt and a storm.)

Disguise plays a less important role in *La dama pastorella* than in *Il talismano.* By pretending to be a shepherd, Fideling persuades one of Rusticone's comrades to tell him the truth about Eurilla's origins. Rusticone finally confesses his deception. Fideling reveals his identity and expresses joy in the aria "Il mio duol più non rammento," and the opera, like *Il talismano,* ends with festive anticipation of a double wedding.

Of the thirty-six complete operas by Salieri that reached the stage during his life *La dama pastorella* is the only one of which a complete or nearly complete score has apparently not survived. Few if any manuscript copies were made, because the opera was never performed, as far as we know, after the first production in Rome during Carnival 1780. Autographs of several numbers are bound together in an order that has nothing to do with their original order in the opera. A few more survive as separately catalogued autographs in the Austrian National Library.[36] From the printed libretto we know that the autograph fragments lack the introduzione, the finale of part 1, and several arias and ensembles.

Salieri probably disassembled the autograph of *La dama* with the intention of reusing some of it in *La cifra.* But the autograph of *La cifra* does not seem (on the basis of an examination of the paper) to contain any leaves taken from the autograph of the earlier opera. Salieri, if he revised parts of *La dama* in preparation for use in *La cifra,* may have copied them into the autograph of *La cifra* and then discarded the marked-up portions of *La dama* (which now served no useful purpose).

Da Ponte as Arranger

Although Da Ponte claimed credit, on the title page of the libretto printed for the 1788 production of *Il talismano,* for the "many changes" made in Goldoni's libretto, some of these had been made by an anonymous poet when Salieri and Rust set the libretto to music in 1779. (Out of respect for Goldoni the libretto printed for the Milanese production presented his original intact, with changes made at the instigation of Salieri and Rust relegated to an appendix.)

36. The autograph sources are listed in the appendix.

Da Ponte made very few changes in act 1, probably because this allowed Salieri, who had already composed act 1, to reuse his old music.[37] Parts of act 1 in the autograph score of the Viennese version show signs of being Salieri's original setting of the libretto, into which have been introduced changes made in 1788. For example, we know from the 1788 libretto that Da Ponte gave a duet to Lindoro and Sandrina in act 1, scene 7, placing it in the middle of Goldoni's original scene and omitting the recitative of which the rest of the scene had originally consisted. In the autograph score, however, we find Goldoni's entire scene set as simple recitative (presumably for the 1779 version), followed by the duet.

Da Ponte's changes in Goldoni's acts 2 and 3 go much further, as we might expect from the fact that Salieri had not already set these acts to music. Da Ponte omitted entirely the first eight scenes of act 3, leaving this act only a tiny appendage to acts 1 and 2, which he expanded largely by increasing the length of Goldoni's finales.

In turning the Roman intermezzo *La dama pastorella* into a full-length opera buffa, Da Ponte raised the number of characters from five to six by adding Sandrino, a young shepherd who loves Rusticone's daughter Lisotta (Lisandra in Petrosellini's original); Lisotta falls in love with Sandrino rather than with Milord Fideling's friend Leandro (Corifeo in Petrosellini's original). He made the revelation of Eurilla's identity more complicated than in *La dama* by introducing a message in code (hence the opera's title) that indicates the location of a letter revealing Eurilla's identity. The letter is in a box: precisely the location of the documents that disclose Carolina's identity at the end of *Il talismano.* By incorporating an element of *Il talismano* into *La cifra* Da Ponte perversely managed to make two similar operas even more similar.

La cifra and the Viennese Version of *Il talismano:* Music

Of the cast that created the Viennese version of *Il talismano* in 1788 we know nothing, but a report of the premiere of *La cifra* in the *Gazzetta universale* of Florence leaves us well informed about its original cast:

> On the 11th of this month [December 1789] a new Italian opera buffa entitled *La cifra* was performed for the first time in this Imperial Royal Court Theater. . . . The large audience was pleased by the book, the music, and the performance, the following actors having distinguished themselves: Sig. Ferrarese, well known for her celebrated singing; Sig. Benucci, recognized for his talents in the comic art; Sig. Vincenzo Calvesi; and finally Sig. Bussani, who showed herself in this opera, as in many others, worthy of unanimous applause.[38]

37. Della Croce/Blanchetti, 494.

38. Nel dì 11. del corr. fu rappresentata per la prima volta in questo Cesareo R. Teatro di Corte un'Opera buffa italiana intitolata la *Cifra* Poesia del Sig. Abate da Ponte Poeta del Teatro Imperiale, e musica del Sig. Salieri primo Maestro di Cappella di S. M. Imperiale. Il numeroso Pubblico è rimasto sodisfatto del libro, della musica, e dell'esecuzione; essendosi distinti i seguenti Attori, cioè la Sig. Ferrarese già conosciuta per

EXAMPLE 13.9 *Il talismano,* act 2, "Fra l'orror di quelle piante," mm. 12–22 (D-F, Mus. Hs. Opern 503)

Amid the horror of this forest I gave expression to my laments.

We know from Salieri's annotations to his autograph score that Ferrarese sang Eurilla (soprano). Benucci presumably sang Rusticone (bass); Calvesi, Milord Fideling (tenor); and Dorotea Bussani (Francesco Bussani's wife), Lisotta (mezzo-soprano). All of these singers created roles in Mozart's *Così fan tutte* a little more than a month after singing in the premiere of *La cifra.*

Given the close parallels between the comic librettos that Salieri set to music in 1788 and 1789, one would expect to find musical parallels, and there are many. The music of both Carolina in *Il talismano* and Eurilla in *La cifra* reflects the two sides of their personalities. Lindoro and Milord Fideling express their passion for Carolina and Eurilla in much the same mezzo-carattere musical language, while Salieri's depictions of Pancrazio and Rusticone are both products of the buffo-caricato tradition.

Carolina's music can be cheerful and rustic, as in "Quantunque vecchierella," a charming Allegretto in 3/8 time. It can also be grand and heroic, as in the rondòlike showpiece "Fra l'orror di quelle piante," whose opening melody is notable for its expressive chromaticism (ex. 13.9). As so often in Viennese opera of the 1780s, the clarinet appears here as an emblem of nobility.[39] The aria's concluding fast section reaches an emotional peak at the words "Piango, grido, e più m'affanno"; Salieri took Carolina and a solo clarinet into F minor and then into D♭ major. Eurilla's sweetness and nobility likewise find timbral expression in clarinets, which Salieri frequently combined with

il suo celebre canto; il Sig. Benucci cognito abbastanza per la sua abilità per l'arte comica; il Sig. Vincenzo Calvesi, e finalmente la Sig. Bussani, che in quest'Opera, come in molte altre si è dimostrata degna di un applauso universale (*Gazzetta universale,* 1790, p. 5 [article dated Vienna, 21 December 1789]).

39. From the autograph we can see that Salieri originally scored the aria for oboes rather than clarinets.

EXAMPLE 13.10 *La cifra,* act 2, "Alfin son sola" (accompanied recitative), mm. 1–4 (A-Wn, Mus. Hs. 16514)

EXAMPLE 13.11 *La cifra,* act 2, "Alfin son sola," mm. 32–35

~Milord . . . oh heavens!

bassoons and horns. These instruments announce her entry (with Sandrino) in the sextet in the first act of *La cifra.* Clarinets and bassoons are featured prominently in the recitative preceding her rondò in act 2. The chromatically inflected melody, with its sighing appoggiaturas (ex. 13.10), seems to express something unspoken; but Eurilla's emotionally neutral words do not at first express the feelings to which the instruments allude. Only later, when the opening melody returns, do Eurilla's words make its meaning clear: she is thinking about the nobleman she loves (ex. 13.11).

From the beginning of his career Salieri had written beautiful lyric-tenor melodies; he did not fail the singers who created Milord Fideling and Lindoro. Fideling's aria "Quelle sembianze amabili" begins with a tender melody in moderate tempo (Andante un poco sostenuto) and triple meter and concludes with an Allegro in duple meter. Carolina's lover introduces himself with a similar aria, "Guida l'industre amante." A lovely minuet-like tune, Andante sostenuto, accompanied by a tonic drone played by oboes and bass (ex. 13.12), may have impressed Mozart. Its first two measures reappear in the same key at the beginning of Vitellia's first aria in *La clemenza di Tito.* Salieri's

EXAMPLE 13.12 *Il talismano,* act 1, "Guida l'industre amante," mm. 1–8

⁓The industrious lover draws all lines to the vanishing point, until he reaches the center to which Love invites him

aria, like Mozart's, concludes with faster music in duple meter. Chromaticism and a sudden shift in register nicely underscore the word "ferito" (wounded; ex. 13.13).

For Pancrazio's aria "Padre son e son tutore" (*Il Talismano,* act 1) Salieri chose the buffo-caricato key of D major, with music whose comic conventions (including falsetto, as Pancrazio imitates his daughter Sandrina) go back to the first half of the eighteenth century. Pancrazio has another buffo showpiece in act 2, again in D. "Al dottore Cincinnato" begins, quite unusually, with patter (ex. 13.14). In the middle of this aria Salieri nicely conveyed Pancrazio's anger and stubbornness with another original idea. Pancrazio says "No," not to any particular pitch but rather "Un Nò arrabiato senza musica."[40] Salieri used the same effect at the end. Pancrazio repeats "No" at the final cadence of the vocal part, but instead of singing it on the expected pitch D, he shouts "Un Nò senza musica e più arrabbiato di prima," before the orchestra provides a tonic chord. Rusticone's

40. These instructions are in the manuscript consulted in the course of this study, D-F, Mus. Hs. Opern 503 (a copy from the Sukowaty workshop).

EXAMPLE 13.13 *Il talismano,* act 1, "Guida l'industre amante," mm. 55–63

So many beauties that have wounded my heart.

EXAMPLE 13.14 *Il talismano,* act 2, "Al dottore Cincinnato," mm. 1–3

Take this immediately to Doctor Cincinnatus

arias are equally entertaining essays in the comic style. "L'anno mille settecento" (*La cifra,* act 2), for example, is remarkable for its long uninterrupted stretches of patter.[41]

When, in the finale of act 1 of *Il talismano,* Perillo impersonates a notary, he sings in a monotone similar to the one used by Despina when disguised as a notary in the second-act finale of *Così fan tutte* (ex. 13.15). *La cifra* also features a scene in which monotone is used as a comic device. In the finale of act 2, Leandro, singing every word

41. For a discussion of "L'anno mille settecento," with an extensive musical example, see John Platoff, "The Buffa Aria in Mozart's Vienna," *COJ* 2 (1990): 105–12.

EXAMPLE 13.15 *Il talismano,* act 1, finale, mm. 110–17

Here I am, at the command of the most illustrious, wisest, wisest, and most illustrious governor.

EXAMPLE 13.16 *La cifra,* act 2, finale, mm. 355–63

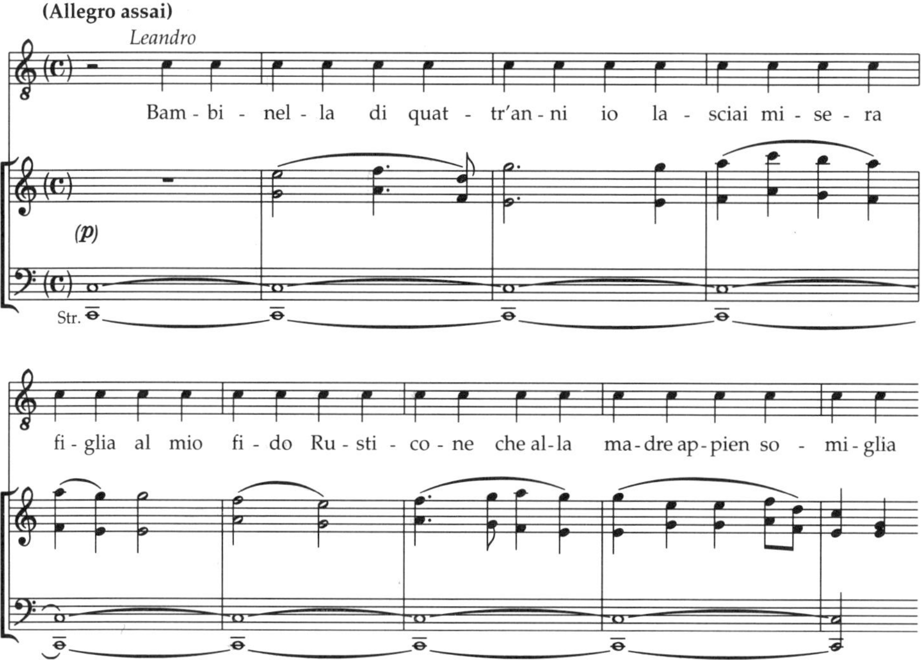

I left a little baby, four years old, a poor daughter, to my faithful Rusticone, who hardly resembled the mother.

on the same pitch, reads the manuscript that, in revealing Eurilla's identity, leads to a happy ending (ex. 13.16).

For an opera that includes gypsies among its characters *Il talismano* has remarkably little folklike color—instrumental, melodic, or harmonic. The gypsy choruses have energy and charm (especially "Viva, viva Carolina," at the beginning of act 2, with its opening five-bar phrase; ex. 13.17), but little that one could easily associate with the gyp-

EXAMPLE 13.17 *Il talismano,* act 2, "Viva, viva Carolina," mm. 3–7

Long live Carolina, highest honor of the troupe

EXAMPLE 13.18 *Il talismano,* overture, mm. 1–8

sies. One passage that Salieri might have intended to sound exotic is the beginning of the overture. A full orchestra including trumpets and timpani, 2/4 meter, monophonic texture, the surprising leap down to F♯ in measure 4 (instead of the expected A), and the fleeting tonicization of B in the following measure—together all these elements give the overture the sound of "Turkish" music and by extension, perhaps, convey something of the opera's gypsy background (ex. 13.18).

La cifra, in contrast, frequently evokes its pastoral setting through the same musical devices that Salieri had used in his first pastoral opera, *L'amore innocente,* and in his most recent, *Il pastor fido.* The introduzione, which Salieri described in annotations to the autograph as "completely pastoral in style," begins with a short orchestral passage in which compound meter, drones, a melody that features a repeated alternation between the fifth degree and the third, birdlike twittering in the oboes and flutes, harmonic stasis, and the key of G combine to produce a vivid picture of rustic tranquility (ex. 13.19).

The peace is interrupted by a hunt, depicted musically by a pair of horns "sopra il

EXAMPLE 13.19 *La cifra,* introduzione, mm. 1–6

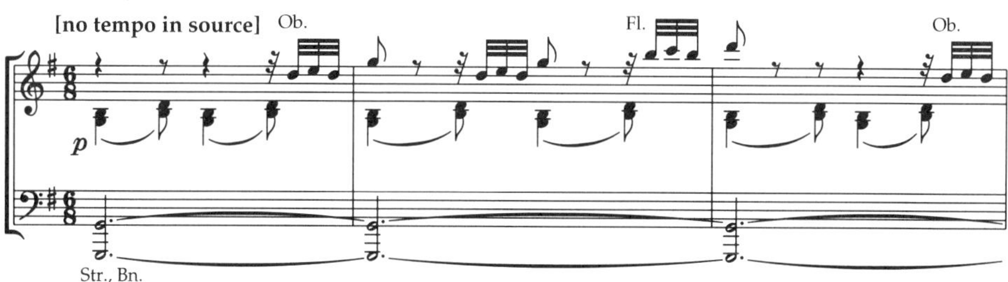

(*Continued on next page*)

EXAMPLE 13.19 *(continued)*

teatro," which means in this case offstage, since the horns are instructed to play pianissimo and the hunters (Fideling and Leandro) have not yet appeared. The combination of pastoral and hunting music in this opening scene anticipates the opera's central problem, the interaction of peasantry and nobility. Martín's *Una cosa rara* is also pervaded by the musical evocation of the pastoral and also begins with an aristocratic hunting party. Salieri and Da Ponte may have reworked *La dama pastorella* in the hope that *La cifra* would appeal to the Viennese for some of the same reasons that *Una cosa rara* did.

It was probably in direct reference to the Martín's operatic style that Salieri incorporated a canon, one of the Spaniard's favorite devices, into the second-act finale of *La cifra.*[42] Salieri's canon, in nine parts (three groups of three), outdoes Martín's canons in contrapuntal complexity but not in melodic charm.

While horns convey the excitement of the noble hunt, oboes sound often in connection with the rustic characters in *La cifra.* Among several fine oboe solos is the lyrical melody that serves to link declamatory dialogue in the duet for Lisotta and Sandrino in act 1, "Un abbraccio, idolo mio." Winds play an important role in the overture as well, calling attention to a tune that will reappear at the drama's dénouement. In the second-theme area a melody accompanied by a drone is played by oboe (flute in the recapitulation) and bassoon in thirds and sixths. This melody does not appear in the overture to *Der Rauchfangkehrer,* in other respects almost identical to that of *La cifra* (see ex. 9.9). Salieri introduced it here so that audiences would recognize it when they heard it near the end of the opera. Leandro, reading the letter that explains that Eurilla is really Olimpia, is accompanied by a drone and a tune whose familiarity contributed to the sense of resolution that Salieri sought as his opera neared its close (see ex. 13.16). Mozart, of course, had tied the overture to the second-act finale of *Don Giovanni* by using the Andante in D minor in both. He and Salieri were probably inspired by Martín, whose overture to *Una cosa rara* begins with a melody (accompanied, like Salieri's, by a drone) that returns at the end of the opera ("Su, su cacciatori," at the beginning of the finale of act 2).

The most brilliant orchestral display in *La cifra* involved the revival and partial re-

42. Link, "The Viennese Operatic Canon," where Salieri's canon is transcribed.

writing of an old aria. In *L'amore innocente* Guidalba anticipates her wedding celebration by listing, in a big catalogue aria, both the rustic instruments that she wants to ban from her wedding and the more sophisticated instruments that she wants to hear (the text of the aria is quoted in chap. 3). In *La cifra* Lisotta, another ambitious and unscrupulous country girl, looks forward to *her* wedding with Milord Fideling. Salieri recognized an opportunity to reuse "Non vo' già che vi suonino." He removed it from his eighteen-year-old pastoral operetta, leaving there a note that the aria had been transferred to *La cifra* and transposed down a third.

Salieri did more than transpose the aria from C to A. He changed the text, introducing an instrument, the clarinet, that had become much more common in Vienna since 1770. He scored the revision more heavily than the original version, reflecting more realistically the panoply of instruments listed in the text. The 1789 version requires an orchestra of trumpets, horns, flutes, oboes, bassoons, clarinets, timpani, and strings. The aria opens with a nine-measure orchestral introduction, a brilliant march for full orchestra that is later identified with the urban instruments. This is Salierian orchestration at it most recklessly exuberant. His use of trumpets in A (with which he had already experimented in *Il ricco d'un giorno*) is further evidence of his long-standing interest in expanding the trumpet's orchestral role (fig. 13.2).

Lisotta enters, singing a pastoral melody in 6/8 meter, Un poco andante, accompanied by a tonic-dominant drone. Trumpets, horns, and flutes play the colorful drone; oboes, violas, and bassoons double Lisotta's melody as she lists the instruments that she would rather not hear at her wedding. The march returns, now in E, and she sings of the instruments that she prefers. With the mention of each instrument the orchestra responds with a musical illustration, one of the more inventive being Salieri's depiction of the hammer dulcimer by means of the violins alone, playing a melody "con la costa d'arco" (with the side of the bow).

Showpieces for Ferrarese

Although Ferrarese rose to prominence as a singer of opera seria, she was more versatile than the typical opera seria soprano. The comments in the London press about her performances in comic operas make it clear that she not only sang serious arias effectively but could do so within a comic opera, performing less noble arias as well as dialogue in recitative and ensembles (including finales), and interacting almost constantly with other characters, even wholly comic ones. In *La cifra,* the second of the three operas that Da Ponte conceived for her (in addition to the pasticcio *L'ape musicale*), he and Salieri gave her ample opportunity to display (in the words of a London critic) "the versatility of that genius which is equally admirable in the laughing, and the melting strain."[43]

43. *Morning Post and Daily Advertiser,* 14 March 1786.

FIGURE 13.2 *La cifra,* autograph score, beginning of "Non vo' già che vi suonino," showing a very rare use of trumpets in A as part of a massive orchestral sonority. Musiksammlung, Österreichische Nationalbibliothek, Vienna.

Ferrarese projected Eurilla's nobility most powerfully in the rondò "Sola e mesta fra tormenti," to be discussed in chapter 14. She had two arias in addition to her rondò: a big, two-tempo number in act 1, "Deh tergete, sì tergete," and, in act 2, a short but intensely lyrical cavatina, "Lo voglio bacciare." About "Deh tergete" and the recitative that precedes it Salieri wrote in his annotations: "taken together, they are serious and in character; the end in particular is of great effect." The scena not only reflects Ferrarese's talents and experience but depicts Eurilla's personality and state of mind. "Sola e mesta" is one of the opera's musical high points; "Deh tergete" is more effective musical theater, encompassing both sides of Eurilla's character—her noble blood and her peasant upbringing—and vividly portraying the conflict between them.

Da Ponte provided Salieri with a twelve-line poem in ottonari arranged in three quatrains, identical in these respects to the texts of many two-tempo rondòs. It was presumably Salieri who expanded the poem by inserting a rhyming couplet within the third and final stanza (in brackets below). The twelve-line version appears in the libretto printed for the first production; the fourteen-line version appears in the autograph score.

Deh tergete, sì tergete,
Padre mio, le molli ciglia,
O farete ancor la figlia
A quel pianto lagrimar.
S'io son docile e amorosa,
Sallo il ciel, voi lo sapete,
E amorosa ognor vedrete,
Che saprò mi conservar.
Padre . . . Padre . . . ah perché ancora
Va l'affanno in voi crescendo?
Giusto ciel! io nulla intendo,
[A quel pianto, a quel lamento,
Mille dubbi in petto io sento,]
Sento il core palpitar.

[Please dry, yes dry your tearful eyes, father, or you will make your daughter weep again in response to your sorrow. If I am obedient and affectionate, heaven knows it and you know it; and you will always see that I will be able to remain affectionate. Father, father, why does your suffering continue to increase? Just heaven, I understand nothing, in response to that sorrow and that lament, I feel a thousand doubts in my breast, I feel me heart beating.]

The rondòlike features of the poem suggested to Salieri a musical form closely related to the two-tempo rondò but differing from it in crucial respects. He stayed close enough to rondò form to set up expectations in his listeners; then he departed from convention to give them something more dramatic.

Salieri could easily have adopted the duple meter and gavotte rhythms so closely associated with this kind of text, but instead he chose to begin in pastoral 6/8. The simple accompaniment, with downbeats marked off in the bass, offbeat chords in the strings, and a drone played by the horns and bassoons, gives this music a rustic sound that is at the same time delicate and refined. The several C♯s that urge the melody forward as it nears the cadence return later in the aria, serving thus as a unifying device (ex. 13.20).

EXAMPLE 13.20 *La cifra,* act 1, "Deh tergete, sì tergete," mm. 1–11

(*Continued on next page*)

EXAMPLE 13.20 *(continued)*

After the slow section in A-B-A form, the tempo accelerates to Allegro assai, the meter switches to duple, and a transition leads from the tonic, C, to the dominant of the dominant (to be followed, presumably, by a melody in G). The listener, expecting an open cadence on V followed by a melody in C, is disoriented. After a grand pause, Eurilla launches immediately into a melody in neither C nor G. On the words "Giusto ciel!" she boldly outlines a descending triad in E♭ major (ex. 13.21). This is a remarkable moment. A well-behaved shepherdess is transformed before our eyes into a noble heroine who cannot understand what is happening to her. Salieri took a theme that the audience from long familiarity with the two-tempo rondò and related arias expected to hear in the tonic and forcibly lifted it a minor third to the key described by Galeazzi as "heroic, extremely majestic, grave, and serious."[44] This is one of several sudden third modulations in the opera that Salieri associated with the strong, heroic, and noble part of Eurilla's personality.

EXAMPLE 13.21 *La cifra,* act 1, "Deh tergete, sì tergete," mm. 37–48

Salieri regained C major by way of V of C minor, and then firmly reestablished the tonic with a short transition passage based on melodic and harmonic ideas from the slow section; prominent here is the C♯ with which Salieri colored the opening melody. His transformation of a melody originally in 6/8 into one in duple meter echoes a similar transformation in the fast section of Diana's rondò in *L'arbore di Diana* and anticipates a memorable passage in Vitellia's rondò "Non più di fiori" in Mozart's *La clemenza di Tito.* Here it serves as yet another device for the portrayal of Eurilla's identity crisis: duple meter is, in this aria, unmistakably associated with Eurilla's noble side. A setting

44. Quoted in the original and translation in Steblin, *A History of Key Characteristics,* 110–12.

of "Giusto ciel," closely related to the theme in E♭ but now in C major, is followed by a closing passage nicely bound to what came before by the appearance again of C♯ in the vocal line. A series of dramatic leaps—including one of almost two octaves, from high A down to B below middle C—is followed by a prolongation of 6/4 harmony over which Eurilla sings a coloratura passage that takes her up to high C: a kind of metrical cadenza leading to the final cadence.

The finale to act 1 of *La cifra* offered Ferrarese a good chance to show off her skills as an actress. Salieri was justifiably proud of its scope and variety, describing it as "a mixture of buffo, mezzo carattere, and serio. Hunt, storm, wind, rain, thunder, lightning: all these things, I hope, are not badly expressed in the music. Much commotion on stage, suitable scenery, and precision in everything will astonish the eyes and delight the ears to no small degree."

The finale closely follows the text of the finale to the first part of *La dama pastorella.* A chorus sings of the joys of hunting with music in fast tempo and the key of D major. A shift to the subdominant—the rustic key of G major—triple meter, Larghetto, with a dialogue between oboe and flute, accompanies Eurilla's entrance; G major continues as the other rustic characters sing. They are interrupted, as in the introduzione, by a hunting fanfare played—more brilliantly than in the introduzione—by trumpets, timpani, horns, and oboes.

D major returns, and the hunters begin shooting (Da Ponte replaced the bows and arrows of Petrosellini's finale with guns). Salieri specified the exact location of the shots by the symbol "I" below the bass, which he had used to indicate the timing of gunfire in *Axur.* D major is replaced by B minor as a wounded wild boar attacks the hunters and they flee in terror. The scene must have reminded Viennese audiences of the beginning of *Una cosa rara,* where a wild beast threatens the royal hunt, also to the sound of music in the minor mode.

A sudden modulation by a third, from B minor to G major, focuses our attention on Eurilla (ex. 13.22). Her nobility gives her the same courage that the queen displays in Martín's hunt. Eurilla stands firm as the boar charges, but it is a pity that at this dramatic moment Salieri found no musical idea more interesting than his favorite descent from the second degree to the third (at "difendermi potrei"). As Eurilla lifts a gun and takes

EXAMPLE 13.22 *La cifra,* act 1, finale, mm. 231–85

(Continued on next page)

EXAMPLE 13.22 (*continued*)

(*Continued on next page*)

EXAMPLE 13.22 (*continued*)

(*Continued on next page*)

EXAMPLE 13.22 (*continued*)

EURILLA: What an uproar, what confusion! What horrible fear! I feel the forest shaking. Heavens, what should I do? If I had a musket, I could defend myself . . . Here it is . . . Heaven seems to have answered my prayer. The angry beast approaches: I will discharge my weapon. What a lucky shot, oh God, what happiness! OFFSTAGE CHORUS: The wild beast has already fallen. Who was the one who killed it?

aim, another third modulation and a dramatic ascending scale convey her strength and nobility. By moving suddenly from G to B♭ she anticipates the shift from F to A♭ at a climactic moment of her rondò "Sola e mesta." She shoots the boar dead; her shot coincides with a unison A, which serves as the dominant of D, the key in which, to the accompaniment of trumpets, she celebrates her triumph with an aristocratic three-measure phrase ("mi sento consolar").

The shooting of the wild boar is the most important event of finale; but Da Ponte, following Petrosellini, extended the finale by introducing another event: a storm depicted at great length with many changes of tempo and several changes of key. Among the orchestral devices used by Salieri to convey the storm's power is one, in the final section in D major, that he had experimented with in *Les Danaïdes* ("Oui, qu'aux flambeaux des Euménides") and that he almost certainly learned from French opera: long drumrolls synchronized with rushing sixteenth-note scales in the strings.

"The Music Is, in Itself, Almost Action"

Both *Il talismano* and *La cifra* found success in Vienna, other German-speaking cities, and occasionally elsewhere. Zinzendorf expressed his approval, saying of *Il talismano,* "I liked Salieri's music very much,"[45] and of *La cifra,* "it is indeed very rich in nicely varied spectacle."[46] The Burgtheater kept both operas in the repertory until 1791. They were frequently performed in Germany during the 1790s, mostly in German translation; and both circulated widely in manuscript copies, in printed piano-vocal scores, and in arrangements for wind ensemble and string quartet.[47]

A long and detailed review in the *Berlinische musikalische Zeitung* of a production of *La cifra* in Berlin in 1793 begins with this warm assessment of the opera and its composer:

> Rarely has a comic opera made such a universal sensation in the Berlin public as this one, which was given in the Royal National Theater for the first time on 25 February and already several times thereafter. And with good reason. Expression of feeling, sweetly flowing melodies, fire and strength, imagination pleasingly arranged, ensembles calculated for their theatrical effect, daringly surprising yet unforced transitions, richness of harmony, and, what is of most importance, beautiful handling of the orchestra characterize Salieri's music. Salieri

45. Zinzendorf, 12 September 1788, quoted in Michtner, 413.

46. Zinzendorf, 11 December 1789, quoted in Angermüller, *Leben,* 2:221.

47. On the sources see Angermüller, *Leben,* 1:58–70 and 1:179–91. Among the purchasers of Salieri's music was Archduke Francis, who patronized the Viennese copyists Lausch and Sukowaty. From Lausch he bought a piano-vocal score of *Il talismano* in November 1788, from Sukowaty a full score of *La cifra* in 1790 (receipts in HHStA, HKF, Kart. 2 and 3).

is an excellent composer for the theater, in tragedy as in comedy; he draws vigorously; his characters live and maintain their strength; and the music is, in itself, almost action.

Among the numbers singled out for special praise was the finale of act 1, which the critic ranked among the best ever written, "whether we judge it from the point of view of its masterly plan or of its skillful development of surprising turns of event and of painterly representation."[48]

Da Ponte and Salieri in Conflict

Da Ponte's increasing responsibility and authority in the Burgtheater during the last two years of Joseph's reign meant that the music of his collaborators—Mozart and Martín as well as Salieri—was heard with great frequency. But it also strained relations between Da Ponte and Salieri.

Shortly after the failure of the first version of *Il pastor fido,* Da Ponte assembled a pasticcio to be performed during Lent by and for the benefit of the Italian troupe. *L'ape musicale* (*The Musical Bee*), a satire about opera in which members of the company sang favorite pieces from the Burgtheater repertory, was a financial success but a disaster for the poet's relations with several members of the troupe and with Salieri. Da Ponte chose the singers for the production, giving pride of place to Ferrarese and leaving out, among others, Salieri's protégée Cavalieri.[49] The quarrel that resulted did not completely separate the librettist and the composer: the second version of *Il pastor fido* and *La cifra* both reached the stage afterward. It took some time before Da Ponte's resentment came to the surface. In 1791, having been dismissed from the post of house poet and looking for colleagues to blame for his misfortune, he called Salieri his "primary enemy."

48. Kaum hat eine kom. Oper eine so *allgemeine* Sensation in dem Berliner Publikum gemacht, als diese, die auf dem Königl. Nat. Theater zum erstenmal den 25sten Febr. und schon öfter gegeben worden ist. Und das mit allem Rechte. Empfindungsausdruck, süße fleißende Melodieen, Feuer und Kraft, glückliche Komposition der Phantasie, auf Theatereffekt kalkulirtes Ensemble, kühne überraschende, wiewohl ungezwungene Uebergänge, Fülle der Harmonie, und, was mit die Hauptsache ist, schöne Instrumentalarbeit charakterisiren diese Salierische Musik. *Salieri* ist ein treflicher Theatercomponist, sowohl im tragischen, als komischen; er zeichnet kräftig, seine Charaktere leben und halten sich, und die Musik ist fast an sich selber schon Action. . . . Und das *Finale* des ersten Akts is sowohl in Absicht des meisterhaften Plans, als der künstlichen Ausführung, der überraschenden originellen Wendungen, und der malerischen Darstellung, mit einem Wort, wegen alles dessen, was es so äusserst effektvoll macht, eins der ersten, die je von einem Künstler geschrieben worden sind u. s. w. (*BmZ,* 1793, pp. 18–19 [article dated 9 March]).

49. Da Ponte, 136.

14

MOZART AND SALIERI

Mozart settled in Vienna in 1781, fifteen years after Salieri, who was six years older. A young, brilliant, and ambitious musician eager to win fame and fortune, Mozart sought patronage from both the public and Joseph II, who personified the success and recognition that he longed for. He wrote his father only eight days after his arrival: "Well, my chief object here is to introduce myself to the emperor in some becoming way, for I am absolutely determined that he shall get to know me. I should love to run through my opera [*Idomeneo*] for him and then play a lot of fugues, for that is what he likes." [1] Mozart evidently hoped to participate in Joseph's chamber sessions, often devoted to the playing of Italian serious operas from the score.[2] He may have coveted the very position that Salieri, as one of the emperor's Kammermusici, had occupied since 1774. Mozart's pianistic career flourished during his early years in Vienna, but in his efforts to win imperial patronage he ran into a serious obstacle.

An orphan befriended by the emperor when he was only sixteen, Salieri had been a member of Joseph's chamber-music group since shortly after his arrival in Vienna in 1766. Joseph had watched over Salieri's career from the beginning, encouraging him and helping him. The emperor's letters to his ambassador in Paris show how deeply he cared about Salieri and his success. But Mozart exaggerated when he complained that the emperor "cares for no one but Salieri." [3] Just as Joseph gave Casti as well as Da Ponte a chance to write librettos for the opera buffa troupe, so he allowed no composer—not even Salieri—a monopoly over the composition of new operas for the Burgtheater. He

1. Mozart to his father, 24 March 1781, in *MBA*, 3:99.

2. But in writing that he wanted to play *for* Joseph rather than *with* him, Mozart showed that he did not understand the collaborative nature of Joseph's musical sessions.

3. Mozart to his father, 15 December 1781, in *MBA*, 3:179.

probably liked to see his musicians and other theatrical personnel vie with one another to win his and the public's favor. One of his first major opera buffa commissions, resulting in *Il re Teodoro in Venezia,* left both Salieri and Da Ponte out. Furthermore, Joseph's impulsiveness and unpredictability meant that Salieri could never feel completely safe as a permanent member of the emperor's musical staff. Less than a year before Mozart's arrival in Vienna Salieri had hurried back from Italy, afraid that he had lost the emperor's favor. Nor did Joseph refrain from criticizing Salieri's music, as, for example, when he confided to Count Mercy, in connection with the failure of *Les Horaces,* that Salieri could sometimes be "un peu trop baroque en cherchant l'expression dans la musique."

Mozart quickly achieved his goal of introducing himself (or better, reintroducing himself) to Joseph, who witnessed several of his public performances at the piano, applauding him warmly and commissioning *Die Entführung.* During the last decade of Joseph's life Mozart received more imperial patronage than any Viennese musician except Salieri. The emperor commissioned from him three full-length operas—two Italian, one German—and a one-act German opera. The Burgtheater presented a fifth opera that had been commissioned and performed elsewhere; on the performance of *Don Giovanni* in Vienna Mozart received a fee of 50 ducats, the only instance during the period 1782–92 of a composer receiving a fee for a work first performed outside Vienna.[4] One of the first actions that Joseph took in his reorganization of the court musical establishment in 1787–88 was to give Mozart an important musical position at court, that of Kammercompositor.

Yet Mozart remained below Salieri in the court hierarchy, where the principle of seniority was rarely challenged. He must have suspected that he would always be subordinate to the older composer. At the same time, clearly aware of the extent to which his talent surpassed Salieri's, Mozart resented the Italian's position at court. He rarely mentioned Salieri's name in his letters except in a tone of disappointment or resentment. Salieri, for his part, rarely expressed his opinion of Mozart or of Mozart's music; this reticence is consistent with his tendency to avoid comment on the music of his contemporaries. "The greatest musical diplomat" may have thought it prudent to keep his opinions of Mozart to himself. When Rochlitz, editor of the *Allgemeine musikalische Zeitung,* visited Salieri in 1822, the aged musician, who must have assumed that anything he said about Mozart would appear in print, called *Figaro* his favorite among Mozart's operas. But Rochlitz was apparently unable to learn more about Salieri's views of this or any other opera of Mozart.[5]

4. Edge, "Mozart's Fee," 224.

5. Letter from Friedrich Rochlitz to Gottfried Christoph Härtel, 9 July 1822, *AmZ* 30 (1828): cols. 5–16; quoted in translation in Thayer, *Salieri,* 166–69.

Salieri gave his students more candid assessments. Hüttenbrenner, who studied with Salieri at the same time that Schubert did, wrote: "He spoke often to me in confidence, because I was as devoted to him as a child."[6] Salieri's remarks included judgments of Mozart as an operatic composer. Hüttenbrenner recalled that Salieri regarded Gluck as Mozart's superior:

> He considered Gluck to be the greatest opera composer. He alone knew how to depict character in music most perfectly, and how to produce the greatest effects with the fewest notes; while in recent times one is left unmoved by the biggest masses of sound, because of their too frequent use. Of Mozart he always spoke with the most extraordinary respect. He, the incomparable one, came often to Salieri with the words: Dear Papa, give me some old scores from the Court Library. I would like to look through them with you. In so doing he often missed his lunch. One day I asked Salieri to show me where Mozart died, whereupon he led me to the Rauhensteingasse and pointed it out. It is marked, if I remember right, with a painting of the Virgin. Salieri visited him on the day before his death, and was one of the few who accompanied the corpse.[7]

Hüttenbrenner's account does not ring completely true; it is hard to believe that Mozart, only six years younger than Salieri, would have called him Papa (which was how some of Salieri's students, including Hüttenbrenner, did in fact address him). But that Salieri spoke about Mozart with respect, while at the same time showing a clear preference for Gluck in the realm of opera, should not surprise us.

Hüttenbrenner remembered Salieri pointing to a particular passage in *La clemenza di Tito* as an example of where Mozart failed to reach Gluckian perfection:

> Salieri, who wrote fifty-two operas, bore no grudges against Mozart, who put him in the shade. But where he could detect a weakness in Mozart he pointed it out to his students. Thus one day Salieri, when I was alone with him, argued that Mozart completely mishandled the final scene of the first act of *Titus*. Rome is burning; the whole populace is in tumult; the music should also storm and rage. But Mozart chose a slow, solemn tempo and expressed more horror and shock. I did not allow myself to be led into error by Salieri, and agree even today with Mozart's view.[8]

It is ironic that Salieri rejected exactly that part of *Tito* that appealed most vividly to the Romantic mind.[9] His attitude helps to explain why most of his own operas disap-

6. Hüttenbrenner to Ferdinand Luib, 7 March 1858, in Hüttenbrenner, "Erinnerungen," 142–43.

7. Anselm Hüttenbrenner, "Kleiner Beytrag zu Salieri's Biographie," *AmZ* 27 (1825): cols. 796–99; quoted in Angermüller, *Leben*, 3:6*; English translation in Thayer, *Salieri*, 177–78.

8. Hüttenbrenner to Luib, 7 March 1858, in Hüttenbrenner, "Erinnerungen," 142; English translation in Braunbehrens, *Salieri*, 226.

9. For some nineteenth-century views of the first-act finale see John A. Rice, *W. A. Mozart: La clemenza di Tito* (Cambridge, 1991), 128–30.

peared from the repertory in the early nineteenth century, just as *Tito* was finding new audiences.

Turning suddenly to *Don Giovanni,* Hüttenbrenner wrote ambiguously: "As far as I know, Salieri missed only one performance of *Don Juan.* This work must have interested him especially; but I did not know that he ever expressed himself enthusiastically about it."[10]

In the absence of other evidence we may assume that already in the 1780s Salieri recognized the craftsmanship and originality of Mozart's music. We may assume too that he felt threatened by this newcomer who was so eager to impress the emperor, and that he sought to defend his prerogatives as Joseph's chamber musician and operatic music director.

Cabals

Salieri and Mozart were rivals, but whether the resentment and jealousy they both justifiably must have felt led them into activities that seriously damaged the other's career we do not know. Mozart and his father frequently expressed suspicion that Salieri was involved in secret machinations—"cabals"—to keep Mozart's operas off the stage or to hasten their departure. But such suspicions were a commonplace of operatic production. Salieri probably feared cabals as much as Mozart did. Joseph II was confident of the success of *Les Danaïdes,* but only "if there is no cabal," as he put it to Count Mercy. Da Ponte accused Casti's supporters of circulating malicious criticism of *Il ricco d'un giorno* that contributed to the failure and early withdrawal of Salieri's opera. Much later, in 1799, Salieri was to be prevented by an "opposing party" from taking a bow after the second performance of *Falstaff.*[11]

Mozart's success with *Die Entführung* and his close relations with several members of the German troupe put him in an awkward position when Joseph abandoned Singspiel in 1783 and established an opera buffa company. In writing to his father shortly before the arrival of the Italians, he set himself up as a defender of German opera and announced his rather odd project of writing a German opera for himself.[12] The quality of the new troupe and its success with the public caused him to rethink his position, and he looked forward to writing an Italian opera. But one continues to sense in his letters feelings of resentment and suspicion toward various members of the Italian troupe.

10. Hüttenbrenner to Luib, 7 March 1858, in Hüttenbrenner, "Erinnerungen," 142; English translation in Braunbehrens, *Salieri,* 226. Hüttenbrenner may have made these somewhat incoherent comments in answer to a specific question from his correspondent, or perhaps in reaction to a statement that Salieri had enthusiastically praised *Don Giovanni.* That, at any rate, would explain the odd use of the past tense of the verb *wissen* (I did not know).

11. "The Diaries of Joseph Carl Rosenbaum, 1770–1829," ed. Else Radant, *Haydn Yearbook* 5 (1968): 58.

12. Mozart to his father, 5 February 1783, in *MBA,* 3:255.

"Italians are rascals everywhere," wrote Leopold Mozart in 1775; Wolfgang, perhaps without realizing it, inherited his father's prejudice. He seems at times to have thought of the entire Italian troupe as a cabal arrayed against him. Salieri, as the company's music director, personified the machinations that Mozart, like his father, hated and feared.

Mozart's ties to former members of the Singspiel troupe led to his first musical contribution to the opera buffa company and also gave rise to some of his first suspicions that Salieri was leading a cabal against him. For the Viennese production of Anfossi's *Il curioso indiscreto* (Rome, 1777; first performed in Vienna on 30 June 1783) he wrote replacement arias for two German singers who had been among the original cast of *Die Entführung* and who were now making their debuts as members of the Italian troupe.[13] He wrote to his father of the controversy that arose from these arias:

> Now you must know that my enemies were malicious enough to announce from the outset: "Mozart wants to correct Anfossi's opera." I heard it. So I sent a message to Count Rosenberg that I would not hand over my arias unless the following statement were printed in both German and Italian as an addendum to the libretto.
>
> [In Italian:]
>
> Note
>
> The two arias on p. 36 and p. 102 have been set to music by Signor Maestro Mozart, to suit Signora Lange, those written by Signor Maestro Anfossi having been written not in accordance with her abilities, but for another singer. It is necessary to make this known so that honor may go to whom it is due, without the reputation and fame of the well-known Neapolitan being harmed in any way.
>
> It was printed, and I handed over the arias, which brought inexpressible honor to both me and my sister-in-law. So my enemies are quite confounded! Now for a stunt by Salieri that did harm not so much to me as to poor Adamberger. I think I wrote you that I made a rondò for Adamberger. During a short rehearsal, before the rondò had been copied, Salieri took Adamberger aside and told him that Count Rosenberg did not like to see him replacing an aria and therefore advised him as a friend not to do it.

Adamberger followed Salieri's advice; but later it turned out that Rosenberg had nothing against his singing an aria by Mozart, who concluded: "it was only a trick on Salieri's part."[14]

Mozart did not tell his father the whole story. The composition of replacement arias was an essential part of operatic life in the eighteenth century. Salieri himself wrote many during the 1770s, his student and assistant Weigl many more during the 1780s and

13. Federico Pirani, "'Il curioso indiscreto': Un' opera buffa tra Roma e la Vienna di Mozart," in *Mozart: Gli orientamenti della critica moderna,* ed. Giacomo Fornari (Lucca, 1994), 47–67.

14. Mozart to his father, 2 July 1783, in *MBA*, 3:276–77.

1790s. None, as far as we know, caused controversy of the kind described by Mozart. If the Italians resented Mozart, it was probably because of his having pointedly written arias for German singers only, as if to show that only Germans could perceive weaknesses in Anfossi's six-year-old opera (an opera that had all but disappeared from Italian theaters by 1781).[15] If he had had Salieri's diplomatic skill Mozart would have realized that from the Italians' point of view his teaming up with Adamberger and Lange could have been interpreted as a German cabal, organized against what was clearly the weakest opera that the Italian troupe had presented so far.[16]

Michael Kelly remembered Mozart as being "touchy as gun-powder"[17]—we can see as much in his overreaction to alleged grumblings about his replacement arias. The sarcastic note that he added to the libretto could only increase the Italians' resentment (if they had indeed given any thought to Mozart's arias before the note was printed). Mozart reveled in his triumph; but it was a Pyrrhic victory. One can easily imagine how members of the Italian troupe who were Mozart's enemies only in his imagination might learn to dislike him.

Mozart may have suffered from cabals in which Salieri played a role, but evidence of such activities and of Salieri's role in them is of course slim. Leopold Mozart wrote to his daughter shortly before the premiere of *Figaro:* "It will be surprising if it is a success, for I know that very powerful cabals have ranged themselves against your brother. Salieri and all his supporters will again try to move heaven and earth to bring down his opera. Herr and Mme. Duschek told me recently that it is on account of the very great reputation which your brother's exceptional talent and ability have won for him that so many people are plotting against him."[18] Leopold's attitude to Viennese operatic politics had not changed much since he had failed to have *La finta semplice* performed eighteen years earlier. But the fate of *Figaro* contradicted Leopold. Despite its great length and complexity Mozart's opera was a success, performed nine times during 1786 and revived for twenty-nine more performances in 1789 and 1790. Salieri's *Il ricco d'un giorno* and *Il pastor fido,* in contrast, received only six performances each before being dropped from the repertory.[19] The cabal against Mozart, if there was one, was less powerful than Leopold imagined. As for Salieri's role, we should keep in mind Constanze Mozart's statement (discussed below) that he became hostile to Mozart only much later, as a result of the success that Mozart achieved with *Così fan tutte* after Salieri had given up his projected setting of the same libretto.

15. A list of productions in Pirani, "'Il curioso indiscreto,'" shows that the opera was performed frequently in Italy from 1777 to 1780, but rarely thereafter.

16. *Il curioso indiscreto* had been preceded by *La scuola de' gelosi,* Cimarosa's *L'italiana in Londra,* and Sarti's *Fra i due litiganti.*

17. Kelly, *Reminiscences,* 130.

18. Leopold Mozart to his daughter, 28 April 1786, in *MBA,* 3:536.

19. Hadamowksy, *Hoftheater,* 1:92, 96, 105.

Mozart's Development as Composer of Opera Buffa, 1783–86

Shortly after the Italian troupe's inauguration Mozart expressed hope, in a well-known letter to his father, that Da Ponte would write a libretto for him after finishing his collaboration with Salieri on *Il ricco d'un giorno:* "Then he has promised to make a new one for me. Who knows now whether he can keep his word later—or wants to? For you know well how charming [*artig*] the Italian gentlemen are to your face. Enough, we know them! If he is in league with Salieri, I will never get anything from him. And I would like so much to show what I can do in an Italian opera as well!"[20] In the last sentence the word "auch" (rendered above as "as well") is important. It shows that Mozart thought of his projected opera buffa as a sequel to *Die Entführung* in his campaign to impress Joseph and the Viennese. Having demonstrated his skill (and surpassed Salieri) in the composition of German opera, he now hoped to do the same with opera buffa.

Of course Da Ponte, as the emperor's handpicked librettist, was "in league with Salieri," on whose recommendation Joseph had chosen Da Ponte in the first place.[21] But the failure of *Il ricco d'un giorno* caused relations between Da Ponte and Salieri to cool. Mozart's suspicions, like his father's concerning *Figaro,* turned out to have no foundation. Although Da Ponte's responsibility for the revision of *Lo sposo deluso* for Mozart has not been proven, it was probably he who collaborated with Mozart on this ill-fated project, reworking an anonymous Roman intermezzo.[22] The opera remained incomplete, as did Mozart's setting of a libretto by Giambattista Varesco, *L'oca del Cairo.*

Cabals, real or imagined, had nothing to do with the failure of these operas to reach the stage. Mozart's unwillingness or inability to brings these projects to fruition must be considered against the background of the success of Joseph's troupe, which fully exposed Mozart to the genre of opera buffa for the first time since he had reached musical maturity. Joseph's company forced Mozart to reconsider his view of the genre, as he learned at first hand what worked and what did not on the comic stage.[23]

In May 1783 Mozart asked his father to communicate to Varesco, librettist of *Idomeneo,* a proposal that they collaborate on a comic opera for the Burgtheater. Looking forward to setting "a new libretto for seven characters," he stated his requirements with exactness: "But the most important thing is that the whole should be really comic; and, if possible, should introduce two equally good female roles, one of which must be seria, the other mezzo carattere, but both parts equal in excellence. But the third woman can be entirely comic, and so can all the male ones, if necessary."[24]

20. Mozart to his father, 7 May 1783, in *MBA,* 3:267–69.

21. Heartz, *Mozart's Operas,* 127.

22. Alessandra Campana, "Il libretto de 'Lo sposo deluso,'" *Mozart-Jahrbuch* (1988–89), 573–88.

23. Andrew dell'Antonio, "'Il compositore deluso': The Fragments of *Lo sposo deluso,*" in Sadie, 403–12; Neal Zaslaw, "Waiting for Figaro," in Sadie, 413–35.

24. Mozart to his father, 7 May 1783, in *MBA,* 3:267–69.

This passage is often quoted by scholars who point out how the specifications correspond to one or more of the operas that Mozart wrote later in collaboration with Da Ponte. But one can look at the passage differently. Nothing here suggests that Mozart wanted anything substantially different from the librettos he had set in 1768 in Vienna (*La finta semplice*) or in 1775 in Munich (*La finta giardiniera*), or indeed from those written by Goldoni in the 1750s. In the rigidity and specificity of his requirements we can sense that Mozart's conception of opera buffa was still circumscribed by conventions that, during the second third of the eighteenth century, had grown out of the popularity of Goldoni's librettos. Why, for example, did the opera have to have seven characters, four men and three women? Simply because a great many of Goldoni's most successful librettos (*L'Arcadia in Brenta, Il mondo della luna,* and *Le pescatrici,* to name just a few) had casts of four men and three women.

Three years almost to the day after Mozart wrote this letter, *Figaro,* a work that corresponds little to his earlier specifications, reached the stage of the Burgtheater. About a year and a half after that he presented *Don Giovanni,* whose cast of characters comes close to what he had asked from Varesco (the commendatore, an "extra" fifth male character, was originally portrayed by the singer who created Masetto); but it conspicuously ignores Mozart's "most important" requirement, "that the whole should be really comic."

Varesco and Da Ponte (if it was he who arranged the libretto of *Lo sposo deluso*) provided Mozart with what the composer, in 1783, thought he wanted. *L'oca del Cairo* (the text of which survives only in part) and *Lo sposo deluso* are both heavily dependent on Goldonian convention.[25] *L'oca* has eight characters, *Lo sposo* seven, most of whom belong to the types so effectively exploited by Goldoni. Sempronio and Don Pippo, stupid old men, answered Mozart's need for buffi caricati. Pairs of sincere young lovers—Celidora and Biondello in *L'oca,* Emilia and Annibale in *Lo sposo*—serve as parti di mezzo carattere. A servant girl, an opera singer, a tutor, and other stock characters fill out the casts. Although they contain a fair number of ensembles, both librettos are dominated by arias. In the first act of *Lo sposo,* for example, a quartet is followed by six arias that introduce all but one of the characters. A terzetto breaks into the succession of arias, after which the seventh character sings an aria.

Mozart might have been able to set these librettos to music and bring them to the stage earlier in his career; but now, as he became intimately familiar with one of the best buffo troupes in Europe and a repertory that included some of the finest modern operas, his works in progress must have looked increasingly unattractive to him. Mozart's letters to his father concerning changes that he wanted Varesco to make in *L'oca del*

25. On the libretto of *L'oca del Cairo* and its derivation from Francesco Cieco's chivalrous romance *Il Mambriano* see Jane E. Everson, "Of Beaks and Geese: Mozart, Varesco and Francesco Cieco," *ML* 76 (1995): 369–83.

Cairo represent his changing view of opera buffa: one has the feeling that Varesco would never be able to meet Mozart's requirements because these requirements themselves evolved so quickly.

Shortly after initiating the project, Mozart wrote something that should have warned him that he was going in the wrong direction: Varesco "has not the slightest knowledge or experience of the theater."[26] The later success in Vienna of two new operas, *Il re Teodoro in Venezia* and *La grotta di Trofonio,* could have served to demonstrate to Mozart the necessity of working with a clever poet who had, if not extensive theatrical experience, at least good theatrical instincts, and the usefulness of having this poet close at hand during the composition and production of an opera buffa. (This lesson Salieri had learned much earlier, from his intensive collaboration with Boccherini in the early 1770s.) Collaboration by post made revisions of the libretto difficult and time consuming, and it left the librettist out of the important work, normally supervised by him, of staging the opera. Never again would Mozart work with a librettist who had "not the slightest knowledge or experience of the theater." Never again would he collaborate by post, trying to stage a new opera without the librettist's active participation.

Early in his work on *L'oca* Mozart made another ominous remark. After discussing some of the more ridiculous aspects of the libretto in a letter to his father, he made fun of Varesco's plot with a pun: "In any case, I must tell you that my only reason for not objecting to the whole goose story [*die ganze gans=historie*] altogether was because two people of greater insight and judgment than myself have not disapproved it, namely you and Varesco."[27] In light of Mozart's earlier dismissal of Varesco's theatrical knowledge and experience, Leopold should have taken this falsely modest statement as an insult. Wolfgang himself had approved the silly story, probably because of his conviction that comedy had to predominate in an opera buffa, which he reiterated on 21 May ("The main thing must be the comic element, for I know the Viennese taste")[28] and again on 6 December ("the more comic an Italian opera the better").[29] What could be more comic than a lover finding his way into a tower where his beloved is imprisoned by hiding inside a mechanical goose?[30]

Mozart said nothing about ensembles in his initial specifications for Varesco, and the relatively few ensemble texts in *Lo sposo* suggest that he made no special requests for en-

26. Mozart to his father, 21 June 1783, in *MBA,* 3:275–76.

27. Mozart to his father, 6 December 1783, in *MBA,* 3:294.

28. Mozart to his father, 21 May 1783, in *MBA,* 3:270.

29. Mozart to his father, 6 December 1783, in *MBA,* 3:295.

30. Mozart himself may have unintentionally suggested to Varesco the use of Francesco Cieco's goose. His pun "die ganze gans=historie" recalls his almost obsessive repetition of the word "ganz" in his letter to Leopold of 7 May 1783. He expressed preference for a "ganz Neues" libretto, mentioned that Da Ponte was writing a "ganz Neues" libretto for Salieri, and specified that Varesco's libretto be "recht *Comisch* im ganzen," that the two main female roles be "ganz gleich," but that the third woman could be "ganz Buffa."

sembles from the arranger of that libretto either. Yet Viennese opera buffa of the 1780s was largely a comedy of ensembles, and Mozart seems to have become increasingly aware of their importance during the period in which he worked on *L'oca* and *Lo sposo.*

As Mozart rethought the second act of *L'oca* on 6 December 1783, he imagined the effect of an ensemble where Varesco had not placed one: "At this point a good quintet would be very suitable, which would be the more comic as the goose would be singing along with the others."[31] A few weeks later he again suggested the addition of an ensemble. In imitation of Goldoni Varesco had written for two different characters contiguous aria texts with the same meter and number of lines, and next to the second had instructed the composer to set both poems to the same music. Mozart himself had composed a song pair in *La finta giardiniera.* But the operas sung by Joseph's company must have avoided song pairs, to judge by Mozart's letter of 24 December 1783: "for one singer to echo the song of another is a practice which is quite out of date and is hardly ever made use of."[32] He suggested that Varesco write a duet instead, thus replacing a feature of the libretto that was typical of Goldonian opera with a feature typical of Viennese opera of the 1780s. But he did not follow through with his intended change, because soon after writing this letter he gave up entirely on *L'oca.*

Mozart never rejected Goldonian dramatic values and techniques, of course.[33] But *Figaro, Don Giovanni,* and *Così fan tutte* use Goldonian conventions selectively, for special effect. In none of them did Mozart start with an assumption that "the more comic an Italian opera the better." During his collaboration with Da Ponte from 1785 to 1790 Mozart worked within a new conception of opera buffa shaped less by Goldoni's librettos than by the operas performed by Joseph's troupe.

Salieri and *Don Giovanni*

Two fine operas by Paisiello, *Il barbiere di Siviglia* and *Il re Teodoro in Venezia* (both based on French rather than Italian literary sources) inspired Mozart and helped shape his new conception of opera buffa.[34] So did Salieri's operas, several of which Mozart must have known intimately by the mid-1780s. *Don Giovanni* in particular benefited from Mozart's knowledge of Salieri's scores, especially *La grotta di Trofonio,* performed twenty-two times in the Burgtheater during the two years preceding the first performance of *Don Giovanni.* We can hear Paisiello's spirit in *Figaro;* in *Don Giovanni* we can hear Salieri's just as clearly. *La grotta,* a work described by Salieri as belonging to the

31. Mozart to his father, 6 December 1783, in *MBA,* 3:294.

32. Mozart to his father, 24 December 1783, in *MBA,* 3:297.

33. Goldin, *La vera fenice,* 77–163; Heartz, *Mozart's Operas,* 230; Kunze, "Elementi veneziani nella librettistica di Lorenzo da Ponte."

34. Alfred Einstein, *Mozart: His Character, His Work* (New York, 1945), 425–27; Dent, *Mozart's Operas,* 107–8; and Heartz, *Mozart's Operas,* 127–28, 140–51.

"stile magico-buffo," moves swiftly from sinister darkness to cheerful brightness; the musical depiction of both these aspects of the drama is echoed in *Don Giovanni.*

Da Ponte, by referring to Casti's poetry in the libretto for *Don Giovanni,* probably encouraged Mozart to find inspiration in Salieri's music. Da Ponte's text for the chorus "Giovinette che fate all'amore" owes much to Casti's quartet "Il diletto che in petto mi sento," in which Plistene and Dori express their carefree philosophy while the serious Artemidoro and Ofelia comment disapprovingly. Both poems are cast in decasillabi with alternating piano and tronco lines; they begin with a line in which the three most important words end with the same vowel; they include a line in which the word *che* is repeated; and they make the same point that one should enjoy one's youth while one can:

Casti:

DORI, PLISTENE: Il diletto che in petto mi sento,
Che contento, che gioia mi da!
Si distacci ogni tristo pensiero,
Finché siamo sul fior dell'età.

[The delight that I feel in my breast, what happiness, what joy it gives me. May every sad thought disappear while we are in the prime of youth.]

Da Ponte:

ZERLINA: Giovinette che fate all'amore
Non lasciate che passi l'età.
Se nel seno vi bulica il core,
Il remedio vedetelo qua.
Che piacer, che piacer che sarà!

[Young women who flirt, do not let youth slip away. If your heart flutters in your breast, you see the remedy there. What pleasure, what pleasure it will be!]

Mozart followed Salieri in setting the decasillabi to fast music in compound meter, with an opening melody whose long strings of eighth notes repeat the scale degrees 3-4-5 (ex. 14.1). But the "cleverly cockeyed" phrase structure of Mozart's melody makes it more interesting and memorable than Salieri's.[35]

Another cheerful melody by Salieri that Mozart may have remembered when composing *Don Giovanni* was the minuet-song that, as sung and danced by Storace, de-

35. Allanbrook, *Rhythmic Gesture,* 258–59. Allanbrook writes of Mozart's seven-measure phrase: "underneath there lies a vague nonentity of a gigue tune, once the repetitions are stripped off to expose the regular period structure." The four-measure gigue tune that she reveals is very close to Salieri's.

EXAMPLE 14.1 Salieri, *La grotta di Trofonio,* act 1, "Il diletto che in petto mi sento," mm. 1–5

lighted audiences in London as well as Vienna (see fig. 11.5). Modern commentators, when they discuss Elvira's "Ah fuggi il traditor," tend to mention Handel in connection with its syncopations and odd phrase lengths.[36] But the aria that Ofelia sings on leaving Trofonio's cave was a more accessible model. It has many of the same rhythmic eccentricities as "Ah fuggi il traditor" and an opening melody very close to Elvira's.

"Ah fuggi il traditor" is no carefree minuet-song. Mozart developed musical material much like Salieri's into an aria that in craftsmanship and emotional depth far surpasses "La ra la ra." Salieri wrote a fine, original melody, but he did very little with it except repeat it. In Mozart's brilliant mind the bass line came to contrapuntal life; the tonal spectrum opened up; and Salieri's idea (or one similar to it) grew into a splendid portrait of an angry, eccentric, yet passionate woman.

Mozart's exploration of the demonic in *Don Giovanni* finds an important precedent in *La grotta.* If Salieri's musical emphasis on the dark, threatening aspect of Trofonio's magic was inspired in part by his experience with *Les Danaïdes,* then *La grotta* can be thought of as a conduit through which French musical culture entered Viennese opera buffa in general and *Don Giovanni* in particular.

Here again an allusion by Da Ponte to Casti's libretto may have pointed Mozart in the direction of Salieri's music. Near the end of *La grotta* Trofonio invites the newly reconciled lovers to spend their honeymoons in his cave:

Posso un fausto vaticinio
  Far pel vostro matrimonio
  E impetrarvi il patrocinio
  Di Proserpina e Pluton.

[I can make an auspicious prophecy for your marriage and obtain for you the protection of Proserpina and Pluto.]

Da Ponte echoed Casti's ottonario tronco at the end of *Don Giovanni,* having Zerlina, Masetto, and Leporello say of Don Giovanni:

36. See, for example, Allanbrook, *Rhythmic Gesture,* 235.

Resti dunque quel birbon
Con Proserpina e Pluton.

[May that rascal remain with Proserpina and Pluto.]

Mozart knew French opera; and he knew the Italian operas in which Gluck incorporated elements of tragédie lyrique. He learned much from both, as *Idomeneo* clearly shows. He knew Gluck's *Don Juan,* and its dance of the furies helped to shape the end of *Don Giovanni.*[37] But none of these could serve as a model for the integration of the demonic into opera buffa, which is precisely what *La grotta di Trofonio* could do well. It showed that allusions to the supernatural and extensive use of the minor mode were compatible with comic opera and that buffo singers such as Benucci could convey menace as well as comedy. For a composer who had recently written "the more comic an Italian opera the better," *La grotta* served as a useful lesson to the contrary.

The importance of the minor mode in *Don Giovanni* as a symbol of Pluto's realm may owe something to Salieri's emphasis on the minor in *La grotta.* Each opera begins with a slow introduction in the minor mode that anticipates a terrifying moment later in the opera. The key of D minor in Trofonio's incantation in act 1 enhances the effect of the offstage male chorus (spirits of the cave), as it does in the finale of act 2. D minor gives way to D major during the course of that finale, as the danger of the supernatural fades. Mozart used the same minor key for his depiction of the confrontation between Don Giovanni and the stone guest, the same offstage male chorus, and the same modal transformation during the second-act finale.

In one of the less tragic but no less dramatic parts of *Don Giovanni,* the masked ball at the end of act 1, one can sense Salieri's influence as well. The absence of ballroom scenes from most previous operatic versions of the Don Juan story may have to do with the important role of the dinner to which he invites the stone guest. This is the *festa* in which the story culminates; librettists and composers may have felt that a ball earlier in the opera could only weaken the effect of the dinner scene at the end. Incorporating a ball into their version of the story in spite of the potential problems that it might cause, Da Ponte and Mozart built on a tradition of ballroom scenes in opera buffa, introduced to Vienna through the many ballroom scenes in Goldoni's librettos.

Although Goldoni usually placed balls at the ends of acts, he tended not to incorporate dancing into finales, which he conceived as ensembles more of conversation than of action. In *La fiera di Venezia,* in contrast, Salieri and his librettist Boccherini made their ball an integral part of the second-act finale. Their experiment, discussed in chapter 6, must have been familiar to Mozart, who wrote variations on one of the minuets that accompanies the dancing in Salieri's finale. Any chance that he might, by 1787, have forgotten Salieri's ballroom scene or that Da Ponte might have been unfamiliar with it

37. See Brown, *Gluck,* 443.

was eliminated by a revival of *La fiera* by Joseph's opera buffa company in 1785. (Zinzendorf singled out the second-act finale of *La fiera* as "très amusant" when he attended a performance on 7 October 1785.)[38]

If the ballroom scene in *La fiera* represents the integration of social dance into the finale and the expansion of both beyond Goldonian parameters, the ballroom scene in *Don Giovanni* takes that expansion further by incorporating into the finale not only dance but also various events that immediately precede the ball. Da Ponte and Mozart conveyed very dramatically the anticipation, excitement, and uncertainty felt by their characters before the ball. Various episodes are interspersed with musical foreshadowings of the ball in the form of dance music played by an offstage orchestra ("da lontano" according to Mozart's instructions). When the ball finally begins in a room that Da Ponte, using a Goldonian phrase, described as "Sala illuminata e preparata per una gran festa di ballo," the audience will already have briefly heard most of its dance music.

Salieri had allowed his audience a similar sense of recognition by using the ballroom scene's A-major minuet and the forlana in the overture to *La fiera* (second and third movements, respectively). By incorporating their anticipations of the ball into the finale itself, Da Ponte and Mozart greatly enhanced the finale's dramatic realism and complexity.

Da Ponte, like Boccherini, departed from Goldoni's practice of naming only one dance in the stage directions for his ballroom scenes. The minuet gives way in Salieri's finale to the more popular, energetic forlana; in Mozart's finale the minuet is joined, in simultaneous performance, first by the contredanse and then by the "Teitsch," the German dance, each of which is more energetic and more popular than the previous dance. With its fast tempo, 3/8 meter, and scalar runs of four sixteenth notes Mozart's Teitsch resembles Salieri's forlana (the Teitsch marks its modulation to D major with an ascent from D to A identical to the beginning of Salieri's D-major forlana). In each finale a popular dance provides a nobleman with opportunity to make a romantic or sexual proposition. While others dance the forlana, Ostrogoto declares his love to the woman he thinks is Falsirena and suggests that they leave together; while Leporello forces Masetto to dance the Teitsch, Don Giovanni guides Zerlina off the dance floor.

The dancing itself lasts much less time in Mozart's opera than in Salieri's, in which 208 colorful measures of dance music unfold in three different keys and three different orchestrations (to speak only of the G-major minuet and its trios, not the A-major minuet and the forlana). Mozart wrote only 62 measures of dance music, all in G major and all accompanied by oboes, horns, and strings. The minuet with which the dance begins plays continuously throughout. We hear it first with repeats and then without: exactly the pattern of repetition to which Salieri's subjected his G-major minuet before

38. Quoted in Michtner, 397.

the trio in C is first performed (see the layout in chap. 6). Mozart presented his minuet a third time, incomplete: Zerlina's cries for help interrupt the dancing before the minuet is finished. Salieri's ball moves forward in real time, more or less; Mozart's occurs in a kind a surreal temporal compression.

Mozart limited the tonal and instrumental variety and the length of his ball so as to expand it in other, unexpected directions: spatial, contrapuntal, and metrical. Salieri's merrymakers dance to a single orchestra, as we know from Boccherini's stage directions, which call specifically for an "orchestra con suonatori" to appear on stage during the ball. Salieri, as far as one can see from the autograph score, wrote no music specifically designated for the musicians on stage; his stage musicians were evidently only for show. Mozart, in contrast, required three different orchestras on stage, each playing a different dance. With dazzling contrapuntal and polyrhythmic ingenuity, he arranged his three dances so that stage orchestra 2 begins the contredanse while stage orchestra 1 is still playing the minuet; both of these orchestras continue while stage orchestra 3 joins in with the German dance.

Salieri's expansiveness in orchestrational and tonal variety and in length and Mozart's expansiveness in textural, contrapuntal, and spatial complexity have the same goal: a building up of tension, which is released suddenly by unexpected and violent action (Calloandra slaps Grifagno; Zerlina, off stage, cries for help) and a simultaneous cessation of dance. Mozart's ball and his minuet end together at this moment of violent surprise. Salieri's minuet ends too; but, in accordance with the more leisurely, naturalistic pace with which his dances are laid out, the ball continues with the forlana.

A second climax, an unmasking, occurs later in each finale and succeeds in finally bringing Salieri's dancing to an end. By having Ottavio, Anna, and Elvira take off their masks almost simultaneously, Mozart and Da Ponte recreated the moment in which Boccherini and Salieri, during the forlana, had Calloandra unmask to confront her fiancé: "Ah riconoscimi, o traditor!" Don Giovanni's accusers cry out: "Traditore, traditore!" in a vocal unison as threatening as the orchestral unison that accompanies Calloandra's words. Each unmasking leads, within a few measures, to a grand pause (in Salieri's finale this is the end of the forlana), followed by a passage in a new tempo and key in which characters respond to the surprises that have occurred during the masked ball.

Don Giovanni is the most Goldonian of Mozart's late opere buffe: the only one in which Goldoni's categorization of roles—parti serie, parti buffe, and parti di mezzo carattere—is closely followed.[39] Also Goldonian is the ballroom scene with which act 1 comes to its brilliant conclusion. But the integration of ball and finale so memorably realized by Mozart was more likely to have been inspired by Boccherini and Salieri than by Goldoni. The ballroom scene in *La fiera di Venezia* showed how effectively the finale

39. Heartz, *Mozart's Operas*, 200.

could work as an ensemble in which physical activity—not only dancing but coming and going, changing costumes offstage, slapping, unmasking, fainting—is an essential ingredient. By concluding act 2 of *La fiera* with a great orchestrally accompanied number that is pervaded by the rhythms, movements, and intrigues of the masked ball, Boccherini and Salieri helped to lay the dramaturgical and musical foundations on which Da Ponte and Mozart built Don Giovanni's "gran festa di ballo."

Salieri's *Così fan tutte*

During the summer of 1829 the organist, choirmaster, and composer Vincent Novello and his wife Mary, both ardent lovers of Mozart's music, traveled to Salzburg and Vienna with the intention of interviewing Mozart's widow and aged sister and as many others who had known Mozart as they could find.[40] The Novellos' most valuable informant was their first. Constanze Nissen, previously Constanze Mozart, resident in Salzburg since 1820, spoke with the Novellos several times. She seems, at sixty-six, to have been of sound mind and body. Many of her statements, as paraphrased by the Novellos, can be verified by other sources; others have the ring of truth.

Among the many subjects that the conversations touched was Salieri's attitude toward Mozart, which caused Constanze to make a reference to *Così fan tutte.* Both Novellos were intrigued enough by the reference to record it in their notes. Mary paraphrased Constanze as follows: "Salieri's enmity arose from Mozart's setting the *Così fan tutte* which he had originally commenced and given up as unworthy [of] musical invention."[41] Vincent paraphrased Constanze at greater length, and interpreted her words differently: "Salieri first tried to set this opera but failed, and the great success of Mozart in accomplishing what he could make nothing of is supposed to have excited his envy and hatred, and have been the first origin of his enmity and malice towards Mozart."[42]

Biographers of neither Mozart nor Salieri have taken much notice of Constanze's declaration. This may be partly because, if one believes Mozart, Salieri began to act with malice toward him as early as 1783 (the episode involving Anfossi's *Il curioso indiscreto*) and partly because scholars have been unable to find evidence to support Constanze's statement. But such evidence has recently come to light in the form of a manuscript

40. *A Mozart Pilgrimage, Being the Travel Diaries of Vincent and Mary Novello in the Year 1829,* ed. Nerina Medici di Marignano and Rosemary Hughes (London, 1955). The following discussion of a discovery made jointly by Bruce Alan Brown and me in Vienna in July 1994 is based largely on our article "Salieri's *Così fan tutte,*" *COJ* 8 (1996): 17–43. I am grateful to Brown and to Cambridge University Press for permission to publish our findings here.

41. Novello and Novello, *A Mozart Pilgrimage,* 127.

42. Novello and Novello, *A Mozart Pilgrimage,* 127.

in Salieri's hand that records his attempt to set to music the libretto that its author Da Ponte entitled *La scola degli amanti* but that later, as set to music by Mozart, came to be known as *Così fan tutte.*

The Austrian National Library's huge collection of Salieri's autograph manuscripts includes, among works catalogued as "terzetti," settings of the first two numbers of Da Ponte's *La scola degli amanti:* "La mia Dorabella" and "È la fede delle femmine."[43] Salieri composed the terzetti on two different kinds of paper, at least one of which Mozart also used. "La mia Dorabella" is on the paper that Mozart used in parts of *Così* and in several other works composed from 1789 until shortly before his death, the first completed and dated one being the aria "Schon lacht der holde Frühling," K. 580 (17 September 1789).[44] Salieri also used the paper in parts of the autograph score of *La cifra,* first performed on 11 December 1789.

Mozart completed *Così* shortly before its premiere on 20 January 1790: in his thematic catalogue he dated the opera "im Jenner." He was already at work on *Così* in December 1789, when he entered in his catalogue the aria "Rivolgete a lui lo sguardo," describing it as having originally been written for Benucci to sing in *Così.* Salieri probably composed *La cifra* during the period immediately before its premiere on 11 December 1789. It is unlikely that he would have begun composing *Così* after the completion of *La cifra* because by then Mozart had probably already begun to work on his setting of Da Ponte's libretto. Assuming that Salieri was busy with *La cifra* from the beginning of November until the premiere, he probably began and then broke off the composition of *La scola degli amanti* sometime between the completion of *Il pastor fido* (first performed on 11 February 1789) and the beginning of November 1789.

There are some good reasons why Da Ponte might have intended the libretto of *La scola degli amanti* for Salieri rather than Mozart. This was Da Ponte's original title; and he never departed from it even when referring, many years later, to Mozart's setting. The title and several aspects of the plot are reminiscent of the opera with which Joseph's comic troupe introduced itself in 1783: *La scuola de' gelosi.* Did Da Ponte intend *La scola degli amanti* as a kind of sequel to *La scuola de' gelosi:* the second in a series of "scuola-operas" by Salieri?[45]

Alfonso gives his first lesson in the fidelity of women in the terzetto "È la fede delle femmine," paraphrasing an aria by Metastasio ("È la fede degli amanti," in *Demetrio*).

43. A-Wn, Mus. Hs. 4531.

44. Watermark no. 100 in Alan Tyson's catalogue of watermarks in Mozart's autograph scores, in *NMA,* Serie 10, Supplement (Kassel, 1992), 47–48.

45. In view of the frequency with which French playwrights used the word *école* in the titles of plays, the infrequency with which Italian librettists used the word *scuola* in titles is surprising. When Da Ponte wrote *La scola degli amanti* only a handful of librettos beginning with *scuola* had been performed (see Sartori 21348–93). These included, as it happens, a libretto entitled *La scuola degli amanti* (by Giuseppe Palomba), performed with music by Giacomo Tritto in Naples in 1783.

Earlier in his career (in *La secchia rapita, Der Rauchfangkehrer,* and *Prima la musica*) Salieri had shown himself more partial than Mozart to Metastasian quotation and parody.

Mozart's *Così,* both text and music, contains several references to his previous Viennese opera buffa, *Figaro,* including the motto itself, adopted from the words "Così fan tutte le belle" sung by Basilio.[46] The decision to incorporate this particular motto into *La scola degli amanti* was made, probably on Mozart's suggestion, late in the compositional process, well after Salieri had given up on the opera.[47] It was probably also Mozart who turned the motto into the opera's primary title, placing Da Ponte's original title in a subsidiary position. The printed announcement of the opera's first performance referred to it as COSI FAN TUTTE, / O sia, / LA SCOLA DEGLI AMANTI (the alternative title in letters much smaller than those of the primary title). With this change of title Mozart obscured the libretto's references to *La scuola de' gelosi:* he put his personal stamp on the libretto by choosing a title that refers to one of his own operas rather than to one of Salieri's.

In composing his first opera buffa, *Le donne letterate,* Salieri sketched the introduzione as one of his very first steps. He seems to have done the same in the composition of *La scola degli amanti* twenty years later. Confronted with a libretto that began with at least two terzetti in rapid succession, he apparently considered these, together with the intervening dialogue in recitative, to share the function of an introduzione. He began composition with two of these terzetti and some recitative between them, probably first setting to music the text that interested him most—the Metastasian paraphrase. Having completed "È la fede delle femmine" he turned to the first terzetto, "La mia Dorabella," but left the number incomplete.

Alfonso's paraphrase of Metastasio is a joke; Salieri, like Mozart, responded to it with playful music (Mozart wrote "scherzando"). Salieri seems to have been more concerned than Mozart that his audience hear and understand Alfonso's words. Mozart gave Alfonso six measures of cut time, Allegro, to get through three lines of verse without a single rest; in Salieri's setting (ex. 14.2) Alfonso goes through the same three lines in six measures, but in slower tempo. His jovial tune in compound meter divides the old verses neatly into two-measure phrases. Mozart's Alfonso makes up for the haste with which he begins his joke by slowing down to emphasize the punch line ("dove sia nessun lo sa"), which Salieri allows to pass with less emphasis.

Mozart, in his setting of "La mia Dorabella," gave Ferrando and Guilelmo much the same music. Salieri differentiated them more clearly (ex. 14.3). The tenor Ferrando has a lyrical melody in which conjunct and disjunct motion are nicely balanced. After singing the first two lines of text to regular two-measure phrases, he declaims lines 3 and 4 ("Fedel quanto bella / il cielo la fé") in a single, four-measure phrase whose beauty

46. Heartz, *Mozart's Operas,* 234.

47. Alan Tyson, *Mozart: Studies of the Autograph Scores* (Cambridge, Mass., 1987), 190, 197.

EXAMPLE 14.2 Salieri, "È la fede delle femmine," mm. 1–13 (A-Wn, Mus. Hs. 4531)

DON ALFONSO: The faith of women is like the Arabian phoenix, which everyone says exists, but no one knows where it is. FERRANDO: The phoenix is Dorabella! GUILELMO: The phoenix is Fiordiligi!

EXAMPLE 14.3 Salieri, "La mia Dorabella," mm. 1–35 (A-Wn, Mus. Hs. 4531)

FERRANDO: My Dorabella is not capable of that. Heaven made her as faithful as she is beautiful. GUILELMO: My Fiordiligi cannot betray me. I believe her constancy and beauty are equal. DON ALFONSO: My hair is already gray; I speak *ex cathedra* . . . but let these quarrels end there.

reflects the words. Guilelmo responds with a mostly triadic line characteristic of the buffo caricato that he is. Alfonso, trying to reconcile his quarreling friends, sings a melody that brings together elements of their tunes ("Ho i crini già grigi" recalls "La mia Fiordiligi"; "finiscano qua" recalls "il cielo la fé").

Why did Salieri give up the composition of *La scola degli amanti?* According to Mary Novello's interpretation of Constanze Nissen's statement, he found Da Ponte's text to be "unworthy [of] musical invention." According to Vincent, he "could make nothing of" the libretto. Neither of these explanations is consistent with Salieri's personality. During his long career he set several weak librettos. We have no evidence (other than one interpretation of Constanze's statement) of his ever having rejected a libretto because of its poor quality. This does not mean, of course, that he never did; but he certainly was not as selective as Mozart when it came to choosing librettos. Salieri's decision to leave *La scola degli amanti* incomplete probably had less to do with the quality of the libretto than with his state of mind in 1789, which seems, on the basis of evidence discussed in chapter 13, to have been characterized by artistic indecisiveness, a relatively low level of creative energy, and varying degrees of dependence on earlier music. After the failure of *Il pastor fido* and his falling-out with Da Ponte during Lent 1789, he may simply not have felt up to the task of composing another new Italian opera, preferring to recompose an old one (*La dama pastorella*).

Once Salieri began an opera he almost always finished it. After he broke off the composition of *L'isola capricciosa* in 1779 it lay unfinished until 1792, when he completed it as *Il mondo in rovescia*. In 1780 he began *Semiramide* for Naples; two years later he finished and presented it in Munich. He might have finished *La scola degli amanti* too (doubtless he kept the fragments with that possibility in mind), had Mozart not taken over the libretto and created from it an opera that Salieri could not equal. That Mozart, in doing so, excited Salieri's "envy and hatred" is not outside the realm of possibility.

Rondòs for Ferrarese

Despite being older than Mozart and having written many more operas, Salieri had much to learn from Mozart. But he seems to have been slow to do so, perhaps because so few of Mozart's opere buffe were performed in the Burgtheater until quite late in the 1780s. Only one full-length opera by Mozart, *Figaro*, was performed in the Burgtheater during the first five years of the opera buffa company. But during the last two years of Joseph's reign—the period of Da Ponte's greatest influence—Salieri had ample opportunity to hear and learn from Mozart's Italian operas. The Burgtheater presented not only a revival of *Figaro* but a new production of *Don Giovanni* and the premiere of *Così*. With the departure of Martín y Soler at the end of 1787 Salieri and Mozart emerged more clearly than ever as the two principal composers of the Viennese court theater. Writing for the same prima donna, Ferrarese, and setting to music words of the same librettist (even setting the same words to music, in the case of *Così fan tutte*), Mozart and Salieri absorbed certain aspects of each other's music, and both composers benefited from this interaction.[48]

When preparations were being made to revive *Figaro* in 1789, with Ferrarese in the role of Susanna, it was decided to replace the garden aria in act 4, "Deh vieni non tardar," with a rondò. Mozart, observing the convention that encouraged composers to place a rondò for the heroine of an opera buffa shortly before the opera's last finale, had originally intended to write a rondò for Storace, the first Susanna, in this spot; but he had abandoned it in favor of the seemingly simple, charming "Deh vieni."[49] With Fer-

48. The following is largely derived from my article "Rondò vocali di Salieri e Mozart per Adriana Ferrarese," in Muraro, *Mozart*, 1:185–209.

49. Heartz, *Mozart's Operas*, 151–52; John Platoff, "'Non tardar amato bene' Completed—but Not by Mozart," *Musical Times* 132 (1991): 557–60.

rarese in the role of Susanna, Mozart agreed to eliminate "Deh vieni" in favor of a brilliant virtuoso aria, the rondò "Al desio di chi t'adora."

In "Al desio" Mozart created a rondò that in many respects follows the rigid conventions of the form, as exemplified by "Ah sia già de' miei sospiri," the rondò that Salieri had added to *La scuola de' gelosi* for its Viennese revival of 1783 (see chap. 11). The text, almost certainly by Da Ponte (the opening line is borrowed from the second finale of *Don Giovanni,* where Donna Anna sings it),[50] is a twelve-line poem consisting of three quatrains of ottonari:

Al desio di chi t'adora,
    Vieni, vola, oh mia speranza!
    Morirò, se indarno ancora
    Tu mi lasci sospirar.
Le promesse, i giuramenti,
    Deh! rammenta, oh mio tesoro
    E i momenti di ristoro
    Che mi fece Amor sperar!
Ah ch'omai più non resisto
    All'ardor che il sen m'accende
    Chi d'amor gli affetti intende
    Compatisca il mio penar.

[To the longing of the one who adores you, come, fly, oh my hope! I will die if you let me languish any longer in vain. Oh my treasure, remember the promise, the vows, and the moments of comfort for which Love makes me hope. Ah! I can no longer resist the passion that burns in my breast. May those who understand the effects of love pity my suffering.]

"Al desio" consists of two parts, one in slow tempo and one in fast:

[Larghetto]	Allegro
A-B-A	C-D-E-D-F

The first quatrain of the text is set as a melody in duple meter (A; ex. 14.4). This is followed by contrasting material (B), a setting of the second quatrain. Then melody A returns. The fast section, also in duple meter, begins with a transition (C) that ends on the dominant; this is followed by the principal melody of the fast section (D); then a contrasting episode (E), a repetition of the principal melody, and closing material (F). "Al desio" differs in form from "Ah sia già" in one respect only: in Salieri's rondò the tempo change occurs after rather than before the transition passage C.

50. I am grateful to Richard Armbruster for pointing this out to me.

EXAMPLE 14.4 Mozart, *Le nozze di Figaro* (1789 version), act 4, "Al desio di chi t'adora," mm. 1–11 (*NMA*)

The conventionality of "Al desio" does not keep it from being Mozartean in many ways. By composing the aria in F major, the key of "Deh vieni," Mozart integrated it into the beautifully balanced tonal plan of *Figaro*.[51] He refrained from exploiting the full extent of Ferrarese's voice, making the vocal style of "Al desio" consistent with the rest of Susanna's music. His use of wind instruments is particularly beautiful, and richer than is normal in Italian rondòs of the period. The score includes a sextet of winds: two basset horns, two bassoons, and two flutes. Playing for the most part together in a group and often in antiphony with the strings, the winds give this aria an extraordinary sonority. (The basset horn was one of Mozart's favorite instruments, partly because of its use in the music of Viennese Freemasonry and partly because of his friendship with the great clarinetist and basset horn player Anton Stadler, also a Mason. Salieri, not a Mason, as far as we know, seems to have called for the basset horn in none of his operas.)

Mozart's rondò was a success in Vienna, if Zinzendorf's reaction is representative. He wrote in his diary on 7 May 1790: "To the opera *Le nozze di Figaro*. The duo of the two women and Ferraresi's rondo pleased as always."[52]

While the second version of *Figaro* continued to be performed during the second half of 1789, Da Ponte and Salieri brought *La cifra* to the stage. Ferrarese sang Eurilla, a role that suited her well. As discussed in chapter 13, Eurilla is a noblewoman brought up as a shepherdess, whose growing love for a nobleman begins to stir her noble blood. But she cannot understand her feelings; and her confusion reaches its climax just before the finale of the second and last act, in a solo scena with rondò, "Sola e mesta fra tormenti."

Da Ponte's text is a typical rondò poem in twelve ottonari:

Sola e mesta fra tormenti
  Passerò languendo gli anni,
  E farò de' miei lamenti
  Campi e selve risuonar.
Mi vedrò la notte e il giorno
  Neri oggetti all'alma intorno,
  E una barbara speranza
  Che vorrei, né so lasciar.
Ah perché spietato Amore,
  Nel mio core entrasti mai,
  Perché vidi i cari rai,
  Onde appresi a sospirar?

[Alone and dejected, I will pass the years languishing among torments, and I will make the fields and forests resound with my laments. Night or day, everything will be black to my

51. Heartz, *Mozart's Operas*, 150.
52. Zinzendorf, 7 May 1790, in *MDL*, 321.

senses, [made so] by a cruel hope that I want to give up but cannot. Ah, why, unmerciful Love, did you ever enter my heart? Why did I see the dear eyes from which I learned to sigh?]

The structure of Salieri's aria follows the conventions of rondò form as closely as does that of "Al desio," differing from Mozart's aria most importantly in lacking the transition between the two main themes, A and C:

Un poco lento	Allegro–Non tanto allegro–Più allegro
A-B-A	C-D-C-E

As in "Al desio" (and many other rondòs), melody A is a setting of the first quatrain; contrasting material B is a setting of the second quatrain. After repeating melody A, Salieri had the choice of writing a transition in the slow tempo (as he had in "Ah sia già de' miei sospiri") or shifting directly to the fast tempo (as Mozart did in "Al desio"). He did the latter.

The similarities between "Sola e mesta" and "Al desio" suggest that Salieri knew Mozart's aria (hardly surprising) and that he drew inspiration from it. Salieri set his rondò in the same key as Mozart's. The elaborate writing for winds in "Al desio" finds an echo in the even larger wind ensemble in Salieri's aria: pairs of flutes, oboes, clarinets, bassoons, and horns. Mozart accompanied the beginning of the main theme of the slow section with winds alone; Salieri went further in the same direction, accompanying his slow theme with two horns alone (ex. 14.5).

The opening themes themselves have similarities that go beyond the melodic conventions—such as those that encouraged the use of duple meter and gavotte rhythm—that helped to shape both melodies. They are identical in their vocal range (from middle C to A an octave and a sixth higher). Susanna's opening idea reappears, lightly varied, in the second measure of Eurilla's tune. The accompaniments too are close. The two horns

EXAMPLE 14.5 Salieri, *La cifra*, act 2, "Sola e mesta fra tormenti," mm. 1–12

(Continued on next page)

EXAMPLE 14.5 *(continued)*

with which Salieri accompanied Eurilla's rising line F–G–G–G♯–A are almost identical to the horn parts within the wind sextet that accompanies Susanna's F–G–G–A.

Mozart's melody culminates in an ascent from D to tonic F, with offbeat chords in the violins and bass descending from B♭ to G to F. After quickly touching its highest point, A, the melody descends to the final cadence. Salieri's melody reaches a similar climax, with the same descent in the bass and offbeat chords. But Salieri interrupted Ferrarese's movement upward toward A by having her sustain F for two and a half measures, then incorporating the A into a cadenza-like descent. He further delayed her arrival on F by delving first into her lower register. Salieri amplified and dramatized Mozart's closing gesture, making fuller use of Ferrarese's virtuosity and range.

This is not the only part of "Sola e mesta" in which Salieri, without the limitations imposed by an existing role, could exploit the talents of his prima donna more fully

EXAMPLE 14.6 Salieri, *La cifra,* act 2, "Sola e mesta fra tormenti," mm. 59–66

than Mozart. The vocal range that he required of Ferrarese in "Sola e mesta" represents an extension of a semitone in both directions beyond that in "Al desio." He made good use of one of Ferrarese's vocal specialties, having her leap between her highest and lowest notes.

The arias also differ in structure and proportions. Most of the musical interest of "Al desio" is concentrated in the long slow section, and especially the episode (part B). Salieri made his episode six measures shorter than Mozart's; it lacks the intricate interweaving of voice and winds that gives Mozart's episode its richness. But Salieri's fast section is much longer and more complex than Mozart's; it includes several changes of tempo and a sudden, dramatic modulation by a third, from tonic F to A♭ (at the beginning of part D: ex. 14.6) that recalls the move from G to B♭ when Eurilla confronts the wild boar in the finale of act 1. There is no tonal gesture of this kind in Mozart's aria, but sudden shifts of a third within a rondò were nothing new for Salieri. He had experimented with one in "Amor, pietoso Amore" (*Il ricco d'un giorno*), a rondò in A that moves abruptly to C.

In the autograph of *La cifra* we find the following comment by Salieri concerning his scena for Eurilla. It is possibly unique among his annotations in mentioning the name of a singer: "Instrumental recitative 'Alfin son sola' and Rondò 'Sola e mesta fra tormenti': Pieces in the high serious style, but suitable for the person who sang them and for the situation in which she finds herself, and above all because they were composed for a famous prima donna [in a footnote: 'Mad. Ferraresi'], who could perform them most perfectly, and won the greatest applause."[53]

Ferrarese and her admirers did not have to wait long for another brilliant role. Two months after the premiere of *La cifra* she became the first Fiordiligi in *Così*. Again Da Ponte saw to it that she had a rondò, which he placed, as usual, in the second act, furnishing the composer and singer with yet another classic rondò poem, "Per pietà, ben mio, perdona." Just as Salieri seems to have learned from "Al desio di chi t'adora," so Mozart in turn seems to have learned from "Sola e mesta." Fiordiligi's rondò, indeed, resembles Eurilla's more closely than it does Susanna's. And it resembles "Sola e mesta" in precisely those respects in which Salieri's aria differs from Mozart's earlier rondò.

In the slow part of "Sola e mesta" Salieri wrote an episode six measures shorter than the analogous episode in Mozart's "Al desio." In "Per pietà" Mozart shortened the episode by another six measures: it lacks most of the repetition of words, the tranquil lyricism of the analogous passage in Mozart's previous rondò. Instead of the elaborate transition with which Mozart returned to the principal theme of the slow section in "Al desio," in "Per pietà" he ended the episode with just a simple cadence on the dominant, as Salieri did in "Sola e mesta."

While the episode in the slow section underwent progressive diminution in the three rondòs, the final part of the fast section became progressively longer and more elaborate, growing from thirty measures in "Al desio" to forty-one in "Sola e mesta" to forty-eight in "Per pietà."

The vocal style of "Per pietà" is also closer to that of "Sola e mesta" than to that of Mozart's earlier rondò. We find the same dramatic leaps that Salieri exploited in Eurilla's aria. Here too Mozart went beyond Salieri, extending Ferrarese's voice yet again a half step in both directions. Just as Salieri's opening melody reminds us of the opening of Mozart's "Al desio," so the opening of "Per pietà," in its leaps from the tonic down to the fifth scale degree and back to the tonic, reminds us of the beginning of "Sola e mesta." By transposing the leaps down a semitone Mozart emphasized more effectively than Salieri the beauty of Ferrarese's low register (ex. 14.7).

One of Salieri's best ideas was to accompany the beginning of his slow section with two horns alone. Salieri's two horns appear in Mozart's "Per pietà," but not at the beginning. Salieri was content to repeat the melody of the slow section literally, without any variation, when it returned after the episode. His practice reflected the Italian assumption that it was the performer's job, not the composer's, to vary a rondò's melody. Mozart, in contrast, almost always varied the melody or its accompaniment in some interesting way, such as the delicate pizzicato that accompanies the slow melody of "Al

53. Salieri's annotations in the autograph of *La cifra* are transcribed in Angermüller, *Leben*, 3:53–55; Angermüller, *Fatti*, 107–8; and Swenson, 149–50.

EXAMPLE 14.7 Mozart, *Così fan tutte,* act 2, "Per pietà ben mio perdona," mm. 1–2

For pity's sake, my love, forgive

desio" on its return. In "Per pietà" he introduced Salieri's horns. Having allowed the horns a short solo in the slow section, he made them a crucial part of the fast section, their virtuoso display going far beyond anything Salieri dared to ask.

One important aspect of Salieri's rondò finds no counterpart in "Per pietà": the sudden shift from F to A♭ in the fast part. Compared to "Sola e mesta" Mozart's rondò is harmonically tame. The color and virtuosity of the winds and brass, particularly the horns, compensate for its lack of tonal complexity. This does not mean that Mozart had no interest in the kind of harmonic surprises exploited by Salieri. Mozart's last rondòs, those of Sesto and Vitellia in *La clemenza di Tito,* are full of abrupt and daring modulations that differentiate these arias clearly from those he wrote for Susanna and Fiordiligi.[54] "Deh per questo istante solo," in A major, contains two sudden modulations by a third. When Sesto sings "Disperato io vado a morte" in C he reminds us of Eurilla singing "Fra tormenti" in A♭. It was from arias like "Sola e mesta" that Mozart learned the effectiveness of sudden third modulations in the fast section of a rondò and their usefulness for the expression of heroic pathos.

Mozart's "Al desio" and "Per pietà," in spite of having been composed less than six months apart for the same singer, and within the parameters of a very conventional form, are quite different. The differences are easier to understand if we think of "Sola e mesta" as a transitional work, inspired by and in turn inspiration for Mozart: an aria that demonstrated to him the strength of certain alternatives to his own previous attempt to write a rondò for Ferrarese and encouraged him to take these alternatives further than Salieri. These rondòs show us two composers contributing to an evolutionary process effecting large-scale form as well as melody, accompaniment, and instrumentation. As rivals for the patronage of Joseph II and the Viennese public Salieri and Mozart must have mistrusted and resented one another; but their rondòs for Ferrarese suggest that, as musicians, they respected and learned from one another.

54. "Compared to Vitellia's 'Non più di fiori' the two Rondeaux of 1789 are as tame animals to wild ones" (Heartz, "Mozart and His Italian Contemporaries: 'La clemenza di Tito,'" 283). And Sesto's "Deh per questo istante solo" is no less wild than Vitellia's rondò; see Heartz, *Mozart's Operas,* 323–27; and Rice, *W. A. Mozart: La clemenza di Tito,* 91–95.

Beyond Opera Buffa: *Axur, Tito,* and *Die Zauberflöte*

In his last two operas Mozart explored genres other than opera buffa. He may have found inspiration in a work that, despite having been written for Joseph's opera buffa company, departs in most respects from the conventions of opera buffa. Echoes of Salieri's *Axur* in *Tito* and *Die Zauberflöte* suggest that Mozart's last operas would have been quite different had Salieri not written *Axur* three years earlier.

Flexibility of form, many ensembles (including finales), integration of chorus (including offstage chorus) into ensembles—*Tito* and *Die Zauberflöte* share these feature with one another and with *Axur.* The offstage chorus singing "Ah" on a diminished seventh chord in the first finale of *Tito* recalls Salieri's offstage choral "Ah" that interrupts the second love duet in act 1 of *Axur* (see ex. 12.7). The arrival of the three ladies near the beginning of *Die Zauberflöte,* where Tamino's C-minor cadence leads directly to A♭ major sustained over two measures, looks back to the interruption of the C-minor cadence in the trio near the end of *Axur,* also with two measures of A♭-major harmony, as Axur's slaves cry out for help.[55] A transition in *Tito* linking Vitellia's rondò in F, "Non più di fiori," to the following G-major chorus, "Che del ciel, che degli dei" reminds one of the transition with which Salieri linked the male quartet and the concluding chorus in the finale of act 3 of *Axur* (exx. 14.8 and 14.9). Both passages involve a sudden shift in tempo from fast to moderate (Salieri's "Mezzo allegro del doppio" pre-

EXAMPLE 14.8 Salieri, *Axur re d'Ormus,* act 3, "Non partir, la scelta è ingiusta" (finale), mm. 117–29

(Continued on next page)

55. For the passage from *Axur* see Rice, "The Operas of Antonio Salieri," 218.

EXAMPLE 14.8 *(continued)*

sumably requires a tempo half that of the previous Presto). Both feature march rhythms, antiphonal effects at the beginning (Salieri's horns answer oboes; Mozart's strings answer brass and timpani), and fast scales at the end. The harmonic destination of both transitions is the dominant of the following chorus, reiterated by the whole orchestra in unison and ending with a grand fermata. The similarity in conception and

EXAMPLE 14.9 Mozart, *La clemenza di Tito,* act 2, "Non più di fiori," and transition to chorus "Che del ciel, che degli dei," mm. 180–89 (*NMA*)

(*Continued on next page*)

EXAMPLE 14.9 (*continued*)

function of these transitions shows that Mozart had much to learn from Salieri; but that similarity also calls attention to the extraordinary craftsmanship of Mozart's music, which is more concise, more purposeful in its harmony, and more muscular in its voice leading than Salieri's.

Axur had its origins in Beaumarchais's assumption that "an opera is neither a tragedy nor a comedy but participates in both and can embrace all the genres." *Die Zauberflöte* illustrates this conception of opera as clearly as *Axur.* Mozart's opera, called a "dramma eroicomico" when performed in Dresden and Prague in Italian translation,[56] shares with *Axur* an exotic setting, a solemn temple scene, and several splendid crowd scenes. The themes of abduction and rescue are common to both operas. Tamino and Pamina match Atar and Aspasia in goodness, nobility, and fidelity, while Papageno far surpasses Biscroma as a purveyor of comic relief. The priest-ruler Sarastro combines the offices of King Axur and Arteneo, high priest of Brahma. (Invocations of Brahma in *Axur* are echoed in another Viennese Singspiel of the period, Wenzel Müller's *Das Sonnenfest der Braminen,* 1790.) The trombones that contribute to the grandeur of the first version of *Axur* sound again in *Die Zauberflöte.*

A few weeks before his death Mozart invited Salieri and Cavalieri to attend a performance of *Die Zauberflöte* as his guests. He wrote to Constanze:

> You cannot imagine how charming [*artig*] they were and how much they liked not only my music, but the libretto and everything. They both said that it was an *operone* ("big opera"), worthy to be performed for the grandest festival and before the greatest monarch, and that they would often go to see it, as they had never seen a more beautiful or delightful show. He listened and watched most attentively and from the overture to the last chorus there was not

56. Sartori nos. 10699–701.

> a single number that did not call forth from him a bravo! or bello! It seemed as if they could not thank me enough for my kindness.[57]

When *Die Zauberflöte* reached the stage *Axur* was less than four years old, but it had already become closely associated with the Habsburg monarchy. First performed in celebration of the wedding of Archduke Francis, it became quickly known as Joseph's favorite opera. Leopold II chose to make his first appearance in the Burgtheater during a performance that celebrated Franz's second wedding in September 1790. *Axur* was one of several operas performed in Frankfurt in celebration of Leopold's coronation as emperor. When, less than a year later, Salicri praised *Die Zauberflöte* as an opera "worthy to be performed for the grandest festival and before the greatest monarch," was he perhaps acknowledging its kinship to *Axur*?

57. Mozart to his wife, 14 October 1791, in *MBA*, 4:161–62. Note Mozart's use of "artig" to describe Salieri. On 7 May 1783, expressing doubt as to Da Ponte's sincerity, he wrote to his father: "sie wissen wohl die Herrn Italiener sind ins gesicht sehr artig!"

15

LEOPOLD II, TOMEONI, AND THE TRIUMPH OF NEAPOLITAN OPERA BUFFA

As an old man in the United States Da Ponte wrote an autobiographical poem that, in an English translation by his daughter, fondly recalls the "brilliant days" of Joseph's reign, mourns the emperor's death, and expresses hostility to his successor, the "tyrant" Leopold II:

> But ah! in darkness set these brilliant days;
> Relentless Death my blooming chaplet tore,
> And sunk in tones of deepest woe my lays.
> All Austria then the garb of sadness wore,
> A Tyrant filled his throne, and nought for me,
> Save life, remained of all that charmed before.[1]

When relentless death struck Joseph down on 20 February 1790, Da Ponte was not the only theatrical artist who mourned him. Da Ponte's gracious prince had smiled on Salieri, and on Mozart too. They must have shared the poet's sense of loss.

With Joseph's death began the most unproductive year of Mozart's adult life. During this year of financial crisis, illness, and artistic uncertainty he began many pieces only to abandon them after a few measures. The emperor's death was followed by a disrup-

1. Sheila Hodges, *Lorenzo da Ponte: The Life and Times of Mozart's Librettist* (London, 1985), 103.

tion of Salieri's musical output even more extreme. After several years in which he had produced at least one opera a year, he brought no new operas to the stage during 1790 and the four years that followed: this was the longest period without the production of a new opera since the beginning of his career. And with the operas that he presented thereafter he was never able to capture such a large share of the repertory as he had in the 1780s.[2]

Leopold II as Theater Director

Joseph's brother and successor was born in Vienna in 1747. As the second son of Maria Theresa and Francis of Lorraine to survive to adulthood, he inherited the grand duchy of Tuscany from his father in 1765. Under the name Pietro Leopoldo he ruled Tuscany from 1765 to 1790. Twenty-five years in Italy shaped his musical tastes and habits of musical patronage. By the time he returned to Vienna in March 1790, a few weeks after his brother's death, he had clear ideas about how a ruler should contribute to and manipulate the musical institutions of his subjects, and about how the theater should be used to enhance the sovereign's prestige.

Leopold's ideas about musical theater differed considerably from Joseph's. When the grand duke visited Vienna in 1784 he recorded mixed feelings about his brother's theater and its management:

> The court theater is composed of a good troupe of German actors and a good troupe of Italian opera buffa. The orchestra is good, and the above troupes perform on alternate days throughout the year; there are no ballets. The audience for the German plays is very small. It is completely at the cost of the court, which pays all these people, of whom there are twice as many as necessary, very well; the whole is an amusement of Count Rosenberg, who directs it, and under his direction the famous intriguer and abusive abbé Casti; as for the German company, the emperor's valet Strack takes part in the intrigues.[3]

With such attitudes one would expect Leopold to make changes in the management and policies of the court theaters on his arrival in Vienna. But it was not until the second year of his reign that he began to shape Viennese theatrical and musical life.

During 1790 Leopold took no active role in the running of the Burgtheater. Rosenberg maintained control; Salieri maintained his position as music director; Da Ponte

2. This chapter is based primarily on Rice, "Emperor."

3. "Relazione del Viaggio e Soggiorno fatto da S. A. R. in Vienna nel Luglio 1784," 454–55, HHStA, Sb, Kart. 17; quoted in Rice, "Emperor," 73.

continued to influence decision making. Theatrical policy remained in most respects unchanged from what it had been during the last years of Joseph's reign. Few new singers were hired. Of the six singers who made up the original cast of *Così fan tutte,* the last opera written for Joseph's troupe, at least five remained in imperial employ through Leopold's first year in power. (Luisa Villeneuve, the first Dorabella, left sometime before the beginning of the theatrical year 1791, but it is not known exactly when).[4]

Repertory during the first year of Leopold's reign largely reflected the tastes of the 1780s, but also looked to the future.[5] The single work most often performed during the theatrical year 1790 was an opera newly imported from Naples. Guglielmi's *La pastorella nobile,* performed twenty-four times, anticipated the popularity that Neapolitan opera buffa would enjoy during the 1790s. Close behind were two Josephinian works: *Il re Teodoro in Venezia* and *L'arbore di Diana,* performed twenty-three times and twenty-two times, respectively. Of the seven works performed eight or more times, six were written for Joseph's troupe: those mentioned above plus *Figaro* and three operas by Salieri, who was the only composer to have more than two operas performed: *Axur, Il talismano,* and *La cifra.* But apparently neither he nor Mozart received encouragement from the court to compose new operas for the Burgtheater.

Leopold's appointment of Count Wenzel Ugarte as Musikgraf in January 1791 marks a crucial turning point in the direction of Viennese musical theater, from a policy of continuity with the recent past to a policy of reorganization and innovation in which Leopold played an important role. The appointment was but one manifestation of a thorough reorganization of the government bureaucracy inaugurated by Leopold during his second year, by which he hoped to gain closer control of all elements of government. He wanted to take government out of the hands of the principal ministers and establish close links with the bureaucracy that was actually carrying out imperial policy.[6]

The office of the Musikgraf had been unfilled since 1775, that is, since just before Joseph's theatrical reorganization. Leopold announced his decision to appoint a Musikgraf in a letter to Obersthofmeister Prince Starhemberg dated 15 January 1791. Starhemberg, jealously guarding the prerogatives of his office, and suspicious that the emperor wanted to run the court theaters through Ugarte, wrote to Leopold, reminding him that the Musikgraf, when the position had been filled, had always been subordinate to the Obersthofmeister. Starhemberg's fears were well founded. Leopold returned his letter with a note in the margin: "Musikgraf Ugarte will indeed be under the direction

4. Villeneuve does not appear in the payment records for the theatrical year 1791 (HHStA, GH, Rechnungsbuch 1791).

5. This paragraph is based on the calendar of performances in Hadamowsky, *Hoftheater,* vol. 1.

6. Ernst Wangermann, *From Joseph II to the Jacobin Trials,* 2d ed. (London, 1969), 107.

of the Obersthofmeister; but in matters concerning the direction of the theater he will be under my authority alone."[7]

The Fall of Da Ponte and Ferrarese

Having consolidated control of the theater, Leopold moved it quickly from the state in which Joseph had left it. Among his first important changes was the dismissal of Da Ponte and Adriana Ferrarese; both left the Burgtheater at the end of the theatrical year 1790.

It is probably no coincidence that they were dismissed so soon after Leopold's appointment of a Musikgraf answering directly to him in theatrical business. Da Ponte, who more than anyone else (except perhaps Salieri) represented the policies and ideals of Josephinian opera buffa, had to be removed if Leopold was to move Viennese theater in a new direction. His intrigues and his friendship with Ferrarese, furthermore, involved him in disputes that a court beset with serious external and internal threats could not abide.

An amusing example of the hostility and controversy that Da Ponte inspired, the anonymous pamphlet *Anti–da Ponte* (Vienna, 1791) rails at great length against the poet and his works. The pamphlet reaches its climax with a mock trial at which he is accused of incompetence by literary figures whose works he adapted for the stage and by composers with whom he collaborated.

> Guarini confronted Da Ponte with extraordinary reproaches for having made a mess of his beautiful poem, *Il pastor fido*. . . .
>
> Now Beaumarchais spoke. The vehemence with which he began his accusations suggested that he must have been badly mistreated by Da Ponte. He asserted that Da Ponte had completely misunderstood his play *La Folle Journée ou Le Mariage de Figaro*, for otherwise he would not have made such a changeling of it. But Da Ponte's treatment of his *Tarare* was unforgivable. Above all he had played the ignoble trick of omitting any mention of Beaumarchais's name on the playbill. On account of his ambition to be taken for the author of a well-written play he concealed the name of the true author. Da Ponte learned from the gypsies something that required no courage, at least no courage of a good kind: how to steal children, how to disguise them and cripple them. Tarare was the hero of the drama. He was its center, around which everything was organized: the mainspring and the object of all the elements of its plot. Da Ponte, on the other hand, gave the drama another name in order to make it unrecognizable, and made Axur, king of Hormuz, the main character. In act 1 Da Ponte allowed the audience to see the abduction of Aspasia. Yet in act 2 he informs the audience again, in a stale narrative, of what it already has seen. Here he makes his clumsiness as clear as day; for a good poet has a character narrate only what could not be represented on stage. Moreover,

7. HHStA, OMeA, Akten 1791, no. 165; quoted in Rice, "Emperor," 366–68.

said Beaumarchais, Da Ponte wrongly eliminated many things, changed many characters, left out important matters and moving ceremonies; in a word he deformed the whole drama to such an extent that Beaumarchais could no longer recognize it as his own child.

Shortly thereafter Da Ponte's musical collaborators came to the witness stand:

Salieri and Mozart loudly complained about the tasteless, clumsy, and incoherent librettos that he had repeatedly given them to set to music. They were often forced to summon all their art in order to give something harmonious to the public, in spite of the barren words. But they now made an irreversible decision not to write another note on a text by Da Ponte.[8]

The "irreversible decision" attributed to Mozart and Salieri by this pamphleteer was exactly the decision made by Salieri after the failure of *Il ricco d'un giorno* in 1784, according to Da Ponte: Salieri "solemnly swore he would rather allow his fingers to be cut off than set another verse of mine to music."

Ferrarese, through whom Da Ponte, Salieri, and Mozart had infused Viennese opera buffa of the late 1780s with the spirit of opera seria, was as closely associated with Jo-

8. *Guarini* machte dem *da Ponte* ganz ausserordentliche Vorwürfe darüber, daß er ihm sein schönes Gedicht *Il Pastor fido*, so sehr verstellt habe. . . .

Nun kam *Beaumarchais* zur Rede. Die Heftigkeit, mit welcher er seine Vorwürfe anfieng, ließ vermuthen, daß er von dem *da Ponte* gräulich müsse mißhandelt worden seyn. Er bestand darauf, *da Ponte* habe seine Stück *La folle journée ou le mariage de Figaro* gar nicht verstanden, denn sonst würde er keinen solchen Wechselbalg drausgemacht haben. Aber die Art, mit welcher *da Ponte* seinen *Tarare* behandelt hatte, konnte er ihm gar nicht verzeihen. Ueberhaupt hätte er einen unedlen Streich darin begangen, daß er seiner (des *Beaumarchais*) auf dem Anschlagzettel mit keinem Wörtchen gedacht habe, und bloß aus Ehrgeitz, für den Autor eines wohlgerathenen Stückes angesehen zu werden, habe er des wahren Verfassers Namen verschwiegen. *Da Ponte* habe etwas (wozu freylich kein Muth gehöre, wenigstens nicht von der guten Art) den Zigeunern abgelernt; fremde Kinder zu stehlen, sie zu verstellen, und zu Krüppeln zu machen. *Tarare* sey eigentlich der Held des Stückes; der Mittelpunkt, um den sich alles bewege, die Triebfeder und Absicht aller Handlungen.—*Da Ponte* hingegen habe dem Stücke, um es unkenntlich zu machen, einen andern Namen gegeben, und den Axur König von Ormus zur Hauptperson gemacht. Im 1ten Akte lasse *da Ponte* vor den Augen der Zuschauer die Aspasia entführen, dem ungeachtet mache er hernach im 2ten dem Publikum das, was er schon gesehen hat, durch eine fade Erzählung noch einmal bekannt; wodurch er seine Ungeschicklichkeit klar an Tag gegeben habe, indem ein guter Dichter nur das erzählen laße, was nicht vorgestellt werden könne. Ferner sagte *Beaumarchais,* daß *da Ponte* manche Sachen unrichtig ausgedrückt, manchen Personen eine Wendung gegeben, wesentliche Dinge und rührende Ceremonien ausgelassen, mit einem Worte das ganze Stücke so verunstaltet habe, daß er es unmöglich für sein ächtes Kind anerkennen könne. . . .

Salieri und *Mozart* beklagten sich laut über den geschmacklosen, holpernden und unzusammenhängenden Operntext, den er ihnen mehrmal, um ihn in Musik zu setzen, vorgelegt habe. Sie hätten oft aller ihrer Kunst aufbiethen müßen, um dem Publikum, der dürren Worte ungeachtet, etwas harmonisches zu liefern. Allein sie hätten auch jetzt den festen Entschluß gefaßt nicht, eine einzige Note mehr zu einem *da Ponti*schen Text zu schreiben (*Anti–da Ponte* [Vienna, 1791], 47–51; I am grateful to Bruce Alan Brown for sharing with me his transcription of these passages).

sephinian opera as Da Ponte. It is not surprising that Leopold, as one of the first actions in his transformation of Viennese opera buffa, should replace her with a prima donna whose talents were completely different from hers. Her relations with Da Ponte, moreover, made it natural for the emperor to dismiss the two of them together, which he did at the end of Carnival 1791. *Der heimliche Botschafter,* a handwritten newsletter, announced on 25 March 1791: "The Italian court poet Abbé Da Ponte has been dismissed and in a few days will leave for Italy in the company of Madame Ferrarese."[9] Ferrarese made her last appearance on the stage of the Burgtheater on 13 April, singing the role of Flora in the cantata *Flora e Minerva,* with music by Weigl and a text by Da Ponte; she left for Venice soon thereafter.[10] By 8 May Da Ponte himself had withdrawn from the city to Mödling, a village near the Wienerwald, where he entered into a correspondence with one of Leopold's secret informants in an unsuccessful effort to salvage his reputation and his job.[11]

Da Ponte's memoranda found their way into police files, where they have remained.[12] They include a list of his enemies, the first of whom was Salieri (fig. 15.1). The poet's rambling and somewhat incoherent accusations against his former collaborator probably contain some truth, but they are more valuable as a record of his own bitterness and confusion:

> Principal enemy: Sig. Salieri
>
> 1 Because he alone dominates in the theater.
>
> 2 Because he ruins the operas of the other composers, whenever he likes, without anyone opposing him.
>
> 3 Because he distributes operas, performances, and roles according to his own ulterior motives.
>
> 4 Because he assigns prima-donna roles to Cavalieri, whom I have recommended to be pensioned off.
>
> 5 Because he has no one under his eyes who criticizes his shortcomings in respect to the company, the management, and the public.
>
> 6 Because of his fear of a gentleman who knows about all his weaknesses.

9. Quoted in Hodges, *Lorenzo da Ponte,* 112.

10. The playbill announcing the performance of Weigl's *Flora e Minerva* on 13 April 1791 (A-Wth) contains the following notice: "NB. Mad. Ferrarese wird heute das letzte mal vor einer hohen Noblesse und einem hochansehnlichen Publikum in dem Part der Flora sich hören zu lassen die Ehre haben." In a letter dated Vienna, 18 June 1791, Da Ponte informed Casanova that Ferrarese had left Vienna for Venice; see *Carteggi Casanoviani: Lettere di Giacomo Casanova e di altri a lui,* ed. Pompeo Molmenti (n.p., [c. 1916]), 1:265.

11. The story of Da Ponte's fall from favor and departure from Vienna is told in detail in Otto Michtner, "Der Fall Abbé Da Ponte," in *Mitteilungen des Österreichischen Staatsarchivs* 19 (1966): 170–209.

12. Several are transcribed in Michtner, "Der Fall Abbé Da Ponte."

Informazione pel Sig.e Baron de Styber.

Primario nemico Il Sig.e Salieri.

1 Per dominar solo in teatro.

2 Per rovinar a piacere l'opere degli altri
Maestri, senza aver chi gli si opponga.

3 Per distribuir a tenore de' suoi secondi fini
opere, recite, e parti.

4 Per far cantare la Cavalieri da prima
Donna, ch'io aveva proposto di pensionare.

5 Per non aver sotto gli occhi chi gli rimpro=
veri i suoi mancamenti verso la compagnia,
verso la Direzione, verso il Pubblico.

6 Pel timore d'un galantuomo, a cui son
note tutte le sue debolezze.

7 Per aver detto più volte pubblicamente che
al cembalo non bisogna aver un maestro
di cappella, ma un cembalista.

Suoi canali il Principe di
Rosemberg.

Secondo nemico il Sig.e Thorvart.

1 Per avergli parlato chiaro sui veri interes=
si teatrali.

2 Per avergli offerto i drappi di seta a miglior
prezzo, e l'illuminazione a due fiorini
meno per sera di quel che paga la Direzio-

FIGURE 15.1 "Primario nemico Il Sig. Salieri," a list of accusations against Salieri in Da Ponte's hand, probably compiled in 1791. Vertrauliche Akten, Haus-, Hof-, und Staatsarchiv, Vienna.

7 Because he has said publicly several times that at the keyboard one needs not a music director but rather a keyboard player.

Banned from Vienna and its environs in June 1791, Da Ponte traveled south to Trieste; there his struggle to keep his post culminated the following month, when he confronted Leopold, who was returning to Vienna from a long Italian trip. During an audience lasting an hour and a half, and described in detail in his memoirs, he pleaded with the emperor to rescind his dismissal.[13] Like much of Da Ponte's memoirs, his account is almost certainly a mixture—as entertaining as it is self-serving—of fact and fiction, with his enemies depicted in the worst possible light. But some of what he wrote was corroborated by Leopold's subsequent statements and actions.

Da Ponte explained to the monarch why he had not come forward directly to Leopold in Vienna to defend himself during the previous winter. He simply was not able to penetrate the army of functionaries and ministers who blocked his way to the throne; the culprits were Rosenberg, his secretary Johann Thorwart, and the newly appointed Musikgraf, Ugarte. Leopold was sympathetic, criticizing those cited by Da Ponte: "Rosemberg [the Italian version of his name] knows little about managing a theater. And I have no need for his poets [Casti in particular is meant here]; I have found one more to my taste in Venice [Giovanni Bertati]." The emperor characterized Ugarte as a bureaucrat with no will of his own, and indeed this may be exactly why he chose him as Musikgraf: "Ugart is a bag of straw. He does everything he is told to do; and the last man who speaks to him is always right." He dismissed Thorwart with a simple "Oh birbante!" (rogue). And Salieri came in for Leopold's harshest criticism: "Oh, I don't need you to tell me about Salieri. I know him well enough. I know all his intrigues, and I know Cavalieri's too. He is an insufferable egoist who wants success in my theater only for his operas and his mistress. He is not only your enemy, but the enemy of all the composers, all the singers, all the Italians; and above all, my enemy because he knows that I know him. I don't want either his German woman or him in my theater any more."

Leopold stated his intention to take personal control of the theater: "Now I am director and impresario; and my Count Sack-of-Straw needs to do nothing; I, I will command, and we will see if things go better." Da Ponte, encouraged by Leopold's hostility to his persecutors, asked the emperor to reinstate him. Leopold hedged, for surely Da Ponte was among those representatives of the old order he wanted to replace. Da Ponte's account comes to a climax as it describes how, falling to his knees, he begged Leopold to reconsider. The emperor repeatedly ordered him to rise, finally offering him a hand and bringing him to his feet. He said that he would do what he could, but promised nothing.

13. Da Ponte, 148–54.

Leopold's Theatrical Plan

In March 1791 Leopold, together with his brother-in-law and sister, the king and queen of Naples, had left Vienna for Italy. The emperor had opportunities to observe singers and dancers during his visits to Venice, Florence, Milan, and Trieste. But it was especially in Milan that he gave serious thought to the theaters of Vienna and the changes that he wanted to make. A biography of Leopold published anonymously in 1796, by a writer hostile to the emperor and sympathetic to the ideals of the French Revolution, described his recruitment of singers and dancers in Milan within the context of flagrant promiscuity, "constant amorous adventures of the night." In addition to the skimpily dressed women who visited the emperor's quarters, "a constant round of female dancers and singers besieged the palace, seeking employment in Vienna, for among the serious concerns occupying the mind of His Imperial Majesty was that of recruiting personnel of both sexes for the theaters of Austria." [14]

Late-eighteenth-century critics of royalty liked to accuse their rulers of extravagant sexual escapades (Leopold's sister Marie Antoinette suffered the same kind of accusations); there is no reason to take this critic completely seriously. But Leopold did make important decisions about the Viennese theater on his Italian tour.

On 15 July 1791, just before returning to Vienna, the emperor wrote to Ugarte, declaring himself ready to begin his transformation of Viennese theater. He instructed his Musikgraf not to engage new personnel or extend contracts with those already in court employ and to prepare a memorandum summarizing the present state of the theaters.[15] On his return to Vienna later in July he responded to Ugarte's memorandum (which does not seem to have survived) with a detailed outline of his plans for far-reaching changes in the repertory and personnel of the court theaters.[16]

A New Theater?

Leopold began his outline with a reference to plans for the renovation or replacement of the Burgtheater, putting off any definitive decision on the matter. He referred to an architect named Moretti, who had drawn up plans for a theater to be built on the site of the imperial stables (the Stallburg, which still stands). The plans doubtless originated in the feeling that the Burgtheater did not represent the court in the grandiose manner

14. [Francesco Beccatini], *Vita pubblica e privata di Pietro Leopoldo d'Austria Granduca di Toscana poi Imperatore Leopoldo II* ([Milan], 1796), 295–96; quoted in Rice, "Emperor," 76.

15. HHStA, HP, Bd. 78b, fols. 113v–114r; quoted in Rice, "Emperor," 370–71.

16. Leopold's memorandum survives in the form of a rough draft under the title *Entwurf zu einer Allerhöchsten Resolution über den Vortrag des Musikgrafen Grafen v. Ugarte,* HHStA, HP, Bd. 78b, fol. 197–202; in Rice, "Emperor," 372–77.

proper to it. The theater was small; it had always been a makeshift building, originally a tennis court, restored every few years but never entirely satisfactory. In 1793 Johann Friedel complained that "the interior disposition does not betray the presence of a great court . . . the boxes are small, poorly decorated, and illuminated still worse . . . one must go early to get a place given the niggardly space of the hall." [17]

Joseph Sartori, author of a laudatory account of Leopold's reign, referred to plans for a new theater: "The court architect from Florence was called to Vienna to make various improvements on the pleasure palaces Schönbrunn and Laxenburg. The emperor expressed the wish to build a theater suitable for the capital based on a model already completed." [18] The architect Moretti to whom Leopold referred in his plans may be the "Hofarchitekt von Florenz" referred to by Sartori, but no architect of that name is known to have worked in Florence during Leopold's reign. That Moretti did indeed prepare a magnificent model we know from Zinzendorf, who examined it on 12 November 1791: "From there to the Josephstadt . . . at the residence of Chevalier de Moretti . . . to see the model of the big theater to be built in place of the Stallburg. It is superb. The stage 45 feet wide, 65 feet high in the parterre, the stage 80 feet long. The shape is that of a bell; five floors." [19]

Moretti's theater was never built, probably owing both to the shortness of Leopold's reign and to the precarious financial situation in which the court found itself. Sartori puts the theater project among several plans that were kept from being realized by lack of funds.

Ballet and Opera Seria

Turning from the building to the performances he wished to see take place within it, Leopold briefly referred to his plans for establishing a permanent ballet troupe in the Burgtheater after a decade in which ballet had no regular place on its stage. Clearly in charge of every detail of this important repertorial shift, he had chosen the dancers and negotiated their contracts; and he had decided when the troupe was to make its debut. He did not mention the name of his newly appointed ballet master, Antonio Muzzarelli, who had performed often in Florence during the 1780s and whose work he knew well.

Later in the outline Leopold turned to opera seria, which he planned to reintroduce to Vienna along with ballet, with the help of the seria singers Cecilia Giuliani and Vincenzo Maffoli. This is the only place in the outline where he named works to be per-

17. [Johann Friedel], *Vertraute Briefe zur Characteristik von Wien* (Görlitz, 1793), 2:45; quoted in translation by Daniel Heartz, "Nicolas Jadot and the Building of the Burgtheater," *Musical Quarterly* 68 (1982), 17.

18. Joseph von Sartori, *Leopoldinische Annalen*, 2 vols. (Augsburg, 1792–93), 2:128.

19. Zinzendorf, 12 November 1791; quoted in Harbecke, "Das Tagebuch des Grafen Karl von Zinzendorf," 137.

formed: Sebastiano Nasolini's *Teseo a Stige* and Alessio Prati's *La vendetta di Nino*. Both had been first performed in Florence. Leopold's decision to have them performed in Vienna was based on his own knowledge of them. He took on himself the responsibility of finding a male soprano for the opera seria troupe, "for without him the opera cannot take place."

Leopold called for a nightly alternation of Italian opera and German spoken drama in the Burgtheater, with opera buffa alternating with opera seria. He commanded that ballet be coordinated (*concertiret*) with opera seria, meaning probably that dancers were to perform during an opera rather than during intermission or after an opera (the normal Italian practice) and that the dance was to be thematically related to the opera. But two paragraphs later he clearly called for entr'acte ballets as well, to be performed with both comic and serious opera.

It was important for Leopold that the newly formed ballet and opera seria troupes make their debuts together, at the beginning of November 1791. He wanted his innovations to have as strong an impact as possible, to unfold not as isolated events but as a coordinated sequence of exciting premieres. One part of the reorganization left unmentioned in the outline was the return of the Kärntnertortheater to active duty as a court theater, equal in status to the Burgtheater. From the inauguration of Leopold's theatrical program on his name day, 15 November 1791, the two theaters opened simultaneously. Ballets, spoken plays, and operas alternated between them, as they had during the first half of the 1770s.

Salieri

Leopold showed in this outline that he was quite serious when, in his audience with Da Ponte in Trieste, he criticized those who ran the Burgtheater. More than anything else he wanted to eliminate superannuated personnel and officials who represented the old order. Thorwart played an important role in Rosenberg's theatrical administration. Leopold had called him a "rogue," according to Da Ponte; the emperor singled him out in the outline as particularly undesirable: "The Court Secretary Thorwart is to have no further influence in theatrical business." Francesco Bussani, whom Leopold had called "that rascally intriguer" in Trieste, played some kind of supervisory role within the Italian troupe. Leopold called for him to be removed from his position of authority: "Bussani will from now on no longer have any say in the direction of the theater or in the distribution of roles."

The next paragraph deals with the musical direction of the theater. Many corrections and interpolations in the manuscript make the passage difficult to read and suggest that Leopold had not yet made up his mind about this part of his theatrical reorganization. What he seems to have decided, at least provisionally, was this: "Kapellmeister Salieri will on 1 November certainly remain at the post he now occupies, but he will at the same time be relieved of the direction of the theater; Weigl, and when he is indisposed, Umlauf, will alone have to remain, but only to accompany [i.e., to conduct rehearsals and performances], without any say in the distribution of roles, or [in the management of] the troupe."

Salieri, so strongly entrenched in the court hierarchy and so highly regarded throughout Europe that Leopold probably did not think seriously about removing him altogether, was to remain as Hofkapellmeister. But he was to relinquish the post of operatic music director. Leopold assigned to Weigl the tasks of rehearsing and conducting operatic performances. Again his changes are consistent with attitudes ascribed to him by Da Ponte, who quoted him as saying of Salieri: "I don't want either his German woman or him in my theater any more."

Leopold had disposed of Cavalieri earlier in his outline: "Cavalieri is to be retired as of 1 November." She was not the only singer closely associated with Salieri whom Leopold wanted to get rid of. Maria Anna and Therese Gassmann, the daughters of Salieri's teacher, had studied singing with Salieri and had recently joined the troupe under his protection. Leopold wrote: "To the two Gassmanns I grant an increase in salary of 200 Gulden each, in view of their circumstances and of the service rendered by their father, but they are to be relieved of any further singing in the theater."

Mosel put a better face on the transfer of responsibilities from Salieri to Weigl:

> Having returned to Vienna [from the coronation ceremonies in Frankfurt and Pressburg, October–November 1790], Salieri asked for and received, after twenty-four years of almost uninterrupted and laborious effort, his dismissal from the direction of operas, in exchange for which however he was assigned a calmer and easier duty, to compose a new opera for the court theater every year. His place in the opera house was bestowed on "his dear and valiant pupil" Joseph Weigl, chosen from among many other candidates, in order, as the monarch was pleased to express it, "to honor the master through the student."[20]

Weigl's own account of the reorganization reveals another side of the story:

> During my absence [in August 1791, when Weigl was at Eszterháza] a great change happened at the court theater. The Emperor Leopold wanted the opera to be run as in Italy. Specifically he found it demeaning that such famous men as Salieri should have to perform at the keyboard; such masters should only have to concern themselves with composition, at their leisure. When I came back here I heard from my teacher himself that he would perform no

20. Mosel, 138.

> more theatrical services from then on, and that consequently I would have to take care of everything. That was in fact the command I received from Count Ugart, with the added instruction that the music director at the keyboard would compose no more operas in the future; he could certainly display his talent in [the composition of] symphonies and other pieces, but for the composition of operas famous composers would be engaged, as Kapellmeister Cimarosa was at that time engaged. What a thunderbolt for me, that I could compose nothing more! Through the withdrawal of my teacher I did indeed receive his position, but my earnings remained the same and my spirits were dashed; but I had to yield, and hoped for a lucky break.[21]

The requirement that Weigl write no more operas for the court theaters was implied in Leopold's outline, where he specified carefully that Weigl's responsibility in the theater was "only to accompany." This prohibition may have resulted from the complete failure of his *La caffetiera bizzarra,* performed in September 1790, in celebration of the arrival in Vienna of the king and queen of Naples; or it may simply reflect Leopold's preference for operas imported from Italy.

Leopold's shifting of the responsibility for supervising rehearsals and directing performances did not in fact represent much of a change. As Salieri's assistant, Weigl had been doing these tasks since the mid-1780s. Leopold's unstated goal was probably the removal of Salieri from the day-to-day management of the theater: the scheduling of operas, the assigning of roles, the hundreds of small decisions that, together, defined the theater's character. The emperor may have had the same goal in mind when he removed from the theater singers closely associated with the Hofkapellmeister and when he circumscribed Weigl's operatic activities.

A Coronation Opera for Prague

Salieri had opportunity in 1791 to demonstrate to Leopold his talent in a genre of which the new ruler was especially fond: opera seria. Shortly before the emperor wrote to Ugarte of his plan to reorganize the court theaters, Domenico Guardasoni, impresario of the Italian opera in Prague, signed a contract with the Estates of Bohemia in which he promised to produce an opera seria for the celebration of Leopold's coronation as king of Bohemia, scheduled to take place on 6 September 1791. Guardasoni agreed in the contract to engage "a famous composer" to write the music. He tried, unsuccessfully, to persuade Salieri to take on the task. Writing to Prince Anton Esterházy, probably in August 1791, Salieri stated that he had been asked to write the coronation opera. The letter gives us a rare opportunity to see him in a state of some anger and indignation:

21. Weigl, "Selbstbiographien," 55–56.

Your Highness!
Immediately upon the return of the Italian opera company, which had the honor to serve Your Highness in the recent magnificent celebration at Eszterháza, I was informed that someone had written to Your Highness that I had been opposed to allowing the prompter of the imperial theater to leave for Eszterháza, which caused some inconvenience at the rehearsals for this celebration and cast the most humiliating suspicions on me.

The person who made such a statement must certainly be unaware that I have been the younger Weigl's teacher for seven years; that I am proud of his talent as well as his behavior; that I myself gave him and had him set to music a poem by a famous poet for the work composed for Eszterháza, a poem that I had begun to set myself; that in order to leave my student enough free time to finish his music in the allotted time and to be able to do honor on such a glorious occasion both to himself and to his teacher, I fulfilled his duties in the court theater, even to the extent of attending the minor rehearsals of the opere buffe in his place, when the activities of my particular position did not prevent me; and finally that I refused—without regret, however—to write the opera that is being prepared for the coronation of Bohemia, for which opera the impresario of Prague visited me five times to beg me to accept the commission, even showing me two hundred zecchini, an engagement that I could not accept because I alone was attending to the affairs of the imperial theater.

Such sacrifices are strongly in contrast to the accusations brought against me. That the person who made me author of the inconvenience that happened, or at least could have happened, is ignorant of these details, or would like to be ignorant of them, would surprise me little or not at all; but it is my duty to make Your Highness aware of my conduct in this affair, because an honest man, an artist, head of a family that receives those few hours left to him by his duty to give without self-interest to his fellow man whatever benefits he has received in the same manner from others, cannot and must not be indifferent to the way in which he is perceived by others.

I know that the true instigator of this disturbance has been discovered by the troupe, but I am uncertain if this is known to Your Highness; and that is the reason that I have decided most respectfully to write an explanation, which I beg Your Highness to accept as a sign of that profound veneration with which I ask permission to call myself Your Highness's

Most humble and devoted servant
Antonio Salieri
First Music Director
of the Imperial Court of Vienna[22]

The celebration to which Salieri referred was the installation of Prince Anton as lord protector, which took place on 3 August 1791. In the absence of Haydn (in London), the prince commissioned Weigl to write a cantata for the occasion, *Venere ed Adone* (the "famous poet" was Casti). The operatic commission that Salieri turned down went, of course, to Mozart, and resulted in *La clemenza di Tito.*

22. Transcribed and discussed in "Acta musicalia," *Haydn Yearbook* 15 (1984): 153–57.

Salieri's operas were popular in Prague, having represented an important part of the repertory there since the early 1770s. Guardasoni knew many of them, and he knew Salieri personally. In his early years as a singer he had created the fine role of the lovelorn misogynist Cavaliere di Ripafratta in *La locandiera.*

If Salieri had written a coronation opera for Prague, he would not have been the first Viennese Kapellmeister to do so. Vice-Kapellmeister Fux had written the opera performed in Prague for the coronation of Charles VI in 1724, *Costanza e fortezza.* Tradition-conscious officials organizing the coronation of Charles's grandson in 1791 may well have been aware of the precedent represented by Fux's commission.

Considering not only musical taste in Prague but also Guardasoni's personal acquaintance with Salieri and his music and the ceremonial tradition of the Viennese court, it is hardly surprising that the impresario asked Hofkapellmeister Salieri to compose the coronation opera. But why did Salieri decline the commission?

That he was busy attending to the court opera during Weigl's work at Eszterháza may be only part of the reason. He must have been keenly aware of the Italianate taste of Leopold and Empress Maria Luisa. Already in 1772 Leopold's mother Maria Theresa had included Salieri among Viennese composers whom she compared unfavorably with Italian composers. Nineteen years later his identification with Viennese music was stronger than ever. If he felt that he would be unable to please the royal family, he was probably right. By refusing to write the coronation opera he avoided the cold reception that the court gave Mozart's *Tito.*

Neapolitans and Neapolitan Opera in Vienna

Leopold's transformation of Viennese musical theater was largely an "Italianization" of personnel and repertory. In the realm of opera buffa, the transformation was more specifically a "Neapolitanization" that reflected not only the emperor's operatic tastes but also the influence wielded in Vienna during his reign by the Neapolitan royal family.

The claim that Viennese opera was "Neapolitanized" during Leopold's reign may come as a surprise to those who believe that Neapolitan opera, in the general sense in which that term is sometimes used, had been a dominant force in the Burgtheater throughout the life of Joseph's opera buffa troupe. True, many operas by composers born or trained in Naples were performed by Joseph's company. But relatively few of these operas were actually written for Neapolitan theaters.

Neapolitan opera in this narrow sense was rare not only in Vienna but in the rest of Europe. The Neapolitan writer Ferdinando Galiani was not alone in regarding it as a genre to be enjoyed in Naples only. In 1771, having boasted to Madame d'Epinay of "the peak of perfection to which Piccinni has raised our comic opera," he continued: "Have no fear that Neapolitan comic operas will come to France. That has never happened;

they do not get even to Rome. You will have Italian comic operas like *La buona figliuola* but no Neapolitan ones."[23] Two years later he praised Paisiello's most recent Neapolitan comic operas but did not send them to France because they were "too Neapolitan."[24]

From the success of Piccinni and Paisiello outside Naples we must conclude that the composer was a relatively unimportant part of what made Neapolitan opera buffa such a problematic export. Neapolitan librettos seem to have been perceived as significantly different from those created in Rome, Venice, and elsewhere in Italy. The dialect typically spoken by one or more characters in Neapolitan librettos may have been regarded as a stumbling block to their appreciation outside Naples. But even with the dialect translated into Tuscan, Neapolitan operas had to overcome prejudice before they could win over the Italian public. The impresario who presented Cimarosa's *Il falegname,* one of the most widely performed Neapolitan opere buffe of the early 1780s, at the Teatro S. Moisè in Venice in 1784 thought it necessary to warn the audience: "This opera is certainly not one of the best planned or adapted to the taste of an intelligent public like the one in this city, for the work is by a Neapolitan poet and written for the Neapolitan theatre, where they take no notice either of the way characters are drawn or the manner of performance."[25]

Joseph II considered Neapolitan opera buffa unsuitable for Vienna. When Paisiello's early comedy *Don Chisciotte della Mancia* (Naples, 1766) was performed in Vienna in 1771, the emperor complained (in a letter to Leopold quoted in chap. 7): "there are many jokes, so crowded together one after another that by the end they become boring." Twelve years later, on a tour of Italy largely devoted to hearing singers and collecting scores and librettos for his troupe, he visited Naples and the nearby royal residence of Caserta. He sent the libretto of Cimarosa's "Chi dell'altrui si veste presto si spoglia" to Rosenberg with a letter implying that it was for the count's entertainment alone: "It is in the Neapolitan genre, and by no means suited to our theater."[26] With a few exceptions, he kept Neapolitan opera off the stage of the Burgtheater. Of the sixty-two operas presented by the troupe from its inauguration in 1783 to Joseph's death seven years later, only six were imported from Naples. When one looks only at the opere buffe most popular in Vienna, Neapolitan operas almost fade from view. Among the fourteen operas performed more than twenty times, only one, Cimarosa's *Il falegname,* had been first performed in Naples.

That operas imported from Naples came to dominate the Viennese repertory during Leopold's reign must have had something to do with the arrival, in September 1790, of King Ferdinand and Queen Carolina of Naples to celebrate the triple marriage that

23. Quoted in translation (used here) in Michael F. Robinson, *Naples and Neapolitan Opera* (Oxford, 1972), 187.

24. Robinson, *Naples and Neapolitan Opera,* 187.

25. Robinson, *Naples and Neapolitan Opera,* 188.

26. Joseph to Rosenberg, Caserta, 31 December 1783, in *Joseph II,* 39.

brought even closer together two already closely related families: the Habsburgs of Vienna and the Bourbons of Naples. The Neapolitan royal family stayed in Vienna during most of the period from September 1790 to March 1791, dominating the social life of the city and influencing its musical life as well.[27]

The most important of the weddings was that of Archduke Francis to Princess Maria Theresa of Naples. Before the wedding Queen Carolina sent her brother the emperor a description of her daughter that mentioned her musical abilities: "elle sait la musique bien, le clavecin, chant, et un peu de harpe; elle danse bien."[28] Maria Theresa maintained her musical interests in Vienna. She went to the theater often; she accepted dedications from Kozeluch, Beethoven, and others; she corresponded with several composers, including Ferdinando Paer and Joseph Eybler; and she commissioned works from, among others, Michael and Joseph Haydn. But her musical tastes must have been thoroughly Neapolitan when she arrived in Vienna in 1790.

The Neapolitanization of the Viennese repertory had begun a few months earlier. Paisiello's *Nina, ossia La pazza per amore* and *La molinara,* and Guglielmi's *La pastorella nobile,* all three first performed in Naples between 1788 and 1790, received their Viennese premieres in 1790. In less than a year three Neapolitan operas reached the stage of a theater that had witnessed the performance of only six during the previous seven years. *La pastorella nobile* went on to become the opera most often performed in Vienna during Leopold's reign.

These operas are light, delicate works, in turn sentimental and gently comic. Their plots, which lack the complex interplay of comic and serious characteristic of many Viennese operas of the 1780s, revolve around the sweet young woman referred to in the title. Serious or mock-serious characters, such as Eugenia in *La molinara,* are of little importance in the drama; and their music offers few opportunities for singers trained in serious opera fully to display their virtuosity. The two-tempo rondò, so much a part of Josephinian opera buffa, is completely absent.

Da Ponte's first reaction to the rising tide of Neapolitan opera was to make operas imported from Naples closer to his own conception of opera buffa. In collaboration with Weigl he rewrote much of *Nina.* In *La pastorella nobile* he expanded the role sung by Ferrarese (Donna Florida), adding to the score, among several other numbers, a rondò by Weigl for her to sing, "Ah se un core all'infedele."[29]

At the end of 1790 Da Ponte wrote a long memorandum to the theater administration (presumably Rosenberg).[30] In it he criticized strongly the recent decision to fire

27. Dexter Edge, "Mozart's Reception in Vienna, 1787–1791," in Sadie, 89–93.

28. Maria Carolina to Leopold, 21 April 1790, HHStA, Sb, Kart. 19.

29. On the first Viennese version of *La pastorella nobile* and Weigl's rondò see Rice, "Emperor," 124–31.

30. Transcribed in Michtner, "Der Fall Abbé Da Ponte," 187–92; reprinted in Michtner, *Das alte Burgtheater,* 441–43.

Ferrarese and hire two new sopranos: Irene Tomeoni Dutillieu, a specialist in Neapolitan opera buffa, and Cecilia Giuliani, a specialist in opera seria. Contending that he never had anything but the theater's interests at heart, he predicted that Ferrarese's departure would have ruinous consequences for the theater. In so doing, he showed himself completely at odds with the ongoing Neapolitanization of Viennese opera buffa.

Da Ponte's claim that the title role of *La molinara* "is written divinely for her [Ferrarese's] voice" is dubious. It is not surprising to learn from him that others had tried to keep Ferrarese from singing Rachelina, the miller's daughter. The role, like the title roles in *Nina* and *La pastorella nobile,* makes no great technical demands but requires a pretty voice and a charming, lively actress who can sing with simplicity and naiveté. It is difficult to imagine how Ferrarese, whose ability to sing in an artless manner Mozart doubted, could have put across an aria like "La Rachelina molinarina" (ex. 15.1). With its very limited compass (one octave), folklike melody, lack of coloratura and dramatic leaps, and simple accompaniment, this song requires none of Ferrarese's strengths; yet this is precisely the kind of music that Viennese audiences found so delightful as they discovered the simple pleasures of Neapolitan opera buffa. Ferrarese sang it, but characteristically did not limit herself to Paisiello's music. She added a rondò, "Ah brillar la

EXAMPLE 15.1 Paisiello, *La molinara,* act 1, "La Rachelina molinarina," mm. 9–32 (full score, ed. Aldo Rocchi [Florence, 1962])

(Continued on next page)

Rachelina, the miller's daughter, comes to pay her respects to her lord. I would say more to you, but that would not be proper, for I know . . . I would like . . . it is not right. I am simple, shy, and my modesty makes me silent.

nuova aurora," taken (no doubt with Da Ponte's approval) from Cimarosa's serious opera *Idalide.*[31]

Da Ponte admitted that Tomeoni "is a fine singer where *gran canto* is not required." He did not realize that Leopold favored the kind of comic opera in which Tomeoni excelled. He rightly pointed out that Giuliani was unsuited to opera buffa; unlike Ferrarese she had no experience in comic opera and no interest in experimenting with it. He did not know that Giuliani would come to Vienna not to join the opera buffa troupe but to form part of the core of a new opera seria troupe. Emperor Leopold loved *gran canto,* but he expected to hear it in opera seria, not opera buffa.

Tomeoni in Guglielmi's *La bella pescatrice* and *La pastorella nobile*

The arrival of Neapolitan operas was followed by the arrival of Neapolitan singers. Tomeoni, the most important of these, had sung almost exclusively in Naples between 1787 and 1791, in comic operas by Cimarosa, Guglielmi, Anfossi, Sarti, and others. During winter or early spring 1791 she came to Vienna with her husband, Pietro Dutillieu, a minor composer of opera and ballet. She made her debut at the beginning of the theatrical year 1791 in Guglielmi's *La bella pescatrice,* in the title role that she had created in Naples in 1789. Zinzendorf was delighted. "The new actress Irene Tomeoni is infinitely pleasing," he wrote on opening night. "She is gay, petulant; she has an agreeable voice; she was charming, especially in her *déshabillé de pecheuse.*"[32]

Tomeoni was not a singer of outstanding virtuosity. Zinzendorf called her voice "agreeable." Ignaz Castelli remembered her as "lovely to look at, and she brought together in her performance in the Italian opera pretty singing and skillful acting. In the opera *Die Müllerin* she was outstanding."[33] Ernst Moritz Arndt, a visitor to Vienna in 1798, wrote: "Tomeoni is the prima donna, a charming, amusing little thing whom Nature must have made in a cheerful mood. She remains (as women do more easily than men) within the boundaries of tradition and good taste, and always pleases, whether she conceals her mischief in serious roles or displays all her comic skills and naiveté in cheerful ones."[34] Tomeoni specialized in the portrayal of sentimental yet charming heroines, descendants of Cecchina in Piccinni's *La buona figliuola;* she moved her audience with the simplicity of her song, her innocence, and playfulness. She excelled in roles in which Ferrarese could not.

31. *Ah brillar la nuova aurora. Rondo per il Clavicembalo . . . cantato dall Sig. Feraresi nell'Opera La Molinara, del Sig. Paisiello* (Vienna, [1790]). The text of this aria appears in the Vienna libretto dated 1790.

32. Zinzendorf, 26 April 1791; quoted in Rice, "Emperor," 181.

33. Ignaz Castelli, *Memoiren meines Lebens,* 4 vols. (Vienna, 1861), 1:222.

34. Die Tomeoni ist die erste Operistin, ein kleines drolligtes und niedliches Wesen, das in einer heitern Laune der Natur gemacht seyn muß. Sie bleibt, wie es Weiber leichter thun, in den Linien der Sitten und Schicklichkeit, und gefällt immer gleich sehr, sie mag nun in ernsteren Rollen ihren Schalk verstecken, oder in muntern alle ihre natürliche Drolligkeit und Naivität aufbieten (Ernst Moritz Arndt, *Reisen durch einen*

The role of Dorinda in *La bella pescatrice* suited her well. In the aria "Mi parea che sola sola" we can see clearly the kind of character that Tomeoni could portray with great effectiveness. The music is in A major, evidently one of Tomeoni's favorite keys. A above the treble clef was normally treated by composers as her highest note. A major in addition had a light, playful connotation for late-eighteenth-century musicians such as Galeazzi, who described it as "perfectly harmonious, expressive, tender, playful, bright, and cheerful."[35] It was thus a perfect key for Tomeoni.

Everything in "Mi parea" is reduced to the utmost simplicity (ex. 15.2). The accompaniment is light; there are no harmonic surprises. Vocal range is limited to a minor ninth, from G♯ above middle C up to A. The lineage of Guglielmi's opening melody can be traced back to Cecchina's lament "Una povera ragazza," archetypical of this kind of simple, sentimental song (ex. 15.3). When Dorinda moves toward the dominant (at "Ti narrava") she again reminds us of Cecchina, with her breathless pauses and tender sighs ("Sì, signora, sì, padrone").

EXAMPLE 15.2 Guglielmi, *La bella pescatrice,* act 1, "Mi parea che sola sola," mm. 12–26 (vocal score, Vienna, ca. 1791)

(*Continued on next page*)

Theil Teutschlands, Ungarns, Italiens, und Frankreichs in den Jahren 1798 und 1799, 4 vols. [Leipzig, 1804], 1:248–49).

35. Steblin, *A History of Key Characteristics,* 111.

EXAMPLE 15.2 *(continued)*

I thought I was walking all alone back there. You came, my beloved, and consoled me. I told you, I spoke to you about the love that was setting me on fire

But Dorinda is no defenseless damsel. Zinzendorf praised Tomeoni's petulance, and that side of the singer's personality is clear in "Mi parea." There is an ironic edge to Dorinda's naiveté. The Allegretto non molto, accompanied by pizzicato strings, is so lighthearted that we cannot take too seriously the apparent pathos of the opening slow section. The concluding Allegro moderato is full of gentle, cheerful mockery (ex. 15.4).

EXAMPLE 15.3 Piccinni, *La buona figliuola,* act 1, "Una povera ragazza," mm. 5–14

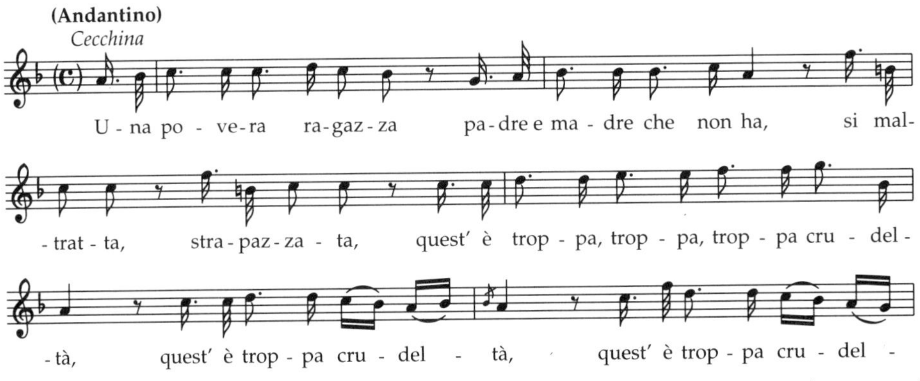

(Continued on next page)

EXAMPLE 15.3 *(continued)*

- tà. Sì, si - gno - ra, sì, pa - dro - ne, che con vo - stra per - mis -
- sio - ne, vo - glio an - dar - me - ne di qua.

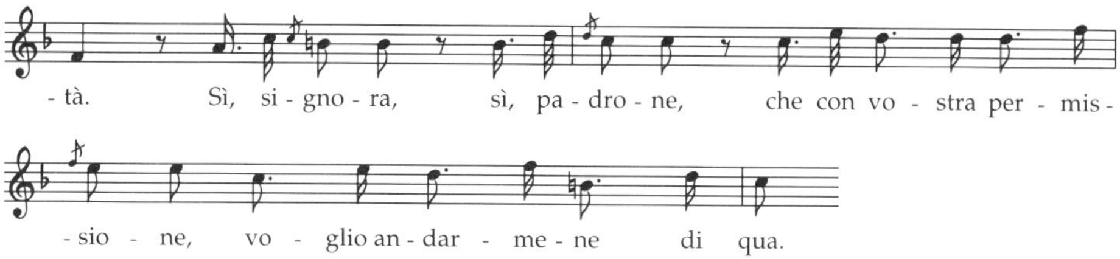

A poor girl who has no father and mother, so mistreated, so ill used, this cruelty is too much. Yes, my lady; yes, sir, and with your permission I want to go away from here.

EXAMPLE 15.4 Guglielmi, *La bella pescatrice,* act 1, "Mi parea che sola sola," mm. 131–38

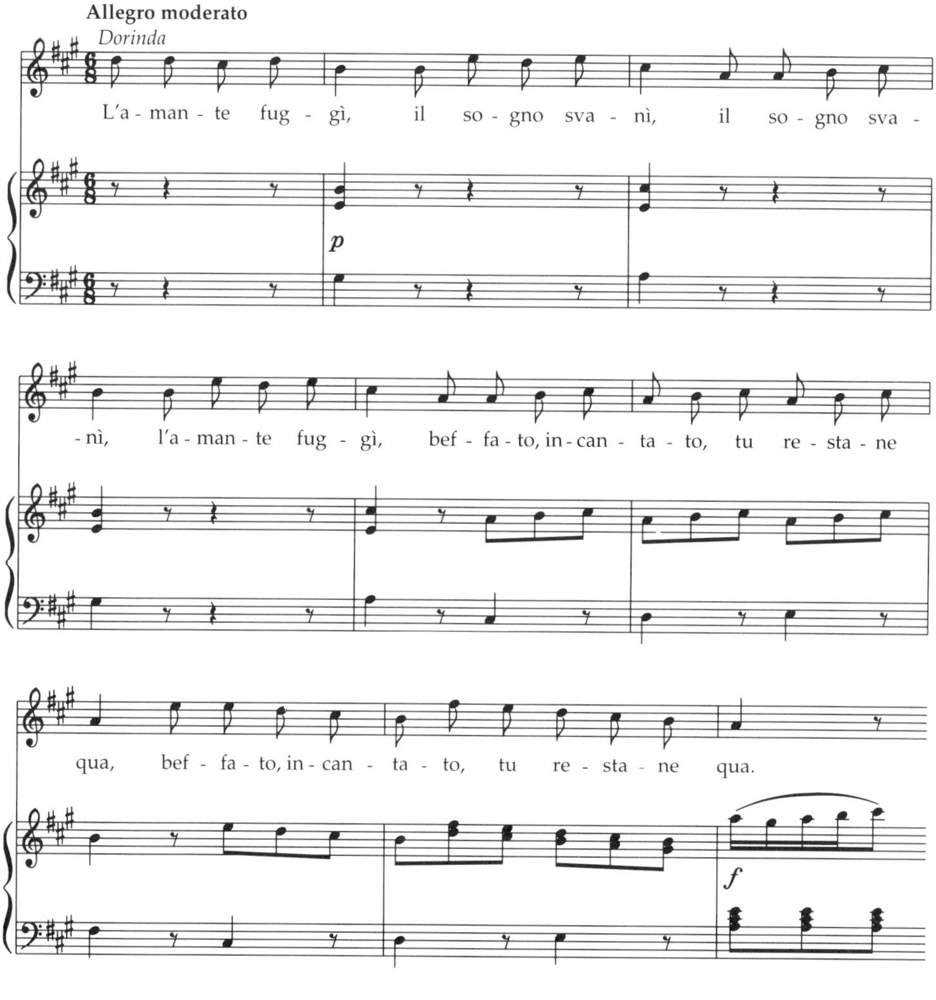

Allegro moderato
Dorinda
L'a - man - te fug - gì, il so - gno sva - nì, il so - gno sva -
- nì, l'a - man - te fug - gì, bef - fa - to, in - can - ta - to, tu re - sta - ne
qua, bef - fa - to, in - can - ta - to, tu re - sta - ne qua.
p
f

The lover fled, the dream disappeared; laughed at and enchanted, you stay here.

FIGURE 15.2 Irene Tomeoni in the title role of Paisiello's *Nina.* (Photo courtesy of Bildarchiv der Österreichischen Nationalbibliothek, Vienna.)

Mad: Irene Tomeoni
dans le Role le Meuniere

FIGURE 15.3
Irene Tomeoni as Rachelina in Paisiello's *La molinara.* (Photo courtesy of Bildarchiv der Österreichischen Nationalbibliothek, Vienna.)

An engraving shows Tomeoni in Paisiello's *Nina,* which she sang in Vienna from 1794 (fig. 15.2). Coltellini created Nina in 1789, but visually as well as vocally Tomeoni fit the part: her pretty face and figure, adorned with a simple dress and a bouquet, made her a perfect Nina. Another engraving bears the inscription "Mad. Irene Tomeoni dans le Role de Meuniere" (fig. 15.3), that is, in the role of the miller's daughter in *La molinara,* her interpretation of which Castelli so fondly remembered. The picture captures some of Tomeoni's simple, rustic charm. "La Rachelina molinarina" (see ex. 15.1) suited Tomeoni's voice and stage personality as obviously as it mismatched Ferrarese's.

Following up Tomeoni's success in *La bella pescatrice,* the Burgtheater revived *La pastorella nobile* in July 1791. The title role of Eurilla (previously overshadowed by Ferrarese's portrayal of Donna Florida), was assigned to Tomeoni, who had created it in Naples in 1788. If Zinzendorf's reaction is typical, she was the center of attention. "In the evening I went to see Tomeoni in *La pastorella nobile,*" he wrote on 5 August.[36] Leopold and his daughter-in-law Maria Theresa attended the same performance; she wrote to her husband Francis: "Yesterday I was . . . in the theater with your father. It was *La pastorella nobile,* in which Tomeoni received great applause."[37]

Eurilla's aria "Quel visino a me volgete" must have delighted the Viennese in Tomeoni's interpretation. As in "Mi parea" Tomeoni's character enchanted men with her sweet song. Again the key is A major. A light, simple accompaniment with parallel thirds in the violins also reminds one of "Mi parea." Frequent rests within words convey Eurilla's hesitation and feigned awkwardness. When Eurilla moves toward the dominant there is something faintly voluptuous in her undulating tritones (ex. 15.5). They remind one again of Dorinda's "Mi parea" (ex. 15.6) and Cecchina's "Una povera ragazza" (ex. 15.7). Andantino amoroso gives way to Allegro, and Eurilla sings a melody of childlike simplicity that suits well her childlike words (ex. 15.8). If "uccellino" (little bird) conveyed in the eighteenth century the same double-entendre as it does today, this would be in keeping with the delicate combination of innocence and sexuality so much a part of Tomeoni's character. The tune's gavotte rhythm reappears in many melodies written for Tomeoni, including several by Salieri.

EXAMPLE 15.5 Guglielmi, *La pastorella nobile,* act 1, "Quel visino a me volgete," mm. 47–50 (A-Wn, K.T. 338)

No, there is no difficulty

36. Zinzendorf, 5 August 1791; quoted in Rice, "Emperor," 148.

37. Maria Theresa to Francis, HHStA, Sb, Kart. 30; quoted in Rice, "Emperor," 182.

EXAMPLE 15.6 Guglielmi, *La bella pescatrice,* act 1, "Mi parea che sola sola," mm. 27–30

When the count arrived in the nick of time and you fled back there

EXAMPLE 15.7 Piccinni, *La buona figliuola,* act 1, "Una povera ragazza," mm. 39–40

Yes, my lady; yes, sir

EXAMPLE 15.8 Guglielmi, *La pastorella nobile,* act 1, "Quel visino a me volgete," mm. 91–104

(*Continued on next page*)

EXAMPLE 15.8 (*continued*)

In the midst of this and that I am confused, a poor little girl, and my poor little heart, like a little bird, jumps and flutters in my breast.

Tomeoni's success in Vienna was acknowledged by Emperor Leopold in his memorandum to Ugarte of 27 July 1791: "Tomeoni can, since she pleases the public, be engaged for two years with an addition of 100 ducats to her present [annual] salary; likewise her husband can be engaged for two years with 300 ducats pay as composer of opera and ballet." Leopold was willing to go to great expense to keep Tomeoni, even creating a new position for her husband, a composer of only modest ability and achievement. Her raise made her one of the two most highly paid singers in Vienna, with a salary (4,500 Gulden) equal to that of Giuliani, prima donna of the opera seria troupe, and higher than that of the veteran comic bass Benucci.

Cimarosa's *Il matrimonio segreto*

One of the first native fruits of Leopold's Neapolitanization of Viennese opera buffa was Cimarosa's *Il matrimonio segreto,* first performed in the Burgtheater on 7 February 1792.[38] Cimarosa, Neapolitan by birth and training, was in the employ of the Neapolitan court at the time of the premiere. He wrote the prima buffa role of Carolina for

38. The following discussion is based on a vocal score, ed. Franco Donatoni (Milan, 1984), and the libretto printed for the first production (Vienna, [1792]).

Tomeoni. The name Carolina itself was surely meant as a tribute to Leopold's sister, Queen Carolina of Naples.

The librettist was not a Neapolitan but a Venetian, Giovanni Bertati, engaged by Leopold to replace Da Ponte. In his first libretto for Vienna Bertati seems to have set out to write a recognizably Viennese drama. He followed Da Ponte in choosing a spoken play of some literary merit as the basis for his libretto.[39] His libretto has much of the elegant symmetry of *Così fan tutte:* six characters, three men and three women, the secretly married couple, Paolino and Carolina, in the midst of misunderstandings made intelligible by the artfully balanced way in which they are presented, with each of the newlyweds attracting the amorous attention of an older admirer.

Yet even with all the ways in which Bertati's libretto is similar to, and probably indebted to, librettos written in Vienna during Joseph's reign, *Il matrimonio segreto* departs from Viennese tradition and reflects the tastes not of Joseph's but of Leopold's Vienna in almost entirely lacking the interaction of serious and comic in which Viennese librettists and composers excelled. The opera's few serious moments—most notably Carolina's accompanied recitative in act 2, "Come tacerlo"—are short lived. Carolina sings no rondò. Bertati could have fashioned a parte seria out of Elisetta, and indeed he provided her with an aria in the serious style, "Se son vendicata." But through most of the opera there is nothing serious or noble about Elisetta. Bertati wanted his audience only to laugh at her pretensions and snobbery. Even while it reminds us of earlier Viennese operas, *Il matrimonio segreto* comes close to the Neapolitan ideal of opera buffa. It appealed to the same tastes as *La pastorella nobile* and *La bella pescatrice;* and the three operas won applause in Vienna for many of the same reasons, not the least being Tomeoni's central place in all three.

Both Bertati and Cimarosa had written for Tomeoni in the past. We might expect the role of Carolina to have fitted her well, and indeed it did. Carolina is not a noble heroine of the kind that Ferrarese portrayed so well, but a pretty young woman rather like those whom Tomeoni had portrayed in Guglielmi's Neapolitan comedies. She describes herself well in her single aria, "Perdonate, signor mio," as she charms herself free of Count Robinson's amorous advances with the same feigned modesty that Rachelina conveyed in her entrance cavatina in *La molinara:*

> Perdonate, signor mio,
> S'io vi lascio e fo partenza.
> Io per essere Eccellenza
> Non mi sento volontà.

39. On the literary background of *Il matrimonio segreto* see Winton Dean, "The Libretto of 'The Secret Marriage,'" *Music Survey* 3 (1950): 33–38; and Francesco Degrada, "Dal *Marriage à la mode* al *Matrimonio segreto,*" in *Il palazzo incantato: Studi sulla tradizione del melodramma dal barocco al romanticismo,* 2 vols. (Fiesole, 1979), 2:19–41.

Tanto onore è riservato
A chi ha un merto singolare,
A chi in circolo può stare
Con buon garbo e gravità.
Io, meschina, vo alla buona,
Io cammino alla carlona,
Son piccina di statura,
Io non ho disinvoltura;
Non ho lingua, non so niente,
Farei torto veramente
Alla vostra nobiltà.
Se un mi parla alla francese,
Che volete ch'io risponda?
Non so dire che *Monsiù.*
Se qualcun mi parla inglese,
Ben convien che io mi confonda.
Non intendo che *addidù.*
Se un poi vien qualche tedesco,
Vuol star fresco, oh, vuol star fresco,
Non intendo una parola.
Sono infatti una figliuola
Di buon fondo, e niente più.

[Forgive me, sir, if I leave you and depart. I feel no wish to be "Your Excellency"; such an honor is reserved for one of special merit, one who can circulate in high society with good manners and gravity. Poor me, I go about with no formality, and carelessly; I am small of stature, I am not at ease, I have no languages, I know nothing at all: I would truly be a discredit to your nobility. If someone speaks to me in French, what do you want me to respond? I can say nothing but *Monsiù.* If someone speaks English to me, I would certainly be confused: I understand only *addidù.* And if some German man appears, he will be in a fix for sure: I do not understand a single word. I am indeed a girl of good character, and nothing more.]

Carolina's final words remind us of the title of *La buona figliuola;* like Guglielmi's Eurilla and Dorinda, Carolina is a descendant of Piccinni's mezzo-carattere heroine. These words also reflect the personality of Tomeoni, of whom Zinzendorf wrote: "she is said to be good, and well behaved."[40] Carolina's confession that she knows not a word of German reminds us that Tomeoni had been in Vienna less than a year when she created the role of Carolina. Bertati's text, in short, describes the singer for whom it was written as vividly as the character she portrayed on stage.

The same can be said for Cimarosa's music. He chose the key of A major, used by Guglielmi for Tomeoni's arias in both *La bella pescatrice* and *La pastorella nobile.* The

40. On la dit bonne et sage (Zinzendorf, 30 April 1791).

aria begins Larghetto con moto in cut time, with a melody of folklike simplicity, very narrow compass, and gavotte rhythm (ex. 15.9). A modulation from E major to C major lends special charm to the naive melody that follows (ex. 15.10). A return to A major coincides with a switch to 6/8 meter, Non tanto allegro, for a charming, rustic conclusion that repeats the last two lines of text over and over.

"Perdonate, signor mio" exploited and communicated Tomeoni's skills as perfectly as it expressed Carolina's character. It is one of the many dramatic and musical delights of *Il matrimonio segreto,* which, performed for the first time only three weeks before the emperor's untimely death, represents the high point of what was new in Viennese opera buffa under Leopold II.

EXAMPLE 15.9 Cimarosa, *Il matrimonio segreto,* act 1, "Perdonate, signor mio," mm. 1–23 (piano-vocal score, ed. Franco Donatoni [Milan, 1984])

(*Continued on next page*)

EXAMPLE 15.9 *(continued)*

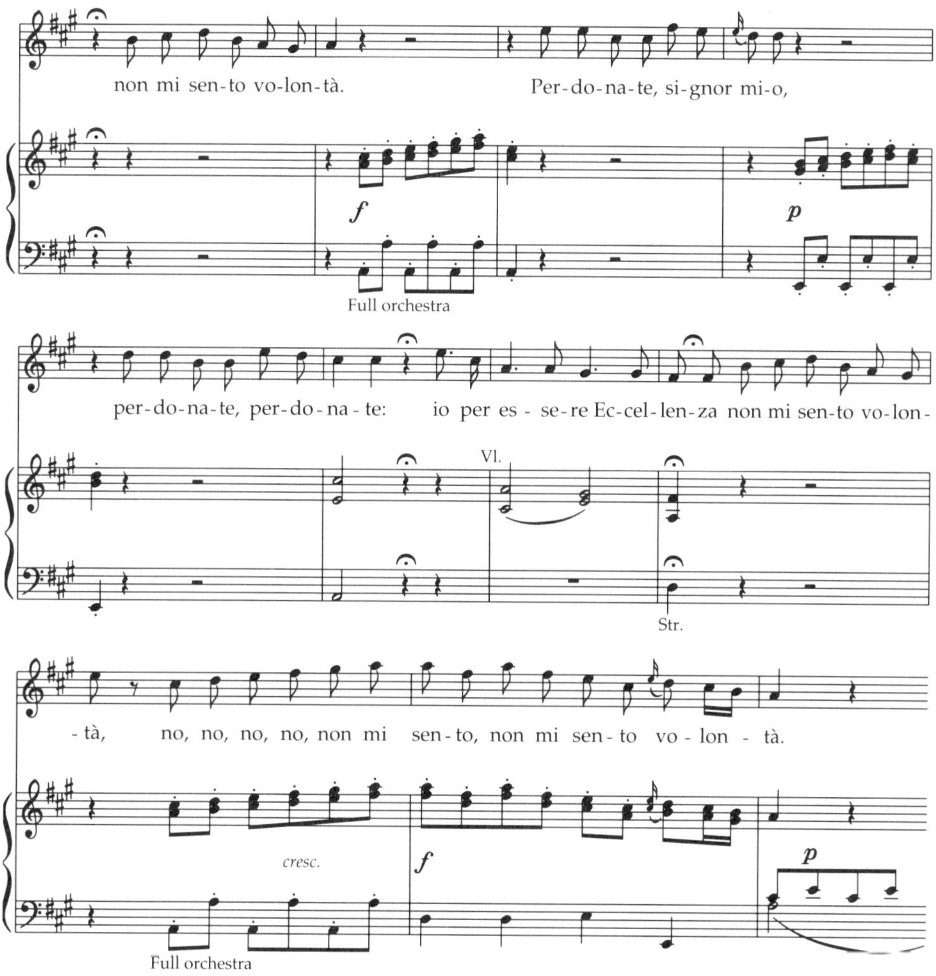
non mi sen-to vo-lon-tà.
Per-do-na-te, si-gnor mi-o,
Full orchestra
per-do-na-te, per-do-na-te:
io per es - se-re Ec-cel-len-za non mi sen-to vo-lon-
Vl.
Str.
- tà,
no, no, no, no, non mi
sen-to, non mi sen-to vo - lon - tà.
cresc.
Full orchestra

EXAMPLE 15.10 Cimarosa, *Il matrimonio segreto,* "Perdonate, signor mio," mm. 63–75

vo - stra no-bil - tà.
Full orchestra

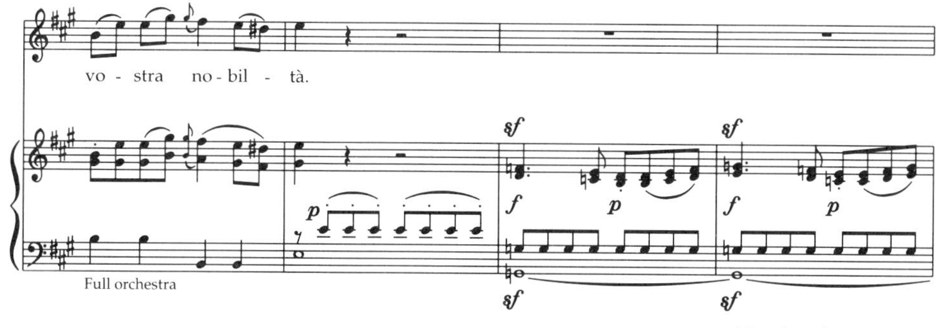

(Continued on next page)

EXAMPLE 15.10 (*continued*)

The opera outlived the emperor, its success linked to Tomeoni's. In 1793 the *Berlinische musikalische Zeitung* published a report on Italian opera in Vienna, bestowing its most enthusiastic praise on Tomeoni and her portrayal of Carolina:

> One must see and hear for oneself how enchantingly Mad. Tomioni sings and acts in the opera *Il matrimonio segreto*. . . . With an inimitable charm she *acts* the first trio of this opera. Her disguised innocence and her bitter irony, which she is able to express with unusual naturalness, united with her beautiful voice, raise this terzetto to the most beautiful piece of comic music that one can ever hear. Just as naive and extremely attractive is her performance of the following aria ["Perdonate, signor mio"], in which she tries to convince the count of her innocence.[41]

41. "Italienische Theatermusik in Wien," 134; quoted in Rice, "Emperor," 441.

Effects of Leopold's Theatrical Reorganization on Viennese Opera Buffa

Curiosity was mixed with indignation as Berlin's *Musikalisches Wochenblatt* followed Leopold's reorganization in a series of often inaccurate reports from Vienna during fall 1791. The editors expressed disappointment in the news (a false rumor, as it turned out) that Salieri had left the service of the court:

> *Vienna.* It is said that Kapellmeister *Salieri* has taken his leave, and that in his place *Cimarosa* has been summoned. As for the former no specifics are known for certain, but it is believed that his next place of residence will be Paris, where he has already written three operas, and consequently has access to a considerable pension. Some would believe that the origin of his dissatisfaction was the erection of a new court theater, in which the boxes will be organized for card playing. [A footnote comments further:] This is what the Italians would have done in Germany with their operas! Can one wonder if a man like *Salieri,* who can bind all the power of German music to the sweet Italian style, will not submit to such contemptible abuse?[42]

The report that Cimarosa was to replace Salieri had no basis in fact, though it was repeated by Gerber's *Lexicon der Tonkünstler* and often thereafter.[43] Cimarosa did enjoy a temporary appointment in Vienna: he received a very large salary of 3,150 Gulden for unspecified services performed between 1 April and 30 September 1792.[44] But he did not take Salieri's place as Hofkapellmeister or Weigl's as music director of the Italian troupe.

The article correctly interpreted Leopold's reorganization as favoring Italian music and musicians. But the changes were more complicated than that. Italian opera had of course enjoyed a dominant role in Viennese music for a long time. What changed during Leopold's reign was the role of Viennese composers in the court's Italian opera troupe. Composers of Italian opera who lived in Vienna—Gassmann in the 1760s; Gassmann and Salieri in the 1770s; Salieri, Mozart, and Martín in the 1780s had played a crucial role in shaping the operatic repertory. By all but ignoring Viennese composers, Leopold encouraged audiences in the court theaters to associate Italian opera with Italian composers only.

Leopold's theatrical reorganization of 1791 initiated a decade in which the achievements of Josephinian comic opera were largely forgotten in Vienna. Between 1792 and 1797 the court theaters performed none of Mozart's three Da Ponte settings. But they did not single Mozart's operas out for exclusion. Most of the operas that enjoyed suc-

42. *Musikalisches Wochenblatt* (Berlin), 1791, p. 15; quoted in Rice, "Emperor," 347.

43. Ernst Ludwig Gerber, *Neues historisch-biographisches Lexicon der Tonkünstler* (Leipzig, 1812–14), 4: col. 7.

44. Court theater account book in A-Wth, Sign. M 4000; payment made during the week of 28 April–4 May 1792.

cess in the 1780s were spurned in the 1790s. Of Salieri's, only one, *Axur,* survived the change of theatrical taste that took place during Leopold's reign.

The 1790s were dominated instead by operas first performed during Leopold's reign, works representing the values toward which Leopold, his court, and his singers steered the Viennese public. *La bella pescatrice,* which had introduced Tomeoni to Vienna, remained in the repertory throughout the decade. It was performed fifty times between 1791 and 1799, a total that does not include many performances of the first or second act as part of a composite program. (Such programs were a common feature of the court theaters during the 1790s.) Even more popular was *La molinara,* another Neapolitan vehicle for Tomeoni, which reached an extraordinary total of 125 complete performances. *Il matrimonio segreto* also met with lasting success, performed fifty-five times between 1792 and 1800.[45]

Tomeoni sang in Vienna for the rest of her career (she retired in 1805), exerting the influence of her voice and stage personality on the repertory and on the composition of new operas, including several by Salieri in which she created roles.

By encouraging the importation of comic operas from Naples and commissioning a new opera from an Italian composer who was in Vienna only for a short time rather than from composers resident in Vienna, Leopold II established a pattern that was followed during the last decade of the eighteenth century. His theatrical reorganization and Mozart's death left Salieri as the lone Viennese operatic composer with an established reputation and a record of distinguished achievement. Salieri and Weigl maintained the tradition of Viennese opera in Italian until the end of the century, but few of their operas achieved the popularity of *Il matrimonio segreto* or of the Neapolitan operas in which Tomeoni shined so brightly.

45. Hadamowsky, *Hoftheater,* vol. 1.

16

WITHDRAWAL AND REEMERGENCE, 1792–96

The administration of the court theaters changed repeatedly during the years following Leopold's death, but his reorganization and introduction of new genres and personnel continued to influence Viennese musical life. Italianate pantomime ballet, serious opera, and comic opera of the kind championed by Leopold all enjoyed success during the 1790s and beyond. They formed an important part of the musical milieu in which Salieri lived out the last phase of his career as a composer of operas.

Francis, Leopold's son and successor, took over the ballet troupe assembled by his father. Ballet attracted many of the most important Viennese composers, who might, if Joseph had still been emperor, have written opere buffe instead of ballets. Beethoven, Kozeluch, Weigl, and Hummel wrote ballet scores as Vienna once again became a center of theatrical dance.[1] Although Leopold's opera seria troupe did not survive his death, the genre gained in popularity during the 1790s. A production of Sarti's *Medonte re di Epiro* in 1794 preceded by less than a year the rehiring of its librettist, De Gamerra, as the court theaters' house poet. Salieri's former collaborator had written many successful serious librettos but very few comic ones. Performances of Giovanni Battista Borghi's *La morte di Semiramide* in 1797 and of Cimarosa's *Gli Orazi e i Curiazi* in 1798 were followed in 1801 by the premiere of Paer's *Achille,* written especially for Vienna on a libretto by De Gamerra.

Of operatic composers active in Vienna during the 1780s only two, Salieri and Weigl, continued to write operas during Francis's reign; but neither of them composed much

1. Robert Haas, "Zur Wiener Ballett-Pantomime um den Prometheus," *Neues Beethoven-Jahrbuch* 2 (1925): 84–103; John A. Rice, "Muzzarelli, Kozeluch e *La ritrovata figlia di Ottone II* (1794): Il balletto viennese rinato nello spirito di Noverre," *Nuova rivista musicale italiana* 24 (1990): 1–46.

during the first two years of that reign. According to Mosel, Leopold's theatrical reorganization left Salieri with the obligation of writing one opera per year for the court theaters. Salieri was slow to put this agreement into practice. He presented no new works between 1790 and 1794. One of the two operas that he wrote between 1790 and 1792, his setting of Casti's libretto *Catilina,* did not come to performance. The other, *Il mondo alla rovescia,* he had actually begun during his Italian tour of 1778–80; and the completed opera was not performed until 1795.

The production of *Il mondo alla rovescia* marked a resurgence of Salieri's creativity. During 1795 and 1796 he completed and staged three more operas. Two comedies, *Eraclito e Democrito* and *Il moro,* won modest applause. But with *Palmira regina di Persia,* a heroicomic spectacle on a grand scale, Salieri achieved success that rivaled that of *Axur.*

Few of the operas written by Salieri during the 1790s enjoyed long runs. Viennese audiences of the 1790s, unlike those of the previous decade, generally preferred their Italian opera imported from Italy, and especially the Neapolitan operas introduced to them by Leopold. They went to see *La molinara* and *Nina* night after night throughout the decade and into the nineteenth century. Only a few operas written for the Viennese court theaters, such as *Il matrimonio segreto* and Weigl's *L'amor marinaro* (1797), won similar popularity. The success of these operas (measured by the number of performances in Vienna) far exceeded that of *Palmira,* the most often performed of Salieri's late operas.

Operatic Reorganization under Emperor Francis

The massive court subsidies that Leopold's theatrical reorganization and expansion required continued into Francis's reign. During the first year alone the new emperor instructed the court treasury to transfer to the theater management at least 95,000 Gulden.[2] Such subsidies could not be continued for long, especially at a time when the young and inexperienced emperor was being steered by foolish advisers into a calamitous war with revolutionary France. In the fall of 1792 (the same fall that saw the arrival of Beethoven in Vienna) Francis set up a commission to consider the idea of leasing the theaters to an independent impresario: of returning, in other words, to the way the court theaters had been run during Salieri's first decade in Vienna.

Francis sent the commission's report to a man who had had little to do with Leopold's theatrical reorganization, Prince (formerly Count) Rosenberg. In a letter of 6 Oc-

2. Francis authorized the following payments to the theater management in 1792: 10,000 Gulden on 28 March, 20,000 Gulden on 29 May, 10,000 Gulden on 24 August, 15,000 Gulden on 22 September, and 40,000 Gulden on 18 November, according to memoranda in HKA, Österreichisches Camerale, Abt. 67.

tober 1792 the emperor praised Joseph's theater director for having "directed the theater management with so much insight into the public amusement and with so much economy" and asked him to evaluate the report.[3] Four days later the prince, apparently eager to get back into the theater business, submitted a detailed critique of ongoing theatrical policy and of the report. He argued that Francis could avoid leasing the theaters if he was willing to grant the theatrical management an annual subsidy of 25,000 Gulden. To back up his claim he proposed a plan for the future management of the theaters.

Rosenberg envisioned an Italian opera troupe of fourteen singers, whose types and salaries he listed. By making no mention of serious opera, he implicitly called for a refocusing of the court's operatic activities on the genres so successfully cultivated during his management of Joseph's troupe: comic and heroicomic opera.

> As far as the Italian opera is concerned, a completely new organization must be established. My plan would be as follows:
>
> | | | |
> |---|---|---|
> | One prima donna di mezzo carattere | | 4000 fl. |
> | One prima donna buffa | | 4000 |
> | Two primi buffi | 4000 | |
> | | 3000 | 7000 |
> | Two tenors | 4000 | |
> | | 3000 | 7000 |
> | Two seconde buffe | 3000 | |
> | | 2000 | 5000 |
> | Two secondi buffi | | 4000 |
> | Two men for minor roles | | 4000 |
> | Two women for minor roles | | 2000 |
> | One poet | | 1200 |
> | One music director | | 1000 |
> | One prompter, with assistants | | 800 |
>
> This [organization] has the advantage that each production is automatically double cast, and thus cannot be interrupted by illness, and (as under my [former] management), new operas can be rehearsed and performed more often.[4]

3. Sie haben die Ober Direction der Schauspiele mit so vieler Einsicht zum allgemeinen Vergnügen, und mit so besonderer Oekonomie geführt (HHStA, GH 1792, Kart. 1, fol. 5; see also Franz Dirnberger, ed., *Burgtheater in Dokumente* [exhibition catalogue; Vienna, 1976], 16).

4. Bei der italienischen Opera müste ein ganz neuer Status reguliret werden, mein Plan hinzu wäre dieser:

eine Prima donna di mezzo car	4000 fl
eine prima buffa	4000

Rosenberg did not discuss repertory in any detail, but he did refer disapprovingly to the abandonment of operas that had been popular during the 1780s (and for whose creation he had been partly responsible): "many fine old works, such as *Arbore di Diana, Grota di Troffonio, Rè Theodoro,* etc."[5] He mentioned these in a discussion of costs of scenery, suggesting that the unnecessary destruction of old scenery made revivals more expensive than they should have been.

Francis, impressed by Rosenberg's analysis, asked him to take up the duties of theater director.[6] But Rosenberg, sixty-nine years old, seems to have been less effectual than his proposal led Francis to hope. His short theatrical regime (from November 1792 to July 1794) was marked by stagnation: few new operas were produced, few new singers engaged, and Salieri's almost complete absence from Viennese operatic life continued.

Comic operas imported from Naples dominated the repertory to the same extent as during the last few months of Leopold's reign. Tomeoni continued to use *La molinara* and *La bella pescatrice* as vehicles for the display of her talent and charm. Among the relatively few operas to join the repertory were two first performed in Naples: Marcello di Capua's *La donna bizzarra* and Guglielmi's *Il poeta di campagna.*

Salieri was represented under Rosenberg's management by one opera only. The Hofkapellmeister revived *Axur* in April 1793. Later that year, on 15 September, *Axur* returned in a new version: in four acts instead of the original five, and with ballet incorporated into the action.[7] Salieri received a substantial fee of 225 Gulden for the revision.[8] The

---

zwei primi Buffi	a 4000	
	3000	7000
zwei Tenori	a 4000	
	3000	7000
zwei 2de Buffe	a 3000	
	2000	5000
zwei 2^{di} Buffi		4000
zwei Männer per l'ultime parti		4000
zwei donne per d°		2000
ein Poet		1200
" Kapellmeister		1000
" Souffleur samt gehülfen		800

Dadurch erwächse der Vortheil, daß dieses Spektakl a double partie zugleich besetzet, und also durch vorwaltende Krankheiten nicht unterbrochen würde, und wie unter meiner Verwaltung öfters neue Opern einstudiret, und gegeben werden könnten (report from Rosenberg to Francis dated 10 October 1792, HHStA, GH 1792, Kart. 1, fol. 6 ff.).

5. viele gute alte Stücke, als *arbore di Diana, grota di Troffonio, Rè Theodoro* p.

6. Francis to Rosenberg, 10 November 1792, HHStA, GH 1792, Kart. 1, fol. 39.

7. A playbill (A-Wth) for the performance of 15 September 1793 announces that *Axur* will be performed in four acts, "Mit einigen Veränderungen und eingemischten Ballet."

8. A-Wth, M 4000, May 1793.

initial revival (during April) coincided with the Viennese debut of Marianna Sessi, a young soprano who had just begun to make a name for herself in Italy as a singer in serious opera. Her engagement in Vienna (presumably as "prima donna di mezzo carattere," to use Rosenberg's terminology) represented a challenge to Tomeoni ("prima donna buffa") and a return to the Josephinian ideal of opera seria singing and acting in the context of opera buffa. That Sessi should make her Viennese debut in Joseph's favorite opera suggests that Rosenberg intended eventually to replace or at least to supplement the Naples-oriented comic repertory left by Leopold with one more closely modeled on that of the 1780s. Another Josephinian opera, *Una cosa rara,* returned to the court theaters shortly after *Axur* but survived only three performances.[9]

An article published in the *Berlinische musikalische Zeitung* in 1793, "Italienische Theatermusik in Wien," presents a useful picture of the state of Italian opera in Vienna during the early years of Francis's reign. In its evaluation of the Viennese troupe the most enthusiastic praise (quoted in chapter 15) goes to Tomeoni, reflecting the importance of her position in Viennese opera during the 1790s.

Only one serious opera (beside the partly serious *Axur*) was performed in the court theaters during 1793: Bianchi's *Il disertore.* Yet the article describes Sessi and the tenor Vincenzo Maffoli as engaged to sing in opera seria. Both singers were indeed opera seria specialists, and Maffoli had come to Vienna in 1791 to sing in Leopold's opera seria troupe; but during 1793 they had no choice but to sing in comic opera.

Sessi's singing impressed the Viennese more than her acting, according to the article, which contains interesting information about her portrayal of Aspasia:

> Signora Sessi, who looks very beautiful on the stage, is engaged for the first roles in the serious opera. Her voice is certainly not as strong as Tomioni's, nor is it as bright and clear, yet this singer also has her value. She comes from a good school and performs with much truth, exactness, and precision. Her technique is brilliant. She has few ugly notes and sings fewer through the nose, as Tomioni does occasionally (but only very rarely). A pity that her embellishments are a little weak. For she always sings the same cadenza in every aria and the same embellishments at every fermata. But she performs the *passaggi* in bravura arias with great assurance and vivacity, and the beautiful, full lower range of her voice is occasionally very pleasing and enhances the brilliance of such arias.
>
> Her acting, however, leaves much to be desired. For example, when, in *Axur* (one of her main roles), she fell in a faint and lay motionless for almost a minute, she must have felt, or so it seems, that the arrangement of her hair did not show her at her best. Without ado she rose a little, put her hair in order, and then fell, *da capo,* in a faint! In other parts of Germany one would laugh out loud at this; but the Viennese public, whose enthusiasm is for music only, hardly seems to notice this mistake.[10]

9. Hadamowsky, *Hoftheater,* 1:24.
10. "Italienische Theatermusik in Wien," 134–35; in Rice, "Emperor," 441.

The article mentions *Il matrimonio segreto* much more often than any other opera, not only because the "Viennese public cannot hear and see this opera enough," but also because in it, apparently, the troupe appeared at its best. Only a few other operas are named more than once; of these, *Axur* is the only one by a Viennese composer, written for Joseph's troupe and representing operatic values of the Josephinian decade.

The article praises a single composer, so enthusiastically that it tempts us to believe that a personal friend of his wrote it:

> The First Hofkapellmeister is the famous *Salieri,* an artist now almost the only one of his kind, the first of all the Italians, who travels his own path, which has soared up to the highest summit of art (in his genre), who is able to discuss his art rationally, on an intellectual level, and demonstrates thereby what an artist can do when he goes to work with *intelligence* as well as with *feeling.* He is a man with his own heartfelt emotions, full of knowledge of the theater, and equally strong in the comic and the tragic: a rare talent! He follows closely in the footsteps of our great German *Gluck,* as his *Axur* and *Les Danaïdes* demonstrate; of his comic genius *La scuola de' gelosi, La cifra,* and *La grotta di Trofonio* are good examples. He is still a young man; what masterpieces can we not still expect from him![11]

This encomium (whose praise of Salieri's ability "to discuss his art rationally" reminds one of what both Beaumarchais and Da Ponte wrote of their collaborations with him) sounds a little hollow in the context of an article that otherwise almost ignores Salieri's music, and thereby reflects his withdrawal from Viennese operatic life.

Italian Opera under Baron Braun

Rosenberg's theatrical regime did not last long. In 1794, reduced to desperate financial straits by the war against France, the court was forced to go ahead with leasing the theaters to Baron Peter von Braun, a wealthy businessman.[12] In a contract signed on 22 July 1794, Braun, like his predecessors who had run the theaters between 1766 and 1776, promised to present operas, ballets, and spoken plays. Francis and his court (in particular his music-loving wife Maria Theresa) continued to exert influence over theatrical matters; Braun could have expected no less, dependent as he was on a court subsidy of 40,000 Gulden per annum. But the transfer of the court theaters to Braun's control

11. "Italienische Theatermusik in Wien," 139; in Rice, "Emperor," 442. Salieri received similar praise in an anonymous article, "Ueber den Stand der Musik in Wien," in *Wiener Theater Almanach für das Jahr 1794* (Vienna, [1794]), 180–81: "Er gehört unstreitig unter die vortrefflichsten Componisten unsrer Zeit; seine Manier ist gross und original; er hat sich göstentheils nach dem unsterblichen Ritter Gluck gebildet."

12. "Veränderungen beym k. k. Hoftheater," in *Wiener Theater Almanach für das Jahr 1795,* viii–xxii.

FIGURE 16.1 Domenico Mombelli, who created the role of Alcidoro in *Palmira regina di Persia.* Engraving by José Cardini. (Courtesy of Civica Raccolta Stampe "A. Bertarelli," Castello Sforzesco, Milan.)

marked the end of the age in which Habsburg monarchs could, if they wanted to, play the role of impresario.

During 1794 important changes occurred not only in the administration but also in the personnel of the court theaters. Several great singers, including the serious tenor Domenico Mombelli and the buffo caricato Carlo Angrisani, joined the troupe. Braun brought back to Vienna De Gamerra, a theatrical poet who had been active there during the 1770s and had collaborated several times with Salieri.

Mombelli (fig. 16.1) began singing leading tenor roles in opera seria in Italy in 1780 or shortly before.[13] From 1783 to 1786 he sang at San Carlo in Naples. In 1786 he traveled north to Vienna, where he became a member of the opera buffa troupe: yet another opera seria singer contributing his virtuosity and dramatic talents to Viennese comic opera. He sang in Italy from 1789 to 1794, winning praise from the composer Johann Friedrich Reichardt, who considered several tenors for engagement in Berlin: "Mombelli has a very pleasant, resonant voice, especially in the lower range, and sings with

13. Sartori, Indici, 2:439–40.

FIGURE 16.2 Carlo Angrisani. The Latin inscription reads: "Most expert in the science of music and unrivaled in comic song." Angrisani created leading roles in many of Salieri's late operas. Engraving by A. Verico after a drawing by F. A. (Felice Angrisani?). (Courtesy of Civica Raccolta Stampe "A. Bertarelli," Castello Sforzesco, Milan.)

feeling and expression; his appearance and action are pleasing and impressive. . . . I liked him more than all the others."[14] In 1794 Mombelli returned to Vienna, probably as a replacement for Maffoli (who fell ill during Carnival 1794 and died less than a year later).[15] He went on to create the important role of Alcidoro in Salieri's *Palmira.*

Angrisani (fig. 16.2) sang in northern Italy as a comic bass from about 1784.[16] He must have been extraordinarily versatile, having portrayed no fewer than three different characters in *Il re Teodoro in Venezia.* During the 1790s he specialized in the roles of Alfonso in *La bella pescatrice,* the count in *Nina,* and Count Robinson in *Il matrimonio segreto.* Since all of these operas were favorites in Vienna, Angrisani must have been a welcome addition to the troupe. Benucci ended his long service to the opera buffa

14. *Monbelli,* hat eine sehr angenehme und klingende Stimme, besonders in der Tiefe, und singt mit Gefühl und Ausdruck, auch ist seine Gestalt und Action angenehm und bedeutend. . . . Mir hat er vor allen andern gefallen (from a report by Reichardt on Italian tenors dated June 1790, in *Musikalische Monathsschrift* [Berlin, 1792], 82–83).

15. Weigl, "Selbstbiographien," 56.

16. Sartori, Indici, 2:22–23.

company at the end of Carnival 1795; Angrisani was probably intended to replace him as Vienna's principal buffo caricato. He created important roles in most of Salieri's late operas: the count in *Il mondo alla rovescia,* Alderano in *Palmira,* Orgone in *Il moro,* the title role in *Falstaff,* Tullo in *Cesare in Farmacusa,* and Cicala in *Angiolina.*

Ernst Moritz Arndt, visiting Vienna in 1798, gave Angrisani a mixed assessment, criticizing him for exactly the same reasons that Sonnenfels had scolded Carattoli thirty years before: "Angrisani is the hero of the comic opera and at the same time a good singer. The public has taken him under its protection, and he can allow himself every license, and does so only too often. However easy and natural his expression, as if he were born on the stage, he often becomes a Hanswurst and descends to clowning that can amuse only children, and even to something worse: an indecency that a well-bred audience should not allow." [17]

Mombelli and Angrisani joined a troupe that included two first-rate sopranos, Tomeoni and Sessi, and two others whose careers were closely tied to Salieri's: Gassmann's daughters Maria Anna and Therese. Leopold II had ordered in 1791 that the Gassmann sisters be dismissed; but the dismissal, if it ever took effect, was short lived. Therese, the younger sister, could sing music that demanded high range and agility; she later successfully portrayed the Queen of the Night (fig. 16.3). Maria Anna, weaker than Therese, never found a secure place on the stage. Most of her roles were in Salieri's operas. He probably cast her in minor roles out of loyalty to her and to her father's memory.

Shortly after Braun took over the theaters De Gamerra replaced Bertati as theatrical poet. He had left Vienna sometime after the failure of his last collaboration with Salieri, *Daliso e Delmita.* Always drawn to centers of theatrical activity, he went to Naples, where his work as a librettist was limited to serious operas, Paisiello's *Pirro* being the most celebrated. During the French Revolution he may have flirted with revolutionary politics, to judge from a letter in which Leopold II urged his brother Ferdinand not to engage him as librettist for La Scala, describing him as "very dangerous." [18] But De Gamerra's politics did not keep him from returning to Vienna after Leopold's death. In 1794 he was engaged a second time as house librettist for the court theaters, and during the next decade he collaborated with Salieri and Weigl on several operas while also providing librettos for Viennese operas by Paer, Peter Winter, and Johann Simon Mayr. He may have made the first Italian translation of *Die Zauberflöte.* [19]

17. Angrisani ist der Held der komischen Oper und zugleich ein guter Sänger. Das Publikum hat ihn einmal in Schutz genommen, und er darf sich alles erlauben, und thut es oft nur zu sehr. So leicht, so natürlich und wie auf dem Theater gebohren er sich zeigt, so ein Hanswurst wird er oft, und erniedrigt sich zu Possen, die nur Kinder ergötzen können, und oft noch zu schlimmeren Zoten, die ein gesittetes Publikum durchaus verbieten müßte (Arndt, *Reisen,* 248).

18. Leopold to Ferdinand, 10 January 1791, HHStA, Sb, Kart. 20; quoted in Rice, "Emperor," 180.

19. Candiani, *Libretti e librettisti italiani per Mozart,* 47–95.

FIGURE 16.3 Therese Rosenbaum, née Gassmann, as Queen of the Night. Florian Gassmann's younger daughter, having studied with Salieri, enjoyed success in the court theaters as a high coloratura soprano. She created the role of the marchesa in *Il mondo alla rovescia.* (Photo courtesy of Bildarchiv der Österreichischen Nationalbibliothek, Vienna.)

Although we might have expected De Gamerra, as house poet, to supervise the staging of operas, Braun distributed these duties more widely than normal. In July 1795, at the end of his first year of administration, he paid four members of the Italian troupe—De Gamerra, Weigl, and the tenors Mombelli and Viganoni—100 Gulden each "for the supervision of staging."[20]

Like the impresarios who managed the court theaters from 1766 to 1776, Braun engaged court musicians as resident music director and composer. Weigl continued to occupy the position of music director assigned him by Leopold; in exchange for an annual salary of 1,050 Gulden, he undertook not only to direct rehearsals and performances but also to compose an unspecified number of operas and ballets.[21] Braun paid a smaller salary—800 Gulden—to Salieri, who agreed to compose two operas per year for the court theaters.[22]

20. für Besorgung der Regie (A-Wth, M 4000).

21. Payment records for September 1994, A-Wth, M 4000.

22. This arrangement can be deduced from payment records for August 1794, at the beginning of Braun's tenure as impresario: "Dem Salieri K. K. Hoff Kapellmeister von den jährl. verwilligten 800 fl. für Componirung der Musick, für 2 ital. Opern, pro Augusto 1794—66 [fl]. 40 [xr]" (A-Wth, M 4000).

Il mondo alla rovescia

Salieri's agreement with Braun led to his return, after a hiatus of four years, to active duty as a composer for the court theaters. He brought three new operas to the stage during 1795: more than in any single year since his Italian tour of 1778–80.

The first product of Salieri's renewed theatrical activity, *Il mondo alla rovescia,* was performed in the Burgtheater on 13 January 1795. He had begun the opera much earlier. In Italy in 1779 he had collaborated with Mazzolà on an opera that was to be called *L'isola capricciosa,* but they suspended work when Salieri's contract was annulled by the death of the impresario who had commissioned it.[23] Mazzolà spent part of 1791 in Vienna, serving as theatrical poet between Da Ponte's dismissal and Bertati's arrival.[24] It was probably then that he and Salieri resumed work on *L'isola capricciosa,* revised and retitled *Il mondo alla rovescia.* In January 1792 the theatrical management paid Salieri 200 Gulden "in the name of the poet Mazzolà" for the libretto. Eight months later Salieri received 900 Gulden (twice the regular fee) for the opera.[25] But more than two years passed before *Il mondo* finally came to the stage. Normally composers were paid for their music only after an opera was performed; Salieri's success at extracting an unusually large fee for an unperformed opera is one of many examples of his financial acumen. If, as is likely, he submitted this opera to Braun in partial fulfillment of his agreement to provide two operas per year, he was in effect paid twice for it.

The musical richness of *Il mondo* owes much to the example of Mozart's operas, which, despite their absence from the court theaters for most of the 1790s, influenced composers who knew them well. Weigl openly declared: "I always had Mozart's excellent instrumentation in my head."[26] Salieri, as far as we know, never acknowledged Mozart's influence. But *Il mondo* and the operas that followed show that his debt to Mozart was as large as Weigl's.

Mazzolà borrowed title and premise from Goldoni's *Il mondo alla roversa, o sia Le donne che comandono,* first performed in Venice in 1750, but otherwise the librettos are different. In the distant past a group of European women, tired of submitting to men, fled Europe and founded a society in which women rule in both love and war. They defend their island with an army led by female officers. The generala, the elderly lady general, was sung by a buffo caricato, the bass Pietro Mazzoni. (Much earlier in his career Salieri had used a comic bass to portray an old woman: Ortensia in *La finta scema.*) Un-

23. Mosel, 66–67, 144.

24. Rice, *W. A. Mozart: La clemenza di Tito,* 32.

25. A-Wth, M 4000, entry for January 1792: "Dem Salieri Anton, im Namen des Poeten Mazzola für Komponirung der Poesie zur Opera Il Mondo all Rovecio—200 [fl]." Entry for September 1792: "Dem Salieri Anton für Componirung der Opera Il Mondo alla Rovescia—900 [fl]."

26. Weigl, "Selbstbiographien," 54.

der her command are the colonnella (the lady colonel, soprano, sung by Tomeoni) and the adiutanta (the lady adjutant, soprano, Maria Anna Gassmann).

Some of the island's men belong to a quasi-religious order reminiscent of the Vestal Virgins of ancient Rome, the Casti Colombi (Chaste Doves), supervised by a kind of high priest, the gran colombo (bass, Felice Angrisani, brother of Carlo Angrisani). Others, reduced to the activities of European women, embroider, make lace, and fend off the sexual advances of the female military officers. The men include two named after flowers: the generala's nephew Amaranto (amaranth; created by the tenor Giovanni Prada) and the dressmaker Girasole (sunflower; created by the tenor Gaetano Lotti).

In his first aria Girasole describes the behavior of the island's women. The text is Goldonian not only in featuring a catalogue (in this case a long list of verbs) but also in generalizing about women:

Girandole le femmine
  Lusingano, contrattano,
  S'aggirano, s'appiattano,
  Subornano, insolentano,
  Si vantano, ed inventano.

[Hovering about, the women flatter, bargain, wander, lie in wait, bribe, insult, boast, invent.]

Also reminiscent of Goldoni is the colonnella's first aria, "Non v'è stato più giocondo," a song in praise of a soldier's life. The text recalls Tagliaferro's "Star trombette" in *La buona figliuola* and Figaro's "Non più andrai"; and Salieri's music in C major, orchestrated with trumpets, recalls the settings of military aria texts by Piccinni and Mozart. But instead of being sung by a bass or baritone, "Non v'è stato più giocondo" is sung by a soprano.

The colonnella tries to seduce Amaranto with a lyrical love song whose key (A major) and absence of coloratura suited Tomeoni. The opening melody, carefully crafted to make the most of Tomeoni's limited tessitura, shows Mozart's influence in the chromatically enhanced climax at the repetition of "guardate." But the nobility of the colonnella's amorous appeal is undercut by Amaranto, who, as a pertichino, replies with flirtatious indignation; short, pert phrases, consisting mostly of sixteenth notes, have (in the context of an opera buffa) a distinctly feminine character: they might have been sung thirty years earlier by one of Piccinni's chambermaids or Fischietti's peasant girls (ex. 16.1).

This "world upside down" is put into a state of tumult by the arrival of a couple of noble Europeans: an attractive but ridiculous count (bass, Angrisani) and a marchesa (soprano, Therese Gassmann). The generala and the colonnella fall in love with the count, who happily flirts with both but is naturally attracted to the character sung by

EXAMPLE 16.1 Salieri, *Il mondo alla rovescia,* act 1, "Pietà, perdono," mm. 1–21 (A-Wn, Mus. Hs. 16180)

COLONNELLA: Have pity, forgive me, my beloved. If you reject me I will die of grief. Do not look at me with such harshness. AMARANTO: I will call people if you continue to be so insistent here in this room.

the pretty Tomeoni rather than the one sung by a bass. Salieri was to exploit in several later operas the comic pairing of Tomeoni and Angrisani.

Act 2 opens with a depiction of workers in an arms factory. In the chorus "Sull'incudine sonora" Salieri periodically added his customary symbol "I" below the bass. He explained in a note: "On the first three measures one will hear, in time with the music, the sound of files and saws. Then, at the signs under the bass, one will see and hear the workers hammering a red-hot iron from which come fiery sparks."[27] He enriched the sound of this scene further by means of an onstage wind ensemble—pairs of horns, oboes, clarinets, and bassoons—whose music he notated at the end of the autograph.

A European fleet threatens the island. The generala, smoking a pipe and studying plans of the fortress, discusses its defense with her officers. Left alone with the count, she tries to kiss him, but he resists. He later sings a love duet with the colonnella and then a comic duet with the generala, "Alle nozze questa sera." The comedy of this number comes partly from its being sung by two basses, one dressed as a woman. Its effect is en-

27. NB. sulle tre prime battute si sentirà a rigore di musica come uno strepito di lime e di seghe. Sulli segni poi notati sotto il Basso, si vedrà, e si sentirà batter dalle Fabbre sopra un ferro rovente, dal quale sortiranno faville di fuoco.

EXAMPLE 16.2 *Il mondo alla rovescia*, act 2, "Alle nozze questa sera," mm. 8–21

At the wedding this evening we want to be happy. With my dear wife, amid wine both white and red, I want everyone to understand my rare ability as a singer.

hanced by the freshness of Salieri's music. The count's opening melody shows the composer breaking away, again under Mozart's influence, from buffo-caricato formulas. At the cadence one might have expected the succession of two-measure phrases to continue and the melodic line to double the bass; Salieri instead extended the last two phrases to three measures and adopted the melodic grandiloquence of serious opera (ex. 16.2). In *Così fan tutte* Mozart had treated his buffo caricato Benucci in much the same manner (see Guilelmo's opening melody in the trio "Una bella serenata").

The marchesa finds Amaranto attractive. But as a European she cannot at first bring herself to take the lead in their courtship, which features a musical device that Salieri had learned from Goldonian opera buffa and had used in several of his early operas: conversation represented by two short songs with identical music but different words. Amaranto sings "Spuntar il sol d'Aprile"; the marchesa responds with the same music in "Di fiero colpo il core." Such song pairs (which Mozart rejected as old fashioned in 1784) had largely fallen out of use in the 1790s. These may have been among the pieces that Salieri wrote in the late 1770s for *L'isola capricciosa.*

Eventually the marchesa proposes marriage to Amaranto. Alone, she expresses her happy anticipation in a brilliant concertante aria that Salieri borrowed from one of his early operas. Such borrowings made particular sense in the case of Therese Gassmann, who, as Salieri's former student, had probably sung his early coloratura arias as part of her training. But Salieri seems to have been uncertain about which aria to reuse. In his autograph he wrote only a brief note: "dell' Europa coll'oboe obb," that is, the aria from *Europa riconosciuta* with oboe obbligato. Gassmann was apparently to sing the great concertante aria "Quando più irato freme," written for Fransziska Danzi Lebrun and (probably) the oboist Ludwig August Lebrun (see ex. 8.3). But the text as it appears in the libretto of *Il mondo* suggests that she sang another old concertante aria instead. "Sente l'amica speme," sung by Elizabeth Wendling in *Semiramide,* with elaborate solos for flute, oboe, and bassoon, had originally been sung by Cavalieri (with a text beginning "Vedo l'amiche insigne") in the cantata *La sconfitta di Borea* (1775).[28] In the fragmentary autograph score of *Semiramide* the text of Wendling's aria (as it appears in the libretto) has been crossed out and a new text added. Instead of beginning with a Metastasian storm simile—

> Sente l'amica speme
> Già ritornar in petto,
> Nocchier, che con diletto,
> Vede calmato il mar

[The sailor who sees with pleasure the sea growing calm feels friendly hope already returning to his breast.]

—the aria now begins with a more personal statement of feelings—

> Sento l'amica speme
> Che mi ritorna in seno,
> E placido sereno
> A me mostrando va.

[I feel friendly hope returning to my breast and showing me a peaceful serenity.]

This second text is precisely that which appears in the libretto of *Il mondo.* The twenty-year-old aria must have suited Gassmann's high soprano voice as well as those of the Queen of the Night that she later sang in the Kärntnertortheater; she performed it again with German words in two different cantatas by Salieri.[29]

The count and the marchesa try to flee the island with their lovers. As a change of scene presents a picturesque seashore, a boatmen's chorus depicts with lyrical words ("Tranquilla e placida") and music the calm sea over which they hope to escape. The on-stage wind ensemble that accompanied the workers at the beginning of the act returns here, adding color and warmth to the scene. In a beautiful canonic quartet, the couples pray that Love will second their escape. With its triple meter, appoggiaturas at the ends of four-measure phrases, and moderately slow tempo, "Amor che in sen m'infondi" is a fine example of the Viennese operatic canon. Imitation dissolves into homophony as all four lovers address Love together, the intensity of their prayer enhanced by Mozartean chromaticism and appoggiaturas (ex. 16.3).

28. Della Croce/Blanchetti, 530–31.
29. Della Croce/Blanchetti, 530.

EXAMPLE 16.3 *Il mondo alla rovescia,* act 2, "Tranquilla e placida," mm. 78–110 (canon)

(Continued on next page)

EXAMPLE 16.3 (*continued*)

(*Continued on next page*)

In the finale of act 2, dominated by a battle between the invading Europeans and the female army defending the island, the sound of gunfire, used by Salieri in *Axur* and *La cifra*, plays an important role. The bass drum, which at one point rolls continuously for fourteen measures, further increases the battle's excitement and noise.

One might expect an opera begun in 1779 and finished (at least paid for) in 1792 to show signs of having been conceived for a cast different from the one that finally per-

EXAMPLE 16.3 *(continued)*

COLONNELLA, MARCHESA, AMARANTO, CONTE: Love, who inspires my heart with such lively and sweet passion, may your favor, Love, help me escape. GENERALA: Love does not favor you

formed it in 1795. Some of the music that Salieri wrote or reused for the colonnella in particular was little suited to the singer who finally created the role. He seems to have originally thought of the colonnella as a high coloratura soprano. One of her arias is a setting of a text from *Didone abbandonata,* "A trionfar mi chiama." This heroic aria in D major, accompanied by trumpets, oboes, and strings, requires a soprano who can sing brilliant coloratura up to high E and can sustain a note, in competition with trumpet fanfares, for four measures. The aria includes a cadenza for soprano and instrumental soloists, in this case oboe and two trumpets. High coloratura and a written-out cadenza, characteristic of Salieri's early operas, in a setting of an aria text by Metastasio suggest that Salieri wrote the aria much earlier than 1792 and inserted it here because its text made sense. Having been intended for Aeneas, the poem suits the colonnella's masculine persona. But the music could hardly have suited Tomeoni's voice less.

More evidence that Salieri originally thought of the colonnella as a high coloratura soprano is a note in his autograph that he intended to incorporate into her part the aria "Ah se foss'io smarrito," which Clementina Baglioni had sung in one of his earliest operas, *L'amore innocente.* The aria has a high coloratura vocal part and an oboe solo of the kind that young Salieri delighted in intertwining with his soprano lines.

Salieri's autograph records his efforts to adjust the role of the colonnella for Tomeoni. He directed the copyist to transpose "A trionfar mi chiama" from D down to C and simplified some of the coloratura. And he abandoned altogether the idea of reusing

EXAMPLE 16.4 *Il mondo alla rovescia,* overture, mm. 68–75

"Ah se foss'io smarrito," crossing out its title and replacing it with the title of another aria, "Aura che intorno spiri," which follows in the manuscript.[30] This aria's moderate tempo (Un poco andante) and lyricism were much more suited to Tomeoni than was "Ah se foss'io smarrito"; the simple coloratura took her only up to B♭.

The overture to *Il mondo* also contains old music. It begins with an attractive theme that Salieri borrowed from the overture to *Don Chisciotte alle nozze di Gamace:* music almost as old as "Ah se foss'io smarrito" (see ex. 5.4). Salieri quoted the old overture literally up to measure 16, enriching the orchestration (originally oboes, horns, bassoons, and strings) with flutes, clarinets, trumpets, and timpani. He substituted a new fanfare for horns in the bridge passage, and the rest of the overture is mostly new. The second theme, a jaunty march with pizzicato accompaniment, brings the overture up to date (ex. 16.4). Salieri was later to use this music yet again. Although he provided his late opera buffa *Angiolina* with a new overture (which can be found in the autograph), the overture to *Il mondo* also served as an overture to *Angiolina:* it appeared in a piano reduction under the title "Overture de l'Opera Angioline ou Le Mariage par le bruit pour le Piano-Forte." Whether the old overture replaced the new one or vice versa we do not know.

Il mondo had little success. Zinzendorf, who attended the premiere, referred to Salieri's opera with a word, *sot,* that he rarely used in his comments on operas: "Stupid opera. The men as women, the women as men. Beautiful music."[31] The rest of the audience seems to have agreed more strongly with his criticism of the plot than with his

30. The text corresponds only in part to the poem "Aura che intorno spiri" in Mazzolà's *L'isola capricciosa,* from which Mozart extracted the text for his concert aria "Aura che intorno spiri," K. 431.

31. *Il mondo alla rovescia.* Sot opera. les hommes en femmes, les femmes en hommes. Belle musique (Zinzendorf, 13 January 1795).

praise of the music. Although the premiere attracted a respectable number of paying spectators (box-office receipts: 427 Gulden, 11 Kreuzer), attendance at subsequent performances fell sharply (receipts for the second night: 240 Gulden, 15 Kreuzer; for the fifth night: 46 Gulden, 54 Kreuzer).[32] Much of the court theaters' audience paid by subscription, so that daily box-office receipts do not tell us how many people attended a particular performance. But it is probably safe to deduce from the declining receipts that *Il mondo* was a flop. After seven performances it was dropped from the repertory, never to be revived.

Mosel blamed the failure largely on the libretto, which seems to have touched a raw nerve for him as well as Zinzendorf. After praising several numbers for their musical strength, he criticized *Il mondo* more harshly than any other opera by Salieri:

> Although the plot seems to be comic at the beginning, since the men and women exchange roles not only in their occupations but also in their emotions and behavior, it is precisely because of this that the opera can never interest the audience without obliterating tender feelings. If laughter is aroused by men, occupied with feminine activities, adopting the modesty and coyness of girls, yet on the other hand it is repugnant, even shocking, to see women and girls pursue and besiege men with their amorous proposals and caresses. This idea belongs among those that are amusing as long they remain in the imagination, but when they are presented before one's eyes they not only lose all comedy but become unbearable. Moreover one cannot describe the development of the plot as anything other than wretched.[33]

Success with Proven Formulas: *Palmira regina di Persia*

Salieri resumed his collaboration with De Gamerra shortly after the failure of *Il mondo alla rovescia.* But the first product of their reunion, a Goldonian comedy entitled *Eraclito e Democrito* (first performed on 13 August 1795) was no more successful than the two operas on which they had collaborated in the mid 1770s.[34] Finally, on 14 October 1795, they triumphed, producing what turned out to be the most successful of Salieri's late operas.

In setting *Palmira regina di Persia* in an exotic, Middle Eastern court, mixing comic and serious elements, and calling for large choral forces and spectacular scenic effects, Salieri and De Gamerra may have hoped to recapture the success of an earlier opera whose title included the name of a Middle Eastern sovereign, *Axur re d'Ormus.* They came close to doing so. Box-office records for the initial run show that *Palmira*—unlike *Il mondo alla rovescia*—drew steadily larger audiences during the first two weeks.[35] The Viennese court theaters performed *Palmira* thirty-nine times between

32. A-Wth, M 4000.
33. Mosel, 145.
34. On *Eraclito e Democrito* see Della Croce/Blanchetti, 285–86, 501–3.
35. A-Wth, M 4000.

1795 and 1798. In German translation it was performed in theaters throughout Germany into the early nineteenth century.

Like *Axur, Palmira* is based on a French libretto. In 1787, around the time of the premiere of *Tarare,* Salieri agreed to collaborate with Désiré Martin on another French opera, *La Princesse de Babylone.* He promised to complete it on his return to Vienna but apparently failed to make much progress. In a letter to Martin of 16 August 1789 he played for time, stating that he had completed most of the first act despite being "extremely busy" with the direction of Joseph's opera buffa troupe.[36] The outbreak of the French Revolution in the same year led to further delays. Salieri's letter of 24 January 1791 shows "the greatest musical diplomat" trying to reconcile his obligations to Martin, his interest in French opera and his growing realization that he, as the Habsburgs' Hofkapellmeister, would be unable to bring a new work to the stage of the Opéra in the foreseeable future:

> I deeply regret that my silence has caused you restlessness, but what could I write to you, Sir, in the uncertainty of things related to our business? I have already heard fear expressed that your great theater will be destroyed; and I am delighted to hear that at present this fear is entirely dissipated. But you see, Sir, that as for me, I am in a very delicate situation, being unsure of things that could, if I returned to Paris in these circumstances, have the most serious consequences for my interests (for I must think of them) and even for my honor: for on what basis should I ask for or hope to obtain from my court permission to make this journey? What assurances have I of the time that I will be given; or even if I will be given any? If I were in Vienna master of my time and of myself, I would not hesitate much, despite the uncertainty on all these points, before spending five or six months in Paris; perhaps we would not need that much time to have our work performed, but this "perhaps," in my situation, this "perhaps" troubles me greatly.
>
> As for the progress of the musical setting of our poem, the imperial coronation and that of Hungary, which have taken place recently, along with a thousand other things that have had to be done before and after for the king of Naples, have made me lose much time. Nevertheless, do not fear, Sir, on that account; I would catch up. But again it is impossible for me to tell you when I will be able to bring this work to Paris, for the reason that I have given above. Beyond that, put yourself in my position, Sir; study the whole situation, and you will see that patience is still indispensable, at least on my side."[37]

Salieri eventually gave up the composition of *La Princesse de Babylone,* but he did not forget Martin's libretto. Probably by analogy with the derivation of *Axur* from *Tarare* he decided to present in Vienna an Italian version of Martin's drama.

36. The letter is quoted in chap. 13.

37. Salieri to Désiré Martin, 24 January 1791, in Jullien, *La Cour et l'opéra,* 169, Angermüller, *Leben,* 3:58–59, and Angermüller, *Fatti,* 129–30.

Palmira is loosely based on Voltaire's story "La Princesse de Babylone" (1768), a pseudo-oriental tale very much in the style of Ridley's "Sadak and Kalasrade," the story behind Beaumarchais's *Tarare.* According to the pronouncement of an oracle, Formosante, princess of Babylon, will marry the man who can bend the bow of Nimrod and slay a ferocious lion. Three men take up the challenge: the pharaoh of Egypt, the shah of India, and the great khan of the Scythians. Voltaire delighted in his descriptions of the arrival of the suitors with their vast retinues. A fourth man, whose identity is unknown, arrives on a unicorn, accompanied only by a valet. In this mysterious man beauty and strength are united: "le visage d'Adonis sur le corps d'Hercule."

Only the fourth man can bend the bow, and only he succeeds in killing the lion. But then, on hearing that his father is dying, he suddenly disappears. A second oracular pronouncement—"Your daughter shall not be married until she has traversed the globe"—sends Formosante on a long voyage in search of the mysterious man who will eventually become her husband. Voltaire's description of this voyage takes up most of the story and provides the narrator, as in *Candide,* with much opportunity for social criticism, especially when Formosante travels through Europe and learns of its strange, exotic customs.

De Gamerra's libretto is based almost entirely on the first few pages of Voltaire's story. He omitted the bow of Nimrod and Formosante's travels, the latter being much more effectively narrated than depicted on stage; he changed Voltaire's lion into a monster that has been terrorizing Persia. The high priest (bass, the role created by Felice Angrisani) makes an oracular pronouncement: one of the kings who seek the hand of Princess Palmira (soprano, Sessi) will kill the monster and thereby win Palmira. By casting Sessi as Palmira, De Gamerra and Salieri allowed her to build on the success that she had achieved as Aspasia since the revival of *Axur* in 1793.

The kings arrive: first timid Egyptian Alderano (bass, Carlo Angrisani) and boastful Scythian Oronte (bass, Ignaz Saal), both comic characters; then brave, handsome Indian Alcidoro (tenor, Mombelli). Alcidoro and Palmira are already secret lovers; they express their passion in the duet "O del cor speme gradita." By placing this love duet near the beginning of the opera Salieri and De Gamerra may have reminded audiences of the two love duets for Atar and Aspasia in act 1 of *Axur.* Palmira tells her father, King Dario (bass, Johann Michael Vogl),[38] that she loves Alcidoro; but he insists that the competition go forward. After Alderano's cowardice is made known and Oronte fails in his attempt to kill the monster, Alcidoro triumphs; the opera ends with celebration of his impending marriage to Palmira.

The overture has very little in the way of exotic color (ex. 16.5); in this it resembles the rest of the opera, from which "Turkish" musical elements are almost entirely absent.

38. Vogl later won fame as one of Schubert's most effective vocal collaborators: he gave the first concert performance of "Erlkönig."

EXAMPLE 16.5 *Palmira regina di Persia,* overture, mm. 1–27 (A- Wn, Mus. Hs. 16183)

But the opening measures establish a sense of place by referring simultaneously to two Middle Eastern operas with which Salieri's audience was familiar. The initial three chords are deployed in exactly the same rhythm—half note, half note, dotted half note—as at the beginning of the overture to *Axur.* The ascending melodic line, D-F♯-B, differs from the melodic line at the beginning of *Axur* (also D-F♯-B) only in that the first interval here is a rising third rather than a falling sixth. By harmonizing that rising third with a falling third in the bass (D-B), Salieri may have also reminded his listeners of *Die Zauberflöte,* which begins with the same progression (E♭-G in the treble, E♭-C in the bass). Instead of using conventional "Turkish" music to announce the opera's Middle Eastern setting, Salieri referred in the overture to a specifically Viennese tradition of heroicomic operas in exotic settings.

Salieri scored the D-major overture for an orchestra that includes horns in E♭, which, as one might expect, are rarely heard. But they do contribute crucially to a surprising shift, at measure 20, from tonic D to B♭, which is quickly reinterpreted as the Neapolitan sixth of A. Salieri had used abrupt digressions to the flat sixth scale degree to great dramatic effect in *Les Danaïdes* and *Tarare* (in the overture that also serves as the overture to *Axur*); but such a shift in the middle of an exposition, as here, was an unusual departure from convention. The entry of the horns in E♭ on the B♭ chord adds to the surprise and focuses the audience's attention on it.

Salieri's extensive use of accompanied recitative in *Palmira* reminds one of *Axur.* The free-flowing alternation of accompanied recitative, vocal solos, and chorus contributes to the cohesion of several scenes, including the first. The overture in D is followed directly by the marchlike chorus "Nume eterno" in B♭, one of Salieri's favorite tonal juxtapositions. "Nume eterno," which contains a solo for King Dario, leads without a break into an accompanied recitative for Dario, which is followed, again without a break, by the chorus "A poco a poco," in F. An orchestral transition leads to an accompanied recitative for the high priest, which is followed by the celebratory chorus "Oh non sperato felice evento," in D. The vigorous cadences at the end of this chorus, which coincide with the end of the opera's first scene, represent the strongest musical punctuation to this point in the opera. That the cadences are in D major helps us hear them as the conclusion of a tonal progression that began with the overture.

Rivalry among the suitors for the honor of first battling the monster takes up much of the opera, beginning with a spectacular scene in which the three kings introduce themselves to Dario and Palmira. After a chorus in praise of Dario, Alderano arrives on a camel, Oronte on an elephant, and Alcidoro on a horse, each singing an aria as he presents gifts. For the Viennese production both the camel and the horse were real, but our sources are silent about how the elephant was represented.

De Gamerra's stage directions for this scene describe one of several elaborate sets required in the opera, scenery whose inspiration can be traced back, ultimately, to the fantastic descriptions in Voltaire's story: "A magnificent courtyard, oval in shape, with a great triumphal arch at the back that allows a view of a vast piazza full of people. At the top of the hall a gallery full of spectators, from which hang colorful tapestries. The ceiling of the hall is painted blue, sprinkled with gold stars representing constellations and the planets. At the right is the throne."[39]

Also contributing to the monumentality of this scene is its opening chorus, one of many in the opera—choruses of people, priests, Palmira's handmaidens, soldiers—that enhance its splendor and again remind us of *Axur.* Especially close to Salieri's earlier Middle Eastern opera is the final chorus, "Ogni riva d'un eco giuliva," whose decasillabi caused him to echo the rhythms of the last chorus of *Axur* (also based on decasillabi), "Qual piacer la nostr' anima ingombra."

Act 2 begins with a temple scene much like the one in *Axur,* complete with a high priest and chorus of priests. The suitors anxiously await a ruling from the high priest as to the order in which they will face the monster. In the charming unaccompanied quartet sung by King Dario and the three suitors, "Silenzio facciasi" (ex. 16.6), Salieri successfully exploited the interest that audiences had shown in an a-cappella duet in *Eraclito e Democrito,* "Imparate anime amanti."[40]

EXAMPLE 16.6 *Palmira regina di Persia,* act 2, "Silenzio facciasi" (complete)

(*Continued on next page*)

39. Magnifico Terreno di figura ovale con grand' Arco di trionfo nel fondo, che lascia libera la veduta d'una vasta piazza all'intorno ripiena di Popolo. Nella sommità del Salone Galleria ricolma di spettatori, dalla quale pendono dei coloriti tappeti. La volta del Salone è dipinta d'azzurro seminato di stelle d'oro rappresentanti le costellazioni e i pianeti. Alla destra trono (act 1, sc. 10).

40. In his annotations to the autograph of *Eraclito e Democrito* (transcribed in Angermüller, *Leben,* 3:79–81; Angermüller, *Fatti,* 103–4; and Swenson, 167–69) Salieri wrote: "The duettino without instruments, 'Imparate anime amanti,' is simple, as it must be, but perhaps precisely because of its having no accompaniment it attracted the audience's full attention and was always repeated."

EXAMPLE 16.6 (*continued*)

Let there be silence: sleep has fallen into a mystic's heart; uncertain and mute, I stand here waiting. When will he wake up? What will happen?

When the high priest designates Alderano as the first to fight the monster, Oronte terrifies the Egyptian prince with a big buffo aria, "Sopra il volto sbigottito," in which he depicts in words and music the dismembering of poor Alderano by the monster. Already in *La finta scema* De Gamerra had taken the Goldonian catalogue aria in a new direction with a detailed description of the activities of a cook (pounding meat and grating cheese); twenty years later he took the catalogue aria further, listing in gruesome detail the parts of Alderano's body as they lie on the ground, about to be eaten by the monster:

Qui la testa al suol si vede,
Là una spalla, il collo, un piede;
Qui il ventricolo, lì un occhio,
Qua un polmone, là un ginocchio;
Qui le braccia e le cervella,
Là una costa, e le budella;
Qui un'orecchia, il naso, un dito,

Lì . . . oh che pranzo saporito
Sul sbranato corpo vostro
Dolcemente farà il mostro,
E ve l'auguro del cor.

[Here you see the head on the ground, there a shoulder, the neck, a foot; here the stomach, there an eye; here a lung, there a knee; here the arms and the brains; there a rib and the entrails; here an ear, a nose, a finger; there . . . what a tasty dinner the monster will calmly make of your mutilated body; and I wish it for you with all my heart.]

Salieri's setting of this aria, while in some respects maintaining buffo-caricato traditions, differs as significantly from his early comic arias as De Gamerra's catalogue differs from the Goldonian catalogues that inspired it. The aria consists of a slow section followed by a fast one. The Andante un poco sostenuto features a melody whose duple meter and dotted rhythms are reminiscent of melodies written much earlier for comic basses and baritones (ex. 16.7). The melody's references to the minor mode by way of G♭ and C♭, which reflect the text's preoccupation with death, are not new to Salieri's comic vocabulary. What markedly differs from his earlier approach to the buffo style is the accompaniment, both instrumentation and harmony.

EXAMPLE 16.7 *Palmira regina di Persia,* act 2, "Sopra il volto sbigottito," mm. 1–21

(Continued on next page)

EXAMPLE 16.7 (*continued*)

Over your astonished face, over your weak and bewildered brow, and on those pale cheeks death is painted with a dark funereal color.

Even before Oronte sings, the orchestra announces with a jagged unison (horns, cellos, and basses) that avoids the tonic E♭ that this aria will go beyond buffo convention. Audiences used to hearing buffi caricati accompanied by an orchestra of strings augmented by oboes, bassoons, horns, and sometimes trumpets and drums must have been surprised to hear clarinets, bassoons, and horns accompany Oronte's opening melody. If he had used this tune during the 1770s or 1780s, Salieri would almost certainly have harmonized the first four measures I–V–I. But in 1795 he chose a more quickly moving, far-reaching harmonic progression, enriched with secondary dominants, that avoids cadences to the tonic. Instead of a V–I cadence at measure 7, we have to wait until measure 21, the end of the slow section, for the cadence. It was probably from Mozart's operas (the slow introduction of the overture to *Die Zauberflöte*, for example, uses some of the rich harmonic material that reappears in Oronte's aria) that Salieri learned to extend his harmonic vocabulary during the 1790s.

Palmira differs from *Axur* in the extent to which it exploits the skills and background in opera seria shared by the singers who created the two romantic leads. The big formal showpieces composed by Salieri for Sessi and Mombelli exceed in length and complexity the numbers that Salieri wrote for the singers who created the roles of Atar (probably Vincenzo Calvesi) and Aspasia (probably Luisa Laschi). The clear difference between the music written for Atar and that written for Alcidoro is perhaps related to the fact that Calvesi was a mezzo-carattere tenor who had rarely sung in serious opera, whereas Mombelli, although he sang mezzo-carattere roles in Vienna, had devoted his career in Italy to serious opera. Laschi likewise had much less experience in opera seria than Sessi.[41]

Alcidoro's role culminates in a great rondòlike aria that he sings shortly before going off to fight the monster, "Luci amate in tal momento." Like most rondò texts this one consists of ottonari, but eleven rather than the usual twelve. And rather than pleading for pity in the poem's last sentence, as so many heroes and heroines do in their rondòs, Alcidoro promises that he will return victorious from his combat with the monster:

Luci amate in tal momento
    Uno sguardo per pietà.
Sì, voliamo al gran cimento;
    Animar di più mi sento.
    Ah che in faccia al suo tormento,
    Trema il piè . . . partir non so.
Ma che tardo? alla vittoria
    L'amor mio col ciel m'invita;
    Quando sia che torni in vita,
    Deh le dite che fra poco
    Il suo bene, il suo tesoro,
    Il suo tenero Alcidoro
    Vincitor ritornerò.

[Beloved eyes, at this moment a glance, for pity's sake. Yes, let us fly to the great battle; I feel myself inspired. Ah, my foot trembles in the face of her torment . . . I cannot leave. But why delay? My love and heaven encourage me to victory; when she should return to life [Palmira has just fainted], tell her that in a short time her love, her treasure, her gentle Alcidoro will return victorious.]

The tender melody in A major with which Salieri set the opening couplet is very similar to an A-major tune sung by the tenor Lindoro in Gassmann's *La contessina* of 1770 (in the duet "Contessina, mi permette"), but the clarinet solo woven into the accompanimental fabric of "Luci amate" gives it a modern flavor. Typical of the rondò is that the following text, the quatrain beginning "Sì, voliamo," is set to contrasting musical material. We expect this passage to be tonally unstable; but we do not expect Salieri's sudden modulation by a third, from a half cadence on the dominant, to C major (ex. 16.8). Third modulations have a place in many rondòs, including several of Salieri's; but they usually occur later, in the fast section. ("Amor, pietoso Amore," in *Il ricco d'un giorno*, another two-tempo aria in A, also features a sudden modulation to C, but after the main

41. Sartori, Indici, 2:360, 609.

EXAMPLE 16.8 *Palmira regina di Persia,* act 2, "Luci amate in tal momento," mm. 1–23

(*Continued on next page*)

EXAMPLE 16.8 (*continued*)

theme of the fast section.) By bringing the modulation forward to the slow section Salieri enhanced its effect, just as he had done with the surprisingly early tonal detour in the overture.

Alcidoro returns to A major and the opening melody. The tonally unstable transition that follows the repetition of the opening theme gave Salieri opportunity to introduce the trumpets in D, which have been silent since the beginning of the aria. As Alcidoro begins to think of victory, the sound of trumpets in festive D major helps to convey his feelings.

The scenic requirements of *Palmira*—magnificent Middle Eastern buildings and live animals on stage—were partly responsible for its success. Zinzendorf's comments after attending an early performance (in the very crowded Burgtheater on 22 October 1795) are typical of favorable reactions to the opera in that they focused more on how the opera looked than how it sounded. He clearly enjoyed the performance in spite of uncomfortable conditions in the theater: "To the new opera *Palmyre, Reine de Perse*. . . . Duchess Aremberg came into my box and took sick during the second act on account of the excessive heat. . . . The spectacle is lovely, the scenery beautiful, and the costumes of La Sessi and Mombelli very pretty; the camel and the horse went very well."[42] At another performance he listened as well as looked: "In the evening to the opera," he wrote on 5 November. "*Palmyra*. Beautiful music, beautiful scenery. La Sessi sang well."[43] But later, on 9 February 1796, he had his eye on the animals again: "In the evening to the theater. *Palmyre*. The camel kneeled at first."[44]

Palmira once again offered a live camel when it was revived in German translation by the Theater an der Wien in 1803. In his *Eipeldauer Briefe*, a lively, satirical commentary on Viennese life in local dialect, Joseph Richter wrote of this production:

> I have seen among others the opera *Palmira*, which is being performed at the Theater an der Wien. Well, dear cousin, there the eyes certainly get their fill. There is the most beautiful scenery, and a live camel, and elephants and dragons and giants, and our own jolly Schikaneder himself rode out a couple of times on the camel, and thus became a camel-knight [a pun in German: *gritten . . . Kameelritter*]. As soon as the camel appeared, everyone clapped and cried "Vivat!" The camel thanked the audience, making a deep bow with the rider still on his back; little had the good beast dreamed that he would become an actor.[45]

Sung in German by a cast that included Emanuel Schikaneder (as the cowardly Egyptian King Alderano, to judge from Richter's account), *Palmira* at the Theater an der Wien must have reminded Viennese of *Die Zauberflöte* even more clearly than the court theaters' original production. The Theater an der Wien kept *Palmira* alive after it had ceased to be heard in the court theaters.[46] The young French composer Louis

42. au nouvel opera *Palmyre, Reine de Perse*. . . . La Duchesse d'Aremberg y vint dans ma loge et se trouve mal au second acte de la chaleur excessive. . . . Le Spectacle est beau, les decorations belles, les habillemens de la Sessi et de Mombelli tres jolis, le chameau et le cheval vont tres bien (Zinzendorf, 22 October 1795).

43. Le soir a l'opera. *Palmyra*. Belle musique, belle decoration. La Sessi chante bien (Zinzendorf, 5 November 1795).

44. Le soir au Spectacle. *Palmyre*. Le chameau s'agenouilla d'abord (Zinzendorf, 8 February 1796).

45. Quoted in Swenson, 211.

46. *Palmira* was performed fifty-nine times in the Theater an der Wien between 1803 and 1816; see Anton Bauer, *150 Jahre Theater an der Wien* (Vienna, 1952), 272.

FIGURE 16.4 Set design by Giorgio Fuentes for a production of *Palmira* in Frankfurt, 1797. (Courtesy of Goethe-Museum, Frankfurt.)

Herold, visiting Vienna in 1815, saw one of the last performances of *Palmira*. He called it "a fine work by the great Salieri," and commented: "Everything is calculated for the stage: the short numbers, very concise and vigorous, often delightful phrases."[47]

As *Palmira* spread to other German-speaking cities during the late 1790s, its scenic element continued to account for much of its success. A production in Frankfurt with sets by Giorgio Fuentes was particularly splendid (fig. 16.4). Goethe, in a letter to Schiller of 14 August 1797, wrote at length of the scenery:

> Yesterday I saw a production of the opera *Palmira*, which, taken as a whole, was given a very good and suitable performance. I especially had the pleasure to see a part that was completely perfect: namely the scenery. It is the work of a Milanese who is presently in residence here. . . .
>
> The scenery for *Palmira* represents an example from which one could extract a theory of theatrical painting. There are six sets, which follow one another in two acts, without the return of any one of them. The variety and transitions between them are very cleverly achieved. . . . The colors are faultless and the style of painting extremely free and yet precise; all the tricks of perspective, all the charms of the arrangement of objects along lines converging to vanishing points are apparent in this work. In its infinite detail one can discern the

47. Della Croce/Blanchetti, 287, citing A. Pougin, *Herold* (Paris, 1906), 27.

studies of a great school and the tradition of many lifetimes; and one can well say that this art stands here at its highest level.[48]

John Quincy Adams, who spent a short time in Berlin during the late 1790s as the American government's diplomatic representative, attended a performance of *Palmira* on 18 May 1798. We learn from his diary that again scenery played an important role in the production: "At the play in the evening—*Palmira, Princess of Persia,* a German translation of an Italian opera. The scenery was magnificent, the music pretty good, the performers tolerable, the house small and very badly lighted. The royal box in front of the stage was as full as it could hold. The King, Queen, and all the younger part of the royal family were there. . . . Play over before nine."[49]

Those who noticed the similarities between *Palmira* and *Axur* did not object. In 1804 *Palmira* was performed in Warsaw, where *Axur* was well known. A critic pointed out the relationship between the operas, but singled out for praise a piece in *Palmira* quite different from anything in the earlier opera, the a-cappella quartet "Silenzio facciasi": "it did not go unnoticed by connoisseurs that its resemblance to *Axur* is that of a good, free copy. The scene with the quartet without instruments was always especially excellent."[50]

The popularity of *Palmira* is reflected in the large number of manuscript copies and printed vocal scores in which the opera—individual numbers as well as the complete work—circulated. A printed arrangement of the opera for string quartet and many manuscripts of arrangements for wind ensemble are further evidence of its appeal. These include several arrangements for three basset horns by Anton Stadler which until recently were assumed to have been Stadler's own compositions.[51] Paul Wranitzky, concertmaster in the Burgtheater and a prolific composer, included a transcription of "Silenzio facciasi" in an elaborate "Quodlibet Symphony" that assembles arrangements of favorite operatic numbers by Weigl, Paisiello, and Mayr.[52] Salieri himself took advantage of the popularity of the a-cappella quartet by reusing it in a context in which its references to silence and sleep made good sense. When Baron Braun built a "Temple of the Night" in the park of his country house near Vienna he commissioned Salieri to write wind music to be played in it.[53] The resulting "Armonia per un tempio della notte," a pleasing Andante un poco sostenuto in E♭ for pairs of oboes, clarinets, bassoons, and horns, quotes "Silenzio facciasi" in its entirety.

48. *Der Briefwechsel zwischen Schiller und Goethe,* ed. Siegfried Seidel, 3 vols. (Munich, 1984), 1:381–83.

49. *Memoirs of John Quincy Adams comprising portions of his diary from 1795 to 1848,* ed. Charles Francis Adams, 12 vols. (Philadelphia, 1874), 1:216; quoted in Thomas Bauman, *North German Opera in the Age of Goethe* (Cambridge, 1985), 266.

50. "Die Oper der Polen," *AmZ* 14 (1812): cols. 323–31; quoted in Swenson, 238–39.

51. Pamela Weston, "Stadler, Anton (Paul)," in *NG,* makes no mention of Salieri's opera in referring to Stadler's basset horn trios.

52. Jan LaRue, "A 'Hail and Farewell' Quodlibet Symphony," *ML* 37 (1956): 250–59.

53. Della Croce/Blanchetti, 555–56.

17

SALIERI'S LAST OPERAS AND THE END OF VIENNESE ITALIAN OPERA

From the middle of the seventeenth century until the beginning of the nineteenth, librettists and composers resident in Vienna wrote operas in Italian for Viennese rulers and their subjects. They contributed to a tradition of innovation and excellence that made Vienna a leading center of Italian opera. That tradition, maintained during the 1790s largely by Salieri and his former student Weigl and brought to a final brief flowering by Paer at the turn of the century, died out shortly thereafter. Its end coincided with that of Salieri's career as composer of operas.

Viennese Italian opera faced competition on several fronts. A growing sense of national and cultural identity led Viennese audiences increasingly to favor opera in German and to expect composers resident in Vienna to write operas in German. A German opera troupe returned to the court theaters in 1795. As during the days of Joseph's Singspiel company, German opera of the 1790s and early nineteenth century was often Italian or French opera in translation. Audiences enjoyed performances in German not only of authentic Singspiele but also of Mozart's opere buffe and the latest opéras-comiques from Paris. Viennese music lovers did not tire of Italian opera; but instead of a constant supply presented by a competent but hardly stellar resident company, they came to prefer isolated seasons that featured the most popular Italian composers and the most expensive and brilliant singers.

German Opera in the Court Theaters and the Revival of Mozart's Opere Buffe in German Translation

The court theaters presented no operas in German, as far as we know, during the early 1790s. But they came under increasing pressure to do so. *Die Zauberflöte,* which continued to draw crowds to Schikaneder's Theater auf der Wieden throughout the decade, enhanced the popularity and prestige of German opera. Nationalistic and patriotic feelings aroused by war with France also favored opera in German and fed an anti-Italian current in Viennese popular opinion. Writing of Viennese opera in a Berlin journal in 1793, an advocate of German opera put the debate in nationalistic terms by accusing Prince Rosenberg, director of the court theaters, of being a "sworn enemy of the Germans" who "cannot bear to hear anything that is not Italian." [1]

Braun, in one of his first acts as impresario, brought German opera back into the court theaters. Out of the existing troupe, which already included several singers who could perform in German, he made two overlapping companies by adding several more German singers, some of whom could also sing in Italian. The result was a troupe that could present operas in both Italian and German. He appointed Franz Xaver Süssmayr, former student of Mozart and—more recently—of Salieri, music director of the German opera, which made its debut on 11 May 1795 with a performance of Wranitzky's *Die gute Mutter.* Its early repertory included Umlauf's old *Die pücefarbnen Schuhe* and Dittersdorf's *Der Apotheker und der Doktor.* But probably the most popular opera of the period was Johann Schenk's *Der Dorfbarbier,* a Singspiel of which the Viennese could not tire. It was performed 169 times between 1795 and 1809.[2]

Der Dorfbarbier probably owed its success more to the fine comic actors who performed it night after night than to its music.[3] Together with Karl Friedrich Weinmüller, who sang the title role, the comedian-singer Friedrich Baumann (as Adam) delighted Viennese audiences with comic acting that, to judge from Castelli's memoirs, represented a revival of the Hanswurst tradition of improvised comedy that Maria Theresa had temporarily stifled:

> I am unable to describe the pleasure that this *Dorfbarbier,* and Baumann in it, afforded. It was no longer a performance: it was rough comic nature itself. A prompter was completely unnecessary, for the two principal characters, the village barber and Adam, hardly spoke a word that was written beforehand, but extemporized the whole play. It was a competition between two comedians, a private game that they played together, in which however the audience

1. Fürst *Rosenberg,* . . . der ein abgesagter Feind der Deutschen ist und durchaus nichts hören kann, was nicht italienisch ist (*BmZ,* 1793, p. 141 [article dated 12 October]).

2. Hadamowsky, *Hoftheater,* vol. 1.

3. *Der Dorfbarbier,* ed. Robert Haas, vol. 66 of *DTÖ.* The opera is briefly discussed in Winton Dean, "German Opera," in *NOHM,* 8:456.

played the liveliest role. Crudities of all kinds were not lacking, but the audience did not mind, wanting for once to laugh until it could laugh no more.[4]

Der Dorfbarbier is a one-act opera consisting (in addition to the spoken dialogue) of fifteen numbers: ensembles (the first of which Schenk labeled "Introduzzione"), arias, and Lieder, which differ from the arias in their folklike melodies and simple, usually strophic form. The frequent use of 6/8 meter in moderate and fast tempos (beginning with the overture) reminds one of Martín y Soler. The folksy charm of Schenk's Lieder is easy to perceive in Adam's "Der Teufel hol' die Schererei," in which a comically repetitive alternation of G and A is enlivened by a crescendo in the orchestra. Folk music of a more exotic kind is evoked in Suschen's "Mädchen kann man leicht betören," labeled by the composer Allegretto alla Polacca. This, one of the first vocal polonaises, vigorously exploits rhythms that long echoed in Europe's ballrooms, opera houses, and salons (ex. 17.1).

After an absence of several years from the repertory of the court theaters, Mozart's operas returned at the end of the 1790s. The opere buffe had been performed in German translation, and usually in bowdlerized versions, in the Theater auf der Wieden

EXAMPLE 17.1 Schenk, *Der Dorfbarbier,* "Mädchen kann man leicht betören," mm. 11–18 (*DTÖ,* vol. 66)

(*Continued on next page*)

4. Castelli, *Memoiren,* 1:223–24.

EXAMPLE 17.1 (*continued*)

One can easily delude girls by praising them to their face. If men swear fidelity to you, do not believe the dissemblers.

and elsewhere in Germany during the 1790s; Braun's German troupe brought these versions inside the walls of Vienna. *Figaro* returned first, in July 1798.[5] *Don Giovanni* was revived in December 1798. The German singers presented *Così fan tutte,* as *Mädchentreue,* in 1804. These were joined by Mozart's German operas. *Die Zauberflöte* was performed at the Kärntnertor for the first time in 1801. Although audiences preferred the production that they had grown used to in Schikaneder's theater, that did not keep Braun from staging *Die Entführung* later the same year. Mozart's operas henceforth represented an important part of the German troupe's repertory, helping to raise its musical standards above those of the Italian troupe.

The beauty and dramatic power of Mozart's Italian operas were apparent to Viennese audiences despite the clumsy arrangements in which some of them were performed. Had they been revived in Italian, they might have served as a potent symbol of what Viennese composers could achieve in Italian opera and thereby encouraged Salieri and Weigl to continue (and younger composers such as Beethoven to begin) to write Italian opera; but because Mozart's operas were now performed in German, they hurt rather than helped the cause of Viennese Italian opera. Viennese composers, if they were to follow in Mozart's operatic footsteps, would henceforth be expected to write operas in German.

Mozart's operas may have dampened the enthusiasm with which Salieri's new operas were received. A performance of *Figaro* on 2 January 1799 surely affected the way listeners heard Salieri's *Falstaff,* performed for the first time the following evening. The *Allgemeine musikalische Zeitung* reviewed excerpts of *Falstaff* as published in vocal score. Finding "nothing great" but "pleasing, fluent melodies and light harmony throughout" and dismissing several numbers as "fairly inconsequential" or "only for the theater," the review seems to judge Salieri's music by Mozartean standards.[6]

5. This and the following dates are from Hadamowsky, *Hoftheater,* vol. 1.

6. *AmZ* 2 (1799–1800): col. 93.

French Opera in Vienna

Having reminded the Viennese of the greatness of Mozart's comic operas and strengthened Mozart's reputation as a composer of German rather than Italian opera, the German troupe revealed to them for the first time French opera of the 1790s, with its exciting and heroic rescues, its disguises and comic subplots, and its many novel musical effects.

The return of French opera to Vienna coincided with an important political event. During the 1790s Viennese theaters reflected the state of war between Austria and France by consistently avoiding French opera, even in German translation. The Treaty of Lunéville, signed on 9 February 1801, led to a period of peace between France and Austria. During this interlude French opera invaded and quickly conquered Vienna.

Cherubini's *Médée* and *Les Deux Journées* brought into the court theaters during the first decade of the nineteenth century the brilliance and pathos that the Revolution had encouraged in opéra-comique. The extraordinary popularity of Cherubini's opéras-comiques in Germany at the beginning of the nineteenth century is reflected in the almost idolatrous praise that appeared in the *Musikalisches Taschenbuch auf das Jahr 1803,* published in Penig (near Chemnitz), which goes so far as to call Cherubini *heilig,* holy:

> No words can express Cherubini's universality and originality, his individuality and holiness. Just as his *Medea* is the highest expression of the tragic, so his *Lodoiska* is the highest representation of the heroic, his *Elisa* of the romantic, his newest comic opera of the comic, his *Wasserträger* [*Les Deux Journées*] of one and all. Every one of his works is a new wreath that glorifies him and documents irrefutably his versatility and universality. Every detail of his works demonstrates his originality: every measure and every phrase. Every tone in its place is evidence of his elevated artistic sensitivity. And in the inexhaustibleness of his melodic and harmonic invention and in the unity of the whole and the variety of detail he is unique; in his wonderful representation of the sublime, the heavenly, and the godly, he is holy.[7]

Above all Cherubini's other operas the Viennese adored *Les Deux Journées,* on a libretto by Jean-Nicolas Bouilly. First performed in Paris in 1800, it arrived in Vienna in

7. Keine Worte sind im Stande, Cherubini's Universalität und Originalität, seine Einzigkeit und Heiligkeit auszusprechen. Wie seine Medea der höchste Ausdruck des Tragischen, so ist seine Lodoiska die höchste Darstellung des Heroischen, seine Elisa des Romantischen, seine neueste, komische Operette des Komischen, sein Wasserträger des Einen und Allen. Jedes seiner Werke ist ein neuer Kranz zu seiner Verherrlichung und documentirt unwiderlegbar seine Vielseitigkeit und Universalität. Von seiner Originalität zeugt jede Einzelnheit seiner Producte, jeder Tact und jede Periode. Jeder Ton an seiner Stelle ist ein Beweis seines höchsten Kunstgefühls, und in der Unerschöpflichkeit an neuen Melodieen und Harmonieen, in der Einheit im Ganzen und Mannichfaltigkeit im Einzelnen ist er einzig; durch seine wunderbare Darstellung des Hohen, Himmlischen, Göttlichen heilig (*Musikalisches Taschenbuch auf das Jahr 1803,* ed. Julius and Adolph Werden [Penig, [1803]], 122–23).

1802, receiving an unprecedented double premiere in two different translations. *Graf Armand, oder Die zwey unvergeßlichen Tage* reached the stage of the Theater an der Wien on 13 August; the following night *Die Tage der Gefahr* was performed at the Kärntnertor. By the end of the decade the court theaters had given their version 140 times. Beethoven, who considered Cherubini the greatest living composer, called Bouilly's libretto one of the best that he knew.[8]

Many elements of *Die Tage der Gefahr* contributed to its popularity. Its glorification of friendship, patriotism, and married love appealed to the same sensibility that found Bouilly's *Léonore* and its Italian and German versions (as set by Paer and Beethoven) so moving. Its mixture of comedy and pathos, typical of post-Revolutionary opéra-comique, found ready acceptance among audiences who knew *Axur* and *Die Zauberflöte.* Bold modulations, offbeat accents, and rich orchestration (which, however, idiosyncratically avoids trumpets) offered Viennese audiences attractive novelty. Act 2 begins with a coloristic effect of great originality. An orchestral unison (including the piccolos that Salieri hated), fortissimo, is followed by a diminuendo that involves a gradual silencing of the instruments until only the double basses are heard. In the mysterious pause that follows, a distant bell tolls. The effect must have stirred Romantic sensibilities; Weber echoed it in the Wolf's Glen scene in *Der Freischütz.* Occasional chromaticism, although some of it may have been inspired by Mozart, sounded new and fresh in Cherubini's hands. One chromatic passage, at the very beginning of the overture (ex. 17.2), gives the violas a more important harmonic role than they were used to. Mendelssohn claimed in 1834 that the first three measures of Cherubini's overture were worth more than Berlin's entire operatic repertory.[9] The water carrier Mikéli represented for early-nineteenth-century audiences a new kind of hero: an ordinary working man, a father, poor yet dignified, risking imprisonment and death to save his fellow man. In Mikéli's great aria "Guide mes pas, ô providence," the secondary dominant harmony in measure 5 helps to transform a seemingly ordinary melody into a memorable expression of heroism and idealism (fig. 17.1).

The success of opéra-comique in German translation threatened even the inroads made by authentically German opera, in the form of the spectacular magic operas put on by Schikaneder in the newly opened Theater an der Wien. When *Das Labyrinth* (a sequel to *Die Zauberflöte*) was performed in 1803, Richter commented ironically in his *Eipeldauer Briefe:* "in the midst of many wonderful decorations the elegant audience forgot that our own dear Schikaneder was the opera's daddy, and clapped and applauded as much as if the opera had been imported from Paris."[10] The success of a Ger-

8. Alexander Wheelock Thayer, *Life of Beethoven,* ed. Elliot Forbes (Princeton, N.J., 1967), 346, 683.

9. Mendelssohn to Eduard Devrient, 5 February 1834, in *Meine Erinnerungen an Felix Mendelssohn-Bartholdy und seine Briefe an mich,* by Eduard Devrient (Leipzig, 1869), 168–69.

10. Quoted in Kurt Honolka, *Papageno: Emanuel Schikaneder, Man of the Theater in Mozart's Time* (Portland, Oreg., 1990), 194.

EXAMPLE 17.2 Cherubini, *Les Deux Journées,* overture, mm. 1–3 (engraved full score, Paris, *ca.* 1800)

man version of *Palmira* in the same theater caused Richter again to think of French opera and to refer to Salieri jokingly as "an old master": "As often as they give the opera, the theater is full of people; and it is no French music, but Italian; but I think an old master wrote it, and so it must please."[11]

Paer in Vienna

One of the most skillful Italian composers to rise to prominence in the 1790s, Ferdinando Paer composed several operas for the Viennese court theaters between 1799 and 1801. He conducted performances of these operas and others that he had written for Italian theaters; but the accuracy of the often-repeated statement that he held the position of music director in the Kärntnertortheater from 1797 is suspect for several reasons. That such a position existed at all is unlikely because until 1810 the court theaters shared the same repertory. Paer's operas were performed in the Burgtheater as well as the Kärntnertortheater. His association with the court theaters probably began not in 1797, when he was still busy writing operas in Italy, but after Lent 1798. His wife, the soprano Francesca Riccardi, made her Viennese debut on 26 April 1798 in Paer's *Gl'intrighi amorosi.* Joseph Carl Rosenbaum, a Viennese music lover who later married Therese Gassmann, mentioned Riccardi's debut in his diary without saying whether Paer conducted the performance; but he probably did.[12]

11. Quoted in Swenson, 211.

12. Rosenbaum, "Diaries," 41. In a letter of 19 December 1798 Paul Wranitzky wrote a description of the Viennese musical scene for the music publisher André of Offenbach (quoted in its entirety, in English translation, in Landon, *Haydn,* 4:332). He included Paer among many "composers in Vienna," but mentioned no position; Weigl, on the other hand, he described as "Kapellmeister at the Italian opera."

FIGURE 17.1 Cherubini's *Les Deux Journées,* beginning of Mikéli's aria "Guide mes pas, ô providence" in an early full score (Paris, ca. 1800).

Paer seems to have served the impresario Braun as a kind of composer in residence: the last in a long line of Italian musicians who lived in Vienna and wrote Italian operas for its court theaters. At the same time, the brevity of his residence in the Habsburg capital looks to the future: to the short visits of great nineteenth-century Italian composers such as Rossini and Donizetti. Only twenty-seven years old when he arrived in Vienna, Paer eagerly sought to integrate into the Italian operatic language of the 1790s some of the most characteristic features of Mozart's operas and of post-Revolutionary opéra-comique.

Elements of French rescue opera are obvious in *Camilla, ossia Il sotterraneo* (Vienna, 1799), to a libretto by Giuseppe Carpani inspired by Marsollier des Vivetière's *Camille, ou Le Souterrain* (set to music by Dalayrac in 1791).[13] Paer skillfully expressed the pathos of a wife imprisoned by a husband who believes her to be unfaithful, the heroism of her rescuer, and the comedy of his servant with musical styles ranging from the tender supplication of Camilla's prayer "Clemente ciel, che ai misteri" to finales and other ensembles that derive their musical dramaturgy largely from opera buffa. The trio "Una campana antica" would not sound out of place in a comic opera by Cimarosa. Another trio, the beautiful canon "Sento che quelli sguardi," may have served as a model for Beethoven's canon in *Fidelio;* but it also depends on the Viennese tradition of opera buffa canons to which Salieri had contributed fine examples (ex. 17.3).

Paer's grand, somber *Achille* (Vienna, 1801) features striking combinations of instrumental and vocal music. The overture, which begins with a very long slow introduction,

EXAMPLE 17.3 Paer, *Camilla,* act 1, "Sento che quelli sguardi" (canon), mm. 1–17 (piano-vocal score, Hamburg, n.d.)

(*Continued on next page*)

13. The following remarks are based on a vocal score (Hamburg, n.d.) and on Gian Paolo Minardi, "Paër semiserio," in Muraro, *Mozart,* 1:349–52.

EXAMPLE 17.3 (*continued*)

ADOLFO: I feel that those looks speak to my heart but I cannot interpret such sweet speech. CAMILLA: After so many years I see you again, my son, but I cannot speak your name. DUKE: Crowds of sweet emotions

leads directly to a male chorus, which in turn flows into the opera's first solo, Achilles' "Speme, fermezza e gloria." Act 1 includes a ninety-five-measure instrumental "battaglia" that may well have accompanied pantomime. Beethoven greatly admired the funeral march in C minor in the finale of act 2, music remarkable for, among other things, its use of woodwind mutes: both oboes and clarinets play the march con sordini. The opera ends with the orchestra alone playing an Allegro maestoso of eighty-four measures.[14]

Living in Vienna at precisely the time when Mozart's Italian operas returned to the stage in German translation, Paer could hardly have ignored them; and one hears their influence strongly in *Achille.*[15] Briseide's "No, che viver non poss'io," a big two-tempo aria in F major, recalls "Non più di fiori" (Vitellia's rondò in *La clemenza di Tito*) in its combination of key, tempo, meter, and melodic style.[16] In keeping with the latest Ital-

14. The opera can be studied in a vocal score (Hamburg, n.d.). Part of the funeral march is quoted in Dean, "Italian Opera," 388.

15. Mozartean aspects of *Achille* have been pointed out in Daniel Heartz, "Mozarts 'Titus' und die italienische Oper um 1800," *Hamburger Jahrbuch für Musikwissenschaft* 5 (1981): 255–66; and Dean, "Italian Opera," 387–401.

16. "No, che viver non poss'io" is discussed and parallels between it and "Non più di fiori" pointed out in Heartz, "Mozarts 'Titus' und die italienische Oper um 1800."

EXAMPLE 17.4 Paer, *Camilla,* act 2, "Oh! momento fortunato!" mm. 1–4

⁓Oh happy moment! Finally I will see my joy!

ian fashion, Paer introduced a chorus into the aria, which, like many heroic arias of the 1790s (including "Non più di fiori" and several by Salieri) modulates suddenly to a key related by a third, in this case D♭ major, in the fast section, as Briseide expresses anguish in exclamations that echo Vitellia's "Infelice! qual orrore!"

Achille, which has no male soprano role, helped usher in the age in which the heroic tenor replaced the musico in Italian serious opera. The Viennese, although they flocked to hear the musici Marchesi and Girolamo Crescentini during their several guest appearances in Vienna between 1797 and 1806, found pleasure in opera seria even without male sopranos. *Achille* was performed fifty-nine times in Vienna between 1801 and 1804.

Paer had a talent for delightful melody, often decorated with strings of dotted notes or triplets. He shared with several composers active at the turn of the century a tendency to emphasize a melody's high point with a single syncopated half note. Camilla's exultant "Oh! momento fortunato!" is typical of Paer's melodic style (ex. 17.4). In *Sargino* (Dresden, 1803; first Viennese performance in 1807) Pietro sings a comic tune with some of the same features (ex. 17.5). It may have impressed Weber, who conducted *Sargino* in Prague in 1814. In *Der Freischütz* Max sings the words "Durch die Wälder, durch die Auen" to a melody very similar to Pietro's.[17] *Leonora* (Dresden, 1804; first Viennese performance in 1809), makes effective use of musical reminiscence (a precursor of Berlioz's *idée fixe* that Paer probably learned from Cherubini, Dalayrac, and other composers of opéra-comique). An attractive melody in the overture's slow introduction comes fully to life only when reharmonized over a resounding pedal point (ex. 17.6). This tune later becomes identified with Leonora herself; it reappears in her scena "Esecrabil Pizzarro," as she thinks of her beloved Florestano, and again in the dungeon scene, as she gives him bread.

17. The parallel is drawn in Martin Ruhnke, "Opera semiseria und Dramma eroicomico," *Am* 21 (1982): 268.

EXAMPLE 17.5 Paer, *Sargino,* act 1, "Ma venite," mm. 21–28 (piano-vocal score, Leipzig, n.d.)

~Observe the doctor, who will cure you completely.

EXAMPLE 17.6 Paer, *Leonora,* overture, mm. 17–22 (piano-vocal score, Leipzig, n.d.)

Salieri's Last Italian Opera Company

Confronted with artistic challenges from many directions, Salieri stood resolutely by comic and heroicomic Italian opera and by the musical and dramatic techniques that had served him well for thirty years. He did so in collaboration with many of the singers for whom he had composed since the mid-1790s. Angrisani continued to serve as his principal buffo caricato. Tomeoni, with whom Salieri had worked only sporadically in the past, became his prima donna, and Giuseppe Simoni, a former singer of opera seria recently arrived in Vienna, became his primo mezzo carattere. After working closely with De Gamerra during the mid-1790s Salieri turned to a new librettist, Carlo Prospero Defranceschi, who was to be his last collaborator in the production of Italian opera.

Paer's arrival in Vienna led to an important change in the Italian troupe. By writing most of his prima-donna roles for his wife, Francesca Riccardi, Paer made her the troupe's leading female singer. Tomeoni continued to sing the Neapolitan operas in which she had earned her reputation, relying for new roles mostly on Salieri and Weigl. The years of Paer's residence in Vienna were also those in which Tomeoni worked most closely with Salieri. His last three Italian operas to reach performance in Vienna—*Falstaff, Cesare in Farmacusa,* and *Angiolina*—all have major roles for Tomeoni, who also took over roles written for other sopranos. When *Palmira* was revived in 1798, she sang the title role, created three years earlier by Sessi.[18] Although Tomeoni, on her arrival in Vienna in 1791, had represented an alternative to the kind of opera in which Salieri excelled, by the end of the 1790s she had become one of his closest allies.

Simoni (fig. 17.2), of Bohemian birth (his name may originally have been Joseph Simon), had sung in Italy since the early 1780s.[19] He never reached the top rank of opera seria tenors. Benedetto Frizzi wrote: "The tenor Simoni, whom I heard in Trieste, did not have a bad voice; but his manners and his singing seemed to me suited more for the choir loft than for the theater [più da Coro che da Teatro]."[20] Frizzi was perhaps referring to Simoni's less-than-vivid acting, which Arndt witnessed shortly after the singer's arrival in Vienna: "Among the Germans Herr Simoni is also a good singer; but one must listen only; for acting that is clumsier and more stilted than his cannot be imagined."[21] One of Simoni's first Viennese roles was Alcidoro opposite Tomeoni's Palmira; he went on to create roles in Salieri's *Falstaff* and *Cesare in Farmacusa.*

Salieri's *Il moro,* an opera buffa first performed in 1797, was the last product of his collaboration with De Gamerra, who remained at his post of theater poet for several

18. Rosenbaum, "Diaries," 31 (entry for 1 January 1798).

19. In the libretto recording one of Simoni's earliest appearances in Italy (Turin, 1783) he is referred to "Giuseppe Simon boemo" (Sartori no. 16585).

20. Frizzi, *Dissertazione,* 85; Frizzi, "Singers," 381.

21. Unter den Teutschen ist noch Herr Simoni ein guter Sänger; aber man muß ihn bloß hören; denn stolpernder und stelzenfüßiger, als seine Aktion, läßt sich kaum etwas denken (Arndt, *Reisen,* 249).

FIGURE 17.2 Giuseppe Simoni as Floreschi in Mayr's *Lodoiska.* Simoni went on to create the role of Ford in *Falstaff* and the title role in *Cesare in Farmacusa.* Engraving by Johann Niedl after a painting by Johann Ziterer. (Courtesy of Civica Raccolta Stampe "A. Bertarelli," Castello Sforzesco, Milan.)

years thereafter but wrote few librettos.[22] He seems to have saved his energy for the genre in which throughout his career he had found most success, collaborating with Paer on *Achille* and, two years later, with Johann Simon Mayr on *Ercole in Lidia.* Salieri, meanwhile, found another poet.

Like so many of his previous literary collaborators, Defranceschi had little experience as a librettist, and especially little as a librettist of comic opera, when he began to work with Salieri. A lawyer by training (like Goldoni), he came to Vienna from Prague, where he had worked with the impresario Guardasoni in bringing several German operas—heroicomic spectacles in the tradition of *Die Zauberflöte*—to the stage in Italian translation.[23] These included Franz Anton Hoffmeister's setting of Schikaneder's *Der Königssohn aus Ithaca* (a "große heroisch-komische Oper" first performed in Vienna in 1795), which Defranceschi turned into *Il principe d'Itaca,* a dramma eroicomico per musica.[24] On the title page he described himself as "graduate of law, and translator of

22. On *Il moro* see Della Croce/Blanchetti, 288–89 and 504–5.
23. Thomas Bauman, "Defranceschi, Prospero," in *NGDO.*
24. Sartori no. 19102.

Il sacrificio interrotto and *L'Amore e Psiche.*" His transformation of Winter's *Der unterbrochene Opferfest* into a dramma eroicomico was performed in Dresden in 1798[25] and probably earlier in Prague.

From Elizabethan Comedy to Goldonian Opera Buffa: *Falstaff*

Salieri and Defranceschi presented their first work, *Falstaff, ossia Le tre burle,* in the Kärntnertortheater on 3 January 1799. One of the first operas to derive its plot from *The Merry Wives of Windsor, Falstaff* was not, however, the first Viennese opera buffa based on Shakespeare. Da Ponte had found the story of *Gli equivoci* (performed in 1786 with music by Stephen Storace) in *A Comedy of Errors.* Less than two years after the successful premiere of *Falstaff,* Salieri and Defranceschi turned again to Elizabethan comedy. *Angiolina, ossia Il matrimonio per sussurro,* first performed at the Kärntnertor on 22 October 1800, is loosely based on Ben Jonson's *Epicoene, or The Silent Woman.*[26] With the exception of some elements of plot, however, *Falstaff* and *Angiolina* have more to do with Goldoni than with Shakespeare or Jonson.

Falstaff departs from Shakespeare's play most noticeably in his omission of the young lovers Ann and Fenton. This allowed Defranceschi and Salieri to focus their attention on five characters: Master Ford (tenor, the role created by Simoni) and Mistress Ford (soprano, Tomeoni); Master Slender (baritone, Ignaz Saal) and Mistress Slender (mezzo-soprano, Luigia Miloc), based on Shakespeare's Master and Mistress Page; and Falstaff himself (bass, Angrisani). The cast is completed by Falstaff's servant Bardolf (baritone, Gaetano Lotti) and Mistress Ford's maid Betty (soprano, Maria Anna Gassmann).

The opera begins with a ballroom scene of the kind that Goldoni and his followers delighted in. Almost thirty years after staging *La fiera di Venezia,* with its complex dance-finale, Salieri returned to the carnivalesque pleasures of the ball. The minuet that accompanies the dancing of Falstaff and Mistress Ford (ex. 17.7) shows that Salieri's ability to write memorable minuet tunes, already apparent in *Don Chisciotte alle nozze di Gamace* (1771), had not deserted him. His favorite trumpets in B♭ add to the festive sound of the orchestra here and in several other numbers. His fondness for chorus is apparent in the important role for chorus in the ball and elsewhere in *Falstaff.* The key of B♭ and the trumpets return at the end of the finale of act 1, helping the audience notice the similarity between melodies in the finale (at the words "Così va: chi a' sogni crede") and in the introduzione (at the words "No, non v'ha piacer maggiore"). Salieri had used the recurrence of a similar combination of musical elements to frame act 1 of his first comic opera, *Le donne letterate.*

25. Sartori no. 20397.

26. On *Angiolina* see Della Croce/Blanchetti, 299–300 and 506–10.

EXAMPLE 17.7 Salieri, *Falstaff*, act 1, introduzione, mm. 152–59 (A-Wn. Mus. Hs. 16191)

Salieri and his librettist carefully differentiated Mistress Slender and Mistress Ford. The former, on reading Falstaff's amorous letter, is outraged; she can think of nothing but revenge and expresses her anger in the quasi-serious "Vendetta, sì, vendetta!" Mistress Ford, on the other hand, reacts to her letter, and to the news that Mistress Slender received an identical one, with laughter.

Mistress Ford's cheerfulness (so much in keeping with the singer who created the role) wins Mistress Slender over. The two women express their surprise in the lighthearted canonic duet "La stessa, la stessissima," accompanied by a single oboe and strings. Salieri wrote of this piece: "It makes an effect that some will perhaps not see in the score, but that all will feel in the theater." Especially pleasing is the sudden acceleration of text declamation at the words "Malgrado la mia collera" (ex. 17.8). The canon in the vocal parts underlines the meaning of the text: the music that the women sing, like the letters they received from Falstaff, is indeed *la stessa, la stessissima.*

Salieri's charming duet caught the attention of some of Vienna's leading pianists. Just two months after the premiere of *Falstaff* Artaria announced the publication of Beethoven's variations on "La stessa, la stessissima."[27] Beethoven used only the accompaniment, not the canonic vocal parts, as his theme, which he seems to have taken directly from the piano-vocal score published shortly after the premiere.[28] On 25 March 1799, about three weeks after Artaria advertized Beethoven's variations, Josepha Auernhammer played her own variations on "La stessa, la stessissima" as part of her annual Burgtheater concert.[29]

27. *WZ*, 2 March 1799.
28. *RISM* S 503 and S 513; see ex. 17.8.
29. Morrow, *Concert Life*, 301.

EXAMPLE 17.8 *Falstaff*, act 1, "La stessa, la stessissima," mm. 9–21 (piano-vocal score, Vienna, 1799)

The same, the very same to the comma; only the names are different. Despite my anger, I can hardly keep from laughing; this is indeed bizarre.

The women's decision to punish Falstaff leads to an important scene that has no parallel in Shakespeare—and one that must have delighted Viennese audiences—in which Mistress Ford comes to Falstaff disguised as a German girl who speaks a comic mixture of German and Italian. Falstaff, of course, finds this unknown *Mädchen* attractive, and tries to communicate with his own linguistic mixture:

FALSTAFF: Mein Jungfer
Ich sag in confidenz:
Von deutsch nit haben viel intelligenz:
Vor das ich dir preghieren,
Nostra lingua du will mit mich parlieren.
MISTRESS FORD: Mein Herr! io poco posso
Vostra lingua parlar.
FALSTAFF: Du nur probieren.
Ich bissel deutsch, tu bissel nostra lingua,
A bissel pantomime,
A bissel discretion . . . assicurieren,
So tres bien mitanander explichieren.

Mistress Ford responds to Falstaff's advances in her pretty bilingual aria "O! die Männer kenn' ich schon," whose sweet, childlike melody, gavotte rhythms, limited range (an octave and a fourth), and jolly triplets in the accompaniment are all characteristic of arias that Guglielmi and Cimarosa had written for Tomeoni (ex. 17.9).

EXAMPLE 17.9 *Falstaff*, act 1, "O! die Männer kenn' ich schon," mm. 9–24 (A-Wn, Mus. Hs. 16191)

Oh, I already know men! As soon as they see a girl: "You are charming, you are lovely, you are pure and without blemish, oh, you are such an angel!"

FIGURE 17.3 The "scena tedesca" in *Falstaff* depicted on the title page of a piano-vocal score of excerpts from the opera (Vienna, 1799).

The "scena tedesca," depicted on the title page of the Viennese piano-vocal score (fig. 17.3), partakes of a tradition of multilingualism and comic attempts to speak in foreign languages that goes back to Goldoni. Angrisani's linguistic potpourri may well have reminded older Viennese of Carattoli's portrayal of Tagliaferro in *La buona figliuola,* just as Tomeoni's aria may have reminded them of the bilingual trio in *La fiera di Venezia,* "So wie bei den deutschen Tänzen." Having translated at least three German librettos into Italian, Defranceschi certainly knew enough German to cobble together the "scena tedesca." Salieri, for his part, sprinkled his German conversation with Italian and French: he was used to communicating in the manner proposed by Falstaff to Mistress Ford.

As is so often the case with music written for Tomeoni, the "scena tedesca" has associations with the singer herself. Tomeoni's linguistic troubles as an Italian newly arrived in Vienna and her subsequent progress in learning German had been followed by the Viennese in her musical performances. As Carolina in *Il matrimonio segreto* ("Perdonate, signor mio") she made a special point of her complete ignorance of German: "Non intendo una parola." By 1798 she had learned enough German to be able to make

EXAMPLE 17.10 *Falstaff,* act 1, "Nell'impero di Cupido," mm. 7–12

In Cupid's realm I am a Caesar, an Achilles

use of it in concert. A cantata that Weigl presented at his benefit concert on 30 March 1798, "Die Gefühle meines Herzens," was apparently bilingual. According to a playbill, "Mme. Tomeoni and Herr Angrisani will sing not only Italian but also German."[30] The spectacle of Italians singing in German in Weigl's cantata, nine months before the first performance of *Falstaff,* may have suggested to Salieri and Defranceschi the idea of these same singers, in the roles of Mistress Ford and Falstaff, amusing the Viennese with a "scena tedesca."[31]

By 1799 Angrisani had established himself firmly as Benucci's principal successor in buffo-caricato roles. Salieri, having written parts for Angrisani in *Palmira* and *Il moro,* had learned how to exploit his voice and acting. Much of Angrisani's music in *Falstaff* is in the traditional comic-bass key of D major, including "Nell'impero di Cupido." This brilliant aria begins with a melody that fits neatly into the same D-D octave that had framed buffo-caricato melodies since the 1760s, accenting the high D with the syncopated half note that graces many melodies of Paer and Weigl (ex. 17.10). Falstaff makes fun of the heroic a-b-b′ melodic structure, exactly like Baggeo in *Le donne letterate* (see ex. 4.11) and Lena in *Don Chisciotte* (see ex. 5.1). As he boasts that he is as much a hero as Achilles and Caesar, he comically contradicts what the audience knows and sees of him (and by naming these particular heroes Angrisani amusingly antici-

30. Morrow, *Concert Life,* 296.

31. Salieri wrote another German scene for Tomeoni later in *Falstaff.* It survives in an autograph fragment (A-Wn, Mus. Hs. 4489), where it is preceded by an explanation in Salieri's hand: "L'opera seguitava prima così, e si è abbreviata perche Madama Tomeoni non ha avuto coraggio d'imperar una seconda scena in lingua tedesca" [The opera originally continued as follows, but it was shortened because Madama Tomeoni did not have courage to learn a second scene in the German language]. See Richard Armbruster, "Zur Kölner Fassung von Salieris 'Falstaff oder Die drei Streiche,'" in *Antonio Salieri: Falstaff* (program book, Cologne, 1995).

This was not the last time that Tomeoni sang in German. On retirement in 1805 she bid farewell to her admirers in their own language, according to Joseph Richter, *Eipeldauer Briefe,* ed. Eugen von Paunel, 2 vols. (Munich, 1917–18), 2:199: "She wished thereby to show that she loves us Viennese, and that during the seventeen years in which she sang in our city, she also learned German, which seems to be a rare occurence."

pated two forthcoming operas: Salieri's *Cesare in Farmacusa* and Paer's *Achille*). Later in the aria Salieri gave Angrisani an opportunity to display his ability to sing patter and—still a favorite with the composer—falsetto. As Angrisani imitated Tomeoni singing her German aria, he reminded the audience that he too had sung in German at Weigl's benefit concert.

Salieri wrote the lyric-tenor role of Master Ford for Simoni, of whose background in opera seria he made good use in a passionate accompanied recitative ("Ah vile! Ah seduttore!") and in arias expressing rage, grief, and joy. In a reversal of the venerable opera buffa custom that delayed the entrance of an important female character until she appears alone to sing a cavatina, Ford does not appear until scene 4, when he sings the cavatina "Vicino a rivedere."

Simoni brought out Salieri's lifelong love of concertante winds. "Vicino a rivedere" is nicely orchestrated with solo flute and oboe, which Salieri had frequently assembled in virtuoso display during the 1770s. "Or degli affannosi palpiti," a two-tempo show-piece later in act 1, features one of the few extensive clarinet solos in Salieri's operatic oeuvre. Although he may have written it partly in answer to a big clarinet solo in Weigl's *L'amor marinaro* of 1797, the combination of clarinet solo, key of A major, and rondò-like structure brings to mind Mozart's portrayal of Sesto in *La clemenza di Tito* ("Parto, ma tu, ben mio" features a magnificent clarinet solo; "Deh per questo istante solo" is a rondò in A). The most dramatic moment in Ford's aria follows a cadence in the dominant, E. The whole orchestra, reinforced with trumpets (playing in the aria for the first time), enters in C (ex. 17.11). In several earlier operas Salieri had delayed the entrance of trumpets for dramatic effect (trumpets in keys other than the tonic make surprising entrances in Curiace's "Victime de l'amour" in *Les Horaces*[32] and in Alcidoro's "Luci amate in tal momento" in *Palmira*); he had often exploited sudden shifts of key up or down a third, including moves to C within arias in A. Here he effectively combined both of

EXAMPLE 17.11 *Falstaff*, act 1, "Or degli affannosi palpiti," mm. 48–58

(*Continued on next page*)

32. Rushton, "Salieri's *Les Horaces*," 275.

EXAMPLE 17.11 *(continued)*

. . . faithful passion. Ah! All at once my heart is rent by shame, anger, and love!

these devices. Sesto's A-major rondò likewise shifts suddenly to C, but it does not reinforce the tonal surprise with an instrumental one.[33]

Like most if not all of Salieri's operas composed after *Tarare, Falstaff* contains old music. Persuaded finally of his wife's fidelity, Ford expresses his joy in an aria, "Ah ch'a idea così gradita," whose melody, in the same key of B♭, Salieri had used twenty years earlier in Italy. Near the end of *La dama pastorella* (another opera set in Britain) Milord Fideling, having discovered that his beloved Eurilla is really the noble Olimpia, expresses happiness in the aria "Il mio duol più non rammento." The gavotte rhythms and coloratura of the tune in which the aria culminates (at the words "Cari amici non resisto") suit Ford as neatly as Fideling, and the melody fits well into the composer's late musical style. "Ah ch'a idea" continues with a modulatory passage (at "Puro in seno") that would not be out of place in an opera by Rossini, yet it follows naturally from the tune that Salieri wrote in 1779 (ex. 17.12).

Like many of Salieri's late operas, *Falstaff* demonstrates his familiarity with Mozart's music.[34] The plot has much in common with that of *Le nozze di Figaro.* Both operas revolve around a faithful wife and a jealous husband who thinks his wife is having an

33. Mozart saved his trumpets, silent since the beginning of act 2, for a later moment: the transition from Vitellia's rondò "Non più di fiori" to the chorus "Che del ciel, che degli dei" (see ex. 14.9).

34. This paragraph is based on Richard Armbruster, "Die Anspielungen auf Mozarts *Le nozze di Figaro* in Antonio Salieris *Falstaff* (1799)," *Studien zur Musikwissenschaft* 44 (1995): 209–88.

EXAMPLE 17.12 *Falstaff,* act 2, "Ah ch'a idea così gradita," mm. 1–18

Ah! I feel my heart rejoice at such a delightful idea, and I feel my soul exult with joy and happiness. First love, pure in one's heart

affair. Such parallels, and the fact that *Figaro* was being prepared for revival by the German troupe just as Salieri was working on *Falstaff,* may have encouraged the composer to incorporate elements of Mozart's handling of similar dramatic situations. The scene in act 2 in which Falstaff tries to avoid Ford's jealous anger by disguising himself as a woman is particularly reminiscent of *Figaro* in dramaturgy and music. A sequence of ensembles (the duet "Per carità, celatevi," the trio "Prima ancor che master venga," and the duet "Che vedo?") calls to mind the sequence of ensembles at the end of Mozart's act 2 (the trio "Susanna, or via sortite," the duettino "Aprite, presto aprite," and the finale, which begins with a duet for the count and countess). The sequences are similar in their tonal planning (Salieri: G-C-E♭; Mozart: C-G-E♭) and share some telling details of melody, harmony, and texture.

The overture to *Falstaff* is one of several by Salieri that anticipate the action and atmosphere of the opening scene. This "Allegro di contradanza" is a loosely constructed rondo in D major, 2/4 time. (In casting his overture in this form Salieri may well have imitated the overture to Weigl's *L'accademia di Maestro Cisolfaut* of 1798, a charming rondo.) Salieri explained in his autograph that in the opera's opening ballroom scene the words "si torni di nuovo a ballar" imply that the guests have already danced. This gave him the idea of writing "an overture somewhat in the form of a series of contredanses; and the audience heard the effect immediately and applauded it." Although this overture is completely different from the overture to *Armida* of 1771, its function—the musical depiction of action taking place just before the drama begins—is the same. Salieri was not the first Viennese composer to incorporate a *contredanse en rondeau* into the overture of an opera buffa. Gassmann had done so in his last opera, *La casa di campagna* (1773), which, like *Falstaff,* includes a ballroom scene. The third and final movement of the overture is a rondo in 2/4 meter labeled Tempo di contradanza.

Salieri's annotations allow us a glimpse at the composer at work on the opera during rehearsals, adding to an aria near the end of the opera a detail that contributed greatly to its success: "The aria 'Reca in amor la gelosia' is in a meter used little in music [i.e., novenari], nevertheless well set to music, it seems to me, and in an unusual manner. But it would have remained of little interest to the audience, I believe, without the idea of the echo: an idea that came to me after the first rehearsals, and became a natural way of representing the scenery of the forest and the nocturnal setting. The echo therefore caused the aria to be heard with the greatest attention and approval."

Echoes were of course nothing new on the operatic stage, but they are rare in Salieri's oeuvre. Having discovered how much his audience liked this effect, Salieri and Defranceschi made sure to use it in their next opera, *Cesare in Farmacusa.* Tullo and Gigi, looking for one another on a deserted stretch of coast, call out each other's names; but at first they hear only echoes of their own voices.

The first performance of *Falstaff* was a success, despite being scheduled a day after a performance of *Figaro* on the same stage. Joseph Carl Rosenbaum wrote in his diary:

"at about 5 o'clock to the Kärntnerthortheater, where Salieri's opera *Le tre burle* was given for the first time; it was received extraordinarily well. Many numbers were repeated, one duet three times over [probably 'La stessa, la stessissima']. After the opera Salieri had to appear twice before the public, and the whole cast was called out."[35] *Falstaff* continued to win applause, performed twenty-six times before being dropped from the repertory in 1802.

The reaction to *Falstaff* among audiences and critics increasingly familiar with and appreciative of Mozart's operas was mixed. Discussions of the opera in the *Allgemeine musikalische Zeitung,* while not making direct comparisons between Salieri and Mozart, found something lacking in Salieri's opera. When *Falstaff* was performed in Dresden less than a year after its Viennese premiere, a critic distinguished between "higher music" and music whose only function was to entertain. Salieri's opera belonged in the second category; Mozart's, presumably, in the first. The concept of opera as "art," not simply "entertainment" (which would lead eventually to the distinction between opera and operetta) was beginning to make itself felt in this review, but the critic was not fully convinced of the concept's validity: "In Dresden Salieri's opera *Falstaff* . . . was given several times, but generally not to the applause that this witty composition, full of levity and naturalness, deserves. Its many humorous moments . . . ensured applause from that part of the audience that is unfamiliar with higher music and wishes only to be cheerfully entertained."[36]

Cesare in Farmacusa

Between the productions of his two Elizabethan opere buffe, Salieri presented a dramma eroicomico: the last of several operas whose generic designations had advertised, since *La secchia rapita* of 1772, a mixing of comic and serious. *Cesare in Farmacusa,* first performed in the Kärntnertortheater on 2 June 1800, appealed to the same tastes as *Axur* and *Palmira;* it offered audiences an exotic setting, plenty of choruses, and the grandeur, pathos, and vocal virtuosity of serious opera enlivened with buffo antics.

Cesare was well received in Vienna. Zinzendorf attended the premiere and wrote in his diary: "The scenery beautiful, the music by Salieri beautiful and the story rather amusing and varied."[37] The *Allgemeine musikalische Zeitung* confirmed the opera's success: "Salieri's new, recently introduced opera, *Cesare,* increases in popularity every day. The first finale in particular is admired as a masterpiece."[38]

35. Rosenbaum, "Diaries," 57.

36. *AmZ* 2 (1799–1800): col. 174; quoted in Swenson, 185–86.

37. Le soir au Spectacle: *Cesare in Farmacusa* nouvel opera. Les decorations belles, la musique de Salieri belle et le sujet asses amusant et varié (Zinzendorf, 26 June 1800).

38. *AmZ* 2 (1799–1800): col. 783; quoted in Swenson, 201.

Impresarios in Germany quickly took up *Cesare.* In Dresden a critic noticed similarities between *Cesare* and the most famous of Salieri's earlier heroicomic operas but was not bothered by them: "If one is occasionally reminded too distinctly of *Axur,* that is too pleasant a reminder for us to wish to criticize the composer too harshly, especially since the opera also has masterly passages that belong to it alone."[39] A production in Berlin (in a German translation by the prolific Georg Friedrich Treitschke) won praise from the *Allgemeine musikalische Zeitung.* Salieri, whose *Falstaff* that journal had criticized for its lack of "higher music" and for its appeal to audiences interested only in "entertainment," could now read that *Cesare* pleased connoisseurs: "The plot is serious and heroic, with a variety of comic elements. Since the music, from the overture to the ending, is strong and original, it pleased knowledgeable listeners and will surely win the applause of the public (which up until now has been unenthusiastic), especially since theatrical spectacle of various kinds has been brought into the production."[40]

Defranceschi, perhaps inspired by Casti's *Catilina,* found his subject in the history of late republican Rome. The story of young Julius Caesar's capture by pirates is told by Plutarch, whose statements that Caesar laughed at the amount of ransom that the pirates demanded and that they treated his threats as jokes are probably what led Defrancheschi to think of this episode as material for a dramma eroicomico:

> on his voyage back [to Rome, in 75 B.C.] he was captured near the island of Pharmacusa[41] by some pirates. . . . First, when the pirates demanded a ransom of twenty talents, Caesar burst out laughing. They did not know, he said, who it was that they had captured, and he volunteered to pay fifty. Then, when he had sent his followers to the various cities in order to raise the money and was left with one friend and two servants among these Cilicians, about the most bloodthirsty people in the world, he treated them so highhandedly that, whenever he wanted to sleep, he would . . . tell them to stop talking. . . . However, the ransom arrived . . . and, as soon as he had paid it and been set free, he immediately manned some ships and set sail . . . against the pirates . . . and he captured nearly all of them. He took their property as spoils of war and put the men themselves into the prison at Pergamum. . . . [Later he] took the pirates out of prison and crucified the lot of them, just as he had often told them he would do when he was on the island and they imagined he was joking.[42]

Defranceschi rewrote the violent end. A Roman army arrives while Caesar is still on Pharmacusa; in the finale of act 2 Caesar joins in the battle against the pirates and, having defeated them, destroys their fortress with a spectacular fire.

39. *AmZ* 4 (1801–2): col. 368; quoted in Angermüller, *Leben,* 3:107, and Swenson, 210.

40. *AmZ* 7 (1804–5): col. 111; quoted in Swenson, 215.

41. Pharmacusa is a small island in the Aegean Sea, south of Miletus (Matthias Gelzer, *Caesar, Politician and Statesman* [Oxford, 1968], 23).

42. Plutarch, "Caesar," trans. Rex Warner, in *Fall of the Roman Republic* (Baltimore, 1972), 244–45.

Salieri made Caesar a tenor and assigned the role to the former opera seria singer Simoni. Despite the laughter mentioned by Plutarch, Caesar is mostly serious, with long and expressive accompanied recitatives and vocal writing that exploits Simoni's many years of experience in Italy. Salieri conveyed Caesar's nobility and bravery on his first appearance. As the opera begins, the pirate fleet has just safely reached shore after a storm. Salieri described the disembarkation in great detail in his autograph (the annotations in this score are, in length and scope, second only to those in the autograph of *Axur*):

> The pirates who are to sing the opening chorus are the first to disembark and arrange themselves in a line to the audience's left. After their appearance, the two leaders of the pirates, Nicanore and Megistone, appear; they sing the first four verses of the introduzione with the others: "Salvi siam," etc. Then they too come on shore, and following them, one or two at a time, the slaves recently captured by them.
>
> Most of these slaves are Caesar's followers, and all find themselves, once on shore, arranged on the right side of the stage, a moment before singing the verses "Qual colpa nostra o Numi," etc. Then, on the verse "Di noi che mai sarà," Caesar appears on board the ship, in the midst of pirates, and in this condition he sings his first solo.[43]

"Qual colpa nostra, o Numi" (within the ensemble "Giuro a Pluto") is a mournful chorus in D minor (ex. 17.13). Caesar, appearing suddenly on the ship (probably at the back of the stage), interrupts the chorus. He expresses his authority and heroism by confidently asserting a new key, B♭, and by replacing the two-measure phrases of the chorus with noble three-measure phrases. Instead of beginning the melody on the downbeat (coinciding with the B♭ in the bass), Salieri shifted the first note forward to the third beat of the previous measure, a kind of syncopation that Mozart had used effectively in writing for noble characters, especially in *Don Giovanni* (for example, Donna Anna's "Fuggi, crudele fuggi" in her duet with Don Ottavio; and Donna Elvira's "Non ti fidar" in the first-act quartet).[44]

Caesar's aria "Sovra l'alme più inique e più nere," later in the opera, confirms his heroic stature. The key of C and an orchestra that includes trumpets contribute to the

43. I Pirati destinati a cantar il primo Coro, discendono i primi dal Bastimento, e si mettono in fila dalla parte sinistra del pubblico. Dopo di essi, compariscono sul bordo della nave li due capi Pirati (Nicanore, e Megistone) li quali cogli altri cantano di colà li primi quattro versi dell'Introduzione—*Salvi siam* etc—poi discendono a terra anch'essi, ed in seguito discendono, uno o due per volta li schiavi da loro nuovamente predati.

La maggior parte di questi schiavi saranno del seguito di Cesare e tutti si troveranno a terra schierati alla parte destra, un momento avanti di cantare i versi—*Qual colpa nostra o Numi* etc—Sul verso poi, che dice:—di noi che mai sarà?—Cesare comparisce sul bordo del vascello in mezzo ad alcuni Pirati ed in questa situazione canta tutto il suo primo solo.

44. See Allanbrook, *Rhythmic Gesture*, 225–26, 247–48.

EXAMPLE 17.13 *Cesare in Farmacusa,* act 1, "Giuro a Pluto," mm. 71–87 (A-Wn, Mus. Hs. 16513)

CHORUS: What fault of ours, oh Gods, has incited your wrath? What cruel destiny awaits us? What will become of us? CAESAR: Cease your complaints, your words of sadness.

majesty of the opening section, marked Grave; so does the three-phrase form of Caesar's melody and the extension of the third phrase to five measures. The opening melody, by favoring G above middle C, suggests that Simoni could sing that note with particular beauty. Near the end of the aria Caesar sustains the same G four measures, but perhaps in recognition of Simoni's age Salieri wrote very little coloratura for the veteran tenor.

Defranceschi, following Plutarch, gave Caesar two servants, whom he made lovers: Tullo and Gigi. Angrisani's Tullo is a conventional *parte buffa.* Tomeoni's Gigi is the sweet young charmer that she excelled in portraying. Salieri could count on Angrisani and Tomeoni, who had worked together as a comic team in *Il mondo alla rovescia* and *Falstaff,* to provide most of the comedy in this dramma eroicomico.

Tullo reveals himself to be a buffo caricato near the beginning of the opera, as he thanks Jupiter sarcastically for having saved him from the storm only to leave him in the hands of pirates. In writing of this number Salieri offered an insight into the relation between pathos and comedy in late-eighteenth-century opera. "Messer Giove, obbligatissimo" is a comic aria "despite the character's sad situation; but one knows that

EXAMPLE 17.14 *Cesare in Farmacusa,* act 1, "Per dirvi schietti schietti," mm. 1–19

To tell you my most sincere feelings, I will say . . . that is, I would say . . . I do not know how to explain.

when the buffo weeps in the theater, the audience must laugh." To avoid being consigned to hard labor Tullo tries to persuade the pirates, in his aria "Per la musica vocale" (with Gigi, Nicanore, Megistone, and Nerbote as pertichini) that he has many artistic talents: he can sing, play the flute, and dance. Naturally he demonstrates all of this on stage. The idea is much like that of "Delle sue dote fisiche," an aria that Angrisani sang in *Il moro,* except that Orgone boasts of his daughter's skills while Tullo boasts of his own. In showing how his vocal prowess exceeds Orpheus's, Tullo indulges in coloratura that is very atypical of the eighteenth-century comic bass but anticipates some of the elaborate vocalization demanded by Rossini from his comic basses (such as Mustafà in *L'italiana in Algeri*).

Gigi's personality emerges just as clearly in "Per dirvi schietti schietti," a big aria in F major that perfectly exploited Tomeoni's talents. The opening words themselves may have reminded Viennese audiences of a role that Tomeoni had made her own: that of Rachelina in Paisiello's *La molinara.* In her cavatina "La Rachelina molinarina" (also in F) Tomeoni sang the words "Son schietta schietta, vergognosetta" (see ex. 15.1). A light accompaniment frames Gigi's pretty melody, with its small range and small amount of simple coloratura. Short instrumental interjections enhance the music's charm (ex. 17.14). The aria ends, like so many of those written for Tomeoni, with a rollicking Allegro in compound meter.

Caesar and his comic servants match wits against the pirates. Nicanore finds Gigi attractive, inflaming the jealous anger of his fiancée, the *piratessa* Termuti. The finale of act 1, praised as a masterpiece in the *Allgemeine musikalische Zeitung,* dramatizes the cultural differences between the pirates and their Roman prisoners. It begins with the pirates celebrating their successful voyage. Salieri, assuming the role of stage director, described the scenery and action in great detail:

> The stage will be adorned with many trophies and banners of various nations, all attached in a symmetrical pattern to the wings at the back. In the middle, also in the back, a large cask on a kind of wagon will be visible, from which all the pirates will fill their large, silver-plated tankards. Care will be taken that those of the two principal pirates and of Termuti will be gilt, so as to distinguish them from the others.
>
> The scene will open on the first note of the orchestra, at which point the signal will be given for a loud beat on the Turkish bass drum; the beat will be repeated at the repetition of the chorus.
>
> All the pirates will drink and cease drinking at the same time, as the music indicates. At the back of the stage it will possible for a line of slaves to be visible as witnesses of the pirates' celebration.
>
> When the pirates repeat the words "Si beva, si tracanni" [let us drink, let us swill] they must show themselves to be half drunk, and must leave in that state.[45]

The pirates accompany their drinking with a kind of vaudeville in E♭ major whose monophonic texture and unexpected tonal shifts, especially from major to minor and vice versa, give it a "barbaric" character. Nicanore sings a vigorous melody that modulates to C minor and then to the dominant of G minor. All the pirates respond in G minor, but suddenly modulate back to E♭ (ex. 17.15).

Caesar, Tullo, and Gigi are shocked by the crudeness of this music. Having decided to give the pirates an example of beautiful Roman music, they sing a prayer to Venus: a lyrical Andante con moto that alternates between moments of serene beauty and silliness. A graceful gavotte tune, predominantly homophonic except for a short imitative passage, culminates in coloratura for Caesar and Gigi over Tullo's bass. An instrumen-

45. La decorazione sarà adornata di molti Trofei, e bandiere di differenti nazioni, il tutto attaccato con simetria alle quinte del fondo. In mezzo, parimenti nel fondo, si vedrà una gran Botte sopra una specie di carro, dalla quale tutti li Pirati empiranno di vino i loro inargentati e grandi boccali. Si avrà l'avvertenza di far che quelli delli due principali Pirati, e di Termuti, per distinzione sieno dorati.

La scena si apre sulla prima nota dell'orchestra nel qual punto si farà dar un gran colpo di Tamburo turco, colpo che si replicherà anche alla represa del coro.

Tutti li Pirati beveranno, e cesseranno di bevere nello stesso tempo secondo che accenna la musica. In fondo della scena si potrà far vedere una fila di schiavi come spettatori delle Fasta dei Pirati.

Quando i Pirati ripetono le parole: *Si beva, si traccani* devono mostrarsi tutti mezzo ubriachi, e in tal guisa partire.

EXAMPLE 17.15 *Cesare in Farmacusa*, act 1, finale, mm. 44–56

NICANORE: For him who aspires to great deeds, for him who has a strong spirit, there is no fate worthier than that of the pirates. CHORUS: Long live the pirates!

tal interlude undercuts the apparent seriousness of the prayer by having Tullo imitate a clarinet on nonsense syllables, probably falsetto.

The pirates reject the Romans' music: "Che scempiataggini . . . che insulse inezie . . . che stomachevole puerilità!" [What stupidities! What inane trivialities! What nauseating childishness!]. Tempers flare; Caesar promises vengeance on his captors, while the other Romans marvel, in asides, at his bravery and the pirates comment on his impudence and arrogance. In the finale's climax Salieri gave Simoni plenty of opportunity to show off his apparently brilliant G above middle C and used that pitch to make Caesar the center of attention for both the characters on stage and the audience. At one point Caesar sings six successive half notes on G.

The storm that threatens the pirate's fleet at the beginning of the opera is not in Plutarch. Salieri may have urged his librettist to introduce it, because it gave him an opportunity to reuse a fine piece of music unknown in Vienna: the storm overture to *Europa riconosciuta* (see ex. 8.1; fig. 17.4), reorchestrated to take advantage of instruments, such as the clarinet, that were unavailable in Milan in 1778. As usual, the composer said nothing about this borrowing in his annotations.

Salieri's instructions on the activity that takes place during the overture show that he clearly remembered how, under Verazi's direction, the overture to *Europa* had accompanied an elaborate pantomime. Some of his instructions, indeed, are amazingly close to Verri's description of the beginning of *Europa* (quoted in chap. 8). Salieri evidently hoped to reconstruct Verazi's spectacle:

> Very loud thunder serves as a signal to the orchestra to begin the sinfonia and to the director of scenery to raise the curtain. The stage is almost dark, and represents a storm at sea.

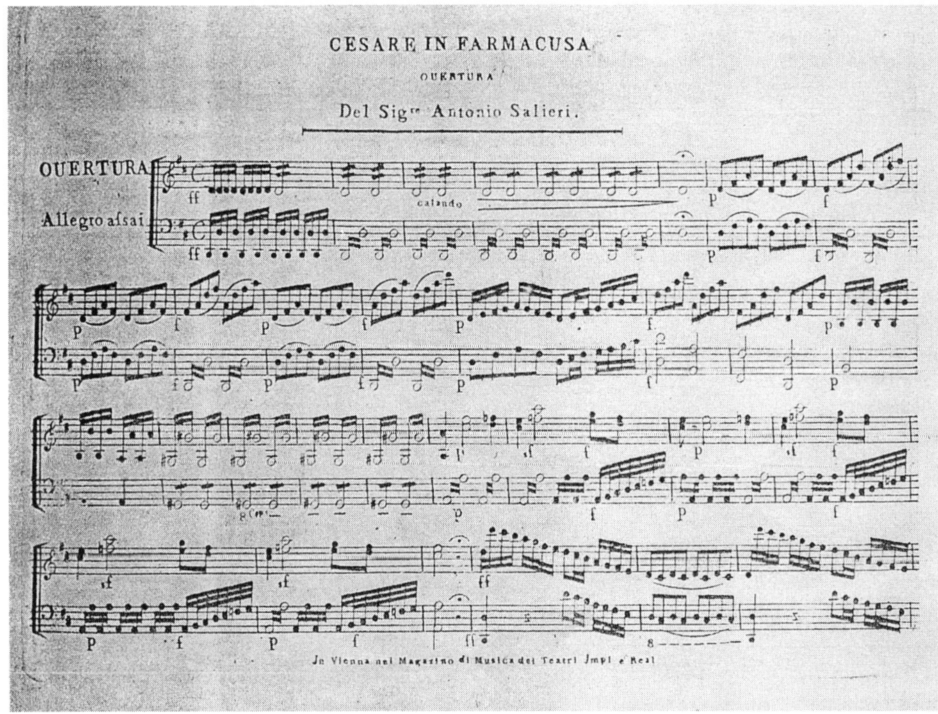

FIGURE 17.4 Overture to *Cesare in Farmacusa,* borrowed from *Europa riconosciuta.* Piano-vocal reduction by Joseph Patzelt (Vienna, n.d.).

> One sees ships passing back and forth in continuous agitation, loaded with people who through their gestures plead for help, all of which one sees clearly only by means of frequent flashes of lightning. On the twenty-ninth measure some pirates of low rank enter from the interior of the island; on the beach they show with gestures that they are afraid of the dangers besetting the ships. One of these pirates orders the others to go with him. A few moments later they all return with some long ropes. The end of one of these ropes will be thrown in the sea, but sideways, in such a way as to show that they want by this means to pull to shore one of the boats that is closest to land, which will appear in the audience's view only toward the end of the sinfonia, that is, in the moment at which the strength of the storm begins to wane. In that moment the stage brightens.[46]

The overture ends, as in *Europa,* on an open cadence; here it is followed by a chorus of pirates celebrating their escape from the storm (Salieri's instructions for the performance of this scene were quoted earlier). The combination of the key of D, duple meter, and a melody that often doubles the bass places this chorus in the realm of opera buffa. By juxtaposing the chorus and the tumultuous overture, which lacks even a trace

46. Quoted in Angermüller, *Leben,* 3:104, Angermüller, *Fatti,* 99–100, and Swenson, 199–201.

EXAMPLE 17.16 *Cesare in Farmacusa,* act 2, finale, mm. 164–83

of buffo qualities, Salieri projected right at the beginning of the opera his heroicomic intent.

The overture is not the only part of *Cesare* that looks back, beyond *Axur,* to the 1770s. Salieri returned to a device that he had learned from Viennese opera of the 1760s and had used frequently in his own early comic operas: the incorporation of melodic material into the accompaniment of simple recitative. When Tullo, looking for Gigi near the beginning of the opera, decides to climb a cliff for a better view, the bass depicts his ascent with a two-octave scale of staccato eighth notes.

Not that all of *Cesare* looks to the past. Some of the opera's most up-to-date music accompanies the battle near the end. In the brilliant military march we can see that Salieri on occasion could match the melodic freshness of Weigl, Paer, and Cherubini. The chains of dotted notes remind one particularly of Paer, but this melody also anticipates quite strikingly the second theme of the overture to *L'italiana in Algeri* (ex. 17.16).

The Dissolution of the Italian Troupe and Salieri's Retirement from Operatic Composition

More than twenty years after helping to celebrate the opening of La Scala in Milan with *Europa riconosciuta* Salieri was invited to provide another inaugural opera for a new theater in another Austrian-governed Italian city. During spring 1801 the Imperial-Royal Theater of Trieste opened with productions of Mayr's *Ginevra di Scozia* and Salieri's *Annibale in Capua,* on a libretto by the Venetian Antonio Simone Sografi.[47]

After supervising performances of *Annibale* Salieri returned to Vienna, a city in which resident composers no longer felt much encouragement to write operas in Italian. He came close, nevertheless, to finishing another opera buffa. But when it was decided (by whom we do not know) not to perform *La bella selvaggia* Salieri left the opera incomplete. Where the aria "Il più costante affetto" should have been in the autograph are blank pages, placed there by Salieri presumably in the hope that he would compose the aria for some future production.[48]

Salieri's failure to finish and stage *La bella selvaggia* reflects the precarious state of the Italian troupe during the first years of the nineteenth century. The success of *Palmira,* first performed a few months after the debut of Baron Braun's German troupe, revived public appreciation for Italian opera, according to a biographical sketch of Salieri published the following year;[49] but that revival seems to have been short lived.

In 1800 Braun asked to be relieved of the obligation (to which he had agreed in his contract of 1794) of presenting Italian opera. Emperor Francis wrote to his Oberstkämmerer Count Colloredo: "Baron Braun is to be informed that he is certainly free to give up the Italian opera as long as he strives to present good German plays and Singspiele."[50] The Italian troupe survived, but such threats cannot have helped its morale or that of the composers associated with it. In 1801 Paer accepted a position at the court theater in Dresden, where Italian opera was evidently on a stronger footing than in Vienna. Salieri remained, but he wrote no more Italian operas.

During the late 1790s Braun had introduced to Vienna a new way of presenting Italian opera: he engaged a single great musico and organized a series of performances around him, the repertory being based on the principal singer's roles in the most celebrated contemporary opere serie.[51] In 1797 Girolamo Crescentini presented, among other works, Nicola Antonio Zingarelli's *Romeo e Giulietta.* A year later Marchesi (who had anticipated this way of organizing performances when he appeared in a single

47. On *Annibale in Capua* see Della Croce/Blanchetti, 300–303 and 510–13.

48. *La bella selvaggia* is discussed briefly in Della Croce/Blanchetti, 303–4 and 514–15.

49. Diese Oper [*Palmira*] ward mit ausserordentlichen Beyfall aufgenommen, und belebte den Geschmack des Publikums an Italienischen Opern, der bereits nur zu sichtbar erloschen war ("Nachrichten vom Leben und den Werken des k. k. Hofkapellmeisters, Anton Salieri," in *Wiener Theater Almanach für das Jahr 1796* [Vienna, [1796]], 98).

50. Dem Baron Braun ist zu bedeuten, daß ihm allerdings gestattet sei, die Italienischen Opern aufzugeben, jedoch habe er sich zu bestreben, gute deutsche Schau- und Singspiele zu geben (annotation [signed by Francis] to a proposal by Oberstkämmerer Colloredo, HHStA, GH, Kart. 3 [1799–1805]).

51. This paragraph is based largely on a study of cast lists in *Theaterzettel* (theatrical posters) preserved in A-Wth.

opera seria in Vienna in 1785) sang Zingarelli's *Pirro* and Mayr's *Lodoiska.* He returned to Vienna in 1801, as did Crescentini in 1804. The success of these guest appearances did not bode well for the future of the Italian troupe. The musici overshadowed members of the permanent company with whom they shared the stage, and their presence in Vienna must have suggested to Braun the idea of engaging for a limited time not just one singer but an entire troupe. Singers of Italian opera did not have to be on his permanent payroll for the Viennese public to enjoy occasional seasons of Italian opera.

Braun finally dismissed the Italian troupe in the midst of a series of momentous political and military events that must have played a role in his decision. The peace with France concluded at Lunéville broke down in 1805. The French army occupied Vienna on 13 November 1805; about three weeks later Napoleon crushed the Austro-Russian alliance at Austerlitz. Humiliated, Emperor Francis sued for peace; less than a year later he abdicated the throne of the Holy Roman Empire, which on 6 August 1806 ceased to exist.

Since the seventeenth century, Italian opera had helped project the image of Vienna as the cosmopolitan capital of a multinational empire. The Italian operas of Antonio Draghi, Antonio Caldara, Gluck, Salieri, and Mozart had represented a cultural *lingua franca* accessible to all of the monarchy's multilingual elites. Emperor Francis, born in Florence, might have been expected to support Italian opera as actively as his father before him. But now that he was emperor of Austria, at the head of a government whose army was helpless and whose treasury was almost empty, it made little sense for his court theaters to cultivate Italian opera. With a performance of Francesco Gardi's *La donna ve la va* on 20 March 1806 the Viennese opera buffa troupe, having performed more or less uninterruptedly since 1783, took its final bow.[52]

Italian opera continued to be performed, but sporadically. Viennese audiences enjoyed several opere buffe during the second half of 1809, and in 1811 opere serie by Cimarosa, Paer, and Giuseppe Nicolini. Five years later they witnessed the first performance in Vienna of operas by Rossini. Salieri attended the Viennese premiere of *Tancredi,* not as an active participant in the production but as a less-than-enthusiastic member of the audience.[53]

New operas by Viennese composers were conspicuously absent from the repertory of these isolated seasons of Italian opera. They had turned from Italian to German opera even before the dissolution of the permanent Italian troupe. Weigl's *L'accademia del maestro Cisolfaut* was the last Italian opera that he wrote for the court theaters. Later he won remarkable success with several Singspiele: *Die Uniform, Ostade,* and above all

52. The data on performances in this and the following paragraphs are from Hadamowsky, *Hoftheater,* vols. 1, 2.

53. See chap. 1, n. 18.

Die Schweitzerfamilie (performed 218 times between 1809 and 1836, not counting performances of a single act). Adalbert Gyrowetz joined the court theater staff in 1804, almost exactly at the time that Salieri stopped writing operas. Braun probably engaged him with the intention of replacing Salieri as resident composer. Gyrowetz made his compositional debut with a German opera, *Selico,* which reached the stage within a month of the first performance of Salieri's last opera. Over the next three decades he composed many operas, serious and comic, almost all in German. Among the most popular were *Agnes Sorel* (performed 124 times between 1806 and 1816) and *Der Augenarzt* (96 times between 1811 and 1817).

Italian operas were occasionally commissioned by and first performed at the Kärntnertor. (At the end of 1810 it became the permanent home of the court opera, ancestor of today's Staatsoper, which stands in roughly the same place.) Rossini came to Vienna in 1822 to present *Zelmira,* especially composed for this visit (although the premiere had taken place in Naples shortly before), and several other operas. Donizetti presented the premieres of *Linda di Chamounix* in 1842 and of *Maria di Rohan* in 1843. Gyrowetz made the piano reduction of *Zelmira.* That a court Kapellmeister should be reduced to such a menial task may have reminded him that although Italian operas were still performed in Vienna, the great age of Viennese Italian opera was long over.

Salieri had been immersed since the beginning of his career in Viennese Italian opera: first as Gassmann's student and apprentice, then as composer and music director, then as Hofkapellmeister under Emperors Joseph II, Leopold II, and Francis II. He was only fifty years old in 1800, as the end of Viennese Italian opera drew near; we might think that he could adapt to new operatic tastes and conditions, just as he had adjusted earlier in his career to the tastes of Italy and Paris. Personal tragedy, especially the death of his wife Therese in 1807, contributed to his inability or unwillingness to adapt again. Political instability and war, conditions that seem to have inspired Beethoven's creativity, had the opposite effect on Salieri, to judge from Mosel's explanation of his withdrawal from operatic composition:

> The tumultuous, eventful time, which deeply affected every sensitive person who was loyal to his prince and country, took from our master the peace of mind necessary for the practice of his art; he was no less affected by the deaths in rapid succession of his many children and finally the loss of a wife to whom he was attached with a love that was pure and selfless, and in whom he found his life's happiness; these losses gradually choked off the enthusiastic pleasure that he had formerly felt in working for the public.[54]

The evolution of musical style took Viennese opera in directions that Salieri was unwilling, or unable, to follow. On this point Mosel quoted the composer directly: "From

54. Mosel, 178.

that period I realized that musical taste was gradually changing in a manner completely contrary to that of my own times. Eccentricity and confusion of genres replaced reasoned and masterful simplicity."[55]

The circumstances both political and musical to which Mosel and Salieri alluded had to do with France. Paris of the ancien régime, with its dynastic links to Vienna, had given Salieri some of his greatest triumphs, in the glow of which he had declared admiration for French musical taste and hope that he would never have to write another Italian opera. Post-Revolutionary France, in contrast, was his enemy as well as Austria's. He could have no dealings with a republic that had put to death Queen Marie Antoinette, his patroness and the sister of Joseph II; nor could he appreciate and imitate the operatic music produced in Paris during the years after the Revolution.

France invaded Austria militarily and musically in the early nineteenth century, and Salieri suffered from both invasions. The city walls within which he had lived in comfort since his arrival in Vienna and which had represented the invincibility of his Habsburg patrons since the defeat of the Turks in 1683 could not stop French troops from occupying Vienna in 1805 and bombarding it in 1809. The operas of Cherubini and Dalayrac won Vienna over no less easily.

While Beethoven embraced Cherubini's music, Salieri rejected it. In doing so he did not win the approval even of his most faithful student, Hüttenbrenner, who wrote: "Salieri went too far when he told us that Cherubini's operas are orchestral music with a vocal accompaniment."[56] Unwilling to learn from Cherubini, Salieri found himself increasingly isolated from the mainstream of Viennese operatic life.

Salieri's attempt to follow Viennese composers and audiences into German opera led to the Singspiel that turned out to be his last opera. With Treitschke, who had translated *Cesare* into German, he produced *Die Neger,* first performed in the Theater an der Wien on 10 November 1804. It was withdrawn after a few performances, rejected by an audience that, in the words of one critic, was "increasingly learning to appreciate the work of Mozart and Cherubini."[57] Beethoven's *Fidelio* suffered the same fate when it was first performed a year later, during the French occupation, in the same theater; and a critic compared Beethoven unfavorably to the same composers whose operas Salieri was unable to equal.[58] Beethoven, twenty years younger than Salieri, tenaciously revised his opera (with Treitschke's help) and presented it again to the public; Salieri allowed his opera to disappear from the repertory without a trace.

55. Mosel, 173.

56. Hüttenbrenner, "Erinnerungen," 123.

57. *AmZ* 7 (1804–5): cols. 174–75; quoted in Swenson, 218.

58. "The melodies [of *Fidelio*] . . . lack that happy, clear, magical impression of emotion which grips us so irresistibly in the works of Mozart and Cherubini" (*Der Freymüthige* [26 December 1805], quoted in translation in Thayer, *Beethoven,* 387).

During the last two decades of his life Salieri wrote no operas. He devoted himself to his duties as Hofkapellmeister and to the teaching of singing and composition. Although Viennese audiences no longer expected or wanted to hear new operas in Italian by Viennese composers, Italian vocal music had not yet lost its place among the genres in which every well-rounded composer was expected to have some expertise. Beethoven, Schubert, and many other young composers came to Salieri for instruction in the setting of Italian texts to music, learning what he had learned from Metastasio himself about the musical declamation of Italian operatic poetry.

APPENDIX: A CHRONOLOGICAL LIST OF SALIERI'S OPERAS

The list includes generic designation (from libretto, when available), number of acts, librettist, place and date of first performance, and principal sources consulted in the course of this study.

La vestale, composed 1768. Probably unperformed; all sources apparently lost.

Le donne letterate (commedia per musica, 3 acts, Boccherini), Vienna, Burgtheater or Kärntnertortheater, Carnival 1770. Libretto: Vienna, 1770 (copy in US-Wc); score: A-Wn, Mus. Hs. 17833.

L'amore innocente (pastorale per musica, 2 parts, Boccherini), 1770, place and exact date of first performance unknown. Libretto: Vienna, 1770 (copy in A-Wn); scores: A-Wn, Mus. Hs. 16510 (autograph), and D-Dlb, Mus. 3796/F/1.

Don Chisciotte alle nozze di Gamace (divertimento teatrale, 2 parts, Boccherini), Vienna, Kärntnertortheater, 6 January 1771 (?). Libretto: Vienna, 1770 (copy in A-Wst); score: A-Wn, Mus. Hs. 17835.

Armida (dramma per musica, 3 acts, Coltellini), Vienna, Burgtheater or Kärntnertortheater, 2 June 1771. Libretto: [Vienna], 1771 (copy in A-Wst); scores: A-Wn, Mus. Hs. 17837 and Mus. Hs. 16517 (autograph, heavily revised).

La fiera di Venezia (commedia per musica, 3 acts, Boccherini), Vienna, Burgtheater or Kärntnertortheater, 29 January 1772. Libretto: [Vienna, 1772] (copy in A-Wn); scores: A-Wn, Mus. Hs. 17185 (autograph, heavily revised), Mus. Hs. 17838, Mus. Hs. 1048, and K.T. 157.

Il barone di Rocca Antica (dramma giocoso per musica, 2 parts, Petrosellini), Vienna, Burgtheater or Kärntnertortheater, 12 May 1772. Libretto: [Vienna, 1772] (copy in A-Wst); score: A-Wn, Mus. Hs. 16511 (autograph).

La secchia rapita (dramma eroicomico, 3 acts, Boccherini, after Tassoni), Vienna, Kärntnertortheater, 21 October 1772. Libretto: Vienna, [1772] (copy in US-Wc); score: A-Wn, Mus. Hs. 17841.

La locandiera (dramma giocoso per musica, 3 acts, Poggi, after Goldoni), Vienna, Kärntnertortheater, 8 June 1773. Libretto: [Vienna, 1773] (copy in A-Wst); scores: A-Wn, Mus. Hs. 16179 (autograph) and Mus. Hs. 17840.

La calamita de' cuori (dramma giocoso, 3 acts, Goldoni), Vienna, Kärntnertortheater, 11 October 1774. Libretto: [Vienna, 1774] (copy in A-Wst); scores: A-Wn, Mus. Hs. 16508 (autograph) and Mus. Hs. 17839.

La finta scema (commedia per musica, 3 acts, De Gamerra), Vienna, Burgtheater, 9 September 1775. Libretto: [Vienna, 1775] (copy in A-Wn); score: A-Wn, Mus. Hs. 17842.

Daliso e Delmita (azione pastorale or dramma per musica, 3 acts, De Gamerra), Vienna, Burgtheater, 29 July 1776. Libretto: Vienna, 1776 (copy in A-Wn); score: A-Wn, Mus. Hs. 16186 (autograph).

Europa riconosciuta (dramma per musica, 2 acts, Verazi), Milan, Teatro alla Scala, 3 August 1778. Libretto: Milan, [1778] (copy in Us-Wc); score: A-Wn, Mus. Hs. 17836.

La scuola de' gelosi (dramma giocoso per musica, 2 acts, Mazzolà), Venice, Teatro S. Moisè, Carnival 1779. Libretto: [Venice, 1779] (copy in US-Wc); score: A-Wn, Mus. Hs. 16615 (autograph, heavily revised), Mus. Hs. 17845, and K.T. 411.

La partenza inaspettata (intermezzo, 2 parts, Petrosellini), Rome, Teatro Valle, Carnival 1779. Libretto: Rome, 1779 (copy in US-Wc); score: A-Wn, Mus. Hs. 16607 (autograph).

Il talismano (dramma giocoso per musica, 3 acts, Goldoni), Milan, Teatro alla Cannobiana, 21 August 1779; acts 2 and 3 by Rust.

La dama pastorella (intermezzo, 2 parts, Petrosellini), Rome, Teatro Valle, Carnival 1780. Libretto: Rome, 1780 (copy in D-Mth); scores: A-Wn, Mus. Hs. 16186, Mus. Hs. 4487, Mus. Hs. 4539, Mus. Hs. 4541 (autograph fragments).

Der Rauchfangkehrer (musikalisches Lustspiel, 3 acts, Auenbrugger), Vienna, Burgtheater, 30 April 1781. Libretto: Vienna, [1781] (copy in US-Wc); scores: A-Wn, Mus. Hs. 16611 (autograph, overture missing), reproduced in facsimile, New York, 1986, and Mus. Hs. 16518.

Semiramide (dramma per musica, 3 acts, Metastasio), Munich, court, Carnival 1782. Libretto: Munich, 1782 (copy in D-Mbs); scores: A-Wn, Mus. Hs. 16605 (fragmentary autograph), and D-Mbs Ms. 2523.

Les Danaïdes (tragédie lyrique, 5 acts, Du Roullet and Tschudi, after Calzabigi), Paris, Académie Royale de Musique, 26 April 1784. Score: Paris, n.d., reproduced in facsimile, Bologna, 1969.

Il ricco d'un giorno (dramma giocoso, 3 acts, Da Ponte), 6 December 1784. Libretto: Vienna, 1784 (copy in D-MHrm); scores: A-Wn, Mus. Hs. 16609 (autograph) and Mus. Hs. 17846.

La grotta di Trofonio (opera comica, 2 acts, Casti), Laxenburg (?), summer (?) 1785; Vienna, Burgtheater, 12 October 1785. Libretto: Vienna, [1785] (variant 1 in A-Wn, variant 2 in I-Rsc); score: Vienna, [1786?], reproduced in facsimile, Bologna, 1984.

Prima la musica e poi le parole (divertimento teatrale, 1 act, Casti), Schönbrunn, 7 February 1786. Libretto: Vienna, [1786] (copies in D-MHrm and I-Rsc); score: A-Wn, K.T. 359.

Les Horaces (tragédie lyrique, 3 acts, Guillard, after Corneille), Paris, Académie Royale de Musique, 7 December 1786. Score: A-Wn, Mus. Hs. 17953 (autograph).

Tarare (opéra, 5 acts, Beaumarchais), Paris, Académie Royale de Musique, 8 June 1787. Libretto: Beaumarchais, *Oeuvres*, ed. Pierre Larthomas and Jacqueline Larthomas, Paris, 1988; score: ed. Rudolph Angermüller, Munich, 1978.

Axur re d'Ormus (dramma tragicomico, 5 [later 4] acts, Da Ponte, after Beaumarchais, *Tarare*), Vienna, Burgtheater, 8 January 1788. Libretto: Vienna, [1788] (variant 1 in A-Wn, variant 2 in I-Rsc); scores: A-Wn, Mus. Hs. 17049 (autograph, heavily revised), Mus. Hs. 17832, and K.T. 50.

Cublai, gran kan de' Tartari (opera eroicomica, 2 acts, Casti), begun in 1787; never performed. Score: A-Wn, Mus. Hs. 16188 (autograph).

Il talismano (commedia per musica, 3 acts, Goldoni, revised by Da Ponte), Vienna, Burgtheater, 10 September 1788. Libretto: Vienna, [1788] (copies in D-MHrm and I-Rsc); scores: D-F, Mus. Hs. Opern 503, and A-Wn, Mus. Hs. 16604 (autograph).

Il pastor fido (dramma tragicomico per musica, 4 [later 3] acts, Da Ponte, after Guarini), Vienna, Burgtheater, 11 February 1789. Librettos: Vienna, [1789] (4-act version, copy in D-MHrm), and Vienna, [1789] (3-act version, copy in I-Rsc); score: A-Wn, Mus. Hs. 16606 (autograph).

La cifra (dramma giocoso, 2 acts, Da Ponte, after Petrosellini, *La dama pastorella*), Vienna, Burgtheater, 11 December 1789. Libretto: Vienna, [1789] (copy in I-Rsc); scores: A-Wn, Mus. Hs. 16514 (autograph) and K.T. 83.

Catilina (opera tragicomica, 2 acts, Casti), composed in 1792; unperformed until 1994. Score: A-Wn, Mus. Hs. 16512 (autograph).

Il mondo alla rovescia (dramma giocoso per musica, 2 acts, Mazzolà), Vienna, Burgtheater, 13 January 1795. Libretto: Vienna, [1795] (copy in A-Wn); score: A-Wn, Mus. Hs. 17180 (autograph).

Eraclito e Democrito (commedia per musica, 2 acts, De Gamerra), Vienna, Burgtheater, 13 August 1795. Libretto: Vienna, [1795] (copy in A-Wn); score: A-Wn, Mus. Hs. 16190 (autograph).

Palmira regina di Persia (dramma eroicomico, 2 acts, De Gamerra, after Martin, *La Princesse de Babylone*), Vienna, Kärntnertortheater, 14 October 1795. Libretto: Vienna, [1795] (copy in US-Wc); score: A-Wn, Mus. Hs. 16183 (autograph).

Il moro (commedia per musica, 2 acts, De Gamerra), Vienna, Burgtheater, 7 August 1796. Libretto: Vienna, [1796] (copy in A-Wn); score: A-Wn, Mus. Hs. 16181 (autograph).

I tre filosofi, 1797, comic opera, unfinished.

Falstaff, ossia Le tre burle (dramma giocoso per musica, 2 acts, Defranceschi, after Shakespeare, *The Merry Wives of Windsor*), Vienna, Kärntnertortheater, 3 January 1799. Libretto: Vienna, [1799] (copy in A-Wn); score: A-Wn, Mus. Hs. 16191 (autograph).

Cesare in Farmacusa (dramma eroicomico, 2 acts, Defranceschi), Vienna, Kärntnertortheater, 2 June 1800. Libretto: Vienna, [1800] (copy in A-Wn); score: A-Wn, Mus. Hs. 16513 (autograph).

Angiolina, ossia Il matrimonio per sussurro (opera buffa, 2 acts, Defranceschi, after Jonson, *Epicoene*); Vienna, Kärntnertortheater, 22 October 1800. Libretto: Vienna, 1800 (copy in A-Wn); score: D-F.

Annibale in Capua (dramma per musica, 2 acts, Sografi), Trieste, Teatro Nuovo, 20 May 1801. Score: A-Wn, Mus. Hs. 9994.

La bella selvaggia (opera buffa, 2 acts, Bertati [?]), composed 1802; never performed. Score: A-Wn, Mus. Hs. 16610 (autograph).

Die Neger (Oper, 2 acts, Treitschke), Theater an der Wien, 10 November 1804. Score: A-Wn, Mus. Hs. 16182 (autograph).

BIBLIOGRAPHY

Archival Sources

BUDAPEST — Magyar Országos Levéltár (National Archives of Hungary)
Keglevich papers (P 421, V/15–22)

KLAGENFURT — Kärntner Landesarchiv
Rosenberg papers

VIENNA — Bibliothek des Österreichischen Theatermuseums (formerly Theatersammlung der Nationalbibliothek)
Burgtheater Theaterzettel (playbills), 1776–1806
Hoftheater Kassabuch (account-book), 1789–97, Signature M 4000

Haus-, Hof- und Staatsarchiv
Generalintendanz der Hoftheater, Akten, Kart. 1–3; Rechnungsbücher, 1776–92
Handarchiv Kaiser Franz, Kart. 1–6
Handbilleten-Protokoll
Hofmusikkapelle, Akten, Kart. 1
Interiora, Kart. 86 (alt 108)
Obersthofmeisteramt, Akten, 1791; Protocollum 46 (1788–89); SR, Kart. 369
Oberstkämmereramt, Akten, 1781–90
Sammelbände, Kart. 7, 10, 17, 19, 20, 30, 53
Tagebuch Zinzendorf

Hofkammerarchiv
Hofzahlamtsbücher
Österreichisches Camerale, Abt. 67

Wiener Stadtarchiv
Totenbeschauprotokoll, 1774

Eighteenth- and Early-Nineteenth-Century Journals and Newspapers

Allgemeine musikalische Zeitung. Leipzig, 1798–1812.

Berlinische musikalische Zeitung. Berlin, 1793.

Gazzetta toscana. Florence, 1779, 1785.

Gazzetta universale. Florence, 1790.

Gazzetta urbana veneta. Venice, 1789.

Morning Chronicle. London, 1798.

Morning Post and Daily Advertiser. London, 1786.

Musikalische Monathsschrift. Berlin, 1792.

Musikalisches Wochenblatt. Berlin, 1791.

Times. London, 1791.

Wiener Zeitung. Vienna, 1770, 1775, 1788.

Eighteenth- and Early-Nineteenth-Century Almanacs (in Chronological Order), Published in Vienna Unless Otherwise Specified

Genaue Nachrichten von beyden kaiserlich-königlichen Schaubühnen. Ed. J. H. F. Müller. 1772.

Theatralkalender von Wien, für das Jahr 1772.

Theatral-Neuigkeiten. Ed. J. H. F. Müller. 1773.

Theatralalmanach von Wien, für das Jahr 1773.

Almanach des Theaters in Wien. 1774.

Theatralalmanach von Wien, für das Jahr 1774.

Geschichte und Tagbuch der Wiener Schaubühne. Ed. J. H. F. Müller. 1776.

Taschenbuch des Wiener Theaters. 1777.

Allgemeiner Theater Allmanach von Jahr 1782.

Wiener Musik- und Theater-Allmanach auf das Jahr 1786.

Wiener Theater Almanach für das Jahr 1794.

Wiener Theater Almanach für das Jahr 1795.

Wiener Theater Almanach für das Jahr 1796.

Musikalisches Taschenbuch auf das Jahr 1803. Ed. Julius and Adolf Werden. Penig.

Other Primary Sources

Adams, John Quincy. *Memoirs of John Quincy Adams comprising portions of his diary 1795 to 1848.* Ed. Charles Francis Adams. 12 vols. Philadelphia, 1874–77.

Alfieri, Vittorio. "Vita di Vittorio Alfieri da Asti scritta da esso." In *Opere di Vittorio Alfieri,* ed. Vittorio Branca. Milan, 1968.

Anti–da Ponte. Vienna, 1791.

Arndt, Ernst Moritz. *Reisen durch einen Theil Teutschlands, Ungarns, Italiens, und Frankreichs in den Jahren 1798 und 1799.* 2d ed. 4 vols. Leipzig, 1804.

"Auszug eines Schreibens aus Wien vom 5ten Jul. 1790." In *Musikalische Korrespondenz der teutschen Filarmonischen Gesellschaft,* 28 July 1790, cols. 27–31. Reprinted in Angermüller, *Leben,* 3:55–58.

Beaumarchais, Pierre-Augustin Caron de. *Oeuvres*. Ed. Pierre Larthomas and Jacqueline Larthomas. Paris, 1988.

Beccatini, Francesco. *Vita pubblica e privata di Pietro Leopoldo d'Austria Granduca di Toscana poi Imperatore Leopoldo II*. Filadelfia [Milan], 1796.

Berlioz, Hector. *Mémoires*. Ed. Pierre Citron. Paris, 1991.

Bogusławski, Wojciech. *Dzieie Teatru Narodowego*. Warsaw, 1820. Reprinted in facsimile, Warsaw, 1965.

Burney, Charles. *A General History of Music*. Ed. Frank Mercer. 2 vols. New York, 1957.

———. *The Present State of Music in France and Italy*. Ed. Percy A. Scholes, London, 1959.

———. *The Present State of Music in Germany, the Netherlands, and United Provinces*. Ed. Percy A. Scholes. London, 1959.

———. *Music, Men and Manners in France and Italy, 1770* (an edition of Burney's manuscript journal). Ed. H. Edmund Poole. London, 1974.

Calzabigi, Ranieri de. "Dagli archivi milanesi: Lettere di Ranieri de Calzabigi e di Antonia Bernasconi." Ed. Mariangela Donà. *Am* 14 (1974), 268–300.

———. *Scritti teatrali e letterari*. Ed. Anna Laura Bellina. 2 vols. Rome, 1994.

Casanova, Giacomo. *Carteggi Casanoviani: Lettere di Giacomo Casanova e di altri a lui*. Ed. Pompeo Molmenti. N.p., [c. 1916].

Castelli, Ignaz. *Memoiren meines Lebens*. 4 vols. Vienna, 1861.

Charrière, Isabelle de. *Oeuvres complètes*. Ed. Jean-Daniel Candaux et al. Amsterdam, 1979–84.

Da Ponte, Lorenzo. *Memorie*. Ed. Cesare Pagnini. Milan, 1960.

Devrient, Eduard. *Meine Erinnerungen an Felix Mendelssohn-Bartholdy und seine Briefe an mich*. Leipzig, 1869.

Dittersdorf, Carl Ditters von. *Lebensbeschreibung seinem Sohne in die Feder diktiert*. Ed. Norbert Miller. Munich, 1967.

Favart, Charles-Simon. *Mémoires et correspondances*. Ed. A. P. C. Favart. 3 vols. Paris, 1808.

Frizzi, Benedetto. *Dissertazione di biografia musicale*. N.p, n.d.; but probably Trieste, 1802. Excerpt in "Benedetto Frizzi on Singers, Composers and Opera in Late Eighteenth-Century Italy." Ed. John A. Rice. *Studi musicali* 23 (1994): 368–93.

Gebler, Tobias Philipp von. *Aus dem Josephinischen Wien: Geblers und Nicolais Briefwechsel während der Jahre 1771–1786*. Ed. Richard Maria Werner. Berlin, 1888.

Gluck, Christoph. *The Collected Correspondence and Papers of Christoph Willibald Gluck*. Ed. Hedwig and E. H. Mueller von Asow. New York, 1962.

Griesinger, Georg August, *Biographische Notizien über Joseph Haydn*. Ed. Franz Grasberger. Vienna, 1954. Translated by Vernon Gotwals in *Haydn: Two Contemporary Portraits*, Madison, Wis., 1968.

Grimm, Friedrich Melchior. *Correspondance littéraire*. 16 vols. Paris, 1877–82.

Hoffmann, E. T. A. *Briefwechsel*. Ed. Friedrich Schnapp. 3 vols. Munich, 1967–69.

Hüttenbrenner, Anselm. "Anselm Hüttenbrenners Erinnerungen an Schubert." Ed. Otto Erich Deutsch. *Jahrbuch der Grillparzer-Gesellschaft* 16 (1906): 99–163.

"Italienische Theatermusik in Wien." *BmZ*, 1793, 131–39.

Joseph II. *Joseph II. und Leopold von Toscana: Ihr Briefwechsel von 1781 bis 1790*. Ed. Alfred von Arneth. 2 vols. Vienna, 1872.

———. *Joseph II., Leopold II. und Kaunitz: Ihr Briefwechsel.* Ed. Adolf Beer. Vienna, 1873.

———. *Joseph II. und Graf Cobenzl: Ihr Briefwechsel.* Ed. Adolf Beer and Joseph von Fiedler. 2 vols. Vienna, 1901.

———. *Geheime Correspondenz Josefs II. mit seinem Minister in den Österreichischen Niederlanden Ferdinand Grafen Trauttmansdorff, 1787–1789.* Ed. Hanns Schlitter. Vienna, 1902.

———. *Joseph II. als Theaterdirektor: Ungedruckte Briefe und Aktenstücke aus den Kinderjahren des Burgtheaters.* Ed. Rudolf Payer von Thurn. Vienna, 1920.

Kelly, Michael. *Reminiscences.* Ed. Roger Fiske, London, 1975.

Khevenhüller, Johann Joseph. *Aus der Zeit Maria Theresias: Tagebuch des Fürsten Johann Josef Khevenhüller-Metsch, Kaiserlichen Obersthofmeisters, 1742–1776.* 8 vols. Vienna, 1907–72.

Klopstock, Friedrich Gottlieb. *Briefe 1776–1782.* Ed. Helmut Riege (Hamburger Klopstock-Ausgabe). 3 vols. Berlin, 1982.

Kraus, Joseph Martin. "The Travel Diary of Joseph Martin Kraus." Ed. and trans. Bertil van Boer. *JM* 8 (1990): 266–90.

Maria Theresa. *Briefe der Kaiserin Maria Theresia an ihre Kinder und Freunde.* Ed. Alfred von Arneth. 4 vols. Vienna, 1881.

Meine Empfindungen im Theater. Vienna, 1781.

Mosel, Ignaz von. *Ueber das Leben und die Werke des Anton Salieri.* Vienna, 1827.

Mount Edgcumbe, Richard Earl of. *Musical Reminiscences of an Old Amateur.* 2d. ed. London, 1827.

Mozart, Wolfgang Amadeus. *Mozart: Die Dokumente seines Lebens.* Ed. Otto Erich Deutsch. Kassel, 1961.

———. *Mozart: Briefe und Aufzeichnungen.* Ed. Wilhelm A. Bauer, Otto Erich Deutsch, and Joseph Heinz Eibl. 7 vols. Kassel, 1962–75.

———. *New Mozart Documents: A Supplement to O. E. Deutsch's Documentary Biography.* Ed. Cliff Eisen. Stanford, Calif., 1991.

Müller, Johann Heinrich Friedrich. *Abschied von der k. k. Hof- und National-Schaubühne.* Vienna, 1802.

Novello, Mary, and Vincent Novello. *A Mozart Pilgrimage, Being the Travel Diaries of Vincent and Mary Novello in the Year 1829.* Ed. Nerina Medici di Marignano and Rosemary Hughes. London, 1955.

Pezzl, Johann. *Skizze von Wien.* Ed. Gustav Gugitz and Anton Schlossar. Graz, 1923.

Plutarch. "Caesar." Trans. Rex Werner. In *Fall of the Roman Republic.* Baltimore, 1972.

Richter, Joseph. *Eipeldauer Briefe.* Ed. Eugen von Paunel. 2 vols. Munich, 1917–18.

Riesbeck, Johann Kaspar. *Briefe eines reisenden Franzosen über Deutschland an seinen Bruder zu Paris.* Ed. Wolfgang Gerlach. Stuttgart, 1967.

Rosenbaum, Joseph Carl. "The Diaries of Joseph Carl Rosenbaum 1770–1829." Ed. Else Radant. *Haydn Yearbook* 5 (1968), whole issue.

Schiller, Friedrich. *Der Briefwechsel zwischen Schiller und Goethe.* Ed. Siegfried Seidel. 3 vols. Munich, 1984.

Sonnenfels, Joseph von. *Briefe über die Wienerische Schaubühne.* Vienna, 1884.

Türk, Daniel Gottlob. *School of Clavier Playing.* Trans. Raymond H. Haggh. Lincoln, Nebr., 1982.

Weigl, Joseph. "Zwei Selbstbiographien von Joseph Weigl (1766–1846)." Ed. Rudolph Angermüller. *Deutsches Jahrbuch der Musikwissenschaft* 16 (1971): 46–85.

Secondary Sources

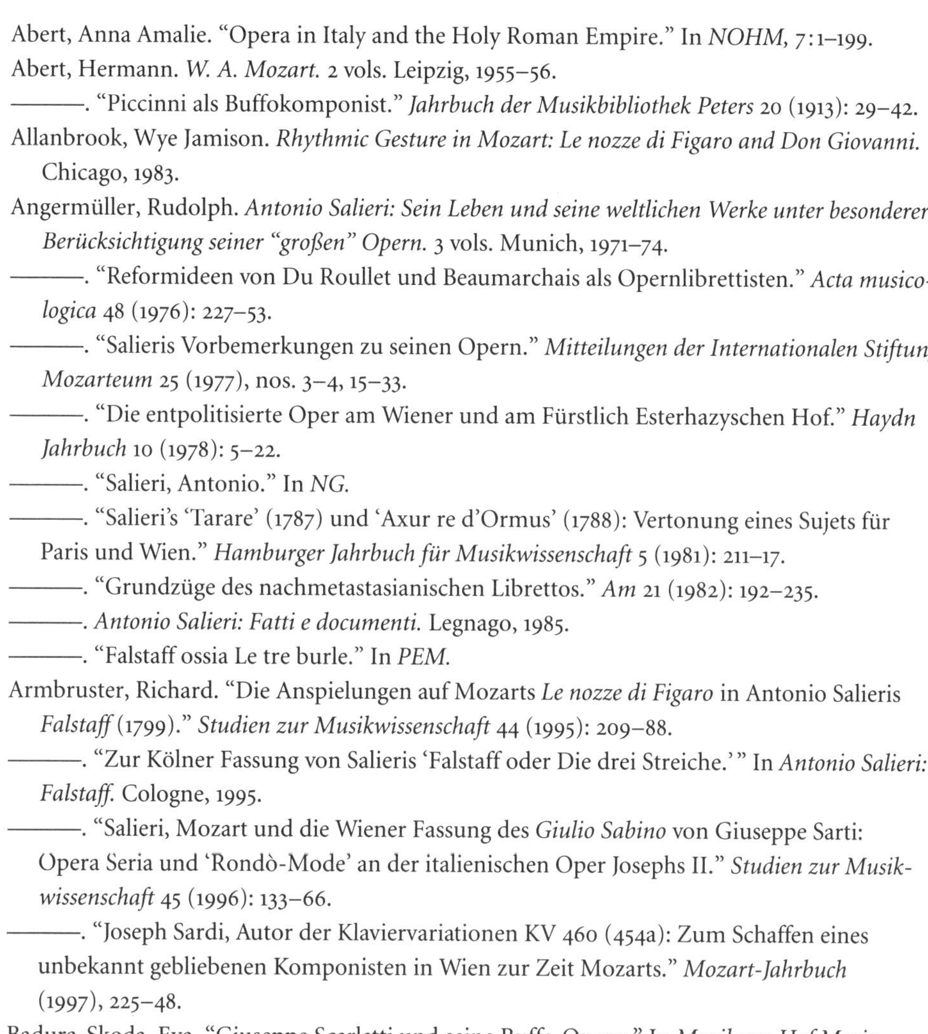

Abert, Anna Amalie. "Opera in Italy and the Holy Roman Empire." In *NOHM,* 7:1–199.

Abert, Hermann. *W. A. Mozart.* 2 vols. Leipzig, 1955–56.

———. "Piccinni als Buffokomponist." *Jahrbuch der Musikbibliothek Peters* 20 (1913): 29–42.

Allanbrook, Wye Jamison. *Rhythmic Gesture in Mozart: Le nozze di Figaro and Don Giovanni.* Chicago, 1983.

Angermüller, Rudolph. *Antonio Salieri: Sein Leben und seine weltlichen Werke unter besonderer Berücksichtigung seiner "großen" Opern.* 3 vols. Munich, 1971–74.

———. "Reformideen von Du Roullet und Beaumarchais als Opernlibrettisten." *Acta musicologica* 48 (1976): 227–53.

———. "Salieris Vorbemerkungen zu seinen Opern." *Mitteilungen der Internationalen Stiftung Mozarteum* 25 (1977), nos. 3–4, 15–33.

———. "Die entpolitisierte Oper am Wiener und am Fürstlich Esterhazyschen Hof." *Haydn Jahrbuch* 10 (1978): 5–22.

———. "Salieri, Antonio." In *NG.*

———. "Salieri's 'Tarare' (1787) und 'Axur re d'Ormus' (1788): Vertonung eines Sujets für Paris und Wien." *Hamburger Jahrbuch für Musikwissenschaft* 5 (1981): 211–17.

———. "Grundzüge des nachmetastasianischen Librettos." *Am* 21 (1982): 192–235.

———. *Antonio Salieri: Fatti e documenti.* Legnago, 1985.

———. "Falstaff ossia Le tre burle." In *PEM.*

Armbruster, Richard. "Die Anspielungen auf Mozarts *Le nozze di Figaro* in Antonio Salieris *Falstaff* (1799)." *Studien zur Musikwissenschaft* 44 (1995): 209–88.

———. "Zur Kölner Fassung von Salieris 'Falstaff oder Die drei Streiche.'" In *Antonio Salieri: Falstaff.* Cologne, 1995.

———. "Salieri, Mozart und die Wiener Fassung des *Giulio Sabino* von Giuseppe Sarti: Opera Seria und 'Rondò-Mode' an der italienischen Oper Josephs II." *Studien zur Musikwissenschaft* 45 (1996): 133–66.

———. "Joseph Sardi, Autor der Klaviervariationen KV 460 (454a): Zum Schaffen eines unbekannt gebliebenen Komponisten in Wien zur Zeit Mozarts." *Mozart-Jahrbuch* (1997), 225–48.

Badura-Skoda, Eva. "Giuseppe Scarlatti und seine Buffa-Opern." In *Musik am Hof Maria Theresias,* ed. Roswitha Vera Karpf, 57–75. Munich, 1984.

Balsano, Maria Antonella. "L'ottava di *Così fan tutte.*" In *Liedstudien: Wolfgang Osthoff zum 60. Geburtstag,* ed. Martin Just and Reinhard Wiesend, 279–91. Tutzing, 1989.

Balthasar, Scott. "Paer, Ferdinando." In *NGDO.*

Bauer, Anton. *150 Jahre Theater an der Wien.* Vienna, 1952.

Bauman, Thomas. *North German Opera in the Age of Goethe.* Cambridge, 1985.

———. *W. A. Mozart: Die Entführung aus dem Serail.* Cambridge, 1987.

———. "Mozart's Belmonte." *EM* 19 (1991): 557–63.

———. "Defranceschi, Prospero." In *NGDO.*

———. "Salieri, Da Ponte, and Mozart: The Renewal of Viennese Opera Buffa in the 1780s." In *Internationaler Musikwissenschaftlicher Kongress zum Mozartjahr 1991 Baden-Wien: Bericht,* ed. Ingrid Fuchs, 65–70. Tutzing, 1993.

Beales, Derek. *Joseph II.* Vol. 1, *In the Shadow of Maria Theresa, 1741–1780.* Cambridge, 1987.

Benaglia Sangiorgi, Roberto. "I melodrammi giocosi dell'Abate Casti poeta cesareo e successore del Metastasio a Vienna." *Italica* 36 (1959): 101–26.

Bergh, Herman van den. *Giambattista Casti (1724–1803): L'Homme et l'oeuvre.* Amsterdam, 1951.

Betzwieser, Thomas. *Exotismus und 'Türkenoper' in der französischen Musik des Ancien Régime.* Laaber, 1993.

———. "Exoticism and Politics: Beaumarchais' and Salieri's *Le Couronnement de Tarare* (1790)." *COJ* 6 (1994): 91–112.

Biagi Ravenni, Gabriella. "Calzabigi e dintorni: Boccherini, Angiolini, la Toscana e Vienna." In *La figura e l'opera di Ranieri de' Calzabigi,* ed. Federico Marri, 29–71. Florence, 1989.

Biggi Parodi, Elena. "La fortuna della musica di Salieri in Italia ai tempi di Mozart." In *Convegno,* 41–71.

Black, Jeremy. *The British Abroad: The Grand Tour in the Eighteenth Century.* New York, 1992.

Blümml, Emil Karl, and Gustav Gugitz. *Alt-Wiener Thespiskarren: Die Frühzeit der Wiener Vorstadtbühnen.* Vienna, 1925.

Bollert, Werner. "Antonio Salieri und die italienische Oper." In *Aufsätze zur Musikgeschichte,* 43–93. Bottrop, 1938.

Braunbehrens, Volkmar. *Mozart in Wien.* Munich, 1986. Translated by Timothy Bell as *Mozart in Vienna, 1781–1791,* New York, 1989.

———. *Salieri: Ein Musiker im Schatten Mozarts.* Munich, 1989. Translated by Eveline L. Kanes as *Maligned Master: The Real Story of Antonio Salieri,* New York, 1992.

Brizi, Bruno. "Uno spunto polemico Calzabigiano: *Ipermestra o Le Danaidi.*" In *La figura e l'opera di Ranieri de' Calzabigi,* ed. Federico Marri, 119–45. Florence, 1989.

———. "Da Ponte e Salieri: A proposito dell''Axur re d'Ormus.'" In *Omaggio a Gianfranco Folena,* 3 vols., 2:1405–29. Padua, 1993.

———. "Libretti e partiture: A proposito dell''Axur re d'Ormus' di Lorenzo da Ponte (Salieri) e del 'Telemaco' di Marco Coltellini (Gluck)." In *L'edizione critica tra testo musicale e testo letterario,* 437–42. Lucca, 1995.

———. "Il *Parere* di Salieri sull'*Axur re d'Ormus.*" In *Varietà d'harmonia et d'affetto: Studi in onore di Giovanni Marzi per il suo LXX compleanno,* ed. Antonio Delfino. Lucca, 1995.

Brown, A. Peter. "Haydn and Mozart's 1773 in Vienna: Weeding a Musicological Garden." *JM* 10 (1992): 192–230.

Brown, Bruce Alan. "*Le pazzie d'Orlando, Orlando Paladino,* and the Uses of Parody." *Italica* 64 (1987): 583–605.

———. *Gluck and the French Theatre in Vienna.* Oxford, 1991.

———. *W. A. Mozart: Così fan tutte.* Cambridge, 1995.

Brown, Bruce Alan, and John A. Rice. "Salieri's *Così fan tutte.*" *COJ* 8 (1996): 17–43.

Campana, Alessandra. "Il libretto de 'Lo sposo deluso.'" *Mozart-Jahrbuch* (1988–89), 573–88.

Candiani, Rosy. *Libretti e librettisti italiani per Mozart.* Rome, 1994.

Carter, Tim. *W. A. Mozart: Le nozze di Figaro.* Cambridge, 1987.

Celletti, Rodolfo. "La 'Leonora' e lo stile vocale di Paer." *Rivista italiana di musicologia* 7 (1972): 214–29.

Chandler, Tertius, and Gerald Fox. *3000 Years of Urban Growth.* New York, 1974.

Charlton, David. "Salieri's Timpani." *Musical Times* 112 (1971): 961–62.

———. *Grétry and the Growth of Opéra-Comique.* Cambridge, 1986.

Clark, Caryl. "Intertextual Play and Haydn's *La fedeltà premiata.*" *Current Musicology* 51 (1993): 59–81.

Claudon, Francis. "A propos de 'Falstaff': Shakespeare, Salieri et le renouveau du théâtre européen à la fin du XVIII siècle." In Muraro, *Mozart,* 1:297–310.

Colombati, Claudia. "'Les Deux Journées' di Cherubini: Dalle idee rivoluzionarie allo stile neoclassico." In Muraro, *Mozart,* 1:325–42.

Cooper, Martin. "Opera in France." In *NOHM,* 7:200–256.

Cumming, Julie E. "Gluck's Iphigenia Operas: Sources and Strategies." In *Opera and the Enlightenment,* ed. Thomas Bauman and Marita McClymonds, 217–40. Cambridge, 1995.

Dean, Winton. "The Libretto of 'The Secret Marriage.'" *Music Survey* 3 (1950): 33–38.

———. "French Opera." In *NOHM,* 8:26–119.

———. "German Opera." In *NOHM,* 8:452–522.

———. "Italian Opera." In *NOHM* 8:376–451.

Degrada, Francesco. "Dal *Marriage à la mode* al *Matrimonio segreto.*" In *Il palazzo incantato: Studi sulla tradizione del melodramma dal barocco al romanticismo,* 2:19–41. Fiesole, 1979.

De Guidi, Piero Giorgio. *Antonio Salieri.* Legnago, 1985.

Della Chà, Lorenzo. *Lorenzo da Ponte: I libretti d'opera viennesi, 1783–1791.* Parma, 1999. Forthcoming.

Della Corte, Andrea. *Un italiano all' estero: Antonio Salieri.* Turin, 1936.

Della Croce, Vittorio, and Francesco Blanchetti. *Il caso Salieri.* Turin, 1994.

Dell'Antonio, Andrew. "'Il compositore deluso': The Fragments of *Lo sposo deluso.*" In Sadie, 403–12.

Dent, Edward J. *Mozart's Operas.* London, 1947.

———. *The Rise of Romantic Opera.* Cambridge, 1976.

Dirnberger, Franz, ed. *Burgtheater in Dokumente* (exhibition catalogue). Vienna, 1976.

Donath, Gustav. "Florian Leopold Gassmann als Opernkomponist." *Studien zur Musikwissenschaft* 2 (1914): 34–211.

Edge, Dexter. "Mozart's Fee for *Così fan tutte.*" *Journal of the Royal Musical Association* 116 (1991): 211–35.

———. "Mozart's Viennese Orchestras." *EM* 20 (1992): 64–88.

———. Review of *Concert Life in Haydn's Vienna,* by Mary Sue Morrow. *Haydn Yearbook* 17 (1992): 108–66.

———. "Mozart's Reception in Vienna, 1787–1791." In Sadie, 66–117.

Einstein, Alfred. *Mozart: His Character, His Work.* New York, 1945.

———. *Gluck.* Trans. Eric Blom. New York, 1972.

Emery, Ted. "Goldoni's *Pamela* from Play to Libretto." *Italica* 64 (1987): 572–82.

———. *Goldoni as Librettist: Theatrical Reform and the Drammi Giocosi per Musica.* New York, 1991.

Engländer, Richard. "Domenico Fischietti als Buffokomponist in Dresden." *Zeitschrift für Musikwissenschaft* 2 (1919–20): 321–52, 399–422.

Everson, Jane E. "Of Beaks and Geese: Mozart, Varesco and Francesco Cieco." *ML* 76 (1995): 369–83.

Folena, Gianfranco. "Goldoni librettista comico." In Muraro, *Venezia,* 2:21–32.

Gallarati, Paolo. "'Axur re d'Ormus': Appunti sulla drammaturgia di Salieri." In *Convegno,* 33–39.

Gallico, Claudio. "Da 'L'Arcadia in Brenta' a 'La diavolessa' di Goldoni e Galuppi: Una via alla riforma dell'opera italiana." In *Galuppiana 1985: Studi e ricerche,* ed. Maria Teresa Muraro and Franco Rossi, 143–52. Florence, 1986.

Gelzer, Matthias. *Caesar, Politician and Statesman.* Oxford, 1968.

Geyer-Kiefl, Helen. *Die heroisch-komische Oper ca. 1770–1820.* 2 vols. Tutzing, 1987.

Gianturco, Carolyn. *Mozart's Early Operas.* London, 1981.

Gidwitz, Patricia Lewy. "Vocal Profiles of Four Mozart Sopranos." Ph.D. diss., University of California, Berkeley, 1991.

———. "'Ich bin die erste Sängerin': Vocal Profiles of Two Mozart Sopranos." *EM* 19 (1991): 565–79.

Girdham, Jane. *English Opera in Late Eighteenth-Century London: Stephen Storace at Drury Lane.* Oxford, 1997.

Goehring, Edmund J. "Despina, Cupid and the Pastoral Mode of *Così fan tutte.*" *COJ* 7 (1995): 107–33.

Goldin, Daniela. *La vera fenice: Librettisti e libretti fra Sette e Ottocento.* Turin, 1985.

Gugitz, Gustav. "Die Totenprotokolle der Stadt Wien als Quelle zur Wiener Theatergeschichte des 18. Jahrhunderts." *Jahrbuch der Gesellschaft für Wiener Theaterforschung* (1953–54), 114–45.

Haas, Robert. "Zur Wiener Ballett-Pantomime um den Prometheus." *Neues Beethoven-Jahrbuch* 2 (1925): 84–103.

Hadamowsky, Franz. *Die Wiener Hoftheater (Staatstheater) 1776–1966.* 2 vols. Vienna, 1966–75.

———. "Die Schauspielfreiheit, die 'Erhebung des Burgtheaters zum Hoftheater' und seine 'Begründung als Nationaltheater' im Jahr 1776." *Maske und Kothurn* 22 (1976): 5–19.

———. *Die Josefinische Theaterreform und das Spieljahr 1776/77 des Burgtheaters.* Vienna, 1978.

———. *Wien, Theatergeschichte: Von den Anfängen bis zum Ende des ersten Weltkriegs.* Vienna, 1988.

Hager, Manuela. "Die Opernprobe als Theateraufführung: Eine Studie zum Libretto in Wien des 18. Jahrhunderts." In *Oper als Text: Romanistische Beiträge zur Libretto-Forschung,* ed. Albert Gier, 101–24. Heidelberg, 1986.

Hansell, Kathleen Kuzmick. "Opera and Ballet at the Regio Ducal Teatro of Milan, 1771–1776: A Musical and Social History." Ph.D. diss., University of California, Berkeley, 1980.

Harbecke, Ulrich. "Das Tagebuch des Grafen Karl von Zinzendorf und Pottendorf als theatergeschichtliche Quelle." Diss., University of Cologne, 1969.

Heartz, Daniel. "The Creation of the Buffo Finale in Italian Opera." *Proceedings of the Royal Musical Association* 104 (1977–78): 67–78.

———. "Vis Comica: Goldoni, Galuppi and *L'Arcadia in Brenta* (Venice, 1749)." In Muraro, *Venezia*, 2:33–73.

———. "Mozart and His Italian Contemporaries: 'La clemenza di Tito,'" *Mozart-Jahrbuch* (1978–79), 275–93.

———. "Mozarts 'Titus' und die italienische Oper um 1800." *Hamburger Jahrbuch für Musikwissenschaft* 5 (1981): 255–66.

———. "Nicolas Jadot and the Building of the Burgtheater." *Musical Quarterly* 68 (1982): 1–31.

———. "Traetta in Vienna: *Armida* (1761) and *Ifigenia in Tauride* (1763)." *Studies in Music from the University of Western Ontario* 7 (1982): 65–88.

———. "Coming of Age in Bohemia: The Musical Apprenticeships of Benda and Gluck." *JM* 6 (1988): 510–27.

———. *Mozart's Operas.* Berkeley, 1990.

———. *Haydn, Mozart, and the Viennese School, 1740–1780.* New York, 1995.

———. "When Mozart Revises: The Case of Guglielmo in Così fan tutte." In Sadie, 355–61.

Heinzelmann, Josef. "*Prima la musica, poi le parole:* Zu Salieris Wiener Opernparodie." *Österreichische Musikzeitschrift* 28 (1973): 19–28.

———. "La grotta di Trofonio." In *PEM.*

———. "Prima la musica, poi le parole." In *PEM.*

———. "Tarare / Axur re d'Ormus." In *PEM.*

———. "Catilina." In *PEM.*

Henze-Döhring, Sabine. *Opera seria, Opera buffa und Mozarts Don Giovanni: Zur Gattungskonvergenz in der italienischen Oper des 18. Jahrhunderts.* Laaber, 1986.

Hodges, Sheila. *Lorenzo da Ponte: The Life and Times of Mozart's Librettist.* London, 1985.

Holmes, William C. "Pamela Transformed." *Musical Quarterly* 38 (1952): 581–94.

Honolka, Kurt. *Papageno.* Salzburg, 1984. Translated by Jane Mary Wilde as *Papageno: Emanuel Schikaneder, Man of the Theater in Mozart's Time.* Portland, Oreg., 1990.

Hunter, Mary. "Haydn's Aria Forms: A Study of the Arias in the Italian Operas Written at Eszterháza, 1766–1783." Ph.D. diss., Cornell University, 1982.

———. "'Pamela': The Offspring of Richardson's Heroine in Eighteenth-Century Opera." *Mosaic* 18 (1985): 61–76.

———. "The Fusion and Juxtaposition of Genres in Opera Buffa, 1770–1800: Anelli and Piccinni's 'Griselda.'" *ML* 67 (1986): 363–80.

———. "Text, Music and Drama in Haydn's Italian Opera Arias: Four Case Studies." *JM* 7 (1989): 29–57.

———. "Some Representations of *Opera Seria* in *Opera Buffa.*" *COJ* 3 (1991): 89–108.

———. "Buona figliuola, La." In *NGDO.*

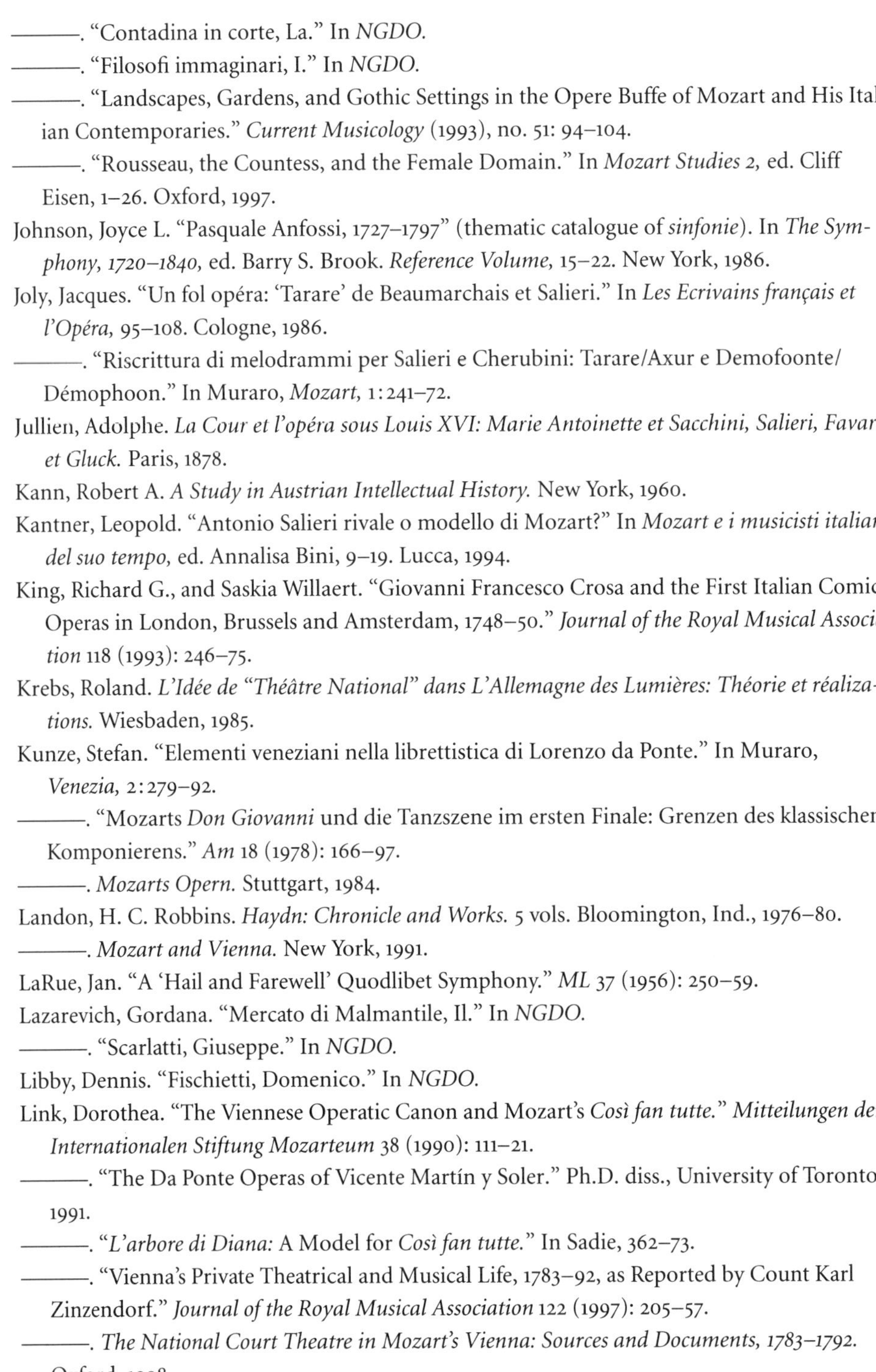

———. "Contadina in corte, La." In *NGDO.*

———. "Filosofi immaginari, I." In *NGDO.*

———. "Landscapes, Gardens, and Gothic Settings in the Opere Buffe of Mozart and His Italian Contemporaries." *Current Musicology* (1993), no. 51: 94–104.

———. "Rousseau, the Countess, and the Female Domain." In *Mozart Studies 2,* ed. Cliff Eisen, 1–26. Oxford, 1997.

Johnson, Joyce L. "Pasquale Anfossi, 1727–1797" (thematic catalogue of *sinfonie*). In *The Symphony, 1720–1840,* ed. Barry S. Brook. *Reference Volume,* 15–22. New York, 1986.

Joly, Jacques. "Un fol opéra: 'Tarare' de Beaumarchais et Salieri." In *Les Ecrivains français et l'Opéra,* 95–108. Cologne, 1986.

———. "Riscrittura di melodrammi per Salieri e Cherubini: Tarare/Axur e Demofoonte/ Démophoon." In Muraro, *Mozart,* 1:241–72.

Jullien, Adolphe. *La Cour et l'opéra sous Louis XVI: Marie Antoinette et Sacchini, Salieri, Favart et Gluck.* Paris, 1878.

Kann, Robert A. *A Study in Austrian Intellectual History.* New York, 1960.

Kantner, Leopold. "Antonio Salieri rivale o modello di Mozart?" In *Mozart e i musicisti italiani del suo tempo,* ed. Annalisa Bini, 9–19. Lucca, 1994.

King, Richard G., and Saskia Willaert. "Giovanni Francesco Crosa and the First Italian Comic Operas in London, Brussels and Amsterdam, 1748–50." *Journal of the Royal Musical Association* 118 (1993): 246–75.

Krebs, Roland. *L'Idée de "Théâtre National" dans L'Allemagne des Lumières: Théorie et réalizations.* Wiesbaden, 1985.

Kunze, Stefan. "Elementi veneziani nella librettistica di Lorenzo da Ponte." In Muraro, *Venezia,* 2:279–92.

———. "Mozarts *Don Giovanni* und die Tanzszene im ersten Finale: Grenzen des klassischen Komponierens." *Am* 18 (1978): 166–97.

———. *Mozarts Opern.* Stuttgart, 1984.

Landon, H. C. Robbins. *Haydn: Chronicle and Works.* 5 vols. Bloomington, Ind., 1976–80.

———. *Mozart and Vienna.* New York, 1991.

LaRue, Jan. "A 'Hail and Farewell' Quodlibet Symphony." *ML* 37 (1956): 250–59.

Lazarevich, Gordana. "Mercato di Malmantile, Il." In *NGDO.*

———. "Scarlatti, Giuseppe." In *NGDO.*

Libby, Dennis. "Fischietti, Domenico." In *NGDO.*

Link, Dorothea. "The Viennese Operatic Canon and Mozart's *Così fan tutte.*" *Mitteilungen der Internationalen Stiftung Mozarteum* 38 (1990): 111–21.

———. "The Da Ponte Operas of Vicente Martín y Soler." Ph.D. diss., University of Toronto, 1991.

———. "*L'arbore di Diana:* A Model for *Così fan tutte.*" In Sadie, 362–73.

———. "Vienna's Private Theatrical and Musical Life, 1783–92, as Reported by Count Karl Zinzendorf." *Journal of the Royal Musical Association* 122 (1997): 205–57.

———. *The National Court Theatre in Mozart's Vienna: Sources and Documents, 1783–1792.* Oxford, 1998.

Lippmann, Friedrich. "Haydns 'La fedeltà premiata' und Cimarosas 'L'infedeltà fedele.'" *Haydn-Studien* 5 (1982): 1–15.

Loewenberg, Alfred. *Annals of Opera, 1597–1940.* 3d ed. Totowa, N.J., 1987.

Lühning, Helga, "Die Rondo-Arie im späten 18. Jahrhundert: Dramatischer Gehalt und musikalischer Bau." *Hamburger Jahrbuch für Musikwissenschaft* 5 (1981): 219–46.

Mann, Alfred. "Johann Joseph Fux's Theoretical Writings: A Classical Legacy." In *Johann Joseph Fux and the Music of the Austro-Italian Baroque,* ed. Harry White, 57–71. Aldershot, U.K., 1992.

Marinelli, David Newton. "Carlo Goldoni as Experimental Librettist: The *Drammi Giocosi* of 1750." Ph.D. diss., Rutgers University, 1988.

Martinotti, Sergio. "'Falstaff': Per un altro ritratto di Salieri." In Muraro, *Mozart,* 1:273–96.

Mattern, Volker. *Das Dramma giocoso "La finta giardiniera": Ein Vergleich der Vertonungen von Pasquale Anfossi und Wolfgang Amadeus Mozart.* Laaber, 1989.

———. "Les Danaïdes." In *PEM.*

McClymonds, Marita P. *Niccolò Jommelli: The Last Years, 1769–1774.* Ann Arbor, Mich., 1980.

———. "Mattia Verazi and the Opera at Mannheim, Stuttgart, and Ludwigsburg." *Studies in Music from the University of Western Ontario* 7 (1982): 99–136.

———. "Transforming Opera Seria: Verazi's Innovations and Their Impact on Opera in Italy." In *Opera and the Enlightenment,* ed. Thomas Bauman and Marita McClymonds, 119–32. Cambridge, 1995.

———. "Verazi's Controversial *Drammi in Azione* as realized in the Music of Salieri, Anfossi, Alessandri, and Mortellari for the Opening of La Scala, 1778–1779." Forthcoming.

Michtner, Otto. "Der Fall Abbé Da Ponte." *Mitteilungen des Österreichischen Staatsarchivs* 19 (1966): 170–209.

———. *Das alte Burgtheater als Opernbühne von der Einführung des deutschen Singspiels (1778) bis zum Tod Kaiser Leopolds II. (1792).* Vienna, 1970.

Minardi, Gian Paolo. "Paër semiserio." In Muraro, *Mozart,* 1:343–58.

Morrow, Mary Sue. *Concert Life in Haydn's Vienna: Aspects of a Developing Musical and Social Institution.* Stuyvesant, N.Y., 1989.

Muresu, Gabriele. *Le occasioni di un libertino (G. B. Casti).* Messina, 1973.

———. *La parola cantata: Studi sul melodramma italiano del Settecento.* Rome, 1982.

Nettl, Paul. "Forlana." In *Musik in Geschichte und Gegenwart,* ed. Friedrich Blume. Kassel, 1949–86.

Noiray, Michel. "Roi e le fermier, Le." In *NGDO.*

Osthoff, Wolfgang. "Mozarts Cavatinen und ihre Tradition." In *Helmuth Osthoff zu seinem siebzigsten Geburtstag,* ed. Wilhelm Stauder, 139–77. Tutzing, 1969.

———. "Die Opera buffa." In *Gattungen der Musik in Einzeldarstellungen: Gedenkschrift Leo Schrade,* ed. Wulf Arlt, Ernst Lichtenhahn, and Hans Oesch, 678–743. Bern, 1973.

———. "Gli endecasillabi villotistici in *Don Giovanni* e *Nozze di Figaro.*" In Muraro, *Venezia,* 2:293–311.

———. "Comicità alla turca, musica classica, opera nazionale: Osservazioni sulla 'Entführung aus dem Serail.'" In *Opera & libretto,* ed. Gianfranco Folena, Maria Teresa Muraro, and Giovanni Morelli, 2 vols., 2:157–74. Florence, 1990–93.

Page, Janet K. "'To Soften the Sound of the Hoboy': The Muted Oboe in the 18th and Early 19th Centuries." *EM* 21 (1993): 65–80.

Page, Janet K., and Dexter Edge. "A Newly Uncovered Autograph Sketch for Mozart's 'Al desio di chi t'adora' K 577." *Musical Times* 132 (1991): 601–6.

Pendle, Karin. "Opéra-Comique as Literature: The Spread of French Styles in Europe, ca. 1760 to the Revolution." In *Grétry et l'Europe de l'opéra-comique,* ed. Philippe Vendrix, 229–50. Liège, 1992.

Pestelli, Giorgio. *The Age of Mozart and Beethoven.* Trans. Eric Cross. Cambridge, 1984.

Petrobelli, Pierluigi. "Goldoni at Esterhaza: The Story of His Librettos Set by Haydn." In Badura-Skoda, 314–18.

Petty, Frederick C. *Italian Opera in London, 1760–1800.* Ann Arbor, Mich., 1980.

Pirani, Federico. "L'opera buffa tra Roma e Vienna al tempo di Giuseppe II: Cantanti e repertori." In *Mozart, Padova e La Betulia liberata,* ed. Paolo Pinamonti, 407–16. Florence, 1991.

———. "'Il curioso indiscreto': Un'opera buffa tra Roma e la Vienna di Mozart." In *Mozart: Gli orientamenti della critica moderna,* ed. Giacomo Fornari, 47–67. Lucca, 1994.

———. "*I due baroni di Rocca Azzurra:* Un intermezzo romano nella Vienna di Mozart." In *Mozart e i musicisti italiani del suo tempo,* ed. Annalisa Bini, 89–112. Lucca, 1994.

———. "Operatic Links between Rome and Vienna, 1778–1790." In Sadie, 395–402.

Pirrotta, Nino. "Causerie su Beaumarchais e la musica teatrale." In *Scelte poetiche di musicisti: Teatro, poesia e musica da Willaert a Malipiero,* 309–21. Venice, 1987.

Pistorelli, Luigi. "I melodrammi giocosi di G. B. Casti." *Rivista musicale italiana* 2 (1895): 36–56, 449–76.

———. "I melodrammi giocosi inediti di G. B. Casti." *Rivista musicale italiana* 4 (1897): 631–71.

Platoff, John. "Music and Drama in the Opera Buffa Finale: Mozart and His Contemporaries in Vienna, 1781–1790." Ph.D diss., University of Pennsylvania, 1984.

———. "Musical and Dramatic Structure in the Opera Buffa Finale." *JM* 7 (1989): 191–230.

———. "The Buffa Aria in Mozart's Vienna." *COJ* 2 (1990): 99–120.

———. "'Non tardar amato bene' Completed—but Not by Mozart." *Musical Times* 132 (1991): 557–60.

———. "Tonal Organization in 'Buffo' Finales and the Act II Finale of 'Le nozze di Figaro.'" *ML* 72 (1991): 387–403.

———. "How Original Was Mozart? Evidence from *Opera Buffa.*" *EM* 20 (1992): 105–17.

———. "A New History for Martín's *Una cosa rara.*" *JM* 12 (1994): 85–115.

———. "Myths and Realities about Tonal Planning in Mozart's Operas." *COJ* 8 (1996): 3–15.

———. "Catalogue Arias and the 'Catalogue Aria.'" In Sadie, 296–311.

Price, Curtis, Judith Milhous, and Robert D. Hume. *Italian Opera in Late Eighteenth-Century London.* Vol. 1, *The King's Theatre, Haymarket, 1778–1791.* Oxford, 1995.

Rabin, Ronald J. "Mozart, Da Ponte, and the Dramaturgy of Opera Buffa: Italian Comic Opera in Vienna, 1783–1791." Ph.D. diss., Cornell University, 1996.

Raynaud, Michael Louis. "A Guide to Antonio Salieri's *Axur re d'Ormus.*" Master's thesis, University of Houston, 1992.

Reichenberger, Teresa. "Joseph Weigls italienische Opern, mit einem biographischen Nachtrag." Diss., University of Vienna, 1983.

Rice, John A. "Sense, Sensibility, and Opera Seria: An Epistolary Debate." *Studi musicali* 15 (1986): 101–38.

———. "Emperor and Impresario: Leopold II and the Transformation of Viennese Musical Theater, 1790–1792." Ph.D. diss., University of California, Berkeley, 1987.

———. "Rondò vocali di Salieri e Mozart per Adriana Ferrarese." In Muraro, *Mozart,* 1:185–209.

———. "Vienna under Joseph II and Leopold II." In *The Classical Era,* ed. Neal Zaslaw, 126–65. London, 1989.

———. "Muzzarelli, Kozeluch, e *La ritrovata figlia di Ottone II* (1794): Il balletto viennese rinato nello spirito di Noverre." *Nuova rivista musicale italiana* 24 (1990): 1–46.

———. "An Early Handel Revival in Florence." *EM* XVII (1990): 62–71.

———. *W. A. Mozart: La clemenza di Tito.* Cambridge, 1991.

———. "The Operas of Antonio Salieri as a Reflection of Viennese Opera, 1770–1800." In *Music in Eighteenth-Century Austria,* ed. David Wyn Jones, 210–20. Cambridge, 1996.

Robinson, Michael F. *Naples and Neapolitan Opera.* Oxford, 1972.

———. "Three Versions of Goldoni's *Il filosofo di campagna.*" In Muraro, *Venezia,* 2:75–85.

———. "Mozart and the Opera Buffa Tradition." In *W. A. Mozart: Le nozze di Figaro,* by Tim Carter, 11–32. Cambridge, 1987.

———. *Giovanni Paisiello: A Thematic Catalogue of His Works.* Vol. 1. Stuyvesant, N.Y., 1991.

Rosselli, John. *Singers of Italian Opera: The History of a Profession.* Cambridge, 1992.

Ruhnke, Martin. "Opera semiseria und Dramma eroicomico." *Am* 21 (1982): 263–75.

Rushton, Julian. "Music and Drama at the Académie Royale de Musique (Paris), 1774–1789." Doctoral diss., Oxford University, 1970.

———. "Salieri's *Les Horaces:* A Study of an Operatic Failure." *Music Review* 37 (1976): 266–82.

———. *W. A. Mozart: Don Giovanni.* Cambridge, 1981.

———. *Classical Music: A Concise History from Gluck to Beethoven.* London, 1986.

Salter, Lionel. "Footnotes to a Satire: Salieri's 'Prima la musica, poi le parole.'" *MT* 126 (1985): 21–24.

Sartori, Claudio. *I libretti italiani a stampa dalle origini al 1800: Catalogo analitico con 16 indici.* 7 vols. Cuneo, 1990–94.

Schindler, Otto G. "Das Publikum des Burgtheaters in der Josephinischen Ära: Versuch einer Strukturbestimmung." In *Das Burgtheater und sein Publikum,* ed. Margret Dietrich, 11–95. Vienna, 1976.

———. "Der Zuschauerraum des Burgtheaters im 18. Jahrhundert." *Maske und Kothurn* 22 (1976): 20–53.

Schneider, Herbert. "Vaudeville-Finali in Haydns Opern und ihre Vorgeschichte." In Badura-Skoda, 302–9.

Smith, Patrick J. *The Tenth Muse: A Historical Study of the Opera Libretto.* New York, 1970.

Sommer-Mathis, Andrea. *Tu felix Austria nube: Hochzeitsfeste der Habsburger im 18. Jahrhundert.* Vienna, 1994.

Steblin, Rita. *A History of Key Characteristics in the Eighteenth and Early Nineteenth Centuries.* Ann Arbor, Mich., 1983.

Steptoe, Andrew. *The Mozart–Da Ponte Operas.* Oxford, 1988.

Stewart, Pamela D. "Le *femmes savantes* nelle commedie del Goldoni." *Yearbook of Italian Studies* 7 (1988): 19–42.

Strohm, Reinhard. *Die italienische Oper im 18. Jahrhundert.* Wilhelmshaven, 1979.

———. "Zur Metrik in Haydns und Anfossis 'La vera costanza.'" In Badura-Skoda, 279–95.

Swenson, Edward Elmgren. "*Prima la musica e poi le parole:* An Eighteenth-Century Satire." *Am* 9 (1970): 112–29.

———. "Antonio Salieri: A Documentary Biography." Ph.D. diss., Cornell University, 1974.

Szabo, Franz A. J. *Kaunitz and Enlightened Absolutism, 1753–1780.* Cambridge, 1994.

Thayer, Alexander Wheelock. "Half a Dozen of Beethoven's Contemporaries: II. Antonio Salieri." *Dwight's Journal of Music* 23 (20 February–26 November 1864): 185–347. Edited as *Salieri, Rival of Mozart,* ed. Theodore Albrecht, Kansas City, Mo., 1989.

———. *Life of Beethoven.* Ed. Elliot Forbes. Princeton, N.J., 1967.

Tyson, Alan. *Mozart: Studies of the Autograph Scores.* Cambridge, Mass., 1987.

Viale Ferrero, Mercedes. "Torino e Milano nel tardo Settecento: Repertori a confronto." In Muraro, *Mozart,* 1:99–138.

Walton-Myers, E. H. "Antonio Salieri's 'La cifra': The Creation of a Late Eighteenth-Century Opera." Ph.D. diss., Northwestern University, 1977.

Wangermann, Ernst. *From Joseph II to the Jacobin Trials.* 2d ed. London, 1969.

———. *The Austrian Achievement, 1700–1800.* London, 1973.

Weaver, Robert Lamar, and Norma Wright Weaver. *A Chronology of Music in the Florentine Theater, 1751–1800.* Warren, Mich., 1993.

Webster, James. "Mozart's Operas and the Myth of Musical Unity." *COJ* 2 (1990): 197–218.

———. "The Analysis of Mozart's Arias." In *Mozart Studies,* ed. Cliff Eisen, 101–99. Oxford, 1991.

———. "Understanding Opera Buffa: Analysis = Interpretation." In *Opera Buffa in Mozart's Vienna,* ed. Mary Hunter and James Webster, 340–77. Cambridge, 1997.

Weimer, Eric. *Opera Seria and the Evolution of Classical Style, 1755–1772.* Ann Arbor, Mich., 1984.

Weiss, Piero. "Carlo Goldoni, Librettist: The Early Years." Ph.D diss., Columbia University, 1970.

———. "La diffusione del repertorio operistico nell'Italia del Settecento: Il caso dell'opera buffa." In *Civiltà teatrale e Settecento emiliano,* ed. Susi Davoli, 241–56. Bologna, 1986.

———. "Cocchi, Gioacchino." In *NGDO.*

———. "Goldoni, Carlo." In *NGDO.*

Weston, Pamela. "Stadler, Anton (Paul)." In *NG.*

Wignall, Harrison James. "L'avversario imperiale di Mozart." *Nuova rivista musicale italiana* 28 (1994): 1–16.

Wilson, W. Daniel. "Turks on the Eighteenth-Century Operatic Stage and European Political, Military and Cultural History." *Eighteenth-Century Life* 9 (1985): 79–92.

Wlassack, Eduard. *Chronik des k. k. Hof-Burgtheaters.* Vienna, 1876.

Woitas, Monika. "'. . . Bewegungen von unvergleichlicher Sinnlichkeit . . .': Auf den Spuren des berühmt-berüchtigten Fandango." In *De editione musices: Festschrift Gerhard Croll zum 65. Geburtstag,* ed. Wolfgang Gratzer and Andrea Lindmayr, 203–18. Laaber, 1992.

Zaslaw, Neal. *Mozart's Symphonies: Context, Performance Practice, Reception.* Oxford, 1989.

———. "Waiting for Figaro." In Sadie, 413–35.

Zechmeister, Gustav. *Die Wiener Theater nächst der Burg und nächst dem Kärntnerthor von 1747 bis 1776.* Vienna, 1971.

INDEX OF SALIERI'S WORKS

Page numbers in italics refer to musical examples, those in boldface type to illustrations.

GENERAL INDEX

WEST ORANGE PUBLIC LIBRARY
46 MT. PLEASANT AVENUE
WEST ORANGE, N.J. 07052

782.1092 Rice, John A.
SAL Antonio Salieri
RIC and Viennese Opera

4/99

DEMCO